# PSYCHIATRIC CRIMINOLOGY

## A Roadmap for Rapid Assessment

# PSYCHIATRIC CRIMINOLOGY

## A Roadmap for Rapid Assessment

John A. Liebert, MD
Psychiatrist, Scottsdale, Arizona, USA

William J. Birnes, JD, PhD
Chairman of Sunrise Community Counseling Center
Los Angeles, California, USA

CRC Press
Taylor & Francis Group
Boca Raton London New York

CRC Press is an imprint of the
Taylor & Francis Group, an **informa** business

CRC Press
Taylor & Francis Group
6000 Broken Sound Parkway NW, Suite 300
Boca Raton, FL 33487-2742



Printed on acid-free paper
Version Date: 20160603

International Standard Book Number-13: 978-1-4987-1417-4 (Hardback)



**Visit the Taylor & Francis Web site at**
**http://www.taylorandfrancis.com**

**and the CRC Press Web site at**
**http://www.crcpress.com**

Printed and bound in the United States of America by Publishers Graphics,
LLC on sustainably sourced paper.

# Contents

# Foreword by David Boyd

Dr. Liebert was a classmate of mine at McGill University Faculty of Medicine, and, although we pursued very different career pathways after graduation from the "then-most international medical college in North America," our paths would cross later in life. I realized that we had common interest and experience in emergency medical care, public safety, and the healthcare delivery systems. John asked me to review the latest book he has authored with William Birnes, PhD. This will be their latest of four books addressing the needs and solutions across the spectrum of social, political, and socioeconomic crises in public health and safety. They write on important and perplexing issues that confound society, clinical and public health experts, law enforcement officials and politicians in both practice and academic discourse. Uniquely, in this new book the authors not only document with research-based evidence and multiple case studies the needs and solutions to today's new epidemics, but they present convincingly the benefits of their solutions.

Dr. Liebert and I shared the unique opportunity to learn neuroscience at McGill's Montreal Neurological Institute. We learned from the legendary pioneers; in neurosurgery by Dr. Wilder Penfield, neurology by Dr. Herbert Jaspers and psychology research by Donald O. Hebb, PhD. These great scientists and excellent teachers literally wired our brains for future growth and comprehension that is now of increasingly critical importance. Dr. Liebert became a psychiatrist and continues to practice psychiatry and psychotherapy based on complex psychopharmacotherapeutics from the solid foundation of neuroscience he learned at McGill.

As our med-class president I recognized a group of class colleagues who trained and excelled in their initial chosen fields and subsequently had the secondary vision, energy, and perseverance to explore and succeed at another new and broader societal impacting career. I recognized my classmates who took the road less traveled who made a major impact in a different condition or field and awarded them McGill Med-Class 1963 Percival Pott Virtuous Physician Award. This award was based on the discovery by a solo practitioner, Dr. Pott, of scrotal cancer occurring in the young male chimney sweeps of eighteenth century London. He recognized for the first time an occupation caused cancer, and fought in Parliament to regulate this child abuse and eradicate a lethal disease.

I selected Dr. Liebert for this award for his pioneering work in addressing our public health and safety epidemics of suicide, violence, and invalid diagnostics for both chronic psychiatric impairment within 22% of our population and common medical errors with altered states of consciousness causing both death and chronic disability within the emergency services system.

My career started as a general surgical resident with a special interest in injury and became aware of report "Accidental Death and Disability, *The Neglected Disease of Modern Society*" (Accidental Death and Disability, 1966). I conceived the idea that we needed intensive care Trauma Units in selected hospitals and these should be arranged in large geographic regions with upgraded prehospital emergency medical services. I convinced Illinois Governor Richard B. O'Gilvie to support a Statewide Trauma Center and Emergency Medical Services System in 1971 (Flashner and Boyd, 1971). Invited to Congress to testify on our experiences, I argued for a similar national program based on our model. I authored the clinical and programmatic aspects of the Emergency Medical Services Systems Act(s) of 1973 (PL-93-154), 1976 (94-573), and 1979 (96-142). Subsequently I was appointed the National EMSS director by President Ford, and served under the Carter and Reagan administrations. Based on the proven Illinois model I established 304 contiguous regional trauma and EMS systems that covered every state and territory of the United States. Within each state I developed an EMSS "Lead Agency" in the State Health Authority to appropriately and flexibly implement the operational EMS components to support essential clinical systems for

- Major trauma
- Burns
- Spinal cord injuries (SCI)
- Acute cardiac attacks
- Poisonings and clinical toxicology
- High-risk infants and mothers
- Psychiatric and behavioral emergencies

All of these important clinical problem areas could be and were supported by the organization and public health orientation established from the instructive regional trauma systems. These were used as the basis for access and uniquely developed interventions for all of the other acute clinical programs.

I recognized early in my career as a trauma surgeon that consistent emergency psychiatric evaluation and treatment was inadequate or nonexistent in most of our developing trauma regions. During an interview with an emergency department nurse in one of our well-functioning trauma centers, I asked, "How do you handle psychiatric emergencies?" She replied, "We have much improved our program for trauma and the other types of emergencies, but not for psychiatric cases. Once we drug them and restrain them and put them in the back cubical, we don't know what to do for them." Unfortunately this was true for both the privileged and disenfranchised patients. Assessment, diagnosis, and treatment were not available or were extensively delayed. In the other clinical areas I identified a knowledgeable and expert specialty physician and we would work out how to provide the emergency services system for that clinical area.

What did exist was primitive emergency room practices and complex interactions with law enforcement, social service and referral agencies. These are slow and dissatisfying. Large numbers of agitated and mentally disorganized patients clogged the inadequate facilities in hospitals severely impacted by a lack of a systems approach. Although psychiatry is not my field of expertise, I could not help but recognize that something better needed to be done. I included psychiatric patients as an important group who could benefit from our success in a comprehensive and regionalized Emergency Medical Services System.

I needed to find an interested psychiatrist; however, I found none. I did a national search through our growing body of "systems" experts that participated at our regional and national technical assistance (TA) conferences. We did as was our custom and asked the local conferees to point out their leaders which they did. I got the same result. Many were psychiatric nurses and social mental health workers and a few psychiatrists. In 1983 we published our landmark text, *Systems Approach to Emergency Care* (Boyd, 1983). This textbook laid out the conceptual development of EMS Systems in the United States. It presented chapters on the seven critical patient groups identified for regional EMS planning and the transferability of the "systems methods" for varied emergent medical conditions. We included a chapter on "Systems Approach to Behavioral Emergencies" (Resnik and Hudak, 1983).

"For each clinical category an in-depth knowledge of the incidence, demography, epidemiology, and clinical aspects associated with these critical patient categories is mandatory to address EMS regional planning and operations. General as well as specific planning for a regional EMS response for the overall patient population and particularly for the critical target patient groups provides a system of care for both routine critical medical conditions and other emergencies so that all would receive better care and benefit from sound regional EMS system planning and operations. Responsive region wide system plans and operations in both the general and critical care areas provided a basis and an opportunity for evaluating these goals and impacts with an aim toward prevention" (Boyd, 1982). For psychiatric and behavioral emergencies, we need to find leadership psychiatrist and mental health workers and introduce them to systems and the experience of trauma surgeons, nurses, and hospital administrators. Psychiatric systems like trauma should not be centralized but developed nationally and within a regional concept that anticipates the many obvious differences of urban, suburban, rural, and remote areas in the country. Each of these regional conditions share common demographics and cultures that need compatible rules and guidelines for psychiatric and behavioral emergency medical services.

Dr. Liebert picked up on these concepts during his second career as a traveler working in emergency psychiatry from Maine to San Diego and many sites in the Midwest, both remote and inner city. He correctly reiterates in his books to date that the Emergency Medical Services System has saved millions of lives and prevented chronic disability in many millions more; he states, "dialing 911, I assure you, was not a presidential edict. It was a fight all the way from local hospital campuses fearful of sicker patients arriving at their ERs and thus escalating their DOA rates to vested interests afraid of a regionalized system of best practices that, as simply the case in medicine and public health, always follows discoveries. One is now shocked to see the blood soaked surgical tables at Guy's Hospital in London and the sink where surgeons washed their hands after surgery! Then came Dr. Joseph Lister who translated the bacteriological discoveries of Pasteur into best surgical practices—namely aseptic surgical practices, now taken for granted."

As Dr. Liebert and Dr. Birnes consistently assert in their various publications and books, the public institution of Psychiatry today is like surgery returning to colonial practices in denying the translational research of aseptic best clinical practices. Today hardly any informed citizens of this country would tolerate such denial and ignorance in the name of a budgetary shell game that shifts public psychiatry to law enforcement as the authors correctly point out in case after case. The emergency services gateway that was modernized with implementation of the Emergency Services Act nearly 50 years ago is open and will accept rational "Systems" concepts to their local behavioral health problems. The scope of both public health and safety now covers a broad spectrum of fragmentation from community services to academia. Criminal justice or health and social sciences simply cannot embrace the systems concepts under their current departmental and disciplinary structures. The scope of this new textbook extends from the battlefields in Iraq to the streets of American cities; from solitary confinement in primitive jails to emergency departments swamped with both non-emergent and emergency care and with school health and counseling services confronting unprecedented violence and suicides on campus with a system made for the silent generation of the '50s.

*Psychiatric Criminology: A Roadmap for Rapid Assessment*, should be a first step for both college departments responsible for educating our new clinicians and public safety officers, as well as public health and safety officials in active roles. As of now there is no strategy in place. I included behavioral emergencies as a major category for our national modernized Emergency Medical Services System decades ago. As Liebert and Birnes assert, it is time to read again what I said back then and start doing it. It certainly has worked for trauma, heart attacks, and strokes.

Dr. Liebert practices at the cutting edge of psychopharmacology one day in North Scottsdale, Arizona, but he must see the disenfranchised psychiatric patient in Sheriff Joe's jails the next day in Phoenix; he reports in his latest textbook this strange and threatening dichotomy of managing malfunction of our brain's neuronal pathways, both in the twenty-first century and seventeenth century, that he personally experiences every week as a practicing psychiatrist. Read the book—better yet, for professors with students hungry for understanding the current public health and safety crises of our land, adopt this textbook for your course, and remember rapid assessment is critically important. Trauma care, whether surgical or neuropsychiatric, is an amazingly complex and demanding field. Every case is different. People get shot differently, they are critically injured in varying ways and you have to know your field, to think fast and have a pre-planned rapid, accurate response to the situation.

Dr. David Boyd, MDCM
Fellow American College of Surgeons, author of Emergency Services Act and founder of The National Emergency Medical Services System

## REFERENCES

Accidental Death and Disability. 1966. *The Neglected Disease of Modern Society.* Division of Medical Sciences, National Academy of Science, National Research Council, Washington, DC.

Boyd, D. 1982. The conceptual development of EMS systems in the United States, Part II. *Emergency Medical Services* 11(2), 26–35.

Boyd, D. R. 1983. The history of emergency medical services (EMS) systems in the United States of America. In: Boyd, D. R., Edlich, R. F., Micik, S. H. (eds), *Systems Approach to Emergency Medical Care,* Chapter 1. Norwalk, CT: Appleton-Century-Crofts, pp. 1–82.

Flashner, B. A. and Boyd, D. R. 1971. The critically injured patient: A plan for the organization of a statewide system of trauma facilities. *Illinois Medical Journal,* 139, 256–265.

Resnik, H. L. P. and Hudak, C. J. Jr. 1983. Systems approach to behavioral emergencies. In: Boyd, D. R., Edlich, R. F., Micik, S. H. (eds), *Systems Approach to Emergency Medical Care,* Chapter 10. Norwalk, CT: Appleton-Century-Crofts, pp. 181–200.

# Foreword by Cloyd Steiger

When I became a homicide detective in 1994, the first murder I was assigned was the killing of a seven-year-old girl named Angelica. Angelica lived in a ramshackle, hastily-erected shelter with her mother, who was otherwise homeless. Gang members fired guns indiscriminately in the structure. Angelica, asleep inside, was struck and killed by one of the bullets. She should have not been there, but in a safe, secure home.

During my 36-year career with the Seattle Police Department, including 22 as a homicide detective, I saw the violence committed against and by the homeless population. Many of the people I've encountered were homeless veterans. I've seen these veterans murdered on the streets, and other times I've arrested them for murder.

I've investigated the senseless murders of innocent victims by psychotic people, seemingly at random on the street, from a baseball fan walking back to his car after a game being stabbed by a deranged suspect who'd been in and out of the court systems, to a soccer fan meeting the same fate on the street by different, but equally deranged individual. I investigated several mass-shootings committed by the mentally-deranged, including the Café Racer shooting by Ian Stawicki, detailed by Dr. Liebert in this book.

The common denominator in these cases is the revolving door failure of the psychological evaluation process.

Police officers are often the first contact with people suffering from severe psychological impairment; many are dangerous. Even when these people are taken in for involuntary mental evaluation, they are released after a few hours, with little or no evaluation actually done. Is this because of concern for the rights of the patient, the lack of facilities or both? By pushing a seriously mentally ill person out of the door and back onto the street you do a disservice both to them and the public at large.

Dr. Liebert is a passionate advocate for humane and effective treatment for the invisible population on the streets of America, and a tireless advocate for taking care of the American veteran who volunteered to serve their country, only to be later pushed into oblivion by the government they served.

Cloyd Steiger
Chief Criminal Investigator
Washington Attorney General
Homicide Investigation Tracking System

# Authors

**John A. Liebert, MD,** completed his residency training in psychiatry at the University of Washington and served as chief resident at the Seattle VA Medical Center. He practiced psychiatry in Bellevue, Washington for 25 years before becoming an author while traveling the country as a locum tenens psychiatrist. In that capacity he practiced in every type of point of entry to the health-care system and studied a broad spectrum of patient populations from Eastport, Maine, to San Diego, California, with every region of Wisconsin and California—rural and inner city—in between. He served on both the clinical faculty of Harvard at Cambridge Hospital and the forensic psychiatry team at the Security Housing Unit (the SHU) of Pelican Bay Prison, California.

Following his last assignment performing fitness-for-duty examinations on troops returning to Joint Base McChord/Fort Lewis from the surge in Iraq, he returned to private practice in Scottsdale, Arizona, where he specializes in the diagnostics and treatment of psychiatric disorders via evidence-based criteria demonstrated online at www.digitalclinician.com.

He is a Master of Psychopharmacology from The Neuroscience Education Institute of Carlsbad, California with membership for both continuing education and consultative services with the Massachusetts General Hospital Psychiatry Academy of Harvard University. He combines psychopharmacotherapy with psychotherapy in treatment and has extensive training and clinical experience in both treatment modalities.

Dr. Liebert completed his premedical training at Amherst College, Massachusetts, with a BA in English and received his MD CM degree from McGill University Faculty of Medicine in Montreal, Quebec. He completed a rotating medical-surgical internship at Santa Clara County Hospital in San Jose, California, where it was customary for interns to manage the emergency room alone for two months. He was drafted for the Vietnam War during internship and served as the flight surgeon in a unique air transport mission with the 7th Logistics Squadron. Following his military service, he completed his training in psychiatry and neurology at the University of Washington. He is licensed for practice of medicine in Arizona and Washington State and a member of both the King County Medical Society and Washington State Psychiatric Association. He is the Consulting Board Psychiatrist for the American Investigative Society of Cold Cases and recipient of the Percivall Pott Virtual Surgeon Award from McGill University, based on his discoveries in the field of medicine as a solo practitioner. (Pott, an eighteenth century solo practitioner in London, discovered cancer in chimney sweepers.) In addition to this book, he has authored three books with attorney and investigative reporter William Birnes: *Suicidal Mass Murderers: A Criminological Study of Why They Kill* (Taylor and Francis/CRC Press) based on the Virginia Tech massacre and anthrax attacks associated with the events of 9/11; *Wounded Minds: Understanding and Solving the Growing Menace of Post-Traumatic Stress Disorder* (Skyhorse Press) based on the Fort Hood rampage murders by Nidal Hassan, the Great Bear Lake suicidal mass murder by Los Angeles Police Department Officer Christopher Dorner, and the Afghanistan atrocities of Sergeant Robert Bales from Joint Base McChord/Fort Lewis; and *Hearts of Darkness: Why Kids Are Becoming Mass Murderers and How We Can Stop It* (Skyhorse Press) based on the Sandy Hook Elementary School, Tucson Safeway Plaza, Utoya Island/Oslo, and Aurora Theater suicidal rampage murders.

**William J. Birnes, JD, PhD,** is the chairman of the Board at the Sunrise Community Counseling Center in Los Angeles, a New York Times bestselling author, and a National Endowment for the Humanities Fellow. He was a member of a research team for the U.S. Department of Justice on cold case sexual offender data analysis and a coauthor, with Dr. John Liebert, of *Suicidal Murderers, A Criminological Study of Why They Kill, Wounded Minds, Hearts of Darkness*, and, with Robert Keppel, of *Serial Violence, The Grisly Business Unit, Signature Killers*, and *The Riverman*. His first work in this field was *Serial Killers* with coauthor Joel Norris. His book, *Dr. Feelgood*, was an Los Angeles Book Award finalist.

# 1

# Through a lens darkly

We live in the age of the all-seeing eye of the video camera, surveillance cameras on ATM machines, at convenience stores, at street corner locations, and on mobile phones of all types. The all-seeing eye of the video camera captures events of every type from children diving into swimming pools, to piñata events at birthday parties, to police interactions with citizens on freeways, country roads, and city streets. And the all-seeing eye of the video camera has become part of our daily lives, turning up in the most inconvenient ways on the evening news. And so it was all the way back in 1992, when Los Angeles Police Department (LAPD) officers chased, cornered, restrained, and then beat Rodney King with their batons in such a way that even LAPD Chief Darryl Gates said publicly that he was "disgusted" by what he saw. Whether Rodney King was acting strangely because he was mentally ill or because he was high on a particular drug, we do not know. But, we do know that as a result of that videotape the officers involved were tried, acquitted by a California jury, and became the poster images for the Los Angeles (LA) riots after their acquittal.

The cameras keep on recording as if the citizenry wants to maintain a public record of police interactions that may go swiftly and horribly awry. Interactions between police and citizens caught on random cell phone videos galvanize our attention because the camera frames the moment, takes a slice out of reality, and in a McLuhanesque moment of clarity, isolates it and raises it to a form of art where it becomes cathartic to individuals watching it and to their entire communities. Is it any wonder that demonstrations break out in the streets after each shocking event bursts into our collective consciousness? This is new. This is how technology now moves the politics of policing and the justice system.

One of the most recent examples of this took place in North Charleston, South Carolina, when passerby Feidin Santana noticed what seemed to be an altercation between North Charleston police officer Michael Slager, a 5-year veteran of the department with at least two citizen complaints against him for excessive force, and motorist Walter Scott, an African American whom Slager said he stopped because a taillight was out on Scott's Mercedes. Then through the dashboard cam on Slager's police unit, we see Walter Scott fleeing. Slager catches up to him and then the two men seemed to be struggling, and Santana, as he told NBC news anchor Lester Holt, felt that things were going to go down very badly.

Thus, he aimed his cell phone camera at the pair and captured on video Scott struggling with Slager and then running away as Slager aimed his weapon at the fleeing individual and fired eight shots into his back. Scott went down, Slager handcuffed him, seemed to drop a device beside his body, and called for backup. Scott died from his gunshot wounds.

At first, Officer Slager filed a report indicating that he made a routine traffic stop for a taillight violation, at which point, Scott exited the car and struggled with the officer for his Taser, then ran away. At that point, Slager said, he felt justified in firing his weapon, because he believed his life had been in danger. The police report, Santana said, appeared in the newspaper, but because Santana was an eyewitness and what he saw contradicted what the police report said, he was very disturbed as well as frightened for his own safety. But after much soul-searching, he told Lester Holt and then MSNBC's Chris Hayes, Santana turned over to Scott's family the video he had taken of the officer shooting the fleeing Walter Scott in the back. From the victim's family, the family lawyer sent the video to *The New York Times* (NYT), who published the story and the video, after which publication, the South Carolina Law Enforcement Division opened an investigation, and Officer Slager was arrested and charged with murder.

He is now in jail awaiting trial (Schmidt and Apuzzo 2015). According to the NYT story, Walter Scott had been arrested numerous times in the past, mostly for failure to pay child support and at least once for assault and battery. Anthony Scott, Walter Scott's brother, told the NYT that Walter Scott might have believed he was about to be arrested again because he owed child support. Nevertheless, commentators have pointed out, the U.S. Supreme Court has held—and this is current and established law—in *Tennessee v. Garner* (471 U.S. 1 [1985]) that using lethal force against a fleeing suspect is unconstitutional unless that suspect poses a threat to life. The ruling states that the Tennessee law authorizing use of lethal force was, "unconstitutional insofar as it authorizes the use of deadly force against, as in this case, an apparently unarmed, nondangerous fleeing suspect; such force may not be used unless necessary to prevent the escape and the officer has probable cause to believe that the suspect poses a significant threat of death or serious physical injury to the officer or others." Hence, when Scott fled Slager, regardless of Scott's belief that he might have been arrested for failure to pay child support, Slager's use of lethal force was a crime.

It is likely, Santana and the Scott family have said, that this case might never have come to light but for the video that Santana took with his cell phone, an ever-present device, an all-seeing eye. There is no escape from a cell phone camera, which also brought to light the case of Eric Garner on Staten Island, New York, in July 2014.

In another recent case, Freddie Gray was arrested by Baltimore city police, shackled and cuffed after being swarmed and tackled, and then, with his legs dangling loosely, dragged off to a police van. Shortly after his arrest and while in police custody, Gray died from a severed spinal cord. What happened to him in that van and in police custody? All the camera sees is a limp and shackled Freddie Gray dragged off by police. But the resulting fury of the African American community in West Baltimore fueled the worst riot in Baltimore since 1968. Now, however, the Baltimore medical examiner ruled Gray's death a homicide, and State's Attorney Marilyn Mosby announced that all six Baltimore police officers who arrested Gray, an arrest she alleged was unlawful because it was absent probable cause, will be charged with manslaughter in Gray's death. One wonders if the officers' defense, however, will assert *Terry v. Ohio* (1968), in which the Supreme Court ruled that officers may stop and frisk an individual without violating that individual's Fourth Amendment protection against unreasonable search and seizure if they believe that a crime is likely afoot. When Freddie Gray fled the police and was chased by a bike patrol officer, Lieutenant Brian Rice, was that flight cause enough to afford Rice and fellow officers who joined the chase the legitimacy of their arrest? Mosby announced that because Gray's fatal injuries took place while in police custody in a police van transporting him to the police station, during which he was not belted in as the law requires, the officers were responsible for the injuries that caused Gray's death. In a related story concerning one of the charged officers, Lieutenant Brian Rice, who was on bike patrol on April 12 and pursued Gray, according to the Associated Press, Gray had been hospitalized in 2012 for concerns about his mental health and had his guns seized by county sheriff's deputies because of fears he was acting irrationally.

Then there was the death of Eric Garner on Staten Island, who was allegedly illegally selling individual cigarettes—"loosies"—on a street corner when he was confronted by New York City Police Department (NYPD) officers trying to arrest him. He claimed he was doing nothing wrong and tried to walk away from the confrontation and then was placed into a choke hold from which, according to the New York Medical Examiner, he died. The case has been ruled a homicide by the Medical Examiner's office. A grand jury found all officers not guilty, sparking outrage in New York and engendering yet another crime, the point-blank cold-blooded murders of two uniformed NYPD officers, Rafael Ramos and Wenjian Liu, by a mentally ill man, Ismaaiyl Brinsley, who, on the run from shooting his girlfriend in Baltimore, had vowed revenge for the killings of Garner and Ferguson's Michael Brown. This case, among others—particularly white police officers shooting black citizens—has initiated a movement to require all police officers to wear cameras in order to know what really does happen in their encounters with citizens.

We do not know whether Garner, the father of six and a neighborhood fixture, was even borderline mentally ill, but it is clear from the video shot by a bystander that he was reacting strangely—at least behaving unexpectedly to officers—to the police confrontation as he sought to talk his way out of an arrest. The police swarmed him while one officer placed him in a choke hold, a maneuver that is illegal under NYPD procedures, took him to the ground, and, as Garner, an asthmatic, screamed he could not breathe, kept him in the choke hold while other officers piled on until Garner lost consciousness. Other officers did nothing to revive him. The Emergency Medical Technician (EMT) responders did nothing to revive him. This video of Garner's arrest and death has galvanized world opinion and resulted in demonstrations around the United States. Of course it did because the camera lens memorializes the event, raises it to a level of catharsis in the viewer's mind. We realize in that moment that police were crushing his chest as he screamed, "I can't breathe" 11 times, that Eric Garner could have been any one of us, believing himself to be innocent yet struggling for at least one breath under the weight of a swarm of arresting officers. And no amount of explanation by the police union or by the officer's own attorney can wipe away what millions of people saw, repeated over and over again on news channels around the world, with their own eyes. We ask, could this confrontation have turned out another way?

Of course, we know that we are only seeing what the camera has captured. What transpired before and what happened afterward are not captured on the processor embedded in the smartphone's digital imaging device. But what makes this a cathartic event is the medium itself, by framing and elevating it to a form of theater. Like a stage play that depicts only what the audience can see within the frame of the stage and the invisible fourth wall, the events preceding and subsequent are defined by the events portrayed. Thus, even though authorities may exclaim that, "we don't know the whole picture," they miss the fact that what we do not see carries far less impact than what we do see. And that is the problem with seeing police confrontations through a camera lens.

For months, the public at large did not know the full story of the death of Michael Brown in Ferguson, Missouri, even as protestors, some of whom were violent, crowded the streets and the Department of Justice pursued its investigation. Maybe the conflicting stories of eyewitnesses to the shooting were confusing even to the St. Louis County grand jury that refused to indict Officer Darren Wilson as did the Department of Justice after its review of the case. But the camera captured the uncovered corpse of Michael Brown lying unattended in the street as if he were a piece of roadkill carrion and not a human being. And that was infuriating. If you were an African American resident of Ferguson watching the way authorities treated Brown's body, depriving it of the dignity you would give to your own pet who had died, you, too, would experience a seething rage because how they treated Brown would be how they treated you regardless of the cause of death. No amount of official explanation could explain away the perception that in the eyes of the authorities, Brown was considered by them to be less than human. And this is not the way to govern or seek respect from those whom you expect to be governed.

After reviewing the events in Ferguson, including the results of the grand jury hearings, and after an initial U.S. Department of Justice probe of the events subsequent to a visit to Ferguson during the demonstrations by Attorney General Eric Holder, according to CNN, the Attorney General "said this week he expects to announce the results of the department's investigation of the shooting death of Michael Brown and a broader probe of the Ferguson Police Department before he leaves office in the coming weeks" (Perez and Jaffe 2015). Local departments may complain about federal review and intervention in their operations, but, looking at the events in Ferguson and the police department's response to them, sometimes the local departments are their own worst enemies. After the shooting of Michael Brown, the department's decision to leave his body lying in the middle of the street for hours is not just an example of extreme incompetence, it is bad police work and demonstrates to the community that the police whom they licensed to serve instead demonstrate complete contempt. Why humiliate the community you are supposed to serve, which humiliation is perceived as racial bias? And that is one of the reasons the Department of Justice (DoJ) launched a broad probe into the Ferguson police department and found endemic racism there, including a pattern of what amounts to financial extortion of the city's African American citizens by the police and court system. In the aftermath of this disclosure, the state has taken over the justice administration of the local court to remedy the problem.

In the wake of the DoJ report, other people began leaving the Ferguson administration, including Police Chief Thomas Jackson and City Manager John Shaw, both of whom resigned after the report became public. After the announcement of the chief's resignation, residents engaged in more protests, during which a man identified by police as 20-year-old Jeffery Williams shot and wounded two St. Louis police officers. Williams, who was arrested, explained that he was not shooting at the officers. Instead, he told police, he had been in a dispute with another individual and took shots at him from across the street. But the shootings were alarming just in themselves and broke into the national consciousness, even causing President Obama and Attorney General Holder to condemn them. The shootings, though, if motivated by rage and frustration at the police, fall into the category of the assassination of two NYPD officers by a mentally ill individual who fled from police in Baltimore, stalked the officers on a Brooklyn street, and killed both of them before killing himself. It was a murder/suicide, and it could have portended a wave of police shootings, the very worst thing community police departments fear.

As *Washington Post* columnist and MSNBC analyst and guest host Jonathan Capehart wrote on March 16, 2015, after reviewing the DoJ report and the grand jury testimony that exonerated Ferguson police officer Darren Wilson, "'Hands Up, Don't Shoot,' was built on a lie." The evidence, he wrote, showed that Wilson did, indeed, receive the report of a strong-arm robbery at a local store and that Brown had gone for Wilson's weapon while they struggled through the car window and that after the two were outside the car, Brown charged Wilson and refused to stop or obey Wilson's commands. Hence, Wilson shot him in self-defense.

Another aspect of this overview of police/community relations came from the special panel of experts assembled by President Obama to come up with recommendations for establishing a greater level of trust between police and the communities they protect. Based in part on recommendations put forward by aviation experts who applied their oversight of the aviation industry and the types of accidents that sometimes occur therein, their suggestions included independent investigations of police shootings by outside counsels. The panel also called for better training to help police deal with stressful situations. In addition, the panel called for better and more complete record-keeping about police use of lethal force, and they called for use of police body cameras. These, the panel and the president said, would not only provide for independent review of police use of lethal force, but would protect police from false claims of abuse. The panel recognized that these recommendations were a form of prevention to throw light on a growing problem.

Across the country from Baltimore and New York, on July 1, 2014, California Highway Patrol (CHP) Officer Daniel L. Andrew, amid the rush-hour evening traffic on LA's freeway maze, got the call, in response to several 911 calls, of a woman walking barefoot on the shoulder of the 5 Freeway.

"She has no shoes on," one caller said. "She's just standing there with her arms in the air," another said. Two of the callers mentioned trying to help the woman, who was now, we know, named Marlene Pinnock. One woman said she pulled her car next to the woman to ask her something, but that Pinnock started walking faster. Another said she tried to pull over to help, but there was too much traffic. "Honestly, I caught her out of the corner of my eye and I was like, 'Whoa, that's weird,'" the caller said. "And then I couldn't get over—I was several lanes over. I wanted to get over to like, help her off the highway or something."

> 911 Calls Reported Woman Walking on Freeway Before CHP Beating, Nine 911 calls were made in the moments before a woman was beaten by a CHP officer in an incident caught on cellphone. (Jason Kandel and Beverly White, Channel 4, Los Angeles on-air New Coverage)

Had CHP officer Daniel Andrew received any training in handling the resistant or noncompliant mentally ill behaving strangely or even potentially dangerously? The CHP reported that the officer would most likely have had received the standard training in the management of a mentally ill offender the prior month, and it is just as likely that he had experienced his share of tragedy, encounters with the seriously mentally ill, homeless, and mutilation on California freeways. He may have even encountered Marlene Pinnock or her fellow residents under the LaBrea overpass of I-10 in downtown LA. Certainly other police officers had encountered her. She lived in squalor there for a long time, a condition of living making sense through only the narrow legal perspective of a constitutional defense attorney asserting that she had a right to live as she wanted and where she wanted as long as what she did was not a trespass upon the rights of others or did not present a danger to others or to the public safety. Unfortunately Pinnock's walking in traffic on the 10 Freeway did present a danger to drivers who could have been injured in car accidents while trying to avoid hitting her, hence a danger to public safety. She was in extreme danger, herself, too.

According to agency incident reports, when Andrew arrived, the woman ignored him and instead walked right into oncoming rush-hour traffic lanes. The officer ordered Pinnock to stop, but she repeatedly ignored those commands, and then began walking against the flow of traffic and into the traffic lanes. Officer Andrew ordered her off the freeway, but she ignored his order and walked onto the busy freeway and began wandering between the lanes like a stray dog who had run loose into the thick of commuter traffic as darkness was approaching. The officer waited for the opportunity to sprint onto the freeway, and when he did, she resisted, calling him the devil. Was she delusional at that point? On the video, the officer can be seen attempting to hold her arm. Pinnock appeared to try to twist away from him. At that point, the officer took her to the ground and began hitting her with his black-gloved fists as she covered her head with her arms in a defensive posture. After a matter of seconds, an off-duty officer helped subdue Pinnock, but not before the first officer landed at least nine blows.

"She then became 'physically combative,' the CHP report said, and 'a physical altercation ensued'." The video shows the officer pinning the woman to the ground and punching her at least nine times. Technically, because the woman was trying to wrest herself away from the officer, this would be resisting arrest, the CHP has said, because the officer was trying to keep the woman from hurting herself or others by walking into rush-hour traffic.

Officer Andrew later reported that Pinnock was talking to herself. But as speeding cars whizzed by the officer and the woman he was trying to restrain, he had no time to reason with such gross insanity because, probably, he believed that both their lives were in danger, as well as the harm to passing drivers who might swerve to avoid them and cause a serious pileup. But what did he do? More than likely, pumped with adrenaline, he dragged her, fighting him all the way, until safely off the road. She called him "the devil," he later reported, and most likely many other names that made no sense, and despite suspecting she was out of her mind, she likely aggravated him more.

Did the officer know Pinnock had been arrested before for one of the dozen of her prior misdemeanors of trespassing, petty theft, and a battery charge or theft? Theft could have been the charges filed against her for rummaging through a garbage can. What about trespassing? That could have been anything. Battery? A simple battery under California's tort statutes can be filed against an individual for that individual's nonconsensual touching of another person. How dangerous was this person and what was her intent in her resisting arrest? Most likely at least one other California police officer had taken her to LA County Hospital for psychiatric examination under a 5150 Emergency Detention order for grave disability. Might that mean that she was gravely disabled at the moment of her confrontation with the officer—delusional, and oblivious to the flow of traffic? If so, that would have meant she was presenting imminent danger to herself and others.

We can only surmise what her mental state might have been at that moment. However, after Pinnock's several prior arrests, was there ever time or professional expertise to ask her, what did she think she was doing to get arrested a dozen times, mostly in the same neighborhood of downtown LA? And what are the police supposed to do when confronting such a strangely acting individual? Are police officers simply trolling the streets for the helpless to exercise their powers of arrest? We do not believe they are, even though it is probably true that there are psychopathic police officers and ones obsessed with punishing misbehavior. What we do not know is whether CHP officer Daniel Andrew was one of those problem officers. We also do not know for certain his state of mind during confrontations in frantic rush-hour traffic on LA's freeways, but clearly he lost it when finally immobilizing the struggling woman on a safe roadside concrete mat and kept punching her.

A passerby videotaped Andrew delivering sidewalk justice to Pinnock with at least nine punches to the head. After several arrests, probably a few of which were equally dangerous to life and limb, was the officer going to provide the ultimate treatment to save her, himself, and the public's safety? Would he have risked his own life to drag her to safety? Did she do the unforgivable and spit in his face? Whatever the nature of the incident and what psychological issues precipitated it, once captured within the frame of a camera, it became memorialized as a confrontation between a white officer beating up a black woman. Officer Andrew was subsequently exonerated of any criminal liability in this case.

The camera lens is not restricted to police confrontations, but also can be transformational when capturing events during wartime. The photos of U.S. Army prison guards at Abu Ghraib prison in Iraq, standing over piles of naked prisoners, so enraged the Iraqis, as did the sounds of prisoners being tortured, that the seething Sunni residents rose up in fury. We are seeing the results of what we did in Iraq with the rise of ISIS or ISIL, perpetrating violence so beyond the bounds of previous human experience that we are shocked at the level of cruelty. But for the camera capturing the torture and humiliation at Abu Ghraib who knows what might have resulted?

When we look at images of the mentally ill, the dangerously mentally ill, or even those acting strangely so as to be perceived as a threat, through the lens of the camera, often what we see antagonizes us even though the person we see being managed or arrested by the police is incapable of managing himself or herself. What is the nature of these types of individuals and how can society protect them while protecting itself from them? And what are the roles of first responders, emergency personnel, teachers and school counselors and administrators, health-care practitioners, corrections officers, veterans groups, and officers of the court in dealing with these individuals? These are the questions we seek to answer in this study.

## EPIDEMIOLOGY OF VIOLENCE, SUICIDE, AND ALTERED STATES OF CONSCIOUSNESS

Suicidal violence—or, harm to self and others—has reached epidemic proportions in the United States, particularly among teens and young adults, including military veterans. Because of the mainstreaming of the mentally ill and the closing down of public psychiatric facilities, most of the mentally ill are left untreated and have to fend for themselves under unmanaged survival situations. With a large population of the mentally ill at-large on streets, they have frequent encounters with police and public safety officials, resulting in violence. We have witnessed just such violence in states like California, Wisconsin, New Mexico, New York, Arizona, and more recently in Washington, DC. How can we prevent this problem from getting worse?

The cases of Marlene Pinnock and Eric Garner are just the tip of the iceberg in incidents of police confrontations with the mentally ill or with those "acting strangely." To be fair, many times responding officers simply do not know who is actually mentally ill and delusional with auditory hallucinations or who presents a real intentional and perhaps deadly threat. What we do know, from cases dating back to the Columbine High School shooting, is, at the very least, that suicidal violence, harm to self and others, has reached epidemic proportions in the United States, especially among young teens acting out in high school and college. This cohort includes, most disgracefully, combat veterans returning from our Middle Eastern wars with posttraumatic stress disorder (PTSD) or traumatic brain injury (TBI) and, quite inexcusably, waiting for treatment from the Veterans Affairs' (VA) medical centers, but have nowhere to go and nothing to help them support themselves (Liebert and Birnes 2013).

There are many contributing factors to this rise of the mentally ill on the streets and the perceived threats they may pose to emergency responders, particularly police, threats we have documented in our prior *Hearts of Darkness* (Liebert and Birnes 2014) and *Wounded Minds*. The following are contributing factors.

One is the mainstreaming of the mentally ill and the closing down of public psychiatric facilities resulting in many of the mentally ill being left untreated and having to fend for themselves in unmanaged living situations or on the streets. This social crisis is known as deinstitutionalization of the seriously mentally ill, which, in Daniel Moynihan's words, could be considered to have reached its level of maximum feasible misunderstanding: inpatient psychiatric beds are diminishing as fast as new cases needing them present in a growing population that is more distressed on the average since the Great Depression and ensuing World War II. There is no more margin for error in deinstitutionalization. Releasing more patients from the few remaining state institutions for the seriously mentally ill would likely be perceived as a threat to everyone.

After all, one seriously mentally ill homeless veteran, recently returned from Iraq, made it, while brandishing a knife, almost all the way into the living quarters of the president of the United States before he was stopped by an off-duty Secret Service agent before he could get upstairs to the second floor of the White House. Another mentally ill person, Miriam Carey, who insisted on speaking with the president, led multiple Washington, DC, police agencies on a wild chase around the National Mall? She was unarmed but was suffering from delusions of postpartum depression and was ultimately shot dead by Capitol Police with her child sitting right next to her in the car.

In parallel to the social shock of deinstitutionalization that has followed the trend of urbanization—thus the concentration of formerly hospitalized psychotic patients in our city cores—is that of criminalization of mental illness, as presumptively advocated by Thomas Szasz in his book, *The Myth of Mental Illness* (1974). Szasz argues that because there is no such thing as mental illness, it is an invented condition. Attorneys have used it to argue that detention of the mentally ill for forced observation or involuntary commitment is subject to a detainee's Fourth and Fifth Amendment rights to search and seizure and due process. This has resulted in situations where the police and other emergency responders are forced to deal with the mentally ill as violators of the public peace and public safety, effectively criminalizing the mentally ill. The seminal decision creating this situation was the *Lessard* ruling in Wisconsin.

## THE *LESSARD* CASE

The *Lessard* case in Milwaukee, Wisconsin (*Lessard v. Schmidt* 1974, 1975, 1976), resulted from a suit filed on behalf of Alberta Lessard by her court-appointed attorneys, which suit was expanded into a class action on behalf of all residents of Wisconsin 18 years or older, asserting that involuntary commitment of the mentally ill absent a due process hearing was unconstitutional. The federal court held for the plaintiffs in *Lessard*.

In holding for Alberta Lessard, the federal judiciary, while setting aside Wisconsin's involuntary commitment law, ruled in essence that there was no such thing as mental illness and set a new standard for "dangerousness." It held that commitment required a finding that, "there is an extreme likelihood that if the person is not confined he will do immediate harm to himself or others." In so doing, the federal court required that an individual facing a hearing for involuntary commitment be afforded the same constitutional rights afforded to a criminal defendant including, but not limited to, Fourth Amendment protections against search and seizure, Fifth Amendment guarantees of due process, and Sixth Amendment guarantees of right to counsel. Included in this package of rights was also the right to remain silent in the face of an inquiry into an individual's mental health, which was, in essence, a *Miranda* protection to the suspected mentally ill individual, along with an exclusion of hearsay evidence. The court believed that mental illness was simply a label enabling psychiatrists to "shoehorn" certain people into medical diagnosis to "line their pockets" with fees based on the American Psychiatric Association's diagnostic codes (*Diagnostic and Statistical Manual of Mental Disorders*).

Along came sociologists with big data to convince politicians, policy makers, and the judiciary alike that behavior cannot be predicted by psychiatrists and clinical psychologists, particularly in the case of behaviors of suicide and violence. This was also an argument set forth by John Monahan (1994). Monahan has since backed off on his views considerably, recognizing his assertions were based on flawed databases and analytics. He was notably quiet during his attendance at the governors' investigation of the Virginia Tech massacre. His voice, however, is still one given dominance in arguments over preventive detention of such dangerous suicidal psychotic people like Elliot Rodger, who was interviewed by the Santa Barbara County Sheriff's officers, released, and then soon after went on his suicidal mass murder rampage at the University of California, Santa Barbara. The officers who found no abnormal psychology warranting preventive detention for 36 hours for psychiatric examination at the hospital at Ventura/University of California, Los Angeles would likely be supported in his release of this known madman—one who had terrified his own family—by the statistical mystique of John Monahan's treatises. Rodger died with his rights on, which rights were of no help to him whatsoever. Many innocent people were killed. More were seriously injured, and even more were traumatized psychologically for life. And, but for the presentations of data and the arguments of those saying aberrant or dangerous behavior is unpredictable, the Rodger mass murders and prior mass murders in Colorado, Arizona, Virginia, and Texas were all preventable.

Monahan's earlier preachings from large databases and recent retreat to more cautious interpretation of cold numbers from the computer warn us to use caution with analyses and conclusions from databases. In all encounters between clinicians and patients, for example, the individual patient rarely fits cookie-cutter-like into constructs, such as extreme dangerousness, parsed in huge numbers into computers. In fact, rarely does a psychiatrist examine and treat a patient who actually would have been accepted into a large controlled treatment trial. Most real patients would have been excluded for common reasons, such as childhood trauma, and similarly with dangerousness and suicide. Their occurrences are too uncommon in large databases to capture what the clinician is likely encountering with any single patient.

Such operational response to databases—in this case the clinician's turning blind eye to suicidality—is reminiscent of the interpretation of data from North American Air Command following the 9/11 attacks on the World Trade Center. Fighters were scrambled and blindly sent toward the Atlantic, if one stretches one's imagination enough to believe the explanation put forth by the government, only being returned too late to intercept the hijacked jet about to crash into the Pentagon. It is hard, therefore, to assess and predict threats with big databases. We know that. But, as Seymour Halleck sensibly warns in his *Psychiatric Aspects of Criminology* (Halleck and Bromberg 1968), and *Psychiatry and the Dilemmas of Crime: A Study of Causes, Punishment, and Treatment* (Halleck 1971), we must cull out those seriously mentally ill who are more likely than not dangerous to themselves or others. There will be false negatives and false positives. As we have learned from 9/11, such threat assessment will never be 100% perfect. But, in lieu of the fiasco in our nation's military and security response to the attacks of 9/11, are we simply to shut down the radar screens, close North American Air Command, and wait for the attack to find out who our enemy is? Only the lunatic fringe in this nation would buy into such folly, but the public is kept dismayed by the maximum feasible misunderstanding known as deinstitutionalization and criminalization of the seriously mentally ill, along with the deprecating clinical nihilism of John Monahan.

None of those responsible for the demolition of the public psychiatric system or preventive detention of dangerous and suicidal mentally ill has anything to say about the medicalization of presumed organ and system deficiencies of cancer and atherosclerosis. In fact, there is great momentum to predict in order to select the best intervention for the best outcome. Such prediction is at the heart of the Affordable Care Act and the just-enacted Clay Hunt Act for prevention of military suicides, that incentivizes physicians by improving outcomes, rather than increasing utilization of expensive testing or encounters with patients. Nobody argues that to do this, doctors have to diagnose clinical presentations when showing before them. Nobody argues that to get better outcomes, more research has to be done. No ethical researcher, however, is going to draw conclusions about cancer of the lung based simply on everyone who has a cough. Researchers at multiple sites in different regions of the country need to agree on criteria for lung cancer. It is no different with central nervous system and neuropsychiatric impairment. There needs to be reliability of diagnosis for the problem requiring research, such as now, for example, the epidemic of memory loss with aging. That is the purpose of *DSM* manuals. The improvement of criteria that enable researchers to agree on what problem they are studying, whether dementia, suicidal ideation, or first-episode schizophrenia, of which there are 300,000 first psychotic breaks every year in this country.

Should we stop involuntary commitments altogether? Professors and self-proclaimed cable news pundits claim nothing could have been done to have prevented the Santa Barbara suicidal mass murder by Elliot Rodger through preventive detention, an assumption with which we vociferously disagree and will present fact-based evidence in support of our contention. Yet, these same pundits have no problem with their clinical colleagues practicing psychiatry in jail and prisons where, in fact, they are required to predict violence and suicide. This is paradoxical as well as hypocritical. These pundits neglect the very basis of diagnosis which has prediction embedded in it. "For what purpose is differential diagnosis, if not at least partly, to predict clinical course and treatment response?" asks Donald Klein, a dominant figure in the field of treatment science and a prime mover in the improvement of diagnosis and our understanding of psychiatric illness for over half a century. His pioneering work applying both psychological and pharmaceutical approaches to therapy has become standard procedure in the treatment of psychiatric disorders and chronic emotional distress (Klein and Wender 1982).

Like the metaphor of national security threats and preparedness after 9/11, do we simply let life take its course, suffer, and die? Not with cancer, heart disease, infections, and strokes, but that is essentially what has happened in public psychiatry. The courts have seemingly taken the position that aberrant behavior, if not specifically diagnosed by neurology as a disease of the brain, is always a person's choice, either learned or simply idiosyncratic, thus not medical but subject to the law only, and people are dying in great numbers as a result. Suicide now exceeds motor vehicle accidents as a cause of death, and our military veterans and service personnel are committing suicide at the rate of 22 per day, almost one every hour. Almost as seriously, suicide attempts and other forms of violence threaten to drive up cost of health care.

In southeastern Michigan this prevalence has been labeled "The Hidden Epidemic," by the *Detroit Times*, because it cost $42.3 million to save those who try to kill themselves in just one metropolitan area. This cost for medical treatment to spare life and function of suicide attempts alone, therefore, represented about 40% of the $210 million hospital bill to treat violence in Southeast Michigan during the 2 years of 1998 and 1999. Over 10% of direct hospital costs went to treating pediatric victims of violence, or $22.5 million, during 1998 and 1999. Violence against children, in fact, ranked among the top five causes of death for all children under 14, regardless of race. Bullet wounds also took a big share of the bill for hospital care in southeastern Michigan, and fistfights and beatings continue to keep hospitals busy and are the most common form of violence treated in the Detroit metro area. Fifteen years more, with the great recession bankrupting Detroit, has likely made these numbers look relatively small. Detroit has just emerged from bankruptcy, and we will see if that has any effect on the levels of violence there.

Nationally, 10% of homicides are committed by a small percentage of the few million of our population suffering from severe neuropsychiatric impairment and helpless in coping with even minor stresses of life, mostly in our downtowns. This is still a high number of people who are in great need of court-monitored case management under "assisted treatment," most often medicated with mood stabilizers, antipsychotics, or both (Torrey 2010).

## SUICIDAL EPIDEMIC ISSUES

We examine some of the medical and policy issues that we believe have contributed to what is nothing less than an epidemic of suicides and suicide/mass murders over the past 20 years.

## CORRECTIONS FACILITIES

Because of the criminalization of the mentally ill, dumped back into society by the courts and the states, police and corrections officers have become the primary guardians of the mentally ill, often to the detriment of those they are supposed to protect. The Cook County Jail, for example, is now our largest psychiatric inpatient unit nationally. Most police officers, like the deputies clinically evaluating Elliot Rodger, have little or no background in dealing with the mentally ill. There are newly formed special mental health police units in the LAPD and the Phoenix Police Department. Hospitals cannot find enough psychiatric beds to house the mentally ill, even for short periods. And the VA is still desperately trying to scare up the funds to hire more psychiatrists and mental health professionals to deal with the flood of psychiatric cases.

Psychiatry, and particularly preventive emergency psychiatry, has been pushed back into barely visible recesses of our health-care system like a shameful closet case, and the public safety is at risk from severely ill and dangerous individuals capable of committing, as we have seen, horrendous mass violence. They are a small percentage of the severely impaired neuropsychiatric population, but 5%–6% of millions is a lot of people who can do a lot of damage if simply left to their own accord, whether the school kid posting threats on Facebook or the homeless psychotic obeying his command hallucinations to push somebody off the platform into an oncoming subway train.

Pinel, an early founder of modern psychiatric treatment, was credited for removing the chains from seriously mentally ill patients at the Pitié-Salpêtrière in Paris circa the late 1700s. Now, however, public psychiatry has essentially been reset in this country to colonial America because of the criminalization of the mentally ill. For example, incarcerated at Riker's Island, homeless Marine veteran Jerome Murdough died of hyperthermia while on suicide watch for schizophrenia and bipolar disorder, a combination of diagnoses that makes no sense, other than diagnostic sloppiness or ignorance. Nonetheless, he was medicated, presumably with mood stabilizers and antipsychotics that made him more heat intolerant. Unfortunately, auditory hallucinations that drive autistic behavior–disruptive individuals to the jailhouse are treated now with solitary confinement, which makes their disease even worse. This is the practice of psychiatry in the cloak of Corrections Therapy. Murdough died a horrendous death. The Marine Corps is silent regarding his last tour of duty in Asia in 1975. New York City quietly settled with his family for over a million dollars, a sealed settlement, of course, so that nothing changes in the treatment of either the seriously mentally ill, homeless, or veterans neglected by our Department of Veterans Affairs (DVA).

## VETERANS AFFAIRS

The returning combat veteran population, many of whom are suffering from PTSD and TBI, absent health management or support from the VA, are a public health and safety crisis today.

Most veterans lacking timely and easy access to care are dumped into the public safety net with little or no access to treatment or funds to sustain themselves. The Boise, Idaho, Chief of Police is one of a few leaders in the civilian community bringing this surging crisis before those in Congress, which has the power to do something. His letter addresses the issues of the massive, unrecognized, and untreated neuropsychiatric impairment from our war on terror:

> Dear,
> Several Boise Police officers were confronted recently by an armed man later identified as a military veteran. Issues revealed to myself, my officers and the community since then prompts me to share some concerns with you.
>
> On July 28, 2009, Boise Police responded to a call from a woman stating a man with a "machine gun" was at her front door demanding to be let in. Police dispatchers heard gunshots and the woman said the man had broken down the door of the apartment across the hall. As officers arrived, they heard another gunshot and saw the armed man ducking in and out of the broken doorway.
>
> The officers called to the man to peacefully surrender and tried to engage him in conversation, offering help if he would put the gun down. Instead the man used, what appeared to be "military tactics" and a bright light to spotlight the officer's positions and aim a handgun in their direction. Four officers fired. None of the shots hit the man as he used the doorway for cover. After the officers fired, the man surrendered.
>
> In a report released January 13, 2010, the Boise Community Ombudsman wrote: "Considering all that these officers personally witnessed and were told, any reasonable officer in similar circumstances would believe that his life, the lives of his fellow officers, and the life of the calling party were in immediate danger from a deadly threat. Given the totality of the circumstances and the subject's lack of compliance with repeated commands to show his hands and surrender, the use of deadly force in response to this imminent threat to human life was both reasonable and necessary."
>
> The armed man currently sits in the Ada County Jail awaiting sentencing on felony charges. He is George G. Nickel, Jr., 38, a decorated Iraqi war veteran. Unbeknownst to my officers at the time, Mr. Nickel is the sole survivor of an explosion in Iraq that killed

three other Idaho U.S. Army Reservists. Mr. Nickel was awarded the Purple Heart and Bronze Star for bravery in Iraq.

Mr. Nickel has also been diagnosed with traumatic brain injury and posttraumatic stress disorder from his time in Iraq.

Following the media publicity of Mr. Nickel's Iraqi war experience and subsequent revelation of his diagnosis, my office received numerous emails and phone calls from citizens and veterans groups highly critical of the officers' actions. Each citizen wanted to know how the officers could justify shooting at a war hero.

I responded to each call and email. I described our department's Crisis Intervention Team (CIT), a large group of officers specially trained to respond to individuals in emotional or mental crisis. I explained to the concerned citizens that we work with the Boise VA Hospital and local veterans support groups to identify veterans in need and connect them with those who can provide them with services. I also explained that, like our veterans, my officers have chosen to serve and protect their community, and that means taking decisive action when faced with an immediate and violent threat to themselves and fellow citizens. The officers did not know who Mr. Nickel was, nor about his military background, and Mr. Nickel's actions did not give the officers time to find out.

What I cannot explain is how the military identifies and treats psychological disorders, and why there appears to be a lack of such identification and treatment. Mr. Nickel's case may or may not be isolated. I have no way to track the number of veterans who, for any number of reasons, come into contact with my officers. I am aware of a recent case where officers were called to respond to a man later identified as a veteran, armed with a shotgun threatening suicide. Fortunately, that case was resolved peacefully. There are, however, indications that veterans struggling with war-related emotional issues are growing in number and severity. A recent study by the Veteran's Affairs Department (published by the Associated Press, January 11, 2010) shows the suicide rate among young veterans has increased significantly.

I have many veterans in my own police department. I share with them a pride in the service they delivered to their country and the service they continue to provide to the citizens of Boise. I also share with citizens a sincere concern for veterans struggling with combat-related disorders, who are in need of professional assistance and for whatever reason, are not getting it. I have been told by veterans, including my own officers, that there are perceived barriers within the military that inhibit individuals from self-disclosing emotional issues, ranging from fear of being labeled, to being passed over for promotion. Veterans tell me military evaluators screening those leaving the service are overwhelmed with sheer numbers, no time is made for thorough screens, and critical post-combat evaluations are offered but not required.

And sadly, the struggles don't appear to be new. Again, just within my own police department, an employee recently revealed the emotional struggles he was aware of with vets who served in World War II and Vietnam.

Whatever the issues and explanations, I am concerned that without more careful identification and treatment, these individuals may indeed pose a threat to their own safety and that of their families and community. My greatest concern is Mr. Nickel's case is not isolated, and other police officers, not only in Boise but in Idaho and across the nation will be forced to confront a troubled veteran with weapons drawn. Any or all those involved will be chastised for doing what they felt they must for self-preservation or public safety, and worse, the outcome will be lives lost.

One citizen who wrote me said, "These veterans are our people. We need to care for them like they took care of us!"

As a Chief of Police of Idaho's largest and Capital City, I urge you to work with all branches of our military, our Veteran's Affairs groups and VA hospitals, and strive to improve and expand the safety net that must cover our veterans. It is the duty of the country they served to now serve and protect them, and indeed enhance their opportunities as they rejoin civilian life.

Thank you for your time and service you give to the citizens of Idaho.

*Sincerely,*
**Michael F. Masterson**
*Chief of Police*
(www.police.cityofboise.org/home/news-releases/2010/02/chief-urges-idaho-congressional-delegation-to-enhance-services-for-vets/)

Chief Masterson was unaware of the true gravity of the situation at the time of this incident and letter, because the whistle-blower at the Phoenix VA Medical Center had not yet come forward with the fraudulent secret wait lists that proved to be system-wide in sweeping the true scope of the Department of Veterans Affairs' lack of preparedness for the injuries from this war. The double wait lists were used to show operational efficiencies that gained financial bonuses for administrators while hiding the true list that showed recklessly long lists for necessary treatments.

Chief Masterson is referencing the problems or potential problems of nearly 3 million young men and women having served multiple deployments, few of whom did not involve exposure to combat. Only a minority of these veterans receive diagnosis and treatment. One of them was Oscar Gonzalez, discharged at Fort Hood with partial service connected disability of $1600/month—not nearly enough to provide him with adequate shelter and support for his family—who became homeless and finally, in the ultimate explosion of paranoid fear, jumped the White House fence, staggering across the south lawn with one foot seriously blown to pieces from an improvised explosive device (IED) explosion. Like Miriam Carey, a postpartum psychosis patient shot by the Capitol police, Gonzalez was compelled to get "the message" to the president. Fortunately, the president and first family were not home, because Gonzalez got as far as the stairway leading to their living quarters in the East Wing with a knife. What he intended to do is unknown, except that he told the Secret Service he had an urgent message to deliver to the president.

Gonzalez was likely suffering from a malignant form of combat-induced PTSD and likely associated TBI similar to that described in the incident Chief Masterson cites in Boise. Although one of a small minority discharged from the military via a Medical Evaluation Board for PTSD and partial amputation of his foot, he complained of severe back pain and was on one of those VA wait lists before its fraudulent system of rejection was exposed at Phoenix VAMC, when he decided enough was enough. He moved into his car and headed to the White House to tell the president how bad things were.

Although the Secret Service gets much of the headlines on this case, the authors take it far upstream to Fort Hood, scene of two suicidal mass murders associated with deployment. One was perpetrated by Major Hasan, a military psychiatrist, who was being deployed, but should have been labeled "unfit for duty," especially because of his exchange of messages, involving the ethics and morality of jihadi suicide/murder, with a radical Al-Qaeda affiliated sheik, Al-Awlaki. These messages had come to the attention of Army brass, who allowed Hasan to continue in his post at Fort Hood. The Army's explanation for allowing Hasan to continue his messaging and to review soldiers before deployment actually defies credulity: they believed he was studying up on the nature of jihad and suicidal mass murder. The other Fort Hood alumnus was Ivan Lopez, also unfit for duty, whose discharge, unlike Gonzalez, was burdened with indecisiveness and dangerous delay to avoid a potentially expensive Medical Evaluation Board. Lopez, who claimed to authorities he had studied the Adam Lanza mass murder in Sandy Hook, attacked other soldiers at Fort Hood in a mass murder rampage.

Indeed, the Boise police chief is correct and might not know about the stack of files at Madigan Army Medical Center containing Idaho Guardsmen diagnosed with PTSD, facing possible alteration of their diagnosis to noncompensable diagnoses to save the government money on long-term disability payments. Nearly one million young men and women are at risk for being forced out with various discharges that deny them the benefits of treatment and long-term disability support for which they are entitled by their enlistment contracts. A corrupted system getting little attention is cutting that wait list also; that process in this case is claims denials and appeals. The longer the appeal, the more drop out—or drop dead or commit suicide at the rate of one per hour. We describe in detail below what is known about the plight of our veterans and the shear incapacity transformed into corrupt administrative practices and worse medical practices. We detail the solution that is urgent.

The Secretary of Health for our Department of Defense and the Secretary of the Department of Veterans Affairs are either knowingly or not charged with the responsibilities of operating two-headed monsters, neither tolerated nor legal in civilian health-care systems—that is, running a medical care system that is grossly understaffed and short of resources, while also judging the extent of long-term disability from war. This is not only a conflict of interest for these secretaries but a responsibility guaranteed to fail or end up in their forced resignations, one after another, just like the former DVA chief, General Eric Shinseki.

Military/VA health and disability services are run as if they are insurance companies, but they operate on faulty actuarial statistics from either misdiagnosis or avoidance of diagnosing the "invisible wounds of war"—namely, PTSD and TBI. Furthermore, as the nation just learned with congressional investigation of the fraudulent wait lists, they are insurance companies run on cost plus basis. The reserves are the maximum depths of U.S. taxpayers' pockets that can be emptied with political expediency.

Congress had better address the polite and salient pleadings of Chief Masterson. There are malignant cases of PTSD in the Idaho bush too—not just in Boise—cases in which victims can metastasize into self-destructive violence in the absence of treatment. The Idaho National Guard, for example, did a lot of heavy lifting in the War on Terror but has been ambiguously brought into the entitlement tent of their combat peers who were regulars.

We argue that claims examiners must be eliminated from DVA. Medical Evaluation Boards (MEBs) are not only costly, but they are ineffective. Oscar Gonzalez had an MEB, but Navy Yard shooter Aaron Alexis did not. Aaron Alexis was discharged with the delusion that his mind was under the control of low-intensity waves emanating from deep inside some bureau within the Department of the Navy. Without case management for his paranoid psychosis, he was given short shrift by the VA twice before taking matters into his own hands in what is now known as the Navy Yard shooting. It was more than that. It started with reckless endangerment in shooting out tires in Seattle, more reckless endangerment in the Navy—called "pattern of misconduct"—and culminated in a fraudulent discharge process negotiated with a mentally incompetent sailor who accepted an honorable discharge instead of a general discharge stripping him of VA benefits. It is the responsibility of the delegates of the Secretary of Health, Department of Defense to perform MEBs on obviously psychotic soldiers and sailors before dumping them onto Main Street United States. Gonzalez had an MEB. Alexis did not. What was the difference? Apparently none. Thus, the authors have advocated for the immediate cessation of disability exams in the military and VA. Instead the military should simply buy out the contracts of all soldiers recruited with entitlements that cannot be paid without bankrupting the Department of Treasury.

As the VA is already doing, let these discharged veterans get help immediately instead of in prison, jail, homeless shelters, gutters, or, worst of all, after they kill themselves, hopefully without taking anyone with them. The Marine Corps did not officially respond to the family's request for support of Murdough's burial after Rikers Island Jail baked him to death. Ideally, the settlement from New York

City should help them out. But this case points to the need for the government to weigh in immediately to prevent veterans from winding up on street corners or in jail. Veterans should not have to wait in line to sign up for Medicaid. They should be required to carry Platinum Obamacare fully paid for by the Department of Defense (Liebert and Birnes 2013). Perhaps the recently enacted Clay Hunt Suicide Prevention Act will help to ameliorate this situation of military veterans suffering from mental illness so severe that suicide seems their only option. We have to wait to see what the results of the act will be.

## SCHOOL AND CAMPUS PSYCHOTIC BREAKS

There is a generation of teenage and young adult children in college and high school suffering from unrecognized and untreated psychotic illnesses who have immersed themselves in the fantasy worlds of violent online gaming so as to earn psychological satisfaction and rewards from peers from digital perpetration of unbelievable acts of violence (Liebert and Birnes 2014).

Parents of the children killed in the Sandy Hook Elementary School massacre by Adam Lanza are suing, and unlike the two families whose children died in the Virginia Tech massacre who are suing the university, the Sandy Hook lawsuits seek to lay liability upon the defendant manufacturer of the AR-15 assault rifle, regardless of the immunity granted gun manufacturers by Congress, as well as the gun shop that sold the rifle that Lanza wielded. If the lawsuit is not dismissed and there is a settlement, that settlement may be sealed. We may never hear the real story, therefore, of Adam Lanza and his mismanagement, both in public elementary and high school, as well as the state university system of Connecticut, where he matriculated as a precocious student before dropping out. His evolving psychosis was managed as if he were simply a bit weird. The school psychologist was assigned to protect him from bullying, as he slid along the school corridors literally hugging the wall to protect himself from coming into contact with other students while, at the same time, clutching his computer to his chest to protect it as well.

Adam's mother, Nancy Lanza, was allowed to determine the nature of his case management, even though she was probably as delusional as her son. She made sure he knew how to shoot, took him to a gun range, and allowed him plenty of shots. He learned well. Lanza also was studious when it came to warcraft, learning anything he deemed necessary from researching the most grisly of mass murderers like infamous Anders Breivik in Norway and the Unabomber. He was allowed to live in total isolation in what became his basement man cave in Nancy Lanza's large New England colonial, its yellow imitation barn wood prettied up with decorations for the joy of Christmas, well back from the street beyond a broad grassy lawn. He communicated only online, even with his mother. Unlike some mass murderers, he did not need to learn combat skills online, because his mother believed in helping him feel like a man by taking him to the range and allowing him access to deadly weapons. Still, he was able to download the video game, *School Shooter*, in which he likely rehearsed for his rampage through the corridors of Sandy Hook Elementary School. He was allowed total isolation beyond that grassy knoll in Newtown to merge his psychotic mind within the only medium—online warcraft—that hooked his brain cells together, just like Cho did. And like Cho, Lanza studied up on the Columbine massacre along with many more suicidal mass murders since the Virginia Tech massacre. He had all day and all night to lose his mind in the insanity of mass shootings and suicide, all of which are in these games.

For very sick young people like Adam Lanza, there is no boundary between what is the illusion of the video game and his own reality. His mother, whom he had already informed that he could care less if she were gone, would be the first on his execution list. Sandy Hook Elementary School would be wiped out, like the helpless kids and adult patrons on Utoya Island in Brevik's wild game hunt for humans. Lanza performed the challenge of blasting away at people as if they were targets at a shooting range. Then he would commit suicide. Was this a game, or was it reality? From what the investigation has released to date, no professional seemed aware enough of his descent into extreme madness to ask. Or, when he became nonadherent with treatment, nobody was there to take over from a mother who now, in retrospect, was totally incompetent, if not merged psychologically in his psychosis with her own death wish. Shockingly, her estate on probate is $64,000—hardly enough to pay for residential treatment she had shared with friends as a possible solution to her son's growing threats.

The basic problems behind these school shootings and rampage murders continues to be obfuscated by researchers who simply do not believe seriously mentally ill patients can do anything like Cho, Lanza, or Aurora Colorado's James Holmes did, or that they were simply "bad" and not "mad." Except in the rampage murder at Northern Illinois University, which we cover below, none of the suicidal mass murderers were diagnosed before their rampages. Nonetheless, official reports and expert interviews with the press make claims based on their histories of mental illness, which essentially do not exist until after apprehension, if there is serendipitous survival, or upon informal suicide autopsy, if dead—the usual outcome (Liebert and Birnes 2014).

Many of these suicidal mass murderers, like Lanza, Holmes, and Rodger, had access to adequate psychiatric care that could have prevented their rampage massacres. Tucson's Jared Loughner, who shot Representative Gabrielle Giffords, is the only living witness to this testimonial to date, and perhaps Holmes will become one. But if only a small percentage of Americans believe that psychotic behavior and suicide is caused by genetically influenced diabolical learning of the brain's neurocircuitry, there seems little hope that public psychiatry will have any impact. We do not know about private psychiatry, because successful interventions are not reported. That means, as the Boise chief said, it is his officer's responsibility to care for the combat veteran in need. Similarly, with the scores of millions of American youth on campus today, it is considered first and foremost a security matter. In the wake of the massacre at Northern Illinois, where there was a robust history of psychotic illness from adolescence in the suicidal mass murderer, Steven Kazmierczak, a campus safety bill was introduced in Congress that included hiring psychiatrists to evaluate psychotic and suicidal students on campus. The bill died in Senate committee.

The frontline of care for students from Marysville, Washington, to Newtown, Connecticut, will remain the school nurse, some security people, and counselors with minimal training and experience in the management of serious mental illness. This will be occurring in environments where psychotropics are both misunderstood, or in amazing consensus, considered more dangerous than duration of untreated psychosis with their use (Liebert and Birnes 2011).

## GANG-RELATED MASS HOMICIDES AND ANTISOCIAL CRIMES

Conduct-disordered children too often find their best role model for success is the local gangster, oftentimes enforcing his mob from inside the walls of prison.

The plight of Central American children sent unprotected on an extremely dangerous trek the length of Mexico to escape the violence of cartels in their homelands, now has this nation on the ropes fearing they will staff gangs on our own streets. Anyone doubting the police are at war with street gangs missed the recent news of 100 people being shot in Chicago over the July 4, 2014, weekend, most victims being tagged from rival gangs encroaching on others' turf or threatened with extortion that's called "insurance" in the ghetto. Additionally, most of those surviving are too scared to testify.

Like the violence in the Gaza strip, where the local fighters know the terrain and the populace better than the Israel Defense Forces (IDF) and, so far, to Mayor Emmanuel's dismay, are able to hold it against the law enforcement authorities trying to wrest control back to the city. But this is not a decades-long war between citizens of warring peoples, like Israelis and Palestinians. These are kids and young adults who aspire to the same good life in America we all do. It is hard to convince them to stay in their apartments, go to school hungry, and see their families and friends fighting off rats in the hallways when the local street lord pays them $5000 a day to sell drugs and pimp for him.

Child psychiatrists used to call this Conduct Disorder, Socialized Type—as compared to Conduct Disorder, Non-socialized, which we witnessed on the video of CHP Officer Andrew's punching Marlene Pinnock in the face. Was the group of officers from NYPD immobilizing and killing Eric Garner the flip side of the same coin as Andrew and the CHP with Marlene Pinnock—or—Conduct Disorder, Socialized Type? Many experts in psychiatry and clinical psychology would look at it that way, as vulnerable egos merge into collective brutality under stress, as in the atrocities of war.

## INNER CITY SYNDROME

Robbery and assault victimize 3% of Americans every year, and Inner City Syndrome, an indirect health-care cost, has been introduced as a psychiatric defense in felony cases. In fact, violence is apparently so prevalent in urban America that researchers studying the impact from terror of the Atlanta Child Murder Case in a multicity study were unable to differentiate Atlanta's inner-city cohort from control communities not having a child killer on the loose, whether the Atlanta Child Murderer Wayne Williams, Milwaukee's Jeffrey Dahmer, or a hate group like the KKK. Most robberies are drug associated and, therefore, preventable. For $5 billion, enough substance abuse slots could be created to absorb the 80,000 convicts now on waiting lists. They will strike again and, if for the third time, will be wards of the departments of corrections for life. They oftentimes go hand in hand with conduct disorder easily identified and diagnosed by school psychologists with validated testing requiring parental and teacher cooperation. Most criminal offenses today are associated with substance abuse and or illicit drug trafficking. Consider the costs to the noncriminal insured in higher premiums, as taxpayers and metro hospitals cited in the Detroit News study, "Bullet wounds take a big share of bills," for hospital care in southeastern Michigan, and "Fistfights, beatings keep hospitals busy...and are most common form of violence treated." The costs only took into account public expenditures without assessing third-party insurance payments.

## ATTENTION DEFICIT DISORDER

Attention deficit disorder (ADD) afflicts over 20 million Americans in the United States. With few exceptions, as in brain injuries, attention deficity-hyperactivity disorder (ADHD) is a congenital disorder of cerebral dysfunction, formally known as cerebral dysfunction syndrome. Most of these children will not recover, and residual attention deficit disorder will afflict them in adulthood. Of all adolescents with well-diagnosed attention deficit disorder, 50% are arrested for a serious offense, and 25%–45% are arrested for multiple, serious offenses. Conduct disorder in childhood, usually associated with comorbid attention deficit disorder, frequently progresses to antisocial personality disorder in adulthood, generating a prevalence of over 6% of antisocial personality disorder in our population.

Research demonstrates that aggression can be reduced in 60% of this adolescent population. Chronic depression in the mother, spouse abuse, bad schools, and delayed diagnosis in early childhood—all remedial—predict a bad outcome—oftentimes incarceration. A small minority of Americans incarcerated in prisons and jails do not have attention deficit disorder, but state authorities discourage prison doctors from examining for it. Attention deficit disorder is not a difficult diagnosis with current real-time diagnostics. It is a controversial diagnosis, which, when made in childhood, places demands on our schools, but ultimately saves both child and adult lives. Furthermore, when identified in the adult male patient, along with history of childhood conduct disorder, it greatly reduces the risk of imminent violence after release from points of entry to the health-care system. In the female patient, identification with appropriate treatment can dramatically and effectively reduce the morbidity of chaotic family lives they too often create.

Such epidemiological knowledge is imperative for best practices of emergency psychiatry for all those required now to practice psychiatry and clinical psychology on the frontlines. The street landscape of destructive behavioral processes on which you walk, therefore, is, on average, worse than threats of accidents. An increasing number of young black males are being killed, particularly in the inner city. Direct treatment costs for gunshot wounds alone in this country have doubled since 1990 and now exceed $20 billion; this is probably way understated in the latest annual FBI crime statistics, due to underreporting. In the nation's capital, an African American youth has a 10% chance of being shot before turning 18. He has a better chance of protecting himself anywhere as a soldier in the war on terror than within the few miles' radius of our national congressional offices. Homicide is the most common cause of death among black males ages 15–24.

Behavioral neurologist Gary Tucker found high percentages of brain injury and seizure disorders in the prison population, even before they were filled with combat veterans and seriously mentally ill patients with psychoses. Many of the latter cohorts also had high risk for brain injury. Marvin Wolfgang's study of a cohort of 10,000 young males in Philadelphia found that one-half were arrested, and then one-half were rearrested (www.icpsr.umich.edu/icpsrweb/RCMD/studies/7729). Ultimately rearrests cleared all but a small percentage of young offenders from serious crime. Most of the serious violent felonies were caused by a tiny fraction—about 100—of the original cohort. Although this study seems to run parallel to arrest rates with well-diagnosed ADHD, no correlation has ever been found between the two cohorts studied. In fact, no correlation has been examined, because the first arrest with ADHD is not dependent on socioeconomic class. The second, however, is, suggesting that third and subsequent arrests could hold a very high number of youth with undiagnosed ADHD. This is unlikely to be studied, because prisons, even when under court order to examine inmates for psychiatric impairment, do not include ADHD as an index neuropsychiatric impairment.

Although frequently missed as a diagnosis in higher socioeconomic cohorts of children—particularly girls—it is missed en masse in the lower socioeconomic cohort, which is a high percentage of Wolfgang's recidivists. The ultimate correlation between ADHD, antisocial personality, and psychopaths is unknown and unstudied. Thus, we do not know how many of the serious offenders in Wolfgang's research had ADHD. We do know that there is a genetic transmission of antisocial personality disorder from father to son, which disorder can manifest, according to epigeneticists, depending on the nature of the stimuli that the son encounters. Daughters, interestingly, are not antisocial but suffer Briquet syndrome with multiple and debilitating physical complaints. This cohort of peculiar genetic transmission is too small to draw any conclusions, other than speculating that there are conduct disordered children without ADHD who become hard-core, destructive sociopaths. The explanation for the lack of interest in government and academia for such research could, however, lie with the Congress's choking off funding to research into violence, which research was high on the agenda of then Surgeon General Satcher.

Satcher generated significant research before the alleged lobbying efforts by National Rifle Association (NRA)-sponsored politicians fearful that correlation would be proven between violence and gun ownership and by authorizing such research would get a negative rating from the NRA. In other words, the gun manufacturers, for whom the NRA lobbies, feared a negative impact on their bottom line. Therefore, any science about a correlation between firearms and violence was chucked out of Congress like a piece of garbage. However, if we are to recapture the streets from gangsters so that good community policing can protect the innocent forced to reside there, we need such translational research informing on epidemiology of injury and death from unremitting clinical states of human destructiveness. Similarly, the Emergency Medical Services (EMS) legislation made possible by Surgeon David Boyd, must at least be read by politicians before all the hype over Ferguson and West Baltimore results in worse reinventions of the wheel.

We take heart attacks and strokes as part of the responsibilities of EMTs when calling 9/11. What is unknown, however, is that behavioral emergencies were given equal status for translational research and operational interventions, just like heart attacks. But, for David Boyd's category of behavioral emergencies, although prophetically foreseen by Boyd—a surgeon—as a necessary component of emergency medicine and public health and mandated by law, Congress chose not to fund them as a necessary equivalent to cardiac emergencies. Again, the distortions of public perception of aberrant behavior as possibly a product of neuropsychiatric impairment from diabolical learning in the neurocircuitry of many brains, is another foundation stone for much of the death, injury, and psychological trauma of violence in this country, whether suicide, apparently pure violence itself, or murder-suicide, including the current epidemic of suicidal mass murder (Liebert and Birnes 2011).

In light of court decisions, such as the *Lessard* ruling in Wisconsin, and in light of not only the lack of public funding for public emergency psychiatric services, as well as the "new age" denial of the existence of mental illness itself, we find ourselves in a bind. Worse, those tasked to protect society are at a loss to develop coping mechanisms to replace public psychiatry as caretakers of the seriously mentally ill. Are the mentally ill on the streets dangerous? Do they pose a threat to police or to civilians? What types of force can police use to restrain them from causing harm? Is lethal force ever required? What training should police have and should the state provide for the management of the mentally ill?

What we have found, and what we shall explore, is a huge gap between what many in the psychiatric community know and what they can offer to first responders, both in law enforcement and in emergency health care. This is tragic because lives are put in jeopardy every day by those individuals who, because of a mental illness, are divorced from reality, cannot comport their behavior to the strictures of the law, and often cannot understand why police are confronting them. Hence, it is the purpose of this book to close this gap.

## DOCS VERSUS GLOCKS

There was a time in the 1980s when the Center for Communicable Diseases under Satcher funded a productive division that studied violence as a public health issue. And the late Everett Koop, also as Surgeon General, found that violence was a public health issue as well. No more. The NRA took care of that. Congress has all but shut down such research in fear of linkages between easy access to the most lethal of firearms and violence be discovered. This indirect suppression of translational research by well-funded gun lobbies obstructs clinicians in preventing injuries and deaths from violence in their practices. It pales, however, to the Florida Privacy of Firearm Owners Act, signed by Florida Governor Rick Scott in June 2011 and subsequently upheld by the 11th Circuit federal appeals court as a legal restriction imposed by the state on the medical profession. This law prohibits doctors from asking families about access to guns in their homes, the intent of which is really to prevent family practice physicians and pediatricians from discussing gun safety with families. It is as if a misinterpretation of the Second Amendment has trumped content-based freedom of speech from government control under the First Amendment. This Florida law, on its face, seems to violate flagrantly the basic principle of the First Amendment, which protects the freedom of speech from government regulation by any state actor, especially when it comes to the content of that speech, a very strict standard set forth by the U.S. Supreme Court. At least 10 other states have introduced similar bills, but none have passed. In the dissenting opinion in the 11th Circuit, Judge Charles Wilson called the law an infringement of First Amendment rights. "The act prohibits or significantly chills doctors from expressing their views and providing information to patients about one topic, and one topic only, firearms," Wilson wrote. "Regardless of whether we agreed with the message conveyed by doctors to patients about firearms, I think it is perfectly clear that doctors have a First Amendment right to convey that message" (www.politico.com/story/2014/07/federal-court-upholds-florida-docs-vs-glocks-law-109403.html and www.politico.com/story/2014/07/federal-court-upholds-florida-docs-vs-glocks-law-109403.html#ixzz3Z6nfjpdw).

In essence, the 11th Circuit erred by using a backdoor argument to create a second class of citizens in Florida to whom First Amendment rights do not apply. If a hypothetical Joe the Bartender asked one of his patrons, "what kind of guns is your kid hunting with these days? Keep them at home?" Nothing prevents him in advance from asking that question. But if a psychiatric pediatrician asks the same exact question of a parent, he or she could lose his license to practice medicine. Does this infringe upon the Second Amendment's "right to bear arms" clause and is the pediatrician a federal or state actor to whom the Second Amendment applies? Of course not, and as such there is no Second Amendment issue despite the frantic cries from the gun lobby. But does a content-based advanced prohibition against speech by a nonstate actor infringe upon that actor's right to free speech? Absolutely, even though the 11th Circuit's decision is disingenuously couched as a regulation of medical practice. It has created an entirely new class of citizens who do not have the same free speech rights as other citizens not in their class.

Insofar as the 11th Circuit legalized the creation of a second class of citizens that do not have the same equal protection under the law as other citizens not in their class, the court has formalized the state's violation of the Fourteenth Amendment guarantee of equal protection under the law. If Joe the Bartender is protected by the First Amendment to ask a patron about gun ownership, so should Pam the pediatrician be guaranteed the exact same freedom regardless of her profession and the nature of her inquiry.

The court standard for infringing upon a citizen's rights under the First Amendment is to subject the government to a strict standard of scrutiny. In other words, the government must show the court an overriding compelling need to so infringe. In Florida, however, because doctors are not infringing upon a citizen's right to own and bear arms, the Second Amendment is not involved. Therefore, the state has no compelling need to protect the Second Amendment rights of its citizens and thus no compelling need to abridge the First Amendment rights of a particular class of citizens or to deny that particular class of citizens the same First Amendment protections as other groups of citizens.

All of the above are matters of law, not fact, and thus the 11th Circuit erred in its upholding of the Florida Privacy of Firearm Owners Act, which decision should, in a world not governed by the *Twilight Zone*, be overturned by the Supreme Court.

James M. Perrin, president of the American Academy of Pediatrics, responded to recent Florida appeals court rulings vetting the law, "State legislatures should not stop physicians from practicing good medicine. This law has a chilling effect on life-saving conversations that take place in the physician's office. More than 4000 children are killed by guns every year. Parents who own firearms must keep them locked, with the ammunition locked away separately. In this case, a simple conversation can prevent a tragedy. The evidence is overwhelming—young children simply cannot be taught to overcome their curiosity about guns, and to suggest otherwise is, frankly, the height of irresponsibility."

Subsequently, American Medical Association (AMA) President Robert M. Wah also weighed in. "The AMA will continue to oppose governmental intrusions into the clinical examination room and calls on lawmakers to leave determination of what constitutes medically necessary treatment where it belongs—in the hands of physicians and patients," he said in a statement (Sutton 2014).

Florida doctors were urged by the Florida branch of the American Academy of Pediatrics to defy the appeals court ruling and continue best practices of asking about guns in the home. Lawyers are bogged down in this case, judging in the cool light of dawn how doctors' challenges to this law as infringement on their First Amendment Rights conflict with the Second Amendment right to bear arms, which should not be confusing because speaking about firearms is no infringement on the right to bear firearms. But the law simply does not pass the smell test, because why would anyone be afraid of doctors discussing guns at home with families unless the party is concerned, as in the shutdown on meaningful research on violence by Center for Disease Control and Prevention (CDC), that maybe there will be clear and convincing evidence that a gun in the home correlates with death and/or injury from violence, accidental, suicidal, or felony assault? Of course, there should be concern, because evidence is clear and convincing of such a correlation. Studies of violence comparing two demographically similar cities—namely Seattle and Vancouver, British Columbia—show overwhelming evidence that the statistically significant high rate of violence in Seattle, compared to Vancouver, correlates with gun ownership. There is no right to be in possession of a gun in Canada unless hunting, or, in extremely rare cases, where one is permitted to carry a concealed weapon. But beyond the correlation between gun ownership and violence in the home is the basic issue of a state's regulating speech by making certain content illegal: *ab initio* on its face violative of the First Amendment

The travesty of the Florida law and its negative impact upon public health and safety is even more a threat to best practices in psychiatry than pediatrics, because the highest lethality in psychiatric practice is suicide. Psychiatrists simply must know if there is a gun in the home of patients they suspect of being suicidal, because suicide, the 10th leading cause of death in America according to official public health records, takes the lives of nearly 38,364 for an incidence of 10.6 per 100,000 annually. Suicide now officially kills more Americans than automobile accidents, which killed 33,687 Americans in 2010. Deaths from motor vehicle accidents are accurate, but death from suicide is considered by most experts to be underreported. For example, how many single-passenger and wrong lane motor vehicle accidental deaths are completed suicides? Suicide autopsies are needed to provide insight into the state of mind in such motor vehicle deaths. Similarly many overdoses are likely suicidal but ruled accidental, whether illegal abuse or prescription medication misuse. We also need to dissect these national statistics to find trends within demographic groups. Here, there are alarming trends, particularly in the veterans' population which far exceeds most American demographic group trends.

## EPIDEMIC OF SUICIDE

"Suicide has typically been viewed as a problem of teenagers and the elderly, and the surge in suicide rates among middle-aged Americans is surprising. From 1999 to 2010, the suicide rate among Americans ages 35–64 rose by nearly 30%, to 17.6 deaths per 100,000 people, up from 13.7. Although suicide rates are growing among both middle-aged men and women, far more men take their own lives. The suicide rate for middle-aged men was 27.3 deaths per 100,000, while for women it was 8.1 deaths per 100,000" (Tara Parker-Pope 2013).

In the previous decade's report, there was actually a 1% reduction. Some experts speculated that the reduction was the more widespread prescribing of safer and more tolerable antidepressant medications. Less questionably, the suicide rate also correlates with gun ownership. States with high gun ownership, such as Wyoming, have a significantly higher rate of suicide than New Jersey, where there is far lower gun ownership. The correlation between completed suicides with rate of gun ownership in states can logically be explained anecdotally. A man deciding to shoot himself is likely to do it if he has access to a loaded gun. Similarly, the high rate of suicides in active duty military is partly due to their access to weapons, which they are by training, orders, or simply survival habit, likely to keep loaded and ready to fire in an instant. Many an intoxicated man, whether soldier or civilian, will decide to kill himself but not be able to find the means. The next morning he awakens trying to remember why his cupboards and drawers are open. He was prowling the house in a drunken stupor trying to find a gun. He's sober now and not suicidal. The argument that suicide is such a rare event that it is unpreventable is simply rhetorical and is not supported by the facts. Suicide is nearly as common a cause of death as accidents, statistics show. Should we simply put St. Christopher on our dashboards and pray, or start examining public safety crises involving guns as public health crises?

## CRIMINAL JUSTICE AND PSYCHOLOGY

We argue that there is a vital psychological component to interactions between law enforcement/emergency responders and the public, especially members of the public who are either mentally ill or on the borderline between eccentricity and psychopathological behavior. We argue further that unless the discipline of criminal justice recognizes that psychological component, we will see more tragic missteps in places like Los Angeles, New York, Cleveland, Baltimore, and Ferguson. These will result in more distrust between minority communities and the police, engendering the types of reactions that can turn the general public against the police, the first stirrings of which were evident in the shooting deaths of officers in Las Vegas and New York, also by mentally ill but politically deranged individuals. We, therefore, argue not only for better training protocol, but for an understanding that sometimes a citizen may not be able to react to a police command because of a mental illness, which was clearly the case of Marlene Pinnock resisting CHP Officer Andrew's commands in the midst of rushing traffic on a busy Los Angeles freeway.

Here is the problem we face in a nutshell: the law enforcement authorities can only enforce the law in a free society with the consent of those whom they expect to obey the law. Anything less means that the society is no longer free. As Americans we expect nothing less and will put up with nothing less. Thus, watching an unarmed person posing no threat being killed by the bare hands of a swarm of police officers who continue to crush him while he pleads for his life; watching a woman pummeled viciously into submission along a busy freeway; staring at the image of a man's body being left out uncovered in the middle of the street while local residents complain is not just wrong; looking through the aperture of a police body camera lens as a homeless man camping out in the New Mexico desert and being shot to death after surrendering to police rubs against our very grain as Americans regardless of any explanation authorities concoct. Heaven help us if the population itself turns on those we elected to govern. Heaven help us if the social order breaks down because the authorities hired by those we elected to govern are viewed as threats and not protectors. We are seeing this now through the lens of the camera.

## THE NEW NEUROLOGICAL PARADIGM: THE REWIRING OF AMERICA

Amid the spate of what look like police lethal overreactions, of rampage suicide/mass murder school and workplace shootings, of untreated veterans suffering from unremitting states of despair as they decompose, of brutality perpetrated in prisons and violence in hospital emergency rooms, and amid recurring stories of airline pilot suicides, commentators are looking for answers. Unfortunately, they do not come easily. We argue that part of the problem is not just that society is changing all around us, but that we are witnessing an entirely new paradigm shift in the human neurological matrix.

Perhaps beginning with television in the 1950s, but quickly evolving to video games in the 1980s with the advent of the personal computer, and advancing into avatar-driven violent shooter games in the new broadband millennium, our children are rapidly becoming transformed into clients of digital servers, communicating with each other in 140-character Ruby language code, moving their digital images across bloody battlefields, and unleashing their innermost ideations of violence and threats into a world of like-minded server clients. We are both desocializing and resocializing our children at the same time along with ourselves.

But if commentators believe that all this is only taking place inside a digital video matrix, they are wrong. What we learn online, we do online, we bring to life from online. As the famous psychologist Donald Hebbs once said, "neurons that fire together wire together." In essence, as neural networks assemble themselves to allow players to participate in a digital matrix, those very neurons rewire the human matrix itself. As a result, we have new generations of individuals, now reaching the ages when they can wield real, not digital, weapons, who are unloosed on society. Attempt to manage this, however, and we run head on into the freedom of speech and right to bear arms amendments of the U.S. Constitution. Now what do we do? This is one of the problems the authors address in the chapters that follow.

## THE CAMERAS ARE ROLLING

We live in the age of the smartphone camera whose lens sees everything, an age in which a simple police misidentification, which might have been the case in Cleveland, is immediately converted to an Internet meme once the video is uploaded, displayed on YouTube, and spread around the world on Twitter. There is nothing under the radar anymore when it comes to police and public interactions. This is why, to prevent missteps and misunderstandings, to preserve lives, to protect both the police and the public, and to protect the very fabric of American society itself, we need an understanding of the basic psychological issues that inform every instance of police and emergency responder interaction with members of the public, because these interactions are the potential flash points that can turn the public against those hired to protect it.

## REFERENCES

Halleck, S. L. 1971. *Psychiatry and the Dilemmas of Crime: A Study of Causes, Punishment and Treatment.* New York: Harper and Row.

Halleck, S. L. and Bromberg, W. 1968. *Psychiatric Aspects of Criminology.* Springfield, IL: Charles C. Thomas.

Klein, D. and Wender, P. 1982. *Mind, Mood and Medicine: A Guide to the New Biopsychiatry and Understanding Depression.* New York: Meridian Books, New American Library.

*Lessard v. Schmidt*. 1974, 1975, 1976. 349 F. Supp. 1078 (E.D. Wis. 972), Vacated and Remanded, 414 U.S. 473, On Remand, 379 F. Supp. 1376 (E.D. Wis. 1974), Vacated and Remanded, 421 U.S. 957 (1975), Reinstated, 413 F. Supp. 1318 (E.D. Wis. 1976).

Liebert, J. A. and Birnes, W. J. 2011. *Suicidal Mass Murderers*. Boca Raton: Taylor and Francis.

Liebert, J. A. and Birnes, W. J. 2013. *Wounded Minds: The Menace of Post-traumatic Stress Disorder*. New York: Skyhorse.

Liebert, J. A. and Birnes, W. J. 2014. *Hearts of Darkness*. New York: Skyhorse.

Monahan, J. 1994. *Violence and Mental Disorder: Developments in Risk Assessment*. Chicago: University of Chicago Press.

Parker-Pope, T. 2013. Suicide rates rise sharply in U.S. *New York Times*, May 2.

Perez, E. and Jaffe, A. CNN, February 19, 2015, on CNN.com

Schmidt, M. S. and Apuzzo, M. 2015. South Carolina officer is charged with murder of Walter Scott. *New York Times*, April 7.

Sutton, C. 2014. Physician groups slam 'Docs vs. Glocks' ruling, *Tampa Bay Times*, July 28.

Szasz, T. 1974. *The Myth of Mental Illness*. New York: Harper and Row.

*Tennessee v. Garner*. 471 U.S. 1 [1985].

*Terry v. Ohio*. 392 U.S. 1 [1968].

Torrey, E. F. 2010. *Assisted Treatment*. Treatment Advocacy Center.

Wolfgang, M. Delinquency in a birth cohort in Philadelphia, Pennsylvania, 1945–1963. www.icpsr.umich.edu/icpsrweb/RCMD/studies/7729

# 2

# A brief history of managing the mentally ill

We refer to psychiatric traumas resulting from combat, such as Posttraumatic stress disorder, as "invisible wounds of war." The operative descriptor here is "invisible." We cannot see the wound. It does not bleed, is not a palpable bruise, and cannot be reset like a broken limb. But it is nevertheless as painful and as debilitating as a wound from a piece of shrapnel tearing through flesh. The invisible nature of the wound is important as it relates to the entire field of study regarding mental illness. Before modern imaging instruments, psychiatric illnesses were indeed invisible to the naked eye and only identifiable by trained medical personnel who recognized the symptoms. But that does not mean that psychiatric illnesses were nonexistent before Freud. They were simply classified as something else and treated by sequestering the patient, often under the most brutal of environments.

During the Renaissance in England, the most infamous holding facility for the mentally ill was St. Mary's of Bethlehem, whose name was phonetically syncopated to "Bedlam," a term used in modern English to describe often violent chaos. More like a prison than a hospital, St. Mary's of Bethlehem kept patients chained, often ill fed, taunted, and when unfettered, allowed to abuse one another as they were abused by their wardens. Bedlam became a descriptor in Shakespeare's England for a chaotic violent environment, often used comically because the mentally ill were considered to be laughable fools.

Before the French Revolution of the late eighteenth century, psychiatric patients who could not adapt themselves in society were detained in lunatic asylums and restrained with chains. The inflection point of modern psychiatry was the unchaining of these patients by Pinel et al. in the Pitié-Salpêtrière during the French Revolution. Pinel demonstrated that these patients actually could return to the community without threat to society. Of interest is the fact that despite the appalling conditions and management of these patients in the asylums of the eighteenth century, these people were segregated from criminals, although nothing was done for them, except segregation from society.

Moral therapy took over, and the legendary earliest psychiatric leader in America, Benjamin Rush, began the psychiatric institutional movement in America that led to severely disabled patients becoming wards of the state. Rush was a founding member of the Philadelphia Society for Alleviating the Miseries of Public Prisons, known today as the Pennsylvania Prison Society, which greatly influenced the construction of Eastern State Penitentiary in Philadelphia. He took patients from that drudgery and placed them in a "normal" hospital setting. This alone resulted in a number of patients recovering sufficiently to return to society. For this reason his approach is officially referred to as the moral therapy. Rush is sometimes considered a pioneer of occupational therapy, particularly as it pertains to the institutionalized.

In *Diseases of the Mind* (1812), Rush wrote: "It has been remarked, that the maniacs of the male sex in all hospitals, who assist in cutting wood, making fires, and digging in a garden, and the females who are employed in washing, ironing, and scrubbing floors, often recover, while persons, whose rank exempts them from performing such services, languish away their lives within the walls of the hospital." Rush is sometimes considered a pioneer of occupational therapy particularly as it pertains to the institutionalized. In honor of his service to mental health, the American Psychiatric Association uses Rush's image as part of their seal.

By the middle of the nineteenth century, a new movement was underway in Europe and America in which researchers tried to figure out the nature of how what was unseen in the human psyche influenced what was clearly observable. This movement to understand the unseen was not limited to medicine, though. It spread across all disciplines from physics to art to literature as well as to a new science of psychology. From a purely medical diagnostic perspective, researchers sought to explain how aspects of a patient's mind that we could not readily see could be ascertained through a patient's behavior, his or her dreams and memories, and any physical manifestations, such as psychosomatic symptoms. Mesmer, Freud, and Jung were pioneers in this new field of medical science, and their work with patients influenced not only medicine in the twentieth century, but the entire field of human behavior, bringing what had been considered spiritual affliction in the seventeenth century under the scholarly microscope of medical science. By the 1950s, psychology had become part of American culture.

Today, however, we are witnessing nothing less than a counterrevolution in how society deals with the population of the mentally ill, a politicalization of medicine. This is exemplified, in one instance, by the life and death of a mental hospital and the policy rationale for it. This represents the counterrevolution sweeping the nation in the name of fiscal responsibility, more appropriately known as cost shifting from one bureaucracy—Department of Health and Human Services—defeated by political authority to another bureaucracy—Department of Corrections. Any relationship to actual fiscal responsibility, such as, for example, saving the taxpayer any money, is purely accidental. Prison construction and the empire of state corrections boomed with, for a specific example, the closure of Northern State Hospital in Washington State which represented a pre-nineteenth-century type of management of the mentally ill that has been booming under the judicial and philosophical cover from denying the existence of mental illness, the Thomas Szasz argument, now cloaked under guise of fiscal responsibility. If there is no such thing as mental illness, then the mentally ill are not ill, but, rather, criminals who need to be incarcerated because they present a danger to others.

The history of Northern State Hospital is detailed in *Under the Red Roof* (McGoffin 2011) as an example of how treatment of the mentally ill has changed under the rubric of fiscal responsibility. A well-respected state institution for the seriously disabled psychiatric patient that extended Benjamin Rush's revolutionary transformation of public psychiatry from imprisonment to active treatment was closed for financial reasons in 1973. This hospital, under psychiatrist Saul Spiro, had a training program for psychiatrists and incorporated the contemporary medical treatment of psychiatric disorders, including medicating patients with antipsychotics like Thorazine. It was well respected within the Washington State psychiatric community, and its closure in 1973 was bitterly fought out between then State Director of Health and Human Services, Charles Morris, and the Washington State Psychiatric Association.

According to M. J. McGoffin, Morris was brought in from New York to cut state budgets for management of serious psychiatric illness. The closure was abrupt and extremely dehumanizing of the most helpless; patients were inhumanely placed in buses and sent to Seattle in their hospital gowns where they were expected to cope for themselves. Morris expressed no concern for the fate of these helpless and sick people, by now dependent on the institution for their basic needs, although likely, in most cases, functioning vocationally and socially at their highest possible levels at Northern State. Morris was popular with state treasurers anxious to move tax revenue from what was considered dead money in caring for the least able of our society to the general budget that was discretionary and under the governor's control for either pet projects or simply campaign purposes.

"The eventual closure of Northern State Hospital in 1973 was a political decision driven by tight budgets and a focus on forensic populations in other state hospitals. The occasion marked by a busload of elderly, institutionalized chronically mentally ill people delivered to the streets of Seattle with only their original belongings and hospital issued clothing. What became of them may be in a sense unknowable once they were divorced from the community able to care for them." (Tom Read, science-medical writer, 1973).

In its heyday, when society's answer to the mentally ill was to stick them as far out of sight as possible, there was a patient population of 2700 at Northern. The beautiful campus snuggled against the Cascade foothills had its own farm and provided much of its own food. Two things changed all that. Society found a conscience and realized the mentally ill have rights, especially rights to treatment—not just custody. And several medical breakthroughs in the 1950s introduced drugs that could support a disturbed person and help lead him back into society. Patient populations and length of stay started skidding at that point.

Last year metropolitan Seattle's King County was removed from Northern's "catchment" area and 150 patients were transferred to Western State Hospital in five months. As it became apparent that Northern no longer was serving at full capacity, plans for alternate use were developed and put forward by legislators from the four counties it serves—San Juan, Island, Whatcom and Skagit. It was this alternate use that the legislature approved and Gov. Evans vetoed. Under the plan, Northern would have continued as a limited mental hospital, would have continued geriatric services, mental retardation training and alcoholism treatment center. In addition, certain functions already there in leased quarters would have remained. These include two Headstart classes; a department of Public Assistance Office, Sedro-Woolley Senior Citizens Center; an Adolescent Center for the mentally retarded; a sheltered workshop for the trainable mentally retarded; a family planning clinic, and a homemakers' program for women on welfare. The functions, not directly related to the hospital, will remain. A total of $500,000 has been appropriated to maintain the grounds and provide heat. Similar attempts in California to close mental hospitals and shift patient care onto community mental health systems is failing there and may portend failure in Washington State, too.

In the wake of the closure, symbolic of retrenchment in mental health facilities around the country, the state of Washington has given grants to the nearby counties to bolster community mental health centers. Whatcom county in Northern's cachment area was given $200,000, as was Snohomish while Skagit county was given $100,000. In theory, the discharged patients who still require medication and treatment from time to time will receive it at these centers. For those who live in remote areas, a traveling team is envisioned but it is not clear if or when this part of the program will develop.

Morris represented the application, which we argue is dehumanizing, of the concepts of Patient Throughput and Optimization of patient flow, a modern concept under the Affordable Care Act (ACA). But his management process predated the ACA by 50 years. Although the fate of Morris's victims in the arbitrary and chaotic closure of Northern State Hospital is generally reported to be unknown, one of them who had done well there ultimately jumped from a high-rise office building onto a busy downtown sidewalk of Seattle just as offices were closing. His brother committed suicide by walking in front of a city bus. We do not know the fate of those uprooted from their institutional dependency under the red roof of Northern State Hospital, but we know what happened to these two. How costly were just two such horrible suicides and are there others out there who could decompose mentally into potential suicidal mass murderers absent the institutional protection of the hospital? Recent suicidal rampage murders in metropolitan area are strong evidence that there are.

Morris has never made such calculations in his literature following the closure of Northern State Hospital and his retirement. Although Morris never anticipated the fate of patients, he was unwavering in his decision to close Northern State and was uncompromising in the numerous meetings held with him by the Washington State Psychiatric Association. In retrospect, regardless of his personal beliefs, Morris proved an iconic figure of what was to come later—mainly the deinstitutionalization and criminalization of the seriously mentally ill.

All the progress made from post-revolutionary American Psychiatry by another iconic figure in American psychiatry, Benjamin Rush, was erased with the stroke of a pen and cold determination of political expediency, and it was not just in Washington State. Under President Reagan, hundreds of thousands of patients would hit the streets nationally in the 1980s, and only those adjudicated criminally insane after an act—most often murder—would be institutionalized. Ironically, so was President Reagan's would-be assassin, John Hinckley, found not guilty by reason of insanity and soon likely to be released. The rest would have to fend for themselves. Morris was the model. He took on organized psychiatry and arbitrarily and unilaterally returned it to the era of Colonial American punishment of the severely ill psychiatric patient. He proved it could be done. Other states would gain confidence for starting their own shell games, robbing departments of institutions of the billions considered necessary for care of the seriously mentally ill and transferring the proceeds to the general fund. States were almost totally out of the game for the care of the seriously mentally ill and ferociously resist getting back in.

Politicians simply do not understand the nature and history of psychiatry, and they relegate it to the darkest corners of something mystical. They cringe in fear at the image of the catatonic patient who could go from quiet concentration on the chess board to catatonic fury, flipping the table and sending the volunteer to the floor at Northampton Veterans Affairs' (VA) hospital in 1955. Swarmed with white-coated men more suited to the linebacker corps of University of Massachusetts than a therapy environment, Duke, the patient, was bundled in a straight jacket, dunked in ice water to cool him off, and put to sleep with barbiturates.

The tunnels of Verdun Protestant hospital in Montreal were even worse in 1961. Patients grotesquely lay in rancid conditions, gesturing in bizarre fashion to McGill medical students being introduced to their clinical rotation in psychiatry. A professor would put four of them on a stage and demonstrate all the classical psychopathology. He raised the arm of one, and the arm stayed up, motionless. "This is the waxy flexibilitity of catatonic schizophrenia." He then stood beside a man giggling one minute and crying the next. "This is schizophrenia, hebephrenic type." He stepped back from the next man scanning the audience with obvious fear. "This is schizophrenia, paranoid type." Finally, and most mercifully, there was a very pale and frail appearing man who simply sat expressionless, seemingly disengaged from the world. "This is schizophrenia, simple type."

Fortunately, within a couple of years, such bizarre behavior, known as positive signs of schizophrenia, would be hard to find. McGill Psychiatrist, Dr. Heinz Lehman had imported a new drug from France after it was found to turn agitated mice into tranquil animals, seemingly uncaring of their environment. But, unlike Duke's ultimate fate of sleep therapy, they remained awake—just calmed and "tranquil." This was Largactil, now known as Thorazine. It promised miracles—a cure for schizophrenia. It was a miracle, in that patients were not as bizarre and autistically preoccupied by their delusions and hallucinations. It was, however, no cure. All these patients would remain seriously disabled. They were "neurolepticized"—that is tranquilized. As long as they had their medications on a regular basis, they would not suddenly flip the card table over and knock the poor volunteer to the floor.

Straightjackets disappeared, but electroconvulsive treatment would not. It was still necessary on the treatment-resistant cases, but it would become less cruel in its use, sometimes, as in the Catholic Saint-Jean de Dieu Hospital, punitive for aggressive behavior. Patients could be sedated so that they did not feel the shock; their limbs paralyzed with curare-type medication to prevent convulsive spasms and injuries to their arms and legs. Most patients could be moved out of those tunnels and caves of Verdun Protestant and into case-managed outpatient care.

On campus at the Montreal Neurological Institute, secrets of the human brain were being revealed by Wilder Penfield's mapping of the cerebral cortex with electrical stimulation of specific regions of the cerebral cortex in the awake patient. Odd it was, the top of the brain that controlled the toes; the human skeleton was upside down and contralateral on the cerebral cortex. One tiny area, Broca's area, was necessary for speech. Promise was palpable on the McGill Faculty of Medicine Campus. There might not be any aberrant human behavior untraceable to a small nucleus of neurons that could be altered either medically or surgically.

Penfield was interested in epilepsy. Were the bizarre behaviors of schizophrenia electrically traceable to specific areas of the brain? What chemicals were involved in transmission between the billions of neurons in the brain? Harold Jaspers would discover the surprising reciprocal innervation. Some transmission would stimulate a neuron, while another transmission would inhibit it. The brain was extremely complex, but it now could be understood. What McGill needed was a psychiatrist interested in discovering and exploring the secrets of the brain's working as applicable to mental illness, a psychiatrist who would work with the neuroscientists at the Montreal Neurological Institute.

What they got, however, was a plant from the Rockefeller Institute—an individual who did not consider it necessary—or possibly advisable—to share his work with neighboring peers from his redoubt named the Allan Memorial Institute. Dr. D. Ewan Cameron occupied this old steamship owner's mansion and turned it into his own laboratory for experimenting on patients. His treatments were crude efforts to rewire the brain his own way. Cameron destroyed the promise of a consensual study of the brain and its abnormalities in all neuropsychiatric disorders for a team of neuroscientists gathered under one roof, perhaps once in an era. Ewan Cameron, ultimately to be found guilty of brainwashing private patients supported by research funding vicariously routed from the United States intelligence services under the auspices of the Central Intelligence Agency's (CIA) MK-ULTRA program. The heyday of McGill neuroscience was severely tarnished, its greatest neuroscientists sucked into the web of suspicions. Progress in neuroscience was set back decades by the intrusion of Cold War brainwashing experimentation contaminating a unique team effort to discover the cause of neuropsychiatric impairment. Only now are we getting back to where we left off when the Allan Memorial Institute was convicted of brainwashing experiments on patients not given informed consent regarding the procedures Cameron would use on them.

In the universe of psychiatric pharmaceuticals, Thorazine worked with the most grotesque signs of schizophrenia in McGill's other affiliated psychiatric hospital, Verdun Protestant, under psychiatrist Dr. Heinz Lehman. His humane and well designed research translated across national and state borders, and soon there was hope that patients could be deinstitutionalized and live more normal lives with families. But, this could happen only if they could be trusted to take their medications, an issue called "adherence" poorly understood in the initial days of the introduction of Thorazine at McGill. Charles Morris seemed to be indifferent to this anomalous finding in these patients, who usually thought they did not need them. The side effects were also uncomfortable. But, it was full steam ahead for closing institutions because of Lehman's successful introduction of Largactil into North America, thus lulling local governments into a false belief that the drugs were miracle cure-alls allowing them to save money by closing institutions.

The ostensible reason for closing mental hospitals and mainstreaming the mentally ill to save the taxpayer money. It did not work—just the opposite, because the costs of deinstitutionalization would soar but their accounting tracks would prove untraceable. What did it cost to care for a patient in Northern State Hospital for 20 years versus the costs of suicidal rampage murders in Seattle by psychotic men whose families could get them no care decades later? Many of the mentally ill released under Morris's plan likely ended up in prison, even though he was warned this would happen when confronted face to face with just such a specter by experienced psychiatrists knowledgeable about those psychotic patients who were suicidal and dangerous.

Two thousand miles to the east in a suburb of Milwaukee, a schoolteacher would flee in terror under command hallucinations from what she believed to be President Nixon's goons. She was completely insane. Dangling from her apartment, Alberta Lessard would be rescued and committed to the local psychiatric hospital. The two graduates from University of Wisconsin law school appointed by the court to represent Lessard who had challenged her involuntary commitment, read their first psychiatric book—and the only one they admitted to having read. It was *The Myth of Mental Illness* by Thomas Szasz. They took on the delusional Alberta Lessard and defended her from imprisonment by convincing the federal judiciary that there was no such thing as psychiatric disease. They convinced the federal judiciary that psychiatric diagnosis was simply a myth created by medical professionals choosing to specialize in psychiatry to line their pockets by labeling eccentric people with aberrant behavior as medically based. Thus, the court, agreeing with Lessard, established a new standard for commitment based on the concept of imminent dangerousness to others and to self. And this has become the standard, a standard based on the theory that mental illness is not real. Where Charles Morris had reason to close Northern State Hospital so as to save money by medicating patients in the cheapest apartments in the worst parts of town, he now had justification to simply let them go to prison, because under Lessard they were not even sick—just eccentric criminals.

Medic One and the Emergency Services Act would soon come to Seattle at the end of the decade. Under nine categories David Boyd included in the legislation passed by Congress and signed into law by President Ford, behavioral emergencies were included with equal weighting to strokes and heart attacks. This category was not funded, however. As a result, the state hospitals were closed, and the patients were remanded to the streets and to jail, where many ultimately died. The Lessard decision justified this now obviously catastrophic political decision by criminalizing the patients. Finally, behavioral emergencies were not even matters for emergency medical personnel, but, rather, the police. Everything was in place. Deinstitutionalization of the seriously mentally ill now labeled the most severely mentally ill as criminals instead of patients.

Community mental health centers, born of President Kennedy's personal family tragedy of his sister Rosemary's psychiatric disability, would soon be shuttered in the wake of JFK's assassination, a sequelae of deinstitutionalization and criminalization of the mentally ill captured by E. Fuller Torrey in his manuscript, *American Psychosis*. Torrey parallels the death of Community Mental Health to the death of Rosemary Kennedy in private care at a residential care facility in Wisconsin. In just a matter of less than a decade, everything accomplished by leaders from Benjamin Rush to Saul Spiro at Northern State Hospital was gone. Young psychiatrists do not even remember long-term hospital care, community based care, or relative ease of involuntary, if not always well-supervised, legal treatment of the seriously mentally ill. With all the tools of modern psychopharmacology and neurobiological treatments, like deep brain stimulation, their patients are in emergency rooms, fortunate to even have the rare crisis beds for emergency psychiatry. More likely, they are now in jail, prison or homeless on the street.

The money saved by Charles Morris in Washington State was siphoned off into the state department of corrections and governor's general fund. New prisons would be built to house them, they were also built to house victims of the failed "War on Drugs." Portending to be the paragon of civilization in this violent and troubled world, the United States now has more of its citizens in prison than any other nation on earth, and the numbers keep going up thanks to failed federal and state policies for diagnosing, treating and managing the seriously mentally ill and drug dependent populations of our society. We are in a new millennium for almost everything in America, but for public psychiatry we are back in Colonial America and prerevolutionary France. Who are these people with known neuropsychiatric impairment and chronic psychotic diseases? We do not even have a name for them anymore, but in public psychiatry they should be known as "subjects." Their standard of care is certainly not deserving of the identity of a patient, because that assumes medical treatment. Patients like Marine veteran Murdough, who was baked to death in solitary confinement at Rikers Island, are the norm now. Would he have been better off in chains than on psychotropic medication in solitary confinement in jail? Arguably, yes.

With serious mental illness manifesting annually in hundreds of thousands of fulminating psychotic breaks in adolescence and early adulthood—along with the additional burden from neuropsychiatric impairment emanating from a surge in the numbers of geriatric depression and dementias threatening almost epidemic proportions as the Baby Boomers advance into their seventies, the

United States, with its crippled public emergency psychiatric preventive health system, is at risk of being overwhelmed with psychiatric-related crime. And as we wring our hands over the recent murder of three young Muslim students in Chapel Hill, North Carolina—wringing them in concert with pundits who scream "hate crime" from their microphoned pulpits—we should at least pay lip service that the heavily armed perpetrator of this crime might be so insane that the least little infringement upon his sense of paranoid territoriality, focused as it was on a parking space, was enough to set off a mass murder spree. And this may only be one of the early indicators of the surge that is to come, a surge, in the absence of public emergency preventive psychiatry, that will overwhelm our emergency responder services.

## MENTAL ILLNESS AND THE AMERICANS WITH DISABILITIES ACT: *THE CITY OF SAN FRANCISCO V. SHEEHAN*

Passed by Congress and enacted into law by President George H.W. Bush in 1990, the purpose of the Americans with Disabilities Act (ADA) was to protect those with disabilities against discrimination from the government, in public facilities, and in the workplace. Among the various types of physical disabilities covered by the act, including diabetes, the act also covers individuals suffering from mental illness. The act stipulates that a mental illness is a disease that substantially limits one or more of the major life activities of an individual, an individual who has had a record of mental illness, or an individual whom others recognize as having a mental impairment. A mental impairment itself is defined as any "mental or psychological disorder, such as mental retardation, organic brain syndrome, emotional or mental illness, and specific learning disabilities."

Under Title II of the act, state and local governments and the federal government are prohibited from discriminating against any covered individual in the delivery of government services. And this stipulation has become one of the arguments in a California case now at the Supreme Court. In City and County of San Francisco, California et al., *Petitioners v. Teresa Sheehan* (2014), Sheehan was shot by police after she threatened them with a knife after they broke into her room at a group home for the mentally ill. They were responding to a call from her social worker who said Sheehan had threatened to kill her with a knife and then locked herself in her room. The police were asked to transport Sheehan to a hospital for treatment. Sheehan survived the police shooting and then sued them for failing to take into account her mental disability under the terms of the Americans with Disabilities Act, which requires public officials to make reasonable accommodations for people with disabilities. Sheehan argued that police, who were informed that Sheehan was mentally ill and were specifically dispatched to deal with her, should have used all reasonable means to avoid a violent confrontation before drawing and using their weapons. Their failure to do so, Sheehan argued, was a failure to provide those accommodations. The trial court held for the officers. The Ninth Circuit Court of Appeals, however, held, on Fourth Amendment search and seizure grounds, that because the police entered

Sheehan's room forcibly and without a warrant, there was a question of the constitutionality of their entrance. The court recognized that Sheehan, though in the midst of a violent outburst, nevertheless was still accorded her constitutional rights to privacy in the "sanctity" of home and that even though they were called to help her, that did not mean they could transform the intended benefit into criminalizing the mentally ill individual through the use of force and lethal force.

The particulars of the case were that the officers summoned to help the social worker and restrain Sheehan did not have a warrant to enter Sheehan's room. They had called for backup but did not wait for backup, thus exposing themselves to Sheehan's delusional rage after they violated her privacy by breaking into her room. Sheehan retreated into her room after telling the officers she did not wish to be transported to a mental health facility, barricading herself in her room after closing the door behind them and threatening the officers with a knife. The court wrote that the officers, now out of the room, called for backup, "but rather than waiting for backup or taking other actions to maintain the status quo or de-escalate the situation, the officers drew their weapons and forced their way back into Sheehan's room, presumably to disarm, subdue and arrest her, and to prevent her escape (although there do not appear to have been any means of escape available). Sheehan once again threatened the officers with a knife, causing the officers to shoot Sheehan five or six times."

Though the court found that the officers' initial entry into Sheehan's room was a reasonable exception to the Fourth Amendment requirement for a warrant because they were responding to what was deemed an emergency rescue, their secondary entry into the room, whether an emergency or not, was a matter of triable fact. The court held, "We nonetheless hold that there are triable issues of fact as to whether the second entry violated the Fourth Amendment. If the officers were acting pursuant to the emergency aid exception, then they were required to carry out the search or seizure in a reasonable manner. Similarly, if they were acting pursuant to the exigent circumstances exception, they were required to use reasonable force. Under either standard, a jury could find that the officers acted unreasonably by forcing the second entry and provoking a near-fatal confrontation. We therefore cannot say that the second entry was reasonable as a matter of law." Simply stated, the lower court erred in dismissing Sheehan's case because it was not a matter of law that the police were exempted from obtaining a warrant for their second entry. Whether or not their second entry was legal was a matter of fact to be heard by a finder of fact, in other words, the trial court. Therefore, the case had to be returned to the trial court to be heard.

The appeals court also held that because Sheehan had retreated into her room, she was no longer presenting a life-threatening danger to the police, whether or not the shooting was lawful in response to a threat was, again, a triable issue which should have been heard at the lower court. They held, "We further hold that there are triable issues of fact as to whether the officers used excessive force by resorting to deadly force and shooting Sheehan. The shooting was lawful when viewed from the moment of the shooting because at that point Sheehan presented an immediate danger to the officers' safety. Under our case law, however, officers may be held liable for an otherwise lawful defensive use of deadly force when they intentionally or recklessly provoke a violent confrontation by actions that rise to the level of an independent Fourth Amendment violation." Thus, because Sheehan presented a triable issue, that issue should have been litigated by the lower court and not dismissed. That dismissal was a trial court error of law, which the appeals court overturned.

Sheehan's social worker, who called the police, told them that he had filled out an order for a 5150, the 72-hour detention for observation under California law, and showed the officers the order he had filled out. He said she had been off her meds and was acting violently. However, she had no means to escape her room and the premises had been emptied, which meant that she was actually not a danger to anyone else. But when they confronted Sheehan, she said that absent a warrant and absent a subpoena, she wanted to be left alone. This, the court held, should have required a warrant.

After the officers reentered Sheehan's room and found themselves confronted by an angry, knife-wielding individual, they tried to subdue her with pepper spray, but Sheehan, though falling to the floor, still held the knife. She said that although she told the officers she was blinded, they started shooting her. She testified that she had already fallen when an officer fired the final shot. Thus, she said, she could not possibly have been a threat requiring the response of lethal force. She was tried on criminal charges, but the jury hung on the assault charges and found her not guilty on making threats to the social worker. San Francisco elected not to retry her.

In the court's opinion, "Sheehan then filed this 42 U.S.C. § 1983 action against the City and County of San Francisco, Police Chief Heather Fong, Sergeant Reynolds and Officer Holder, alleging violations of her Fourth Amendment rights against unreasonable search and seizure, including a warrantless search and use of excessive force. She also alleged violation of her rights under the Americans with Disabilities Act and state law claims for assault and battery, negligence, intentional infliction of emotional distress and violation of California Civil Code § 52.1. The district court granted the defendant's motion for summary judgment and Sheehan's timely appeal." (ibid).

Although the city claimed sovereign immunity, the court found that immunity does not apply when the city, through its actors, in this case the police, violated the constitutional rights of the claimant. Hence, Sheehan's claim was not barred by immunity. The court then held that although the initial entry into Sheehan's room was reasonable as an exemption to the Fourth Amendment requirement for a warrant, as was the second entry, the use of lethal force by the officers was an issue to be decided at trial. Thus, a trial court should hear Sheehan's claim, the court held, and the trial court's dismissal was reversed.

As to the question of police requirements when dealing with the mentally ill, the appellate court relied on a report presented by expert witness Lou Reiter, a former deputy chief of the LAPD, in which Reiter, described general police practices for dealing with persons who are mentally ill or emotionally disturbed, explaining that officers are trained not to unreasonably agitate or excite the person, to contain the person, to respect the person's comfort zone, to use nonthreatening communications and to employ the passage of time to their advantage. He also cited materials used by the San Francisco Police Department to train officers on 'appropriate tactical actions' to be used when confronting the mentally ill. These materials, which are germane to the excessive force inquiry because they were designed to protect individuals such as Sheehan from harm, see *Scott v. Henrich* (1994), advise officers to request backup, to calm the situation, to communicate, to move slowly, to assume a quiet, nonthreatening manner, to take time to assess the situation and to "give the person time to calm down" (ibid). Reiter further said that there was "no logical reason that the officers did not pull back from the landing outside Ms Sheehan's private residence after their first attempt to enter. The location was a tactical disadvantage for the officers. Both officers knew that Ms Sheehan had refused their entry and made specific comments regarding the necessity for a warrant. They knew that other resources were en-route to their call for backup. Officer Holder's and Sgt. Reynold's [sic] continued conduct exacerbated the confrontation, rather than any effort to [defuse] the agitation." Hence, breaking into the plaintiff's room and shooting her five or six times was excessive force, particularly because it violated the department's own guidelines on dealing with a mentally ill individual.

The court then held that a "reasonable jury" could decide that the officers violated Sheehan's Fourth Amendment rights. Therefore, a jury should hear the case. As to the officers' qualified immunity, the court held that because the officers' second and forced warrantless entry into Sheehan's room with their weapons drawn and prepared to use lethal force and because Sheehan had posed no threat to escape her room or no threat to others, the officers were not protected by immunity and therefore were subject to Sheehan's claim at trial. And finally, looking at the issue of whether the ADA requires police officers, as state actors, to accommodate the needs of the mentally ill, the court held that Title II of the ADA applies to arrests by the police who fail to use accommodation in dealing with the mentally ill. Hence, Sheehan's claim under the ADA on the basis of her mental illness was upheld upon appeal. This is a decision that, unless overturned by the Supreme Court, which granted cert to the city's petition and is now hearing oral arguments, will have precedential value.

## REFERENCES

McGoffin, M. J. 2011. *Under the Red Roof.* Mary McGoffin Publisher, 156 pages.

*Petitioners v. Teresa Sheehan.* 2014. 743 F. 3d 1211—Court of Appeals, 9th Circuit 2014, www.scholar.google.com/scholar_case?case=16826381847214621786&q=City+of+San+Francisco+v.+Sheehan&hl=en&as_sdt=6,39&as_vis=1#p1216.

Read, T. 1973. Science-medical writer. A hospital is dying: A town is grieving. *APA Journal Book Review, Seattle Post-Intelligencer,* May 6.

*Scott v. Henrich.* 1994. 39 F.3d 912, 915-16. 9th Cir. 1994.

# 3

# The misleading statistics of violence and crime

## INTRODUCTION

For those living inconspicuous lives within expensive gated communities, the precipitous drop in the homicide rate in this country and downward trend in violence can probably be reason for comfort and hope. Do we stop recalling defective cars because accidental death is rare? Of course not, but where is the presence of the Centers for Disease Control and Prevention (CDC) for suicidal emergencies, and for behavioral emergencies in general, after the funding and implementation of the Emergency Medical Services Systems Act of 1973 (Boyd, 1983)? It's missing in action, and may remain so as long as gun lobby groups continue to assess the predilections of candidates for senior administrative positions in the public health apparatus using bizarre and biased forms of content analysis.

Although mass murder in this nation is not a new phenomenon, starting with the Richard Speck massacre of nurses in Chicago and the Charles Whitman massacre in the 1960s from the University of Texas Tower, it would, as with any theory of cyclicality of headline events, be irresponsible for both academics and public health and safety officials to simply try surfing the tides of history.

Although Grant Duwe's "A History: Mass Murder in the United States" (2007) provides an important backdrop for understanding "senseless" murders—particularly mass murders, as both cyclical in incidence and primarily familial in the past century—such historical determinism can blind us from malignant social trends. Awareness of these trends may allow us to reverse them, sparing life and severe disability in our youth, veterans, and mentally ill. Duwe suggests that the misperceptions about the phenomenon have occurred because claims-makers in the media report incorrect beliefs repeatedly, and ignore bold statistics demonstrating that the first wave of mass murder spanned the years 1900–1939, followed by a quiescence preceding the second wave beginning in the mid-1960s, almost a half-century before the Seung-Hui Cho murders at Virginia Tech.

Although important in terms of driving policy and investment in resources in both public health and safety, it is a bit like ignoring the impact of the Internet and migration of our population from farm towns to burgeoning cities, thence to the suburbs, on our economy over the past century. Are we to believe that major changes, such as renewed energy independence of the United States or the development of telecommunications, will have little impact on the business cycle, because our economy will cycle regardless of our energy policy or investment in engineering education? Rather than falling back on the Currier and Ives tradition of the family farm as central to our core social values each holiday season, we look at the modern urban or suburban family and pick up those trends in our advertising. Generally speaking, advertising looks forward and not backward, because advertising by its nature encourages consumers to inhabit the life it presents. Hence, social investment in the sentimentality of a bygone era at the expense of understanding the inbound migration to the cities and outbound migration to the suburbs amid accelerated technological change would doom us from a policy perspective with a skewed concentration of farm subsidies for smaller and smaller demographics, while ignoring preparation of our urban youth for a vastly different job market. It is not our purpose to examine the roots of mass murders in the society of our Great Depression leading up to World War II, and the apparent statistical drop-off with the start of World War II. We focus, rather, upon a new millennium whose public health and safety problems are determined by many glaring changes in our society that are likely uncoupled from Arnold Toynbee's deterministic theory of historical cyclicality.

We have a spike in suicides in baby boomers who grew up in the chaotic and oftentimes rebellious Days of Rage in the 1960s, a frightening spike in veterans' suicides, and a very menacing spike in school and campus mass shootings. We are now watching as a new form of suicidal mass murder creeps across social media. The incitement created by social media threatens to turn the silent and brooding hostility among at-risk adolescents, who need to identify socially, into acts of violent mass homicide.

Although it is doubtful that the incidence of psychotic illness has changed in this country or that the prevalence of neuropsychiatric impairment has moved much either way from the 22% discovered by Leighton in the Mid-Manhattan Study (Murphy et al., 2000), certainly the policies and management of both have changed dramatically. These policies and management are for the better with new and better psychotropic medications and the worse with an impassioned counterrevolution to their use on the growing numbers—if not percentages—of our population.

Subgroups of the cohort of 22% of populations of the developed world include millions of patients with chronic and severe psychotic illness like schizophrenia. The nearly 300,000 persons who experience their first psychotic break, particularly those of late adolescent and young adult populations inhabiting colleges and military bases, place a heavy burden on both families and communities. Children with school maladaptation problems can be identified early, and in most cases treated to prevent delinquency leading to criminality filling our jails and prisons, promising to make them worse.

One psychiatric diagnostic entity, Borderline Personality Disorder, is responsible for 6% of emergency room (ER) visits, most often from suicide attempts or other forms of self-harm, such as cutting. Ironically, many of these conditions have subtle, yet specific, brain abnormalities that are detectable with modern imaging studies. Dramatic improvements in effective treatments are being ignored by state and federal governments, who seem more interested in exiting the medical specialty of psychiatry to save money upstream in early identification and treatment. This exodus allows massive public health and safety problems from untreated psychiatric disorders to evaporate visibly downstream to a lethality of primitive management, recycling patients from homelessness to ERs to jails and prisons. In other words, failure to diagnose and remediate early will cost the public more money than it does now in public safety budgets, even though it is more politically correct to claim "law and order" rather than to diagnose and treat. Were patients with early signs of strokes managed in this way, the public would be up in arms. Despite the advances of modern medicine—including psychiatry and clinical psychology—political leadership to reverse trends in public health policy and practices in psychiatry, which could be used to reduce costly mortality and disability from crippling disorders of the brain, is essentially absent.

## COLD CASES OF VIOLENT CRIMES AS THEY RELATE TO CRIME STATISTICS

People are afraid of violence. The residents of one particular elderly couple's exclusive gated community on the Georgia seashore aren't complacent anymore. Random home invasions are purportedly rare, but not so rare that you need not take any precautions. On May 5, 2014, the body of 88-year-old Russell Dermond was found decapitated in the garage of his home in the Great Waters community at Lake Oconee. Eleven days later, two fishermen found the body of Dermond's 87-year-old wife, Shirley, near a dam at Lake Oconee.

This will likely become a cold homicide case. There is neither a single lead nor a motive in this case. There are nearly 200,000 official cold cases in this country. Homicides are rare, but should that number, when filtered through official crime statistics, make us relaxed? Only a fool would believe that, but there are fools who draw conclusions from the science of crime statistics based on felony violence pleaded out or resulting in conviction in a court of law. Only 10% of violent assaults result in arrest, and an even smaller percentage is reported, leaving a tiny fraction of violence parsed into federal crime statistics for purposes of reporting. Strange as it may seem, given the amount of money taxpayers pay for public safety, the statistical facts upon which taxpayers must base their lifestyle are about as valid for predicting their fate as statistics predicting the stock market from day to day. Will the recent July 4th, 2015 weekend in Chicago, when 100 people were shot, reverse the downward statistical trend for violent crime? Of course not, but for the people of Chicago who are in the line of fire, the crime statistics mean very little.

The case of the strange, extremely brutal, and likely cold double homicides of the Dermonds in Georgia is probably an anomaly in crime statistics for those

Table 3.1 Comparative statistics of selected violent crime types (per 100,000 population)

| Type | United States | Germany | Austria | England and Wales | Scotland |
|---|---|---|---|---|---|
| Forcible rape | 26.8 | 9.0 | 0.42 | 2.6 | 2.66 |
| Robbery | 113 | 64 | 9 | 64 | 20 |
| Aggravated assault | 241 | 88 | 47 | 157 | 117 |

fortunate enough to live outside urban areas in upscale gated communities that include both security and traditionally low crime rates. People, however, are still dying and being injured and scarred for life, both physically and emotionally, at high rates from violence in this country. Furthermore, our rates do not compare favorably with other developed Western nations (Table 3.1). Our latest official homicide rate of 4.7/100,000 is 500% higher than the likely more accurate official homicide rate in Germany of 0.9/100,000.

To complicate matters, homicide is likely underreported, as is suicide, because of the number of missing person's cases that are not cleared as either. Even missing persons reports are likely underreported because of the number of illegal immigrants in this country, and fear of the police among many constituent subpopulations in our society. Although violent crime has been trending down for a decade, it is on the rise again. Most importantly, our violent crime rate is in extreme misalignment with other Western developed nations whose official statistics are probably more accurate. We have a serious problem with both underreporting for purposes of official statistics to inform health and safety policies and the official fact that the United States has a huge problem compared to our peer nations. Comparing the U.S. violent crime rates to Germany, for example, the prevalence rates are extremely disparate in all categories.

Numbers as reported per 100,000 populations annually in 2010 by the U.S. Bureau of Justice and the European Sourcebook of Crime and Criminal Justice Statistics are given in Table 3.1.

Furthermore, we do not include assaults without weapons, which the *Detroit News* has reported to be one of the costliest of health-care problems for hospitals. Even so, our official assault rate is 300% higher than the official rate in Germany, which is probably more accurate and also includes assaults without weapons.

## CHILD ABUSE AND STATISTICS

Child abuse is violence, but it does not show up with specificity in Department of Justice violent crime statistics. The magnitude of this endemic injury to mind and body is greatly underreported. The underreported statistics reveal only the tip of an apparent iceberg of child abuse. Similarly we see trends. What has been endemic is likely epidemic. As in school shootings, arguments can be made that they are increasing with the attendance at school. If that were true, why would local police departments be training for them with SWAT teams since

Columbine? Of course, there is something new going on, something ominously visible as epidemic in proportion. In the cases of child abuse and intimate partner violence, awareness is certainly a factor in current opinions regarding their underreporting and in likely epidemic proportions also. Society is changing rapidly, and so are families as a consequence. With these changes come changes in injuries, both psychological and physical (Liebert and Birnes, 2014).

## INTIMATE PARTNER VIOLENCE

Intimate partner violence (IPV) is defined as actual or threatened psychological, physical, or sexual harm by a current or former partner or spouse, and is dependent upon neither sexual intimacy having occurred nor gender of partners. IPV affects at least 10% of Americans, or 30 million adult Americans annually. It is the epidemiological leads generated by these statistics that inform public health and safety research. Because of the prevalence of intimate partner violence, especially among returning combat veterans and even among some police officers who had served in our Middle East wars, this is no time to underfund violence and injury prevention research and development at the CDC. This is the time for translational research to address the problem as an issue of public health, because not only is IPV a crime, its effects on children in violent families damages them as they grow older and try to start their own families. We look at this in the same way we look at controlling any epidemic that threatens public safety.

There were only a few cases of Ebola in this country. Surely the threat of Ebola deserves the attention of our public health agencies, and so does violence. The numbers cited tell the story. Violence and suicide prevention deserve equal attention given to infectious diseases that often contain unambiguous pathology reports divulging causation in the form of a visible lesion. Nonetheless, there is an evidence-based emergency medicine presentation known as "assault." All of these numbers should be informing clinicians what to do at points of entry to our health-care system.

"Assault" has been endemic and a serious public health and safety problem. Now it is likely epidemic and so enormous an epidemiological threat, no longer can it be ignored by either politicians, officialdom, or clinicians at all points of entry to our health-care system. What about suicidal mass murders, which were rare before Charles Whitman shocked the nation, sniping at innocent people from the University of Texas Tower? Now they occur more than once a month, and school shootings so frequently that every school and police department trains for them.

Statistics tend to lull us into brain fog lethargy. They can be helpful of course, because they can indicate trends, but they always need to be put in context so that they don't become obfuscatory. For example, how do the medical diagnoses of injury and death in Detroit compare with the crime statistics? They should correlate 100%, but this is not an ideal world, in fact far from ideal. But, statistics are rarely challenged when they are official. They can lead to therapeutic nihilism in psychiatry itself, where academic pundits drown out voices to the contrary and claim rampage murders are rare, and behavior cannot be predicted.

If not, then simply dump everyone on the street from prison without assessing risks for reoffending. That is what happened in the horrific cases of ex-convict William Spengler's ambushing first responders in Rochester, New York, and ex-convict Alton Nolen's beheading rampage at his workplace in Moore, Oklahoma. Is that really what our society expects for their public safety and public health tax dollars?

Statistics pose the same challenge for police departments, especially officers on patrol on the lookout for suspicious behaviors along their beats. If they cannot predict anything either, then why pay the hundreds of thousands of dollars to put a single new officer in a patrol car for a year? Statistics make psychiatrists and police departments lazy, or they become nihilistic, which justifies moral turpitude. The statistics then spin the public relations of public safety. It is not public safety, but the sense of public safety. Are the violent crime statistics going down in Detroit, too, or do they not trap the escalating medical care costs in Wayne County for treating violence, whether from self-harm or harm to others? How was the Kansas City study constructed to conclude that regularly visible police patrols have no impact on crime in the area they patrol (Kansas City study on regular police patrols to reduce crime, 1974, www.ncjrs.gov/pdffiles1/Digitization/42537NCJRS.pdf)? That was a money saver, but was it a valid conclusion based on solid research? One could conclude from that study, along with the supposedly objective studies of Monahan, that patrol officers cannot predict behavior and prevent major felonies any more than psychiatrists and clinical psychologists can predict behavior. Public officials can take advantage of these studies and essentially hamstring neighborhood policing, which is expensive and troublesome, as the Garner on Staten Island, New York, and Brown in Ferguson, Missouri, cases show. They have hamstrung public psychiatry to the point where the attorney for Marlene Pinnock, a chronic psychotic patient, is her primary guardian after charges were filed against California Highway Patrolman Daniel Andrew. Andrew was seen on video beating the 51-year-old black female, allegedly to keep her from entering rush hour traffic. If statistics are not adequate predictors, but lull us into a belief that they are predictors, it invites the state legislatures, influenced by the gun lobby—or any other lobby—right into the examining rooms of physicians. They don't need to listen to professions after they've digested the executive summary of a statistical report.

## PREVENTATIVE DETENTION

The theoretical basis of preventive detention is built upon a legal construct of predicting imminent harm to self or others. Unfortunately, the nature of psychiatric illnesses often cannot discriminate with such precision between self-harm and harm to others. Those who are likely, because of mental illness, to harm others are just as likely to harm themselves. What is the likelihood of emergency exposure to this pathological destructive process on the front lines of clinical care today, whether the ER, jail, prison, or clinician's office? Is it much less than pulmonary disease? No. In fact more people are disabled from violence and die from murder and manslaughter than from all pulmonary diseases combined. "The $210 million hospital bill to treat violence in Southeast Michigan during 1998 and 1999 ... is only a sliver of the region's actual medical bill for violence. The records that area hospitals supplied to The Detroit News for this analysis did not uniformly include two of the most expensive health care costs, doctors' fees or pharmaceuticals" (Liebert and Birnes, 2011, p. 130).

More problematic is the fact that national crime statistics inform us to relax a little, because the violent felony rate is decreasing. Is that true in Detroit or Chicago, or in impoverished neighborhoods in any of our large cities? How aligned are FBI national violent crime statistics with actual hospital ER diagnoses of assault? Because so few violent felonies are reported to the police, whether or not they are documented by a doctor, and just as few reach plea agreements or convictions in court, the "big data" can be dangerously misleading, resulting in cutbacks in both public safety and public health investments in prevention of injuries and death caused by both suicide attempts and assaults.

Moreover, statistics demonstrate that an active destructive clinical process can rarely be dissected between harm to others and harm to self. The epidemiology looks at the sentinel act; therefore, statistics are either for suicidality or violence. Don't let these separate figures lead you to believe that any of the individuals from these cohorts have not been in both states of mind. It is likely that most have, but were simply clinically trapped in only one of them. Statistics robustly support evidence-based response to both danger to self and danger to others as merging states of mind across the same continuum of human destructiveness. Our nosology confuses us in a potentially dangerous way by constantly dividing violence and suicidality into separate items. In the real world of such poorly defined nosology, such division is not that simple. In fact, it robustly demonstrates comorbidity of violence and suicidality. This is the best of evidence-based medicine you can go with. Suicides and violence are more often than not comorbidly intertwined, although not necessarily always contemporaneously. For that reason, we discuss encounters with violence and suicidality together, as they are best seen as pathologically destructive behavior divided only by technical nosology.

Only a small percentage of patients committed for harm to others were not also suicidal. Population-based studies support this finding, because suicide attempts increase in frequency not only with substance abuse and mental illness, but also with violence. For example, Ismaaiyl Brinsley, the New York suicide murderer who recently killed police officers Ramos and Liu in Brooklyn, made at least two suicide attempts: one right in front of his girlfriend whom he eventually shot before he fled Baltimore for New York, and then he shot himself in the head standing on a Brooklyn subway platform as police closed in. Steven Stack reported that for a one-unit change in the subculture of violence (quantified) index the risk of suicide rose 3.1% (2012). For this reason the term "unremitting clinical states of human destructiveness" is frequently used to represent more accurately the statutes regarding our failed civil laws for involuntary commitment.

### Case study

JK was nearly murdered in a final domestic violence episode in 1989 and was admitted to the hospital for multiple traumatic injuries following multiple presentations at the ER over the years. She had been knocked out with loss of consciousness numerous times. She started using opiates and cocaine to suppress flashbacks, not knowing that they were symptoms of a psychiatric disorder treatable by medication and psychotherapy. She had stopped shooting heroin and cocaine for 7 years. Approaching the silver anniversary of her close encounter with murder in 1989, she started abusing methadone and crack cocaine. After she saw her boyfriend discovering her paraphernalia, she took his 45-caliber handgun, smashed his office window, and tried to shoot him. The safety was on, but she did not know that and kept squeezing the trigger. He chased her home, where he found her in bed trying to shoot herself.

The caveat is: Don't waste time dissecting danger to self and danger to others in emergency psychiatric presentations. When one does that, one will miss JK and many, many others who are in an unremitting clinical state of human destructiveness. Focusing upon one, while neglecting the other, may be a form of medical negligence. In most clinical disciplines, there is a rule to actually prevent medical negligence: "Think like a lawyer, be a lawyer." Practice defensive medicine so that all the aspects of a range of diagnoses are covered. The frontlines of acute and emergency psychiatry today are increasingly dominated by the courts. Involuntary psychiatric treatment units are underwritten and controlled by the courts and legislatures, for example, like in Florida, increasingly penetrate the examining rooms.

Many readers of this article are expected to be trained in criminal justice with less training in clinical disciplines. It is the purpose of this discussion; therefore, to return ethical practices to all front-line professionals responsible for taking care of the seriously mentally ill. Since *Schmidt v. Lessard* 414 U.S. 473 (1974), courts have paralyzed clinicians into withdrawing from decisions to intervene in preventing disasters emanating from unremitting clinical states of human destructiveness, whether more apparently suicidal or more apparently homicidal.

### Additional case studies

This man was more apparently suicidal than violent toward others, but he certainly endangered lives:

> Authorities tracked down a man reportedly armed and making suicidal threats Saturday afternoon and stopped him on Loop 303, blocking the freeway in both directions for almost 5 hours. Just before 2 p.m., Frank

> Schultz, 86, was making suicidal threats at his home when he took off in his vehicle, according to Maricopa County Sheriff's Office spokesman Christopher Hegstrom. Schultz headed south on Loop 303, where deputies and Department of Public Safety officers were able to stop him near Camelback Road, Hegstrom said. He refused to exit the vehicle, and authorities believed he was armed, Hegstrom said. Loop 303 was blocked in both directions between Camelback and Bethany Home roads. At about 6:25 p.m., Schultz was taken into custody without incident, Hegstrom said. No one was injured, and Schultz did not have a gun, authorities said. He is facing two counts of aggravated assault, police said.

In another case, this man was more apparently homicidal. Police obviously questioned whether he was caught in the act of committing a crime, or appearing to have committed a crime, to get shot to death by the police.

> A man was shot and killed in Phoenix early Sunday morning in the area of Northern and 35th Avenues after he fired at police, according to an official. Police responded to a group of condos in the area after receiving a burglary call at about 2 a.m., said Sgt. Steve Martos, a Phoenix police spokesman. When officers arrived, they noticed a man on top of a shed who appeared to be trying to enter or leave a condo on the second story of a building, Martos said. Officers also observed the man was armed. The man did not comply with commands from officers and proceeded to jump off the shed onto the ground. Martos said police believed the man fired shots at officers who then returned fire at the man, hitting and killing him. No other residents or officers were injured during the shooting, according to Martos. Police are investigating the situation and working to determine if the man was in fact burglarizing residences in the area.

The above two cases occurring on the same day in Phoenix highlight the significance of suicide by cop in which an obviously suicidal individual commits suicide by posing a threat or committing an actual assault upon a police officer that causes the officer to shoot him. Thus, what may look like a crime is actually a suicide in which the police officer, in the act of defending himself, is the instrument of that suicide. This is an increasingly recurring crime even when the perpetrator takes his own life as police close in, as in the case of Ismaaiyl Brinsley in Brooklyn, New York. The problem with this type of crime is how it's statistically categorized. It's not necessarily a mass murder if fewer than three people are killed, and more confounding is that it recently had to be four killed. If the officer shoots the perpetrator, can we categorize it as a suicide? Probably not, according to the Federal Bureau of Investigation (FBI). If the perpetrator shoots and wounds the officer, which happened recently in Ferguson during the demonstrations there, is it an attempted homicide on a peace officer even though the individual may have suicidal intent? Suicide by cop is a real crime that needs to be looked at in a separate category and statistically monitored.

## THE *TARASOFF* DECISION

The medicalization of serious mental illness and violent crime has been so publicly demeaned and minimized by pundits from Szasz's "Myth of Mental Illness" to the federal judiciary in the *Lessard* case in Wisconsin, that it is time to hit the refresh button and look at the California Supreme Court decision in the *Tarasoff* case (*Tarasoff v. Regents of the University of California*, 17 Cal. 3d 425, 551 P.2d 334, 131 Cal. Rptr. 14 [Cal. 1976]). In essence, the court in California held that a mental health practitioner, in this case working for the University of California, had a duty to warn and a duty to protect a potential victim from a potential perpetrator of a violent crime who posed a threat to the potential victim, even when disclosing that threat may be a violation of the doctor/patient privilege. Failure to warn or protect would make the practitioner liable for damages in negligence. In Liebert and Birnes (2011), we provide a detailed explanation and history of criminalization of serious mental illness and explain in detail the ramifications of the *Tarasoff* decision. The California Supreme Court, in contradiction to the experts responsible for deinstitutionalizing the seriously mentally ill, ruled health practitioners are nevertheless responsible for the activities of a patient when he or she poses a potential threat.

The justices involved in the *Tarasoff* decision argue for common sense, and ruled that clinicians have "Peculiar Ability," meaning an ability singularly relevant to the expertise of clinicians that enables them to both know what the problem is and how it will unfold. They held that Tatiana Tarasoff would likely be killed by patient, Prosenjit Poddar, and like contagious diseases, such knowledge demands control, for which "psychotherapists," like doctors diagnosing infections, have the power to do.

The recent case of a 62-year-old man admitted through the ER of a suburban St. Paul, Minnesota, hospital highlights the realities of our current frontline of health care. It is being pushed deeper into the wards of hospitals, once considered secure and safe havens for clinicians and patients alike. After 3 days in a medical unit for evaluation of rapid-onset paranoia and confusion, Charles Logan became delirious and attacked nurses with a metal bar. The nurses suffered serious injuries. Another patient who was post-op came out of his room at 2:00 a.m. to witness his nurses lying in a pool of blood, and their assailant running down the hall in a hospital gown. There was no security visible. The patient was ultimately stopped on the street outside the hospital and tased. The Taser did not work, so he was taken down by the police. Reentering the ER, he was pronounced dead. It was as reported, "Behind Maplewood incident, a rising trend of hospital violence: State is seeing a record number of assault claims" (Olson, 2014). In fact, ERs are one of the most dangerous workplaces in the nation, second only to mines.

## ALTERED STATES OF CONSCIOUSNESS AND DEMENTIA

Altered states of consciousness are increasing in frequency, both within hospitals and outside. There are many reasons for this. There are eight million head injuries per year in the United States; the average cost per injury is approximately

$10,000—or, nearly $80 billion per year. Additionally, there are more cases of brain injury, both identified and undiagnosed, from heart attacks, toxic shock syndrome, and other causes, such as combat traumatic brain injuries, that add to this cost. Head injuries are now a priority for not only the military and NFL, but for front-line clinicians. Head injuries are a contributing factor to both the unremitting clinical process of human destructiveness and Alzheimer disease.

Delirium afflicts 10% of all patients admitted to an acute care facility. In the geriatric patient population upward of 80% of acute care inpatients develop delirium. Diagnostic sensitivity and acute medical intervention can save lives and spare brain function, thus improving quality of life and reducing need for institutional care. Untreated delirium, a hidden epidemic in hospitals, causes an increase in both mortality and lifetime disability following discharge for any disease.

Dementia afflicts 50% of patients occupying nursing home beds in the United States, or 600,000 beds at a total cost of $20 billion per year. Many of these patients can be treated with home care resulting in a 15% reduction in primary health-care costs when such care is bundled with innovative housing, board, and clinical care. Unfortunately, such programs are rare today. The burden of progressive dementia ruins families, both psychologically and financially, because it is uninsured by everything but specialized and highly expensive long-term care insurance. It is like floods. Families must take out special policies early in life to relieve the burden from years of progressive deterioration in Alzheimer disease.

## ANTIPSYCHIATRIC BIAS

Western society still lingers under the false assumption that diseases of the mind are simply a concoction of weak-minded people, and that if those suffering from psychological problems would only buck up and stand on their own two feet all of their problems would go away. Nothing could be more false and more dangerous to assume, creating an environment where mental health professionals are not trusted as health-care professionals. The federal government enables this by funding such antipsychiatric bias: E. Fuller Torrey explains how the federal government actually funds antipsychiatry, aggravating regressive and dangerous policies operationally mushrooming for decades. "Court-ordered outpatient treatment is often the only way severely mentally ill individuals can get help" (Torrey, 2015). Yet, as D. J. Jaffe, executive director of Mental Illness Policy Org. and a co-founder with me and others of the Treatment Advocacy Center, wrote in a 2011 *Washington Times* op-ed: "In spite of the risk to public safety and homeland security posed by letting some people with serious mental illness go untreated, the federal agency Substance Abuse and Mental Health Services Administration (SAMHSA) charged with helping them is instead working to see they don't get the treatments they need" (Jaffe, 2011). In other words, SAMHSA supports and funds organizations opposed to court-ordered outpatient treatment. Worse, as Jaffe wrote, SAMHSA has supported the Massachusetts-based National Empowerment Center's annual antipsychiatry "alternatives" conference at which it teaches people with mental illness "how to get off their medications."

Clinicians may be wondering by now why they are not trusted as an MD or allied health professional trying to treat the confused and psychotic patient. Much of that mistrust is centered on the false assumptions that there's no such thing as mental illness or that psychiatric treatment has political implications, inculcating in a patient the belief system of his or her therapist. To that point, psychiatrists visiting former Soviet psychiatric hospitals in 1996 and discussing these matters with staff in the company of translators learned the importance of all legal standards for any clinical intervention. The staff's expressions of subtle laughter can be an expression of recent shame that also points to the fact that to speak or maintain belief against the state was to be insane, because in a perfect society, there could be no psychiatric illness. Therefore, to protest against the perfect state meant that the protestor had to be suffering from a mental disease that required medical treatment and confinement. The remedy for this mental disease was neuroleptics without anticholinergics. The outcome? The outcome was almost always unremitting akathisia—a compelling need to be in constant motion—in psychiatrically normal dissidents.

Akathisia was not a side effect, any more than electric shock therapy (electroconvulsive therapy [ECT]) was therapeutic in "One Flew Over the Cuckoo's Nest," but every psychiatrist belonged to "The School" and simply knew what was expected of him or her in the Soviet Union when dealing with what has been called, Species "Homo Sovieticus." With this dramatic and terrifying prelude to our prescriptive authorities so freshly in our historical consciousness, we should avoid at all costs wearing two hats as doctor and lawyer, particularly as federally employed physicians during these times of varying judgments of civil rights for prisoners of war (POWs) and detainees having no choice but to receive our care. Our advice is that always behaving civilly and humanely is in the best interest of the patient, regardless of whether the patient wants the clinician to like him or her, will go a very, very long way, even when having so quickly to predict that the local judge would agree with you. One should think about what a lawyer may say, but practice medicine first.

We are trying to convince those in special mental health police units, first responders, and those practicing emergency psychiatry, that they must do what is right for the patient and society despite the threat of criminal or civil judgments against them. We must find a way to balance the needs and fears of those confronted by law enforcement with the needs of innocent victims the person may harm.

In light of the epidemic of shootings of unarmed mentally ill individuals—already 150 in the first 6 months of 2015—or of those who cannot comport their behaviors to the law because of a mental illness—financing the Behavioral Emergencies section of the California Emergency Services Act, 2006 is urgent. We know what happens to detainees without rights. We need to be mindful that those who bluster threateningly are often subject to internal voices and delusions and have no capacity to reason or respond to police commands. In light of what we know about human behavior, how can one, even based on threat, predict that a patient, robustly psychotic and pathologically jealous, will or will not kill or injure somebody in the future?

Studies by John Monahan demonstrated that psychiatrists and psychologists are no better at predicting behavior than others, making powers of predictability too poor to strip a person of his or her rights and detain or treat against the patient's will (Monahan, 1981). The authors describe how Monahan has backed away from such a blanket statement, because his statistical universe was too large to account for the 10% of this nation's homicides known to be committed by psychotic people. These homicides are committed by a tiny fraction of what is known as the "seriously mentally ill population." This fraction is most likely composed of people being committed for treatment on an involuntary basis, thus entering the court database open to academia for research.

The importance of the apparent contradiction between the *Lessard* and *Tarasoff* decisions is a no-man's land in which any clinician diagnosing or treating a patient/client is between a rock and hard place. Lean too far to the left, and the clinician faces liability for negligence. Lean too far to the right, and the clinician risks violating the patient/client's rights. There is an equal chance, statistically, of getting sued for both. Therefore, for clinicians, always document competency for informed consent.

## FIRST RESPONDERS AS DE FACTO THERAPISTS

Because most policing policies are driven by crime statistics and responses to perceived threats, there has become a disconnect between otherwise innocent individuals in the throes of hallucinatory states and those who are real criminals. Since deinstitutionalization and the subsequent criminalization of the seriously mentally ill, a somewhat ambiguous legal and sociological construct that retains the word, "illness," remains in every state. Any professional, except sworn police officers, engaging a person who is really a patient becomes a therapist intervening in an illness regardless of that person's profession. California Highway Patrol Officer Daniel Andrew was not a licensed clinician, but he had to act like one to assess Pinnock's mental state, and thus her ability not only to understand his lawful commands, but to comport her behavior to obey those commands. On Staten Island, the emergency medical technicians (EMTs) responsible for a suffering Eric Garner were professional health-care clinicians, but Garner died on their watch while the police swarmed him and compressed his chest and respiratory system, while the EMTs simply stood by. Did Garner have a disease, a mental illness, or was he so fraught with both terror and indignation as police closed in on him that he reacted from fright and flight? Whichever it was, it cost him his life. Are illness and disease synonymous? Until there is a medical or legal distinction, it's best to consider them synonymous. Actually, the precedents for *Tarasoff* are of more significance within emergency psychiatry than is *Tarasoff*'s being synonymous for "Duty to Warn." That is because it redefined "special relationship" for psychiatry. How should crime statisticians catalog Eric Garner's arrest—a felon resisting arrest, a homicide victim, a mentally ill individual as the victim of a tragic accident? In Washington State today, a psychiatrist faces serious charges for not managing a patient who killed two people 3 months after the last appointment with the patient. Such duration of forward prediction was defined as "foreseeable future" in the appeals process and threatens to turn the entire civil liberties construct of "imminent" as sole justification for preventive detention.

In a new decision the Washington Court of Appeals ruled that a psychiatrist potentially can be liable to the victims of a patient's violent acts—even if the patient had not made a specific threat to harm the victims. Unless it is reversed by the Washington Supreme Court or limited by the legislature, the case will significantly expand the scope of liability of mental health providers for acts of their patients.

"The case involved a double murder-suicide in July 2010. After a breakup with his girlfriend, Jan DeMeerleer entered her house, attacked one of her children with a knife, and then shot his former girlfriend and another child to death. A third child was left unharmed. DeMeerleer then left the home and was later found dead from a self-inflicted gunshot wound. DeMeerleer had been a patient of Dr. Howard Ashby, a Spokane psychiatrist, for about 9 years. Over that time he had expressed a variety of depressed, angry, and troubling thoughts, including thoughts of homicide and suicide. Other than a single occasion when he slapped his then-girlfriend's autistic son, however, he had not committed any acts of violence toward others. Dr. Ashby's diagnosis was bipolar affective disorder, possible cyclothymic personality disorder, and some obsessive-compulsive traits. Dr. Ashby was aware that, on and off, DeMeerleer's personal life was in disarray. DeMeerleer's crimes and suicide took place on July 18, 2010. He last saw Dr. Ashby 3 months earlier, on April 16. At that time DeMeerleer told Dr. Ashby that "when depressed he can get intrusive suicidal ideation, not that he would act on it, but it bothers him." He reported that he was mending his relationship with his girlfriend. Dr. Ashby knew that DeMeerleer had a family support network. DeMeerleer's psychiatric medications were continued. Although he did not see Dr. Ashby again before the murders, DeMeerleer was in contact with family and friends. None of them had any indication that DeMeerleer had a plan to kill someone or commit suicide.

Emergency psychiatry is epidemiologically informed regarding violence and has the ability to know likelihood of certain threat risks within certain populations, and hence, medicine's reliance on numbing statistics. We know even far more about the epidemiology of pathologically destructive processes. We know from experience with animals that their expected, or normal aggression, is limited and situational. Aimless aggression in both humans and animals is to a large extent the result of generalized neurobiological factors secondary to increasing disorganization, impulsiveness, lack of control, and irritability. These are necessary, but not always sufficient causes. We also know that there are complex organic, family, psychological, and social factors operating. Is that any different from cardiac disease or diabetes, wherein we know that manifest depression and schizophrenia can cause the emergence of previously unsuspected and latent cardiac and diabetic diathesis, respectively?

Again, clinicians should leave the big data research on predicting behavior to research scientists and should practice their clinical discipline. Statistics will take care of themselves, but clinicians, as Dr. Ashby has learned so painfully late in his career, should understand that they have peculiar abilities for the seriously mentally ill. Simply showing due diligence and documenting the findings will likely

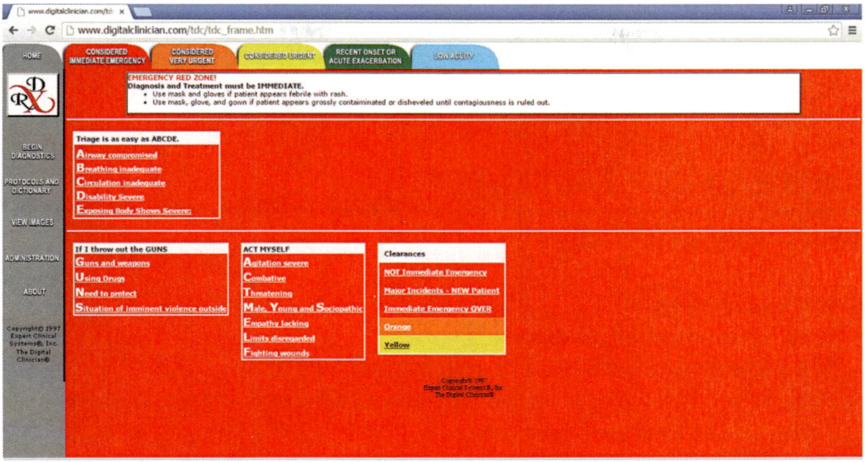


Figure 3.1 Red zone. The five threat levels are as follows: blue level—no threat; green level—minimal threat; yellow level—probable threat; orange level—imminent threat; red level—active threat. (Adapted from Aaron Dale and John Liebert, MD, *Defensive Tactics for Emergency Responders*, www.chall.com; adapted from www.digitalclinician.com for Emergency Medicine Triage.)

stand clinicians in good shape, regardless of outcome. Clinicians already have pattern recognition of aberrant behavior by training and experience. They must use it. Figure 3.1 presents an evidence-based pattern recognition that even the Supreme Court of California will accept as doing one's job and using common sense.

Figure 3.2 serves as an example of how to reduce the number of dangerous people one releases back into society when one has the ability to control them.

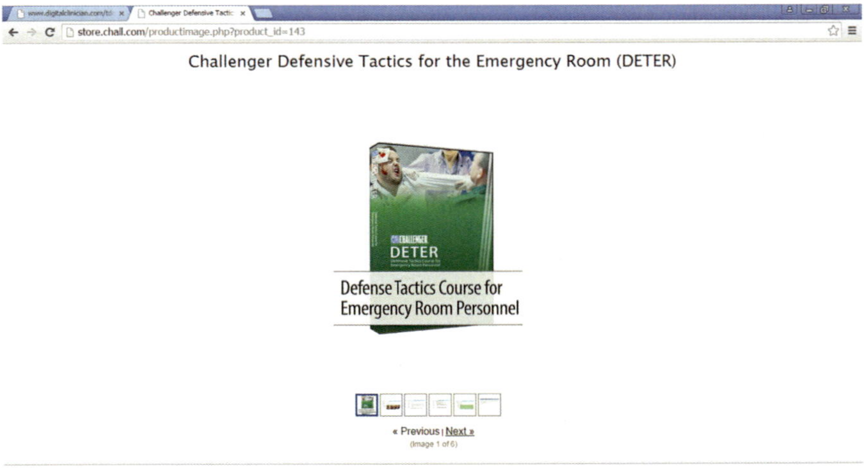


Figure 3.2 The Challenger Emergency Medicine DETER Course. (Faculty Aaron Dale, John Liebert MD and Robert Sweeney.)

That does not mean beating them in the face or taking them down with a choke hold. Even in today's antipsychiatry world of serious mental illness, there are more or less humane means of control available, which we will go into in greater detail below.

## SUICIDE BY COP FACT SHEET

Of the total cohort ($n = 707$),

- 50% had children.
- 100% were armed with weapons.
- 50% had a firearm (33% loaded), and 50% had a knife.
- 100% had confirmed or probable mental health history—67% suffered from depression or other mood disorders.
- 95% were male, with a mean age of 35 years.
- 41% were Caucasian, 26% Hispanic, and 16% African American.
- 37% were single.
- 54% were unemployed at the time of the incident.
- 29% did not have housing at the time of the incident.
- 62% had confirmed or probable mental health history.
- 80% were armed.
- Among the armed group, 60% possessed a firearm of which 86% were a loaded firearm, 7% unloaded, 4% inoperable, and 48% of those with a loaded firearm fired the weapon.
- 26% possessed knives, 19% feigned or simulated weapon possession, and 46% did so by reaching or placing their hand in their waistband.
- 87% of individuals made suicidal communications prior and/or during the incident.
- 36% were under the influence of alcohol (Mohandie et al., 2009).
- Of the cohort, 5% of suicide-by-cop cases were females (9).
- The mean age was 40 years.
- 50% were Caucasian.
- 25% were Hispanic.
- 42% were single (Mohandie and Meloy, 2011).

This brings us to the current and explosive case of the double homicide of New York Police Department (NYPD) patrol officers Rafael Ramos and Wenjian Liu in Brooklyn. Both officers were shot at point-blank range through the front passenger window of their unit by a mentally ill self-described revenge-seeking gunman, Ismaaiyl Brinsley. Brinsley, who had 19 prior arrests, had been fleeing Baltimore police after shooting his girlfriend and then threatening to kill himself by putting a gun to his head. Brinsley had made Instagram threats against the police, claiming it was revenge for the shooting deaths of Michael Brown and Eric Garner. Brinsley then shot himself on a subway platform after running from police, who were pursuing him. Federal crime statistics protocols would not categorize this as a suicidal mass murder even though it was a suicide murder and possibly an attempted suicide by cop, but for Brinsley's fleeing the scene.

Needless to say, the murder of two NYPD officers, neither of whom was Caucasian, but Hispanic and Asian, inflamed the city with the Patrolmen's Benevolent Association (PBA) chief criticizing and blaming both Chief Bill Bratton and Mayor Bill de Blasio. The PBA chief blamed them as if they were responsible for inciting the mentally ill Brinsley to violence, or for criticizing the police for killing an unarmed Eric Garner and thus inciting Brinsley. Brinsley was described by his family as mentally ill, had a long string of arrests, and was manifestly suicidal. He was looking to kill and to die. His incitement was his paranoid delusion in his unremitting state of hopelessness and fury probably fed by the video of Garner's being taken down and held down by the police as he screamed, "I can't breathe." Images have the power to incite, especially among the mentally ill, whose rational behavior is severely compromised if not completely absent. Thus, it was likely Brinsley identified with Garner and through the fog of his delusion, saw himself as a righteous avenger. Brinsley was insane.

What's clear from this is that there may be more Brinsley's out there, festering, lurking, decomposing, and looking for any excuse to engage in an apocalyptic act of murder/suicide. Just look at the lone wolf ISIS-influenced wannabe terrorists. An example is the murders at Charlie Hebdo, the kosher market in Paris, and the synagogue in Copenhagen. Another example is the Fort Hood murders perpetrated by Army psychiatrist Nidal Malik Hasan, who claimed to have been influenced by the American imam Anwar al-Awlaki.

Look at the attack on military institutions in Chattanooga by a drug-abusing, suicidal, depressed Arab American, Muhammad Youssef Abdulazeez. This is a new type of suicidal mass killer, one who, like the Soviet deep cover agent provocateur during the early Cold War, acts as if he or she is an automaton, upon instructions he or she might receive over the telephone or via social media. This type of killer suffers from a type of delusion, whether the result of a mental illness or induced, as in the Soviet deep cover operative, and he or she poses an asymmetric threat to societies wherever he or she is switched on. In the cases of Brinsley and other copacide killers, we must realize we are on the brink of a spate of violence between some citizens and the police that leaders on both sides need to cool down before it gets worse.

## THE MISSING PERSONS CRISIS

One case stands out for dramatically demonstrating what we don't know, we don't know. Human remains were found by fishermen in the Wisconsin River. A determined police detective was able to contract with an anthropology laboratory to reconstruct the skull and ultimately present a virtual image of a person. Amazingly the person was recognized, leading to a tip. There was not even a missing person report. The victim was a Tanzanian student, allegedly here on a student visa. The killer was her cousin and was convicted of murder (Crockett and Zick, 2000).

The National Crime Information Center (NCIC) records show that annual reports of missing persons have increased 600% in the last 25 years to nearly one million now; nearly one-half are children or juveniles under the age of 20. Many are removed because a law enforcement agency located the subject, the individual returned home, or the record had to be removed by the entering agency due to a determination that the record is invalid. Much of the change in statistics is due to population growth, but because cases like Ted Bundy's began with two girls missing from a large picnic, the police are taking missing persons' reports more seriously now. There are 2300 Americans reported missing every day, only a fraction of which can be attributed to abductions or kidnappings by strangers.

A cohort of 48,000 cases reveal the democratic nature of America's missing persons. Slightly more than half—about 25,500—of the missing are men. About 4 out of 10 missing adults are white, 3 of 10 black, and 2 of 10 Latino. Among missing adults, about one-sixth have psychiatric problems. Young men, people with drug or alcohol addictions, and elderly citizens suffering from dementia make up other significant subgroups of missing adults. About half of the roughly 800,000 missing juvenile cases in 2001 involved runaways, and another 200,000 were classified as family abductions related to domestic or custody disputes. Only about 100 missing-children reports each year fit the profile of a stereotypical abduction by a stranger or vague acquaintance. Two-thirds of those victims are ages 12 to 17, and among those 8 out of 10 are white females, according to a Justice Department study. Nearly 90% of the abductors are men, and they sexually assault their victims in half of the cases (Carangelo, 2014).

To further complicate categorization of cases, the FBI designates some missing-person incidents—both adult and juvenile—that seems most dire as "endangered" or "involuntary." For example, the agency deemed Taylor Behl, the 17-year-old college student missing in Richmond, Virginia, to be endangered. Her body was found a month later. A former boyfriend pleaded guilty to second-degree murder. More than 100,000 missing persons, the vast majority of them children, are designated as endangered each year. About 30,000 are deemed involuntary.

## CONCLUSION

Statistics are a tool—a necessary one, but all too often of either little to no use—or worse, distracting the truth to support the funding party's desired objective. We see here that the total number of cold case murders is probably significantly underreported, and that the official distinction between a missing person and a murder or suicide victim is not dependable. Certainly, the upwards of 200,000 cold case murders could be a ballpark number and cries out for solutions. When examining known serial murderers like Bundy and Ridgway, most experts working their cases know these psychopaths killed significantly more victims than have been officially cleared. One of the most egregious examples of skewed statistical constructs is that for mass murder. Some prominent expert statistical analyses remain stable, and therefore, like rabies in this country, endemic—rather than epidemic and accelerating in incidence. This statistical interpretation has likely caused barriers for translational research within the CDC epidemiology division for research on violence, as well as the current example of totally failed institutional preparedness for detection. The uncovering and deactivation of our first successful sleeper cell since 9/11 in San Bernardino was totally missed and remains a mystery. Had the true statistics of suicidal rampage murders, regardless of causation, been properly researched and their statistics known, we could have been better prepared instead of being helplessly inadequate in resources to prevent suicidal rampage murders, as was the case of the Planned Parenthood attack in Colorado Springs, or the politically motivated jihadist suicidal rampage murder in San Bernardino.

Of even more concern is the fact that our demographics could even miss the missing.

A case was cited in Wisconsin where there was no missing person, only skeletal remains found in a river that informed of both a missing person and a murder. Part of the problem is that there are over 40,000 police jurisdictions in this nation, and the Department of Justice depends on their clearance of murder cases and determination of murder investigation of death or missing persons. The standards of reporting are inadequate to provide an accurate statistical basis to inform policy and procedures for homicide investigation, preparedness, preventive psychiatry, and emergency services, all of which are intertwined in providing both knowledge about violent death and security to the public. An example of such failure is the Emergency Services Act of the last century. Although it brought many patients to emergency rooms within the golden hour to save lives from strokes and heart attacks, the mandate for Behavioral Emergency Services was never funded. That leaves us with good intentions and a forgotten law on the books—a law that could save lives and begin to get to the root of an epidemic of certain types of violence—i.e., gang violence, terrorism, and suicidal rampage murders, all of which are epidemic and do not correlate with alleged reduction in violent felony crime.

The original Emergency Services Act mandated equal financing of behavioral emergencies with those of cardiovascular emergencies and major trauma. Although behavioral emergencies were specifically mandated equally with other medical emergencies in the Medic One Law, they were never funded. Let's reverse engineer this conceptual framework, as if it had actually been funded, as were all the rest, for behavioral emergencies. What would the landscape look like from Newtown through Chicago's ghetto to San Bernardino today? Let's dissect Dr. Boyd's conceptual framework piece by piece, reverse engineering each element. Perhaps we can emerge from the jungles bereft of public psych services and failed preparedness and reinvent a more civilized place for all of us to live and shop. Reinvent a safe haven for our children to go to school without having to fear being shot. Statistics are just a tool—they can lie or tell the truth. Obviously, we don't even know what we don't know. We need an objective statistical base, free of political bias, to tell us the truth—not what we are supposed to believe.

## REFERENCES

Boyd, D. R. 1983. The history of the emergency medical services (EMS) systems in the United States of America. In D. R. Boyd, R. F. Edlich, and S. Micik (Eds.), *Systems Approach to Emergency Medical Care*. Norwalk, CT: Appleton-Century-Crofts.

Carangelo, L. 2014. *The Ultimate Search Book: U.S. Adoption, Genealogy, and Other Search Secrets*. Palm Desert, CA: Access Press.

Crockett, R. S. and Zick, R. 2000. Forensic applications of solid freeform fabrication. *International Freeform Fabrication Symposium, University of Texas*, Austin, TX. Retrieved from www.goo.gl/eaA95t

Duwe, G. 2007. *A History: Mass Murder in the United States*. Jefferson, NC: McFarland and Company.

Jaffe, D. J. 2011, September 16. Counterproductive craziness at federal agency. *The Washington Times*. Retrieved from www.goo.gl/p9iJpl

Liebert, J. and Birnes, W. J. 2011. *Suicidal Mass Murderers: A Criminological Study of Why They Kill*. Boca Raton, FL: CRC Press.

Liebert, J. and Birnes, W. J. 2014. *Hearts of Darkness: Why Kids Are Becoming Mass Murderers and How We Can Stop It*. New York, NY: Skyhorse.

Mohandie, K. and Meloy, J. R. 2011. Suicide by cop among female subjects in officer involved shooting cases. *Journal of Forensic Science*, 56(3), 664–668. DOI: 10.1111/j.1556-4029.2010.01686.x.

Mohandie, K., Meloy, J. R., and Collins, P. I. 2009. Suicide by cop among officer involved shooting cases. *Journal of Forensic Science*, 54(2), 456–462. DOI: 10.1111/j.1556-4029.2008.00981.x.

Monahan, J. 1981. *Predicting Violent Behavior: An Assessment of Clinical Techniques*. Thousand Oaks, CA: Sage.

Murphy, J. M., Olivier, D. C., Sobol, A. M., and Monson, R. R. 2000. Incidence of depression in the Stirling County study: Historical and comparative perspectives. *Psychological Medicine*, 30(3), 505–514.

Olson, J. 2014, November 7. Behind Maplewood incident, a rising trend of hospital violence. *Star Tribune*. Retrieved from www.goo.gl/O3HJP8

Stack, S. 2012. The culture of violence and suicidality. In G. R. Hayes and M. H. Bryant (Eds.), *Psychology of Culture* (pp. 201–212). New York, NY: Nova.

Torrey, E. F. 2015, April 3. Bungling the job on substance abuse and mental health. *The Wall Street Journal*. Retrieved from www.goo.gl/N6teOc

# 4

# The drivers of violence-related crime statistics

We may have heard more about Detroit and the crime statistics there. But what is understated in looking at the statistics is that, in reality, over 75% of violent, adolescent offenders have a history of extreme child abuse (Pincus and Tucker 1985). Morbidity figures are further impacted by the 13% of adult women who have been physically abused (Emslie and Rosenfeld 1983) and male rape victims, representing about 8% of male psychiatric inpatients—yet 30% of prison inmates (Liebert 1994). What needs to be done to reduce both direct and indirect health-care costs, aside from the moral dilemma of perpetuating violence through clinical denial and ignorance, is to intervene early in the cycle of abuse. These interventions start in the home, of course, but in dysfunctional and abusive family situations, it will be up to the social authorities. Remember, it is from this cohort of male and female victims of childhood abuse that both malignant character pathology and paraphilias emerge, recycling violence like a perpetual motion machine through institutional processes defying human inventiveness (Liebert 1992).

Despite the political wrangling and inadequate epidemiological studies in domestic violence, it is conservatively estimated that spouse abuse victimizes 6 million women per year (Sadock 1985). Assaults from intimate partner violence are not usually followed by emergency room visits because of threats of reprisal, but there are still multimillions of emergency room visits per year for domestic violence (Friedman 1994). These assaults are preceded by a nonviolent domestic altercation in 90% of cases (Dietz 1986). Diagnostic sensitivity with an appropriate index of suspicion, therefore, may prevent assault and murder when psychosocial interventions are made during the premonitory marital conflagration. Currently, however, intervention rarely occurs until the police are called. In fact, sexism even contaminates the diagnostic process at the points of entry into the health-care system. Abuse is discovered by one-half of female physicians in the first interview, while male physicians usually do not discover it until the third interview, if they ever ask about it (*Psychiatric News* 1994).

## MED-SURG SCREEN

Accurate medical-surgical diagnosis at the point of entry into the health-care system is noncontroversial and self-evident. Nonetheless, over one-half of hospital-admitted psychiatric inpatients and 10% of psychiatric outpatients have physical illnesses that caused or aggravated their psychiatric disorders. Most of these patients have been medically screened before referral. The health-care costs, unnecessary suffering, and risk in the neuropsychiatric, medical, and surgical population are enough to justify objective, computer-supported diagnostics for all identifiable psychiatric patients at points of entry to the mental health and correction systems.

## PSYCHOSIS

Psychosis is debilitating for 0.7% of Americans at either some point or through most of their lives and, along with brain damage and abuse in childhood, remains a major risk factor in violence, such as, but not exclusive to, hate crimes. Ignoring robust research findings on family stress and occupational disability as aggravating factors in this population has generated homelessness and other social disruption as with the Moore, Oklahoma, beheading in the workplace. Psychosis is treatable with access to and availability of adequate psychiatric resources and modern psychopharmacotherapy. Unfortunately, however, despite its inclusion within the seven critical categories targeted under EMS legislation, it was mandated but never equitably funded or supported compared to other categories like "Acute Cardiac."

## SUBSTANCE ABUSE

Alcoholism afflicts 9 million Americans, impacting one-third of all American families. Medical complications fill our hospital beds. Nearly 10,000 babies are born every year in this country with permanently disabling fetal alcohol syndrome. Children who physically survive become victims, now labeled *adult children of alcoholics*, and when they grow up as adult children of alcoholics and become parents themselves, they can be dysfunctional in dealing with their own children. Most arrested males are inebriated, and most deaths in young adults and adolescents are alcohol related; this is an enormous problem on college campuses today. Among alcoholic women, there is a 90% incidence of childhood abuse histories—severe physical abuse (45%) and sexual abuse (66%). Among Vietnam veterans, the incidence of alcoholism associated with posttraumatic stress disorder is 35% (blacks 20%). Veterans from the War on Terror likely mirror the Vietnam population, but statistics are not yet available.

Drug abuse and dependence afflicts over 6% of Americans. Denial at the point of entry to health-care services must be abolished in order to identify this population, usually youthful, before they become violent felons and/or med-surg invalids. The majority of arrested criminals undergoing drug testing are under the influence of cocaine. For $5 billion the substance abuse treatment slots could be doubled. Much of this could be extracted from taxes on addictive products already designated for education and treatment, if anyone could find a way through the bureaucratic maze and find the consuming tax. Substance abuse treatment can reduce the crime rate in America, just as it has in Europe. The Rand Corporation has demonstrated that if just 13% of cocaine abusers reduce their intake, 1% of total market demand, estimated at 330 tons per year, will disappear. But, there are 80,000 convicts on waiting lists for treatment. Under "three strikes and you're out," they represent violent menaces to society if untreated.

Polysubstance abuse among veterans with posttraumatic stress disorder and traumatic brain injury is also common and was associated with the imprisonment of nearly 200,000 combat veterans from the Vietnam War in 1994. It is likely that another 200,000 combat veterans were in jails or homeless because of comorbid substance advice. An increasing percentage of them were already veterans of Desert Storm and the War on Terror. We do not know the current incarceration rates of veterans from the War on Terror, but it is likely back to or exceeding the statistics from 1994.

And, to complicate the cost of associated violence, about one-third of AIDS victims are drug users or sex partners and children of users. Over 100,000 children were likely orphaned by the AIDS epidemic, inseparable from the drug epidemic, by 2000. Obviously substance abuse must be ruled out in all diagnostic assessments. The patient's own presentation is frequently inadequate, but inestimable direct and indirect costs of health care could be impacted by accurate diagnosis of substance abuse disorders that afflict more than 16% of Americans.

## TRAUMATIC STRESS DISORDERS

Because of the escalation in domestic and street violence, concurrent with our legacies of wars, the majority of Americans have been psychologically traumatized with adequate severity to cause illness in any healthy adult. Of this 60% of Americans, including the 35% of all adult females who are child abuse victims, most will acquire partial post-traumatic syndromes during their lifetimes. Nearly 20% of trauma victims—or 10% of all Americans—will develop full-blown posttraumatic stress disorder during their lifetimes. The incidence following rape is 80%; this statistic dramatizes the unique devastation of this crime. With both our delayed diagnosis and neglect of critical incident stress debriefing, a high percentage of these cases will deteriorate into physical illness, unnecessarily taxing medical services and/or character deformity, unnecessarily taxing social services and society itself. Gulf War syndrome may not be delayed like post-Vietnam syndrome, but after Oklahoma City, military clinicians can no longer be complacent about the long-term social consequences of even military victories. For example, Murrah Building bomber Timothy McVeigh was a combat veteran of Desert Storm who later failed an attempt for Special Forces career advancement, as was Mohammed, the Beltway Sniper who co-opted his teenage companion Malvo into randomly firing at innocent civilians and children in his cold-blooded transcontinental sniper rampage.

New cases present every day from old wars, and the War on Terror is filling the beds and cells of Vietnam veterans who are passing away. Suicide rates among Vietnam veterans are suspected of equaling the mortality rate of all Americans; currently one veteran completes suicide every hour of every day! Research on this legacy of war is hampered by selection criteria for cohort study. The sickest survivors are least likely to avail themselves for study due to homelessness, incarceration, "trip-wire"-style residence in the wilderness, and occult suicides. Furthermore, it is from this population of traumatic stress disorders that forensic cases have placed increasing demands on our courts in the form of false memory civil cases and legal defenses for violent felonies. The latter now includes Inner City Syndrome from gang warfare. Posttraumatic stress disorder is a risk factor for both violence and suicide.

These legal statistics highlight the importance of improving standards of both diagnostics and care for this clinical population, a significant part of the high-utilizing population for primary care services. If, for example, psychiatric sequelae of wounds—likely by gunshot—are unexamined in the 50% of jail detentions that manifest them, how will the terminal post-traumatic process of the wound eventually register as social or health cost? There is a massive body of literature on the psychotherapy and biological treatment of trauma victims, most of it encouraging and optimistic, even when no one silver bullet treatment fits all cases. Immersing this population of patients into generic clinical pathways of mental illness and substance abuse, as is too often the current practice, could be considered malpractice. Clinicians must be vigilant for false claims and compensation neurosis but should not overrate their role as guardians of the personal injury gates. It is almost impossible to fake posttraumatic stress disorder in a true therapeutic alliance. It is also extremely difficult to fake multiple personality disorder (dissociative identity disorder) in the hands of a competent psychiatrist today.

Computer-enhanced diagnostics are of particular importance to detect this huge clinical population. Post-traumatic syndromes are not difficult diagnoses clinically. They are politically controversial, generate potential claims for compensation, and arouse the passions of clinicians, clouding diagnostic objectivity. Lives can be salvaged when properly diagnosed. Threats of false memory suits, for example, will reduce clinician sensitivity to the diagnosis, but computer-enhanced diagnosis reduces the shell game of both personal injury recoveries and fiscal exigencies of institutional denial of trauma. In Washington State, for example, psychiatric illness is not compensable as occupationally induced except in rare and exceptional cases; this law has nothing to do with evidence-based medicine, but rather, only lobbying influences to reduce workers' compensation claims.

## SEXUAL ASSAULT

Rape actually victimizes 200,000 women every year for an incidence of 1 sexual assault per 1000 citizens (Dietz 1986); this is a very conservative statistic from actual reports and arrests. Posttraumatic stress disorder will occur in 80% of the victims (Liebert 1987). Psychopharmacology is promising for the treatment of sexual violence (Stein et al. 1992), but, until proven as a preventive tool in sexual violence, presentence diagnostics must be restored within the criminal justice system in order to separate psychopaths from less malignant sexual offenders (Liebert et al. 1979). Certainty of sentencing is of little value without certainty of investigation and prosecution, which cannot replace diligent presentence investigation. Correctional booking offices are processing clinical cases in numbers approaching any point of entry due to deinstitutionalization and criminalization of the mentally ill and drug dependent citizens. The knowledge of predicting dangerousness is advanced, although, like all of medicine, far from perfected. Still, nothing is currently being done to make the diagnostic distinction, crucial for incarceration and probation (Liebert and Birnes 2011). Consequently, thousands of sexual assaults occur that could otherwise be prevented. Furthermore, nearly 50% of assailants are either well known or actually dating the victim at the time of offense. Such statistical knowledge about this frequent and destructive offense places rape within the context of relational adjustment, likely presenting, as does domestic violence, with nonviolent manifestations at a point of entry to the health-care system (Dietz 1986).

The incidence of homicide is conservatively estimated to have declined from 9 murders per 100,000 Americans (Dietz 1986), approaching the mortality rate from suicide, to about one-half that incidence. More alarming, however, is the fact that an increasing number of young males have been killed, particularly in the inner city, where the killed-in-action rate from gang warfare has approached that of Operation Iraqi Freedom. Like suicide, homicide could oftentimes be prevented, because many murders are preceded by clinical presentations at points of entry to the health-care system (Dietz 1986). And, despite the highly publicized war on our streets, 50% of victims, like Nicole Brown Simpson, are still killed in their own homes (Dietz 1986), and over 1000 homicides occurred in the workplace in 1992. This latter rate has escalated, and homicide is now the second leading cause of death in the workplace today. For females it is the number one cause of death in the workplace (Rigdon 1994). Today, the workplace is no longer considered a refuge from human violence but, like our streets, could once again be safe. Timothy McVeigh and infamous arsonists, Keller and Pang, both of Washington State, were not undetectable. Rather, they were undetected prior to going berserk (Liebert et al. 1995).

The incidence of homicide in the United States is conservatively estimated at more than 4 murders per 100,000 Americans and rising. To reiterate, this mortality approaches the halfway mark to the rate of completed suicide, a leading cause of mortality, and approaching the mortality rate of accidents. And, like suicide, homicide could oftentimes be prevented, because many murders are preceded by clinical presentations at points of entry to the health-care system, as in the cases of Aaron Alexis, perpetrator of the Navy Yard massacre; Cho, perpetrator of the Virginia Tech massacre; Holmes, perpetrator of the Aurora Theater massacre; and Eddie Ray Routh who murdered Chris Kyle (the American Sniper) at a Texas gun range, perpetrator of a double homicide killing (Liebert and Birnes 2011, 2013, 2014).

## INNER-CITY VIOLENCE AND CHILD ABUSE

Federal crime statistics reveal that 6,620,000 Americans were victims of violent crime in 1992. Considering that only 10% of violent crimes are recorded through arrest and therefore registered on Federal Bureau of Investigation (FBI) rap sheets, serious, life-endangering victimization likely afflicts close to 20–30 million Americans every year. Have no doubt, America is a violent society. The news from Detroit is probably more realistic, as those injured by human destructiveness will be registered by health-care accounting but oftentimes not by police records. Social indicators for victimization by human destructiveness vary greatly from official FBI statistics, because they account for actual costs registered in social service and health-care offices.

Robbery and assault, for example, victimize 3% of Americans every year, but "Inner City Syndrome," an indirect health-care cost, is now a psychiatric defense in felony cases. In the Atlanta Child Murders case, the nation was shocked by the children's faces on the cover of *Life* magazine, all of whom were listed as victims. That magazine cover erupted into the international news cycle when the Atlanta Child Murder case, now known as Wayne Williams' case, was detected as a drastic change in child homicides in inner-city Atlanta. Wayne Williams was convicted for terrorizing the city of Atlanta, but he did not kill all of the kids whose innocent and smiling faces filled that dramatic *Life* issue's cover page. The *Life* magazine feature really should have been about children being born into trauma in our urban communities—they are mainly black children—and how they either survive or get killed, usually by their families as preadolescents and gangs as teenagers. Scores of them were targeted and shot in Chicago over the July 4, 2014, weekend. Studies of children in the inner cities of other cities during the Atlanta Missing and Murdered Children case found that there was no difference between psychological problems of Atlanta's inner-city poor children—mainly black—and their peers in other cities, despite the highly publicized threat of a monstrous killer on the loose, whether a black serial killer or white supremacist conspiracy to start another civil war.

Victimization by violence is most accurately registered in health-care costs, as reported in Detroit. It is usually a neighborhood drive-by shooting or family matter, at most statistically trapped within our civil legal or cultural tribal systems with punitive response. Many of the murdered children portrayed so dramatically on the cover of *Life* magazine in 1981 were murdered within their own families in clear visibility of neighbors. Other than those cleared with the conviction of Wayne Williams, most are now cold cases. Racial violence terrorized these families through the generations. The press hyped the case as international racial terror. Wayne Williams did terrorize this community, but Wayne Williams was not the product of this underclass he terrorized. He lived in the same neighborhood as the mayor of Atlanta. The majority of these kids, beat officers from the community revealed, were known to have been killed by their families. These children were shot in the head, hung, and beaten to death within their families or by someone well known to their parents.

Too often, these are still family and neighborhood matters such as the case of Jeffrey Dahmer in the inner city of Milwaukee, but such silence is not class bound as with predators like Dahmer and Williams. They came from the suburbs for the predatory opportunism of inner-city chaos. Jon Benet Ramsey, however, was killed in upper-class Denver, and by all accounts it was suspected to be an inside job (Liebert 2014). Serial killer John Wayne Gacy killed his adolescent workers and buried their decomposing corpses in the basement of his middle-class home in Chicago. During their marriage, the late Nicole Brown Simpson, OJ's then wife was repeatedly beaten and ultimately murdered in an upper-class Brentwood neighborhood on the west side of Los Angeles.

These startling statistics do not discount the gray area of a very high percentage of deaths ruled accidental that really were homicides. Such robust mortality statistics mean that clinicians are not likely to be able to step aside from this endemic problem in emergency psychiatry. Clinicians are essentially, by definition, on the frontline facing its monstrous head. And the landscape of destructive behavioral processes is mainly populated by males. Intuitively we know right away, for example, gender determines destructiveness, but we know very little about why. The trend results from 2003 to 2012 showed the vast majority of crimes were still committed by men with around 88% of homicides and 75% of all legal felonies. In fact, a select subgroup of aging, juvenile male offenders (1% of any large male cohort in prospective criminal research) commits 98% of our very serious crimes.

We also know that there is a cycle of violence perpetuating enormous social dysfunction and disruption. There are over a million cases of child abuse presenting for medical treatment annually. Over 4000 children are murdered every year by their parents. That was the really powerful message that Wayne Williams sent to us from Atlanta, despite the news appeal of such occasional and sensational serial killings. And despite the extremely conservative estimates, over 300,000 cases of gross emotional abuse are reported annually. Diagnostic sensitivity with appropriate index of suspicion followed by psychosocial intervention can break this cycle of human destructiveness. Child abuse can be detected, and most victims will not abuse if treated before starting their own families. But, 70% of all abuse victims will abuse their own children if not treated.

## SUICIDE

Suicide, now the ninth leading cause of death in America, takes the lives of nearly 100,000 Americans every year for an incidence of 12 per 10,000 annually, and worldwide, according to a report by Tiesman et al. (2015) and in Holmes (2015). The report, which deals primarily with workplace suicides, according to the Bureau of Labor Statistics' Census of Fatal Occupational Injury data from 2003 to 2010, found that more than 1700 people died by suicide on the job. The statistics get even worse, according to the report, revealing that one in four adults will experience a bout of mental illness during their lifetime. When 25% of Americans find themselves prone to mental illness at some point, either in the workplace or in their personal lives, does this not point to an epidemic? Yet, mental illness is still stigmatized, preventive psychiatric medicine is woefully underfunded, and it is often up to police officers to deal with the mentally ill, too often with lethal force. Moreover, because workplace suicides not only result in trauma on the part of those who witness it or who know the victim, suicidal rampage often involves rampage homicide, a form of mass murder, in which the suicidal individual takes out his rage on those around him, especially perceived persecutors. Therefore, the report, identifying police officers, medical doctors, and soldiers as people with the highest risk of suicide, recommends a more aggressive approach on the part of employers, and the military, to help those with suicidal ideations identify the underlying causes of their distress and to take steps to address these causes by professionals at the workplace.

Youth suicide is approaching epidemic dimensions, too. Yet, many suicides can be predicted and prevented, because 75% of those completed suicides are preceded by a visit to the physician. Victims appear to have wished to discuss their intent but were rarely asked anything about suicidal intent. Untreated depression is a highly lethal disorder. The epidemic of suicides among active-duty soldiers has been well publicized, and a disabled Veterans Administration is going to have a hard time meeting the demand from this at-risk cohort of young adults. Although active-duty suicides are diminishing in incidence, suicides among veterans are not. A U.S. military veteran commits suicide almost every hour—22 suicides a day among those who have put their lives on the line to serve their country.

Although there are numerous false positives in the prediction of future behavior, the lethality of the high-risk suicide patient demands emphasis at all points of entry into the health-care system. Improved suicide prevention would also eliminate post-traumatic syndromes in the survivors left in their wakes. Proven post-traumatic sequellae in a majority of these surviving victims will ultimately compound both the health-care utilization problem as well as the epigenetic transmission of familial psychopathology into future generations.

According to the Detroit News, "The $210 million hospital bill to treat violence in Southeast Michigan during 1998 and 1999 is more than half of what it cost to build the Tigers' new Comerica Park. Still, it is only a sliver of the region's actual medical bill for violence, because the records that area hospitals supplied to *The Detroit News* for this analysis did not uniformly include the most expensive health care costs—doctors' fees or pharmaceuticals. "Repeat victims clog health system….(and) Issue still not health priority." But, they continue, "Violence costs taxpayers (and) Metro Hospitals $210 million." Obviously this not only burdens taxpayers and hospitals financially, but it punishes the nonviolent citizen with higher insurance premiums, because of the large number of insured victims. Detroit is now bankrupt. Violence and suicide are part of the reason.

## REFERENCES

Dietz, P. 1986. Patterns in human violence. *Annual Review*. American Psychiatric Press, Washington, D.C.

Emslie, G. and Rosenfeld, A. 1983. Incest reported by children and adolescents hospitalized for severe psychiatric problems. *American Journal of Psychiatry*, 140, 6.

Friedman, D. 1994. Economics of violence; higher health care costs. *Puget Sound Business Journal*, 15, 16, September 2.

Holmes, L. 2015. *Huffington Post*. www.huffingtonpost.com/2015/03/17/workplace-suicide-rates_n_6879046.html?ncid=newsltushpmg00000003

Liebert, J. 1987. "Sexual manifestations of P.T.S.D." Panel Discussion on Contemporary Issues in Traumatic Stress Disorders, Annual Meeting of the American Psychiatric Association, Chicago.

Liebert, J. 1992. Violence as a manifestation of reliving in post-traumatic syndromes. The Brian Buss Memorial Lecture, Oregon Psychiatric Association.

Liebert, J. 1994. Substance abuse and violence: Twenty years after first pacific northwest conference on violence and criminal justice. *Presentation to King County Medical Society*, September 20.

Liebert, J. 2014. The Atlanta Missing and Murdered Children Case. What Was It? Who Did It? *Annual Conference of The American Investigative Society of Cold Cases*. Fayetteville, North Carolina, June 2014.

Liebert, J., Harris, G., and Wright, C. 1979. Psychiatric assessment in the presentence process. The Probe: Washington Corrections Association, Winter.

Liebert, J., Unis, A., and Wright, C. 1995. The keller serial arson case: Psychopathy or psychobiological diathesis? *International Conference of Psychoneuroendocrinology*. Seattle.

Liebert, J. A. and Birnes, W. J. 2011. *Suicidal Mass Murderers: A Criminological Study of Why They Kill*. Taylor and Francis, Boca Raton, Florida.

Liebert, J. A. and Birnes, W. J. 2013. *Wounded Minds*, Skyhorse, New York, New York.

Liebert, J. A. and Birnes, W. J. 2014. *Hearts of Darkness*, Skyhorse, New York, New York.

Pincus, J. and Tucker, G. 1985. Behavioral Neurology, 3rd edition. Oxford University Press, New York.

Rigdon, J. 1994. Companies see more workplace violence. *Wall Street Journal*, 131, April 12.

Sadock, V. 1985. *Spouse Abuse, Comprehensive Textbook of Psychiatry*, 4th Edition. Williams & Wilkins, Baltimore, Maryland.

Stein, D. et al. 1992. Serotonergic medications for sexual obsessions, sexual addictions, and paraphilias. *Journal of Clinical Psychiatry*, 53, 8.

Tiesman, H. M., Konda, S., Hartley, D., Menéndez, C. C., Ridenour, M., and Hendricks, S. 2015. *American Journal of Preventive Medicine*. March. www.ajpmonline.org/article/S0749-3797(14)00722-3/abstract

Women doctors detect abuse faster than men. *Psychiatric News*, Page 24, April 15, 1994.

# 5

# The Tarasoff decision

The discourse on the medical legal rules for clinical intervention assumes the medical model for conceptualizing certain subgroups of people at risk for self-harm and harm to others. This medicalization of these "syndromes," to be detailed later, is best defined and articulated in the Tarasoff decision, although by no means was it specifically addressing controversies of criminalizing versus medicalizing serious mental illness. Rather, it defined and articulated the medical model for managing the person at risk for violence within the context of an existing therapeutic contract—namely University of California, Berkeley's Cowell Memorial Hospital, and patient Prosenjit Poddar (*Tarasoff v. Regents of the University of California* 1976) (Figure 5.1).

This is such a controversial and complex forensic psychiatric issue that we could devote an entire book to it and become better informed about the law than we are about clinical practice. The good news, however, is that it is extremely unlikely to pertain specifically in very many cases, even though the ruling has been extended to include threats disclosed by family members and has become controlling law in states beyond California. The reason clinicians need to know about it is twofold. First, it was based on case law of physicians having a "special relationship with patients" that contained two broad theses subsumed under legal construct of "peculiar ability" as follow: (1) "unique knowledge about the patient derived from that special relationship"—i.e., clinical assessment—and (2) "ability to prevent a third party from being injured." Second, it has spawned a field of creative law that could put clinicians in a position of having such a special relationship when their patients do injure or kill somebody—hence the previous reference to *Tarasoff* and its progeny.

That is the purpose of citing *Tarasoff* here in order to stress the importance of understanding the concept and process of unremitting clinical states of human destructiveness. Tatiana Tarasoff was killed 2 months after Poddar's release. One of the elements of "special relationship" relied upon here is the "peculiar ability" of the physician when detecting a highly contagious and reportable disease on an outpatient basis that is more likely than not to injure specific and general third parties.

The *Tarasoff* decision held that when patient Prosenjit Poddar informed a psychologist employed by the University of California that he intended to kill

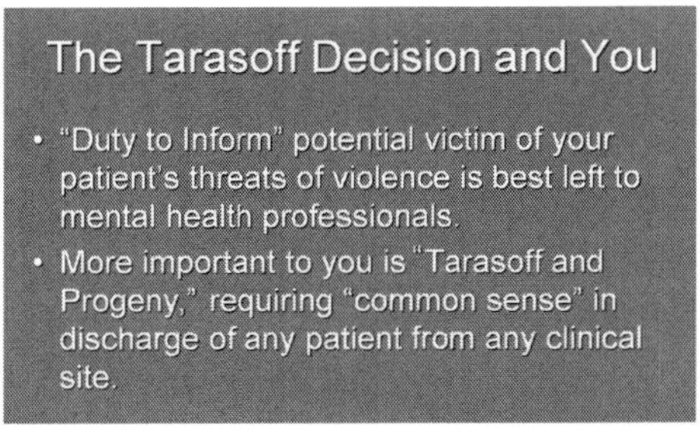
The Tarasoff Decision and You
• "Duty to Inform" potential victim of your patient's threats of violence is best left to mental health professionals.
• More important to you is "Tarasoff and Progeny," requiring "common sense" in discharge of any patient from any clinical site.

Figure 5.1 Alert to *Tarasoff* decision.

Tatiana Tarasoff upon her return from summer vacation, she should have been informed and in some way been protected from that threat by the university. That lethal act occurred 2 months later, but we do not know whether the defendant knew that at the time of disclosure in Berkeley. In fact, it is unlikely that the defendant therapist even knew her name at the time. He was knowledgeable enough, however, about the circumstances of Poddar and Tarasoff's relationship that it was alleged that he should have known her name.

Poddar was a voluntary outpatient involved in psychotherapy. The psychologist, in consultation with others in his department, decided that Poddar should be committed to a psychiatric hospital for observation. The psychologist communicated this decision to the Berkeley Police, who in turn detained Poddar briefly and then released him when, in their judgment, he appeared to be "rational." The director of the Department of Psychiatry at the university's hospital then ordered that no further attempt be made to have Poddar detained. Poddar killed Tarasoff when she returned approximately 2 months later, and her parents sued the psychologist and his colleagues who had been involved in the case for negligent failure to warn the victim, or those likely to warn her—like her family—of the danger. The California Supreme Court, overturning the court of appeals, ruled in favor of the family on this issue and in doing so established the duty for mental health professionals to warn.

After great outcry from the profession and institutions involved, the court, in an unusual move, agreed to a rehearing. The court's definitive decision in the subsequent *Tarasoff* ruling in 1976 exempted the police from potential liability but held that the plaintiff's suit could be amended to provide a cause for action in law against the therapist. In so doing it laid down a standard for outpatient psychotherapists without any recognized power to either detain or predict a patient's movement and actions. The court held, "When a therapist determines, or pursuant to the standards of his profession should determine, that this patient presented a serious danger of violence to another, he incurs a serious obligation to use reasonable care to protect the intended victim from such danger."

The case was settled out of court, and the court did not set down a rigid standard for "reasonable care," realizing that what might be reasonable in one case may not be reasonable in another. It also did not hold the therapist to a perfect standard as judged by the wisdom of hindsight. The court made it very clear, in its amended ruling, that in some cases a warning to the threatened party or some other particular action may be too radical a course to constitute reasonable care. It also indicated, however, that in other cases influencing this decision, warning the victim may not be enough to fill the therapist's obligation. It never held out the possibility that, in fact, warning could exacerbate the clinical process of dangerousness.

Although many psychologists were, and continue to be, outraged by this decision, it can be argued that there is a natural extension in tort law to encompass the fact pattern in *Tarasoff*. First, under the 1928 case, *Palsgraf v. the Long Island Railroad* (1928), the court ruled that any individual owes a duty of care to an individual within a "zone of danger," an individual to whom foreseeable harm may come as the result of an action by the defendant if that individual is in a place where it is foreseeable that harm may come. Then there is an extension that defines a particular responsibility or a "peculiar duty of care" based upon a special relationship established by one party, a defendant, to another, call him or her the plaintiff. For example, defendant Dan, walking by a lake on a summer evening, hears cries for help from Plaintiff Paul, who appears to be drowning. Dan can simply walk on by, ignore the cries for help, and if he is sued by Paul's family members, it is likely a court will dismiss for failure to state a claim. Dan, a passerby, had no duty of care to Paul, who was a complete stranger. However, assume that Dan throws a line to Paul or attempts to swim out to him and then abandons the attempt at rescue. At that point, because Dan began a rescue attempt, he established a duty of care, which duty he breached, thereby making him subject to a suit in tort. Much the same argument applies in *Tarasoff* when the therapist, through treatment, established a special relationship with Poddar that involved a duty of care not only to Poddar, but to Tarasoff, whom Poddar indicated he would murder. The therapist, by not warning Tarasoff, the California court ruled, breached that duty of care, and Tatiana Tarasoff was an individual in a zone of danger to whom foreseeable harm could come. Hence, despite a physician-patient relationship of confidentiality, the court held that it was trumped by basic tort law.

But, we do not know the specific peculiar knowledge the psychologist should have had, even though he considered Poddar imminently dangerous enough to file for emergency detention. Was it transient pathological jealousy aggravated by separation? Very likely, but was the murder derivative of a continuous process of this psychotic state of mind after release from police detention? The diagnosis was paranoid schizophrenia. Thus, most likely this presentation was not transitory but part of a clinical process of human destructiveness unlikely to remit without substantial therapeutic intervention such as hospitalization and/or antipsychotic medication. That is what is important, because it is extremely unlikely that anything like these circumstances apply in standard practices of emergency psychiatry. There was already a body of case law pertaining to practices of emergency psychiatry, where powers to control a patient are inherent in the definition of its best practices previously covered in the clinician's authority to waive informed consent when determining incompetence and a threat to patient and/or others, including the clinician.

*Tarasoff* goes further and defines the psychotherapeutic engagement as medical in nature, with the same special relationship of an MD diagnosing a reportable contagious disease. Furthermore, it assumes a continuous and unremitting process about which all clinicians must now be aware. Poddar was not necessarily imminently dangerous, it turned out; he killed Tarasoff 2 months later. Were there intervening or supervening events to impose new proximate causality, that is intervening events closer to the commission of the crime? Had Tarasoff been warned about Poddar's threats, would that have kept her vigilant and alive? But for a warning from the University of California, Berkeley, therapist, would Tarasoff still be alive? These are still lingering issues that attorneys arguing similar cases should consider. For the most part, however, clinicians must depend on past history of violence for determination of future dangerousness. How can the clinician, even based on threat, predict that a patient, robustly psychotic and pathologically jealous, will or will not kill or injure somebody in the future when the preponderance of studies demonstrate that even psychiatrists and psychologists are no better at doing so than others? Furthermore, is predictability too poor an indicator to strip a person of his or her rights and detain or treat against a patient's will, hence the focus of the *Lessard* decision? We argue that there is no bright red line here.

If, however, this presentation is associated with other acts of violence, particularly within a similar context of the current one, then clinicians are more likely to be held to a special relationship. This may not be specifically a *Tarasoff* case; it may simply be that a doctor is in a situation where clinical knowledge tells him or her that more likely than not a past act of violence will occur again and that his or her patient is in the unremitting clinical state of human destructiveness. This is psychopathology—or, more significantly, neuropsychiatric pathology if there are biomarkers, as in the case of the Texas Tower sniper found to have a brain tumor at autopsy. This latter is, in other words, "disease." Furthermore, unlike the psychologist, clinicians on the frontline who are readers of this book, are likely not outpatient psychotherapists. Rather they are functioning in the role of physicians and professionals held accountable for releasing patients or "special offenders" who committed acts of violence; they, therefore, under special relationship, have been attributed authority based on their "peculiar ability" and have power to control the patient because of the work site, whether jail, emergency room, LaBrea overpass on I-10, or prison.

Consider whether victims of Elliot Rodger's suicidal shooting rampage or the families of his victims have standing to sue the individual sheriff's deputies who did not put Rodger into custody because they believed, acting now in the role of mental health evaluators, that he was a danger. Were they competent to make that assessment? Should they have transported Rodger to a medical facility for an interview and observation? Should the county have called in a psychiatrist or clinical psychologist for a consult? By what medical standards was Rodger evaluated, and did the deputies possess the expertise to make such an evaluation? The record shows that Rodger satisfied the deputies that he was not a danger despite his Internet postings and rants and his parents' concerns. Inasmuch as Rodger's mother also agreed that he seemed to not be dangerous prior to his rampage and her belief might have influenced the deputies' decision, might not any plaintiffs have a cause of action against her? In light of *Tarasoff*, you can see how that ruling might be extended to encompass potential victims as well as those who established a peculiar ability to manage a potential offender.

These cases are extremely complicated, risky, and demanding. I was involved in a case in Ventura County in which the intended victim was likely spared by warning of his release and helping her to protect herself, but an innocent stranger was murdered by him more than a year later. Emergency psychiatry should not in any way be applicable under *Tarasoff* when the peculiar ability applies to a specifically targeted individual, but never say never. It is a big standard setter and will be used, possibly in reverse, in cases of emergency psychiatry—i.e., the use of the term, *Tarasoff and Progeny*. The emergency psychiatrist knew a guy could kill his girlfriend, but should he know this patient would likely kill a stranger months later when no such threats were evident? The court always emphasized the use of common sense. That was not specifically stated, but justices explained the true intent for their controversial ruling in person to clinical professionals after it was reheard and revised. Their warning to an audience of psychiatrists was as follows: when confronted with the patient/client symptomatic of an unremitting clinical state of human destructiveness, use common sense!

How do we define a special relationship in tort? Such a special relationship is defined as follows:

1. "A" (you) has a duty to conduct a relationship with a third person "B" (the emergency patient you encounter) in such a manner as to take reasonable care to
2. Control the conduct of "B" (your patient), in order to prevent "B" from causing harm to another, "C"
3. Just in case "A" (you) stands in a special relationship to "B," such that
4. The nature of that relationship provides "A" (you) with some "peculiar ability" to control the conduct of "B" (the emergency psyche patient) because
5. "A" knows—or should know, constructively—of the necessity and opportunity for controlling "B"

The practice of emergency psychiatry assumes those practicing know the necessity with "B" because they have been designated for such, whether officially or operationally, and both their work site and authority convey the opportunity to do so. It is important for such professionals to connect these dots defining their "peculiar ability," because this puts it as simply as possible. Clinicians might as well take this connection as the law regulating all clinical encounters with patients coming to their attention with either known proclivity to violence or pathological processes they should know more commonly cause or manifest such proclivity.

## PECULIAR ABILITY

All of this was based on case law precedents wherein clinicians failed to take all necessary and appropriate precautions with patients whom they knew—or should have known were either dangerous or in a process of dangerousness and had authority and the knowledge of such authority to detain those patients to prevent harm to others. The necessary elements of this special relationship were peculiar ability to both know the process of dangerousness and invoke their power to control it by not releasing the patient from safe, humane and effective control. On an outpatient basis the court relied upon case precedent of physicians who either should have known or did know their patients suffered contagious diseases and failed to report this to prevent harm to third parties; here, the peculiar ability applies to medical diagnostic knowledge and skills and duty to report—thus control over their patients.

Thus, the legal term "peculiar ability" that includes both authority to control as well as knowledge of such authority to control are key elements of *Tarasoff* and progeny; without the slightest doubt they apply to every encounter in emergency psychiatry that involves either destructive behavior or potential for such. And, that is almost all of emergency psychiatry, with the exception of altered mental states, when emergency medicine, neurology, and neurosurgery presentations are erroneously identified as psychiatric. It is not psychiatrists and clinical psychologists' proven weakness in predicting violence, therefore, that jeopardizes clinical decision making. We know that, under the best of circumstances, to reduce the release of patients who do commit violence upon release to 5% false-positive level of accuracy we are likely to hold about one-third back who will not; those held back would be false negatives. On the surface of such research findings, that is a high price constitutionally for honing our skills and targeting them on prediction of violence in patients having a history of violence that is not very recent. On the surface, however, these statistics again raise the question of how many of those false negatives were really false negatives, in view of the fact that only 1% of violent assaults are reported to the police. Conversely, the question in this study was never asked. Did the false negatives have better aftercare than the false positives?

There are agendas out there with this research when it reaches the courtroom, and research can prove just about anything—i.e., prediction of violence was good, in reducing false positives to 5%. Prediction of violence was no good in predicting violence in 30% who were not violent. These are interesting results, but caveat: they are not valid enough for making laws. If acting as a clinician with the seriously mentally ill, the best practices, ethics, and liabilities of emergency psychiatry and emergency medicine should be known. Unfortunately such practices have been delegated to allied professions, many of which are not even health professions—i.e., corrections officers and probation officers.

One's peculiar ability, therefore, is not based on clairvoyance generated from college or professional experience. It is based on his or her expert knowledge base of both time-determined and epidemiologically informed clinical decision making, as well as knowledge and power of emergency detention. Is the clinician encountering this patient, more probably than not, during an unremitting clinical state of dangerousness? That was not very difficult to determine within the first hour with Marlene Pinnock. It became more difficult after 1, 2, or 3 days of observation on an involuntary psychiatric hold (a 5150). This peculiar ability attributed to a clinician by the courts should apply to self-destructive behavior, too, because the spirit of *Tarasoff* will apply, if not the letter of the law, as in harm to others. We know, for example, that following either a violent suicide or a homicide, loved ones who are not seriously psychologically damaged are the exception rather than the rule. Both events, suicide or homicide, could certainly be construed in personal injury law as harm to others that you could have prevented by your peculiar abilities and authority to control—that is your operational special relationship functioning in the role of a clinician in an emergency psychiatric encounter. And, that is the importance of *Tarasoff*.

What is the jeopardy in emergency psychiatry? Based on a small sampling of 195 claims against 285 defendants between 1975 and 1995, occurrence results were as follows:

1. 59% of them were psychiatrists.
2. 13% were other MDs.
3. 8% were nurses.
4. 23% were nonmedical mental health professionals.

This demonstrates that almost half of the risk for psychiatric malpractice comes outside the specialty of psychiatry. Thus, lack of knowledge of forensic psychiatry provides no protection against malpractice. And, then, when we look at the universe of allegations in this small, but meaningful sample, we find the following occurrences:

- 25% were for improper medical treatment.
- 13% were for violation of patient's rights.
- 11% were for inadequate patient monitoring.
- 10% were for medication-related adverse outcomes.
- 9% were for failure to ensure patient safety.
- 11% were for sexual misconduct and undue familiarity.

## REFERENCES

*Palsgraf v. the Long Island Railroad*. 1928. Ct. of App. of N.Y., 248 N.Y. 339, 162 N.E. 99 [N.Y. 1928].

*Tarasoff v. Regents of the University of California*. 1976. [17 Cal.3d 425 [1976]].

# 6

# The importance of informed consent

Within the no-man's-land we describe between the due process strictures of *Lessard* and the duty-of-care strictures of *Tarasoff*, there is one safe haven, albeit elusive depending on the particular case and the particular patient. This is the haven of informed consent, the consent of the patient to treatment, to observation, even to commitment for a period of time to ascertain whether a diagnosis requires treatment (Figure 6.1).

Medico-legal knowledge of informed consent is crucial for all clinical interventions. Clinicians often cannot spend too much time and energy obtaining this in an emergency. But, they need to know about what they are likely not going to be able to do. Failure to document later why they did what they did without formal informed consent is critical when their social role in any encounter with a citizen is clinical, rather than a police action. Documentation of competency for informed consent, or inability to obtain it in an emergency, will ultimately determine their fate if the case sours.

After Officer Andrew secured the scene of his rescue and safely immobilized his "suspect" on California's I-10 freeway, he could, for example, have called EMTs. Pinnock's behavior should have indicated to him she was a medical emergency and not a criminal. Once the EMTs arrive it is a clinical matter, and further interventions should be considered emergency medicine, both in terms of best practices in that medical specialty and tort law governing it. Under the stress of oncoming traffic and the potential for a disastrous multicar pileup on one of America's busiest freeways, Andrew crossed the line and allowed his raw emotions to become the ultimate court of law for public safety and, perhaps, Pinnock's survival, too. It is a stretch, but in a way, under the pressure of the moment when both parties were in extreme danger, he may have been teaching her a lesson that she could not teach herself by thus substituting his ego for hers, which was obviously too seriously dysfunctional to know the extreme dangers of her behavior.

Police and first responders in extremely dangerous situations, when lives are at risk, sometimes do substitute their egos for those they try to save, because in those moments there is a merging of egos. The problem occurs when, just as

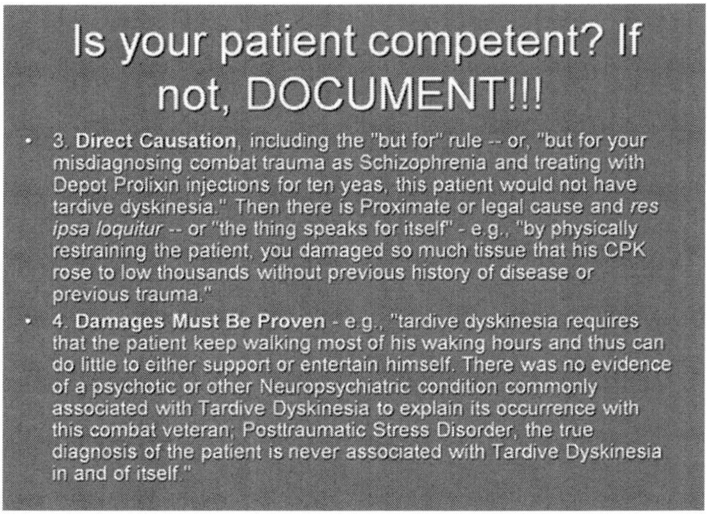
Is your patient competent? If not, DOCUMENT!!!
3. Direct Causation, including the "but for" rule -- or, "but for your misdiagnosing combat trauma as Schizophrenia and treating with Depot Prolixin injections for ten yeas, this patient would not have tardive dyskinesia." Then there is Proximate or legal cause and res ipsa loquitur -- or "the thing speaks for itself" - e.g., "by physically restraining the patient, you damaged so much tissue that his CPK rose to low thousands without previous history of disease or previous trauma."
4. Damages Must Be Proven - e.g., "tardive dyskinesia requires that the patient keep walking most of his waking hours and thus can do little to either support or entertain himself. There was no evidence of a psychotic or other Neuropsychiatric condition commonly associated with Tardive Dyskinesia to explain its occurrence with this combat veteran; Posttraumatic Stress Disorder, the true diagnosis of the patient is never associated with Tardive Dyskinesia in and of itself."

Figure 6.1 Is your patient competent? Document to protect yourself from law suit.

in some reactions to posttraumatic stress disorder, rational behavior is overwhelmed by an autonomic response to stimuli that, in hindsight, appears excessive. All it would take for Officer Andrew to beat Marlene Pinnock to death was a flashback to the bloody carnage to which he may have had to respond at this same intersection days, months, or even years earlier. Just the fading sunlight, rushing sounds from lanes of oncoming traffic, and blast of horns could be the ancillary stimuli to cause Andrew to lose his sense of time and turn from rescuer and public official to sole judge of right and wrong on planet Earth. The sidewalk justice, therefore, could have been delivered in a dissociated state of mind he may not even recall dishing out to a victim who had obviously lost her mind.

Similarly, was Officer Pantaleo's ego so challenged by Eric Garner that he reacted with violence instead of just issuing a summons? Can the same be said for Officer Darren Wilson who could have avoided the physical confrontation with Michael Brown by simply giving him another warning or writing him up a jaywalking citation? Even if Brown badmouthed Wilson, why initiate a potentially physical event when you are alone in a police unit, particularly if Wilson had received the report over his radio of a strong-arm robbery?

We have found that in stressful confrontations, clinicians as well as first emergency responders bring their ego baggage into situations, especially when confronted aggressively. Consider again Darren Wilson's ego when Brown might have dissed him by not walking back to the sidewalk or Pantaleo's ego when Eric Garner pulled his hands away as the officer tried to cuff him during an arrest. Now apply this ego substitution to clinical situations where a medical professional tries to help a potential patient, especially in an emergency room. Although there may not be an initial physical confrontation, the threat of litigation always hangs over their heads. Therefore, in the case of clinicians, informed consent from a patient competent to give it is a must.

Clinicians are all taught that our relationship with patients, whether implied or directly contracted, is to first show all possible respect for the patient's preference as the legal and moral nucleus of the "special relationship," as defined by the California Supreme Court in *Tarasoff*. The elements of informed consent include standards and requirements of information, voluntary state, and competency to provide consent; the lack of the last of these elements, we argue, was the mistake the court made in *Lessard* due to Alberta Lessard's incompetence, by reason of mental illness, to provide consent and to understand the obligations of her rights. These are all issues against which any professional functioning in a clinical role will be going head to head with in emergency psychiatry. This conflict with the unknown patient is to be expected by the very nature of presentations most likely to be encountered. The hypothetical example of an EMT showing up to help Officer Andrew restrain Marlene Pinnock or the EMTs at the scene of Garner's choke hold takedown all serve as instructive examples for purposes of this book. Standards of informed consent embrace both professional—corrections officers at Riker's Island—and material. Thus, they require patients to be reasonable people, and if not, then their incapacity for informed consent must be documented. Such would be the case were an EMT to medically restrain Pinnock roadside during a dire emergency or the corrections officer's isolating Murdough at Rikers by forcing him into solitary confinement for suicide precautions to not document his understanding that the psychotropics he was on could cause hyperthermia in such an environment.

Clearly, this unit of Rikers Island is a medical environment. Murdough's violation of the law—a minor misdemeanor—certainly did not justify solitary confinement as if he were Charles Manson at Pelican Bay Prison Security Housing Unit in California. The failure to monitor him on suicide precautions was negligence enough to be the cause of civil action; the failure to document that he was forced there against his will without his consent is a gross violation of his rights.

Requirements of information in such cases where psychiatry is practiced by law enforcement, firefighters, and corrections officers include diagnosis and nature of condition, the benefits reasonably expected from proposed clinical intervention, nature and probability of material risks, ability to predict results, irreversibility of procedure when applicable, and likely results of no treatment, available alternatives, and risk and benefits of both alternatives and no treatment. Thomas Szasz, who wrote *The Myth of Mental Illness* upon which the *Lessard* court relied, did not practice in high-acuity settings. He was a psychoanalyst who did not have to think about such mundane matters in cases where a patient could have drawn a knife on him or mayhem could erupt at the scene of his clinical encounter with a patient on the psychoanalytic couch. It is easy to be academically abstract in an ivory tower. It is much more difficult to be academically abstract in an inner-city hospital's emergency room when confronted by a suicidal individual wielding a weapon and threatening a rampage murder to satisfy the voices ringing inside his head.

On that California freeway, as Officer Andrew tried to save Pinnock's life, his own life, and the lives of innocent motorists simply trying to get home from work, mental illness was no myth. It was a lethal threat. An EMT should have shown up to assist in the restraint of Marlene Pinnock and should have immediately known she was incompetent for informed consent and that she required his best means of control. In this case, it should have been one of any number of safe and immediately effective injectable tranquilizers. The issue of an EMT's authority to inject this psychotic woman with a tranquilizer—or the issue of whether she was indeed psychotic—is best left to philosophy courses. In the middle of freeway traffic on that fateful evening of July 28, 2014, the issue is saving lives with a minimum of violence. As soon as possible, an EMT should document that Pinnock was incompetent for informed consent and the tranquilizer that should be administered was with the sole intent of preserving the lives of both her and others. It was justified, because it was the safest means to immobilize her for safe transport to the nearest emergency department with access to open beds on a secure inpatient psychiatry unit.

Could the Los Angeles fire department, California Highway Patrol, and individual officers be sued for violating this woman's rights had this procedure been followed? Sure. Would the plaintiff prevail? Not according to evidence-based best emergency medicine and emergency psychiatry practices documented with intention and justification for a clinical intervention. These would clearly demonstrate that she was incompetent for informed consent as a patient. In that last statement, the EMT would have made clear that he understood her rights.

The problem with the New York City Police Department (NYPD) choke hold case is that there simply is no evidence that officers, including EMTs, were the slightest bit concerned about the victim's rights. Garner was simply too different and objectionable in his behavior to be allowed any respect for his rights or bodily safety. And, in the wake of a suicide/double homicide of police officers Liu and Ramos, look where we are now with the Patrolmen's Benevolent Association (PBA) and the mayor and police commissioner all at odds. Look how this entire situation could have been avoided had police simply warned him they were going to get a warrant for him and advised him, absent any bodily contact, to get himself a lawyer, show up in court, or face subsequent arrest under a bench warrant for a nonappearance. Three people would probably still be alive in New York City had they done that. In the cases of Pinnock, Murdough, and Garner, the restraint was dictated by medical necessity—the officers' judgment of these three persons' dangerousness to self and others. They were not terrorists fleeing from an attack that caused harm to others and thus needing to be immobilized without consideration of force needed or addressing their right to know why their lives would be at risk. Two died, and one thought she was being killed and could have died. It is unfortunate today that officers of the law and fire service must practice medicine on our streets, but that is reality—and will remain reality until the federal judiciary reverses *Lessard* and reason is restored to emergency management of the seriously mentally ill simply allowed today to die with their rights on.

Of most importance for emergency psychiatry, whether practiced by MDs or allied professionals, therefore, is voluntary consent to treatment versus competency for informed consent. Assessment of patient's competency is far more complex than noting that a patient is merely irrational or acting in a bizarre fashion.

All of this might seem excessively complex and legalistic for purposes of emergency practices, and, in fact, it is complex. It is so very complex, because, by definition, clinicians in emergency medical incidents are frequently waiving patients' rights to confidentiality—their privileged communications—and their rights to escape the clinician's control, refuse treatment, or both. When emergency situations require that determinations of probable competence be made promptly, refusal of any necessary clinical intervention becomes particularly problematic. Although there is usually a presumption of the patient's competence, clinging to that presumption in the face of life-threatening circumstances will result in the failure to treat some incompetent patients, simply because they resist even the clinician's most basic efforts to assess, i.e., "get out of here, I don't want to talk with anymore of you jerks." You, the clinician, however, knows he's a barbiturate addict in lethal withdrawal.

On the other hand, concluding that all uncooperative patients, like Eric Garner, are probably incompetent is clearly wrong and would lead to overriding the wishes of some competent, if angry and disrespectful, patients. It is not required that a patient show any clinician respect. It is preferable and certainly better, but it is not a requirement as the condition for the patient to be an emergency psychiatric patient under a clinician's care. Was this the reason for the aggressive restraint of Eric Garner? He was belligerent when officers threatened to lay hands on. As a compromise, it is reasonable to begin with the presumption of competence when time does not appear to be of essence. In life-threatening circumstances, however, lowering the threshold at which a determination of probable incompetence is made is necessary. Thus, in an emergency, when a patient does not cooperate with evaluation and there is substantial indirect evidence of impairment of the patient's capacities based on information from caregivers and relatives about the patient's behavior, it is appropriate to conclude that the patient would probably be found incompetent by a court. The EMT knows the guy who just called him a jerk and would not let him prevent a lethal withdrawal from barbiturates would be found incompetent by a judge. His brother brought the Fiorinal bottle with valid amounts and dates. This is a neurological emergency, and the clinician knows that a barbiturate addict in acute withdrawal is also dangerous to himself and others in this state of mind.

Thus, when reviewing the statistical breakdown of psychiatric malpractice, it is important to put one's liability risk for either intervening or not in context of actual liability experience. Insurance records show that 25% of claims of medical negligence in psychiatry were for improper medical treatment, and 13% were for violation of patient's rights. Nearly 10% were for failure to ensure safety. Thus, clinicians can be between a rock and a hard spot, but to be legally and civilly informed about one's role in emergency psychiatry can in all but the most eccentric of circumstances require waiving the patient's rights.

The substance of forensic literature on this subject is the body of "competence" and how the clinician functions in essentially a judicial role in substituting his for the patient's judgment based on immediate preponderance of evidence—there is a 51% chance the clinician's judgment is right within the context of the presenting situation. By this substitution, he is asserting in word and deed that what he is doing is what the patient would consent to were he capable of doing so. What, therefore, are clinicians substituting in the eyes of the judiciary? What will they be judged upon in the event a claim is filed against them for violating a patient's rights?

Let us look at the elements demanded in a full assessment of competency for informed consent in order to know what has been substituted by treating either without or against formal informed consent. What do these terms mean?

Most determinations of decision-making ability, of course, are ambiguous, but few ever reach court. Physicians accept most patient decisions unless they believe that there may be substantial impairment of competence. In the latter case they must estimate the likelihood that a court would find the patient incompetent on the basis of independent assessment. The President's Commission endorsed the approach of allowing physicians to substitute decisions made by family members when physicians decide a patient likely would be found incompetent. And clinicians need to remember that they must be familiar with their own jurisdiction's law and that no assessment will demonstrate perfect competence. The courts will look at determinations of functioning that do not deviate from the average when determining claims of either violation of patient's rights, or, conversely, improper treatment or abandonment. That is, only the patients on the extreme end of the bell-shaped curve are likely to be found incompetent or so ambiguous in competence that clinicians' interventions violate their rights. And courts may also impose a "reasonableness" factor in which they would assess what a reasonable objective third party would do if placed in the shoes of the clinician. And under the Americans with Disabilities Act (ADA), mental illness is considered a disability, and those who suffer from it, particularly those who show up in an emergency room because of their mental illness, are protected by it.

A caveat is that the clinician's conclusion that a patient would probably be found incompetent does not eclipse the necessity for the evaluation process. And, that assessment should also, when freed up with the time to document, include a determination of diagnostic impression of mental disorder and recommendations for treatment when possible. All causes of delirium, for example, should be suspected and ruled out. Effective treatment, even that one Haldol injection, may restore a patient's faculties sufficiently to deprive patients of their decision-making rights if automatically given again, without reassessment, just for mild agitation. Such acute reversal in competence is of major concern to the courts—i.e., "Hey, doc! No more shots. I'm just a little scared now and will be OK when I eat something. I remember what happened now." Give that guy another injection against his will, rather than special ordering him a lunch tray from the cafeteria, and that clinician could be in deep trouble.

While clinically assessing, regardless of pressures of time, clinicians are always determining for purposes of prediction, which is the court's opinion in the event of judicial review—rare as it will be. Better safe than sorry, therefore, and also, "if it's not written down, it didn't happen"—and it either was not considered or not done for purposes of later judicial review.

Failure to treat, negligent treatment, and, conversely, violation of a patient's rights are causes for action against anyone functioning in the role of a healthcare professional; courts may apply the same law to officers in special mental illness units of police departments. The more one respects the law and civil responsibility as a clinician, the less likely one will be to experience judicial review of any emergency psychiatry decision making. Exceptions to informed consent include emergency, patient's privilege in restricting access to information, court-ordered waiver, and incompetence. Documenting any or all will always render one's interventions less vulnerable to retroactive legal challenge, and thus there is less chance of trouble for even the best clinician acting in good faith.

Again, this gets back to determination of competency and "substitution." When clinicians use best practices to detain, or even warn a potential third party, they are predicting that the court would substitute their judgment for that of the patient's judgment, assuming that in a rational state, the patient would not decide to kill or injure another person. Clinicians are therefore serving as a substitute healthy ego for a patient throughout an unremitting clinical process of human destructiveness. Were clinicians not to do so, based on common sense and good clinical assessment and judgment—assumedly documented as such—and the patient injures or kills a third party, they are more likely to be sued for negligence or failure to treat. Such treatment proceeds via substituting their presumably healthy egos for the patients' currently impaired egos. Presumably there is no difference than in principle in such emergency interventions—at least for frontline clinicians faced with immienent harm or mayhem—than when finding patient competent for informed consent by a physician at bedside.

This is a new era, and case law has likely not caught up to standards of clinical practice for mental health officers functioning as psychiatrists determining dangerousness and mental illness, as in the Elliot Rodger Santa Barbara case; psychiatric nurses, as in the Red Arrow Milwaukee Park case; EMTs on site of police misconduct with the mentally ill; jailers titled mental health corrections officers as in Rikers broiling of Murdough, and volunteers now increasingly greeting patients entering emergency rooms. Under such conditions, it would be extremely unlikely that the vast majority of clinicians would be held liable either criminally or civilly for violating patient's rights following detention, although they could be threatened with that many times in the process of doing it. Still, they must know about competency for informed consent, but most have never heard of it.

Whether one's jurisdiction calls this a Section 12 (Massachusetts) or 5150 (California), clinicians are determining and/or signing for emergency commitment up to 10 days, oftentimes a maximum of 72 hours of working days, where failure to hospitalize would create a likelihood of serious harm by reason of mental illness. This is commonly called a *writ of apprehension*. This, once again, requires assessment of competence to be a conditional voluntary patient.

A patient determined to be in need of emergency detention, or actually signed for emergency detention, must be offered a conditional voluntary admission. Acceptance of a voluntary admission can have a significant impact on the course of treatment. Because the admitting physician likely will not be the treating physician, it may be better practice to defer acceptance of a conditional voluntary, where possible, signed upon admission to allow the treating psychiatrist the opportunity to make his or her own assessment of competence. If the person is deemed incompetent upon admission, then his or her conditional voluntary admission should not be accepted and commitment proceedings should be considered. Again, it is the issue of assessing competence, but here it is somewhat simpler. The question is, "does the patient have at least a very basic understanding that he or she is in the hospital for treatment whether or not he or she is accepting treatment, and that if he or she wishes to leave the hospital, that a three-day notice is required, during which time the hospital may petition for commitment?" This is a fairly minimal level of competence. It does not require that the person accept treatment, nor does it imply competence to make treatment decisions. If the patient is deemed incompetent at a periodic review, then the voluntary admission is considered no longer valid and commitment proceedings should be initiated.

Although clinicians will unlikely be doing this in emergency psychiatry, almost by definition, they should know that administration of antipsychotic medications is not covered by emergency detention. Oftentimes called by different names in different jurisdictions, what is required here is clear and convincing evidence that the patient is incompetent to make informed decisions about proposed medical treatment that will more likely than not be of significant benefit to the patient. In this hearing for a detained patient, usually one detained for a total of 17 days, the courts will either agree to substitute the incompetent patient's autonomy allowing medical authority to treat against the patient's will or defer for further observation while detained. Similarly, this can be done through appointment of a guardian who substitutes for an incompetent patient's decision-making authority. If the clinician is unable to present clear and convincing evidence that a patient is incompetent to make decisions about antipsychotic medication that will more likely than not significantly benefit a presenting psychiatric condition, then the court could rule that the patient has the right to make a decision, including a bad decision.

Caution is required in such situations, as was recently demonstrated in Maplewood, Minnesota, wherein a confused and likely delirious patient was allowed to participate in a family conference over his competency to divorce his wife and change his will. The judge would not hear an emergency petition at night, the patient became hyped and later tried to murder his nurses and then died in flight from the hospital after police tasering failed and he had to be taken down on the street. It is clear in retrospect that he should have been medically restrained, whether or not he agreed; such medical restraint is less legally restricted on a medical ward where other patients reside than a psychiatric ward, where other forms of de-escalation are expected prior to emergency restraint, whether medical or physical. This patient, whether competent or not for informed consent, should have been medically restrained in a medical ward before having to be physically restrained by the police on the street outside the hospital—the latter proving fatal.

We only go into these complex medico-legal matters here in order to demonstrate the seriousness with which the courts take both the depriving of a person's liberty by emergency detention and, even more so, administering mind-altering medications against a patient's will. When clinicians restrain, medicate, or admit a patient, therefore, without the patient's consent, they are waiving due process as the exception—as a medical emergency. We have discussed such emergency waiver of due process wherein clinicians substitute their judgment for that of their patients' egos where determinations of competency and informed consent, as likely was the case of Marlene Pinnock, and such medico-legal demands become seemingly oxymoronic. Nonetheless, documentation is necessary, even in the obvious case of Pinnock curbside on I-10.

An evidence-based clinical assessment of dangerousness is necessary in any clinical encounter with an unknown person, particularly if forced custody, restraint or detention are needed.

Ask these questions before releasing a potentially dangerous person, because anyone officially functioning in the role of clinician should be considered to have "peculiar ability" with special knowledge and ability for control as caretaker under *Tarasoff*:

1. Did symptoms of encounter relate to violence or threat of violence?
2. Does the person have a history of violent behavior?
3. If yes, does that person have a history of arrests or violence before age 15?
4. If yes to both, then already, you have a high risk of imminent violence in the event that violence or threats of violence were an element of the presentation you were called to see. And, if symptoms have not been adequately treated, you must not release this person.
5. If symptoms have been adequately treated, is the person likely to comply with prescribed outpatient treatment? With history or likelihood of non-compliance, again, you cannot release this person.
6. But, if yes, does that person have a paranoid disorder?
7. And, again, if yes, is the person male, age 15–35?
8. If so, is he exhibiting soft neurological signs and/or does he have below-average IQ?

   Give one point for each of these factors. And, if possible, try to get a retrospective Conners test from a reliable family member that can be computer-scored for your review within 1 hour. Robust evidence of conduct disorder and cerebral dysfunction syndrome in childhood is, in our opinion, as strong a factor as soft neurological signs and far more valid. What is sometimes done for soft neuro signs with such short assessment time is to have the patients repetitively tap their fingers sequentially while keeping the contralateral hand at rest. Either severe clumsiness in doing so, or, more significantly, adventitious movements, like movement of the leg, emerging facial movements, or inability to suppress movements of contralateral fingers, constitute soft neurological signs. Although these factors do not predict violence, they are more often than not present in those committing recurrent violent acts. And, one is epidemiologically informed and knows that most violent felons have subtle neuropsychiatry findings, although the converse is not true; that is, not all boys that do will be violent. A significantly higher percentage than the normal peer group will be, which is just one factor in your decision making.

9. Does the person have a history of alcohol or drug abuse?
10. If so, is there a history of violence under the influence of substances?

    Again, to be epidemiologically informed, one must know that most offenses are associated with these factors, but, again, most substance abusers are not necessarily at risk for violence. In fact, do we really have any clue whatsoever as to how many violent crimes were prevented by drinking or smoking pot? We are looking for a pattern and one that likely correlates in this person and his cohort with cerebral dyscontrol.
11. Has the person identified a particular victim or class of victims? Here we revisit *Tarasoff*, and considerations of the potentially judged special relationship with the patient. Additionally, revisit the necessity these days to be aware of the higher risk of both gang and domestic violence. The latter was discussed in the red zone and the former in the *Tarasoff* case, where we suspect the deceased was perceived to have either cheated on or rejected her murderer. In a more psychotic version of this, erotomania, the person might have a delusion that a third party is in love with him or her. That was cause of John Hinckley's assassination attempt of President Reagan and Cho's murder of Emily Hilscher at his initiation of the Virginia Tech Massacre.
12. Will the person be likely to come into contact with the identified victim? That was a key finding for liability in the Tarasoff case. The patient/murderer Poddar said he was going to kill Tatiana Tarasoff when she returned from her vacation. It was this statement that likely was most damaging for the treating psychologist. It all but guaranteed contact with the intended victim. Distance, of course, is significant. Is a person in Chicago likely to come in contact with a hated person in Alaska? Possibly, but the psychologist would have been saved by being able to address this matter by saying that the intended victim was not expected to return and had moved to Hong Kong.
13. Does the person have access to firearms? Never forget to ask this in our world of omnipresent handguns today. However, in Florida, such a question posed by a physician is barred by state law. The American Medical Association (AMA) suggests that physicians ask it anyway because to learn that information is in the best interests of the patient, and though the issue of free speech versus state regulation of the medical profession will likely be decided by the Supreme Court, barring a Supreme Court of the United States (SCOTUS) ruling in favor of Florida, your questions may still be protected speech under the First Amendment.
14. Will the patient return to the environment where violence originated? Commonly, a mentally ill patient has become violent in the setting of a residential placement. Do not return him or her there until aggravating factors have been assessed and neutralized. Separating roommates who are delusional about each other is a simple example.

15. Does the person have a stable environment to enter? Evidence is overwhelming that mentally ill patients are more likely to relapse in high emotional intensity living situations than in stable ones, and most of the emergency psychiatry assessments will be on mentally ill patients. If a young adult male is living with his mother and his mother prevents his independence from her for either emotional or economic reasons—two versus only one Supplemental Security Income (SSI) check—the clinician needs to be aware of the potential for another violent incident if that was either in the patient's history or part of the presentation i.e. "assaulted or threatened mother." And, let's be realistic as clinicians. That mother may be buying drugs with his SSI check for both of them and even other parties, too. Addiction has no morality, irrespective of age, gender, ethnicity, filial relationship, or race. Consider, again, the case of Adam Lanza and his mother, Nancy, and the environment she allowed him to inhabit in which his mental illness festered and metastasized into suicidal lethality.
16. Does the patient have a job or training program upon release from your custody? This would provide more structure, self-control and self-esteem, less risk of out-of-control behavior, such as substance abuse, running with a gang, stalking, and the like.
17. Are the person's reasons for release from your custody reasonable? "There's no problem walking on the freeway, because I have been transformed in ethereal way"—you know that is an extreme reason not to release someone in your custody just found walking on a freeway.
18. Can the clinician reasonably come up with a treatment plan? That is unlikely, considering the time constraints of emergency psychiatry. Maybe a frail and demented patient can be safely returned to a nursing home, but, if the clinician believes that a person is at high risk, is there a reasonable treatment plan? That is unlikely.
19. Now, having these answers in hand, if there is a history of violence, particularly with or without arrests before age 15—or there is a likelihood of substance abuse, particularly with violence associated with it, risks of not hospitalizing a patient are very high. Let inpatient psychiatry figure it out. That is why hospitals are paid in the four figures for a bed per night. And, if most of the above are present, again, the risk of not hospitalizing is just too great. Risk is less without a past history of adult or juvenile violence and/or without a history of substance abuse with or without a history of violence under the influence, but, nonetheless, research there shows some risk. In this latter circumstance, the clinician needs to have a really solid plan before releasing this person from his custody (Rofman et al., 1983).

## REFERENCE

Rofman, ES et al. 1983. *Hospital and Community Psychiatry*, Vol. 34, 1, January.

# 7

# Police and psychiatric patient encounters

Because studies have indicated that individuals who are confronted by police are 67 times more likely to suffer from mental illness than people not suffering from mental illness, police need to know with whom they are dealing and what protocols should be in play. Unfortunately, there is precious little in police training manuals and in criminology literature about the problem of confronting and interrogating the mentally ill, especially the mentally ill who present as dangerous. To any individual confronted, even as the result of a simple traffic stop for a missing taillight, as recently in the case in North Charleston, or even a moving violation, the very nature of a police confrontation conveys a threat to that individual. To the mentally ill, largely because they have little or no resiliency to threats or mechanisms for dealing with perceived threats rationally, they are more likely than not to react to threats with hostility usually fear-based. Their aggression, whether accurately understood or not, is sometimes perceived by police to be life-threatening.

Looking at confrontations with the mentally ill from a police perspective, it is assumed that people stopped for questioning or detention should be responsive and complicit with police commands so as to avoid the use of force. Questions like "let me see your ID" or "are you carrying any weapons" are completely legitimate even if police do not explain why. The Supreme Court has ruled that police have the authority to stop and question if officers believe that a criminal act may be afoot. However, though a police stop or a stop and frisk may be legally correct and police mean no threat or hostility, these assumptions are simply not immediately applicable to mentally ill subjects who may be delusional or at least walled in psychologically by a world of their own making. It is one thing to require of an emergency room (ER) clinician the adherence to a protocol for identifying the potentially mentally ill. It is another to ask a police officer, who may believe that every traffic stop or street stop carries with it the potential for a life-threatening incident, to take on the role of a therapist and to make an on-the-spot diagnosis of the subject of his stop. Despite the continuing blur of facts in Officer Wilson's encounter with Michael Brown in Ferguson, clearly there was a verbal confrontation that escalated into a physical confrontation when Brown attacked the officer and reached inside the car for his gun. Should we have expected that Officer Darren Wilson psychologically analyze Brown before shifting his patrol car into reverse to block his flight to avoid a physical confrontation resulting in the use of lethal force? The same can be said about Ezell Ford's death in Los Angeles and Eric Garner's death on Staten Island.

We contend that there should be a "commonsense" protocol that comes into play when police find themselves dealing with individuals acting strangely, whether resisting arrest for an obvious crime, meandering down a busy arterial street, or talking to himself or herself. When a person like Eric Garner screams that he cannot breathe after an officer, working with backup on the scene, places him in a choke hold, and knowing that a choke hold is illegal in New York, the officer should release the hold long enough for his backup to handcuff the suspect. Lives and careers would have been saved. That is common sense. Accordingly, and still mindful that we are Monday-morning quarterbacking, we are deconstructing a number of recent police use of force encounters to see how commonsense emergency protocols might have been adopted so as to save the lives of those detained. The following cases are discussed:

- Ezell Ford in Los Angeles.
- Kajieme Powell in North St. Louis, Missouri.
- Miriam Carey in Washington, D.C.
- Kelly Thomas in Fullerton, California. A homeless, mentally ill man and veteran was beaten to death while in custody.
- Red Arrow Park shooting in Milwaukee, Wisconsin.
- Alfred Redwine in Albuquerque, New Mexico. Police shot a homeless mental and delusional individual whom they perceived to be a threat even though he was asking for help. His offense? Illegal camping.
- Scott Walker in Charleston, South Carolina.
- Freddie Gray in Baltimore.
- In New Mexico, state police shoot at a minivan full of children because they frightened a disturbed woman into fleeing.
- In Phoenix, Arizona, police shoot and kill a mentally ill patient during a routine petition for involuntary commitment. Police responded to an apartment complex for an emergency mental health pickup order.

In this latest case, according to police, 50-year-old Michelle Cusseaux was threatening mental health workers, saying she would show up at the mental health facility where she was supposed to be receiving treatment and shoot the workers. When police arrived at Cusseaux's apartment to pick her up, they said she was agitated and swinging a hammer. "When our officers go to serve mental health pickup orders, they're some of the most dangerous calls to even go on because those people often have mental challenges," said Phoenix police spokesman Sergeant Tommy Thompson. "And that's what we're dealing with at this time" (www.ireport.cnn.com/docs/DOC-1163455).

When officers, including a sergeant, tried to get Cusseaux to come out of the apartment, she opened the door and allegedly had a claw hammer raised above her head. Police said the sergeant fired one shot, striking Cusseaux. Officers administered cardiopulmonary resuscitation (CPR), and the woman later died at a hospital. Police said a weapons examination and information from witnesses confirmed the 48-year-old sergeant fired his weapon only once.

> "All of a sudden, I heard them screaming, 'Drop the hammer, drop the hammer, drop the hammer,'" said Michael Lebay, a maintenance man who witnessed the incident. "This person lunged out at them with the hammer, swinging it crazy, and the officer unfortunately had to shoot. ... When she lunged out at them, she was trying to hit somebody in the head," Lebay said. "The way she was swinging that hammer, if she would have connected, one of the officers would have been seriously hurt. So in my opinion, they had no choice."
>
> *(www.ireport.cnn.com/docs/DOC-1163455)*

> Neighbors said Cusseaux was known around the complex for having bouts with mental illness.
>
> "It's sad because ... mental illness, we need to take care of it," neighbor Linda Garcia said (*Arizona Republic*).
>
> *(www.ireport.cnn.com/docs/DOC-1163455)*

Victor White III, a black youth, was arrested for marijuana possession and allegedly shot himself in the back while handcuffed in a New Orleans police car. Attorney Benjamin Crump, who also represents Trayvon Martin's parents in Florida and is "representing Michael Brown's family in Ferguson, characterized Mr White's death as a 'Houdini handcuff suicide,' a case similar to that of other young minority men who were said to have died of self-inflicted gunshot wounds while handcuffed and in police custody—Chavis Carter, in Jonesboro, Ark., in 2012, and Jesus Huerta, in Durham, N.C., in November" (Reckdahl 2014).

We left discussion of the initial protocols for emergency assessment of dangerousness from the mnemonics "Throw out the 'GUNS' and 'ACT MYSELF' on the Red Screen for Emergency Medical Rapid Assessment" to this chapter, because this is the routine emergency confronting the police. The wild card these days, however, is the unpredictable and seemingly incomprehensible psychotic on the street. The police generally understand and feel confident in encounters with bank robbers. They are crooks, but they are rational, know the game and play it by rules—if not laws—that cops and robbers both understand. As seen, the red screen from www.digitalclinician.com can be used for threat assessment. In the blue zone, the officer is having coffee hearing only non-emergent chatter of old chronic problems that can wait. In the green zone, he is prowling for crimes. In the yellow zone, he unbuttons his holster. In the orange zone, he grips his gun. In the red zone, he has a citizen's face in his gun sight. These are states of awareness.

With the mentally ill however, there are no rules for cops and robbers; so, first of all the policeman must assess the critical issues of life threat and level of consciousness. If and when cleared, any medical/neuropsychological disease can wait for assessment from a well-run clinic. This time-determined rules-set is not cited here in the expectation that policemen should be EMTs, but, if they are public safety officers, it is imperative they know what can be causing strange behavior, whether the person is talking to them, like Eric Garner, or not. Therefore, assuming there is reason to arrest Eric Garner, officers must make sure he can breathe and his heart is pumping adequately. He said he could not breathe, and eventually his heart did stop beating with the takedown and choke hold. He is morbidly obese and perhaps diabetic. Why is he resisting arrest? Is he copacidal? Is he delusional from a medical condition that has sapped his resiliency? If so, are there procedures in place within more forward-thinking agencies to deal with copacidal or delusional individuals who present threatening situations to police, and if so, how do police defuse them?

San Antonio, Texas, now has mental health cops. It will be critically important for them to know emergency medicine. Things will sour on them, and if so, would our tort law be applied to an incident in which they functioned as clinicians? Will police forces that field mental health cops be judged as clinicians under *Lessard* and *Tarasoff*, although that may seem to be a stretch? Police should not be held to the standard of clinician, because when they confront, it is only to defuse and potentially save a person or themselves or others from injury—not to intervene medically. However, it is not possible to predict how courts might rule one day when a policeman's role is so ambiguous as to be titled Mental Health Officer of the Law. For example, one of the clearest illustrations of role confusion imposed upon police officers is clearly visible in the police shooting of a homeless, mentally ill black man in Red Arrow Park, Milwaukee. Officer Christopher Manney claimed there was a struggle when he did a welfare check on Dontre Hamilton sleeping in the park.

"Shots fired. Officer-involved. Guy started beating me. Started hitting me in the head with my own baton," he shouted, according to dispatch audio obtained by Fox News WITI-TV. When the man didn't flinch, he said he continued to shoot. He shot 10 times. "Uh, Starbucks. Starbucks. Help right now. Uh, send me medical too. He's gonna need medical. Shots multiple times to the chest. Black male. He's about 20. Starbucks at Kilbourn and Water. I need medical" (www.wisn.com/news/just-released-911-recordings-capture-moments-after-red arrow-park-shooting/30364470).

Officer Manney was cleared for use of lethal force—he was defending himself from serious bodily injury—but fired for not following procedures for welfare checks of seriously mentally ill? Had he followed the established procedures, perhaps there would have been no violent confrontation, the victim would not have been killed, and Officer Manney would still have his job. But look at the irony here. Welfare checks of the seriously mentally ill offender sleeping in a park? That is a total paradigm shift for modern medicine, wherein the public itself, public safety officials, and the medical community are expected to accept the standards of the court in protecting psychotic people and the public alike from delusions and hallucinations.

It is ironic that decades after a court ruled that Alberta Lessard was not sick, and thus set the constitutional standard for involuntary commitment, a police officer was held responsible for failing to meet the standards of practice of a psychiatric nurse in the case of Dontre Hamilton. These narrow court-imposed definitions of mental illness and the ways of dealing with them are confusing enough for clinicians. Imagine how confusing it must be for the law enforcement and criminal justice communities.

Milwaukee Police Chief Flynn was initially infuriated by the protests of another shooting of a black man by a white officer. The citizens in this city, he said, were "missing in action" in the case of blacks killing blacks in the social chaos of Milwaukee's core. What has never been mentioned is the gross travesty of justice and all civility presuming it acceptable to allow anyone to sleep in a park, particularly a man known to the police to be psychotic, who had already been checked out and cleared of any wrongdoing by two other Milwaukee police officers. If the Milwaukee court ruled correctly in *Lessard* that there is no such thing as mental illness, then why should a Milwaukee cop be fired for failing the standards of practice for a psychiatric nurse checking on a known psychotic patient? Chief Flynn in his moment of peak emotionality over the absurdity of the whole situation did not mention this. Officer Manney is a police officer and not a psychiatric nurse. Red Arrow Park is not any safer a place for a patient to recover from psychosis than it is for recovery from congestive heart failure.

Cases like these, where police are required to confront the mentally ill or at-risk individuals acting strangely, are the progeny of the *Lessard* case, discussed above. No one could have foreseen the chaos that would result from the *Lessard* ruling, which ultimately put the public and the police at risk. The chaos of bloodshed in Red Arrow Park and resounding outcries of injustices of the police killing black males would one day come back to haunt the justice system as we continue to wrestle with the implications of the *Lessard* ruling and the arguments that urged the court to so rule. Dontre Hamilton died, a policeman lost his career trying to protect himself and had to be sacrificed to spare the city from race riots, and both the police chief and the public were outraged by an event that could have and should have been avoided.

"The standard of imminent danger set by Lessard's case would prove to be a tragically inaccurate measure for who was mentally ill and in need of being kept safe. Thousands of people who were sick—but not obviously immediately dangerous—would be set free without proper care. In time, even Lessard would be denied protection she desperately sought. By correcting one outrage, her case had created others" (Kissinger 2011).

It will be the length of an officer's career before the medical ignorance embodied by the *Lessard* ruling will be recognized by the courts and the public. Until then, officers, like Christopher Manney, will be held to standards of professional practice more those of clinical practice, rather than policing. Under *Lessard*, however, they are the ones empowered to deal with the consequences of criminalizing serious mental illness.

Thus, Chief Flynn and others across the country will be forced to create ad hoc mental health cops. The absurd and seemingly contradictory dichotomy of roles for contemporary policing is the headline today, illustrating police interactions with the eccentrics on the street. The new mental health cops do not require a nursing or medical degree even though they are put in the position of dealing with people who might be unable to discriminate right from wrong or who, because of a medical impairment, cannot comport their behavior to comply with police commands. Mental health cops, however, will require knowledge of strange behavior seen on the beat every hour or every minute. Traditional law enforcement on the street is neither social work nor nursing, but is public safety. It is control of behavior that should not be occurring under our rule of law. There is a time for enforcing and a time for dealing with aberrant and minor criminal behavior without confrontation. There is a time when public safety trumps law enforcement. In the arrest of Eric Garner, just as in Red Arrow Park, Milwaukee, this was just such a time.

From the perspective of dealing with those behaving strangely, the last thing needed is an aggressive show of force and overwhelming takedown. Ultimately, this is not a law enforcement or public safety issue, but an ego issue. What possible purpose does it serve, other than proving in the neighborhood who is in charge? Is there not a better way? Certainly these New York City Police Department (NYPD) officers on Staten Island did not intend to kill Eric Garner. It is not asking too much of them to learn some basic facts in the emergency medical procedures for "strange behavior, verbal," if that is the presentation Garner in fact was. The authors question if that was even the case, except from their perspective in his resisting arrest.

The New Orleans case of Victor White is even more ominous, as it hardens the default line polarization of police and the black community. In light of this arrest and death inside a police unit, how does one explain a black youth, arrested for possessing marijuana, committing suicide by gun while handcuffed in a patrol car—and, worse yet, shooting himself in the back? The Garner and White cases are going to evolve as racist confrontations between police and blacks. The others, whether serendipitously black or white, are, in the authors' opinions, primarily encounters between the police and a more likely than not intoxicated Michael Brown strolling in the middle of a busy street or strange behaving citizens in the case of Dontre Hamilton asleep in the park. As such, they must be handled differently to prevent what is routine emergency medicine from converting into disaster medicine. It can happen so fast, as in the hammer swinging patient in Phoenix, when basic rules of triaging patients are ignored.

Sometimes the question is whether police should focus more on public safety or on enforcement, because sometimes the two should be differentiated with different protocols in the hope that there would be different outcomes. There are lots of "strange" people on the street, whether relatively so in the eyes of beholders, as with Garner on Staten Island, or actual, as with Pinnock in Los Angeles. There are a lot of medically ill people like Charles Logan of Maplewood, Minnesota, on the street, too, and there are a lot of dangerous people too, some of whom, as detailed above, want the officer to shoot them. Know the limits of power. Know how to differentiate contemporary public safety from enforcement, because confrontational situations with the mentally ill individual behaving strangely can end very badly if the officer does not understand who and what he or she is dealing with. The 911 tapes of Officer Manney's welfare check of Dontre Hamilton are dramatic proof of such encounters with the unknown person. Pinnock was known to the California Highway Patrol (CHP); Hamilton was obviously not known to Officer Manney although he was known to other officers who had checked him out earlier and cleared him of any wrongdoing and life threat to self. The recordings of those two encounters clearly demonstrate knowledge of the subject going in were vastly different, yet officers' fear, first of being hit by a speeding car on a freeway and second of being beaten by the officer's own baton, resulted in the same catastrophic outcomes.

In the Kajieme Powell case in North St. Louis, only a few miles away from where Michael Brown was fatally shot, folks in the neighborhood knew that Powell was mentally ill. Did police who patrolled that neighborhood know that? When a suspect like Powell is pacing up and down the street talking to himself as if he is in the midst of a conversation with unseen figures, does it not seem like he is hearing voices? And if so, especially if that person asks—or even challenges police—by saying, "shoot me," why would police do that? Would there have been any way to defuse that situation without lethal force, even assuming that Powell was wielding a steak knife, although we could not see it on the cell phone video of that encounter? Similarly with Michelle Cusseaux in Phoenix, was there time for officers to back off, regroup, and return with less lethal force? Our argument is not that police should refrain from defending themselves, but that the entire police protocol of dealing with the mentally ill, dangerous, or individual acting strangely and posing a threat should be reviewed with an eye to understanding the abnormal psychology of the situation so as to avoid bloodshed and maintain the public safety. It also must be viewed within the budgetary practicality of our police forces being grossly undermanned for the largest gun-toting population in the world. We do not want "slow walk" from our police; we want "walk on by" when enforcement is not necessary to prevent foreseeable threat.

In the New Orleans case of Victor White, there appears to be a particularly ominous use of lethal force that only threatens to polarize the police and the black community. The intent for restraining White with handcuffs in the first place—as in the case of the takedown of Garner—will be the first question. Is every citizen in New Orleans found by police to be carrying pot going to be handcuffed and booked into jail? What will be the justification for his being allowed to shoot himself in the back while handcuffed in the patrol car? At first blush, this case, from intent for restraint to justification for his death will not pass the smell test, and, like the case of Garner on Staten Island, simply polarize the police and black community, making public safety more and more difficult to provide in lower socioeconomic communities, more often than not inhabited by minorities, gangs, and the seriously mentally ill. These are tinder boxes that require special attention to police tactics with both minorities and mentally ill alike.

Unfortunately, although not implied to be one and the same, they oftentimes cohabit neighborhoods whose economy is primarily dependent on illegal trafficking in contraband run by crooks from prisons and their gangsters on the streets. No case will be the same. Too often enforcement response in lower-level crimes is namely the arrest requiring hands-on restraint that ignites confrontation. For Officer Manney, he did not know his subject had already had his emergency medical check—also called a welfare check—and was cleared. The officer should have let sleeping dogs lie; Hamilton did not meet the standards for any intervention because he was not immediately dangerous. He was asleep.

He proved to be dangerous, however, when awakened. If police provoke an otherwise nondangerous person, whether intentionally or not, have they crossed a red line when dealing with the mentally ill?

The issue for the police in the case of Miriam Carey in the nerve center of the nation's capitol and Marlene Pinnock's strolling onto I-10 during rush hour in Los Angeles are far different matters. Who would not agree that these two women were not behaving strangely? Yet, the former was shot to death, taking four rounds in her back while her child looked on beside her in the car, and the world watched the chaos of a supposed counterterror right in the heart of the nation's capital. There was no need for secret videos. The whole world was watching and saw the officer carrying the dead mother's child away from the scene. The woman was unarmed, but her erratic behavior, leading Capitol Police on a chase through central DC, was enough to so unnerve them to the extent that, even after she stopped and exited the car, their only response was to shoot her without determining if she was armed or whether there was anyone else in the car. Carey was suffering from a psychotic episode resulting, in part, from postpartum depression.

For CHP Officer Andrew, a brave and heroic rescue ended in totally unnecessary horror as an obviously sick woman pleaded for him to stop beating her, calling him the devil. Following hospitalization she asserted publicly that he wanted to kill her. He may have at the moment out of utter despair and fear, but that was not the intent—this looked like on video a physical form of sidewalk justice for somebody unlikely to gain therapeutically from such shock treatment to her brain.

In the cases of Carey, Pinnock, Garner, Powell, and possibly Michael Brown, officers were confronted with this emergency medicine presentations demonstrated by the template, "Strange Behavior, Verbal." Template 1 is best represented in the emergency medicine literature of "the violently disruptive user of vile language" who, as long as he is talking is rarely violent, therefore needing isolation in the ER to de-escalate him and prevent disruption of emergency care to others (www.challengercme.com/Product?productid=18).

The case of Freddie Gray in Baltimore, in which six police officers have been charged and indicted in Gray's death, also presents a problem for how police react to an individual acting strangely. Gray did not threaten police when Lieutenant Brian Rice on bike patrol first noticed that Gray was holding a knife whose blade he was folding into the handle. Whether he believed it was a switchblade—illegal in Baltimore—or whether he did not know whether it was legal or not and wanted to investigate, when he saw Freddie Gray catch his stare and then run away, that was enough for Rice to pursue him. Under *Terry v. Ohio*, police do not need probable cause to detain and search an individual if they have a reasonable suspicion that a crime is afoot. Hence, if Lieutenant Rice reasonably believed that Gray might have been wielding an illegal weapon, that would have been reason for him to ask to inspect the weapon. Instead, when stopped, Gray resisted, and the result was an arrest and transportation to the police station in a van in which Gray was placed without restraints. This might have resulted in fatal injuries that caused his death. We ask, was there an alternative approach that would have mitigated a confrontational situation in which the police assured Gray that he was not under arrest, but merely was asked to display the knife so they could have ascertained its legality? If Gray had not threatened the police initially, why was there a need for a hostile street confrontation? Police, even when a potential detainee is acting irrationally confrontational, should be trained to back off and try to talk the detainee down, assuring him or her that there is no threat and that all police want to do is talk. As psychiatrists have learned through experience, asking a patient politely for a conversation is the best way to calm a patient's fears, a practice police should adopt (Figure 7.1).

The case of Strange Behavior, Nonverbal, is best represented in the literature of Catatonia and Mutism.

Virginia Tech shooter Cho Seung-Hui presented as Strange Behavior, Nonverbal, and was misdiagnosed as depressed, when, in fact, he was likely preoccupied in his own delusional and hallucinatory world later exploding into the world's consciousness with the Virginia Tech massacre and his bizarre warrior image on NBC News (Liebert and Birnes 2011).

The nonverbal strange behavior is best seen in the case of Unidentified Asian Male (UIAM).

Little was known of UIAM, an Unidentified Asian Male, who lay in catatonic stupor. A medical student insisted on testing for Gegenhalten resistance to movement of a limb. Catatonic stupor immediately converted to catatonic fury. His supervising psychiatrist was backpedaling out of the patient's room

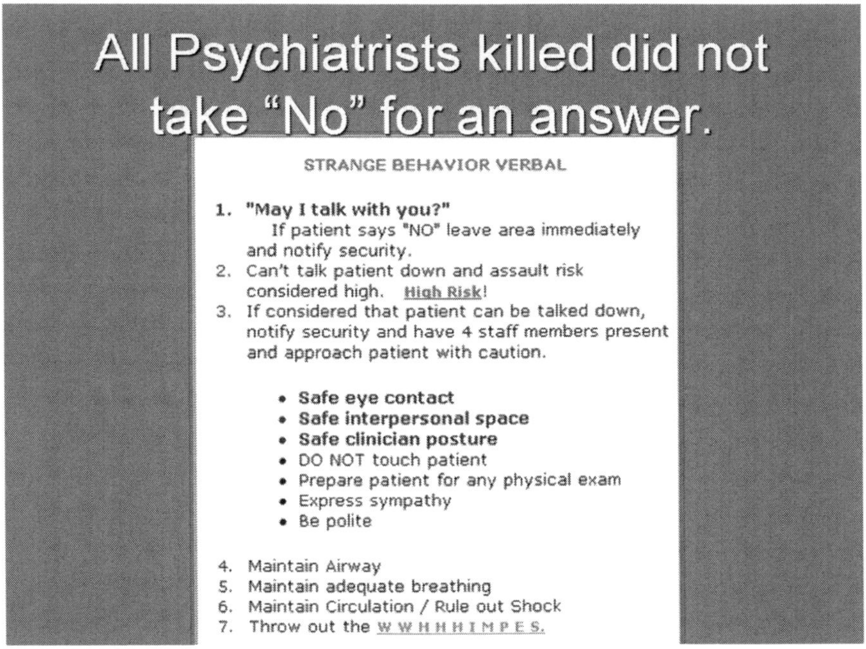


Figure 7.1 Strange behavior, nonverbal. WWHHHIMPES—Wernicke's Encephalopathy, Withdrawal from Barbiturates, Hypoglycemia, Hypertensive Encephalopathy, Intracranial Hemorrhage, Hypoxia, Meningitis, Encephalitis, Status Epilepticus.

with admonitions not to do this. And that medical student soon learned to keep his distance from such a patient, without standing with his feet either parallel or perpendicular to the patient. Keep that imaginary line connecting your toes at a 45° angle with your hands pensively folded across your chest. In this way, you are ready to either backpedal in the event the patient lunges toward you or deflect punches backhand in the event it is too late for you to move—all the while appearing at ease. You most likely know how to stand for a golf or tennis swing and fishing cast. Know how to stand in emergency psychiatry. Oftentimes you cannot tell when such violence will erupt—e.g., catatonic stupor—but as soon as you feel "hyped" by a patient's behavior and are afraid, leave this patient and do not return without three to five staff backed by security. With catatonic stupor, the medical student learned the hard way that there is no time, and all you can do is defend yourself amid the fury until help arrives.

Sometimes there is not even time for that. A clinician once walked behind a patient who was quietly watching TV. The clinician stopped next to the couch to watch it with him, but, for some reason, continued on behind him. The clinician only got 30 feet away from him and turned to see him coming at him like a lion. Instantly the fight was on. By pure coincidence, the clinician was next to the nursing station, and the patient was quickly subdued. The clinician ended up with a black eye. Although this was not the clinician's patient—who was new on the ward—he still knew about someone else's patient who intermittently exploded like this without any warning; this behavior in fact, was the reason for admission.

*Caveat:* Be alert. Know what is going on in your space. Avoid getting sequestered in blind spots where increasing numbers of increasingly violent patients congregate. Points of entry were built for a different era, too. They were built for efficiency and effectiveness with emergency med-surg—not with threatening patients in mind. What should be the takeaway here? Take care of yourself, because you are usually on your own where such patients congregate, oftentimes unknown. In this particular case, however, the patient was known and still got to his clinician violently. Do not get into the patient's intimate space, which greatly expands in extreme paranoia, until you are sure the patient is nonviolent. And even then you have to be on your guard.

Ordinarily, however, your primitive response to a patient's threatened penetration of your safe radius for intimacy is like the nose of a dog for barrier aggression. "Sniff the air" as a cautious dog does, because your gut survival instincts are often as valid as any test; in fact, studies have shown that experiencing white knuckles in interviewing the dehumanized delinquent predicts violence in three out of four cases (www.challengercme.com/Product?productid=18). Additionally, there are specific tell-tale odors picked up sniffing the air that can oftentimes be diagnostic of toxicity, as in the case of an alcoholic beverage or delirium in that Maplewood, Minnesota, hospital that became a blood bath one quiet night and ended with the police killing the patient, Charles Logan (Figure 7.2).

Heed it, because this is the real world. A patient, whether a known psychotic patient or a suddenly delirious patient on a medical-surgical ward or ER unit, may not know he or she is in a hospital and will frequently perceive you as any variety of aggressive threats in any number of dangerous situations he or she has

**Before touching, sniff the air.**

**Protocols and dictionary**

| Odor list | |
|---|---|
| Odor | Possible substance |
| Acetone (sweet, like russet apples) | Ethyl or isopropyl alcohol, chloroform, ketoacidosis, lacquer |
| Acrid (pearlike) | Paraldehyde, chloral hydrate |
| Alcohol (fruitlike) | Ethyl or isopropyl alcohol |
| Ammoniac | Urea |
| Bitter almonds | Cyanide (e.g., in choke cherry or apricot pits) |
| Carrots | Cicutoxin |
| Coal gas (stove gas) | Carbon monoxide (odorless but associated with coal gas) |
| Disinfectants | Phenol, creosote |
| Eggs (rotten) | Hydrogen sulfide, mercaptans, disulfiram (Antabuse) |
| Fecal vomitus | Lower-bowel obstruction |
| Fish or raw liver (musty) | Hepatic failure, zinc phosphorus |
| Fruitlike | Amyl nitrite, ethyl or isopropyl alcohol |
| Garlic | Phosphorus, tellurium, arsenic (breath and perspiration), parathion, malthion, selenium, dimethyl sulfoxide (DMSO), thallium |
| Gasoline | Kerosene, gasoline |
| Halitosis | Acute illness, poor oral hygiene |
| Mothballs | Camphor-containing products |
| Peanuts | RH–787 (Vacor) |
| Shoe polish | Nitrobenzene |
| Tobacco (stale) | Nicotine |
| Urine | Kidney failure |
| Violets | Urinary turpentine |
| Wintergreen | Methyl salicylate |

Figure 7.2 Sniff the air.

encountered in the jungle of the street outside or imagined world of demonic possession. And, of course, you must appear in control without conveying acute fear, but, if you wish to make your living controlling or correcting behavior distasteful to you, then join the Military Police (MP). In the case of this violent subject, the reason the person had the area around the television to himself was because all the other patients were terrified of him, but the clinician, new on the ward, did not know that (Figures 7.3 and 7.4).

## POLICE PROTOCOLS

These protocols are meant for an emergency-room situation where a clinician can safely exit the scene. The Capitol Police could not exit the scene of Miriam Carey's obviously strange behavior when she threatened to breach White House

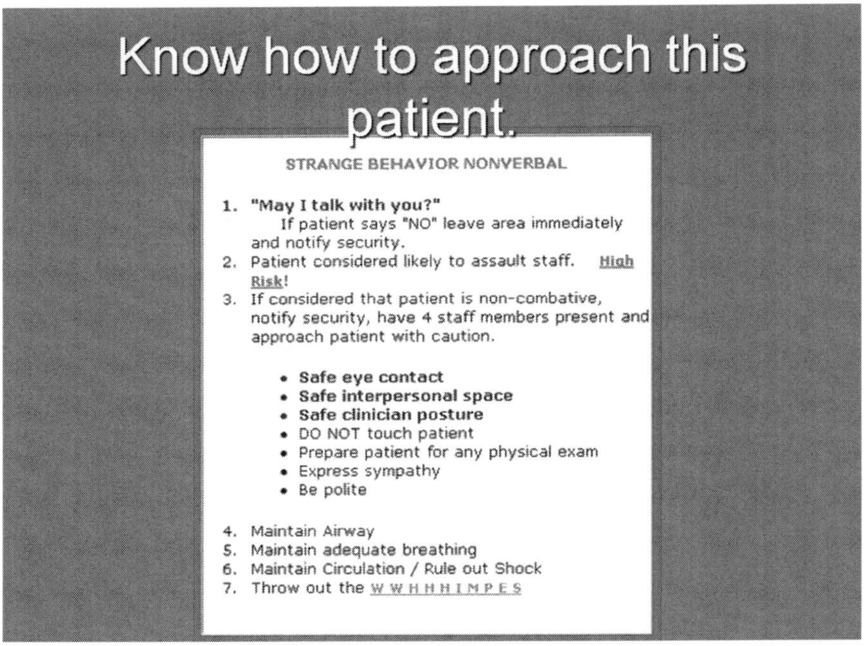


Figure 7.3 Strange behavior, nonverbal.

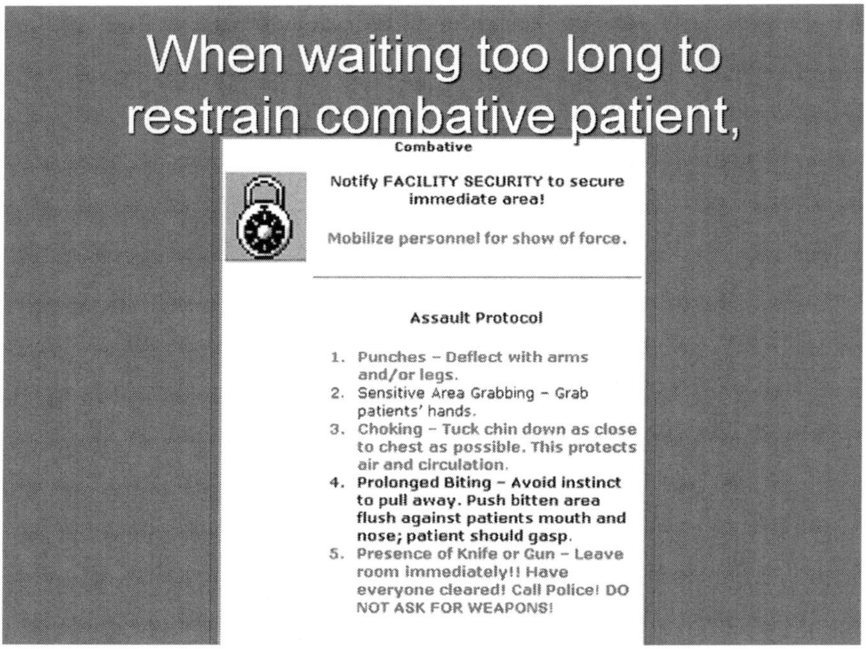


Figure 7.4 Assault protocol.

security boundaries loudly demanding to speak with President Obama, and Officer Andrew could not in good faith avoid engaging Marlene Pinnock on I-10 where they were both trapped by oncoming speeding traffic. It is very likely that officers engaging Eric Garner could have avoided a show of force with no danger to anyone. His violation of the law could have been dealt with differently. Are the police going to use a show of force on every vendor of hot goods on the streets of New York City or for every quality of life incident? That is impossible. Under the Chief Bratton policy of "Broken Window," where apparently minor violations seem to engender aggressive solutions, Garner's case, most likely, could have safely been turned over to detectives working illegal cigarette sales. Wouldn't that crime be of more interest to state authorities who want the taxes paid? Couldn't Eric Garner have been handled by the State Attorney General's office better than a show of force in a political tinderbox with a tradition of racial conflicts with the NYPD? Certainly all those officers restraining Garner, and EMTs observing as he was expiring, were needed elsewhere. Unfortunately for first response, whether enforcement, public safety, or emergency response for life threat, Eric Garner might have looked like a threat, but with deeper understanding, Garner was no threat at all. A summons with a return date for a court appearance and perhaps a confiscation of his contraband by follow-up state authorities was all that was needed. Similarly in New Orleans in the case of Victor White, was aggressive arrest with extreme risk of lethal force really necessary?

Police protocols should require that no lethal force should be used until—or unless—a subject actually wields a weapon or has probable cause of being a life threat to self or others in the foreseeable future. Here is another commonly visible person around the Capitol.

> The United States Capitol was temporarily locked down by law enforcement authorities Saturday after a man committed suicide by gunshot outside the elegant west front of the building, officials said. Witnesses described the suicide victim as a middle-aged male. He fired a single gunshot about 1 p.m., witnesses said, and did not interact with any nearby police officers or bystanders. Capitol Police Chief Kim Dine, speaking at an outdoor news conference near the scene of the shooting, said the victim carried a sign bearing a message about social justice.
>
> The bomb squad was called to investigate a backpack and a roller suitcase near the victim. Nothing threatening was found, officials said. One person near the shooting, Robert Bishop of Annapolis, Md., said he was taking a bike ride around Capitol Hill and had stopped at the west front where he decided to take a selfie. "It didn't sound like a gunshot, it sounded like a balloon pop," said Mr. Bishop, who was about 30 feet away from the victim.
>
> Mr. Bishop said an off-duty Capitol Police officer was the first on the scene and quickly responded by moving bystanders—including a mother and her young daughter, who was visibly upset by the death—away from the immediate area.

It is not known if the Capitol Police may have known him to be a threat, but, if they did, there was cause for confrontation, even if no weapon was clearly visible. For example what was he saying; what did people hear him say? Who was he? Did they know him? What was their gut instinct about him; what aroma, emotional or odoriferous, did he emit? What was he carrying in the backpack and the roller suitcase; should anyone be simply allowed to wander freely in the Military District of Washington with such paraphernalia—particularly if behaving strangely? Every situation is different and must be seen in context; such a situation possibly signaling imminent violence should be far more salient near a critical site in the Military District of Washington, a known and obvious target for terrorists as is Farragut Square behind the White House for psychotics.

In the case of an encounter with a suspicious person who appears to have a weapon, a safe distance between police and the subject must be maintained, even when time consuming and demanding of additional manpower. Discharging weapons should be a last, not a first, resort. That protocol alone would save lives, particularly the lives of the mentally ill who almost always react out of fear that is generated more from distorted stimuli from inside their minds, rather than reality of the external world. In the cases of Carey in DC and Pinnock in LA, however, emergency restraint was immediately necessary. Ideally, Carey should not have been allowed to move her car. With the appropriate training, the police should have decided immediately to follow this emergency medicine protocol (Figure 7.5).

The "G" stands for weapons. When Seattle police tabulated the number of concealed firearms carried by drivers in routine traffic stops after 10 p.m. in downtown Seattle, they found 70% of drivers were carrying concealed firearms, most of them with permits. From this cohort will come many emergency patients, because they are up and doing things, rather than resting at home. We know that states, such as Montana, Texas, and Colorado, have high per capita gun ownership. Many also have had higher male suicide rates than states where per capita gun ownership is lower, such as in Rhode Island. The problem with universal gun wielding is that those who carry weapons are sometimes wont to use them as a first resort because

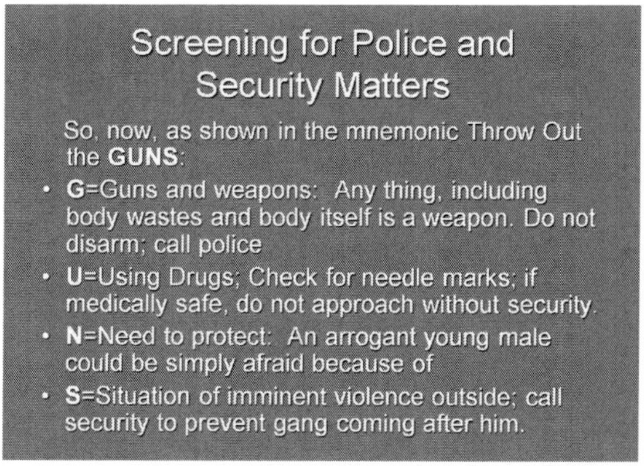
Screening for Police and
Security Matters
So, now, as shown in the mnemonic Throw Out the GUNS:
• G=Guns and weapons: Any thing, including body wastes and body itself is a weapon. Do not disarm; call police
• U=Using Drugs; Check for needle marks; if medically safe, do not approach without security.
• N=Need to protect: An arrogant young male could be simply afraid because of
• S=Situation of imminent violence outside; call security to prevent gang coming after him.

Figure 7.5 Weapons protocol.

of state "stand your ground" laws that both prosecutors and juries tend to misinterpret as licenses to kill. Also, those wielding weapons also feel empowered to make citizens' arrests, believing that gun carrying gives them some form of state-sanctioned authority. Citizens' arrests are dangerous. Authority for use of deadly force is vested in sworn officers only, although "stand your ground" laws risk making enforcers out of anyone, as was the case in the Treyvon Martin case in Florida.

Police are the best trained and experienced in confronting obviously lethal weapons like knives and guns, but ordinary objects in the workspace are also very dangerous. For example, if a patient charges at a first responder, a clinician, or health-care worker, that accelerating patient's body is a missile directed at a target. From preliminary reports allegedly from police sources in Ferguson, this is what Officer Wilson might have feared as 6′6″, 300+ pound Michael Brown, possibly seen as apparently acting strangely or intoxicated aggressively walking down the middle of the street, allegedly ran toward him. Officer Wilson was allegedly wounded in the encounter with Brown—likely slugged in the face by him as they struggled over Wilson's weapon. Pundit heads may argue over the parsing of this encounter with cable news commentators, but once Brown tried to take away Wilson's weapon and they fought over it, that was the signal to Wilson that Brown meant him serious bodily harm, justification for lethal force even though Brown may have tried to flee the scene—and especially after he turned to face and then advance on Wilson. We still argue that the encounter should never have occurred; Wilson should either have issued a summons for jaywalking and driven away, leaving it for the warrant squad to get him into court if he did not show up for his appearance, or called for backup to make a peaceful arrest. And nothing can excuse police for leaving Brown's body in the street like a piece of roadkill. In fact, this incident was more a traffic hazard than a criminal public safety matter; drive on by, call traffic squad and block off the street. Then get Brown, who was simply walking home.

Other missile-type weapons include pictures on the wall and tables separating the clinician from the patient during the information intake process. For example, according to the Federal Bureau of Investigation (FBI) and the Florida State prosecutor's report on the incident, Ibragim Todashev, a friend of Boston Marathon bomber Tamerlan Tsarnaev, who was about to implicate himself and Tsarnaev in a drug-related triple homicide in Watertown, Massachusetts, was himself killed in a police shootout after, according to the FBI and Florida Attorney General's reports, he lunged himself at police just as he was admitting to complicity in that homicide as a confederate of Tsarnaev.

Brian Buss, an Oregon psychiatrist, was killed in Oregon when he tried to talk with a patient who refused to talk with him in the seclusion room of a hospital. The patient picked up a rod and battered Buss to death. Later when the patient's psychosis cleared, he advised the hospital on safety precautions:

1. "Dr. Buss should not have come into the seclusion room alone"
2. But, "once in, he should have left immediately, 'no means no'"

Ordinarily, however, one's primitive animal response to a patient's threatened penetration of his or safe radius for intimacy is a valid signal. Heed it, because this is the real world. A patient's perception, as with the psychotic woman meeting officers with a hammer, can be a variety of aggressive threats in any number of dangerous situations she has encountered in the jungle of the street outside. Or the psychotic perception, as in the case of Brian Buss's murderous patient, was in an imagined world of demonic possession that cleared later with antipsychotic medications. And, of course, the first responder or clinician must appear in control without conveying acute fear. Engendering fear in confronting a suspect might serve to make that suspect more aggressive and resistant, putting him or her into a fight-or-flight mode, thus engendering further force on the part of the police officer or first responder. The results can be deadly, as we have seen with Michael Brown in Ferguson; Michelle Cusseaux in Phoenix; Eric Garner in New York; Ezell Ford in Los Angeles; Kajieme Powell in North St. Louis; Miriam Carey in Washington, DC; Kelly Thomas, a homeless mentally ill man and veteran beaten to death by Fullerton, California, police; James Boyd, a homeless, delusional man shot to death by Albuquerque police while illegally camping and asking for help; and waking up Dontre Hamilton for his "clinically appropriate bed check" on the grass of Red Arrow Park.

## Alfred Redwine in New Mexico

Shortly after the last fatal officer-involved shooting in Albuquerque, the Albuquerque Police Department showed media pictures of the gun they say the suspect had wielded. Late Friday afternoon, 3 weeks later, police released lapel camera video from the officers who were right there when convicted felon Alfred Redwine was shot. Following the shooting, some people doubted whether Redwine had a gun; so, the key was to find the gun in those videos. The video was dark and not of great quality, and there were objects on the ground that were hard to discern.

Over and over again, officers tell 30-year-old Alfred Redwine to "put down the gun." Police say Redwine did not listen and fired a round. In cell phone video, you can see Redwine holding something up to his head, pointing it down, and then it looks like smoke comes out of what may have been a gun. The lapel camera video does not clearly show Redwine before the shooting.

Police said Redwine's gun was in the dirt after he was shot. In this case, the sound may be more revealing than the video.

"Leave the firearm where it is," a lieutenant says.

At one point, feet from Redwine's body, there is what could have been a gun between an officer's legs. Police were shining a flashlight in that area.

In the case of Miriam Carey, the car should have been determined immediately to be a weapon and therefore immobilized, either by disabling the tires—better shoot out the tires with four rounds than Miriam Carey with nineteen. Alternatively, and in a friendly way—despite the intense flow of adrenaline—try to disable the ignition system while distracting the suspect by advising, "Hey, maa'm, I smell something burning. Mind if I open your hood?"

Sound silly? It would have saved her life and kept her child out of the range of fire. Carey was so preoccupied that, given assurances the police would help her talk with the president—but not until that engine gets checked for the bad odor—might have alleviated her psychotic symptoms long enough to get her into custody. In ego-threatening situations to police and first responders in all these cases, law enforcement personnel will find that defusing the situation without violence is actually more ego gratifying to police than opening fire or applying any potentially lethal force.

Here is another headline case that, on the surface of things, does not appear to be a case for talk. Were drugs the issue, as in "U"ser in the case of Michael Brown in Ferguson? Certainly, as can be seen, there is "N" to Protect from "S"ituation outside, whether it was the alleged assailants or the patrolman in a community possibly infected with gangs. But, here one also must immediately triage dangerousness via the mnemonic, "ACT MYSELF." On the surface of things, it appears that the patrolman had no time to Throw Out the Guns, but he probably made an assessment from experience like this emergency psychiatry protocol that police might find helpful. "ACT MYSELF" is another mnemonic that officers, ER personnel, and first responders may find helpful in quickly screening a suspicious person for imminent dangerousness (Figure 7.6). Until proven not dangerous, alert security and do not release without very good cause.

Assume that a patrol officer responding to a combative individual on the street arrives and perhaps is mentally screening for a law enforcement situation. This could be an armed man, a potentially dangerous drug-seeking man, and a signal presentation of a gang or terrorist threat, such as a suspicious thin man with a disproportionately huge chest that means suicide vest until proven otherwise. The officer has, in other words, Thrown Out the GUNS. The person is dangerous, and the officer has judged the person now approached to be, in fact, a potentially at-risk threat who might be considered a potential psychiatric patient. The same applies in the similar set of circumstances to a clinician encountering just such an individual in an ER. It would have sounded idiotic in the era of George Engel's psychiatric interview for the medical setting to first and foremost declare a person at any point of entry a patient instead of a threat before proceeding with psychiatric examination. But, Marlene

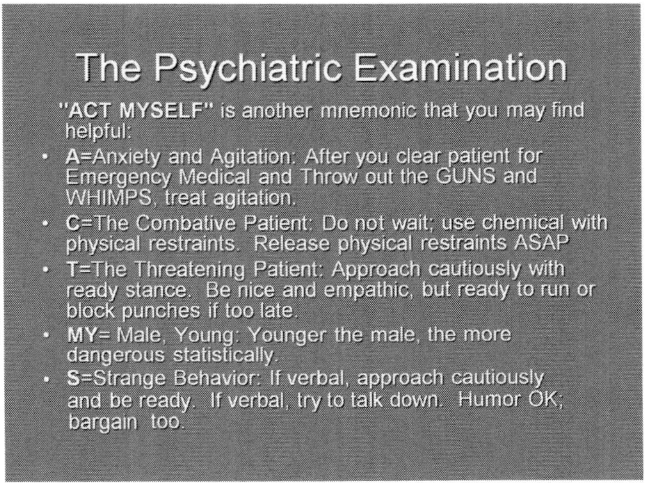


Figure 7.6 Rapid assessment for imminent dangerousness.

Pinnock is an example: noncompliant, clearly delusional, physically resistant to any form of restraint, and incapable of listening to reason as an officer attempts to arrest her for causing a dangerous situation on a California freeway—as well as contain her as a threat to herself or others. In our contemporary health-care and public safety environment, she is more likely to be seriously injured by an officer if not killed. Thus, the street becomes the point of entry to the health-care system, and emergency medicine, along with emergency neuropsychiatry, must, by contemporary necessity, be projected from the ER to the pavement.

## "A" STANDS FOR ANXIETY AND AGITATION

Within the context of the clinical work site, it manifests in most cases as "change" in patient's behavior. For example, the prone patient with a bloody cloth over his forehead gets off the gurney and starts walking around. Clinicians do not know much about that man. However, regardless of how busy and stressed they are, they should be thinking, "anxiety," and approach him with a soft voice and demeanor. At the same time they need to be thinking about the possibility of physical restraint if ultimately necessary, and seclusion. But the mission at the moment in encountering this change in behavior is to deescalate it without using either chemical or physical restraint. What does the patient want? To call his girlfriend and say he is sorry? Urinate? Leave before the cops come, either in reality or imagination?

Clinicians should be supportive. Listen empathically, and try to answer his Questions, even if only silently nodding their heads to convey that they hear him and are interested—even if his words seem nonsensical. There is no need for overpowering anyone unless the supportive approach does not work. It is only then that limits have to be set. If your patient is inebriated, he will not hear much of what is being said. Brown and his accomplice in the strong arm robbery might have been high at the time: "Using." Were they so high that they could not immediately respond to Wilson's command to get out of the middle of the street, or were they simply unresponsive? Wilson said that he had heard the robbery report over the radio but did not know whether they were the perpetrators or whether they were high on a substance. All he saw was a person who seemed hostile to his commands but not brandishing a weapon or posing a threat. This should have been more of a psychological encounter and certainly not a physical one—even an emergency medical encounter, due to possible lethal toxicity to disease or poisoning. How about asking a person who's refusing to obey a lawful police command, "why?" The answer you get might be more instructive than you know, because, if it is pure psychosis, the patient will hear it. In that instance, clinicians should keep everything as simple as possible. Clogged with hallucinations, the patient can process a few words but not a litany. "Mr. Smith, you are in the emergency room in downtown Dallas. You had a bad fall." It is important to provide the patient with his or her whereabouts to answer the question, "where am I?" and answer it even before it is asked so as to break through the fog of confusion as soon as possible. Did CHP Officer Andrews attempt that with Marlene Pinnocks? Did Michael Brown know he was endangering his and other lives walking in the middle of the street? It would be instructive to find that out.

For clinicians in a hospital setting, the alleged risks of intramuscular preparations available today are overblown when compared to risks of unfettered agitation threatening harm to self and others at the work site. When medically treating severe agitation with, without, or against patient consent after judging that unfettered agitation will lead to damage for the patient, staff, and other patients—or all, then even nonconsensual treatment is called for. Reasonable self-defense or defense of third parties will likely trump a lawsuit for battery, a tort that involves nonconsensual touching. One can argue the pros and cons of whether to use chemical restraint or physical restraint first or together, but for the present sake of argument, let us assume that it is best to medicate for agitation and anxiety. Clinicians should document that medical risks—such as acute cardiac arrest—are far outweighed by risks of physical restraints without medicating.

Marlene Pinnock could have been medically restrained by an EMT. This must become standard for emergency services as patients bed down now on the street and park grass instead of institutional settings with medically monitored beds. Such "community mental health beds," such as Red Arrow Park in Milwaukee, are now considered by the courts to be an appropriate level of care. Police are their psychiatric nurses doing what is labeled "welfare checks" for the mentally ill, wherever their hallucinations and delusions lead them to settle in for the night. That is no longer grave disability, unless, of course, they strip buck naked and sleep in the snow. That behavior would undoubtedly result in a hearing before a lawyer for "grave disability," but maybe such an "eccentric, risk-taking person" and his attorney would convince the hearing officer he would wrap himself in two blankets if released. That could be enough in today's insanity commitment hearings (Liebert and Birnes 2011).

Whether the agitated patient is medicated or physically restrained at this point is totally dependent on the clinician's intent and purpose, although the facility's policies and procedures need to be known and also addressed; the states and federal government contradict each other on preference for medical or physical restraint. That is why the hospital needs to develop its own policies and procedures (P&P) that balances the contradictions of federal and state regulation while enabling quality of care within standards of risk assessment. That is why documentation of the clinician's intention and justification for restraint is mandatory, and when done properly and within good faith, as discussed in previous chapters, will minimize liability risk. So, it is important to note that failure of talking somebody down supportively resulted in the decision to restrain. Then the clinician should be prepared to document both intent and justification for what was done to restrain the patient; documentation of intent and justification for what is done will serve well, regardless of outcome. Clinicians are not expected to be clairvoyant and omnipotent, as long as they are acting with intent that can be justified for demonstrating medical competence and good faith. Even if the administration of certain medications or physical restraint could set off a potentially lethal cardiac arrhythmia, the settings now requiring medical intervention are not considered preoperative with anesthesiology backup immediately available. We do not recommend wanton use of chemical restraint, but adverse medical complications for emergency medical restraint are uncommon compared to consequences of withholding them for fear of violating patient rights. They certainly do occur, but so does sudden death under the best of circumstances during elective abdominal hysterectomy and gastrointestinal hemorrhage with stat aspirin in acute coronary insufficiency.

For Administration of Medications in Extreme Anxiety Patients select from following menu:

- Zydis 2.5–10 mg po to prevent cheeking
- Zyprexa 2.5–10 mg po or IM
- Risperdal M tabs 0.5–2 mg po to prevent cheeking
- Risperdal 0.5–2 mg po
- Geodon 5–15 mg IM
- Seroquel 25–50 mg po
- Haldol 0.5–5 mg ± Cogentin 0.5 mg ± Ativan 0.5–2 mg IM. Give in liquid form together to assure compliance or in tablet form if practical
- Ativan 0.5–2 mg po may be surprisingly effective, and certainly should be considered first line when anxiety rather than dyscontrol dominates presentation
- Abilify 2 or 5 mg IM
- Droperidol IM 5 mg in younger patients who have no apparent medical surgical problems or history of cardio/respiratory disease (www.challengercme.com/Product?productid=18)

There is no known evidence-based preference for any of these agents, but they all work well, and experienced emergency physicians have their "armamentarium" of select agents from this group that work safely and well on certain clinical presentations. In this case there is no substitute for clinician's judgment and later documentation of informed consent with intention and justification for selecting one modality of chemical or physical restraint over all others.

## "C": THE COMBATIVE PATIENT

Here is an emergency medicine template for managing the combative patient in an ER. Obviously, the cases discussed here are arrest situations that are far upstream in public health and public safety interventions. Nonetheless, the White House perimeter has a high concentration of severely ill psychiatric patients, and attracts many, too, like psychotic patients Miriam Carey and White House intruder Oscar Gonzalez. The grotto beneath I-10 at La Brea, California, is home to many, too, as is the encampment in San Jose currently being cleared of the homeless. Therefore, the police are caretakers as well as enforcers. This dual role is clearly demonstrated in the Carey and Pinnock cases. It is not in the Garner case. Accordingly, police can take these templates for strange behavior outside the ER, because the public safety officer must not only protect himself, but enforce the law and make an arrest.

According to the grand jury report from Ferguson, Officer Wilson was not confronted with strange behavior, but, rather, jaywalkers in the middle of the street who were hostile. When engaging them he was reportedly attacked. What were the circumstances? Did he stop for a field interrogation because of suspicious activity and simply end up at the wrong place at the wrong time without adequate backup, or did he stop because he had been alerted over the radio dispatch to a strong armed robbery for which they fit the description of the suspects? St. Louis has been innovative in the past for managing its police force for excessive force, at one time ordering the psychological assessment of officers who have a high number of "resisting arrests" booked into jail. How smart is it to have an officer on patrol in such an explosive community when perceptions can be as immediate as a lightning strike as they were in the case of Michael Brown? To date, Officer Wilson was one of those St. Louis metro policemen who had been vetted as being safe—at least by history—to be on patrol, even though he had previously served in a neighboring department where there had been such extreme racial tension between the police and the African American residents the department was shut down. Now, given what we know about the Brown shooting, what could Wilson—or what should Wilson have done other then issue a jaywalking or impeding traffic summons and drive away?

From what we have learned from witness statements and legal reports, we conclude Wilson should have done nothing on his own. If he truly suspected that Brown had robbed a convenience store because he had heard it on the police radio, he should have called for backup after reporting the possible suspect was in sight. He should not have approached a suspect by himself. Certainly, aggressively shifting his cruiser into reverse to block the flight of fleeing felons, possibly high on drugs, was very risky. However, if the infraction was impeding traffic, he should simply have told Brown and Dorian Johnson politely to walk on the curb and then driven on. No need to get into a confrontation with someone as big as Brown, especially if alone in the car. If Brown confronted him, call for backup while trying to talk Brown down.

But we are Monday-morning quarterbacking with an incomplete set of facts and considerable, but conflicting, eyewitness testimony that eclipses the critical moment of this field interrogation. Assuming no new facts, it appears that Wilson did not need to confront Brown or arrest him alone. The priority in this case was public safety, particularly the health of the two apparently young men jaywalking. If they acted drunk or he believed them to be drunk, then he could have suspected the "U" for user. That is not an immediate enforcement need, but it may be a medical emergency. Certainly it was a public safety emergency, but he could not solve that himself with a 300-pound young man and aggressive-appearing companion, later found to be an accomplice to robbery with a criminal history. Had Wilson seen it this way immediately, then hardly anyone in the entire world would have ever known of Ferguson, Missouri.

## THREATENING

When escalation between police and a subject occurs without a weapon, threat assessment for surviving in emergency medicine applies to police as well as to ER personnel (Figure 7.7).

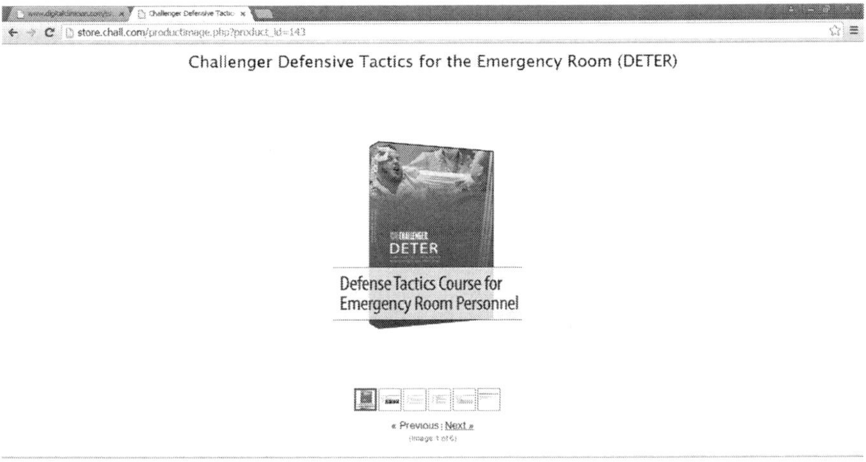


Figure 7.7 Challenger DETER course.

Remember, ERs are the second most dangerous workplace in America—second only to mines. ER staff need protocols for being late in responding to release of violence. Every policeman knows that. What did Wilson believe was the response to assault, once it was too late to prevent? In the case of Michael Brown, we think the answers are 1 and 2 in Figure 7.1: "Leave and call for security"—aka traffic in the case of this Ferguson incident. Again, this may not be the weakened show of force the department wants on the street; it is not ego gratifying in the face of a confrontation, thus perhaps perceived as less than manliness. But that would be a false ego talking. For the individual officer, other than being physically alive, how could things be worse for his future? For the department? Police have to realize that unemployed young men, perhaps seething with anger, are like kindling on a dry day. One spark can start a fire. This street in Ferguson was not a posh upscale suburb but a transitional community, mainly of color and policed by a white minority. Tensions likely have been high between the police and the community for a long time as later proven from racist records obtained by the Department of Justice's investigation of the Ferguson Police Department.

Back in the 1980s, Jayne Byrne, Mayor of Chicago, was concerned enough about race riots caused by encounters between black youth and unprepared police officers when high interest rates in 1982 created what she thought was a tinderbox of unemployed black youth. She was so concerned that she held a policing conference to deal with inflammatory confrontational issues. St. Louis commanders were well represented and openly discussed the crises of phony resisting arrest confrontations in the metro area. The Michael Brown police shooting, therefore, did not occur in a vacuum of Jim Crow justice. This conference addressed the problem of Brown in the context of police/community tensions in St. Louis County, and everywhere America, 34 years before the Brown case took place ("Identification of Problem Police Officers," sponsored by City of Chicago and U.S. Department of Justice, Chicago, 1982).

Nothing has changed. The police in Ferguson face a type of Hobson's choice: either beef up patrol with better backup and training in such volatile encounters or follow less aggressive rules of engagement. Residents who believe themselves to be harassed by the police, underrepresented politically, and distrustful of the local governing body, are not going to stand for being pushed around by ego-challenged police officers. Thus, prudence and a good emergency psychological protocol save lives, protect public safety, and save careers and the public welfare. At least one or two police careers are destroyed from postshooting trauma or worse; state homicide charges or federal charges of violating the rights of citizens. Is this public safety? No, not in the view of many people of color. And the attack by a crazed and suicidal Ismaaiyl Brinsley left two police officers dead and a department so disrespectful of its own civilian command that officers turned their backs on the mayor and police commissioner.

St. Louis alderman Antonio French said, in television interviews in the aftermath of the Brown shooting and the social unrest that followed, that, "It's a textbook example of how not to handle the situation. Ferguson has a white government and a white mayor, but a large black population. This situation has brought out whatever rifts were between that minority community and the Ferguson government" (www.nytimes.com/2014/08/11/us/police-say-mike-brown-was-killed-after-struggle-for-gun.html?_r=1).

Our psychological deconstruction of the events here may seem an overreach in light of the lack of complete reports and the disputable grand jury findings, but, when compared to the other cases covered—Marlene Pinnock, Miriam Carey, Eric Garner, Ezell Ford, and Kajieme Powell—clearly there is a psychological component that law enforcement and criminal justice professionals need to understand before the next similar encounter sparks another catastrophic social fire—one that could easily spread out of control.

## WORKING SMART

Working smart in emergency medicine and even emergency police response means reducing violence and resultant psychiatric and medical complications—or doing everything you can do before laying hands on any person for either seclusion with lockup—the clinical equivalent of jail—or physical and chemical restraint. Thus, as seen in Figures 7.2 and 7.6, "sniff the air" and be prepared with your assessment of threat level. Once you lay hands on that person or administer drugs into a patient who has not been thoroughly worked up, you have moved to the precipice. Many times you can avoid that precipice through your demeanor and a polished, silver tongue.

It has been said about problem police officers who inflame incendiary situations that it is almost always about "booze, broads, and mouth." Think about that when approaching the patient now. Booze raises the risk of violence in your workplace sevenfold with a loud patient. (Your blood alcohol level should be 0.00.) It is almost always about gender—domestic violence, assault, and males—and your mouth can frequently either reduce that explosive eternal triad or escalate it. Clearly, Wilson's verbal exchanges with Brown did not help, nor did Andrew's with Marlene Pinnock.

As in assault protocols presented in this chapter, you either came too late or, like Wambaugh's off-duty cop in *Choir Boys*, you simply were at the wrong place at the wrong time. If not at the wrong place at the wrong time, it is now that you have a last chance to avoid the use of restraint and seclusion—aka jail for the police. We believe that this is what happened to Officer Wilson. Emergency psychiatry, whether played out on the street or in an emergency room, requires the appropriate temperament. This is a dangerous place for control freaks and sadists. Patients representing threat are not the characters of the Old West who can be expected to weigh the force and either attack or retreat. Such a paradigm may fit certain corrections situations, where career criminals and their controllers both know the rules of the game. These two adversaries, however, share one common ideology, and that is to eliminate the unpredictable psycho driven by autistic agendas and getting real rewards from a shared environment, even if it is just a cigarette for assurances not to escape or stir things up. Traditional corrections is far more predictable in regard to threat assessment than many acute care points of entry today.

## The veiled threat

In the case of the Flight 93 hijackers presenting at Holy Cross Hospital in Fort Lauderdale, Florida, during June 2001, with a lesion, Tsonas noted its appearance more carefully than usual because of its unique appearance. It did not seem like the abrasion the two complained of, because the mechanism of injury was not consistent with the lesion. The hijackers said it was caused by accidentally kicking a suitcase months before, but that mechanism of injury did not fit the appearance of what John's Hopkins retrospectively diagnosed as consistent with cutaneous anthrax (Liebert and Birnes 2011).

Here the question would ideally have been, what was this presentation—was it a "local inflammation," and if so from what? Was it "chemical exposure," and if so, what? Was it really a "wound" from accidentally bumping into a suitcase, as reported, or something far more lethal—like an exotic infection, as Tsonas may have even suspected back in June 2001? Most importantly, was this presentation appropriate? Was the collateral witness with the patient appropriate? Now, on a more likely than not basis, we know the answer to that question was definitively "No," and were ERs better informed of bioterror threats in 2001, the FBI should have been notified. The patient was the hijacker of Flight 93; the collateral witness reporting the phony suitcase bump months before was the muscleman and roommate of the hijacker and was on the Central Intelligence Agency (CIA) watch list, and the lesion, within the context of the events of 9/11 was more probably than not cutaneous anthrax. In retrospect, there should have been no treatment and release of this patient, just like there should have been no computed tomography scanning and release of Thomas Duncan from the Dallas ER with Ebola. Was the presentation appropriate? The mechanism of injury months before—kicking a suitcase—did not match the lesion; the presentation was inappropriate.

Figure 7.8 Subject with weapon.

Tsonas needed to seriously ask the question, "is this presentation appropriate," and then follow the protocols of classical emergency medicine triage. "No" is no, and the threat level moves from routine care in the blue zone to the red zone—first alert for bioterror until proven otherwise with two suspected terrorists in an unsecure and potentially dangerous environment where they could not be restrained. This is not intended to fault Tsonas, but he would likely agree that his first impression of inappropriate presentation should not have led to his doctorly impulse to treat a chronic lesion that was not even a medical emergency, but, rather, to follow this protocol, because the patient and his collateral companion were more probably than not armed and dangerous with a lethally contagious infection (Figure 7.8).

In this case, the protocol in emergency medicine for inappropriate history in which mechanism of injury does not match the clinical presentation requires an immediate return to the red zone to begin triaging all over again. Ideally, the Holy Cross Hospital, Florida, ER would have unobtrusively isolated the patient without arousing the suspicsions of the patient and his accomplice in the later hijacking and reported them to the police, who ideally could have determined that neither was in the country legally and that the collateral informant in the presentation had already been identified by the CIA as a terrorist threat. Would this have prevented all the events of 9/11? Very possibly under the best of circumstances in the post-9/11 world, but Tsonas and Holy Cross Hospital were operating in the pre-9/11 world and were ignored in the post-9/11 world. The director of the anthrax investigation associated with the events of 9/11 has sued the federal government for punishing him as a whistle-blower in the investigation, declaring that the person of interest, Bruce Ivins, was only that—and that exculpatory evidence on him was suppressed by the FBI in order to close the case of the anthrax attacks on this nation without clearing them.

> Now, a former senior F.B.I. agent who ran the anthrax investigation for four years says that the bureau gathered "a staggering amount of exculpatory evidence" regarding Dr. Ivins that remains secret. The former agent, Richard L. Lambert, who spent 24 years at the F.B.I., says he believes it is possible that Dr. Ivins was the anthrax mailer, but he does not think prosecutors could have convicted him had he lived to face criminal charges.
>
> In a lawsuit filed in federal court in Tennessee, Mr. Lambert accused the bureau of trying "to railroad the prosecution of Ivins" and, after his suicide, creating "an elaborate perception management campaign" to bolster its claim that he was guilty. Mr. Lambert's lawsuit accuses the bureau and the Justice Department of forcing his dismissal from a job as senior counterintelligence officer at the Energy Department's lab in Oak Ridge, Tenn., in retaliation for his dissent on the anthrax case. (Shane 2015)

## CHILD AND ELDER ABUSE

A victim's spouse in Florida sued the federal government when the anthrax case was closed following the suicide of person of interest, Bruce Ivins. At first, government attorneys defended the US Army and denied Bruce Ivins could have committed all the anthrax attacks; the authors, based on common sense of his job and geographical scope of the attacks, agree with this defense. But suddenly and surprisingly, Attorney General Holder stepped in and withdrew government defense offering multi-million dollar settlement to the plaintiff!

When you encounter an unresponsive or injured child and take a history from the adult presenting with the child, make certain that the historian is reliable and that the mechanism of injury fits the history. Once again, follow the evidence based rules of emergency medicine triage and ask yourself, "Is this presentation appropriate?" (Figure 7.9).

This patient's caretaker or parent from Figure 7.9 should be a "Worried Parent" as in the protocol on the yellow template in Figure 7.10.

If the parent is not worried, then immediately hit the Reassess button, whether on the computerized triage screen or in your head, assume nothing more, and triage in the red zone (Figure 7.11).

We do not know all the ways that adults abuse and kill their children, but we know that they do so in great numbers. Be epidemiologically informed. Violence against children, in fact, ranked among the top five causes of death for all children under 14, regardless of race. And you can bet that these statistics are just as underreported—or even more so—than those for violence between nonfamily members. Public consciousness is being brightened for both the differential cultural and legal values placed on intrafamilial and extrafamilial violence. Our current legal system discriminates against the intrafamilial victim, oftentimes trying to keep it within the civil justice system to maintain both the integrity of the family and the economic support that is most often dependent on the perpetrator himself. But that does not immunize you legally. Certainly it should

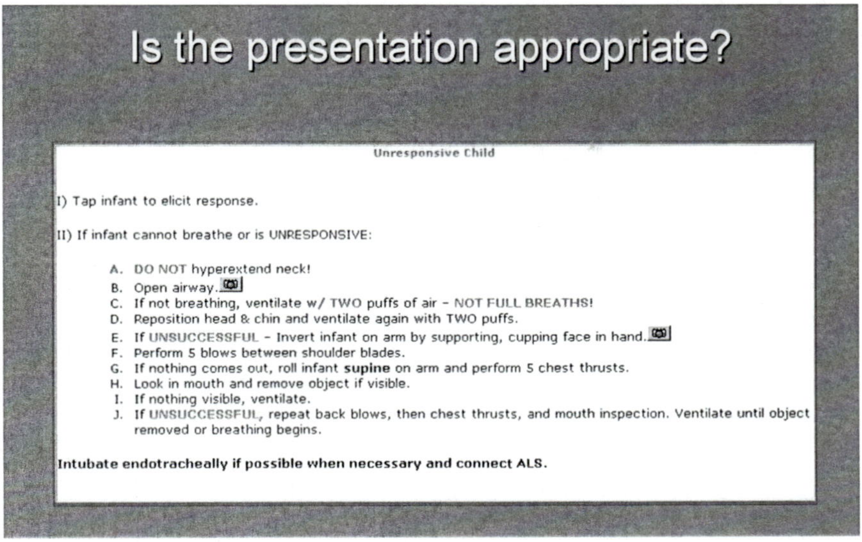


Figure 7.9 Is presentation appropriate?

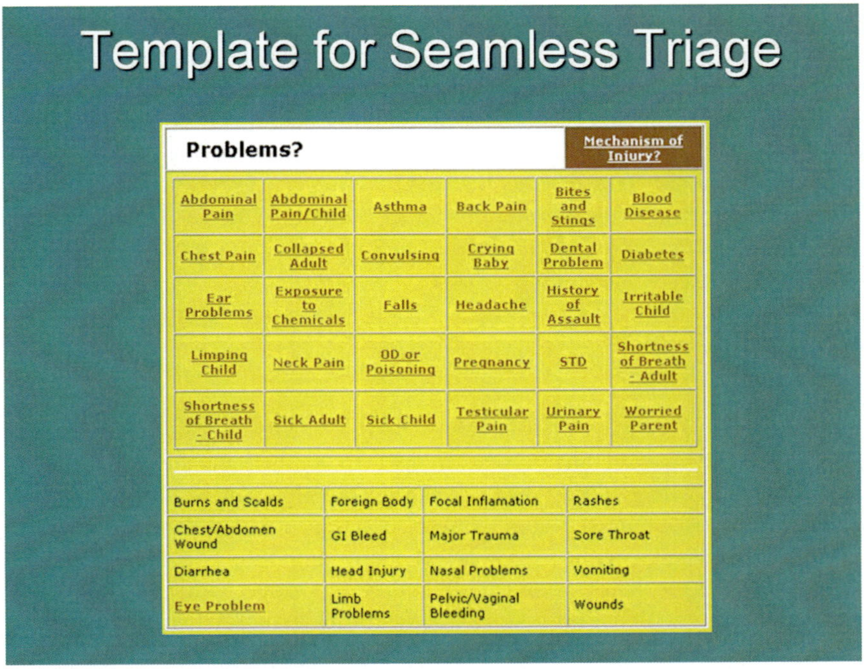


Figure 7.10 Yellow zone.

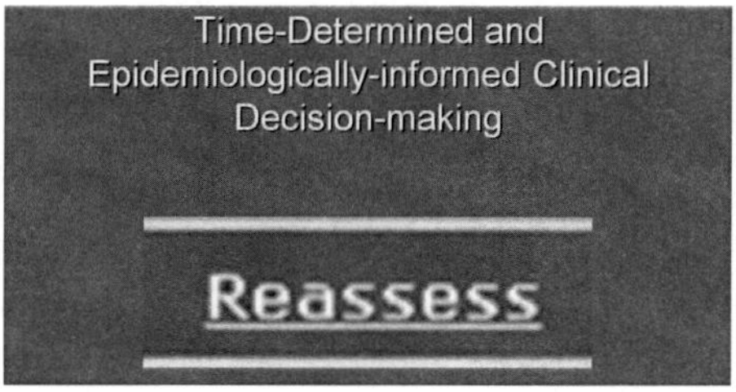


Figure 7.11 Reassess button.

not morally. A clinician, in his or her role of providing such *epidemiologically informed* psychiatric intervention, can be the first line in prevention because it is a possibility, more likely than not, that one day that child will be either a ward of the state or dead. The parents' in-laws may suspect it, but, unlike a clinician, they are not required to have the "peculiar ability" necessary to prevent morbidity and/or mortality in their grandchild. The clinician is the one to whom the court has attributed a special relationship with that family and child, and that special relationship is based on both expectations that the clinician knows the very high risk of death in the case presented in an ER and has the power to control that child's destiny for life, death, or chronic debilitation by statutory reporting.

Accordingly, if a clinician does not feel secure in determining how the mechanism of injury thoroughly explains what can be seen in that exposed child's injured body or that disabled child's emergency presentation, then it is time to think, "what was the source of the history?" The clinician can now assume that absolutely nothing about this history is true if the source provides inappropriate history.

That brings us back, once again, to the red zone of the clinical state of awareness. You are thinking of a deadly destructive process going on. No, these adults are not threatening the clinical site or apparently out of control. They are polite and poised, though maybe too much so for the severity of presentation. On the Triage Screen for Clinical Presentations, they are not "Worried Parents." Only Adult and Children's Protective Services have the capability and authority to determine truth from fiction in these cases.

## Case study

Kay had a large ecchymosed lesion covering the entire left side of her face. Kay was also demented. She perseverated, "help me, help me, help me." She had a sitter who looked very perturbed, and the clinician wondered, after leaving the ward, about the sitter's response to the clinician's interview. The clinician wondered why the sitter worried about something and was not very happy with the medical assessment. Of course he was not happy, because he had been sitting with her for hours listening to, "Help me, Help me." The clinician reported the case through nursing administration as suspected elder abuse, even though the patient was not his patient. The clinician was doing a second opinion for emergency detention of her dementia. The nursing home was investigated, but the nursing director had to be assured that the sitter was not the one the clinician was worried about.

One of the most publicized cases of complaints of elder abuse made it to the U.S. Senate in 2011 when actor Mickey Rooney, who had been a child star at MGM throughout the 1930s and 1940s and who would forever be remembered for his ongoing role as Andy Hardy, testified before a Senate subcommittee about elder abuse at the hands of his stepson for 30 years. Rooney gave a shocking description of physical, mental, and financial abuse at the hands of his caretakers. The Senate hearings showcased the pervasiveness of elder abuse, an issue that affects millions of senior citizens in the United States—regardless of socioeconomic class. Ultimately, a court in Los Angeles County, upon Rooney's petition thereto, ordered a conservatorship over Rooney and appointed an attorney to oversee that conservatorship. Mickey Rooney died at age 93 in April 2014 (Lertzman and Birnes 2015).

Emergency psychiatry, therefore, intervenes when emergency disability and/or emergency exposed body exam raise the suspicion of either partner or caretaker abuse, whether the latter is a child or dependent adult. And, unfortunately it does not matter who that caretaker is, whether professional or family. Dependents of all ages are maimed and killed by all of them. You do not make the determination, not unless you know this family very well, because you cannot assume an accident.

While following the time-determined rules of emergency medicine, you must have a high index of suspicion for elder abuse before simply attending to acute med-surg problems. Caretakers not only abuse their dependent family members, they kill them, too. Ninety percent of perpetrators are family members, and the older or younger the dependent and the closer the filial ties, the higher is the likelihood of injury secondary to criminal assault. Professional caretakers cause most of the other cases, particularly in nursing home settings where staff turnover is high, reflecting bad preemployment screening, occupational burnout, poor violence prevention for the demented, and the resulting and constant infusion of inexperienced staff.

Therefore, in emergency medicine, when examining the severely injured by working smart through epidemiologically-informed clinical decision-making, remember that psychosocial—and your own—denial of elder abuse can kill.

---

The incidence of elder abuse is soaring much higher than demographics of the geriatric population. And, for the dependent adult, the incidence of reported elder abuse of those over 60 is already over one-half million people. In the cohort over 80 years of age, the rate of elder abuse triples. It can be diagnosed, and emergency psychiatry discipline is required for documentation and reporting to prevent further morbidity, suffering, and murder. These are messy situations and run counter to our grain as decent citizens and helpers. We just do not suspect other clinical sites of facilitating such felony assaults on frail and helpless patients, and we respect motherhood. Most clinicians do not "sniff the air" for the "limbic energy" of dangerousness like cops, but this stuff happens all the time, and it is our responsibility to detect and report it. Policemen are no exception.

It is possible that accidents were the cause with any injured children, intimate partner, or dependent adult, but always raise the question in your own mind, "does the mechanism of injury fit the presenting lesion?" In Kay's case, too many doctors assumed that had been checked—why just one side of the face from a fall? It is your legal responsibility to initiate the investigation once you determine that the mechanism of injury, as presented in the patient's history by an accompanying caretaker or significant other, does not fit the presenting disability or exposed body impairment.

Clinicians should always keep in mind the rare Munchausen by Proxy Syndrome, where a parent can intentionally cause illness in a normal child to get pediatric attention. These otherwise normal children can come in repeatedly with deadly hyperglycemia and multiple clinical abnormalities caused by a caretaker, usually the mother, who is either diagnosable or diagnosed as borderline personality disorder. These children can end up in surgery and can be killed before the embarrassing truth is learned. The Munchausen-by-proxy mother wants to be the parent of a seriously ill child and will literally devote her life to creating such a severe pediatric syndrome, like diabetic coma or acute abdomen, to realize her only wish in life. Adults will do this to themselves, too—in Munchausen syndrome.

---

### Case

Mrs R brought her 10-year-old son in for a routine appointment for attention deficit-hyperactivity disorder (ADHD) reevaluation. It was noted that the boy's head had a large abrasion with considerable hair loss which was not recent. When asked about it, she said her boyfriend dropped a spinning fan on her son's head and that it gave him a haircut as well as the healing abrasion. She appeared quite nondefensive about this, and the boy showed little response to her explanation. The mother was convinced to take the boy to the ER just for a checkup, as this was a head injury. Reluctantly she did. The ER called, quite perturbed because of the lack of acuity; "this happened 2 weeks ago. What do you want me to do, skull films without neuro signs? There are none."

After expressing concerns regarding child abuse to the ER, the doctor attending calmed down and said, "Oh, I see—OK. I'll get back to you."

He called back 1 hour later and said that he carefully examined the healing wound and took detailed history from both the boy and mother. "The mechanism of injury fits perfectly with the wound. This was an accident."

The patient was released, and when the mother returned to the doctor's office the following week, she was still a bit perplexed about her child's referral to the ER. She never did know that it was to investigate her and her boyfriend for child abuse. She will likely never know and should never know. Therefore, particularly with the accident-prone female, dependent elder and peculiarly injured child, best document whether mechanism of injury fits the lesion(s).

Perceiving threat from such situations, the simplest time-determined and epidemiological rules in emergency medicine should be instinctive when encountering the threatening patient. They are as follow:

1. Understand potential risks in advance of any treatment—as a surgeon would when entering the operating room (OR) to open up an abdomen. Upon approach, one should be automatically thinking about stabilizing the surroundings to establish security. Every surgical unit is different, and every clinical point of entry receiving the emergency psychiatric patient is different, but, like all ORs, all points of entry can be both stabilized and secured for psychiatric emergencies. The exception, of course, is the newest point of entry to the health-care system—namely the street. The police have to be there in place of psychiatric professionals, yet the rules of engaging the unknown patient remain the same.
2. All psychiatrists killed by their patients failed to heed the advice of Brian Buss's killer: "I don't want to talk with you." His killer meant, "when I say I don't want to talk with you, that means I'm likely to kill you unless you leave now!" We do not know what percentage of the 10% of psychiatrists seriously injured and 40% assaulted by patients in the workplace could get away from a threat or simply felt too omnipotent to accept rejection of patients. So, why did Brian Buss risk his life in Oregon? Always ask first, "May I talk with you?" "No" means "No," and you are asking for a lethal attack by ignoring this patient's warning. These patients are essentially telling you that they cannot tolerate your presence at this point. Indeed, sometimes a lab tech can come in, when you, the treating clinician cannot.

   Many otherwise noncommunicative or intractable patients may have partial awareness of a clinician's presence and are protecting him or her from their demons. They are more likely hallucinating, whether they admit it or not, rather than just being negativistic. Miriam Carey likely was, and certainly Marlene Pinnock was. We do not know what Dontre Hamilton was perceiving, awakened in the park for his welfare check. Obviously, he did not perceive, when awakened, that Officer Manney was simply there to assure his welfare. This issue is even so serious a matter today in psychiatry that we are questioned whether weapon carriage for psychiatrists should be routine. This awakening came as a result of a 2014 shooting death of a threatening patient by a psychiatrist after the patient had murdered another clinician in his presence (Winter 2014). Don't be this officer: "Deputy killed in Minnesota after hospitalized suspect grabs his gun" (www.cnn.com/2015/10/18/us/minnesota-deputy-killed/).

3. Patients who are verbally threatening usually do not physically act out their threats unless intoxicated. Again, one reason for this might be the apparent receptive aphasia of intoxicated patients compared to the autistically preoccupied psychotic patient. They simply cannot listen to you, whereas the non-intoxicated confused and agitated patient can, if you talk softly with few words and set reasonable goals for a therapeutic alliance free of either chemical or physical restraint. "Carl, we need to get your vital signs and some blood tests before we can begin to help you." The psychotic patient could cooperate with you, whereas the intoxicated patient could go berserk on you. In the case of Dr. Buss's killer, he was able to tell interviewers later that he was in no state of mind at the moment the doctor walked in to comprehend reason at any level. In that case the doctor should just leave. And, for police or emergency first responders, best do that if possible on the street, keeping the subject under close surveillance, until adequate support through back up becomes available and the scene is cleared. Patrolman Andrew had no time to do this, he had to physically restrain Marlene Pinnock, and he appeared to be physically capable of doing this. That is still uncertain, because an off duty officer did arrive and helped. Furthermore, police officers in many departments believe that black females are harder to restrain than black males (Identification of Problem Police Officers, "Chicago Police Problem Officer Conference," 1982).

   Was that the problem in the cases of Garner and Pinnock, the former resisting arrest, which may have seemed strange to them, and, conversely, the latter, deceptively hard to restrain, despite mismatch of force on paper? It may have been possible to engage Miriam Carey in a conversation until her weapon—the car—was immobilized. Such restraint, however, would have required immediate recognition that she was listening to another voice and that she was not on the same planet Earth as the officers engaging her in front of the White House. Ideally, an intelligent dialogue would have begun with

> "Ma'am you have really urgent problems to discuss with The President. Let's see if he's home and check how we can get you in touch with him." rather, than, "Ma'am, you cannot see the President, and that's that."

Of course, what transpired at the critical moment before she recklessly slammed her gears into reverse, using Pennsylvania Avenue as a drag strip, is unknown to the public. However, engaging her rather than confronting her with force might have provided time to disarm her—specifically the car being her lethal weapon of murder and mayhem in the nation's capital. There is no evidence that the officers had reason to believe she had other weapons, but she had what amounted to a hostage, her child. They did not give themselves the time to consider that.

4. There is a time after a patient refuses cooperation that he releases fury. Distinguish the genre common to ERs called "fuck-shouters" from the patient who actually threatens flight or fight. The latter hypes a clinician or emergency responder at the approach with his state of arousal and readiness to flee. This may have been more the profile of Eric Garner, Victor White, and Michael Brown than that of the dangerous fugitive from justice. But experienced patrol officers as well as detectives skilled at engaging with a suspect have a street sense. One does not have to grow up and live the life of a street hustler to hear the limbic music for threat assessment.

   Clinicians, especially, should remember where they are and whom they are with when on an open psychiatric ward. This may sound excessive for the presumably secure hospital setting, but the clinician should always try to keep a safe corridor to safety when one knows or senses high acuity on the unit. Of course, all patrol is like this. Could Phoenix, New Orleans, and Ferguson police simply have vacated the field interrogations to prevent imminently escalating their encounters? They are not trained to do so, nor is it in their DNA. But, times have changed; as can be seen in all these cases, tough police officers were not the answer. Milwaukee's Chief Flynn had to back up to that conclusion and fire Officer Manney. A recent study of prosecutions shows minimal risk of felony conviction for officers using deadly force. Is this fair, or does it provide false confidence in enforcing first and worrying about public safety second? (www.nytimes.com/2014/09/04/us/challenges-seen-in-prosecuting-police-for-use-of-deadly-force.html).
5. When verbal release or apparent verbal negotiations collapse, action prevails and there is no more time. At this point in classical emergency triage for emergency medicine, things have moved past behavioral change, where supportive methods can likely be timely. The clinician simply must distinguish that authentic "fuck-shouter," who can be diverted and distracted from the puncher, and waste no time deciding whether to just isolate or restrain immediately. This is the likely scenario preceding the Ferguson, Missouri, disaster. Do not wait and keep talking the acting-out patient down. Did Officer Wilson take offense to Brown's insult when telling him to get off the street and leave his guard down for big Mike to slug him, penetrate through the protective shield of his car, and go for his gun? Action threats must be taken seriously. Reason and rationale always should prevail when verbal communications are operational, but action, by definition, is at best symbolic communication. In emergency psychiatry it is more often than not prelude to mayhem. That was clearly the cases of Carey and Pinnock. It was not at all clearly the case of Garner, or perhaps even the psychotic man, Ezell Ford, recently killed by the Los Angeles Police Department (LAPD) or Hamilton, asleep in the park and already determined by prior patrol to be alive. It appears Wilson did not have to confront Michael Brown and Dorian Johnson for purposes of either their safety or the public's safety. What would have been the consequences were

he to have decided to make this simply a traffic and emergency medical case for apparent drunkenness and low-level criminal investigation by detectives for unarmed robbery, just as suggested in the Garner case? The authors believe, had this sensible and legal procedure been performed with Michael Brown, the world would never have heard of Ferguson, Missouri, nobody would have been injured or killed, and Darren Wilson would still be on patrol, rather than hiding and trying to find a way to support his growing family.

---

If you are practicing emergency psychiatry, you must be both prepared and trained, but you also must have the temperament. That goes for police officers as well. This is a dangerous place for control freaks and sadists because the ill-conceived move at the wrong time can end in violence, which would have otherwise been avoidable. Patients representing threat are not the characters of the Old West who can be expected to weigh the force and either attack or retreat. Such a paradigm may fit certain corrections situations, where career criminals and their controllers both know the rules of the game. These two adversaries, inmates and officers, share one common ideology—that is to eliminate the unpredictable psycho driven by autistic agendas and get real rewards from a shared environment even if it is just a cigarette for assurances not to escape or stir things up. The traditional corrections matrix is far more predictable in regard to threat assessment than many acute care points of entry today. Filling them with psychotics and hypervigilant combat veterans changes the rules of prison, rules long established like cats and dogs in the house. Cons and their guards are equally threatened by the majority of "special offenders" like the Marine Veteran, Murdough, recently baked to death at Rikers. The rules for both cons and their guards have changed drastically, making for a highly toxic and volatile environment. The words of the prosecutor in Seattle are instructive, "there is always room for one more," but should no longer be muttered from any courtroom (Liebert and Wright 1977).

When approaching that emergency psychiatric patient, therefore, one faces a very high likelihood of either of these scenarios occurring. A police officer's approach to the person with a mental illness is of utmost importance, as are his or her verbal and nonverbal communications and positioning. In this country, 3 feet is the safest radius to consider before one is perceived to be penetrating the average person's intimate space. Thus, it is professional caution to keep a buffer zone when trying to talk a mentally ill person down so as to prevent a potentially dangerous incident from taking place.

Could the most sophisticated threat assessment detect brainwashed males' intent on causing maximum carnage without caring for their own lives on earth? It can be said that there is no more dangerous person than a suicidal man—e.g., the man who went berserk in Colorado, crashing, armed to the teeth, into buildings in his sophisticated, homemade armored bulldozer. That is the sentinel case of extreme dangerousness of suicidal patients. Or at least it was until the self-appointed lone wolf suicidal terrorists began to emerge in the United States and other Western countries, having been incited into action via the social media rants of radical jihadist groups.

We can only detect the suicidally dangerous in the same way as we successfully detect other people in our sights who do not belong there, e.g., the parents who have beaten their child nearly to death and—based on mechanism of injury—have been judged unreliable historians because the mechanism of injury does not fit the presenting exposed body impairment or disability. This equals an unreliable historian; a smart point of entry that quietly and calmly shifts to the red zone of states of clinical awareness and discretely isolates this unreliable historian and contains him until returning to Throw Out the GUNS.

## "MY" STANDS FOR YOUNG MALE

Our database to date informs us that we must be more vigilant with the male presenting as patient or collateral companion, but next one needs to look more closely at the patient and assess imminent dangerousness. Elder abuse, child abuse, and intimate partner abuse are all official violence in this nation. But the reportedly descending violent felony rate in this country shines the light on crime in public places that pales in comparison to what goes on behind the apparent sanctity of the neatest picket fences. Jon Benet Ramsey, most experts agree, was brutally murdered by someone inside the family circle (American Investigative Society of Cold Cases Annual Conference 2014). Yet, at the time of this writing, the external threat of kids with insignificant juvenile records from upwardly mobile prosocial American families returning from Africa and the Middle East as adults to blow us up is as high as any time since 9/11. What is going on behind those closed doors in places like St. Paul, Minnesota? We need to know in order to prevent terrorism in this nation; has anyone asked former psychiatrist, Nidal Hassan, what radicalized him to commit what now is officially recognized as an act of terrorism. Of anyone purportedly studying at-risk families in prosaic places such as St. Paul, psychiatrist Nidal Hasan likely holds more leads for understanding than anyone. But, the full thrust of society and government is to kill him without hearing another word from him. Threat assessment is an imperfect science, but it must be performed. And it must be done smartly. Hands-on courses like that produced by Challenger Corporation for Threat Assessment complement traditional training for police, firefighters, and corrections officers now faced with being clinically informed as well as effective enforcers. Challenger Threat Assessment and Defensive Tactics was designed by experts in emergency medicine, martial arts, and psychiatrists specifically for the subject who should be a patient under case management or hospitalized but is not—and therefore is free to roam from street to ER and back to street (Challenger Defensive Tactics for the Emergency Room [DETER], www.challengercme.com/).

Tackling and restraining the hijackers of Flight 93 in the ER of Holy Cross Hospital would not have been smart. Identifying them with the FBI would have been. Identifying the threat of Brown and his accomplice in the strong-armed robbery in Ferguson, Missouri, would have been smart. Engaging them alone on their turf to assert the authority of the law in this day when cities and states cannot afford either gang units or community policing would not be smart.

As for dangerousness and imminent violent suicide, the threat is usually, but not exclusively, male. Prospective studies of a cohort of Philadelphia males in the 1970s demonstrated that, even following multiple arrests, eventually 98% of most serious felonies were committed by just 1% of this male cohort (Wolfgang 1975). And the younger the male, the more dangerous he is, with the exception, probably, of terrorists. The debate over standing versus portable metal scanners due to racial profiling of young males pre-9/11 is now shifting to "threat assessment," a politically correct way of screening young and middleaged males of Middle Eastern descent. The fact is, however, that Europeans, or even Americans with fluent English, are considered as likely a threat for blowing you up in a hospital as a male or female of Middle Eastern descent. It is believed that radical terrorist Muslim groups are recruiting Europeans to blow you up. The Israel Defense Forces (IDF) is training the U.S. military in our own shopping centers to detect the suicide bomber. Although the bomb could be carried by anyone, the terrorist is more likely a young male with a cell phone. The War on Terror presents a new paradigm for combat trauma, because the most dangerous environment in this war is ordinary people in ordinary places such as the marketplace in Baghdad or the Times Square subway station in Manhattan.

Similarly, when examining the list of the most destructive serial murderers and suicidal mass murderers in recent history, they were overwhelmingly young males, from lust murderers, like Ted Bundy and Wayne Williams, to mass killers like Speck in Chicago, Whitman in the Texas Tower, and Aron Alexis in the Navy Yard massacre. It is safe to say that were terrorists and suicidal mass murderers and lust killers restricted to the female gender, such unremitting states of human destructiveness would be rare. For Officer Wilson, the responses to his commands from two young males walking in the middle of the street automatically raised the threat level for him in Ferguson, Missouri.

The "S" in MYSELF stands for sociopathy, and that means a person who violates laws and rules with no regard to the consequences for anyone else, most likely including the rules of civility required to safely and effectively manage an emergency service and any point of entry. No reliability in the history of presentation—or, chief complaint and history not matching clinical presentation means there is no reliability for the patient. And, again, have confidence in your intuition; if you let your instincts take you to the red zone of clinical states of awareness, more often than not, you will go to the right place when pushing that imaginary "Reassess" button in your head. Field interrogations, arrests, bookings, and prisoner classification are now points of entry to our health-care system, and may be the only one for a huge, vulnerable, and high-risk population. It is the only place, for instance, where the perpetrator of the Chinatown Massacre, Willie Mak, surfaced right before the massacre and was briefly incarcerated in the King County Jail! Unfortunately he was released before studying his criminal background and connections to criminal gangs in Hong Kong and his Visa status in Seattle. The question should have been, "what's he in jail for, and what's he in Seattle for?"

When entering our corrections system, life's toll is obvious. There are 15 million adults, or, 1 in 75 men behind bars. There are roughly 20 million detentions per annum in this country. Although they may, like the gangsters on TV, fit the criteria for diagnosis of sociopathic antisocial personality disorder (ASD), they will usually not fit the criteria for Psychopath on the Psychopathic Check List (PCL).

There are emergency psychiatry screens for ASD. But, always trace that time-determined triaging algorithm back up to states of mental disorganization, and even further upstream to neuropsyche brain injury without gross lateralizing signs (Figure 16.5). In 1994 there were 200,000 Vietnam combat veterans imprisoned in this country, most of them for drug-related offenses, and, among Vietnam veterans, the incidence of alcoholism associated with posttraumatic stress disorder is 35% (blacks 20%; for cocaine, reverse the percentages). It is unlikely with all the combat since then that this figure has improved. Gulf War I combat vets were already replacing Vietnam veterans in prison in 1994. And if you see this corrections population, you can find that most of them have subtle neuro dysfunction. Sometimes this dysfunction is hard but called soft. By the time they have reached this point they could be close to meeting the criteria for sociopathic personality disorder or sociopathy. That does not rule out Axis I diagnoses like PTSD, IED (Intermittent Explosive Disorder), or substance abuse and Axis III diagnoses of central nervous system (CNS) dysfunction—i.e., CHI with seizure history, particularly in the War on Terror with the high incidence of traumatic brain injuries.

Emergency responders could get a tip on this by reading tattoos on young males. The more pictorial and decorative they are, the less indicative of being a gangster with sociopathy. Does it say "Mom" or "Hate?" The small telltale tattoo on the hand, however, should alert you to being in the presence of a "marked" gangster. The classically sociopathic men depicted in *The Sopranos* show no guilt or inhibition to satisfy immediate needs. They bond internally, but will not bond with you, unless you meet their needs. Violence can be a routine way of getting what they want, and they will not spare anyone, even those wearing white and working in an emergency room or corrections site. They may not be stupid, but they will be ruthless when they need something. Because sociopaths know no borders and do not differentiate between self and others when it comes to territory, they can be frightening to encounter, whether immediately violent or not. But they will always seek to gratify their needs at the expense of others with no regard whatsoever for others, and that includes emergency responders, healthcare workers, and anyone they perceive can be of service to them.

"E" stands for empathy—Listen to the Limbic Music of Violence as if instinctually—"sniff the air." Studies show that skilled interviewers can feel imminent violence better than any form of verbal testing can predict. Empathy is depicted in Triage Protocol, Strange Behavior, Nonverbal, Figure 7.3. Most likely, if your sense of hype is diminishing rather than escalating as you get closer to the person you are engaging on the street, that person is not violent, at least not to you. Maybe you are just encountering disorganized aggression in the form of agitation with no real target at all, as with Pinnock and Carey, or maybe there is a target—the policeman, because the last arrest was humiliating, painful, and emasculating.

If you cannot empathize with the person, you need to listen to and trust your feelings. More likely than not, you are approaching somebody whose motivation, rational or irrational, is not that of a help-seeking patient who fits in the health-care system. The white-knuckle experience in interviewing that person who speaks of the most bloodcurdling acts or fantasies in his life with inappropriate emotion demands special consideration, including, again, that call to security. Michael Brown was not described as such a person, nor was Johnson, his accomplice caught on video during the robbery. But they were fugitives on the run, whether Officer Wilson knew that at the time or not. And, they might have been high on at least cannabis. If reports of Brown accessing the police car in an attempt to grab Wilson's gun are true, then the officer could likely have sensed threat to his life. At the same time, there was no evidence of threat to anyone else's life. Nobody has said that either Brown or accomplice, Johnson, were imminently dangerous to anyone else at the time of his engaging them. Did Officer Wilson need to stand his ground in the face of insult or expected aggression directed at him? If so, follow the lesson from Brian Buss's killer, roll up the windshield, drive off without the light bar on, and take care of traffic. That would have been a public safety duty. Had Wilson known a crime had been committed, then these two guys were easily found in this community; they were in fact going home to do drugs. Had they merely been suspicious for, perhaps, gang affiliation, then notify police intelligence. There is no evidence to date that a confrontation between a single officer in this hostile community and two strangely behaving young black males was necessary, even in the context immediately post-strong armed robbery. There is no evidence that these two men meandering down the middle of the street posed any threat to anyone, other than Officer Wilson and drivers approaching from both directions.

Sniffing the air and listening for the Limbic Music is also where you may first sense the patient's internalized "perturbation" and "inimicality." This is severe internal preoccupation, almost to the exclusion of being interested in you. Obviously the patient has a lot on his mind but is not there to make you listen or understand his agony. He has decided by this time to kill himself. Associated with a recent history of socially "isolating," this is a serious triad of subtle signs warning of imminent suicide. Do not hesitate to order suicide observation of this patient until securely admitted for safe, humane suicidal observation.

Marine veteran Murdough was baked to death on suicide watch while on psychotropic medications in solitary confinement at Rikers Island. This is not corrections. This is psychiatric malpractice, regardless of the color of the uniform, white, blue, or brown.

And when there is a distinct behavioral change, you should consider such change to be heightened anxiety and agitation. It could be either the beginning of a panic attack, intensification of auditory hallucinations, or onset of agitation in either psychosis or organic brain syndrome. Your position here is important, signifying that you are empathically listening. Try to get to his eye level, rather than towering above him, while positioned in such a way as to deflect punches and escape (Figure 7.4).

Humor can oftentimes defuse a situation; so, this is not the place for the compulsive among us. It is also not the place for clinical ignorance, rigidity, or unprofessionalism. Imagine how much Officer Andrew would like to have that moment back with Marlene Pinnock, roadside on I-10.

"L" stands for limits. You must try to use firm and sensitive verbal limits, but do not wait too long before calling for a show of force from all staff and security to restrain both medically and physically difficult patients .

Any point of entry to the health-care system demands a code of behavior. There is no rationale in due process for tolerating disruptive behavior in this unique and critical setting. Two warnings to cease and desist in any disruptive behavior with clear and concise consequences if defied is as far as you can go at this point. Once you have lost verbal communications with the verbally or nonverbally threatening patient, actions take over. Make them very clear, speaking with a slow and soft voice:

> "You need to stop pacing around so fast, or we will have to stop you from doing that. If you're hungry, we can get a pizza sent up."
> "Joe, You need to stay here on this gurney."

You will know whether you have someone on your hands who is able to hear you or not. Your personality and physical demeanor may put a patient who is fearful of being out of control at ease by showing your jugular with submissive humor. The patient is going to tell you whether he is going with you as a buddy, e.g., regarding that offer to send out for pizza, "Everything on it or just plain?" If that goes in one ear and out the other while the movement increases, you are tuned out. If your "buddy chat" turns ugly, e.g., "Everything on it so it burns your ass good," it is time for restraint. Do not wait, because the risk of physical confrontation is very, very high, particularly with intoxicated patients. We have been talking about ER practices. In these cases it is important to distinguish between the health setting like the ER where containment and restraint are possible without police intervention and nonclinical settings that prohibit the jailer, police officer, or first responder from leaving, as the authors have so often advocated in some deadly police encounters. There are dangerous felons on the run, such as the survivalist who assassinated state patrolmen in Pennsylvania, who simply must be stopped any way possible before they do any more damage.

We are talking about crises involving threats from people who have primary psychiatric disorders and not career sociopaths; we believe this is self-evident to the reader and needs no elaboration. But in the emergency clinical services arena, whether in hospital or outside its boundaries, make certain that there are at least three to five staff with you now and security is on its way, because one of two things is going to happen in this next stage. You will either have the screamer or "fuck-shouter" whom you can redirect and isolate while he is releasing or an acting-out patient who can no longer process words. Your duty now is to deescalate an imminently violent situation through every deal you can legally make before you lay hands on.

Verbal communications have all but failed; this is the precipice where things can go in any way, and very, very fast. You may be successful in asserting yourself with firm authority without precipitating a power struggle, but if the patient is still listening, nobody will call you on the carpet or pick your pockets for ordering out and getting the man the pizza or even his favorite submarine sandwich. Negotiate, negotiate, negotiate. Do whatever is practically possible, but keep that limit clear and concise with reasonable consequences that can be delivered with a show of force from staff and security, through physical restraint, injectable tranquilizer, isolation, or locked seclusion.

In the tiny window of opportunity, quickly base your clinical intervention on knowledge base, imperfect as it is. Think "social, psychological, and biological" elements of violence to formulate your intervention, and then put everything moral and legal on the table within reason and be ready to deliver and defend your solicitation, before deciding you are with the bio of the human beast.

If he can listen and reliable family or peers are available, call on them to assist to quell the situation that may be caused or aggravated by threat of estrangement to a frightened patient. We know all too much now about the psychology of threatened and absolute control. Put yourself in the patient's shoes. Do not frighten him with your fear. Certainly be poised and calmly firm. But, show respect and humanity by honesty, even saying, "We're afraid of you," and perhaps humor that does not humiliate.

Offer a patient a smoke break, because what is there to lose if the patient elopes after lighting up outside with security alerted? Elopement and submitting to a cigarette are less hazardous for everyone than going to the mat with someone you do not know; this, of course, excludes a prisoner brought in by the police, but that should be their primary responsibility when containment is not possible in the medical setting. You do not have custody of these patients. Perhaps you should, but in most cases you do not. And, if he runs and you should have custody, then call the police. Of course, you cannot offer sexual favors to the seductive or hypersexual patient of any persuasion, but you can ask him to wait for a pizza with everything on it or the food of his choice—that is, if he agrees to sit down, not threaten, and wait quietly for it.

This is negotiation, but consequences have to be clear, and then it is necessary to risk restraint, rather than continued talking, as soon as adequate staff and security are with you. If this patient is *"C"ombative*, even if he has not taken the first swing, you are not obligated to wait until the patient actually becomes combative before you take physical control, whether by either medical or physical restraint—or on the street in blue with a Michael Brown, simply drive on by and arrest later. He is going home. He said so and likely was—or certainly not far away to show up later with a warrant on another arrest. In all these encounters with the police cited, such deescalation might be relevant. But, in the cases of Brown and Garner, perhaps it is best to simply walk on by and report the problem at another level.

Many inner city males have been shot; most bookings show scars of gunshot wounds. "F" stands for fighting wounds from gang violence that shoots to wound, rather than kill, until proven otherwise. Alert security and do not release without a thorough psychosocial history of gang affiliation.

And, like that telltale little tattoo "marking" the hand and raising the specter of your chance encounter with a young gangster, evidence of fighting also raises that chance. Any young male with either recent or old bullet wounds needs to be treated differently in the first encounter with an unknown patient. There is a war out there, and if you happen to be working in the neighborhood where gangs are empowered, the evidence of a gunshot wound that is coincidental to a reason for presentation should raise a flag of caution. Combat wounds in the young male should signal antisocial gang lifestyle, as should a limp in an otherwise healthy young male.

It is unfortunate that Officer Wilson learned the whole mnemonic for a dangerous person by prolonging the encounter with Michael Brown, who ultimately fit every element of it. By following evidence-based rules of emergency medicine triaging, however, policemen, as the new caretakers of the mentally ill, are less likely to need to use deadly force. Although few prosecutions succeed against policemen for use of deadly force—thus sparing officers' lives from death sentences or prison—having evaluated nearly 100 postshooting trauma cases and studied the psychopathology of this syndrome—it is evident that, except in extreme cases, there is serious psychopathology regarding officers who find themselves continuously in situations where they have to defend themselves with lethal force.

Every occupation has its psychopaths, and except for the psychopathic officer, the vast majority of officers using deadly force may survive prosecution, but their careers will be dead. Their lives are numbed and controlled by traumatic flashbacks, because the law of Mother Nature holds, even when that of the law does not; police killings are murder for Mother Nature, even when ruled as "good shootings" by the shooting review boards.

Murder is alien to the vast majority of police officers, even when they are saying they can kill somebody if necessary. It is simply not that simple. There is no good shooting, only a righteous one in the eyes of the department investigating it. In summary, following the rules of emergency medicine triage for imminent dangerousness will reduce the risk of killing the mentally ill or strangely behaving individual not on view in commission of the crime, caught after the act of a dangerous felony, or apparently an imminent threat to others or self.

## REFERENCES

American Investigative Society of Cold Cases Annual Conference, 2014. Fayetteville, NC. www.aisocc.com/2014-conference.html

Kissinger, M. 2011. Law creates barriers to getting care for mentally ill. *Milwaukee-Wisconsin Journal Sentinel*, December 10. www.jsonline.com/news/law-creates-barriers-to-getting-care-for-mentally-ill-135387808.html

Lertzman, R. and Birnes, W. 2015. *Mickey Rooney: His Life and Times*. Gallery Books.

Liebert, J. A. and Birnes, W. J. 2011. *Suicidal Mass Murderers: A Criminological Study of Why They Kill*. Taylor and Francis, www.search.yahoo.com/search?ei=utf-8&fr=slv8-w3i&p=cutaneous%20anthrax%23q%3dcutaneouanthrax%20pictures&type=W3i_YT,191,8_4,Search,20120310,18370,0,18,0

Liebert, J. A. and Wright, C. 1977. Proof of identity: The presentence evaluation. *AAFS Annual Meeting*, New Orleans, 1977.

Reckdahl, K. 2014. Father seeks answers in death of son, who police say shot himself while cuffed. *The New York Times*, September 1. www.nytimes.com/2014/09/02/us/louisianian-seeks-answers-in-death-of-son-said-to-have-shot-himself-while-cuffed.html

Shane, S. 2015. Former F.B.I. agent sues, claiming retaliation over misgivings in anthrax case. *The New York Times*, April 8. www.nytimes.com/2015/04/09/us/ex-fbi-agent-claims-retaliation-for-dissent-in-anthraxinquiry.html

Winter, M. 2014. Pa. doctor shoots patient who killed caseworker. *USA Today*, July 25. www.usatoday.com/story/news/nation/2014/07/24/shooting-wellness-center/13113555/

Wolfgang, M. 1975. *Delinquency in a Birth Cohort in Philadelphia, Pennsylvania, 1945–1963*. www.ncjrs.gov/App/publications/Abstract.aspx?id=29557

# 8

# Protecting our greatest natural resource: Our youth in schools

If professionals in clinical psychiatry and psychology, as well as first responders—especially law enforcement personnel—believe that suicidal mass murder rampages happen out of nowhere, which is what so many cable news pundits and national reporters pronounce authoritatively, they are suffering under a false and fatal misconception that promotes an ironically nihilistic, but nonsacrificial response. Most of these suicidal rampage mass murders on campus were predictable and the offenders could have been prevented from committing their crimes, if those charged with providing care to students understood and acknowledged the warning signs of dangerousness. How many times has it come out in the news after a tragic mass murder or suicidal mass murder that the killer was under observation, and both the health-care system—even the justice system—had failed because adequate diagnosis and management were not provided or simply not available on campus?

In a litany of cases since Columbine, we have seen that the perpetrators, most, if not all, of whom were suffering from a mental illness so debilitating they could barely function in society, were evaluated at points of entry into the system. Dylan Klebold and Eric Harris had been called out to the local sheriff; James Holmes in Colorado was under some sort of student counseling at the University of Colorado and Seung-Hui Cho at Virginia Tech had been involuntarily committed for treatment to the university's counseling center that had no psychiatrist, even thought he had to be medicated to insure his safety and that around him. But, all were left free to roam and ultimately commit their suicidal rampage murders. In terms of the field of criminology and its intersection with psychiatry we have to argue that it is clear; there are certain types of offenders, particularly in schools and workplaces, who, when they turn up on official radars as mentally disorganized and threatening, they need to be surveilled—even if not medically or judicially supervised.

## COLUMBINE AS THE TEMPLATE FOR SCHOOL SHOOTINGS

In 1995, two nerdish and neo-Goth students at Columbine High School in Littleton, Colorado captured headlines all over cable and print news when they took revenge on perceived tormentors and jocks believed to have shunned them, murdering a total of 12 students and 1 teachers while injuring 24 others. This was an assault on America's consciousness. The sheer brutality of two kids loose on a suicidal rampage in the sanctity of an upscale high school where our children were considered safe had ended any social delusion of homeland security anywhere. Then the events of 9/11 numbed our minds and souls, and we became wrapped up in wars overseas as the cancer of suicidal school and workplace shootings metastasized throughout the country.

Most Americans may have had forgotten about Columbine, but Seung-Hui Cho remembered it, and although supposedly suffering from "selective mutism"—a George Washington University Child Psychiatry trainee's diagnosis—expressed his admiration of Dylan Klebold and Eric Harris as early as middle school. In a short essay, he bragged he would outdo them. He did just that on the Virginia Tech campus on April 16, 2007, killing 32 and injuring 17 before killing himself. Less than a year later, University of Illinois graduate student, Steven Kazmierczak, went on a suicidal murder spree on the campus of Northern Illinois University in DeKalb, Illinois, killing 5 people and injuring another 21, before committing suicide. It was Valentine's Day, and this otherwise nondescript Chicago scholar would avenge his perceived persecution at Northern Illinois University on the anniversary of Capone's notoriously and celebrated cold-blooded Valentine's Day massacre. He talked a lot about this Chicago execution on campus, and students said they tired of hearing his apparent obsession with mass cold blooded violence; these students could not have imagined, however, that Kazmierczak would end up shooting more of them than the notorious ruthless gangster Capone had shot 79 years before to the date.

## ELLIOT RODGER AND THE ISLA VISTA RAMPAGE

On May 23, 2014, a young man from an affluent California family—one well placed in the state's entertainment industry—went on a shooting rampage in an area next to the campus of the University of California, Santa Barbara. The Santa Barbara Sheriff's report graphically depicts the events of that day when Rodger, who had previously posted his antisocial hatred—then his intentions to go on a shooting spree—stabbed his two roommates to death one after the other as they separately entered the apartment.

Hours passed after the initial murders, during which time Rodger posted a "self-made video," entitled "Retribution," and a 137-page manifesto that he sent to friends and family, in which he described not only his anxiety, but fury at the world. The actions he would take on were justified based on both his inability to relate to others and the way he was ostracized by women. That explains why one of his targets was a local sorority house near campus. He pounded on the door but could not gain entrance; so, he left the sorority house and shot three young women on the sidewalk nearby, killing two of them and wounding a third.

Rodger's spree continued as he drove away and fired a shot into an unoccupied building, likely hoping to kill someone at random before driving on to where he saw a male pedestrian in front of a market, whom he shot and killed. Not satisfied with just shooting, Rodger then saw another pedestrian and ran him over with his car, endangering his life and seriously injuring him. He then continued driving, and, upon seeing two more pedestrians, he shot them as well, wounding both of them.

Rodger continued to shoot at pedestrians whose path he crossed, all of them women, wounding some and missing others. But his spree would not end. He exchanged fire with a Santa Barbara County Sheriff's deputy who shot out one of Rodger's tires, but Rodger kept on driving, again intentionally running over two male pedestrians and seriously injuring both of them, caring less whether they would live, die or simply suffer out their shortened lives. He shot and wounded another pedestrian and then aimed his car at a man riding a skateboard, striking and seriously injuring him. He also struck and injured another man, this victim riding a bike, and then struck another pedestrian. His murder and mayhem resumed as he encountered pedestrians along the sidewalk; he fired rounds from his passing car and wounded them in cold blood as if he were competing for stuffed monkies at a carnival shooting range.

Finally Elliot Rodger was surrounded by units from the Sheriff's Department and exchanged fire with them. This time, the deputies wounded Rodger in the hip, but Rodger was still capable of driving and intentionally struck another cyclist with his car, seriously injuring him. This vicious assault on a total stranger was by coincidence his last attempted public execution, because, while still driving, Rodger turned the gun on himself and shot, killing himself while his vehicle was still moving. It ultimately crashed into another car and finally stopped, miraculously injuring and killing no more.

In a subsequent interview with Peter and Chin Rodger, who were driving back to Santa Barbara from Los Angeles, the sheriff's investigators learned that the parents had read their son's manifesto and were beyond concerned, but they indicated to the investigator that they did not believe their son would hurt anyone. Meanwhile, another detachment of deputies entered Rodger's apartment where they found the bodies of his roommates and one of their friends. Rodger had brutally murdered all three of them.

In the wake of the murders, the Sheriff's Department recovered hundreds of documents, along with megabytes of data from Rodger's computer, and collected statements from Rodger's parents, family, friends, and acquaintances. They amalgamated all of this disparate information into a portrait of a young man who gradually descended into the maelstrom of debilitating mental illness. His spiral was gradual at first but then gained intensity as his sickness worsened. The sheriff determined that Elliot Rodger did not pop up out of nowhere but was the subject of an investigation initiated by his mother via her son's life coach through the local county mental health center. Her request for an intervention was based on Elliot's "disturbing" videos, the report said—videos which he had posted on YouTube. They conducted what they called a "welfare check."

During the welfare check at Elliot's apartment, the police officers interviewed him, looking for any signs of dangerous behavior conforming with the checklist from his LPS (Lanterman Petris Short Manual). But the officers determined that he showed no signs of being dangerous to himself or others and did not make any statements to that effect; they obviously interpreted dangerousness as an overt threat within the context of the LPS manual to determine eligibility for involuntary commitment for emergency psychiatric detention and examination. In particular, the sheriff's officers said, they were calmed down by Elliot's saying that his mother was a "worrywart" and that the videos he had posted only revealed his loneliness and his complaint that he had no friends. Nothing dangerous here, he assured them. According to the deputies, "the suspect was calm, shy, and polite." And after the interview, they contacted Chin Rodger, whose description of Elliot's expressions of loneliness in his video postings comported almost exactly with what Elliot himself had told the investigating deputies. And at the conclusion of the interview, the conversation with Elliot's mother, and a conversation between Elliot and his mother held in the deputies' presence, the deputies concluded that Elliot did not meet the criteria for a 5150(a) detention and restraint order that would have allowed them to take Rodger into custody for a 72-hour "mental health assessment." As a result, there was no further investigation at that time.

After the rampage, sheriff's investigators reviewed their own procedures and revisited Rodger's postings where they discovered a trove of information leading them to further insights about Rodger's state of mind. They discovered that in addition to his being suicidal because of his hopeless remorse at his inability to connect with other human beings, his anger manifested itself in his fascination with Nazi war criminals and propagandists, the most notorious mass murderers in the twentieth century. Rodger's interest in the Third Reich included his study not only of the philosophy of mass genocide, but the techniques of genocide as well, especially those promulgated by Heinrich Himmler and Joseph Goebbels.

In concluding its summary of the Isla Vista mass murders, the sheriff's investigators concluded that Elliot Rodger had planned his attacks well in advance, acquiring weapons and ammunitions, and focusing on targets that were the object of his frustration, particularly the college-age women with whom, he said, he could not connect. He was socially isolated, and as his frustration at his self-imposed isolation increased, he blamed others for his own inability. His hopelessness was palpable, and he found a level of psychological justification for his own suicidal ideations, as well as his homicidal rampage, in the writings of other mass murderers. Ultimately, he turned his ravings set forth in his online manifesto and his Internet video postings into action, working himself up to commit the ultimate act of suicidal mass murder.

The tragedy of preventive psychiatry in this case is that the initial sheriff's investigation relied on the killer's own words to eliminate any suspicions they had about his potential dangerousness. Hence, although they had the authority to hold him under a 5150(a) detention under the California code, they said that his responses to their inquiry assured them that he was dangerous neither to himself nor others. This was a serious mistake. What should have happened in this case was that the sheriff's department, once alerted by Rodger's mother, should have erred on the side of caution and deferred medical examination to nearby Ventura/University of California, Los Angeles (UCLA) Medical Center, which has the psychiatric and medicolegal resources for a minimum of 72 hours of working days to investigate the allegations, thus reducing the risk of missing serious mental illness that policeman do not have. Although the folly of Lanterman–Petris–Short (LPS) delegated such authority to policemen, few officers would agree that they should be the ones making such calls and placing them in the crosshairs of a *Tarasoff*-type review. His threats were specific enough, most likely, to give warning—at least, perhaps to a sorority named in his rantings and manifesto. Whether this officer is liable or not is unclear, but the *Tarasoff* decision resulted from California police also finding Poddar, the killer of Tatiana Tarasoff, no threat also. Certainly, there have been and will be circumstances in which officers have made and will make decisions for probable cause for involuntary commitment of a person for emergency psychiatric evaluation under a 5150, but what training do they have for this? They have none, or they would have gone to medical school or obtained a PhD in clinical psychology instead of applying for the police academy. There is no doubt in the authors' mind that Elliot Rodger would have been held for 72 hours for psychiatric evaluation at Ventura/UCLA and found to be suffering severe Paranoid Schizophrenia. Whether he could have been medicated and kept for an additional 2 weeks under a Riese and 5250 order, respectively, is speculative, but most likely he would have been both "Riesed" and 5250'd by Ventura/UCLA because of their known expertise in the practical operations of managing a *Tarasoff* case from at least one other high profile *Tarasoff* case.

In the wake of these tragedies, politicians from California to Virginia to Illinois were seemingly desperate for solutions. Even former Governor Rod Blagojevich signed an order to upgrade campus safety before he himself went to prison. Soon thereafter, the U.S. House of Representatives passed the Campus Safety Act. Its legislative history is brief: "CAMPUS Safety Act of 2009, Introduced: January 28, 2009 (111th Congress, 2009–2010) Status: Died (Passed House) in a previous session of Congress." Thus, there is no law addressing this problem. But here is the story from an *Esquire* magazine article written by David Vann (2009) about Steve Kazmierczak's mass shooting at Northern Illinois University (NIU) that prompted the congressional activity:

> Valentine's Day. 3:04 p.m. Cole Hall Room 100. The end of class. Intro to Ocean Science. Many of the students are gone, since they had a test two days before. The stage door behind the screen bursts open. Steve walks abruptly onto the stage. He stands for the briefest of moments just looking at the class, and then he raises the shotgun. He fires into the front row of students. (www.esquire.com/news-politics/a4863/steven-kazmierczak-0808/)

Thus begins a narrative describing the chaos that ensued as many students were hit with shotgun rounds. The class, as Steve continued to point his gun and fire, began to flee, rising from their seats and heading for the doorway. However, typical of many mass murders, a sense of denial had set in to other students in a way similar to the James Holmes' mass murder in an Aurora, Colorado, movie theater. There, as in this classroom, some students thought the whole thing was a joke. In the midst of the panic in the front of the class, confusion reigned. Joe Peterson, the class instructor, tried to open a stage door so the students could get out of the line of fire, but the door was locked. The shooter kept on firing two more times as Peterson made repeatedly unsuccessful attempts to yank the stage door open.

Unfortunately for the students, most of them were directly in the shooter's line of fire because of the layout of the auditorium. The aisles were the only way out, and they were clogged with students fleeing. The instructor, however, could not flee. He could only try to take cover behind the stage podium, from which position he could hear the menacing clack as the shooter rechambered his rounds and the shell casings were discarded from the weapon, a 12-gauge shotgun that the shooter had been trained to use as a guard for the Indiana prison system after graduating as the top senior from NIU undergraduate class. Shortly later he had flunked out of NIU grad school, where he was allowed to take simple undergraduate courses. Nobody on campus had a clue how well trained in firearms Kazmierczak was. His academic performance at NIU certainly made absolutely no sense either, and he had hardly been a low-profile student on this large university campus.

Trained to kill with a shotgun after flunking out, Steve was methodical in his fusillade, as he stood in one place, sweeping his gun barrel across his targets as if victorious in a military ambush. He showed no sign of panic and did not rush his fire. Then, he fired three more times, hitting students in the back as they ran down the clogged aisles in their attempts to escape. This was a 12-gauge, so the spread of pellets was very wide, hitting students with each burst of fire and wounding them.

"I had two thoughts during his second reloading," Joe Peterson told *Esquire* magazine. "I remembered that girl at Columbine hiding under her desk who got shot at point-blank range. I also thought, I just got married. I'm not going to do this to my wife."

Joe Peterson finally saw his chance to escape and leaped from the stage, heading toward the aisle. But victims were lying on the ground so that Peterson had to use his hands to "spider-walk" over their bodies. "I was keeping my eyes on him as I went," Peterson said. "I knew not to turn my back on him. I was halfway up the aisle when he turned and looked right at me. He had just reloaded the shotgun, but he dropped it. I didn't see him reach for the Glock. It was so fast, he just suddenly had it, and he fired at me. There was no change of expression, not even excitement. It was like if you're repainting a room at home, painting the walls, and you realize you missed a few spots, it was that mechanical."

Steve Kazmierczak had drawn his handgun and had begun firing 48 rounds into his victims. Joe Peterson felt himself get hit, but fortunately, the layers of clothing he was wearing stopped the bullet before it penetrated his body. He knew at that moment, he told *Esquire* magazine, he was going to get out alive. Others who were hit remembered that they were lying there on the cold floor, either waiting for death or waiting for the massacre to stop. But Steve Kazmierczak kept on shooting, combing the aisles for helpless students who could not escape and, taking his time to aim, mowing them down one by one. The methodical nature of his rampage, in retrospect, was frightening to contemplate.

Student Dan Parmenter was visiting the class that day, Valentine's Day, to sit alongside of his girlfriend, Lauren Debrauwere. Sitting with her in the front row, Dan immediately sought to protect Lauren with his own body, shielding her from the fire, but Kazmierczak shot him five times, killing him before he shot Lauren and then the person sitting next to her on the other side.

Amid what some students felt was an event that stretched forever, even though it was only a couple of minutes, students called out to Kazmierczak to stop shooting. Others pleaded for their lives. But he would not stop, working his way along the rows of the aisles, execution style. Finally, he stepped back up on stage where he put the gun to his head and fired a single round. After all the bursts of fire and heavy smoke, after the smell of spent powder filled the auditorium, there remained an eerie quiet as some of the surviving students picked up their heads to see if they could escape.

Kazmierczak's friend, possibly a girlfriend, later wrote that she wondered why Steve did this. Still in the throes of lingering stress and suffering from nightmares even months later, she still adheres to a belief that on the day of the shooting it was not Steve Kazmierczak up on that stage, it was someone else—not someone she knew.

As quoted in the *Esquire* magazine article cited above, she revealed that she had last seen Steve only 3 days before the shooting.

> She remembered him telling her, "You can write a book about me someday."
>
> "Why would I want to write a book about you?" she asked him.
>
> "I can be your case study," he said.
>
> She was studying criminology; clearly he was contemplating his own end.

But Steve Kazmierczak had left other clues to his intentions, telling his girlfriend on the way to a Marilyn Manson concert they attended, "What do you think happens when you die?"

And months earlier, he told her, "One day I might just disappear and you will never find me. Nobody will ever find me." And even before that he advised her that if anything happened to him, she should not tell anyone about him.

Vann concluded in his article that, "We were told that Steven Kazmierczak, who killed five students and then himself at NIU one year ago, was a sweet, unassuming, overachieving grad student who inexplicably snapped. He was not."

Is reviewing such massacres on campuses across the country in an attempt to explain the shooters' motivations just a case of hindsight with 20/20 vision? If we could have understood what was brewing in the psyches of these suicidal mass murderers, we might have been able to intervene. As Vann's *Esquire* article shows, the ice cold brutality and pure evil of Steven Kazmierczak has become vivid through the eyes of survivors of his rampage shooting at Cole Hall on that fateful Valentine's Day of 2008. Like Cho at Virginia Tech before him and Adam Lanza at Sandy Hook afterward, Kazmierczak destroyed all evidence of his thought processes culminating in this catastrophe by depriving police investigators of the hard drive to his computer and his cell phone. Once again, we are left to search for the pieces of a jigsaw puzzle scattered over acres—even many hundreds of square miles—of turf, many of them missing.

The puzzle gradually takes form and portrays the descent of a young man into hell with many noticing a piece here and a piece there in retrospect but doing nothing. Some pieces are red flags standing in isolation. Steven Kazmierczak had a well-documented history of a psychotic illness from adolescence in Chicago to his final days as a transfer grad student at the University of Illinois in Urbana. He was on the most powerful of psychotropic medications in adolescence, including the antipsychotic Clozaril, reserved for the most treatment-resistant cases of psychotic disorders.

Everything was in threes, right up to the moment of final preparation for murder and mayhem. He carefully arranged three guns neatly beside him at the seedy Travelodge in DeKalb, Illinois, the day before going berserk like a robotic killing machine on a campus where he had actually achieved considerable success just months before. He had won a Deans' Award, the highest honor given to undergraduates at NIU. This success was in reckless defiance of the grim prognosis he carried from months of inpatient psychiatric treatment in Chicago during high school and a psychologically devastating discharge from the army 6 years to the date of his attack on the very people who embraced him as a friend, good student, and even a leader. However, not everyone thought of him that way. He had to get a single dorm room because a roommate called him "Strange Steve" and referred to him as "psycho." But, Steve was an advisor in statistics where he was remembered as extremely helpful to students struggling with the complex math.

Steve was especially noted as professional and patient with frustrated students who simply could not get it. He got it and helped them without a sense of superiority. This absence of ego and superiority was in sharp contrast to his intense attraction to power figures like Hitler, Capone, and Bundy and their absolutely cold-blooded control over humanity. He shared this frightening preoccupation with friends, most of whom did not take it seriously, but who must have seen it as over the top. Among other powerful psychopathological demons struggling to get out of Steven Kazmierczak, the most obvious were wild mood swings and compulsive checking, counting, and hand washing. Threes were his obsessions; compulsive checking had to be obvious to anyone knowing him well, as it was so constant he finally bowed to encouragement to get help at the University of Illinois counselling center. A psychiatrist focused on his severe obsessive-compulsive disorder (OCD) without knowledge of his serious mental illness with four nearly lethal suicide attempts during adolescence and his hospitalization in an army psychiatric hospital with suicide precautions after high school graduation.

The university psychiatrist treated him with a high dosage of Prozac for his OCD and Xanax for his anxiety. It seemed to help, but in a state of crisis, he contacted Navy recruiters in order to return to the military where the structure, he thought, allowed him to cope with his problems without psychotropic medications. As was commonly the case in 2008, he was told by the recruiter to stop his medication and come back later. This was the year of the surge in Iraq and a peaking economy. Soldiers, especially ones already successfully completing phase one of basic infantry training, were not easy to find and recruit. Fearing another encounter with military psychiatry, however, Steve only discontinued his medication and did not pursue reenlistment. Instead, he took his killing skills from both basic military training at Fort Sill and a brief job as a corrections officer in Indiana and immersed himself in wild sex from the Internet and violent video games like "Call of Duty." He read up on Cho's suicidal mass murder and downloaded a video game replicating Cho's methodical killings. He was not reticent in telling acquaintances about his admiration for the Columbine and Virginia Tech massacres. He openly admired the tactics of diversion of explosives at Columbine and Cho's two sentinel murders that preceded his chaining the engineering building, like Cole Hall at NIU, Cho's mysteriously selected target for suicidal mass murder at Virginia Tech.

Steve's girlfriend said he became more erratic in his behavior after discontinuing his medication in southern Illinois with deeper dives in his depression. The war in Iraq was boiling with the surge. He probably could have gone, but he would start his own at his alma mater, which he may have considered to have alienated him through flunking him out of its grad school, its newly installed administration no longer adulating of him and unacceptable responses from old acquaintances via e-mails. He was writing crazy stuff and was losing friends at his alma mater upstate.

> He wrote: "I may have graduated at the top of my college class, but I now understand that book smarts don't translate into common sense. In college, and by past girlfriends, I was often told that I was too smart for my own good. I now understand what was meant by this comment."

A couple of days later, he fought with his former NIU friends on WebBoard, an online discussion forum to which he still had access. They were talking about sex offenders. Online was a gay grad student at NIU who worked with them, and this was a guy Steve respected. But one day Jessica, his girlfriend, was looking around online. She worked in rehabilitating juvenile sex offenders and had found this guy on the list, a former sex offender himself. On WebBoard, Steve exposed the gay man for the hypocrite he believed the man to be. "Disgusting, a horrible, horrible person," Steve thought to himself. Steve was vicious, relentless in his attacks—so vicious, in fact, that former mentor and professor, Jim Thomas, and Steve's friends were shocked by the whole exchange. They would later say that this was not the Steve they knew and could not make any sense of what they were seeing online. Steve went back on meds a few days later, but around this time something primal kicked in. First it was the guns. Then it was sex, and he began surfing the Casual Encounters section of Craigslist.

Does this descent into violence of an individual who seems to have two aspects to his personality—an outward shell of normalcy and benevolence that masks a seething fury—sound familiar? It should. Is there a common denominator for mass murderers on campus, and, if so, is it a legal point for the school's intervention? In researching mass murderers on campuses, we have found that most have dropped out, flunked out, were kicked out of school, or simply disappeared off the simplest radar screen that should be every school's dashboard to monitor students. Most were obviously psychotic like Cho at Virginia Tech, Loughner at Pima College, and Holmes at University of Colorado. Others, like Adam Lanza from University of Connecticut, simply withdrew behind a shell of reclusiveness, withdrawing from any contact—as did Elliot Rodger from Santa Barbara City College. But inside they raged, and the manifestations of that could be seen from time to time bubbling to the surface like lava from a smoldering volcano about to erupt. Our challenge—the challenge of the clinical professions as well as first responders—is to recognize these indicators of violence, and to address them in such a way as to prevent catastrophic results on school grounds and campuses. Identify the at-risk student early, diagnose, and treat—rather than criminalize or avoid medicalizing eccentricity for reasons more philosophical than practical. A student walking on campus at night with a bullhorn yelling, "It's all a scam; Words mean nothing," is not eccentric; he—in this case Jared Loughner at Pima College—was grossly psychotic and responding to his inner world of hallucinations and mushrooming delusions that would later explode in the Tucson Safeway Plaza Massacre, and, without his apprehension, another planned massacre elsewhere in Tucson.

It is not our intention to Monday-morning-quarterback cases like the NIU disaster in order to attribute fault, but, as with all "incidents" in medicine, physicians need to brainstorm in the sanctity of peer review that is immune to discovery for purposes of malpractice. Unfortunately this is unlikely to occur in our current health-care environment of defensive medicine that generates more and more of the "big cases" for personal injury (PI) attorneys. Somehow we need to be able to do this—in this case at NIU, a literal suicide autopsy—without the findings being discoverable. We should not depend on civil trials, like the recent ones against Virginia Tech and University of Colorado, to force testimony from all parties responsible for outcomes when cases sour in murder and mayhem on campus.

Cho killed 32 including himself at Virginia Tech and Holmes 12 in Aurora, Colorado. The president of Virginia Tech was compelled to testify; clinicians with knowledge of Cho were not, because the case was limited to security, rather than failures in psychiatric and clinical psychological evaluation followed by failed student counseling under involuntary commitment to Cook Counseling Center at Virginia Tech. Cho's case even remains under investigation to date—further hamstringing a suicidal autopsy—allegedly for reasons of the continued search for his hard drive and cell phone to shed light on motivation. Such a search will likely only support his postmortem diagnosis of schizophrenia; the intentional and illegal destruction of his commitment hearing records and theft of his clinical records from the university counseling center during the governor's investigation further impedes our understanding of how Cho got loose from Virginia Tech's Cook Counseling center under his court-approved involuntary commitment to that facility (Liebert and Birnes 2011).

With this caveat in mind, let us try the 20/20 hindsight to help prevent a few more such disasters as that caused by Steven Kazmierczak and Cho, because they are epidemic on our campuses—no longer the random and isolated disasters of the Texas Tower disaster in 1966; it is a different era than the 1960s. We can only identify some putative causes for the epidemic of suicidal mass murders, but campuses and military bases are ground zero for them. We need to examine where the alarms were sounding with Kazmierczak to inform public school boards, trustees of all schools, and educational administrators from elementary to graduate schools.

Steven Kazmierczak did not first emerge on the academic stage, both literally and figuratively, when he walked on stage at Cole Hall armed to the teeth that fateful Valentine's Day in 2008. His godfather knew of his bizarre relationship with his mother during elementary school. Steve sat with her, curtains closed during the day for darkness, watching horror movies. Was this her remedy for severe insomnia? Could he leave her to go to bed? Was she suffering from the same psychiatric disorder later diagnosed in her son? Was this not reportable child abuse?

Steve's academic performance was poor in grade school. His parents were called in because he was impulsive and did not check his work, causing him to make so many errors even teachers in a big Chicago public school noticed and brought attention to the problem. Even in my histories of thousands of psychiatric patients, parent-teacher conferences are not common in the childhood patients of even the sickest patients. His third-grade teacher, Ms. Mosher, was the first to pick up on what would later prove to be the diathesis of serious mental illness. This would have been the appropriate setting for the testing President Nixon considered to identify kids at risk for later trouble, Sheldon Glueck's, Unraveling Juvenile Delinquency via their Social Prediction Tables. This may have helped and been indicated in this case, because his childhood behavior was ominous, including cruelty to his dog, whom he swung by his rear legs, smashing the helpless and frail old pug against a shed's wall; firing pellets at passing vehicles, bursting in glee with the "ping" of metallic hits; and exploding canisters of inflammable Drano on a neighbor's porch. For a boy later to prove highly intelligent, his 58th percentile testing score on the Iowa Test was incongruent. Something was wrong with this young boy. Teachers picked up on it and should have ordered a Conners Test that questioned parents, teachers, and the primary care doctor about a child's behavior and ability to concentrate (Figure 8.1).

The police had questioned him about the bombing of his neighbor's house. Nothing was done, because he promised the police and his father to be good. He showed remorse and promised not to set off any more bombs. That was 1994. Perhaps he never used explosives again, but just 14 years later he would commit murder and mayhem in a college lecture hall with a cold, calculated

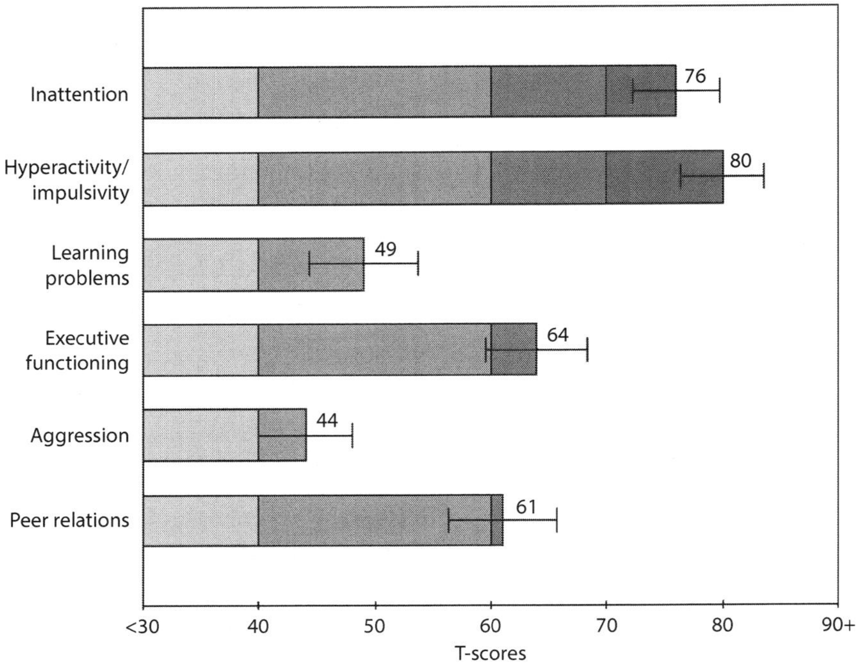


Figure 8.1 Computer-scored Conners Test. (From Conners 3rd edition. Copyright © 2008 Multi-Health Systems. Reproduced with permission from MHS.)

brutality nobody had ever seen before or could imagine. But, nobody knew that in elementary school he already was learning ballistics by firing the slowly propelled pellets well in front of speeding cars, thrilled by the hits from his nearby ambush. Had he not been spiraling into psychotic disease, he already demonstrated what he would later consider the best time of his life, basic military training and learning to shoot at people without emotion. He was arrested again, this time after a neighbor reported him for smoking dope in a car with a friend.

Steve told his girlfriend that he loved school but hated people. He withdrew socially, isolating himself by hiding out in the band room, where he learned to play the sax in order to spend time in this safe space away from other students who intimidated him. A peculiar gesture with his hand often drew abusive responses from peers calling him "a fag." He and another socially awkward boy enabled themselves protection from socializing in school by being called out for concerts. Were school administrators to monitor students in the most basic parameters of performance with modern computerized dashboards for simplest of class population management, the dials for Steve would have either been red hot in the red zones of "full for explosion" or near empty across the screen. They would point in elementary school to a boy destined to either fail or end up in jail. Glueck's probably would have picked up on this correctly. But, their testing would not be necessary as Steve's illness progressed in high school.

A serious failure occurred there when school counselors refused the request of Steven's parents to have him psychologically evaluated. Instead, they were treated as unworthy because of being simply working people who could not afford private help. On April 8, 1997, Elk Grove High School denied Steve's parents to have a case-study evaluation. Instead, in traditional obedience to state treasuries and routine violation of the law, the school acquiesced to quotas on testing at state expense for grossly impaired kids. Skimping on such mandated testing, they committed the critical error that later would blow up hours away in DeKalb by simply handing his parents a handbook on dealing with students with disabilities. That is like a primary care doctor in preventive health handing his patient's family, while the patient is bent over and clutching his chest in crushing chest pain, a brochure on healthy eating to reduce cholesterol.

It is just like the fatal error contributory to Keller's mass murders by serial arson; interpreting a valid and grossly abnormal Minnesota Multiphasic Personality Inventory (MMPI) in a recently addicted patient as needing only a list of foods to eat, as if nutritional counseling has anything to do with psychiatric decompensation.

For Steven, it would get worse in high school where school personnel could not avoid confronting Kazmierczak's descent into psychotic illness. He made four serious suicide attempts that were unequivocally intended to kill himself. These could not be brushed off as gestures to draw attention. High school personnel could not have missed his severe deterioration, because school jocks knew about it, called him "Suicide Steve" and "Crazy Mierzak" in the cafeteria and ripped his tray from under him, smashing it to the floor. Nothing was done for Steven. Nothing was done to the jocks either who severely bullied him in public. Things would get worse, until, at last, the school was off the hook.

Subsequently, Steven became a ward of the state, confined to a public residential psychiatric inpatient facility, and then a halfway house in a crime-ridden neighborhood likely to have complicated his fulminating suicidal depression with Posttraumatic Stress Disorder from gunfire on the street outside and terrorifying nights when he had to blockade his door from assailants looking for former residents without respect for who he was. He was now on the heaviest of antipsychotics and mood stabilizers, including the last resort—Clozaril for Schizoaffective Disorder, a gray zone of serious mental illness that blends the auditory hallucinations, paranoia and delusions of schizophrenia with extreme mood swings of manic depressive illness. Like many patients with this disorder, nonadherence to the medication is the rule rather than the exception; he stopped his medication. Recurrent and severe paranoia are also hallmarks of this disorder, as was likely the case in Wade Page who, like Steven, after discharge from the army following psychiatric hospitalization, committed suicidal mass murder in Milwaukee's Sikh Temple massacre.

Nobody knew about Steven's medication nonadherence with the powerful antipsychotic and mood stabilizer, Clozaril, because he was able to fake adherence with complaints of listed side effects. A sparse crew of low-paid case managers were conned, missing the expectable problem of medication nonadherence with this disorder. They could not stop his failures in social and vocational rehabilitation.

Steven bumped into another resident who hit him. Steven punched the resident in the face so hard he broke his own hand. His mother had already reported Steven as a missing person so that these should have at least qualified for his third reported offense on the police blotter during adolescence, the cutoff point where Wolfgang's research on 10,000 delinquents clearly showed it was time to thoroughly evaluate adolescents before they become that 1% of delinquents going on to commit nearly 100% of serious felonies. Steven Kazmierczak was just such a kid, but Wolfgang could never have imagined just how big a statistical slice of his documented "most serious felonies" this three-time juvenile offender would be good for in 2008!

There is no evidence Kazmierczak even received an MMPI that could have picked up his pathology and detected any efforts on his part to be deceptive—or an SCL-90 that would have graphically profiled what his mother called the police about—his depression. A valid MMPI would likely have shown the 4-6-9 profile of a dangerous man; 4 is for psychopathic deviance. Steven was cruel to animals, committed arson, and suffered bed wetting into adolescence. Whether the last was an adverse reaction to his medication is not known, but, were he to be examined for this triad, dangerousness could be expected in the future. Boys with all three have The Triad, predictive of a near 75% chance of future homicide. Scale 6 on the MMPI is for paranoia, which would more likely than not have been high, and 9 is for manic energy, which also would likely have been high, as his diagnosis was schizoaffective disorder, a progressive serious mental illness distinguished by severe mood swings with episodes of manic excitement and delusional thinking—particularly paranoid delusional thought disorder (Figures 8.2 and 8.3).

Steve was a ticking time bomb in grade school and had already exploded in high school. He already had three significant juvenile offenses, two of which were serious felonies, and four serious suicide attempts that were intended to kill. What more does it take for public authority, whether school, mental health professionals, or the police, to start looking—and looking deep. The Conners, SCL-90, and MMPI are easily administered and should be easily accessible to all school psychologists. He conned staff under state custody in residential care, but it is unlikely he would have been able to con even the average psychologist with these simply and inexpensively administered computer-scored tests.

It stirs one's imagination to wonder what has become of all of Steven Kazmierczak's gothic, socially awkward and asocial acquaintances and friends. We suspect some of the most bizarre and scary among them probably are proud grandparents by now or soccer moms. Some of them likely struggled in their lives. Some may not have survived. It is true, therefore, that weird kids do not very often need Hutschnecker's remedy for adolescent boot camps, but Steve did get a type of it in the form of the cheapest residential public program for the seriously mentally ill in the squalor of the Chicago ghetto where regular threats to his suburbia sense of security soon were wiped out.

He got sicker. Had the school found out early, as they were mandated and legally obligated to do, that Steve Kazmierczak was evolving into serious mental illness, he and his family could have been treated on an outpatient basis far more effectively and for less money than where he ultimately was—namely the lowest form of residential treatment guaranteed to make a sick kid even sicker. And,

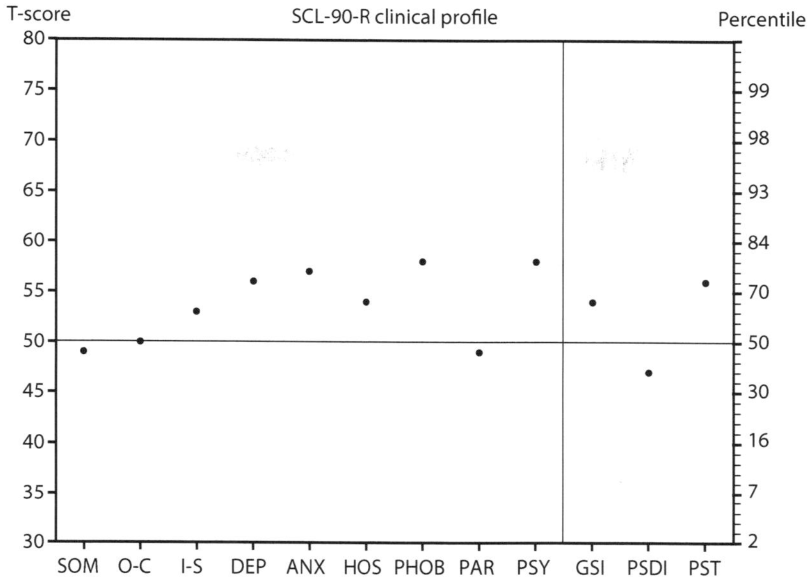


| | | | | | | | | | | | | |
|---|---|---|---|---|---|---|---|---|---|---|---|---|
| T-score: nonpatient | 49 | 50 | 53 | 56 | 57 | 54 | 58 | 49 | 58 | 54 | 47 | 56 |
| Raw score: | 0.25 | 0.30 | 0.33 | 0.54 | 0.50 | 0.33 | 0.29 | 0.17 | 0.20 | 0.36 | 1.14 | 28 |
| T-Score 2: outpatient | 41 | 35 | 38 | 36 | 38 | 42 | 47 | 39 | 39 | 35 | 29 | 38 |
| T-score 3: inpatient | 41 | 37 | 40 | 37 | 40 | 45 | 45 | 38 | 38 | 36 | 35 | 39 |

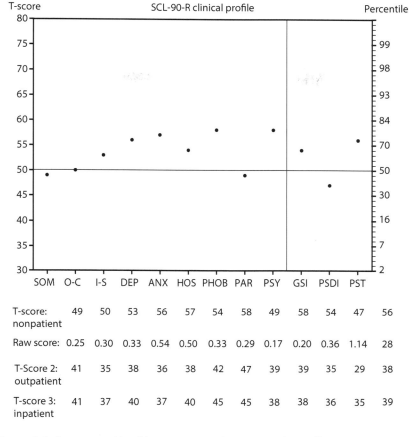

Figure 8.2 Symptom Checklist-90-Revised (SCL-90-R®) Profile Report. (Copyright © 1992 NCS Pearson, Inc. Reproduced with permission. All rights reserved. Portions adapted and reproduced with authorization from the SCL-90-R® test. Copyright © 1975 Leonard R. Derogatis, Ph.D. All rights reserved.)

sicker he got, and graduated into residential treatment as a ward of the state of Illinois. However, just like Cho, he was in no condition to be leaving home for anything. He was so sick that, at the end of his senior year, Steven's parents did not even include his baby picture and a congratulatory note from the family in his yearbook. They were demolished by his mental illness, already discovered but treated ineptly on a shoestring by the State of Illinois.

Steven's parents had even stopped filling in his "School Days" scrapbook years ago. They were afraid of their son. So should have been the State of Illinois, its schoolteachers, counselors and local police, because he would outdo Capone's Valentine's Day massacre to set the record for the biggest massacre in the history of Illinois. Could it have been prevented? Like Cho, he got away on his own, leaving Chicago, and, like Cho, at far-away Virginia Tech, nobody knew who he was outside of Chicago.

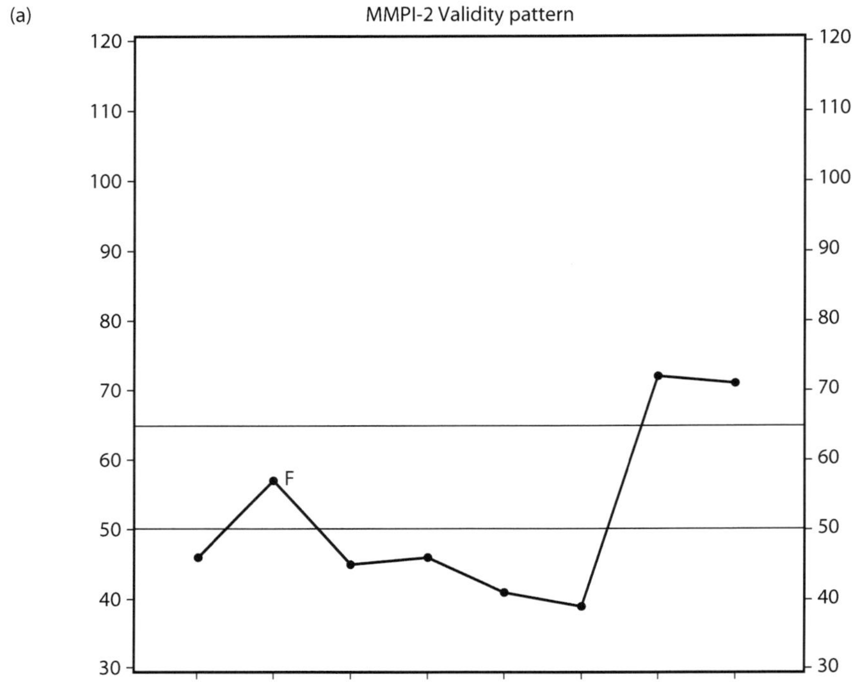


| | VRIN | TRIN | F | $F_B$ | $F_P$ | L | K | S |
|---|---|---|---|---|---|---|---|---|
| Raw score: | 4 | 8 | 3 | 1 | 0 | 1 | 26 | 43 |
| T Score: | 46 | 57F | 45 | 46 | 41 | 39 | 72 | 71 |
| Response %: | 100 | 100 | 100 | 100 | 100 | 100 | 100 | 100 |

| | |
|---|---|
| Cannot say (raw): | 0 |
| Percent true: | 26 |
| Percent false: | 74 |

| | Raw score | T score | Resp. % |
|---|---|---|---|
| $S_1$ - Beliefs in human goodness | 14 | 67 | 100 |
| $S_2$ - Serenity | 10 | 64 | 100 |
| $S_3$ - Contentment with life | 6 | 60 | 100 |
| $S_4$ - Patience/denial of Irritability | 8 | 68 | 100 |
| $S_5$ - Denial of moral flaws | 4 | 58 | 100 |

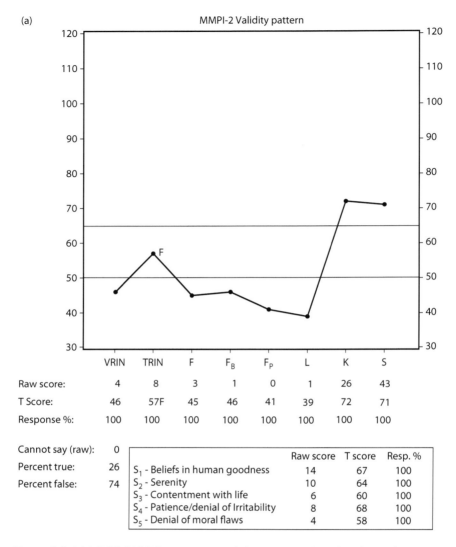

Figure 8.3 (a) MMPI-2 Validity pattern and (b) MMPI-2 Clinical and supplementary scales profile.

*(Continued)*

There was more to come. More bright red flags, more neglect of them, and more disregard for public health and safety in the pseudo righteousness of student and patient privacy. Steven succeeded in deceiving those who should have known better again at the residential treatment facility in Chicago, convincing them that they were not making progress together. The community facility, likely operating on a shoestring in the Chicago ghetto, agreed and cut him loose. There certainly was no shortage of sick souls to fill his space.

(b)

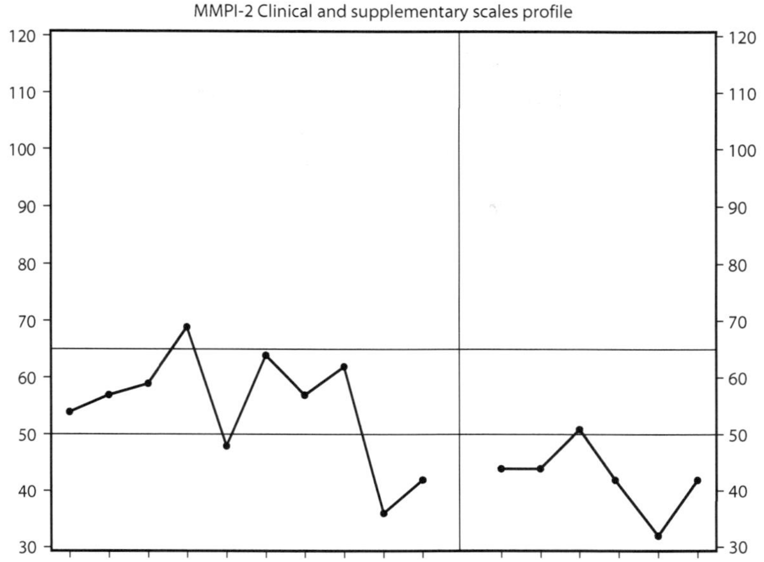


| | Hs | D | Hy | Pd | Mf | Pa | Pt | Sc | Ma | Si | MAC-R | APS | AAS | PK | Ho | MDS |
|---|---|---|---|---|---|---|---|---|---|---|---|---|---|---|---|---|
| Raw score: | 1 | 21 | 25 | 21 | 25 | 14 | 4 | 7 | 8 | 18 | 18 | 21 | 3 | 3 | 3 | 1 |
| K correction: | 13 | | | 10 | | | 26 | 26 | 5 | | | | | | | |
| T score: | 54 | 57 | 59 | 69 | 48 | 64 | 57 | 62 | 36 | 42 | 44 | 44 | 51 | 42 | 32 | 42 |
| Response %: | 100 | 100 | 100 | 100 | 100 | 100 | 100 | 100 | 100 | 100 | 100 | 100 | 100 | 100 | 100 | 100 |

Welsh code: 4+68-3271/50:9# K'+-/F:L#
Profile elevation: 57.3

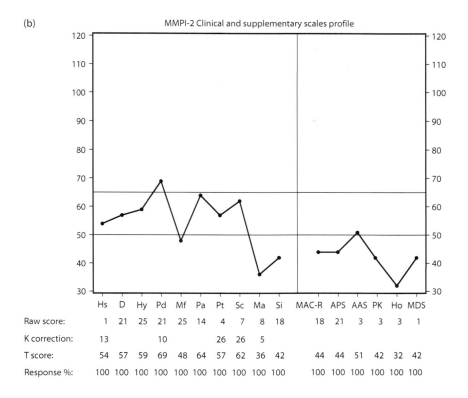

Figure 8.3 (Continued) (a) MMPI-2 Validity pattern and (b) MMPI-2 Clinical and supplementary scales profile.

Somewhat encouraged by his victory over case management and being able to get away without his medication, he hid out at home for awhile doing nothing. Then his fate seemed to have changed when he met his perfect match—the U.S. Army. He entered just pre-9/11 and loved basic infantry training, succeeding well into advanced infantry training in air defense at Fort Bliss—all told 5 months of active duty—far more than required to receive all veteran's benefits at time of discharge. Then for reasons known only to the Department of Defense to this day, he was commanded into the U.S. Army medical center's inpatient psychiatric unit and placed on suicide precautions. It was discovered that he had not been truthful about his history of serious mental illness and was discharged with a general discharge, under honorable circumstances, a common military manipulation that strips sick soldiers of both their benefits and follow-up case management—thus efficiently transferring costs of care back to the community. This is known in the health insurance industry as "cost shifting." It is known in medical practice as dumping, but in reality it is known as a shell game, and it works like this: Where is Steven? Medically discharged from the military? Separated without benefits or followup management by the military? Honorably discharged with full benefits? Early separation? Court martial? Bureaucratically speaking, this is just a game to hide the real reasons for a discharge so that the military is off the hook financially. It is a treacherous game the Defense Department administrators play extremely well, putting mentally disabled veterans into the community where they, their families, and in many cases, innocents like NIU students, faculty, and families become the ultimate victims of bureaucratic violations of the law.

Kazmierczak was well trained in weapons and killing now, but on February 13, 2002, he was taken home and once more dumped on his parents' doorsteps with neither explanation nor advice. This trauma was severe, because he felt successful in the army and was more comfortable than ever with its structure. He would comment that he was mixed with "maggots" in the army and they did not think. For that reason, he was not compelled to use his expressed "special powers" to read minds. "Maggots," he said, had none to read. There came a psychological blindness over him that seemed robotic. He was at ease killing without emotion. It was perfect, until something suddenly went haywire and he was hospitalized once again. Did he make a suicide attempt? Did the army start a security clearance investigation because of his advancing training in a now-post-9/11 military? This question will likely never be answered, but there were anecdotal reports of problems with bunk mates. Was it homosexual panic? By now, reportedly, Steven had already had homosexual relationships. Regardless, the military was over for now. It would come back, however, and once again with the false sense of security of stopping psychotropic medications when recruited for the navy. Ironically, his final and promising reach for a life as a sailor came just before he took his own war to Cole Hall, massacring people once calling him "Psycho" and "Strange Steve" for holing up in a dark room by himself, logging on to macabre music and suicidal mass murder games on the Internet. But nobody thought for a moment, unlike the cases of Cho and Loughner on other large state campuses, that Steven was a real soldier capable of such atrocities. A navy recruiter knew and encouraged him to enlist for the surge in Iraq but told him he had to get off his medications first. So, he did. And that would prove fatal.

There were no more known suicide attempts or cause for arrests at Northern Illinois University. In fact he graduated with the highest award in his class. Steven won the Deans' Award, the highest honor given to undergraduates. But then he was upended. He flunked classes in NIU grad school; significantly, these were easy undergraduate courses and not even graduate level. He failed his LSATs for law school. Was this not somewhat incongruent with his undergrad history of notable success? It certainly was. Once again school administration dashboard dials should have been spinning in the administrative offices of NIU, because something was going wrong. His mother had died from the long debilitation of Lou Gehrig disease. He was likely suicidally depressed, because his relationship with her was likely so ambivalently filled with hate and guilt. As in adolescence and in the public residential treatment of Chicago, a simple MMPI would likely, as in the Keller case, light up the scoreboard of a young man at high risk for suicide and violence, and, in fact a young man with a robust history of florid psychotic disease, schizoaffective disorder (the JAL Triage Algorithm and the case of Paul Keller [Liebert et al., 1994; Liebert and Birnes, 2011]) (Figure 16.5).

It was at that point that NIU should have contacted his father who likely would have informed them of his medical history. Then NIU should have demanded his past psychiatric records from all facilities in Chicago. There were several, all with robust histories and treatments with the highest potency of antipsychotics and mood stabilizers. They should have demanded the psychiatric records from the army, and, if necessary, acted as his advocate to change his discharge from general to medical. Each of the military services maintains a discharge review board with authority to change, correct, or modify discharges or dismissals that are not issued by a sentence of a general court-martial. That could have removed a lot of his stress from having been stripped of his GI schooling benefits so important to him and a major stressor in his academic career. It would have been obvious to any veteran's counselor on such a large university campus that Steven Kazmierczak should be going nowhere, other than to the local Veterans Affairs (VA) medical center, because he clearly was seriously mentally ill in the military for over 90 days and well past the date for early release without any VA benefits. Again, public authorities violated the law with Steven Kazmierczak to save money in the name of "cost shifting" to the community. But, how could social accounting ever assess the costs of these violations of the law in the case management—or lack thereof—for a developing psychotic suicidal mass murderer.

Kazmierczak literally flunked out of the graduate program, just like James Holmes did from University of Colorado. And just like James Holmes, Kazmierczak was simply let go as a star student in rapid descent into lethal psychosis without any debriefing whatsoever. He went from the graduate with the highest award to a flunk out in a matter of a few months. Should that have raised concerns with university administration that something was wrong with this student? It should have, just as it should have at University of Colorado with James Holmes. If the centers for highest standards of human conduct and intelligence cannot be relied upon to even notice a student psychologically collapsing in front of their eyes, they need to do more than beautify their campus with a sculpture to memorialize their negligence manifesting in the Cole Hall massacre. They discarded one of theirs, one who was certainly far above average, but like Holmes, had fallen fast and far off the cliff from its own graduate school in social sciences without anyone apparently taking notice. He flunked out of the very graduate program that prepared students to prevent just the very disaster that was more and more becoming the subtly iconic image of Steven Kazmierczak.

Steven applied for a gun permit and would start accumulating weapons. What was he planning? Would a simple interview by the school psychologist or his Internet history on campus have given any clues? Should such investigations be condition for matriculation under special circumstances when administration can show valid concern for a student and its own student body's safety and welfare? Corporations monitor their employees' Internet usage. Clinics monitor their own doctors' Internet usage. Universities should have the same right when having a valid concern about a student, and there was plenty to be concerned about with Steven Kazmierczak during his drastic fall from best to worst student on campus in such a short period of time. What would they have found? Very likely, a very different Steven would be found than the young man who tutored statistics students and graduates with highest of honors in his class. He wanted nobody to find what he surfed for on the Internet or stored on his hard drive. Would it have proven a lifesaver for him and the student body to discover his secrets? More likely than not it would have been revealing to find out what he did in his isolation in that darkened dorm room, far from any outer milieu ultimately reflecting off him as the best and brightest in his graduating class.

Were the Ebola virus infecting students on campus, would administration be prevented from infringing on student rights to require regular testing and hygienic standards of behavior? What is the difference? Schizoaffective disorder is not really a disease? That is not true, although some, even in academia, still believe in the myth of mental illness. And, even so, it is not contagious. But, suicide is, particularly since Columbine and the events of 9/11, and the university should have known how suicidal this student was, as an undergraduate, a grad student, and ultimately a flunk-out. Was he so pathogenic within the NIU community, or in fact, even Elkhorn K1-12, that NIU, advertising its counseling and health services, could be held liable for doing nothing to prevent this seriously mentally ill patient from committing suicidal mass murder?

> The Northern Illinois University Counseling & Student Development Center
>
> ***Our mission***
>
> The mission of the Counseling & Student Development Center is to support the academic, emotional, social and cultural development of students. Our student-centered programs include counseling, assessment, psychiatric treatment, crisis response, outreach, consultation, training and educational services. We help students address personal challenges and develop the skills, abilities and knowledge to empower them to take full advantage of their college experience. (NIU Handbook for students and parents)

The Supreme Court of California would have ruled that Steven was indeed a danger to himself and to others and could have been identified, diagnosed, and aggressively treated, according to the promotional blurb on the NIU Counseling Center. Back in 1966, the Texas Tower massacre was an isolated disaster. Today, suicidal mass murders by college students no longer are. They are epidemic, and often infect the brightest of the bright on campus. Our own academic institutions must take the lead in curbing this epidemic. Instead, Steven Kazmierczak knew more about the Virginia Tech massacre than any professor, administrator, counselor, and clinician on campus. It would get worse as he migrated south to the University of Illinois, and he continued to deteriorate, accumulate weapons, and get his next psychiatric evaluation, that is the next one that is known following the debacle at Beaumont Army Medical Center, February 2002.

The case of Steven Kazmierczak, although extreme, is a marquee case, covering the landscape of student problems that fit the public health construct for prevention, which follows:

*Primary prevention:* Identification of causation—or etiology—and eliminating it—that is for example, the Ebola virus. Steven Kazmierczak more likely than not carried the most valid diagnosis from his adolescence into his foreshortened adulthood. This was schizoaffective disorder, with severe mood swings and episodes of psychosis presenting as paranoia, likely delusions, and reportedly hallucinations with evidence of a genetic transmission by family history. There is no way currently known to eliminate the cause, because, although strongly genetic in nature, it is not strong enough for genetic counseling or elimination of the genetically determined breakdown. It is known that schizoaffective disorder breeds schizophrenia, strongly evidencing the close connectedness between these two somewhat different disease entities. But, we do not know the converse; does schizophrenia breed schizoaffective disorder? For this patient, therefore, primary prevention is currently an unknown, but his mother's reportedly strange behavior should have been informative to those evaluating him due to its powerful hereditary transmission.

*Secondary prevention:* Early case identification. Here there was a major failure within the school health and community health systems from elementary school through graduate school in the state of Illinois. Kazmierczak stood out in a large public school for his academic failure. He qualified for special evaluation from third grade until graduation school and received none. Juvenile Court should have the intelligence of Wolfgang's famous research, if, in fact, they are in the business of doing anything more than judging severity of punishment to meet the severity of crime—or sparing the rod or not. Certainly, suburban Chicago juvenile court could have done something instead of nothing to prevent the common—a first psychotic break, which is routine psychiatry—from converting to disaster medicine. The state of Illinois school system, as is too often the case with school systems, gambled on fortune by kicking the can down the road.

Sure, Kazmierczak could have simply been one more felon or psychotic in the Cook County Jail and then Joliet Prison, or he might have slipped by with disruptions in life that did not require massive state investments. As it turned out, the decision was made, as part of de facto state policy, not to evaluate Kazmierczak in elementary school, thus backloading a critical psychological evaluation after the fact—a military-style atrocity that killed many and ruined lives—to this unofficial suicidal autopsy.

There was no significant investigation of what went wrong and what might have been done to prevent this disaster in DeKalb. Perhaps it is the myth of mental illness—or, namely that Kazmierczak really was not sick in the first place, but just a dangerous psychopath who flew under the radar screen waiting for his opportunity to kill as many people as possible before the cowardly act of suicide. Certainly, despite appearances to the contrary, wherein the Cook County Jail is now the largest inpatient psychiatric unit in the country, something could have been done at many points along the trajectory of this very sick young man's life.

Here is a brief menu of options along the trajectory. These are practical evaluations that do not require resources that simply are not available. For example, it would be great if every child flagged as Kazmierczak was in elementary school could be evaluated by a child psychiatrist and child psychologist with a social services assessment of his home environment. That is impossible in all but the rare case, such as Adam Lanza, where it could have been done but was not. Instead, Adam Lanza was allowed by the elementary school to behave in a grossly psychotic manner, moving down the hall with his back to the lockers clutching his computer. This strange behavior was known by the school but merely dealt with by close monitoring to prevent bullying. That is amateur psychology and health care. As his father has stated, his son was far, far sicker than simply Asperger disorder. Lanza was grossly psychotic and should have been on antipsychotic medications and under case management to assure adherence to medication; reportedly he was prescribed medications but did not take them. He presented a threat to himself and to others, as clearly was demonstrated in his massacre of Sandy Hook Elementary School children and staff.

The arguments over medical diagnostics informing of need for complex psychopharmacology belong in philosophy courses and not in the real world of schools where lives are in danger. As cited in the time line of Kazmierczak's evolving clinical state of unremitting human destructiveness, there are simply administered, computer-scored tests that can reduce the risk of missing psychopathology such as that in the cases of Adam Lanza and Steven Kazmierczak, manifesting so robustly in elementary school. They are as follows:

The Conners Comprehensive Executive Function Inventory is easily administered to children, along with parents, teachers, and the child's primary care provider. The family, teachers, and family doctor or pediatrician answer simple questions about the child, and the answers are collated and scored by a validated algorithm that prints out a clear and concise graph highlighting problems—such as distractibility, emotional control, behavioral problems, etc. Kazmierczak's parents were denied this simple testing in third grade and high school. That could have led to early intervention to spare his life and many others.

Later on, another computer-scored test could have identified major problem areas, such as aberrant thought processes and depression. This is the SCL-90 which is a symptom checklist that again is collated by algorithm, scored, and presented in graphic form to highlight special problem areas. He would have likely shown spikes in depression, aberrant thinking, obsessive-compulsive trends, and severe anxiety.

It is possible that an MMPI was performed when he was hospitalized multiple times, but there were many legal opportunities for institutions to administer this test for Kazmierczak. The benefit of the MMPI is that it is sensitive to deception with a K scale that identifies the subject's attempt to falsify results or exaggerate them for some reason. At the University of Illinois Counseling Center, such deception was likely to have been detected, because the patient did not want antipsychotic medication. He controlled his evaluation and diagnostics, minimizing the severity of his psychopathology, thus getting what he wanted—nearly minimal psychopharmacotherapy that might relieve his medically naïve friend who had to live with his depression, anxiety, compulsive counting, checking, and hand washing.

Finally, there is the Computer-Assisted Diagnostic Interview by Paul Miller that has been heavily researched at UCLA to zero in on parameters of serious mental illness in a disciplined way so as not to fly by the seat of the pants. Careful interviewing to rule in or rule out specific symptoms and signs that are specific criteria of psychiatric diagnosis insures a higher degree of reliable results. This interview can be performed by a trained layperson and is proven to reduce diagnostic errors that cause different diagnoses of the same problems in the same patient over time. With Kazmierczak we have at least two psychiatrists coming to two widely disparate conclusions—one, serious mental illness of schizoaffective disorder, and the other, a walking wounded man with OCD. That would be like diagnosing a lump in the breast as a malignancy at one center and later diagnosing it as a nonmalignant cyst. Such diagnostic reliability errors are fatal for women with cancer. The diagnostic errors for Kazmierczak's strange behavior and mood symptoms were lethal for both him and an entire community.

There are many other screening tests available, most of which are designed for certain behavioral complexes, but, in most cases, such as that of Lanza and Kazmierczak, just these simply administered, computerized scored tests would likely have made bright red the subtle and not-so-subtle behavioral aberrations of Steven Kazmierczak before the maximum feasible misunderstanding occurred that converted routine outpatient psychiatry in Urbana, southern Illinois, to disaster medicine in northern Illinois on Valentine's Day 2008.

When studying the cases of mass killers with a college history, the exit gate is far more productive than the entry gate for picking up seriously destructive behaviors. The balance must be carefully weighed, but students, parents, and faculty all deserve the safest environment possibly created for them. This does not require a police state that squelches the free spirit and periodic eccentric nonconformity of young people maturing on campus, both emotionally and intellectually. Nor do the authors recommend criminal background checks for all admissions. They would have shown nothing with Kazmierczak at NIU, Lanza at University of Connecticut, Cho at Virginia Tech, and Holmes at University of Colorado. They were not criminals but very sick individuals. But, when a student simply leaves, whether on the administrative dashboard or actually in person, it is time for alarm. For example, nobody to this day can account for the time between Cho's discharge on involuntary commitment to Cook Counseling Center and his return to campus. Had he not returned, would administration or the Cook Center even have known? It is doubtful, until a serious incident, like suicide, would trace his steps from hospital ward back to dorm room! He simply was not tracked, because, other than the hearing officer and crisis counselor committing him, Cho was never really taken seriously as a threat on the campus of Virginia Tech University. Certainly, only a small percentage of students who leave higher education end up killing themselves or others, but let's take a look at those who did:

Sandy Hook's Adam Lanza quit Western Connecticut State University where he should have been known as the highest-risk, precocious student.

Jared Loughner was suspended from Pima College before the Tucson Safeway Plaza massacre.

John Schick was expelled from Duquesne University before his massacre at University of Pittsburgh Medical Center.

James Holmes was flunked out of University of Colorado Neuroscience program before the Aurora Theater massacre.

The older Tsarnaev brother dropped out of Bunker Hill College three times before the Boston Marathon bombings. The younger Tsarnaev brother never paid anything while attending the University of Massachusetts/Dartmouth.

Seung-Hui Cho disappeared following discharge from involuntary commitment at St. Albans Hospital. Nobody to this day knows where he went or how he eventually returned to campus while under involuntary commitment.

Steven Kazmierczak flunked out of NIU's graduate program soon after being awarded honors as its top undergraduate of the year.

Satto Tonegawa, gifted student and son of a Nobel Prize-winning physicist was discovered—by odor—dead in his dorm room at MIT from suicide. He had not been seen on campus for a week.

James Oliver Seevakumaran was found dead in his dorm room at University of Central Florida when campus security entered his room because of failure to pay his room and board. He was found alongside weapons and a backpack of bombs, evidencing a far deadlier suicidal mass murder.

One L. Goh, who was expelled from Oikos University Nursing School and returned to execute seven and seriously wound three, is incompetent to stand trial based on the diagnosis of paranoid schizophrenia.

Terry Sedlacek dropped out of Southwest Illinois College with a severe case of Lyme disease that likely impaired his brain function. He remains incompetent to stand trial for murder of a Marysville, Illinois, pastor in the course of a suicidal mass murder rampage following dropping out of school.

Elliot Rodger dropped out of Santa Barbara City College in 2012. He then killed six and wounded seven in a rampage suicidal murder avenging delusionally perceived rejection by sorority girls at the University of California, Santa Barbara.

Robert Hawkins killed eight and wounded four before killing himself at Von Maur Department Store in Westroads Mall, Omaha, Nebraska, December 5, 2007. A ward of the state with an extensive psychiatric history, he had dropped out of high school without any follow-up from school officials.

Robert Flores, a Gulf War veteran and nursing student, executed three of his professors before killing himself during classes at University of Arizona in October 2002. He was flunking out of college while working as a licensed practical nurse at the Tucson VA Medical Center.

Radcliffe Haughton, a Marine veteran, killed three, wounded four, and killed himself in Azana Spa suicidal mass murder in Brookfield, Wisconsin, October 21, 2012. He had recently dropped out of Milwaukee School of Engineering where he was attempting to complete his prenursing college education.

Suicidal mass murderer Aaron Ybarra attended but did not complete a home-schooling program through Edmonds School District, although enrolled at Edmonds Community College. He had extensive and well-documented history of violence and serious mental illness escalating to suicidal rampage murder at Seattle Pacific University in June 2014.

It may require an investment of money and personnel to debrief such obvious failures on campus before simply cutting them loose in unremitting clinical states of human destructiveness. These may be spun as "random" for a cohort of 20 million students residing on our campuses today, but what has been the cost in human lives, suffering, and post-traumatic syndromes suffered to this day by survivors and loved ones of the dead and maimed? There is no dollar value to be placed on it; according to the *Boston Globe*, "MIT has suffered a spate of suicides over the past two decades, and the parents of one student, Elizabeth Shin, brought a $27 million lawsuit against the school, which was settled in 2006 for an undisclosed sum" (Abel 2011).

We do not need personal injury attorneys to radically alter student health and counseling services from K–12 through high school, college, and grad school. MIT responded to the lawsuit by expanding walk-in mental health services. That sounds good on paper, but where do these services come from? There simply are not enough experienced clinical psychologists and psychiatrists to staff our public school and college campus health and counseling centers, even though college brochures continue to advertise what deceptively appears to be full-service mental health centers on campuses across the country. We know that those counseling centers were totally incapable of addressing and treating the psychotic disorders presented them in the cases of Seung-Hui Cho at Virginia Tech, Jared Loughner at Pima College, and James Holmes at University of Colorado.

It is also not just those missing on paper or person; there are the grossly psychotic students parading the campus who are threatening to students. Both Cho and Loughner were openly perceived as threatening to students. They made their fears known to administration that did nothing to make certain suspect students were discretely surveilled, diagnosed, and treated for obvious serious mental illness. Dylan Quick stabbed 14 students and was known to be grossly psychotic on campus in Houston, Texas, carrying dolls around with him to class; nothing was done until he went berserk. Nobody on campus could have considered Quick's behavior as anything but strange.

Collateral to secondary prevention on campus, we take the same examining lens to the police, who for most part are the only ones seriously preparing to intervene in the epidemic of campus violence incidents. As it applies to police, secondary prevention involves the identification of problem officers, those too quick on the trigger or those who show contempt for members of the public they deal with. Nowhere is this more obvious than in the Department of Justice report on the failures of the police and justice administration in Ferguson, Missouri. Here, the report identified officers and situations where African American citizens were the objects of discriminatory practices when it came to ticketing and minor offenses. The court system routinely extorted money from defendants who were barely able to pay their fines. By identifying the problems and highlighting them in the report, the Department of Justice evaluators sought to prevent more problems before they continued to fester.

This explains part of the psychology of the Wilson/Brown confrontation as not an isolated incident but a result on the ongoing contemptuous treatment by the police and justice administration toward the African American population. It had simply reached the boiling point, and whether Michael Brown was high or not, whether he had committed a strong-armed robbery, he snapped, and the result brought the entire problem to light.

Tertiary prevention is the treatment of those finally identified as being seriously ill. All of these suicidal killings on campus could have been identified early to prevent extended duration of untreated psychosis (DUP) that worsens the prognosis and course of the disease. But, there were points at which treatment could have been provided. In fact, Cho was in treatment, but nobody at the student counseling center had the training, experience and credentials to treat serious mental illness, even though he did present to them for treatment on more than the allegedly single time. James Holmes saw a psychiatrist once at least. We do not know if he really was in psychiatric treatment at University of Colorado. We do know that Steven Kazmierczak was in psychiatric treatment at University of Illinois Counseling Center, but he was only treated for OCD and anxiety. His attending psychiatrist had no knowledge of his serious mental illness and multiple suicide attempts documented in the medical records of the army and multiple inpatient psychiatric facilities in Chicago.

If there is a reason for this psychiatrist—or, as alleged, those evaluating Cho in Virginia—not to have legal access to a student's past medical history, such obstructions should be removed. In the case of Cho, there was no such obstruction due to the basic fact of his emergency detention. At the University of Illinois, there was no known emergency at the time of his visit to the counseling center. The case has clearly been made that clinicians with first encounters with disturbed students must have access to the student's past medical records. Public health and campus safety demand this, and entering students, now in the era of the Affordable Care Act under which medical records are private—but electronic, should prevent the inter-institutional blindness resulting in the NIU massacre. It is a new era, and the rights of students to deny access to their past medical records, if in fact any of them actually did, needs to be abolished at the time of acceptance to the school in the form of a waiver in the event of conditions considered to be serious and complex enough to require clinicians to have access to past medical history. The University of Illinois psychiatrist treated Kazmierczak with a combination of meds only safe and effective for mild anxiety and OCD. Steven Kazmierczak was far sicker, and, in fact, could have become worse on these drugs because of their propensity to light up mania in the case of Prozac and disinhibit impulse in the case of Xanax. The psychiatrist may well be mortified in knowing now what he was confronting in grad student Steven Kazmierczak, but he has to be breathing a sigh of relief—only a trace of Xanax was found at autopsy. Kazmierczak had discontinued Prozac on the advice of his navy recruiter.

These high-profile cases of death and destruction in failing students are only used to highlight the urgency for school boards and trustees of institutions of higher learning to radically shift the paradigm for campus safety and health and welfare of students. It is not feasible to provide the professional resources on campuses to take care of the needs of psychiatric disorders of the millions matriculating today, already prescribed psychotropic medication—upward of 30% of the millions matriculating every year—is the estimate. Furthermore, school boards and trustees need to confront the reality of serious mental illness. There are 300,000 first psychotic episodes of schizophrenia annually in this nation, a disproportionate number of them occurring on high school and college campus simply due to the epidemiology of age for onset—18 through 26 are the peak years for onset of first psychotic break, following which is the most lethal period for suicide. Perhaps the young psychotic student has the insight following the first episode to know that his life is somewhat doomed—thus peak suicidality following first psychotic episode.

Psychiatry cannot give a lot of hope to patients with schizophrenia. Patients can do better these days, but they will not get well, despite the most modern of antipsychotics. Manic depressives can do well, if they take their medication, but, as we see in too many cases, Kazmierczak is an example of a cyclical mood disorder, although of the worst kind known as schizoaffective disorder. These patients oftentimes can do well, if they stay on their medications, but too often, as in his case, they do not and do not want to be on them. Such patients, like Kazmierczak, need assisted treatment that monitors their adherence to taking medications. Then they can do relatively well in life. Kazmierczak considered himself victorious over psychotropics, but to what end? His nonadherence was enabled by too many in positions to know and do more to prevent the catastrophic outcomes that spelled lasting doom on a campus with too many innocent lives taken or ruined. Memorials are only posthumous honor; the list goes on from Newtown, Connecticut, to Santa Barbara, California.

Even Kazmierczak realized that police response to campus and school shootings had improved; so, he was prepared to kill himself early in his rampage murder. What has not improved are school health and counseling services, nor can they be. There simply are not enough trained, experienced, and credentialed clinicians out there to accomplish the mission. But, there is a solution, and that is the newly developed technology of Telehealth whose cost has plummeted with paradoxically equal improvement in quality of both image and real-time voice interaction through video conferencing. There are some campuses so integrated with their colleges of medicine that they can perhaps continue on doing what has always been done—that is, Hall Health Center and University of Washington School of Medicine. But, for most schools, whether Sandy Hook Elementary, Columbine High School, or Northern Illinois University, what is urgently needed is 24/7 on-site nursing services where the at-risk or students in crisis can be brought in or freely enter for evaluation. Instead of a referral off campus for evaluation, a virtual clinic available 24/7 can immediately bring the nurse on duty in contact with live specialists—whichever specialty is needed in real time. There will be a psychiatrist to evaluate the patient real time as the nurse presents his problems for being there. There will be a clinical psychologist who can perform some necessary tests, such as the MMPI or many others deemed necessary. There will be an experienced psychiatric social worker who can assess the situation and immediately explore the family situation and student's history.

In the case of suspected neurological disease, as in the case of Terry Sedlacek with Lyme disease, there can be neurologist who can both test on his own or direct the nurse to test. This is the virtual clinic. It is here now, and the technology is available for every institution from the county community college to Princeton University. It is essential for every school nursing station in this country. It can be done, but decision-making heads must get over denial, philosophical debate on campus over disease model versus existential realities of psychosis and suicide, and radically change a paradigm created for a different era—the 1950s, when kids like the list above, simply did not matriculate.

Additionally, threat assessment teams must have access to students' online surfing and postings for evidence of clinical states of unremitting human destructiveness. It can be done without turning schools into the rigid performers in Pyongyang classrooms under the watchful eyes of the "Great Leader." It can be done when problems present, rather than, as Nixon was considering, to diagnose quiescent problems in children likely to emerge as delinquency in adolescence—then ordering a form of preventive detention for corrections of, for the most part, unidentified problems. Here is how one such system, Awareity, does it in schools.

> Once at-risk students or individuals are identified, the TIPS prevention platform helps college and university threat assessment and behavioral intervention teams monitor these individuals ongoing and ensure appropriate follow-up and intervention, so no individuals slip through the cracks. Taking a step back, the first step in the TIPS process is creating a community approach to safety and prevention—allowing anyone in the campus community (students, parents, faculty, staff, community members, and other stake holders) to report concerning behaviors. Then, as reports come in from different sources, they are all immediately collected and connected so the appropriate personnel on campus are notified and are aware of all reports involving that individual. Once these behaviors and individuals are identified, the threat assessment and intervention process begins. Team members can conduct their investigation, document all steps they have taken, record interview notes, upload information located on social media, coordinate efforts across multi-disciplinary teams, escalate incidents to secondary team members (including legal, campus police, and counselors) if needed, and set reminders and tasks for follow-up.
>
> It appears that in most of the school shooting cases listed above, these individuals were identified as at-risk students, but then were either asked to leave their institution or dropped out, and at that point, the school/college basically stopped all investigation and monitoring efforts. Our clients using the TIPS system

are encouraged to ensure they continue to monitor behaviors and utilize the system to set reminders to check in with that individual, follow-up with new institution or other involved third-parties such as mental health counselors, social workers, and attorneys, schedule calls with parents to ensure the situation is not escalating and behaviors have not become more aggressive.

The TIPS system does allow schools to communicate and work with those outside mental health professionals. Schools who do not have the internal resources can have secondary team members within the system (third-party mental health services) that can be added into specific cases or reports and then the two parties can work together ongoing to monitor individuals. (K. Johnson, Awareity, personal communication)

The implementation of the Awareity TIPS system is best understood in the case of Eastern Kentucky University, where perceived threatening behaviors of students are investigated immediately without barriers to communications. The university understands the disastrous failures of the actions—or inactions—in the cases cited above. Emergencies allow school administration to contact parents, previous institutions attended, and local community agencies, including law enforcement. In all the cases above, such communications could have prevented disasters from occuring, whether on campus or off, but concerns of privacy, or simply ineffectiveness at the administrative level, resulted in little or nothing being done.

For example, Cho's parents said they would have picked their son up, taken him home, and obtained help for him, had they known he had been hospitalized and committed; tragically, they found out about their son's suicidal mass murder the same way the rest of us did—the horrific image of their son attired as some space warrior on NBC News. Similarly, University of Illinois could have found out about Kazmierczak's strange behavior on the NIU campus and his plunging academic failure as a grad student there. Pima College could have worked with University Physicians Healthcare Hospital at Kino Campus, Tucson, Arizona in Tucson and Loughner's parents, instead of simply physically dumping him on his parents' doorstep with no assistance whatsoever; this final action was particularly egregious, because Pima College specifically advertised its excellent liaisons with community agencies when students needed help. Kino/UAZ hospital is among the most accessible psychiatric inpatient facilities in this country. This is similar to the case of Rodger in Santa Barbara where he could have been admitted, evaluated, and treated with good ease of access to Ventura/UCLA Medical Center.

As Katie Johnson states, there was no justification in either of these cases for doing nothing and simply dumping two dangerous psychotic young men back into their parents' laps and hoping the situation would go away. These situations do not go away, but if they do, students can return to campus if presenting followup care information that aligns with tracking information from Awareity tools. All institutions have modern dashboards to track the day-to-day flow of people and processes relevant to mission. What could be more important than simply tracking all students with a modern dashboard to see when they run out of gas, like Holmes at University of Colorado or Kazmierczak at NIU—and even the Boston Bomber brothers.

"Perhaps the best way to explain this is to share this recent article we put together with the assistance of Eastern Kentucky University" (Katie Johnson, client support, Awareity, www.campussafetymagazine.com/article/youve_suspended_a_potential_aggressor_now_what/P3.)

As Johnson states, communication with outside sources, including law enforcement and mental health services, is both necessary and absolutely legal in emergencies involving students. These third parties should, for many schools, include strong 24/7 nursing services with immediate access to a virtual clinic via Telehealth. McGill University Faculty of Nursing has developed just such a virtual clinic for remote worksites that is easily converted for school nursing services by translational research (www.johnliebert.com/johnliebert/pdfs/talisman_arnaert_11%2012%202012_final%20final2.pdf).

This McGill University Telenursing platform for remote worksites should not be restricted to colleges. Violence in schools is impacting lower and lower grade levels. For example, a tip from another student recently prevented a disaster at a grade school in Traverse City, Michigan. The fifth grader not only brought a loaded weapon to class, but he had a hit list of students to kill.

> The START program in Los Angeles similarly monitors student threats. START recently signed a memorandum of understanding with the Los Angeles Unified School District and Los Angeles Police Department to collaborate on students of concern. This partnership allows for a coordinated effort to assist school threat-management teams and enhance intervention strategies. This partnership is the first of its kind in the country, according to L.A. County officials. The program's timely intervention has prevented school tragedies in numerous incidents, the officials said. These incidents vary from a student's verbal threats of violence to bringing a weapon to school.
>
> "One student at one of our middle schools decided to saw off a shotgun at home so he could fit it in his book bag," Beliz added. "Another student saw the weapon and reported it to the teacher. The student is now getting the treatment he needs and we hope to find out why it was done in the first place."
>
> Since the program's inception, teams all over the county have responded to approximately 250 incidents at elementary, middle, high schools and colleges.
>
> "We'll go to a school, evaluate the individual there, then what we'll also do is go to the kid's home and we'll ask to see the bedroom and we'll do a very data-driven assessment," Dr. Beliz said. "We're trying to figure out, what are the triggers here? What are the risk factors? What's really going on and how can we intervene?"
>
> And, to the point of the failing student either dropping out or dropped out, Dr. Beliz asserted the most important reminder to

> break down the silo mentality of school administrations. "We'll stay with these people as long as we can, and it makes a difference, because we're knocking on their door or their therapist's door," he said. "That's the missing piece in some of these school shootings. They were engaged in some sort of way, but dropped out and no one really thought to follow them." (Almeida 2013)

Clearly, if the LAPD can convert threat into successful therapy for a child and parents, then every school in this country can team up with law enforcement and do the same. We cannot depend on luck anymore. It is unconscionable for this nation to do nothing while we have to watch our kids paraded out of school like prisoners, hands up, surrounded by SWAT teams and armored vehicles every week on TV. What kind of learning environment is that? What can such an environment possibly do to enhance emotional development? Let the NRA and gun dealers yell and scream their way to the bank and buy off congressmen. They should not, however, immobilize schools and institutions of higher learning from making their campuses safe. If the University of Eastern Kentucky can do it, then MIT certainly can figure out a way, too. NIU and Virginia Tech have amassed highly lucrative and winning football programs with considerable investment of administrative resources and financial investment. They go to bowl games every year. Thus, they certainly can develop a TIPS system like Awareity and spare this nation from more massacres on our college campuses.

Memorials are posthumous honor. Proactive preventive action is the best memorial, although not, perhaps, as attractive on national TV as having the president of the United States speak on campus, as he did in the wake of the Tucson Safeway Plaza Massacre by Jared Loughner. The nation does not need Air Force One landing anymore for memorial services. TIPS programs like Awareity and START work, whether for the psychotic rampage student behaving strangely on campus, the local drug dealer getting students high, the drunken males—and oftentimes their drunken female companions—destined for sexual assault, the externally unnoticed Kazmierczak who drops off the radar screen to return with a bloody vengeance, or the increasingly high risk of failing students, like the Tsarnaev brothers, preparing for jihad.

Another difficulty has been convincing school administrators whose first impulse is often to expel students who have made threats, even empty ones, that doing so only pushes the problem onto another school or leaves a child at home with free time to surf the Internet and nurse a grudge against the school.

"What we do is, we work with the school to think that through," Beliz said, adding that one of their goals "is to keep the kid in school, because that is their holding environment" (LA Times, March 14, 2013).

Yet the concern for community safety can bump against individual rights, especially when no crime has been committed. At a recent case meeting, Beliz and his team discussed a worrisome high school senior who had made serious threats in school and was now applying to colleges. Could they notify the university where the student eventually enrolled about his behavior? It was, they agreed, murky legal territory, but so are most cases of Homeland Security designed to prevent another 9/11. Institutions, such as schools, cannot simply stand down while students and faculty alike arm themselves for what increasingly appears to be the next disaster, whether Sandy Hook Elementary School in upper class metropolitan New York City or Umpqua College in rural Oregon.

## REFERENCES

Abel, D. 2011. *Boston Globe*, October 27. www.bostonglobe.com/todayspaper/2015/10/27

Almeida, M. 2013. *The New York Times*, www.nytimes.com/2013/03/15/us/in-los-angeles-focusing-on-violence-before-it-occurs.html?pagewanted=all

Liebert, J. A. and Birnes, W. J. 2011. *Suicidal Mass Murderers: A Criminological Study of Why They Kill.* Taylor and Francis, Boca Raton, Florida.

Liebert, J. A., Unis, A., and Wright, C. 1994. The Keller case: Psychopathy or psychobiological diathesis? Presented at International Scientific Conference of The International Association of Psychoneuroendocrinolgy, University of Washington Medical Center, Seatte, Washington.

Vann, D. 2009. Portrait of the school shooter as a young man, *Esquire*, February 12. www.esquire.com/features/steven-kazmierczak-0808-2

# 9

# Special problems of our veterans

*The Nation that forgets its defenders will itself be forgotten.*

**President Calvin Coolidge**

U.S. Presidents, as commanders-in-chief, pay a lot of lip service to our veterans—especially photo ops with heroes from battle. But, as the facts bear out, the federal government does precious little to resolve the problems in the Department of Veterans Affairs despite the pontificating from politicians and the many promises from administrators. In fact, despite the billions of new dollars thrown at the problem and replacement of management held responsible for corrupt practices that covered up dangerously long—even fatal—wait lists system wide, recent audits show that wait lists for appointments remain little changed from the original discovery of the scandal at Phoenix VAMC (www.militarytimes.com/story/military/benefits/veterans/2015/04/09/va-wait-times-continue/25422103/).

Worse, as we have seen, veterans whose neuropsychiatric disabilities, known as the "invisible wounds of war," are left untreated, are winding up on the streets, in jails, or in shoot-outs with police as they attempt to take their own lives, too often risking the lives of others.

With recent scandals illuminating systemic corruption in the Department of Veterans Affairs (DVA) under fraudulent bookkeeping of VHA National Systems Redesign Programs (VE-TAP), one must be able to speak bureaucratese to even begin to understand how this second-largest cabinet-level department—second only to its big brother, Department of Defense—really operates. DVA essentially has no fixed budget, because, when it fails, it gets more money from Congress. After all, it serves our veterans who should be well taken care of. However, they are not. How can Congress deny it more funding when the numbers of veterans relying on the government for the benefits to which they are entitled continue surging to levels never experienced before in this nation?

In the wake of the scandal of the lethal duplicate and secret wait lists for patient appointments, the DVA is rewarded with billions to get even bigger, with new buildings scheduled to be opened 2 years from now to serve veterans who needed treatment years ago. Its 2014 budget is cited as $150 billion, half of which was reportedly nondiscretionary for payment of approved benefits. A large cohort of veterans from that budget suffered the duplicate wait lists in Veterans' Affairs medical centers—or VAMCs—beginning with the discovery of the fraudulent duplicate lists at the Carl Hayden VAMC in Phoenix.

"Over the last three years, DVA has solicited and evaluated thousands of ideas from our employees and stakeholders. We have identified the best and they have formed the basis of today's VBA Transformation Plan. VA has completed over 4.1 million claims since 2009 and provided over $58 billion in disability compensation to 4.3 million Veterans and their survivors in 2012 alone—about $150 million every day. At no time in our history have our Veterans received more direct compensation payments. Still, more work remains," said Allison Hickey, a retired U.S. Air Force Brigadier General, who is VA's Under Secretary for Benefits.

General Hickey described the complex mathematics crippling the bureaucracy to the point where it is barely functioning. "The compensation claims backlog is a decades-old problem. We have studied it carefully and engaged with Veterans Service Organizations and others to determine the right approach, one that we're working hard to implement right now" (www.blogs.va.gov/VAntage/8995/balancing-the-record-on-the-claims-backlog/). But, as veterans keep returning from wars with invisible combat injuries, the backlog and waiting lists only grow.

The Department of Veterans Affairs is a massive employer with accountability only to the president and congressional committees. In other words, they do not have quarterly meetings with analysts who question their finances against the backdrop of either the regulators who could break them for illegal accounting or investors who could break them for management inefficiency. It takes in billions and pays out billions, only, like a casino, the house has to win to pay salaries, pensions, and building and grounds costs never even imagined by a life, loan, and disability insurer or health-care provider which has to survive in the free market. In other words, the cost of running the VA almost precludes it from fulfilling its own mission. As seen in the wake of the most recent scandal emanating from secret waiting lists to showcase management efficiencies in the Phoenix Veterans Administration—along with its Philadelphia Regional Office's falsification of disability claims applications—this giant bureaucracy is simply proving too big to fail. It must be propped up by a Congress screaming about budget deficits. Like many insurance companies that run amok, the CEO—in this case the Cabinet-level Secretary of DVA—was essentially fired with a golden parachute of another federal retirement to supplement his military pension as a Four-Star General. It is like the Wall Street bailout where a complacent government in the heat of a scandal threatening world financial markets, rewarded failure, malfeasance, wild speculative trading, and outright fraud perpetrated by those at the top. As Vice President Biden himself was quoted as Senator about breaches of national security in *The Puzzle Palace*, "if screwing the government, make sure you screw it big to get away with it." It was the beneficiaries of veterans' entitlements who suffered just—like the consumers and investors who were victims of the 2008 financial crisis.

So it is with the VA where the pressure to meet quotas of performance created an atmosphere of fraud. Supervisors generated false performance reports and leaned on their subordinates to maintain silence—even as veterans slowly died—thus reducing the caseload. Inside the VA, as inside *The Puzzle Palace*, who really knows what happens in the hospital beds, the computer entries, the claims examinations, and the medical exams? Actually, nurse practitioners now do the Compensation and Pension (C&P) medical exams for disability determinations. They cannot afford doctors to do them anymore. Or, perhaps, do doctors fear losing their licenses succumbing to pressures of unethical practices in the politics of misdiagnosis, wherein the invisible wounds get contorted with the stroke of a pen—or keyboard—into "preexisting" conditions that are not compensable. Oftentimes these misdiagnoses, driven by financial pressures upstream to reduce entitlement spending for lifetime disability payments downstream, are extremely damaging to the veteran's reputation and future. Pre-existing diagnoses, such as personality disorder or bipolar affective disorder, are such popular diagnostic scams.

Marine Specialist Murdough, who was baked to death in solitary confinement at Rikers Island, was reported in the press for being treated there for Schizophrenia and Bipolar Disorder, two disorders that are all but mutually exclusive. But veterans accumulate diagnoses—too often based on fears of getting them compensated for lifetime disability, rather than diagnostic reliability that requires agreement of multiple examiners. Murdough's diagnosis certainly could not pass this smell test. In addition, there is no concern about diagnostic validity that predicts outcomes with and without certain clinical interventions. Why should they be, as long as the diagnosis denies service connected status, thus dumping him/her into the community for care. The private medical sector is expected to decode the misdiagnosis and provide the care, which it has always done, more or less effectively.

In the most recent catastrophic failure of the VA system, an active Marine reservist named Eddie Ray Routh, reportedly diagnosed with posttraumatic stress disorder (PTSD), schizophrenia, suicidality, and dangerousness was discharged from a VAMC over the vociferous pleadings of his parents. He was so toxic on nine medications or grossly psychotic that the clinicians forcing his discharge could only communicate with him via his mother. He was possibly overmedicated in the hospital, but he was also on the wrong dosage of the major psychotropic he needed for his psychosis—namely Risperdal. There was no room for discussion about discharge. After all, this Marine reservist was a mere grunt who had no power like that of a high-ranking officer. In the most twisted of medical decision making, he was determined to be too unstable for step-down to the lower level of care requested by his parents but stable enough to go home by himself and wait for the proper new dosage of his antipsychotic to arrive by mail. It would have been clear from his commitment to a civilian hospital shortly before that his family was terrified of him, as was his girlfriend. Thus, nobody was going to take care of him at home. In fact his parents sold their house in order to move away from him for security reasons, leaving him alone in a home on the market. This was psychotic Eddie Ray Routh, who 3 days later would murder Chris Kyle, the American Sniper and companion shooter, Chad Littlefield, at the firing range. It was supposed to be a therapy session—one veteran suffering PTSD and taking an antidepressant for that, having allegedly recovered from alcoholism, and another veteran diagnosed with PTSD from the same war, psychotic and not recovered from substance abuse.

How many psychiatrists actually diagnosed Eddie Routh, and how many of them tried to understand the diagnostic assessment of the others in order to reach a consensus? Probably none did this. How many psychiatrists actually tried to make the diagnosis best predictive of interventions? None did, or he would not have been judged fit for duty as an active-duty Marine reservist. Not one of these psychiatrists, however many were there, would have vouched for the safety of this patient carrying assault rifles with comrades. Nonetheless, he was officially fit for duty until realizing himself that he was very mentally ill; that is what he told his sister. Obviously had Christopher Kyle known how dangerous Routh was, he would not have taken him to the shooting range. How could such illogic come from the documentation of supposedly the best of electronic health records ever produced—VISTA (Veterans Information Systems and Technology Architecture).

The system is failing internally. Here is a hypothetical case illustrating just how the system is failing inside the VA claims processing operation. A claims manager—call her Mary—works in a file room stacked with claims applications, some of which date back over 5 years. The order came down from her supervisors to process these disability claims that are currently stacking up—and no more going back 5 years or even more. She must make sure, first, to ascertain whether the veteran is even alive. That would be her first cut, because she can then close the file on claims of the deceased. Next, if there has been a lot of returned mail, she can shred it and thus eliminate another part of the backlog, because the veteran is no longer reachable. As for the rest, the computer systems that have been installed to streamline the claims process simply do not work. Even if she tried to update claims to 2014 in order to demonstrate progress, as ordered to do by her supervisor, it would leave thousands of cases still open and unprocessed. That was the easiest, but it was illegal. Mary complained to the hospital administrator that the computer system redesign does not work, but the administrator referred her on. He was concerned the management inefficiencies in the claims processing would reflect on his overall hospital performance metrics, and so he sent Mary down the chain of command, ultimately ending up with her boss who had ordered her to do update claims in the first place. She filed a complaint with the inspector general. The next day, she had a job change with relocation as punishment. Now she performs menial tasks in a basement office without windows, isolated like an Ebola quarantine contact. She fears losing her pension and needs to hang on in this dungeon, treated as if contaminated. Other whistle-blowers are worse off, she knows, because they were suspended, forced to drain their savings to underwrite protracted lawsuits against the government; DVA has free defense from our Justice Department. The playing field for this nefarious and lethal game is hardly a level one. It is like a scene from *The Titanic*, while deck chairs get moved, new people sit down, and higher-ups get the lifeboats through early retirements (www.theblaze.com/blog/2014/10/15/fired-va-official-escapes-being-fired-opts-for-early-retirement/). Few, if any, have actually been fired without lifetime pensions, as our government leads us to believe in the wake of the wait-list scandal and resultant forced resignation of former Secretary of Veterans Affairs, General Shinseki.

What about those claims under the redesign system and transformation created to help veterans get their claims processed more efficiently and faster? The modernization process has been described as a Trojan horse. The burden is on the veterans, many of whom are brain injured or limited in their mental abilities due to multiple deployments that burned out their brain cells. The questionnaire they get after submitting their initial claim is as laborious and detailed as filing taxes. Most can thus simply be diverted in the first round as incomplete and, therefore, simply discarded so as to reduce the backlog. As a consequence, veterans are simply deleted from the computer system so that the bureaucracy can report that the backlog is being processed away. For those who can complete their applications and thread them through the initial stages of the bureaucratic maze, the next step might be a nurse practitioner for Compensation and Pension (C&P) disability examination.

For the average grunt who stays with the game, there are plenty of new nurse practitioners trained in the language of obfuscation and even some old insurance doctors who are jaded by the endemic failures of the system, but who go along simply to get paid. They are still around, because they know how many disabilities with what grade of rating they can dish out without ending up on the street looking for work themselves. They do not know how to diagnose and treat diseases anymore, particularly the invisible wounds of war that do not bleed in plain sight until it is too late, as in a suicidal gunshot to the head. They just know how to manipulate claimant clinical information to backload everything to childhood—thus, not PTSD, but, rather, a preexisting personality disorder.

Preexisting conditions supersede battlefield injuries, and the claimant is processed out without benefits. Of course, the claimant has the right to appeal. Not surprisingly, such a denial and an appeal list is on separate books, as the million man and woman march to claims examiners simply melts down, hopefully without anyone noticing or being able to speak bureaucratese and comprehend the true functions of DVA lists—delay, terminate, and litigate in a war of attrition—one oftentimes worse than that which they spilled their blood while buddies died in their arms, blown to smithereens by an improvised explosive device (IED).

What may look good on paper, though, for the DVA bureaucracy suddenly becomes a problem for the public safety network and its first responders and police; for the workplace; for prisons and jails and for the families of veterans who are decomposing without any help from The Department of Veterans Affairs. One only has to look at the cases of Aaron Alexis (the Navy Yard shooter); Ivan Lopez (the Fort Hood suicidal rampage mass murder); and Omar Gonzalez (the White House intruder), all of whom were known to the DVA, investigated by law enforcement, and left to wander untreated.

The case of Omar Gonzalez is especially horrendous, because he was a known assassination threat to the president and recently broke into the White House with a weapon, eluding and then overpowering a Secret Service agent before he was stopped by an off-duty agent inside the building. He was allegedly medically retired as an army sniper, but he was also homeless. He reportedly received treatment for PTSD at Fort Hood and was on the wait list for care at the VA for chronic pain from a combat injury.

What are the issues in the case of Omar Gonzalez, who carried a serrated knife capable of beheadings all the way to the staircase leading to the living quarters of the First Family? Gonzalez had been a forward scout in his army division and a sniper with three deployments to Iraq. His career ended in 2012 when medically retired, presumably for partial amputation of his foot from an IED, PTSD, and possibly intense and acute low back pain. The coordination between his military Medical Evaluation Board (MEB) at Fort Hood and the regional VA benefits office was relatively fast, but not fast enough to spare him from divorce. He was discharged in 2012 and was divorced that same year.

Gonzalez was obviously extremely paranoid and likely suffering from the most malignant form of PTSD that breaks down into psychosis when not adequately treated, or lit up with the wrong psychotropic medications. After discharge he carried a .45 handgun at all times. His wife appears to have had no support from either Fort Hood or the VA in helping to cope with her husband's paranoia. He watched her sleep, likely to protect her. When his wife had little choice but to leave him in his oppressive paranoid state, Gonzalez lived alone for awhile off base in nearby Copperas Cove, Texas. His neighbors reported him as getting weird. He installed motion detector lights in his yard that illuminated his neighbors' yards, too, and was always checking on people because he thought he was being watched by the army. He believed that the army had tapped his phone and bugged his house. He was so frightened at night that he patrolled the perimeter of his residence, checking it while he armed himself to the teeth in a residential neighborhood with families, children, and other veterans, many of them hypervigilant from combat, too.

Therefore, although medically retired and included in that nondiscretionary VA budget for security of his benefits payout, he was soon divorced and homeless after returning from Iraq. Symbolic of his journey to hell and back, he brought the same Bible he and his wife brought to the minister to pray for survival on his last deployment. This time, however, it had a camouflage cover and bore the insignia of the First Cavalry Division, a shield with a diagonal stripe and the profile of a horse's head. His deterioration was noticeable to family and friends, as well as his ex-wife. Few who noticed—and many did notice—were not directly or indirectly connected to Fort Hood, the major employer in Copperas Grove, Texas. He turned off his electricity, either because he could not pay his bill or he thought it was part of the government's plot against him. He stopped answering calls. His cell phone was stored in a microwave oven to prevent wireless intrusions from the army. And, now loaded with plenty of firepower, he left his home in Texas and traveled the country in his truck, until arriving in Washington, DC, for his final mission. He believed that "the atmosphere was collapsing and needed to get the information to the president of the United States so that he [The President] could get the word out to the people," prosecutors said (Justin Moyer 2014).

After his arrest the police found two hatchets and a machete, as well as 800 rounds of ammunition in both boxes and magazines in his vehicle nearby. And this was not the first time he had been caught menacing the building. He had been stopped on August 25 for possible threatening behavior while walking along the south fence of the White House with a hatchet in his waistband. He was not arrested then, and on July 19, he was stopped for reckless driving in Virginia and charged with evading arrest and possession of numerous weapons, including a sawed-off shotgun, and a map with the White House circled. Local police informed Secret Service of that traffic stop and the results of the search. Thus, Omar Gonzalez was brought to the attention of the Secret Service. He was also known to the U.S. Army Medical Department (AMEDD) and to the Department of Veterans Affairs. His family reported that he had stopped taking his antianxiety and antidepressant medications, which he must have received from his attending "prescribing provider" at Fort Hood Behavioral Health Clinic. It was then, his family reported, that he started to go downhill. He complained to friends about intolerable back pain and his inability to get an appointment for evaluation and treatment for pain from the local Texas VA medical center, but they deny his being in their system. Why would that be? It could be for many reasons, such as inaccurate bookkeeping or file management. But, it could also be for the mere fact that he had not come in yet.

One has to wonder, how could a decorated combat veteran with such obvious disability fall through the cracks and come close to converting routine chronic medical care into near-disaster medicine and one of the most horrific political assassinations in American history? It is no secret that Fort Hood medical services have been challenged and are way understaffed. It is no secret that medical evaluation boards are controversial in the military, but Gonzalez did complete his evaluation with the VA in relatively timely fashion (see Liebert and Birnes 2013). It is no secret that wait lists for care at VA medical centers have been manipulated to disguise a system that is overwhelmed and incapable of meeting the needs of veterans or the demands of politicians and their appointed leadership in the Department of Veterans Affairs. What is all but impossible to comprehend is the thinking and resultant policies for handling our returning veterans with disabilities, oftentimes medical-surgical combined with severe pain and neuropsychiatric impairment of PTSD and traumatic brain injury (TBI), as in the case of Oscar Gonzalez. Theoretically, the recently signed into law Clay Hunt Act will address some of the issues Gonzalez faced, unless this is more political cover for a failed institution, whether by intent or pure naivety. We can only hope that the suicide prevention purpose of the Clay Hunt Act actually does what it is supposed to and addresses the issue of debilitating PTSD that can metastasize into unrelenting psychosis.

It is not known whether Gonzalez suffered a concussive head injury in Iraq, but it defies medical logic that he could have lost half of his foot to an IED explosion without having experienced a serious concussive injury to the brain (TBI). What we do know is that there had to be a lot of clinicians and claims administrators slicing and dicing his clinical presentation upon his return from Iraq, presumably via air evacuation following an explosive injury to his foot. They had to determine what percentage of his disability was psychiatric and what percentage was partially amputated foot and then, possibly, what percentage was for pain, whether lower extremity or back. The problem is, he was psychotic, or becoming psychotic. Nobody knew about that at Fort Hood? Nobody reported it? Nobody interviewed his wife who would have rapidly made it clear to a psychiatrist, clinical psychologist, or clinical social worker that her husband was suffering a debilitating paranoid psychosis? Was such a professional even made available from Fort Hood Behavioral Health Clinic during his indeterminate wait for an appointment at the local VA medical center? We simply do not know the official disposition of his case. But we do know that he turned up inside the White House, running past Secret Service agents who were unable to intercept him, kn ocking over an agent at the unlocked front door, and being tackled just as he passed the stairway to the second floor living quarters of The First Family by the last defense—an off-duty officer.

How are percentages determined to sum up Gonzalez for 70%–80% final disability? That is almost as deep a military secret as classified information probably concealing the many battles he fought in Iraq. The fact is, it cannot be done with any validity that predicts how a veteran's injuries are going to play out in real life—in this case play out in desperate homelessness, rapidly escalating into clear and present danger to the very nerve center of the U.S. government—namely The White House!

Was this not also the case with Aaron Alexis, the Navy Yard suicidal rampage mass murderer who was offered an honorable discharge in lieu of a general discharge for misconduct? He made two emergency visits to two different VA medical centers just days before his shooting rampage at the DC Navy Yard. Again, his paranoid psychosis was not recognized. The navy, he complained, had implanted an electronic bug in his brain. Gonzalez complained repeatedly of the same kind of mind control by the army, requiring constant vigilance and storage of his cell phone in his microwave oven. These are both severe paranoid delusions that had "dangerousness" written all over them. Both Alexis and Gonzalez needed to be on antipsychotic tranquilizers and not the antidepressants reportedly prescribed for them. They also had to be under close case management with adequate financial means at least to minimally cope with the unique and new demands of an unstructured civilian society that imposes no hourly schedule on free citizens. Soldiers and sailors are not free citizens.

If we take a look at some of the cases where mentally ill veterans are simply dumped into the public sector while their cases inch their way toward resolution in DVA hospitals or regional claims offices, we will see just how desperate the problem is and why this is a major issue for law enforcement and the emergency medical community.

In 2013, Americans were shocked at the murder of decorated Navy SEAL and bestselling author Christopher Kyle (2012) by combat veteran Eddie Ray Routh, whom Kyle was trying to help recover from PTSD by taking him to a gun range. By coincidence, Eddie's mother, after repeatedly rebuffed by VA and community hospitals in her efforts to keep her son hospitalized until stable and safe, desperately asked an acquaintance to help. That acquaintance was Christopher Kyle. Routh, also paranoid and delusional and with almost no impulse control told his sister that he simply coveted Kyle's pickup truck. Or so he said that was the reason for killing both Kyle and his shooting companion, Chad Littlefield, on the shooting range. Routh murdered Kyle and Littlefield in a mental state of fulminating paranoid psychosis (Liebert and Birnes 2013, 2014).

With the release of the Clint Eastwood's *American Sniper* film starring Bradley Cooper, which garnered a huge box office following, the Christopher Kyle case became a media sensation. Critics dumped on the movie as glorifying war and the killing of civilians, especially children. But the movie itself was antiwar, and Kyle, the movie's protagonist as portrayed by Cooper, had deep reservations about some of the people he was ordered to kill as his combat deployments multiplied. By the time he returned home after his final deployment, he was numb inside, suffering from severe PTSD. Part of his own therapy was working with other veterans suffering from PTSD, sharing and articulating the pain so as to keep one another from committing suicide just to stop the mental anguish. Eddie Ray Routh was also reportedly suffering from PTSD, but his mental disease metastasized into a paranoia, a delusion that the very people who were there to help him by taking him to a gun range, Chris Kyle and Chad Littlefield, were actually out to kill him. Thus, he shot them and stole Kyle's pickup truck, only admitting to his sister after the shooting that he was after the pickup truck and took it. And now, Routh sits in a Texas prison after his conviction for first-degree murder, barely having been able to understand the Erath County prosecutor trying to convince a jury that this insane individual actually had the mental capacity for intentional homicide. The media is feasting on this story. But the real story, the failure of the DVA who sacrificed Routh and Kyle and Littlefield, will go underreported. Indeed, war is like a jungle, but the feeding frenzy seems to go on and on. This one is far from over. It has gone from military and VA medical discharge problems to a trial for double homicide in Texas, an exit path for both the Department of Defense (DOD) and the Department of Veterans Affairs (DVA) that are likely free and out of this compounded American tragedy. A grossly psychotic Marine was deemed to be fit for duty. It is doubtful anyone in his unit would have wished to fight with him another day, if in fact Eddie Routh even fought one day with them or was even ever "outside the wire" in Iraq.

We must ask in all these cases—and for the many hundreds of thousands waiting for their veterans' claims examinations and nearly an equal number fighting claims denials for disability, with even greater numbers being hastily mustered out of the military what is the plan? What mechanism can the secretaries for Health in The Department of Defense and Department of Veterans Affairs employ to screen returning combat veterans for psychological disorders so that they can receive some exit counseling, appropriate medications to alleviate their mental anguish and referrals to therapy sessions to keep them talking so that their anguish does not fester into suicidal and homicidal rage?

The recruiting ads are already filling the quarters of televised football games, while the soldiers who fought our war on terror get dumped into their communities with little but directions on how to file a claim if not able to support themselves and their families—or worse, a referral to the nearest homeless shelter. What are these complex procedures understood only in the offices of PEBLO's (U.S. Army Physical Disability Agency) and VA claims evaluations costing the U.S. taxpayer? We know more nurse practitioners and physician assistants are being recruited by DOD and DVA to get through the wait lists, both in the military and in the civilian world, after discharge. Some veterans, like Omar Gonzalez are in both the military and civilian worlds because their MEBs and VA C&P judgments must align to determine metrics of benefits. In Routh's case, it was minimal or nothing. In Alexis's case it was nothing. And in Gonzalez's case it was $1650/month. The costs are enormous, both professionally and administratively, to squeeze out just this poverty level compensation for one or two in three psychotic veterans from such a mammoth and sprawling bureaucracy, seemingly accountable to nobody.

New computer contracts must be awarded to catch up to the backlog of waiting veterans' claims. For what reason is this necessary? Is it to slice and dice clinical presentations that simply do not lend themselves to certain percentages of disability? But, that is the way it has always been done. Thousands of administrators and clinicians are paid a lot to judge applicants like Omar Gonzalez to be 70%–80% disabled. What does that mean for someone too impaired mentally to even hold down a job? Presumably he can find odd jobs to make up the rest to enable him to eat and keep a roof over his head without anything for his ex-wife, forced to leave him for lack of help to just co-exist with him. She may have saved us from even worse disaster. So far, nobody has been seriously injured or killed by her ex, but she could only turn to her local minister for help. Might that payment for her to stick with him be another 15%? But there is only reason—with no justification—for how he was handled by both DOD and DVA to determine he was partially but not totally disabled for life.

Gonzalez was grossly paranoid, lame from a partially amputated foot and in chronic pain every day. What employer would hire him for any amount of money and thus risk workplace violence? Why wasn't Omar Gonzalez 100% service connected? Maybe 100% service connection would have provided the extra benefits he needed to get traction in civilian life and spare his marriage, like his intended medical retirement at age 42. Afterall, he served nearly his entire 20 for normal retirement, and yet he wound up as another evening news headline for babbling pundits who only looked at the failures of the Secret Service instead of the failures of the health and disability services of our departments of Defense and Veterans Affairs which simply left Gonzalez homeless to rot and fester.

Eddie Routh and Aaron Alexis had to be fit for duty to be discharged, one into marine reserves and the other honorably into a navy contracting position on a sensitive naval facility in Washington, DC. But both were grossly psychotic, whether from preexisting disease or combat-induced psychosis. Gonzalez was in heavy combat. There is no clear evidence that either Routh or Alexis were in combat. That does not deter the military from awarding them 100% service connected disability for psychotic illnesses incurred in the line of duty, which they were.

Only the Office of Management and Budget (OMB) from the West Wing and the Congressional Budget Office (CBO) from Congress have the capability to determine the direct costs of discharging these three men and transferring their care in some way to the DVA. The politics of such an audit is politically inconceivable right now, barring further scandals that cost more billions. Presumably the Department of Justice is thoroughly investigating the relationship between the victim and the shooter in the attempted murder at Vancouver (WA) VAMC. In the case of the murder suicide in an El Paso, Texas, VA health clinic, the Department of Justice did investigate, but what did the veteran under investigation mean when threatening the deceased psychologist? "I know what you did." There is plenty of very unhealthy behavior that goes on in behavioral health clinics. What went on at this one that aroused the murderous passions of this suicidal Iraqi war veteran once employed by DVA?

> The doctor who was fatally shot at an El Paso Veterans Affairs clinic had previously filed a threat complaint against his alleged killer, FBI officials said Wednesday.
>
> VA psychologist Timothy Fjordbak, 63, was allegedly shot and killed by Jerry Serrato, 48, on the fourth floor of the El Paso Veteran Affairs Clinic, FBI special agent Doug Lindquist said. Then Serrato "actually went to the third floor, and that's where he took his own life," Lindquist said.
>
> Serrato, who was once in the military, worked at the VA in 2013 as a desk clerk. But the incident that prompted Fjordbak to file a complaint took place in a grocery store, Lindquist said.
>
> "Mr. Serrato approached Dr. Fjordbak, who did not recognize him, and he made a verbal threat," said Lindquist, who paraphrased the threat as: "'I know what you did and I will take care of that,' something to that effect." (Izadi et al. 2015)

This is not an isolated case; VA employees have been crying out for improved Security:

> The murder-suicide in El Paso was one among a long line of violent acts committed on federal health facility grounds. Former chief of police at the Cheyenne VAMC in Wyoming, John Glidewell, told the *Washington Post*, "These are the same issues we have been screaming (begging) for help with the entire 10.5 years I have been with the VA Police." This comes less than a year after a former VA employee shot and wounded an employee at the Dayton VAMC in Ohio. Craig Larson from the VA's Chicago regional public affairs office noted that the facility, like El Paso, did not have metal detectors, a policy that could have been implemented at the local level. Even the Washington DC VAMC did not announce their installing of metal detectors until 2013. (www.blogs.va.gov/VAntage/8995/balancing-the-record-on-the-claims-backlog/)

Then there are the potential indirect costs of intrusions, such as the one perpetrated by Gonzalez. Only by pure circumstances of serendipity were the White House executive staff in the West Wing and First Family spared in the case of Gonzalez, but the Secret Service was not. New security will cost millions. Secret Service executive heads are already rolling. Lawyers must be appointed. Checks must be cut to pay them. And this is all at the taxpayers' expense. Finally Gonzalez will have to be dealt with in federal court. His felony, however, will likely result in his removal from the waitlist at his local VA, which he desperately needed for evaluation and treatment of severe pain. And all of it could have been prevented if only the local police and the Secret Service had done a thorough investigation of Gonzalez and demanded treatment for him at the nearest VA medical center as a court-ordered diversion rather than releasing him back into the public's lap for what had to appear an inevitable catastrophe. How often can we be this lucky? Of course, we were not that lucky with the Navy Shipyard or the American Sniper. This is cost shifting at its worst.

Somewhere, someone has to do the math for the direct and indirect costs of all the ineffectual and meaningless processing that went into the MEB and DVA C&P assessment to award Gonzalez $1652 per month, just about enough to allow him to live homeless in his truck and get well positioned to give the president the message, albeit a psychotic one, that the atmosphere is collapsing. We all might feel like that, from time to time, but few would either think or be capable of actually doing what Omar Gonzalez or Miriam Carey did to try to barge into the White House to deliver their messages personally to The President of United States!

And pursuant to cost shifting, what are the lawsuits over the Navy Yard massacre going to be costing the taxpayers? These are the consequences of where we are. Murders, suicides, lost lives, threats to the president of the United States, suicidal mass murder, mass institutional fraud; the list goes on. Where will it stop? Not with spin from the top, but maybe long enough to stay out of the headlines until the end of another commander in chief's presidential term; then a new Secretary of Veterans Affairs, once again, will be appointed to clean it all up.

There seems no end to the predictable catastrophes emanating from a medical and disability entitlement system long gone awry. A four-star general who boasted of his agency's record in meeting the challenges for accomplishing the impossible, namely eliminating the wait list for veterans claiming disability pensions and others seeking treatment, fell on his sword for the president. Not even he could untangle the mess of the DVA because it was too much of a Gordian knot that he ultimately had to acknowledge. His metrics to justify his accomplishments were the results of cooking the books. He is off with two rich federal retirements, and many underlings had lifeboats not available to more honest whistle-blowing staff trying to help veterans. And the punishment continues, as the inspector general tries to chase it down and save those resisting the dual wait-list scandal.

> Audio of an internal VA meeting obtained by The DC confirms that VA officials in Los Angeles intentionally canceled backlogged patient exam requests.
>
> "The committee was called System Redesign and the purpose of the meeting was to figure out ways to correct the department's efficiency. And one of the issues at the time was the backlog," Oliver Mitchell, a Marine veteran and former patient services assistant in the VA Greater Los Angeles Medical Center, told The DC. "We just didn't have the resources to conduct all of those exams. Basically we would get about 3000 requests a month for [medical] exams, but in a 30-day period we only had the resources to do about 800. That rolls over to the next month and creates a backlog," Mitchell said. "It's a numbers thing. The waiting list counts against the hospitals efficiency. The longer the veteran waits for an exam that counts against the hospital as far as productivity is concerned." (Morrissey 2014; www.dailycaller.com/2014/02/24/va-employees-destroyed-veterans-medical-records-to-cancel-backlogged-exam-requests-audio/)

Fraud is systemic within the Department of Veterans Affairs. Veterans and taxpayers are major victims, because they expect and believe veterans to be receiving the best of care. They are not the only ones. DVA is stocked with high-quality and conscientious staff. Thousands of veterans depend on them and are satisfied with their care. They are victims too, even if they did not blow the whistle and simply tried to do their jobs within a corrupted and outdated system. How could something like this occur in a system that had built-in congressional oversight and best management practices?

This catastrophe in management and delivery of services was not created by the Obama administration. It inherited it from prior administrations, but it was only made worse by the thousands of returning combat veterans from the Gulf Wars. Whether or not the American people came to support those wars, the burden of those returning vets fell squarely upon the Obama administration to manage the problem at the DVA. Then the dam broke when whistle-blowers—first at the Phoenix DVA facility and then others—began talking openly about fraud and the cooking of the books to make it look like the DVA was meeting its quotas. Only it was not. It was cooking the books to satisfy the metrics requirements of DVA superiors. Congress was legitimately and righteously outraged at having been deceived by the DVA. The White House was also furious. Something had to be done, and fast, to satisfy the anger.

The solution has been to replace the DVA secretary, General Eric Shineseki, with another West Point graduate, Robert A. McDonald, only this one a retired chief executive officer (CEO) of Proctor and Gamble. It is no secret that only a skilled marketing person can make it to the top of a company that successfully competes in branded consumer products. But a Fortune 500 CEO also has to understand the basics of top-down management, setting goals, inspiring subordinates to inspire their subordinates to meet those goals, training, and monitoring performance. These were the skills that the administration needed at the DVA. Indeed, he is Army, and he knows the system to a point, but he has no experience in either health-care delivery or disability compensation. He also appears blind to the crisis of homeless veterans, chatting with them in front of TV cameras and lying about his special operations missions, when he was never in Special Forces. And, therein may lie a problem, because the DVA, like it or not, is a health-care delivery system as well as a long-term disability insurance benefits and annuity institution. Former Defense Secretary Robert Gates once complained that the Defense Department was never meant to be an insurance and annuity company. But it is, and it is now up to a new head of the DVA to fix a problem that had been over a decade in the making.

Secretary McDonald got authority to fire the crooks and the laggards. He quickly invited whistle-blowers to come forward. He got $17 billion to build new clinics to open in 2 to 3 years, and to staff them with doctors and nurses. There will be more billions thrown at IT, the catch-all term for fixing everything in a mammoth bureaucracy stacked with papers for claims examinations and monitoring performance of medical centers. The supposed firewall between doctors, nurses, and physicians diagnosing and treating patients and those performing C&P exams will continue to stand immune to corrupting influences scandalizing the Western Army Regional Medical Command when diagnoses were altered and pressure allegedly brought to bear on clinicians to avoid diagnosing compensable service connected disorders like PTSD or postconcussion syndrome from traumatic brain injuries (Liebert and Birnes 2013, the Madigan Scandal).

The Forensic Unit at Madigan Army Medical Center, Tacoma, Washington, made it loud and clear that certain diagnoses like PTSD were too costly for long term disability payments for which soldiers were entitled in through their enlistment contracts in this all volunteer army. Clinicians were intimidated. The psychotherapy clinic was soon shut down, for reasons unrelated to any politics of misdiagnosis, of course. But, likewise, a systemic conflict of interest still exists in the DVA, because the same organization both provides health-care and long-term disability insurance—as well as benefits to survivors. And they do all of this without the truly impermeable firewall they claim they can maintain, while no insurance company in the world would dare make such a preposterous claim. And that was the problem at Madigan, where the forensic psychiatric unit evaluated claims of PTSD, looked for any preexisting psychological condition as a basis to deny applicants' claims, and, when necessary to meet their own quotas to keep costs down, actually reversed psychiatric diagnoses so as to deny claims. When they did that, and they did that systematically, they effectively dumped mentally ill veterans without any real means of support onto the public safety system, where police and the courts would have to deal with them if they broke the law, where hospitals would have to bear the cost of their health care if they showed up in their emergency rooms and where innocent victims would have to deal with any threats they posed or crimes they committed. Thus, taxpayers foot the bill for the DVA to do its job and taxpayers foot the bill for the DVA's shirking its job. Were any of these veterans on the streets of Boise, whose National Guard was serviced for medical care and fitness-for-duty evaluations at Madigan Army Medical Center? In an open letter to Congress, Chief Masterson has literally pleaded with Congress to get soldiers discharged to Idaho—and nationally—treated so that his officers do not have gun battles with them in the streets of Boise (Boise Police Department 2010).

## BASIC CONFLICT OF INTEREST AT THE DEPARTMENT OF VETERANS AFFAIRS

There is no health-care system in the civilian sector that provides both medical insurance and long-term disability insurance to its patients—not the Mayo Clinic, not the Cleveland Clinic. No provider does, because it is unethical, inviting conflicts of interest and bad practices. It is hard enough to diagnose and treat returning soldiers without auditors looking over clinicians' shoulders at every expense and questioning decisions these practicing clinicians believe are diagnostically valid, reliable, and correct. But this is only worse when you are the director of an organization that must function with a built-in conflict of interest that no organization in the private sector has. Can Secretary McDonald bridge—finesse is probably a better word—this conflict, while civilian insurers and providers cannot? Because there never has been a truly impermeable firewall between Division of Benefits and Division of Medical Services in either the VA or DOD, and there never will be, his task will be monumental. War is an uninsurable risk.

The system is funded and staffed on the false premise that a small minority of soldiers are disabled with neuropsychiatric injuries—maybe one in five—according to the Rand Study. The Triangle Study in the 1980s for Vietnam veterans found closer to 50%, including "partial syndromes" that never were defined. In this study, only those veterans not incarcerated—200,000 were in prison at that time and even more in jail—or able to receive the invitation to fly to North Carolina and actually make the transaction to do so were examined. That was a skewed sample, but nobody ever raises the question of who designs the epidemiological studies of the medical disability consequences of war. It is reassuring that our young going to war can take repeated deployments with horrors only symbolically encasing Gonzalez's Bible. Such reassurance, however, is rhetorical only, having no alignment with the harsh realities of combat as spelled out by Keegan in *The Face of Battle: A Study of Agincourt, Waterloo, and the Somme* (January 27, 1983), about whom the late Tom Clancy wrote:

> The Face of Battle is military history from the battlefield: a look at the direct experience of individuals at the "point of maximum danger." Without the myth-making elements of rhetoric and xenophobia, and breaking away from the stylized format of battle descriptions, John Keegan has written what is probably the definitive model for military historians. And in his scrupulous reassessment of three battles representative of three different time periods, he manages to convey what the experience of combat

> meant for the participants, whether they were facing the arrow cloud at the battle of Agincourt, the musket balls at Waterloo, or the steel rain of the Somme.

Tom Clancy called the author "The best military historian of our generation."

How many in the United States actually paid to evaluate and treat Omar Gonzalez listened to his combat experiences? What was it like to step so close to an IED and lose half your foot? Yet, he is an exceptional case. Disputes over an MEB versus discharge without benefits were unlikely in his case like they were in the cases of the Navy Yard/Alexis, the LAPD's Christopher Dorner, and Afghan mass murder perpetrator Sergeant Robert Bales. In addition, there was the double murder committed by Eddie Routh and the murder suicide by former Special Forces trooper and Buffalo Hospital trauma surgeon, Timothy Jorden, all of whose case studies are covered in detail in *Wounded Minds* (Liebert and Birnes 2013). Gonzalez, Alexis, Dorner, Routh, and Jorden were all individuals who should have been thoroughly evaluated by the DVA, assigned treatment regimens, and given the necessary disability to enable them to get support. So should Wade Page, perpetrator of the Sikh Temple suicidal mass murder; he was hospitalized by the army prior to discharge and left to wander the nation until the final catastrophic conclusion of his career in massive blood shed of an apparent hate crime. However, the military simply abandoned these soldiers to the public sector where their crimes resulted in the deaths of innocent civilians, both here and abroad, put the lives of their family members and loved ones at risk, and also endangered the lives of the police who had to track them down. And all of this occurred at taxpayers' expense.

> Recent wars in Iraq and Afghanistan have resulted in many soldiers coming home still engaged in a very private war emotionally, mentally, and physically. When this very private battle escalates, the war comes alive on the home front with tragic consequences seen nationally including suicide and aggression against others. According to SAMHSA, the Substance Abuse and Mental Health Services Administration, of the approximately 11,000 Idaho veterans who have returned from Iraq and Afghanistan, 16.5% suffer from Post Traumatic Stress Disorder and 19.5% have suffered a traumatic brain injury. (Boise Police Department 2014)

The DVA, also in order to remediate the problems of backlog and unfulfilled medical benefits guarantees to veterans, instituted a Veterans' Choice program, a new law, making it possible for veterans to receive private health care if their claims lag for over 30 days. But, according to AP (Daly 2015), only 27,000 have made appointments to get their private medical care, even though the "Choice Cards" have been mailed out to 6.6 million potential beneficiaries. Secretary McDonald acknowledged this is a slow start, but he hopes the new law will help the backlog if the private medical sector can absorb the overflow from the DVA. This is also a stopgap measure to handle the torrent of claims as more veterans return from the Middle East while new VA facilities are being built and more medical personnel are being hired. The program, the government hopes, will also alleviate the pressure on public safety and emergency service which are also heavily burdened by veterans simply dumped, deprived of care and onto the street.

Congress will be taking a huge risk to preserve the status quo and improve things at the edges for health and disability services for our returning and returned veterans. If DVA were in the private sector, it would be taken through Chapter 11 Bankruptcy, if not a Chapter 13, and radically restructured. Expecting Secretary McDonald to correct a system so entrenched with bureaucratic self interest, while charged with a mission impossible, will inevitably haunt us in a few years like the bailouts on Wall Street of 2008. Good money, if no systemically radical improvements are made, will simply pass through like the bad money has—and pass through by the billions. For those incredible numbers of billions in direct and indirect costs, the contracts of this all-volunteer army could be bought out and every veteran and his family could be provided Platinum Obamacare, allowing our veterans the immediate traction needed to receive the medical and rehabilitation services they need wherever they choose to live. The authors spelled out in detail the needs, solutions, and benefits of just such contract buyout in *Wounded Minds: Understanding and Solving the Growing Menace of Post-Traumatic Stress Disorder* (Liebert and Birnes 2013).

Of interest is the fact that even the VA is beginning to recognize this reality and providing private pay for vets on lethal wait-lists.

It is time for drastic change—change that must be brought in by new generations of law enforcement and first responders at federal, state, and municipal levels. Students who sit in criminal justice and psychology classes right now, as well as in law schools and medical schools, must be the bearers of that change, because right now, we are not getting it. President Obama, for all of his good intentions and honest beliefs, simply did not foresee that a Gulf War III is coming. We started it over 10 years ago, and it is here. Who will fight it? Recruiting for this all volunteer army is not as easy as pressing the Refresh Button; in fact, recruiting is far tougher for this all volunteer army now than it was for Operation Iraqi Freedom as the great recession attracted young people with backgrounds promising future unemployment; military service sounded good then. Now it doesn't sound so good, as young people learn of the abuse and war of attrition they face in the event of being wounded or falling ill in line of duty. Must we depend now on illegal immigrants or dreamers to fight this one? A mercenary army like the Hessians? Or is it time to finally address President Eisenhower's advocacy in his final national address for universal military service. For that, there are no entitlements to require a multibillion staff to carve up and slice through. The entitlement is simply that of being a U.S. citizen. The responsibility is to share equally, regardless of socioeconomic status, in defending this nation. Everyone physically and mentally able goes through military basic training upon graduation from high school shows up at basic training without at least a GED or goes to jail. For those wishing to get a college degree, stay in the military and go to college or take ROTC and serve for 2 years as an officer. Conscientious objectors can join VISTA, the Peace Corps, or any other community short-staffed service organization for a 2-year hitch after college and earn back a college loan or go to a community college for free. Take good care of the millions of volunteers from our War on Terror with a special 9/11 fund now, similar to the FDNY, and get on with defending this nation. Bureaucrats in it for self-interest or double-dipping for a second federal pension, get out of the way. It is all of our security and not just yours that is imminently at stake.

## REFERENCES

Boise Police Department. 2010. Chief urges Idaho Congressional delegation to enhance services for vets. News release, February 3. www.police.cityofboise.org/home/news-releases/2010/02/chief-urges-idaho-congressional-delegation-to-enhance-services-for-vets/

Boise Police Department. 2014. Leadership in veterans support network earns Boise Police Department the IACP/Cisco Community Policing Award. News release, September 17. www.police.cityofboise.org/home/news-releases/2014/09/leadership-in-veterans-support-network-earns-boise-police-department-the-iacpcisco-community-policing-award/

Caruso, D. B. 2015. VA makes little headway in fight to shorten waits for care. *The Associated Press*, April 9. www.militarytimes.com/story/military/benefits/veterans/2015/04/09/va-wait-times-continue/25422103

Daly, M. 2015. VA's 'choice' program for health care off to slow start. *AP The Big Story*, February 22. www.bigstory.ap.org/article/578abfae6b034ce99e3bb48f0b70f3ff/vas-choice-program-health-care-slow-start

Izadi, E., Lamohe, D. and Wax-Thibodeaux, E. 2015. FBI: El Paso clinic victim was VA doctor who had filed complaint against alleged killer. *The Washington Post*, January 7. www.washingtonpost.com/news/post-nation/wp/2015/01/06/doctor-shot-presumed-shooter-found-dead-at-el-paso-va-clinic

Kasperowicz, P. 2014. "Fired" VA official escapes being fired, opts for early retirement. *The Blaze*, October 15. www.theblaze.com/blog/2014/10/15/fired-va-official-escapes-being-fired-opts-for-early-retirement

Keegan, J. 1983. *The Face of Battle: A Study of Agincourt, Waterloo, and the Somme*, Penguin Books, London, UK, January 27.

Kyle, C. 2012. *American Sniper*, HarperCollins, New York.

Liebert, J. A. and Birnes, W. J. 2013. *Wounded Minds: Understanding and Solving the Growing Menace of Post-Traumatic Stress Disorder*. Skyhorse, New York.

Liebert, J. A. and Birnes, W. J. 2014. *Hearts of Darkness*. Skyhorse, New York.

Morrissey, E. 2014. VA destroyed records to cover up massive cancellations for wait-list fraud. *HotAir*, June 18. www.hotair.com/archives/2014/06/18/va-destroyed-records-to-cover-up-massive-cancellations-for-wait-list-fraud/

Moyer, J. 2014. Relative: Alleged White House fence-jumper Omar Gonzalez limping in video because he lost part of a foot in Iraq. *Washington Post*, September 14.

# 10

# Corrections psychiatry

When people realize that a huge number of inmates in both state and federal prisons are impaired with serious psychiatric disorders and relegated to solitary confinement absent medications and any form of therapy, where they wither away and die, they are shocked. Unlike the million homeless visible to every day lying in our parks and gutters, prisons are the forgotten sector of society. And yet, the vast majority of those prisoners living in the shadows will someday be released back into society with neither vocational nor coping skills to fit in. We are literally training our incarcerated population, the majority of whom are people of color, and the majority of whom have been sentenced for victimless crimes—mainly drugs—to prey on society when released because they have no other means of functioning. We need to remedy this situation, because we do not need another job creation program like our Department of Veterans Affairs to deliver worst services for more millions needing best medical practices.

---

**Case study: Pelican Bay State Prison, Crescent City, California**

"Lt. Dave Barneburg, lead gang investigator at Pelican Bay, said incarcerated gang leaders commanded a vast network in the prisons and in cities like Los Angeles, Salinas and San Francisco, ordering attacks on rivals and running drug rings and other illegal businesses. One gang, Nuestra Familia, at one point identified *Pelican Bay as its 'White House'*. The gang problem is so tough," he said, "No one has the answer. You do the best you can with the tools you have" (Joyner 2012).

---

The inmate problem in prisons is so severe that prison gangs are able to operate entire financial empires from behind bars—empires whose reach extends into neighborhoods throughout the country. And this is not a new phenomenon, it has been going on for over 50 years and has even corrupted politicians all the way from departments of corrections to state houses and governors' mansions.

Here is a story about the nature of corrections and its showcase healthcare paradigm for a nation, at Pelican Bay, a high-security corrections facility in California. In actuality, Pelican Bay was always a violent institution under the control of the inmates more than prison administrators. But both guards and inmates knew that in order for them to keep the peace and each other alive, they had to get along by going along; that meant compromises for a population of psychotics and desperados mixed mindlessly together for one reason; to keep them off the streets of California ever again—or, it is believed by the public, at least most of them, such as Charles Manson, coming up for parole every year. But, for a new comer to this facility, a psychiatrist, his introduction to what really goes on in high-security death row institutions was a baptism by fire.

Having recovered from a bitter divorce in Arlington, Virginia, Kit Green—not his real name—was seeking new opportunities out west. Although comfortable in his entry-level position as staff psychiatrist at his local VA medical center, he felt so strongly he needed a complete break with the past that he answered a job advertisement for psychiatrists with forensic experience. It was a supermax prison in one of the most beautiful areas of America—the small fishing village of Crescent City, California, right on the Oregon border.

When originally conceived in the late 1980s, there was little direction from Sacramento, whether legislative or executive, into either its design or its ultimate function. There are only brief notes from legislative hearings regarding this massive monument toward a cutting-edge frontier of corrections. Decisions were simply made by default and left to the Department of Corrections (DOC) over design and ultimate use. The California DOC selected this remote parcel of land near the Oregon border in order to separate inmates—expected to be gang members, or "gangstas"—from both their families and affiliates in Los Angeles, San Francisco, and Salinas. Legislators did discuss with some seriousness what to call this gigantic fortress in the pristine Pacific Northwest—Dungeness Dungeon or Slammer by the Sea? Only later would this massive structure of impenetrable cement and steel in the lus—green seaside county of Del Norte be named Pelican Bay Prison. Few citizens would care what went on there, because the worst of the worst were to be off the streets and the administration of Pelican Bay was trusted to do just that: keep them as far away as possible—and, presumably, forever. It was also good for the local economy, drenched in rain with little sunshine to attract anyone but hardy steelhead fishermen. Nobody should be able to escape from Pelican Bay. The original planners, however, did not have the foresight to realize that some prisoners would spend decades there, some of them in what became infamously known nationally as the SHU—or Security Housing Unit, now home to Charles Manson.

It did not work out as expected. Inmates successfully sued the state for violating their Eighth Amendment rights to "cruel and inhumane punishment" in what would be a groundbreaking federal court decision to protect prisoners from excessive force—including burning them and oftentimes needless shootings while in closed spaces preventing escape.

Green knew little about any of this, but the psychiatrist recruiting him to Pelican Bay had convinced him that he had a career position in paradise—no emergency call, good wages and benefits, autonomy of practice, and pristine living conditions outside the wall in the vicinity of beautiful Oregon beaches minutes away. He elected to live on the beach in Brookside, Oregon.

On the Virginia doctor's first morning he awakened to the fog beginning to burn off the tiny harbor, where he saw in the distance surreal silhouettes of tiny fishing boats climbing up the white-capped surf and then disappearing in descent. He had seen this during the Crescent City earthquake of 1964, when boats were being tossed around like paper cups in a fountain's pond. Now it was April 1996, and the court order in the Madrid decision was just kicking in. No more mentally ill inmates in the SHU. Years later he would see this infamous "prison within a prison" on national TV: the notorious SHU with its 1056 cells designed to keep California's worst of the worst in long-term solitary confinement under conditions experts could have told DOC officials would likely cause sensory deprivation syndrome with hallucinations and psychotic states.

These mental decompensations would be much like the findings in normal volunteers subjected to long periods of isolation without alteration in light or environment stimulus. Studies by Donald Hebb, professor of psychology at McGill University decades before, had conducted translational research which was introduced to the British Army in Northern Ireland and other wartime facilities to extract confessions from terrorists and revolutionaries. Hebb, one of the more celebrated psychologists in the late 1940s and 1950s, is known as one of the fathers of hierarchical organizational theory, the basis of modern computer memory organization. Hebb was also alleged to have been involved with research sponsored by the Central Intelligence Agency (CIA) in the 1950s in a program now known as MK-ULTRA because of his formal association with psychiatric colleague with whom he was not even on speaking terms at McGill, Dr. D. Ewan Cameron, now, in fact, known to be funded by the CIA.

The solitary housing units is where the most difficult and violent inmates were caged, but the SHU was not intended to break down gangsters in California—oftentimes just for their own safety from hits out of gangland or instigation of trouble in the yards—or escape. Inmates prevailed in the yards. Psychiatrists were brought in to examine residents of the SHU to assess them for the new syndrome identified by staff psychologists as "The SHU Syndrome." Fortunately, Green was a graduate of McGill University and had studied under Hebb. He probably knew the syndrome better than anyone, but there was more to Pelican Bay and its notorious SHU than sensory deprivation from long-term solitary confinement—lots more.

Like most concentrations of the alienated, dyssocial, and seriously mentally ill that are the focus of this book, Pelican Bay Prison would be a study of the bizarre and oftentimes horrifying realities of the seemingly oxymoronic euphemism, "correctional psychiatry." Could there really be something like that, wondered Green? He recalled the signs over the gates of Monthausen Concentration Camp: "Arbeit Macht Mann Frei"—work makes man free. Could it really be that bad, as rumors had it from the Madrid case, or could a psychiatrist actually use his skills to help humanity, regardless of their sins—and society, regardless of the seeming impossibility of any solution to extreme felony violence? Maybe he could just help support the Constitution of the United States. That is pretty much what the court ultimately settled for in 2011 when the *Madrid v. Gomez* case (1995), an Eighth Amendment case, was finally settled and California agreed to refrain from using excessive force, improving health care, and removing prisoners with mental illness from the SHU. Green would make his contribution to the settlement. He would also have the education of a lifetime that cannot be obtained at any medical school.

As the heavy steel gate clanked shut behind him, Green entered the guard house to get clearance for entry into the prison. His paperwork had already been processed, and he was rather nonchalantly handed an ID tag and a full metal jacket. He did not think it smart to ask what that was for; certainly the recruiting agent had not told him of getting shot. He would, however, quickly find out. The construction of Pelican Bay Prison was like that of fortified castles over the redouts of Wales in the Middle Ages. They were built to be impenetrable. Nobody in and nobody, but the most closely scrutinized, out. That would be an experience of spiritual renewal Green had never felt before; every evening that big steel gate slammed shut behind him and he was free in pastoral El Norte country.

Green would soon learn the rhythms of Pelican Bay, the climaxes of sirens blasting the warning of lockdowns—not escapes or invasions of gangsters rescuing their own. He would learn the psychology of violent men locked out forever from both street wars and their weaponry. And, he would see how these men with no hope made their own weapons in the most ingenious manner. It was a form of genius—mad genius, and Green grew to respect this genius, although being repulsed by it. He soon learned to love his heavy and burdensome metal jacket but was relieved to take it off in the SHU, ironically, one of the safest places on earth he soon came to realize.

Pelican Bay has 1056 cells for solitary confinement. These are the 8 × 10 foot cells made of smooth, poured concrete. They have no windows but only fluorescent lights staying on 24 hours a day. A SHU inmate could expect to be kept for at least 22 hours every day in his "house," only being able to look out through a perforated steel door at a solid concrete wall. Food is delivered twice a day through a slot in the cell door. Occasionally an inmate in the SHU might hear an iron door, even his own, swing open with the touch of a button by a guard in a central control booth. Truly "supermax," one prisoner at a time for a shower or mandatory 5 hours per week of outdoor exercise in a cement yard called a "dog run." The dog run is the length of three cells with a roof only partially open to the sky. The control booth guard has total control with that button and is armed to kill anyone from his six-pod domain that contains eight cells each. The SHU was to be state of the art, modeled after Florence Federal Penitentiary in Arizona. It was one of 21 new prisons built in California in the 1980s and 1990s, but it was different, as who went in would not come out alive until the boss in Sacramento decided it was time—or the sentence was up, which would rarely be the case in the SHU. They were lifers, and all were murderers.

Green heard from a guard the first day about the original sin in designing and constructing Pelican Bay. The threat would not be from escape or invasion. That was the fortress mentality. Basically nobody could be trusted, he learned that first day. Soon after construction, a guard discovered a peculiar aberration in the concrete wall. Under lockdown, construction crews came in and found they could remove a disguised slab of concrete that was the door to a cave filled with weapons. That would be filled and sealed. No more were found—at least that Green heard of. But, the threats were always from the inside, and who outside the walls in this lush green Irish coastal vista cared? Nobody cared. And for one of the top 10 nation-states in the world, at most a handful of its 37 million citizens, and a single Federal Judge, The Honorable Thelton Henderson, would bring new eyes and ears inside this medieval construct draped with international correctional architecture fame—those of psychiatrists like Green under the *Madrid v. Gomez* decision.

It was a rare sunny morning when Green first viewed B yard. All seemed calm. Prisoners mingled in groups probably exchanging war stories of LA sunshine, a rare experience for them here. Most inmates came from a 1-square-mile area of LA, and most of them were ME, Mexican Mafia, and they were there for murder. Nobody admitted murdering anyone to Green. Everybody he interviewed had been framed. Early on in his stint, however, he read their "C" files as well as their medical files. That was until he was politely asked by a DOC psychiatrist from Sacramento not to read the "C" files. The prison medical director even told him she would not want to read them—for good reason. Of the 100 inmates Green interviewed, only a handful had not murdered more than one. Many, he could tell, were probably good for several. There were some gory ones—revenge murders. A girlfriend of a Sureno gang leader was carved up and branded with Norteno markings.

He asked his escort what Norteno markings were and learned what they meant. The escort explained that the main goal of the corrections officers was to keep the gangsters from killing each other even though inmates control the prison yards.

The escort nodded to the yard where men loitered, soaking up the sun before another El Norte downpour—the constant shower treatment for Anderson Street ME gangsters to cool them off. A big black guy started screaming at him from a dog cage at the end of the yard. Green could not understand him, but knew he was looking right at him.

"Crazy. Getting his daily airing. Sometimes they shut up after that."
"He's hallucinating, I think."

The escort shrugged his shoulders. "He's extremely dangerous. So, don't talk with him unless he's in a cage."

"Cage?"

"You'll see. Guys like that don't just walk around here. They're moved in cages on wheels."

"Who's that?" The guard glanced towards the yard. "No that guy in gray coveralls picking up trash. Looks like a senior citizen with all that silver hair."

"He's a trustee. You ever heard of Joseph Remiro. Symbionese Liberation Army?"

Green dialed his mind back to Woodstock and Jimmy Hendricks on stage seeming to light the night sky with raging guitar licks. "Patty Hearst."

"Yup. Lots of celebrities here."

"He's white. I thought they were black."

"No only Field Marshall Cinque, Donald David DeFreeze, was black. He founded it after meeting up with the Vinceremos Brigade in Soledad and then escaped. He would avenge racism. Got Patty Hearst to spread the wealth of her father and join the revolution."

"She was brainwashed."

"So they say. She could have walked but stayed with DeFreeze. Here's the law library. They spend a lot of time in there doing research on their cases for the jailhouse lawyers." He paused for a moment, then stopped, squinting into the sun. "Doesn't help them much, but riots have gone down since it opened."

He saw something, and Green was trying to pick out something in the crowd that would have gotten his attention.

Then the blare of sirens jolted him. The escort almost knocked him to the ground with a back swing to the chest.

"Hit the wall. Back to the wall."

Green stood in the shade still trying to see what was going on in the crowd. The sirens whooped like an air raid.

"It's a fight. You have just a few minutes to stay out of line of fire. Everybody hits the ground now and anyone standing is shot. Don't move."

It was a sight out of a World War II documentary, something that might be seen in a prisoner of war camp. The yard was soon covered with prone bodies. Not a limb moved. Guards with shotguns entered the yard ready to fire at anyone who made a threatening move. They stopped over three bodies and manacled them. The black guy in the cage was yelling louder. That was the only sound as five men paced towards the cell block.

"It's a lockdown. Very common. They get these guys out and then everyone goes to his cell and everything is shut down until we find out what happened here."

"Like"

"Some transaction. There's deals made out there. There's deals gone bad."

Ramirez hadn't even moved and just continued picking up trash.

This was initiation. Tomorrow would be the SHU and its celebrities.

It was 3 days into Pelican Bay, and Green had not been back to the yards. He thought that liking the peace, quiet, and security of the SHU was a bit strange and became impatient, getting soaked in a downpour while all the gates for transit from one unit to another had to be synchronized. An athletic appearing man had just entered the holding area. They both waited, dripping wet, for the last gate to open; the formidable SHU was right in front through the barren, wired causeway. It was something out of *Blade Runner.* They looked at each other.

"How do you like working in the SHU?" Green opened the conversation.

"I actually like working here," the man said.

That clicked and permitted him to say what seemed really crazy. "It's so serene in there." They looked ahead to the monstrous fort through the barbed wire overhang on the steel fences. "I feel comfortable and take off my vest."

"Right, that's the general attitude here. I'm Dr. Shatress, a psychologist here. You must be the new Forensic Psychiatrist. We all know each other in this shower stall, and I did not recognize you."

"I'm Doctor Green." He paused before forcing the matter, but there was not much private time for consultation at Pelican Bay. But people talk to strangers. "You think there is this SHU Syndrome."

"Sure. We like it there because its quiet with a soft light. Security is hundred percent. But we leave everyday. These guys will never see the light of day or even feel this."

"I saw a guy yesterday. I was at one end of a long table and the prisoner was at the other with two guards holding cast iron clubs over his head. He was cuffed to the back of the chair facing me 15 feet away."

"Sure, and he makes one move towards you, and his head is squashed like a rotten pumpkin," the veteran quietly responded, as if, "welcome to Pelican Bay."

There was a loud buzzing and click as the gate began to slide open. They walked in together to what was actually a great place to work as a psychiatrist and psychologist, but hell on earth for lifers.

The bare room was as silent as a chapel after a funeral, but nobody was praying there. Nobody was there; the silence was eerie, as he waited for number six on his list of 30 for examination; Carlos Fernandez. He was dry now, and quick to remove the full metal jacket. Nobody can harm you here, unless you ask for it. This is the safest place on earth, Green thought to himself. Fernandez was a big man with a neatly trimmed mustache and penetrating black eyes. They fixed on him from 15 feet away as the hombre settled into the uncomfortable pose—chest pressed tightly to the chair's back. Fernandez seemed oblivious to the cast iron truncheons over his head.

"I'm Dr. Green. You were told I was going to come to see you? I'm a psychiatrist. 'What are you in here for?'."

Green was surprised. A soft and polite voice replied in articulate English.

"Murder one, but I'm here in solitary for my own protection. There's a contract on me out there."

Green was a bit stunned and thinking paranoia. But, no, this was Pelican Bay; so better believe it.

"How you holding up in here. Not too much to do. Pretty lonely."

He could see the man's eyes watering.

"Not good, doc. My mom she just died."

Fernandez's cheeks were glistening now. It's not like the guards had Kleenex for him.

"You've been down before like this?"

"A lot. Even before I got here. Can't sleep."

"The noise?"

"The noise? Doc there's no noise here at night. Just a constant whirring sound. You get used to that. Noise? That doesn't last long. You seen an extraction, Doc?"

"No, no. I haven't."

"You will. Guys get scared and yell. They get gassed, strapped to a stretcher and are gone."

This guy's no psychopath. Shartress already clued him in. "These are warriors. They are loyal. They are antisocial behavior disorders, but inside their gang armies they are loyal and trusted. They know little of the Euro-American world, other than what they see on TV—a bunch of fools and comedians. They're in a war and they're in business." Indeed they are, he would soon discover.

Green presented his case at the end of the day at the review conference attended by all clinical staff. "It was a clear-cut case of Major Depression. He would have to be transferred to another prison under Madrid."

A skinny, bespectacled young man instantly stood up and strutted to the podium reserved, Green thought, for Sacramento dignitaries. He had the thick "C" file" that Green had not been allowed to see. It had all the secrets. And the man in the dull gray suit and stringy tie hanging sloppily from his collar would have some background information. This was Alex Girrard, head of the California Department of Corrections Gang Intelligence Unit, the CIA of inmates moving around and in and out of California prisons. He did not make any contact with the audience, and simply poked his metal glasses to stick above the bridge of his pointed nose as he opened a 4-inch "C" file, which contained sensitive information for which few should have privy—and most did not wish to either.

In a monotonous but definitive voice that was the last word, he read. "Carlos Fernando. Anderson street address. LA. Life sentence for murder." He looked up and then stared at the presenting doctor to get his attention for the final nail in the psychiatrists' newbie psyche. "Fernando is known to be the biggest shot-caller on the west coast. He's kited twenty from Salinas to Baja with green lights, all executed with clean head shots on the street, in a crowd. All left dead for notice, 'Pay for insurance'."

A young blond woman limped to the podium. She seemed too young to limp, but her face showed signs of battle fatigue. She was chief psychologist for Pelican Bay.

It was pretty matter of fact, and obviously her call. She called the shots, it was clear, for psychiatrists and psychologists in this prison. "Put him out in the run for a week. The fresh air will do him good. Next."

"Next"? What kind of word was that for a clinical conference? But this was no ordinary clinical setting. No prison is today, and nor are emergency detention centers.

Green recalled working in the old Monterey County hospital in Salinas, where the Maginot line was drawn between Nordenos and Sudenos. It was his first case presentation. An elderly Hispanic, who spoke no English, had beaten his donkey in a fit of rage and was sitting right behind him playing cards with a smile on his face, totally oblivious to what he was hospitalized for and what was being discussed about him. Green was at one end of the table and the medical director, a burly white man with short gray hair and size 50 white gown, listened impatiently to Green's academic presentation.

> "OK, he's a keeper. Document your findings and let's Riese him to get him on Haldol."
>
> "What happened to the donkey?"
>
> "The donkey's dead. Next."

Green had completed his list for the SHU and still had time remaining on his temporary contract at Pelican Bay. There was plenty to do. Thus, the director of psychiatry assigned him to the general population in A and B yards. Having experienced the 100% security of the SHU, he was uncomfortable for his personal safety. The director of psychiatry was a bit bemused.

> "Dr. Green, I must say we get a little careless here, because nothing really happens in the lines."
>
> "The lines?"
>
> "I mean the clinics in A and B units. The nurse running those clinics is a corrections officer and is armed."
>
> "I would still prefer to have a guard present in the clinic with me. I'm worth a lot here as a hostage. I know the SHU has the worst of the worst, but the general population certainly has some very dangerous men too."

Director Mallory was a big man at over 6′ 5″. He probably was not a soft target because of his size. Green was 5′ 9″.

Mallory leaned back in his swivel chair and said, "We want you to stay here. We're recruiting and pay well with good benefits. You want a guard today, you got it."

Back in the free fire zone, Green entered the clinic on A unit. The nurse was a muscular 6 footer with shaved head and bulging muscles filling his scrubs. He could not see the gun and assumed it was a shoulder holster.

"Good to have you on board. We have 10 men in the line today. I bring them in when you tell me. No rush. They aren't going anywhere. Take all the time you need."

"And the guard?"

"He's taking care of something right now, but he's assigned here for your line today. Have some coffee while we wait?"

"Sure."

Green looked through the meshed windows. An inmate was standing in front of him, a very distinctive white guy with a handlebar mustache. Green felt the man was staring at him while casually sipping his morning coffee with a sense of peculiar wariness. There was a certain deliberate manner about this guy.

"Dr. Green, Officer Robertson's here now. He'll be standing outside your interview room; so, you hit the alarm and he's right at your door to help."

This officer was his insurance for the day. Green reached out and shook his hand. He liked the big hand and strong grip. "Thanks for helping me. Hope I don't need you."

"If you do, doc, I'll be right here."

"Thanks." He had no more time, because Nurse Stevens came in escorting number 1 on the line. He was not very threatening—a small black kid, about 160 pounds with good grooming and anxious expression.

"James Anderson, I'm Dr. Green."

He shook the man's hand. That is important. Even the worst beast in this prison liked respect, and a handshake meant you saw the prisoner at least as human in this otherwise inhumane environment.

The door closed behind him, and Green motioned for Anderson to sit on the other side of the small table with his back to the wall. Green waited until he was seated and then sat with his own back toward the door with just enough wiggle room to make a rapid escape if things went bad.

"So, Mr. Anderson, you're here for a major felony?"

The voice was soft and cautious. "Murder 1"

"What'd you do?"

"Nuthin. I was framed."

"OK, what were you convicted of."
"Killing a 7-11 clerk."
"How. I mean what were you charged with doing to her."
"Shooting her in the chest."

Green paused to try getting a read on the man's face to see if he was telling the truth or lying. He knew he was lying, but did Anderson know? This inmate was not intimidating and Green thought he could handle him alone.

"Ah, when?"

He had no opportunity to complete the question, when the door blasted open and Robertson literally dove across the table. "Anderson, down on your belly, hands behind your back."

Green was in a state of shock. He wanted to say, "hey no problem with this guy."

Robertson was sitting on the prone man cuffing him. He dragged him out without even seeming to notice Green.

"Doc, you stay here. There's a stabbing in the yard. We're on lock down."

Even after some scares in the military, Green had never really felt this frightened. The door was open, and time seemed to spin in seconds like fast forward. A stretcher almost rolled over his toes. The body of a white male was profusely hemorrhaging from what seemed to be his liver. There was another room next to the clinic. The line was all prone and cuffed. Robertson stood over them while the crime scene just outside the clinic was secured. The yard was cleared. Two guards were standing in the middle of it. One held a bloody shank, while the other finished locking the white inmate in cuffs and foot chains. It was the same guy. The guy with the handlebar mustache. So, why was he staring at the clinic? Green would never know.

The nurse stopped briefly. "That's it for the day, Doc. We're on lockdown. If you want to see patients, then go to B yard."

Green went to B yard, but that was empty too, and the guards were carrying away another inmate. Not too hard to figure out—a double homicide. The whole prison was locked down.

"That's why I come up here from San Francisco." The psychiatrist was a distinguished looking professional dressed in a pinstriped suit with perfectly groomed silver hair.

"I bring a suitcase of novels and read at least one a day up here."

The psychiatrists were all gathered in a lounge outside the director's office. They were all veterans here and accustomed to lockdowns. One of them had just returned from Virginia where Green worked. These were travelers, and most liked Pelican Bay for its downtime—about half of every work week. Perfect to catch up on your reading.

The senior psychiatrist acknowledged Green being new here—at least to the general population.

> "Where you coming from, Dr. Green?"
> "Virginia."
> "Oh, that's nice. What brings you out here?"
> "Just a change of scenes. And yourself?"
> "I'm an analyst."
> "What's your impression of this place?"
> "You ever go to the cell blocks? I walk past the cells. That's the only object relations constancy these prisoners have. Just a person—most know I'm a doctor—or even a psychiatrist. It helps keep their sanity. This is just a zoo here."

The director came out of his office. "There's an extraction going on. I would like you to come and see it."

The cell block was multitiered with an open space kind of like a Hyatt. But this was not Hyatt Regency. It was barren, just gray, whether gray floor, gray ceiling, or gray steel stairs, walkways and cells. A parade of officers introduced themselves before a video camera. That was the only sound, besides the screaming of a man from the upper deck. Green figured he was having auditory hallucinations and was terrified by his voices. The guard could not get him to shut up. Extraction was the emergency psychiatric response in cases like this.

> "I'm Sergeant Rice," the first in the parade reporting to the videotaping. "I will be instructing him about the procedure."
> "I'm Sergeant Ramirez. I will be taking the inmate down if he does not follow instructions."

An officer stepped before the camera with a container. "I will be doing the chemical restraint with Mace if Sergeant Ramirez can't take him down physically."

And so on. Green could not recall how many. He was a bit stunned, having never seen anything like this. Soon the echoes of their boots would interject the rattling of steel on boots with the terrified screams of the inmate far above.

Soon there was only the sound of screams—then an eerie silence. The sole echoes of clanking steel in the vast armory-space told him the inmate did not cooperate; he had about 30 seconds before getting maced.*

The troops in their hazmat combat suits were now approaching. Suddenly, the huge cell block was a dead silence. One could see why. Another stretcher rolled by, a muscular black male bound tightly like a mummy. In fact, he looked dead. He was

* www.prisonlegalnews.org/news/1995/aug/15/pelican-bay-ruling-issued/; www.fedcrimlaw.com/visitors/prisonlore/romano2.html; www.google.com/search?q=Pelican+Bay+Prison+Extraction&rlz=1T4GGHP_enUS474US474&tbm=isch&tbo=u&source=univ&sa=X&ei=8iJAVLeCEenSigL2yoGIDg&ved=0CD0QsAQ&biw=1366&bih=545

unconscious and made no movements. Green had no idea how he was put under so fast. He showed no signs of being maced. He was simply unconscious, perhaps hit, either intentionally or accidentally by the gas gun bullets in the former case or butt in the latter. How was this guy put under so fast? Don't ask and don't tell is the culture in Pelican Bay that one learns fast to survive. And, Green gained trust by not pushing the rules—that is the rule of Pelican Bay, whether they were legal or not. In fact, a guard walked up to him after the extraction. "Doc, I wonder if you would see this guy up in that upper tier." He pointed into the upper corner cell. "Every time I walk by him he's somebody else. I think he has this multiple personality."

Perhaps he did. Green figured, according to the literature, that he should see at least one multiple personality in his entire career. This was probably going to be it, but he politely declined. He had learned that prisoners had weapons good at 30 feet. No mesh could stop them. They had to have pens by law, which they sharpened at the point, slipped them into the milk straw and wetted the missile into a crude but deadly accurate arrow. The power for the cross-bow was the elastic from their underwear pants. Deadly from 30 feet—right into the jugular vein. To make them deadlier, the sharpened tip was dipped in "gas," the feared weapon at Pelican Bay. Gas is urine and feces, incredibly brilliant biological warfare designed for septicemia and death.

> "Thanks, I'd like to see this man, but I have to attend a meeting."

The guard seemed genuinely disappointed. Green thought he actually was concerned about the guy. The guy just extracted? Well, he was going to the infirmary for treatment. He would get a butt-full of Haldol and sedative to shut him up. The cell block was silent, because everyone knew the next could be he.

Pelican Bay holds all of the most violent mentally ill offenders—hundreds of them. They are wheeled around in cages, standing almost invisible behind steel mesh. A psychologist, he heard, actually would wheel several of them together and have group therapy sessions. But, you could not even see them because of the tight steel mesh to stop them from gassing you. Green did see two of them who he knew were there by mistake and got them transferred. That was about all the good he did at Pelican Bay. One was a DUI white guy from El Norte County who was illegally sentenced to Pelican Bay. Nobody is sentenced to Pelican Bay. You are sent there. The other looked like a Hispanic. Hard to tell through the tight mesh, but he spoke Spanish. He also spoke English.

> "Why I'm here?" He seemed desperate for somebody—anyone to listen just for a minute. "I'm Native American. Broke into a liquor store in downtown LA and stole some booze. They thought I was Hispanic—a gangster—and sent me here."

Both were transferred to more appropriate facilities. So, that was good. They might survive to have some life outside one day.

He had one more assignment, teaching a new psychiatrist how to work-up a patient for Madrid in the SHU. The psychiatrist was a child psychiatrist. He asked the initiate what he thought of the prisoner.

> "He shakes. He has classical ADHD."

Yes, he did, and, if you examine all these prisoners, you would find most of them do. In fact Pincus and Tucker found the majority of prisoners—even before the influx of the psychotics into prisons—to be brain damaged from severe head injuries and even epileptic. Green was so interested in this observation that he met with the head of psychiatry from DOC in Sacramento, a nice guy and clearly concerned for inmate health.

> "I know, Dr. Green. This is a big problem, but Sacramento is never going to add ADHD to the list of psychiatric conditions requiring transfer or special accommodation for psychiatric disability."

He knew that, like most serious offenders, ADHD screening can detect causation of conduct disorder early. Treatment, particularly with the family, can reduce incarceration. Wolfgang found that 50 years ago that over 95% of the most serious offenses are committed by 1% of the delinquents he studied. His statistics parallel the findings of arrests with teens with ADHD too closely not to beg research into the association. Of course there is going to be no screening here at Pelican Bay. As his first corrections officer guide told him, "the people want us to keep these people off their streets. That is what we do here, and that is all we do."

Research is desperately needed into possible correlation between Wolfgang's cohort of 10,000 young males and California DOC's cohort of prisoners (*Suicidal Mass Murder*). It is clearly not going to happen in California or anywhere else as long as the people of California, and every state, actually believe that even the supermax fortress of Pelican Bay is going to keep the bad guys off the street or from committing crimes on their streets from prison. Fernandez probably wanted to get closer to LA to enforce insurance on his dealers from Anderson Street or, he was afraid of a hit up north. He had to get to Corcoran down south. Pelican Bay is the White House for gangs and drugs in California.

Fernandez was president then. Now what for this shot-caller? He accepted this as his executive office, a rather drab and unceremonious one, and not oval. It was to be his cell forever, unless he got shanked or agreed to debrief for the gang intel guys and assume a new identity. For el chapos like Fernandez, that is a tough bargain for freedom. The money is too good in prison. He will get out. He is confident in that, and there is some progress. Now there need not be extractions, because the prisoner can be tranquilized in his cell. Gas guns and mace are hardly therapeutic for psychosis. This is very recent, however, and too late for many mentally ill offenders killed or maimed for life by extractions before Madrid required videotaping and some accountability. Solitary confinement for managing auditory hallucinations? Every week one can read of a seriously mentally ill inmate either killed in physical restraint scuffles with guards, or more recently dying. Most recently one medicated with psychotropics sensitizing the body to heat died of dehydration in solitary confinement at New York's infamous Rikers Island jail.

The criminalization of serious mental illness has resulted in a regressive legal and political trend toward a sort of dumb and blind collusion between otherwise adversarial politicians, U.S. Department of Health and Human Services officials at both state and federal levels, along with hospital administrators scared of human rights activists bent on preventing the restriction of anyone's rights without fair trial—after the fact, that is, and not, as in the murder and mayhem of an Elliot Roger, before through his preventive detention. In most headline cases, such a constitutionally correct wait allows burial of the dead and, commonly, the suicidal perpetrator alike. Therefore, after the fact, nothing has to be done except explain to the press and decry another senseless suicidal rampage murder. That, for example, would be the system failure in simply allowing Elliot Rodger to keep preparing for his deadly attack on University of California, Santa Barbara students before killing himself, or simply executing Aaron Bassler in Mendocino County with a police sniper before he killed anymore. Bassler's father had pleaded with mental health authorities and the police to commit his son, because he knew Aaron suffered from schizophrenia. But this was to no avail; Mendocino County never enacted California's Laura's Law that enforced antipsychotic medication under court-ordered and -supervised case management of dangerous psychotics like Aaron Bassler; that, however, was too expensive and costly for Mendocino County. A police sniper's bullet is a lot cheaper; Aaron Bassler is no longer a dangerous psychotic but is unceremoniously 6 feet under instead, legally executed in the bush like a trophy buck. Except this is not really hunting; so, more likely than not, Mendocino County is dealing with postshooting trauma in one of its officers forced to kill in lieu of preventive detention and another million to replace him on the street. Again, it's all about cost shifting; this is not under the authority or budgeting for public care of the seriously mentally ill. In other words, it was a public safety cost, and it was a "good shooting."

Then another really serious problem arises in the public consciousness, all but numbed with atrocities in their own communities by now. This new problem is about those who do not kill themselves or who are not killed in the act of suicidal rampage murders. The circus of a trial in Texas over the sanity and ability to tell right from wrong legally in the double homicide of the American Sniper, for example, requires more than explanation. It will require lifetime detention after the hospital repeatedly refused responsibility for providing necessary care for psychotic active Marine reservist, Eddie Routh, who was obviously so dangerous that nobody who knew him, including closest loved ones, wanted to be anywhere near him! We will not have explanations from the victims in these cases; they are both dead. But, for Kyle and Littlefield's killer, room will now have to be made in state prison or the nearly extinct facility known today as a state psychiatric hospital, almost entirely reserved for those whose dangerousness was ignored until after the fact—in this a double homicide that quite obviously, if reviewing the killer's psychiatric records, was preventable had clinical arrogance, possibly mixed with ignorance of a disease presenting as paranoid psychosis, not stood in the way of hearing desperate pleadings of a family terrified, just like Aaron Bassler's father and Elliot Roger's parents, of their son's untreated psychotic illness.

The suicidal rampage killers who are stopped before their own death, as in the cases of Routh, Gonzalez, Breivik, and Loughner, will require Corrections Psychiatry. Whatever that title bestows upon a clinician, it means that an inmate in jail or prison must be cared for during eruption of psychosis in the course of serious mental illness that, according to the rulings of the court, does not even exist. The shell game that is public psychiatry, endangering families, patients and the public alike, was temporarily and fatefully stalled in the scandalous wake from Rikers Island. The psychiatrists in California, once silent and choosing to remain on the sidelines when Lanterman Petris Short deactivated involuntary commitment decades before, actually dared speak out in favor of bringing back the state hospital for psychotic and suicidal men and women before they kill others and/or themselves.

There can be little room for tolerating murder/suicide every day on the front pages. Police explanations and trials, although seemingly providing closure, are proving to make less and less sense to the reader; quick and sealed multimillion dollar settlements promise no relief, although silencing some victims' family members. What will it take to make another Agnew or Northern State Hospital? Simply put—an most tragically—it will take more gory and "senseless" slaughter and increasingly disturbing public suicides. In the latter case, after all, are we to start reading Freud and actually believe that we want to die—not live and die? Are we simply lemmings racing en masse for the cliff following our basic instincts to procreate and then turn to dust from Freud's "Beyond the Pleasure Principle?" We are not there yet, but the sense of urgency is rising like thick red mercury in an ever more transparent world of TV and cell phone cameras.

As Winerip and Schwirtzfeb (2015) discuss about the brutality at New York's Rikers Island, there was gross incompetence on behalf of staff and administrators in an inmate's death, a mentally ill former Marine who had been confined to an solitary confinement from disruptive behavior most likely caused by fulminating psychotic hallucinations like the apparent wild man caged in the prison yard at Pelican Bay Prison. He suffered as he overheated and finally succumbed; the family was rapidly paid off with one more sealed settlement in the 7 figures.

> A New York State watchdog agency overseeing jails and prisons has found that gross incompetence by medical personnel and correction officers at Rikers Island led to the death of a mentally ill inmate who was found naked and covered in feces after being locked in a cell for six days. (See www.topics.nytimes.com/top/reference/timestopics/people/w/michael_winerip/index.html.)

Is this the urgency necessary for change, or will it take many more headlines like this to say the obvious. The treatment of psychosis and suicidality is simply too complex for corrections guards turned mental health professionals through a quick course in Psychiatry that takes Psychiatrists 12 to 14 years of post-high school education to learn. These are among the most complex and challenging patients in all of medicine to care for, yet our political leaders, public officials, and courts simply refuse to accept that fact. So, then, bring the doctors—even psychiatrists—into places like Rikers Island and Pelican Bay? Just as in the case of preventing suicides and violence on campuses, where are they going to come from? Minimally trained physician assistants rushed through brief postgraduate training in Psychiatry to be supervised at a ratio of 10–1 by somebody hardly more thoroughly trained than a PA—or, maybe 100–1—whatever the cheapest and defensible leverage proponents of least restrictive alternatives can conjure up? This is what is increasingly known as The Dumbing Down of Medicine. And, Pelican Bay or Rikers Island were to be considered by the judiciary the least restrictive? Compared to what? How is this comparable to assisted treatment under court supervision with day care and outpatient management by a psychiatrist—or even a psychiatric inpatient unit of a community general hospital or state hospital not crammed with more psychotic killers already preparing for an Eddie Routh, inevitably headed there by default after failed management in prison. Routh was another victory for Texas prosecutors whose public contempt for psychiatry and psychiatrists is legion; there will be more, as police get better at disrupting suicidal rampage murders before the psychotic can take that last shot saved for himself. Obviously in Mendocino County, the commissioners did not consider the realities of "least restrictive alternatives" under California law—namely Laura's Law. In fact, shooting Aaron Bassler to death in the county's back country proved the most restrictive alternative—namely his execution based on the prediction—already determined to be impossible for anyone with any level of training to do—that he would kill an officer if not pre-emptively executed as soon as a county sniper could finally get a bead on his head and drop him for good. Isn't this how the debacle of shutting down state hospitals began with Lanterman–Petris–Short? Professionals, whether doctors or policemen, are incapable of predicting behavior, whether violent or suicidal behaviors. So, what justified Mendocino County Sheriffs Department's execution of Aaron Bassler based on prediction of his dangerousness—at least to them. Bassler shot at them? But, how did they know he would shoot at them again? So, going back to Monahan's studies on prediction of violence, flipping the coin twice and getting heads does not predict that you get it with the third flip. Yes, the judiciary has inherited a dangerous body of law from Lessard in Wisconsin and LPS in California; it is time they talk it over and decide it is bad law that needs to be reversed, regardless or the cost of reopening and reconstructing psychiatric hospitals, both at the local and state levels; criminalization of serious mental illness has been a public safety and public health disaster! More simply stated, this nation must provide the financing to rebuild a state hospital system that is separate from the forensic hospitals which hold the insane murderers who could not be swept under the rug, along with rational levels of step-down community inpatient, day and outpatient assisted treatment programs staffed with competent and reliable case management having court oversight. The benefits for leaving things the way they are will be only for trial attorneys and prison contractors—not the American citizen, whether sick or well. Criminals do not want the dangerously insane lodged with them for years or life. Prison riots are guaranteed. Most corrections officers do not want to practice psychiatry. They do not know how to, and it detracts from their real job of keeping prisons and the inmates sentenced there safe, while preventing their flight.

The result is abuse of the psychotic patient we only hear about in Draconian-like prisons mandated to torture and kill people who dissent. What kind of human rights is that for the United States? But, unfortunately, that is what we now have, and we have it by the hundreds of thousands, from ex-Marine, Murdough, broiled to death for a petty offense one has to search for to incarcerate somebody, to the growing thousands of our once-heroes made crazy by inexcusably horrible military discharge tactics that will inevitably jeopardize preparedness via escalating and stupid combat redeployments. More than 200,000 combat veterans from Vietnam were incarcerated on drug-associated charges in one year alone, and more likely were in jails. We are no doubt almost there again, as the Vietnam veteran dies off in prison, opening up a cell for once-heroes of our War on Terror "who got a little high and went to jail."

Eddie Routh will likely die in prison, one of many mentally ill veterans abandoned by the DVA, left to fester on the streets until he committed a violent crime, and then left to fester in jail. Eddie Routh should never have been in the community in the first place without closely managed voluntary psychiatric treatment or involuntary assisted treatment with court oversight. And, now he will receive corrections psychiatry, which means that if he acts out in prison, he will wind up in a solitary to listen to his own voices while he decomposes even more—or, per chance and the most devious backdoor tactic of the prosecution—a state hospital for the criminally insane. This cannot last. Cook County Jail being the largest psychiatric inpatient unit in America is not a shocker but rather a disgrace to this country that claims leadership in the world for human rights. Until the psychotics—like Jared Loughner—and petty offenders sick on our streets—like Marine Corporal Murdough—receive modern medical care, our politicians and officers have no credibility telling nations like China and Burma to clean up their acts.

Green had plenty of time to think inside the walls of Pelican Bay Prison; the history of psychiatry came back to him. Pinel revolutionized psychiatry when he proved to the citizens of Paris that the mad incarcerated within the Pitié-Salpêtrière Hospital could be safely unchained and even released into the community. There was plenty of downtime at Pelican Bay to think about everything that happened every day. It was like going to the movies everyday with no schedule. Clearly, Green knew it was worse than what Pinel walked into on the lunatic unit of Pitié-Salpêtrière 200 years ago. Those patients, he knew, were better off than these at Pelican Bay. There is a certain brutal honesty to the execution of the psychotic Michael Boyd in the high desert above Albuquerque. His executioner rushed to the scene of his arrest, already surrounded by 40 armed cops. He said he was going to shoot this lunatic's pecker off. Perhaps he did not get that good a shot, but Boyd was filled with enough lead, mostly in the back, to sink him pretty fast even in a dry wash after the monsoon. That cop is charged with homicide. But one has to wonder what Boyd would have had to endure in a state prison as his mental condition decomposed even further and, like the mentally ill in Titticutt in Massachusetts, whether forced incarceration would have been simply another form of torture in the nonexistent discipline we euphemistically call corrections psychiatry.

Dostoyevsky wrote, "You can judge a society by how well it treats its prisoners." How, therefore, will we be judged, and by whom?

## REFERENCES

Joyner, J. 2012. America's prison culture destroying our future. Outside the Beltway, March 31. www.outsidethebeltway.com/americas-prison-culture-destroying-our-future

*Madrid v. Gomez*. 1995. [N.D. Cal. 1995]889 F.Supp. 1146.

Winerip, M. and Schwirtzfeb, M. 2015. *New York Times*. January 22. www.topics.nytimes.com/top/reference/timestopics/people/w/michael_winerip/index.html.

# 11

# Special problems of the homeless

"The city had to do this," Trufyn said Monday, as he credited officials for taking their complaints seriously. "I don't know where the people went. But everybody is gone from here." Robert Aguirre knows where some of the people who lived in the Jungle went. But he's not saying. With "the Jungle" closed, San Jose is trying to keep other homeless camps from replacing it. The city has conducted four such post-Jungle cleanups. But invariably when one site is swept, another pops up. It's why some advocates for the homeless have adopted the phrase "whac-a-mole"—after the arcade game—to describe what can seem like a largely futile, never-ending process. "If it is a game of whac-a-mole, then it's a game played with people's lives," said Poncho Guevara, executive director of Sacred Heart Community Service, a nonprofit organization that has assisted 12,000 people this year who identified themselves as homeless. "The people who have been swept from the Jungle are just sleeping somewhere else now. We're just shifting people around. The problem isn't going away" (Mark Emmons, memmons@mercurynews.com, 12/23/2014).

Silicon Valley makes the international news every day, but usually it is for gifted people doing better and better; clearing out the homeless encampment, known as the Jungle, turned over the shiny crystal rock with Apple's headquarters for the whole world to see what lives on the slime of nearby waterways of San Jose. Bulldozers with police cars, their blue lights flashing, just cleaned a makeshift tent city from under Coleman Avenue overpass so that Jungle inhabitants didn't move there. It's like a futile hunt for moles on your lawn; fill a hole, detoxify it, and the tents pop up somewhere else. Over 600 tons of garbage and 315 grocery carts were hauled out by city contractors and Santa Clara Valley Water District. This was neither a pretty sight—certainly not one Steve Jobs would have liked the world to see—nor Larry Ellison, whose problem-solving abilities and deep pockets simply are obviously impotent. There are 7500 people sleeping in public spaces like the Jungle and Coleman overpass any given night, most of them inside the city limits of San Jose. The assumption is that they need shelter; that is certainly obvious. But, there is an unspoken rule in basically arresting these human beings. Who are they? Don't ask, don't tell. Federal statistics show that The South Bay has the country's highest percentage of unsheltered veterans, with 80.6% of the 718 homeless vets counted in a January census living in places not meant for human habitation. That is likely a number that misrepresents reality of homeless veterans; in 1994 Congressional Testimony it was reported that there were more than 100,000 Vietnam Veterans sleeping on the streets! Today there is more than half that number and growing—at least officially. But who really asks; with a $100 billion/annum institution under the President's cabinet Secretary of Department of Veterans Affairs, there, of course, should be none! But, how many federal administrators and managers from HUD and DOD to DVA does it take to count the veterans returning from war, only to be discharged to homeless shelters, and find them shelter? Of the people booted from the Jungle, 150 have been helped into subsidized housing and another 64 have rental subsidy vouchers and are looking for places to live. Local authorities consider the numbers are encouraging and hope this can become a blueprint for dealing with other encampments. But, there are still more than 200 homeless sites to be cleared, and like moles, they get cleared and detoxified for the comfort, health and public safety of more fortunate residents comfortably housed in million dollar abodes abutting these sites. Accused by human rights workers that they are chasing desperate people from the only homes they can afford, officials express sensitivity. "We've heard that concern and we think it's great that there are so many compassionate people who are concerned about our neediest residents," Bramson, charged with this miserable assignment, said. "It's just a very difficult problem. And a delicate balancing act because on the other side of the fence—sometimes literally—are frustrated residents who want the city to deal more forcefully with encampments that they say are bringing crime and blight into their neighborhoods. In fact, the city has been receiving an increased number of complaints about encampments this month" (www.mercurynews.com/bay-area-news/ci_27194702/aftermath-jungle-city-is-trying-keep-other-encampments).

San Jose, one of the wealthiest cities in the world is also among the worst for homelessness, and most of the bodies encountered are natives of the county! "San Jose-Santa Clara County homeless numbers among highest in nation," said Mark Emmons (memmons@mercurynews.com, 11/22/13).

They are not transients, a contingency that would make this wrecking project a bit more palatable before the eyes of international TV cameras. They are locals, they were recruited after 9/11 to protect their high school peers or they should be in Agnew State Hospital, which nobody cleaning up this hell hole probably ever heard of.

> Today known as the world famous Sun Microsystems/Agnews Developmental Center, the campus-like setting of the former (Santa Clara County) Agnews Insane Asylum consists of a grouping of numerous reinforced concrete, brick, stucco and tile buildings. They are constructed in large rectangular-shaped plans and designed in a Mediterranean Revival style. The buildings are formally placed within a landscaped garden of palms, pepper trees and vast lawns. (www.nps.gov/nr/travel/santaclara/agn.htm)

As generations pass on, historical reality passes on with it and new pseudo-realities evolve to explain the shameful dichotomy of Dickensian poverty pock-marking the burnished glass landscape of the world's richest city and capitol of Silicon Valley. The homeless population roaming through the streets is often faceless and nameless because we really do not know who these people are as they wander to and from their hiding places in stark contrast to the wealth that sustains our cities. San Jose, like other cities with high populations of homeless, such as Los Angeles, Seattle, San Diego, and New York, are the most prosperous cities in America where their real estate demands the highest prices, but have sparse affordable housing. So has it always been this way and only now visible in the stark and gross reality of the Jungle being swept up like Bourbon Street at midnight after Fat Tuesday?

No, it has not. Even adjusting for growth, San Jose had no homeless problem 50 years ago, but only a handful of homeless simply too drunk in downtown central park to stand up. Santa Clara County Hospital Emergency Room treated few if any homeless people and did not even need a psychiatric inpatient unit. There were few, if any, seriously mentally ill patients brought there. There was not even a psychiatry department at this county hospital, not even a single psychiatrist on staff. Agnew State Hospital was nearby. President Kennedy was still alive. But after he was shot, dying along with him was his concept of a community-based mental health system designed to be implemented nationally, reportedly in response to the personal family challenges of his mentally challenged sister, Rosemary, institutionalized for life in rural Wisconsin, a thousand miles from Hyannis Port.

State hospitals around the country were gradually closed and helpless, psychotic patients dependent on them for years were simply boarded on buses in their hospital garb and sent to the inner cities in what proved to be an almost genocidal sequestration of the mentally ill to life on the streets where they would slowly disintegrate and die. Under the rules set forth by Health and Human Services Director Charles Morris, Northern State Hospital was shuttered. "The occasion marked by a busload of elderly, institutionalized chronically mentally ill people delivered to the streets of Seattle with only their original belonging and hospital issued clothing. What became of them may be in a sense unknowable once they were divorced from the community able to care for them" (McGoffin 2011). Homelessness started in epidemic proportions then in Seattle. It was limited, as in central downtown park, San Jose, to a handful of men in Pioneer Square and Skid Row who were too inebriated to stand up before the closure of Northern State Hospital. But, they now all ended up in the gutters of Seattle's rising steel and glass monuments to high technology.

The tragedy of people turned out of shelters quietly became an extinction event. One jumped off a high rise into pedestrian traffic at rush hour and one walked into a Seattle bus. One was a psychiatric patient. The other was his brother. Then, whether one believes the movie *JFK* or not, the wars began, and post-Vietnam, Gulf War One, Operation Iraqi Freedom, and now, the end of the war in Afghanistan and a new presence in the Middle East generated millions of combat veterans alleged to have none or little post-traumatic syndromes from war—maybe 1/5 on the high side. This, as previously described, is more propaganda than the reality of foreign war. Now there are 20-million veterans, most of whom get inadequate or no care from mega-billion dollar institutions charged with their care (Liebert and Birnes 2013).

Ten percent of the homeless in San Jose are veterans, and, likely similar to other cities, reside in the worst and most threatening unsheltered homeless state. Most are seriously impaired and unfit for duty, whether for combat or reintegration back into civilian society, oftentimes having bad paper discharges that deny them VA benefits. Such denial of benefits leaves them to fend for themselves. In 1994, 100,000 Vietnam veterans were homeless and, denied care back when PTSD was not recognized as a medical entity. They simply, like the deprecatory-labeled moles of San Jose, found a new jungle on the urban streets of America, if escaping the fate of 200,000 incarcerated in prison for drug-related charges (Liebert et al. 1994).

San Jose and Seattle are featured here, because they have had such a profoundly burgeoning of homeless populations that correlate with surges in both the seriously mentally ill and neuropsychiatrically impaired combat veterans simply left at the gate of the state hospital or military base, respectively, to fend for themselves in what is not so euphemistically—but now generically known as the "Jungle." In fact, we encounter them in large cities and small towns all over America—not only on traditional skid rows, like New York's Bowery district or San Jose's "Jungle," but in shopping malls, bus stations, public parks, subway platforms, and stretched across steam vents on wintertime street corners. Sometimes they seem on the edge of violence, gesticulating into thin air, denouncing demons that plague them, and at other times sitting silently as if in a dream state. Sometimes, as in New York's Tompkins Square Park on Manhattan's Lower East Side, they will reach out to the upscale yuppie morning joggers who have gentrified the neighborhood, begging for a cup of coffee, or a hit of something to get them through the pain of the day. If we are the sane in our society, those entrusted with some form of social responsibility as we navigate through our lives and jobs, they are collectively like Marley's ghost reminding us of our sins of omission and neglect—the failures of the very society we try to improve with our own lives. Who are they? They are the homeless, a cross section of our population, from children to aged war veterans, who are almost invisible victims of lifetime trauma, hidden in the shadows of our affluent society.

For the overwhelming majority of the homeless, those who choose to live on the streets as well as those forced onto the streets by economic hardship, severe psychiatric impairment is common, and if not already suffering from posttraumatic stress disorder (PTSD) and other diseases, homelessness will ultimately cause them to acquire it. Those seething internally with rage, like Aaron Alexis from the Navy Yard Massacre and Oscar Gonzalez, the White House Fence Jumper, believing the government is tapping into their minds or invisible enemies are tracking them everywhere are from delusional disorders. But then there are those whose personalities have completely decomposed. They exited the real world and now live in a completely isolative universe generated from their own psyches—or what is left of them. They are the chronic psychotics we see battling and gesturing to their demons, invisible to us, but as palpable to them as a nearby lamppost or, more dangerous, to the policeman mandated to so much as even touch them.

Not to put a moral spin on this, although this is an amalgamation of social, economic, and political issues, it is still a moral issue. America's report card on casting the least capable of its citizens into the streets to fend for themselves with no resources and simply as prey for others, is our collective guilt despite the protestations of pundits from the radical ends of our political spectrum unwittingly absolving our politicians and officialdom of abrogating their responsibilities for caring for the gravely disabled among us. And even worse than our homeless veteran population, once again approaching the six figures of 1994, are the large numbers of homeless children. According to a recent report from the American Institutes for Research and the National Center on Family Homelessness (www.homelesschildrenamerica.org/mediadocs/280.pdf), 1 in every 30 children is homeless, a terrifying statistic for American society that bodes so ill for our future. It is almost beyond contemplation, partly because this number is increasing by 8% annually. If that sounds scary, imagine the impact these homeless children will have on society when they become of age. How many will be at risk for being mentally ill? How many will have to rely on whatever social institutions they can find for the rest of their lives, and how many will have learned to prey on others and will practice what they have learned for the rest of their lives? If by intent and policy—or, hopefully, pure dehumanization of Western society—it will be a large pool of manpower for our infantry in case of another ground war in Asia.

Lawrence Jacobs, professor of psychiatry, University of Washington, prophesied such a scenario for future wars in 1969 (personal communication). He could have been prescient regarding the future, because it was the poor who fought in Vietnam; it is the poor—although a different poor—who make up the bulk of our all-volunteer army today to remedy the disastrous consequences of the Vietnam draft. And it is still the poor who were turned away by the Department of Veterans Affairs (DVA) and the rest of society, only turning up with weapons in shopping malls or inside the White House fence, former cannon fodder now to be recycled to the streets and in America's jails. In San Jose they are likened to moles. Drive them out of one garbage dump and they pop up in another. Nationally, there will be a lot of mole whackers needed to sanitize our streets and vacant lots.

In 2010 the federal government found that 1.6 million people experienced homelessness at some point and were sheltered. A major 1999 report produced by the federal government, the Urban Institute, and leading researchers estimated that there were 2.3 million people who experienced homelessness over a given year. While that figure is still cited, the National Coalition for the Homeless tried to compensate for undercounting and put the figure at approximately 3.5 million.

- There were 57,849 homeless veterans recorded in 2013.
- Among persons in homeless families, 58% were children (130,515).

There were 46,924 unaccompanied homeless children and youth on a single night in 2013. Most (87% or 40,727) were youth between the ages of 18 and 24, and 13% (or 6197) were children under the age of 18. Half of unaccompanied children and youth (23,461 or 50%) were unsheltered in 2013.

This population is very difficult to count with any accuracy; see this Urban Institute brief on the issue (www.huduser.gov/Publications/pdf/ahar.pdf).

In a shocking statistic reported in "Health Day," one out of every four homeless children in the United States "require mental health services" (Preidt 2015; www.health.usnews.com/health-news/articles/2015/02/19/mental-health-woes-common-among-homeless-kids-study-finds).

That is 25% of the population of homeless children in need of some form of mental health treatment. These are children who, if left untreated, will be subject to a duration of untreated mental illness, an illness that can metastasize into a variety of psychoses including toxic-induced, schizophrenia and bipolar disorder, in addition to a variety of personality disorders putting them at risk for felonies, whether victim or perpetrator, or prostitutes, whether chicken hawk male homosexual or female heterosexual. And this cohort of mentally ill children will grow into adulthood and will not only become a drain on already limited public health services, but may well present problems to public safety services, especially the police and juvenile justice officers, and ultimately the corrections system. For those children who reach their later teens and seek to enter the military, what types of preexisting conditions will be exacerbated by our endless wars and continuing deployments and further drain the resources of the DVA?

The report goes on to say that the reading and language skills among children in this cohort, ages 5–6, were "well below average." Imagine the impact of this group, now in kindergarten and first grade, on the public school system, particularly upon school guidance counselors and school psychologists. Now imagine this group, if not remediated, entering later grades as states try to reduce school budgets because municipalities are squeaking as they face the need to increase school taxes while the bulk of American communities age.

This is a generation of abuse victims as well, according to the report. "These children have often been exposed to domestic or neighborhood violence, chronic poverty, inadequate health care and other circumstances that place any child at risk of mental health problems," lead author and professor of psychology Mary Haskett said in the news release. Worse, the researchers continue, "As a result of their exposure to those difficult life circumstances—combined with living in a shelter—homeless children are at a much greater risk of developmental delays, social and emotional problems, and problems at school," said Armstrong, who added that "the scale of the problem is huge" (Preidt 2015; ibid).

Add this cohort of children to the already existing adult homeless population in local communities, and the problems for public services is just about insurmountable without the budgets to provide housing. Simply shooing them away from one place to another does not solve the problem. And besides the public health and aesthetic threat they pose to the more fortunate living comfortably at, for example, the rims of San Jose's Jungle, the homeless are a persistent problem for police and first responders, because many, like LA's Marlene Pinnock or Ezell Ford, are unresponsive to authority, difficult to communicate with, fearful to the point of resisting what would be considered help for their situation, and completely unpredictable in trying situations, particularly when confronted by a policeman with a gun and baton on his belt. Certainly the sentinel case of this was Officer Manney's tragic encounter in Red Arrow Park with Dontre Hamilton, who did not legally meet the standards of immediate dangerousness when asleep, but certainly did when awakened. He was shot to death by a Milwaukee policeman whom he threatened with his baton during a "welfare check," essentially the new euphemistic paradigm of psychiatric nursing of the homeless by policemen.

We have read stories in the news about homeless individuals, some of whom are veterans with PTSD committing crimes, committing suicide by cop, jumping the White House fence in an effort to get their own message to the president or, like Miriam Carey who left her home in a delusional state, driving a car like a Formula One race car driver around the Capitol just to get in to see the president. But the case of Ian Stawicki is an interesting and poignant illustration of the extreme dangerousness posed by homelessness, especially the homeless veteran with military skills and an untreated mental illness.

## THE CAFÉ RACER

Kurt Geissel is Seattle's host and caretaker to those needing an escape from their routine of grading papers, writing software programs, discouragement from not selling that certain smash-hit play, or missing recording stardom of Seattle's Grunge Rock scene. This was his Café Racer, known for quirkiness where anyone could feel at home. A distinctive artist with a characteristic shock of white hair, he was known for his ability to create a living room atmosphere for human beings with little in common but wanting to be there.

This was not Seattle's Skid Row. These were not defeated men and violated women surviving life's harsh realities and monotony in shared grandiose delusions as in Eugene O'Niell's "Iceman Cometh." They were simply people gathered in a special space to communicate with others who may be very different in career and background, but with shared love of a place, the funky milieu of the Café Racer in Seattle's hip university district where people enjoyed the company of others in a room away from a stressful world of both home and work. Café Racer features jazz improvisation and a venue for rock bands left behind when Seattle's flourishing Grunge Rock scene went global. Bring your guitar and play it into an open mike on an open stage.

Geissel treats everybody with respect and makes each guest feel at home. Not, of course, for everyone, but home to some in the University District. But, there is a broad spectrum of human needs in this community. Café Racer offered refreshment, good conversation in a relaxed environment, free live music, comfort food, wine, beer, and spirits in a place where anyone could go with his board game or guitar without feeling intimidated and unwanted. A few came for breakfast and stayed until the last band went silent and lights went dark. Seattle is a coffee town. The Racer Café was a special coffeehouse catering to those desiring something different than the national design stamp of a Starbucks, Tullys, and Seattle Coffee on every corner.

One patron, welcomed until he simply disrupted Geissel's special reinterpretation of "Cheers," was Ian Stawicki, a homeless veteran attracted to Seattle by its grunge rock scene of the 1990s. He was irritable and belligerent, but Geissel even took him home to cool him off. Café Racer could be just so tolerant, because Geissel was an artist who incubated and kept alive the creative spirit in people, whether graying grunge rockers, struggling guitarists, or simply folks bringing their own board games to play in a home away from home. One day, however, Geisell had to decide it was either the atmosphere of Café Racer or the intimidating volatility of Stawicki confronting his patrons with inexplicable wrath. Stawicki was known as the "Spider Wolf," a homeless veteran discharged from the army for disciplinary reasons in his late teens and a regular at Café Racer until he was forced to leave one day and told not to return. It was a rare event when Geisell asked a patron to leave, especially one he tried to personally help.

Ian Stawicki somehow communicated to his family that he had awakened one Wednesday morning in a uniquely good mood with plans to help his girlfriend's mother move into a new home in Tacoma. But first, he was going to stop for coffee. Stawicki's sunny mood was a welcome change for his family. The 40-year-old had been erratic, argumentative, and full of rage for years, but especially so recently, according to his father. His uniquely good mood had nothing to do with Seattle's being in full bloom, but, like all too many in the Pacific Northwest, the final decision had been made. Rejected from what may have been his only home—or maybe because he was always on guard because of his delusion of being an agent of the Central Intelligence Agency (CIA)—Stawicki was ready for his own mysterious fate. Breakfast guests were gone for jobs, leaving some regulars behind in the late midweek morning following Memorial Day weekend, 2012. It is a beautiful time in Seattle, because most everything that has flowers bursts into bloom out of the months of cloudy mist, with bright rhododendrons, magnolias, and azaleas. There is promise of a warm summer to come with the snowcapped mountains that ring the city beginning to pierce the seemingly perpetual overcast dome like ice cream cones.

Stawicki walked in that quiet morning at 11 a.m. and was told he was not welcome and was to leave. In defiance of orders to leave the premises, he took a seat at the bar and suddenly pulled out two .45s and shot one patron. He did not order anything. He was death embodied. The body slumped to the floor like a heavy sack of sand blocking the entrance. Some patrons fled through the rear exit as one patron stood his ground and threw a bar stool at Stawicki, then charged him medieval style with shield allowing some friends a distraction—just enough to escape through the entrance blocked with a corpse. Stawicki then paced behind the bar stools and executed three more with head shots and shot the chef. Stawicki left as casually as he entered, sporting in cold blood the hat of one of his victims, maybe an old acquaintance from his grunge rock days. He had had a social relationship with a couple of victims, but that relationship was long gone, probably because Stawicki was too volatile, paranoid, and threatening to comfortably be around anymore. They may have known too that he was no CIA agent. Stawicki was simply out of his mind.

Arriving at this bloodbath, Seattle police set up their command post nearby in the University District. Then another homeless veteran, miles away downtown, caught a patrolman's attention leaning over a woman soaked with blood. Jason Yori came to Seattle for different reasons than Stawicki. His wife had died, and he was attracted by the movie *Sleepless in Seattle*. He quickly ended up homeless and largely sleepless in Seattle himself. A somewhat iconic figure in downtown Seattle, police knew him well for drunkenness, but now a dry drunk preaching sobriety with his cardboard sign for salvation on 7th and Pine. He was hanging out that morning in Freeway Park, an overpass landscaped to soften the noise and exhaust of I-5 traffic below. It was a pleasant respite from sleeping on the streets and was now in full bloom.

Then Yori heard something that instinctively he ran toward. It was a gunshot. Somebody just got shot. Seemingly fearless, he ran to the scene where Gloria Leonidas, a married mother of two, had dropped off a friend and was planning to rejoin him after paying to park. At that ordinary moment in everyone's life, a man grabbed and started beating her. Desperate to survive, she fought while a bystander called 911. She may have knocked one gun to the ground. That was the one that may have jammed. The other .45 did not, and that was the shot bringing Yori to the rescue.

> "I ran up to her right away and there was just a massive pool of blood there," said Yori, 58, who helped along with other bystanders. "I didn't know anything about her, so I spoke to her as a human being who was in the wrong place at the wrong time." Knowing she was dead, he gave her last rites. "I felt really special to be able to do that—for us to be there when nobody else was there with her." (www.seattlepi.com/local/article/Police-credit-felon-for-helping-at-3601132.php)

Yori saw Leonidas's black Mercedes SUV drive off but did not get a good look at the driver. A hospital worker from nearby Virginia Mason Clinic, however, did. The carjacker with the distinctive hat gave her the finger. She jumped from her car and, along with a couple, ran to the hemorrhaging lady and attended to Leonidas. But, as Yori probably knew from battle, "Her eyes were fixed and dilated, and when your eyes are fixed and dilated there's no sense in going further."

A crowd gathered. Medics and the police came. The woman in scrubs from a nearby hospital was giving Mrs. Leonidas CPR as Yori held her. The first officer on the scene knew it was too late to save her. Knowing Yori, he told him to leave, thinking he was part of the problem. Another officer who knew him well told him to help keep bystanders away, which Yori effectively did. Mrs. Leonidas was rushed to Harborview Hospital where she was dead on arrival (DOA). A detective, however, immediately recognized the sketchy description of the carjacker and handgun caliber as matching the mass murder uptown at the Racer Café. Yori stayed to give the detective a statement. The command post mobilized as the Seattle police became aware that a mass murderer was endangering the entire city. The deadly rampage did not end until nearly 5 hours later when, confronted by police miles away in West Seattle, Stawicki dropped to his knees and shot himself in the head. For Stawicki, he would control Seattle on his terms from morning to late in the day and then go out on his own terms, once again leaving reporters and the public to wonder again, what was his motive?

The other homeless veteran, Jason Yori, became something of an unsung hero, however. He thanked his jailers for sobering him up. For two decades he had slept on the streets or in dumpsters for cover. He was in and out of jail for three confirmed felonies, all drug cases, and a criminal trespass conviction. Before he sobered up he had given CPR to another homeless man. A homeless buddy told him to get away because the cops were coming "and things could end badly."

> "I said, 'No, man. You don't do that to somebody'."

No longer under Department of Corrections supervision, he said he was not sure how police would respond to him at the murder scene. But, he was reforming, working to set up a tent city for homeless veterans. Department of Veterans Affairs and the Navy said nothing about Yori—especially dodging the question, "what was this veteran doing on the streets for twenty years?" Officers with the Department of Corrections' Northwest Community Response Unit, forced, instead of DVA, to handle Yori's case in rougher times, said his actions were commendable. Yori gives them credit, too, for helping him stay sober and conviction-free for years.

On a most somber note, however, Jason Yori went to Seattle First Presbyterian Church across the freeway bridge downtown and prayed for Mrs. Leonidas. Discovered there later by reporters, he was told she had two young children. "Yori's striking blue eyes welled with tears. 'I got to thinking, what would it be like to come home expecting your wife to be there, expecting your mom to be there and all of a sudden, she'd been shot'. Later that night, he tried to overcome sleepless in Seattle as he usually does in the church's doorway. For this spring day with everything in bloom and scents of summer finally to come, it was one of the bloodiest for citizens in the Queen City's history. For Stawicki the final decision had been made, and for that he felt good. This would be the last day of his life. Spring in Pacific Northwest, but ironically, it is also the peak time for suicide, usually one of the highest annual rate in America."

> Police credit homeless felon for helping at tragic shooting. Ian Stawicki killed Gloria Leonidas and four others in Seattle. (McNerthney 2012)

Stawicki's family struggled to make sense of the violence. But, those who knew Stawicki say his history is dotted with clues, including failures, social rejection, episodes of apparent delusions, spasms of violence, and a strong interest in guns. Walter Stawicki, 65, believes that his son grew more and more lucid in the hours following the shootings, realizing what he had done, and killed himself to take responsibility. He said that his son was a gentleman, but regrets he didn't act to have his son committed for mental-health care. "I recognized the patterns. I saw him as being manic-depressive."

Ian Lee Stawicki was born in Santa Barbara, California, the first of Walter and Carol Stawicki's three children. The Stawicki family settled on Seattle's Beacon Hill to be close to Carol Stawicki's family. Ian Stawicki showed signs of autism and had learning disorders. He struggled to read, write and focus his attention, his father said. Stawicki went to alternative schools before obtaining a GED diploma. He joined the Army at 17 and was stationed at Fort Drum, New York, and did training in Panama. But Ian Stawicki suffered a head injury from a grenade concussion during a training exercise and was discharged two years later. For its part, the Army has no record of his ever serving in the Army. If he enlisted at 17, perhaps he used a pseudonym.

Following discharge at 19, presumably with the tell-tale and high-risk general under honorable conditions that stripped him of VA benefits, he started his civilian career with likely traumatic brain injury. He never had a career, except for a delusional one as a CIA agent. Jobless, Ian Stawicki began a string of odd jobs, commercial fishing in Alaska and working as a roadie for local bands. His family moved west of the Cascade Mountains to cattle town, Ellensburg, after his military discharge. They settled in a ramshackle property north of the Central Washington University campus where they would see their son sporadically. But, Stawicki was a wanderer, living in Oregon and Washington.

His main interest was Seattle's punk-rock music scene, later transitioning into the late Grunge Rock scene of Pearl Jam. A girlfriend following him in the rock scene described him as charming but paranoid. He was a skilled marksman. He had to have learned weapons in the military. Charming, but a little off, said Jamie Pflughoeft. He was paranoid. "He slept with a gun under his pillow and was a skilled marksman," she said. "I felt like he would protect me. I never felt like he would hurt me in any way," said Pflughoeft, who said she hadn't seen Stawicki nearly two decades" (Sullivan and Martin 2012).

Stawicki started arming himself in his early twenties, all with permits. Stawicki was known to be a violent man, but the state always let him go for lack of witnesses willing to testify when victimized by his explosive assaults. One such witness was a girlfriend who had her nose broken by Stawicki when she tried to stop one of his rage attacks. He smashed her in the face with the phone when dialing 911. His brother said Stawicki blinded him with a similar knockout punch to the face. These were major felony assaults, but charges were always dropped. Law enforcement knew he was dangerous and likely was not surprised he could do something this horrific; they expressed their concerns when prosecutors always dropped charges simply waiting until there would be better evidence to do something about his delusional need to protect from foreign espionage services and obvious dangerousness on the street. They would never get their chance.

Stawicki had no problems purchasing weapons with a permit, using his residential address, "homeless." A girlfriend would later testify that, although feeling secure with him, he was always armed and saw the world as imminently threatening. He was, in other words, extremely paranoid. And, he was explosive. His family was afraid of him. Girlfriends were afraid of him. And the most tolerant of innkeepers in Seattle was so afraid of him that Stawicki was told not to return because of his explosive outbreaks of rage.

> Stawicki, described as a real loud mouth, adopted the nickname Spider Wolf and tried to fall in with a crowd of musicians and

artistic regulars at Café Racer, including Joe Albanese and Drew Keriakedes, two of the shooting victims who socialized with him on a couple of occasions and distanced themselves as they learned more about Stawicki's strange and potentially dangerous behavior. Café Racer owner Kurt Geissel saw it, too, as did other nearby businesses knowing his threatening presence on the streets. "Everybody has their own personality and their own quirks and we don't try to fault people for who they are," Geissel said. "Everyone has a bad day. But he was consistently not all there" (www.seattletimes.com/seattle-news/seattle-shootings-day-of-horror-grief-in-a-shaken-city/).

Walter Stawicki also had seen his son's behavior recently devolve. He told his girlfriend that he was actually married and the father of six, and told others that he was on a CIA death squad, his father said. Though his son had long battled mental illnesses, his father didn't think there was anything they could do to get him help. Andrew Stawicki said that his brother, a victim of earlier assault, didn't want to talk about his delusions. His family never pushed to have Stawicki committed, because they'd never heard him threaten to hurt himself, Walter Stawicki said. Now, Walter Stawicki regrets he didn't force a mental-health intervention, even if it meant lying to say his son posed an imminent risk. "We let him down and we let a lot of other people down, too, by not effectively being able to intervene. I'm grieving for him, I'm grieving for his mother, I'm grieving for his brother. I'm grieving for six other families.... One of the things I flagellate myself with is: You should've kept coming back at it. Just because the door didn't open, keep banging at the door. Keep banging at the door," he said. Walter Stawicki himself never felt in imminent danger with his son. "We were more worried in the way he was going to get himself in trouble with his mouth and his actions and get killed under a bridge someplace," he said. He knew his son wasn't bad; he was suffering. So when he once read his son described as a cold-blooded perp, he was taken aback. "People don't understand the difference between an evil person and a mentally-ill person who does an evil deed, ... To say that was a cold-blooded stance was to say that the demons were my son. My son had a moral compass, but he didn't have an awareness of where he was going with those deeds that morning. He did when he killed himself." He cleaned up his mess. Stawicki now gives one advice to parents of other adult children who suffer from severe mental illness: "Lie. If you've got someone that's a ticking time bomb, lie", said Stawicki. "Lie and say they are or have been an imminent threat right now. You know, "I"m afraid to go back in the house after you leave, officer. He's going to pull something out of the, you know, and kill me. Please don't leave. Take him away.... Lie. Lie your ass off" (Gross 2013).

KIRO Team 7 Investigators learned Stawicki's run-ins with police started well before the domestic assault on Roulette's daughter. "In 1989, he was arrested in Seattle for carrying a slide-out locking blade, according to court documents. Charges of carrying a concealed weapon were dropped. In Kittitas County in 2010, Stawicki was charged with assaulting his brother. Charges were dropped then, too. Despite those arrests for violence and weapons issues without any convictions, Stawicki was allowed to keep his concealed weapons permit. Records show that at the time he opened fire inside the Racer Café on Wednesday, he legally held permits for three .45 caliber handguns and three more 9 millimeter handguns. Roulette said he was always armed. 'He saw the world as a potentially dangerous place—an unfriendly place where bad things happened—and he felt like he needed to be protected, so he was armed and ready to take care of things himself, protect himself if need be,' she said. Another common theme that ran through all the police reports: Stawicki constantly listed himself as homeless or unemployed. Seattle shooter had permit for 6 handguns" (www.mynorthwest.com/11/695899/Father-of-Cafe-Racer-shooter-wants-changes-for-mentally-ill).

People should understand, especially professionals in law enforcement and health care, that when stepping over that body of the homeless man, woman, or child before the sun comes up, remember that every step is a footprint in the snow of human destructiveness, not civil rights. The state's inability to deal with its homeless population is nothing less than institutional-sponsored neglect and ultimately the potential for institutional violence. There are only victims of violence sleeping on the streets, and whether one encounters a Stawicki or a Yori is purely a matter of chance when stepping over that body en route to work. In 1999, there was a series of incidents involving individuals with untreated mental illness becoming violent. In two similar assaults in the New York City subway, a man diagnosed with schizophrenia pushed a person into the path of an oncoming train. Andrew Goldstein, then 29, while off medicines, pushed Kendra Webdale to her death in front of an oncoming N train at the 23rd Street station. Kendra's Law is named after her.

During the course of court-ordered treatment, when compared to the 3 years prior to participation in the program, Assisted Outpatient Treatment (AOT) recipients experienced far fewer negative outcomes. Specifically, the Office of Mental Health (OMH) study found that for those in the AOT program: 74% fewer experienced homelessness; 77% fewer experienced psychiatric hospitalization; 83% fewer experienced arrest; and 87% fewer experienced incarceration. The related findings of the independent evaluation were also impressive. AOT was found to cut both the likelihood of being arrested over a 1-month period and the likelihood of hospital admission over a 6-month period by about half (from 3.7% to 1.9% for arrest, and from 74% to 36% for hospitalization) (Treatment Advocacy Center, www.treatmentadvocacycenter.org/solution/assisted-outpatient-treatment-laws/kendras-law-successes#sthash9OdmXso3.dpuf).

But the subway violence continues. "A violent parolee was being sought Monday for allegedly pushing a Bronx dad to his death in front of a subway train—as the motorman apologized to the victim's family for not being able to stop in time." The victim was Wai Kuen Kwok, 61, who was randomly pushed in front of a D train at the East 167th Street station in Highbridge at about 8:45 a.m. Sunday as his horrified wife looked on, the sources said. According to the *NY Post*, the suspect was identified as homeless Kevin Darden, who has more than 30 arrests, including for trying to set his brother's house on fire. The 34-year-old vagrant, who has done at least one stint in prison, was most recently arrested Nov. 9 in Midtown for pickpocketing, sources said.

The motorman described the scene of the tragedy as he tried, but could not, stop the incoming train in time, saying, "I would like to apologize to the family. There was nothing I could have done. I see a body flying across the tracks. I placed the train in emergency. The train doesn't stop right away. All of my passengers were crying with me. They were consoling me. They told me it wasn't my fault." Muriel, a 23-year MTA veteran, said he was so shaken that passengers had to help him out of his subway cab so he could look at Kwok to see whether he was still alive, as is procedure.

He said Kwok's wife, Yow Ho Lee, ran to him and cried uncontrollably into his chest. "She spoke to me in broken English. She said, 'Help me! Help me! Help me! Call someone!'" he recalled. "I told her police and EMS are en route."

Muriel noted that it was the third time he has had the bad luck of striking a person with a train. He said he took off from his job for eight months to deal with trauma after the second incident in 2013, in which a man also died. He returned to the job only because of his daughter's college bills, he said.

Darden, Kwok's killer, is believed to have hopped on a city bus to escape the scene. He got off a few blocks away and headed straight into a bodega, where he bought a 50-cent "loosie" cigarette and smoked it outside, witnesses said. "He seemed calm. He seemed relaxed," said Deimer Alvarez, 24, a worker at the New Yemen Deli on Jessup Avenue. "But maybe that's why he bought the cig—to relax."

Melik Gregory, a construction worker, said he recognized the alleged killer from surveillance video that cops released. "When I saw the video, I said, 'I've seen that guy before! That's the guy that's always walking around the neighborhood asking for change'," Gregory recalled.

Darden had been arrested in Texas for allegedly pouring "an ignitable substance" inside his brother's Texas home in 2011, according to the Longview News-Journal with additional reporting by Amanda Lozada and Laurel Babcock" (www.nypost.com/2014/11/17/suspect-in-custody-in-deadly-subway-push/).

The tragedy is that a homeless mentally ill man, who was in and out of prison or local jails, remained free to cause havoc and take lives. He was certainly a danger to others, a lethal danger, but probably also a danger to himself if he had not been caught. Now, authorities can only hope that a judge will sentence this multiple violent offender and murderer to a life sentence without the possibility of parole where, perhaps, as a result of whatever therapy he receives in prison, he will be able to unravel the mysteries of his life and, at least, help doctors understand how to intervene in the lives of others like he to prevent the deaths of future innocent victims.

This was New York City that had legislated solutions to such acts by the criminally insane to prevent them via Kendra's Law. The irony of the Stawicki case is that it took place in Seattle, home of 911 and the gold standard for emergency medical services (EMS). But, although laying claim to being one of the most humane and civilized of cities in this country, Seattle has one of the worst community mental health and involuntary commitment systems of any city. Psychiatrists evaluating the seriously mentally ill do not even have a chance to examine them before they are picked up by courthouse bus in West Seattle and whisked away to Harborview Hospital where they wait for hours to go before the judge. The rare patient returns in the nearly empty bus for detention and emergency psychiatric evaluation under probable cause. Thus, the chart is simply slid before the attending psychiatrist to sign for discharge. If a doctor argues that he or she has not had a chance to see the patient before signing a discharge order, a nurse administrator will assure him that when the patient is discharged and back on the street, if he survives, he will be back and the doctor can see him next time. And that is the procedure at Harborview when it comes to community preventive mental health medicine.

Harborview is a revolving door, a training ground for young trial attorneys grabbing charts early in the morning before the attending psychiatrist even has a chance to see their clients. They succeed nearly 100% of the time. Who can prove imminent dangerousness claimed by a truck driver last night when a homeless man walked in front of his truck with a sign advising him to prepare for the Judgment Day, which the driver believed was in fact imminent for at least one, if not both of them.

The Washington Psychiatric Association fought week after week with the director of the Health and Human Services Department to halt the arbitrary and capricious closing of Northern State Hospital. The fallout is now the material of state history in "Under the Red Roof." It was contested by the state psychiatric association as potentially genocidal, in that Morris had no plans for safe shelter and treatment of these sick and helpless wards of the state. Northern State Hospital's administration was well respected by resident psychiatrists training at the University of Washington, oftentimes doing training tours there to learn the most humane and safest treatment and management for the most seriously mentally ill. These were not the criminally insane. These were simply the sickest, like the scores of cases we have cited, who needed a therapeutic community for the long term—perhaps life. Just a "bug house," it was said when shuttered. So, how are these patients doing in prison? Very badly, as we will see. Northern State may be history; it is also the template for the next revolution in psychiatry—one that must come to stop the bloodshed and man's inhumanity to man.

Northwest to Southwest, however, nowhere is the problem of homeless threatening public safety so grave as in Albuquerque, New Mexico, where the recent execution-style killing of a homeless "camper" has brought the Department of Justice (DoJ) inside the city's police department with its own man supervising the chief. Albuquerque has come under DoJ scrutiny due to its high per-capita rate of police shootings, two to three times that of Chicago and New York City. In spring 2014 the police were called to extract a known psychotic homeless man from the high desert hills behind an exclusive residential district. This department has a psychiatrist and crisis team, but, instead, 41 street cops from different departments showed up to arrest one mentally ill man. Whether merely a nuisance or a perceived threat to local high desert residents of means, James Boyd had to go. He was not camping. This, for James Boyd, whatever his personal reasons, was "his bush," the southwest homeless phrase for "home." Like Stawicki, he also was known to have a grandiose delusion of being a high-level CIA agent on an enemy hit list. If one accepts his premise, then there is some logic in selection of his "bush," a sort of rampart backed against the desert highland scrub.

Having just served 10 years in prison for behaviors common with his diagnosed and untreated schizoaffective disorder, he had two pocket knives for protection in the event of attack from an infuriated homeowners' vigilante, mountain lion, or pack of coyotes. Those pocket knives were about the only thing rational about James Boyd.

> It was during incarceration that Boyd's attorney, Todd Holmes, was introduced to Boyd's alter ego, Abba Mobus Abaddon, an amalgamation of God and the Hebrew term for a bottomless pit. Throughout the rest of his life, Boyd identified with that alias as his true persona and dismissed the name he was given at birth as the operative name bestowed on him by the CIA. He signed court documents as Abba Mobus Abaddon, told judges to address him by that name, opened a MySpace account under that moniker, and told his limited circle of confidantes to refer to him as Abba. In 2005, Boyd sought to legally change his name to "GOD aka ABBA Mobus Abaddon GOD", but did not follow through with the action (Malone and Chacón 2014).

Officer Keith Sandy was aware of whom he would be encountering en route to Boyd's bush. Sandy had been fired from the New Mexico State Patrol for fraudulently billing for off-duty work while on duty. He was not to be armed and on the street. But, he was, and he was already notorious for cowboy policing when getting the call to back up other police attempting to remove James Boyd from his bush. He was ready to finish the job. Sandy was not known to shy away from dangerous and delicate situations. In fact, he seemed to have thrived on them. Perhaps that is why they called on him. He would end it. He did not know, however, his encounter with Boyd would be recorded.

> Sandy responded to the scene on March 16th where Boyd refused to come down from a makeshift campsite in the foothills near Tramway and Copper. At the scene, Sandy saw former colleague State Police Officer Chris Ware. Sandy didn't realize it, but Ware's dash cam was rolling and picked up their conversation.
>
> Sandy: "What do they have you guys doing here?"
> Ware: "I don't know. The guy asked for state police."
> Sandy: "Who asked?"
> Ware: "I don't know."
> Sandy: "For this f***ing lunatic? I'm going to shoot him in the penis with a shotgun here in a second."

Ware: "You got uh less-lethal?"
Sandy: "I got..."
Ware: "The Taser shotgun?"
Sandy: "Yeah."
Ware: "Oh, I thought you guys got rid of those?"
Sandy: "ROP's got one...here's what we're thinking, because I don't know what's going on, nobody has briefed me.."

"Two hours later he's escalating the situation so he can do just that," Boyd's family attorney, Kennedy said in an exclusive interview with 4 Investigates. "It's chilling evidence and stunning that he has not been criminally indicted. He says to a state police officer 'that f'ing lunatic, I'm going to shoot him in the penis.' It's crystal clear and he says it with contempt in his voice" (Nathanson 2014).

After flash-bangs went off in the wrong place, failing to immobilize him, Boyd stooped down to gather his bedding and surrender in his standoff with 41 armed police. He was seen to have two pocket knives, which most homeless are known to carry. They were considered a threat to the dog, which allegedly by mistake was set on Boyd, now begging not to be hurt. As Boyd turned away from the officers, in cold blood Sandy and another officer shot three rounds each, hitting him three times, twice in his side and back and once on his arm. Then they shot bean bags at him after being shot in the back three times. The officers claimed they did this in case Boyd was simply playing dead and might rise up like a wounded grizzly and charge them. He was bitten for good measure, and then cuffed and taken to the hospital where he later died. It was a frustrating 2-hour standoff in the desert hills for 41 armed policemen, but Boyd did surrender and certainly was taught the lesson of a lifetime—one that would be rapidly shortened. It was over. He was going back to jail, where he had been many times before for his delusional behaviors as a threatened undercover CIA superagent.

"Of course it's not a joke [to say he's going to shoot him in the penis] because he went forward and actually shot him," family attorney, Kennedy, said. "Clearly he has complete disregard for people suffering from mental disabilities. He calls him an expletive lunatic and then in the next breath says I'm going to shoot him in the penis. What is so mortifying about this shooting, and thank goodness we have a tape to show exactly what he did—which is instead of shooting him in the penis, he shoots him in the lower back. So had James Boyd not turned around at that moment to set down his bags, he would have been shot in the penis." (www.infowars.com/im-going-to-shoot-him-in-the-penis-says-cop-before-executing-camper/; Ramirez 2015)

In April, APD internal investigators asked Sandy about what he meant by the "shooting in the penis" comment. In an internal investigation transcript, Sandy is quoted saying,

> Jokingly, just kind of locker room banter, just told him, you know, "Don't worry. I'll shoot him in the pecker with this and call it good."
>
> But a few minutes later, the transcript shows that Sandy recanted his statement. The investigator asked, "Did you say anything to Chris Ware about shooting him in the pecker?"
>
> Sandy responded, "I don't...no, I don't think I did."
>
> In the transcript, Sandy gave the internal investigators a lengthy explanation how the officers working in the Albuquerque Police Repeat Offenders Program (ROP) often make cruel and crude jokes. In fact, Sandy described the hostility among his peers getting so bad that the officers adopted a "safe word". When officers use the safe word, CHINA, all jokes must stop. Sandy told investigators he was merely making a crude joke when he said he wanted to shoot Boyd in the penis". ... "We've developed this multi-tiered society where we treat people like James Boyd as disposable humans," McCall said. "I would hope that the people who care about James Boyd now will remember that this could be a positive legacy for this guy who was a forgotten member of our society living on the fringe when he was alive" (Malone and Chacón 2014).

To emphasize the politics of the homeless, Sandy was placed on administrative leave with full pay and allowed to carry his gun. He is now retired at standard retirement pay. The city attorney later stated that there would be no investigation, because she did not have powers of investigation and always had to take officers' statements at their word. The mayor recently made a statement denouncing the brutal neglect of a man's rights. That again is strange. This was cold-blooded murder. Training such police officers licensed to kill in psychiatry makes about as much sense as training them to tell the difference between an inner-city teen in a hoodie from an armed felon gangster. Is that a 6-hour sensitivity training course instead of 12–14 years higher education required to become a psychiatrist? In all the investigations, prosecutions, civil actions, and finally costs to bury homeless dead, the question is never asked, why are these people sleeping in the desert instead of the security of a hospital bed, as in *Under the Red Roof*, or a safe and humane halfway house under medical supervision? The answer has been clear for decades: institutional neglect, a new form of institutional violence, which is simply cheaper, although the damaging effects of 10 years in prison for schizophrenia are not considered a health-care cost in this era of criminalization of psychosis.

When the costs of this neglect are tabbed up, from whose budget does the James Boyd wrongful death case ultimately get paid? At further cost, now the federal government supervises the Albuquerque Police Department and criminal investigation has been initiated. The upscale residents are rid of their nuisance, at least for now, as are the upscale residents whose Silicon Valley residents are the Jungle. There are no messy homeless people to litter the landscape as they enjoy their morning lattes. However, there will be plenty more disabled psychotics to replace Boyd at his vacant bush called home.

Some of the homeless will find it secure from delusional enemies. Others with grandiose delusions will find it of Biblical significance, waiting to see the burning bush and die from dehydration. Is this what Thomas Szasz was expecting when he demedicalized psychosis in his *Myth of Mental Illness*? He knew little of serious mental illness as a psychoanalyst rarely entering a psychiatric hospital (Liebert and Birnes 2013)? Was this what the federal court in Wisconsin was expecting when they freed Alberta Lessard from a psychiatric institution for a life of jail, homelessness, and prison? We argue that the self-proclaimed experts on the mentally ill, who never treated a psychotic, and the very institutions who rule on the disposition of those who cannot care for themselves, have caused more damage than they realize when they helped to criminalize the mentally ill so that ill-trained police can confront them in the bush, on a freeway, or in a public park.

For such tragic encounters between the police and psychotic homeless people, Chief of Milwaukee Police had this to say when tested to his limits following the shooting of a homeless man, Dontre Hamilton, by his officers. Flynn noted that each year in Milwaukee, 80% of homicide victims, 85% of aggravated assault victims, and 80% of shooting victims who survive shootings are African American.

> "Now, they know all about the last three people who have been killed by the Milwaukee Police Department in the course of the last several years. There's not one of them that can name one of the last three homicide victims we've had in this city," Flynn said. "But this community is at risk alright, and it's not because men and women in blue risk their lives protecting it. It's at risk because we have large numbers of high-capacity, quality firearms in the hands of remorseless criminals who don't care who they shoot."
>
> Flynn then told reporters that he was going directly from the meeting to the crime scene where there was a dead 5-year-old child and that he takes these types of crimes "personally."
>
> "We are responsible for the things that we get wrong," he said of his police department. "We've arrested cops, we've fired cops and so on. But the fact is, the people here, some of them, who had the most to say, are absolutely MIA when it comes to the true threats facing this community. It gets a little tiresome, and when you start getting yelled at for reading the updates on the kid who got shot, yeah you take it personally, OK?" (Howerton 2014)

Way too many of these psychotic patients confronted by police are homeless, yet such grave disability in the psychotic population is defended as a constitutional right rather than outlawed as a public health and safety threat to all Americans, particularly the sick and helpless. Chief Flynn is correct: the police can pay somebody hundreds of thousands of dollars to teach crisis intervention, but what good is that going to do for those whom the police shoot because the victims were either incapable of understanding police commands shouted at them by panic-stricken officers or they, like Boyd, simply moved too slowly as they tried to surrender?

> "The system doesn't need more cops trained to be mental health professionals, it needs more mental health professionals trained to be mental health professionals," department spokesman Lt. Mark Stanmeyer wrote in an email.
>
> Even if the officer involved in Wednesday's shooting had the critical incident training, it would not have changed the outcome, Flynn said during a news conference.
>
> "It's important training. It's very useful training, but when there's a sudden eruption of violence, there's no time to employ it," he said. (Kissinger and Luthern 2014)

The police protect far more homeless people than they kill. Even in the darkest days of the Seattle Police payoff scandal (Chambliss 1988), beat men on Skid Row often nurtured the homeless derelicts like their babies. Robbing one of them after cashing his Supplemental Security Income (SSI) check for the conveniently located state package store in Pioneer Square guaranteed the harshest of sidewalk justice. Seattle police officers would even go undercover and lie on Skid Row inviting robbery. For those predators, punishment was greater than the shock of robbing a cop.

That was another era, and like the Bowery, only the curious walked First Avenue, the original Skid Row named for skidding logs from mountainside forests into Puget Sound. Today's Skid Row is an amalgamation of tourists strolling from Pike Place Market in search of an avant garde restaurant, felons released with a one-way bus ticket from the penitentiary, homeless kids trying to survive selling sex, veterans mustered out of local military facilities without benefits or money for housing, and psychotic people once humanely housed at Northern State Hospital.

Seattle's homeless were perfect prey for serial lust killer Gary Ridgway, the Green River Killer (Keppel and Birnes 1997, rpt, 2003), who is known to have killed more than 50 women over two decades. Borderline in intellectual assets, Ridgway had it easy with homeless girls. Not known for his reticence, Ridgway, now in prison, almost brags about how easy it was to get prostitutes into his car. He was less threatening than most in their environment and probably gave them a Biblical pitch from his amateur preacher disguise. But most, he knew, were homeless, addicted to drugs, and needed the money. "I would talk to them and they'd get in," Ridgway told his police interrogators.

Dave Reichert, now a U.S. Congressman, lived and breathed this case as lead detective in the late 1980s, combing through piles of files brought in as leads. With legendary Seattle detective Robert Keppel as his chief consultant on the Green River Task Force, he took complaints personally that not enough was being done because the victims were seemingly all prostitutes.

"The victims were young women deserving of sympathy who had families, no matter how dysfunctional. He said detectives would talk to one young woman along Pacific Highway or on the street in downtown Seattle and would be collecting her remains two weeks later. That was the reality of living through this case," he said. "It was death every day" (Harger 2013).

And so it is on the streets of America, whether high-profile shootings by police, sexual predators, disease, drugs, or alcohol. A standard psychiatric history of a new patient includes a question to determine history of psychological trauma, "have you ever been a victim of crime or violence?"

Sometimes when there is a pause, an additional question has to be asked regarding child or sexual abuse as a child. Reichert paints the portrait of homelessness, although referring specifically to Ridgway's victims now estimated at just south of 100. There are a lot of cold cases from Ridgway, but the sheriff's office has closed the cold case investigative office. These are forgotten people who may not be missed by anyone. Runaways, hypervigilant combat veterans, and hallucinating psychotics are not missed on any given day because they are usually recognized by someone when killed in dramatic way, the Albuquerque Police or a Green River Serial Murder Case.

When the Philadelphia Police Department visited Bundy on death row while confessing to some of his known murders in Washington State, they turned around and went home in despair. They had so many missing women on their rolls that they did not know where to start questioning Bundy. Where the line is drawn between missing persons and cold murder cases has been revolutionized by the Bundy case. Few are simply missing; many are killed because they either will not allow protection—such as shelter with strict rules—or simply are not sheltered. In the Berkeley hills they live communally, families and singles alike. They sell whatever they can scrounge from the city streets to buy necessities and marijuana to take "home" into the verdant hills of the East Bay. They are flocks who are a little better protected from the wolves, but most homeless people are destined to die early from disease or violence. None can escape violence; all meet the psychiatrist's first criterion for psychological trauma—crime and violence, most often preceding homelessness.

Forgotten warriors, discarded mental patients, and children and women escaping violence and sexual assault at home inevitably will be traumatized many times again on the street. In discussing institutionalized violence 50 years ago, we discussed prison riots and concentration camps under the Third Reich. Now we must study and solve homelessness as institutionalized violence. Whatever official and politician dissociates homelessness from either failed adult and child protection services, veterans and military health and disability services, and total collapse of public psychiatric services has to be in total denial or deliberately robbing human and social service budgets to increase discretionary spending for governors or DC bureaucrats.

Homelessness is the visibly rising red mercury on our thermometer of social breakdown and a culture of violence. The United States has little claim to exporting its civilization as long as a million of its citizens are bleeding from the red claws and teeth of the wilderness that are now Main and First Street, America.

Here we see a policeman fired for improperly handling a case of a schizophrenic patient lying in a Milwaukee Park; first he did not know that the patient had already been checked before by police and did not have to recheck the patient. Worse, when handling the patient, the officer was suddenly faced with unexpected violence and shot him multiple times. The Department of Justice is overseeing the Albuquerque Police Department for executing a psychotic man living in the hills above an exclusive residential neighborhood. Instead of sending their special police unit trained in crisis management backed up by a psychiatrist, they call in 41 officers in what appears overkill.

A suicidal mass murderer's father in Seattle is advising families to lie to the police about how imminent their loved one's violence is so that they take the patient to the hospital before going on a rampage or harming the family again.

The Boise Police Chief is begging Congress to do something about untreated veterans, many of them homeless and hypervigilant, because he's afraid his officers are going to kill them. Young girls are on the street without family support for many reasons—oftentimes escaping sexual abuse at home. They must trade sex for basic means of survival; they are prostitutes then. Lust killers like Gary Ridgway and Jeffrey Dahmer asserted they were easy prey. Obviously they were—and are.

After Michael Brown is killed in the streets, the president goes on national TV advocating for better discriminating powers of beat cops to distinguish the armed gangster in a hoodie from the kid in a hoodie who is menacing but not an armed gangster. Is this the conversation we should be having about violence on our streets—particularly homelessness? First, any man and woman entering basic training becomes the responsibility of the Department of Defense following weapons training to kill. Merely dumping them on the street to avoid taking responsibility for whatever failures led to their discharge (i.e., psychosis, drugs, mental defect or combat trauma) simply kindles the institutional violence known as homelessness in this country. The federal government takes credit for making maximum effort to reduce the homelessness rate of veterans. In 1994 Congress heard testimony about the growing epidemic of homelessness in the veteran population (Liebert et al. 1994). Twenty years later the problem is just as bad as it was then; many have died and been replaced by newly discharged veterans stripped of benefits for one reason or another on their discharge papers; most were good enough to fight for their country but not good enough to help before dumping them outside the garrison gates with the address of the nearest homeless shelter (Liebert and Birnes 2013). Insubordination and substance abuse are all that is needed to dump them outside the garrison gates with impunity.

We wake up to the news that our nation is losing its superpower status. President Coolidge warned, "the nation that forgets its defender will itself be forgotten." This nation could hardly fulfill President Coolidge's admonition fast enough as bodies stack up on our streets. Then there are families or single mothers raising children on the street, and a Good Samaritan veteran sleeping on the steps of a church in downtown Seattle after giving last rites to a murdered mother of two. He is planning to build a tent city for homeless veterans while

San Jose is literally chasing the homeless away with bull dozers. This sounds like sociology. It is simply the sign of failed governance from statehouses to the White House and up Pennsylvania Avenue to Capitol Hill. None of these people should be sleeping on the streets, anymore than murderers should be allowed access to the White House.

In a country that boasts about its health care, people should not be allowed to bleed to death anywhere if they so choose, and psychotic patients should not be allowed to wander barefoot into rush-hour traffic. Gangsters should not be on the street. They should be screened for remedial problems, rehabilitated, or incarcerated until no longer dangerous—if that can realistically be expected to happen. Three strikes and out without judicial discretion for indeterminate sentencing after thorough presentence assessment, including psychological and/or psychiatric examination, must go away. It is proven over and over again every day in every state to have been simply politically motivated prosecutorial rhetoric doomed to fail (Liebert et al. 1978).

Delusional patients who are so incompetent for informed consent that they believe they are on the run as CIA agents—thus justifying their being armed or perching in the desert above a residential community with families and children—should be in long-term hospital care or under careful supervision in the community with safe, healthy residential living quarters followed, if and when possible, by supervised day care programs and assisted treatment monitoring their mood-stabilizing and antipsychotic medications. Szasz is for philosophy classes and not for judges and policemen unless, that is, society is willing to tolerate another Sandy Hook, another Tucson massacre, another rampage at University of California, Santa Barbara—or, more to the point of this chapter, another bloody May in Seattle. There are safe and legal means for segregating the safe from the dangerous, the helpless from the lazy, and the psychotic from the eccentric in our society. The arguments can roil the Ivory Towers of secure campuses that then awaken to the horrors of violent suicide, rape, or murder emanating in their classrooms or from esteemed alumni returning to universities like Northern Illinois with previously invisible delusions that drive bloody vengeance nobody could detect from escalating hostility in distant emails from down state, prelude to massacre at NIU. The scope of the homeless problem in this nation can be seen in cold metrics or human life that follows. It is no more a constitutional issue than any of our rights to bear arms and thus open carry an AK 47 on the street with a bandolier full of gleaming brass ammo slung over our shoulders.

## REFERENCES

Chambliss, W. 1988. *On the Take*, 2nd edition. Indiana University Press.

Gross, A. 2013. Café Racer gunman's father: I 'should've kept coming back at it.' *KPIU 88.5*, May 30. www.kplu.org/post/cafe-racer-gunmans-father-i-should-ve-kept-coming-back-it

Harger, C. 2013. Search goes on for Green River victims with or without Ridgway, KOMO News.

Howerton, J. 2014. Milwaukee police chief explodes on protesters for willfully ignoring crime's 'Greatest Racial Disparity' after being verbally attacked in meeting. *The Blaze*, November 19. www.theblaze.com/stories/2014/11/19/milwaukee-police-chief-explodes-on-protesters-for-willfully-ignoring-crimes-greatest-racial-disparity-after-being-verbally-attacked-in-meeting

Keppel and Birnes. 1997. *The Riverman*, Pocket, rpt, 2003.

Kissinger, M. and Luthern, A. 2014. More training sought after fatal shooting by Milwaukee police. *Milwaukee, Wisconsin Journal Sentinel*, May 2. www.jsonline.com/news/milwaukee/autopsy-planned-thursday-on-man-shot-by-police-at-red-arrow-park-b99260307z1-257512561.html

Liebert, J. A. and Birnes, W. J. 2013. *Wounded Minds*. Skyhorse, New York.

Liebert, Woods and Shay. 1994. *Congressional Testimony*. www.ebooksread.com/.../page-14-viewpoints-on-veterans-affairs-andrelated-issues—hearing-before-the-subcommit-tin.shtml

Liebert, Wright and Harris. 1978. The Washington State Presentence Unit. *American Academy of Forensic Sciences*, New Orleans.

Malone, P. and Chacón, D. J. 2014. In death by police bullets, Boyd has become a cause. *Santa Fe New Mexican*, April 5. www.santafenewmexican.com/news/local_news/in-death-by-police-bullets-boyd-has-become-a-cause/article_a356df2a-55ba-5ca8-aac1-432f63640bf0.html

McGoffin, M. J. 2011. Under the Red Roof: One Hundred Years at Northern State Hospital, Mary McGoffin, Sedro-Woolley, Washington, June 12.

McNerthney, C. 2012. *SEATTLE Post-Intelligencer*, June 1.

Morris, C. *APA Journal Review*, www.facebook.com/pages/Under-the-Red-Roof-One-Hundred-Years-at-Northern-State-Hospital/178087148914280

Nathanson, R. 2014. James Boyd's dark journey. *Albuquerque Journal*, March 30.

Preidt, R. 2015. Mental health woes common among homeless kids, study finds. *HealthDay News*, February 19. www.consumer.healthday.com/mental-health-information-25/child-psychology-news-125/mental-health-woes-common-among-homeless-kids-study-finds-696448.html

Ramirez, C. 2015. KOB Eyewitness News 4, Albuquerque, NM, www.kob.com/article/stories/s3573906.shtml#.VHN1cY10zIU

Seattle shootings: Day of horror, grief in a shaken city, *Seattle Times*, May 31, 2012. www.seattletimes.com/seattle-news/seattle-shootings-day-of-horror-grief-in-a-shaken-city/

Sullivan, J. and Martin, J. 2012. Gunman: A life full of rage, a shocking final act. *The New York Times* (*Seattle Times* staff reporters Jack Broom, Hal Bernton, Mike Carter, Susan Kelleher, Jayme Fraser, and Lynn Thompson, and news researchers Miyoko Wolf and Gene Balk contributed to this report.) www.seattletimes.com/html/localnews/2018328041_stawicki01m.html

Treatment Advocacy Center. Assisted outpatient treatment: Results from New York's Kendra's Law. www.treatmentadvocacycenter.org/solution/assisted-outpatient-treatment-laws/kendras-law-successes#sthash9OdmXso3.dpuf

# 12

# Role of occupational psychiatry for frontline public safety and health officers

With specific reference to police psychology, we examine the role of psychiatrists in helping frontline emergency responders do their jobs better, counseling them on the necessary resiliency required to bring through tough confrontations, and helping analyze the psychological factors at work in day-to-day dealings with citizens. For the purposes of our argument, Occupational Psychiatry plays an important role in training frontline responders across a wide variety of agencies from law enforcement to rescue to emergency room personnel to recognize their own emotions and reactions as well as the recognitions of warning signs of mental illness in others. We suggest that frontline responders, especially police, need more training and comprehensive management in making judgment calls about dealing with the mentally ill, particularly in shoot/no shoot situations.

No one questions the demands and unique stresses of frontline work in health care and public safety. Whether social services investigating child or adult abuse, police encountering suspicious activity on the street, or emergency medical staff when overwhelmed with either a multicasualty incident (MCI) or threat from a strange-behaving patient first encountered prehospital or unanticipated direct admit to the emergency room (ER), frontline health and public safety personnel endure extraordinary stress in their line of duty. Most people are not surprised that burnout in frontline public safety, social services, and emergency health-care services is higher than in their own jobs, but better ways must be found to keep experienced personnel for the duration of their careers, and keep them effective until the very end. We lose too many well-trained, experienced, and effective frontline personnel from burnout. The tide of such costly loss, both financial and protective for our society, must be turned. The public knows that they are mainly good people out there trying to do these jobs but understands the stresses, both physical and psychological, that weigh upon them. It is also known that occupational stress is correlated with three specific work conditions:

1. Physical danger
2. Lack of control over work environment
3. Ambiguity of policies and procedures in administrative chain of command

## PHYSICAL DANGER

The fear generated by physical danger is almost always determinant of how police will respond to a situation. Despite the drama of crime fighters on TV, it is also known that the major function of a police officer is to control, whether controlling a beat during a shift, a critical incident—like a domestic violence call—or particularly—in the face of being confronted with a firearm. Although our culture is changing, studies show that police officers harbor racially discriminatory beliefs that can influence their actions to control, whether for better or worse. This was attested to recently by Federal Bureau of Investigation (FBI) Director James Comey, who, in an address at Georgetown University, said, "All of us in law enforcement must be honest enough to acknowledge that much of our history is not pretty. At many points in American history, law enforcement enforced the status quo, a status quo that was often brutally unfair to disfavored groups" (Dionne 2015).

Obviously, not all cultures and subcultures within our society view the police in the same way, whether black and poor or Muslim Arab and rich. Most police officers, even in racially conflicted environments, are able to perform their functions of control without making critical incidents worse, regardless of their prejudices and biases. These millions of potentially incendiary encounters every year are not known; only those that sour hit the headlines.

We know that all of this failed in Ferguson, Missouri, on August 9, 2014, ending the year with the worst urban riots since the Rodney King incident in 1992. There is no doubt that the parties to the incident in Ferguson had vastly different perceptions of behaviors to be expected from a white police officer in a patrol car encountering two young black males walking down the middle of a busy city street. This is particularly true if the two teenagers, one of whom was shot and killed, believed that the police officer confronting them was aware that they were fleeing a strong-armed robbery.

What happened the morning of August 9? Who were the parties to what happened, and what threat did they pose? What did they look like? What other police and emergency resources were in the area at the time? What were the perceptions of each of the parties in the Brown/Wilson encounter, and when Wilson put his unit in reverse and confronted Brown physically, what were his and Brown's respective stress levels controlling their reactions to one another? These are the key questions governing the psychology of that encounter, and they go well beyond typical law enforcement. Although these questions may seem mundane and routine, they are not. And, too often, the police officer is not as clearly informed of circumstances faced than is possible (Liebert et al. 1989, 1991).

Police are at particular risk for the entire spectrum of occupational risk factors, but in no occupation is dangerousness in tandem with lack of knowledge for sudden encounters with citizens so constant an occupational stressor. Police shootings occurring out of fear, and exacerbated by lack of knowledge of anticipated threat, are the ones likely to be bad shootings—whether adjudicated as such or not. They are swept up by the news cycle, sending them viral within minutes, and, if interracial, civil disorder should be expected. Thus, the Wilson/Brown interaction did not go the way it should have for any of the parties. Big Mike and Dorian Johnson should have simply turned around, said nothing, and walked on the sidewalk instead of the middle of the street. Wilson should have issued a jaywalking summons and driven away. That is not what happened, and Wilson's effort to control the situation failed. The situation was dangerous and he lost control of it.

Police work demands control of people usually not wishing to be controlled and oftentimes armed and/or dangerous. Such demands for control make law enforcement dangerous, hence raising issues of risk, both physical and psychological, as well as job stress that builds, depending on the number and degree of control situations an officer faces. For example, an average citizen encountering Brown and Johnson walking down the middle of a street on a hot afternoon might simply drive on by. But Officer Wilson could not. He had to control a situation that turned out uncontrollable. This is the risk factor for law enforcement: how much control is enough? There is no red line for that, except after the fact when the case sours. Certainly the Ferguson Police Department (FPD) has had thousands of incidents like this involving young black males either acting defiantly or intoxicated. They have had people of all races jaywalking, some, simply in a rush, and some mentally disturbed or intoxicated. Most were handled as best as possible with minimal danger to lives of citizens and officer alike. This one obviously was not. The risk factor here, although seemingly invisible when Wilson commanded Brown and Johnson to get out of the street, suddenly became apparent when Brown defied the command and rapidly escalated when Wilson felt his authority challenged.

## NATURE OF POLICE COMMAND

Ambiguity of command in all occupational situations is a critically important risk factor for stress on any job. A pharmaceutical salesman is told that his product is no longer covered by a couple of insurance companies. His market rapidly shrinks. He cannot expand his market by overselling another product, because physicians will complain. His company can get into big trouble for pushing products rather than informing physicians of pros and cons of a new product. His sales go down, and he is threatened with demotion. His partner was fired because a medical director complained he was bringing too many lunches to the clinic, overselling, and disrupting staff performance and patient flow in the clinic. What is he to do, sell more and run the risk of getting in trouble or simply keep quiet and lose the $50,000 bonus needed for his kids' college tuitions next year?

Such ambiguities occur in all occupations—particularly when there is high level of public exposure or value—such as therapeutic agents. Nowhere, however, is it more a constant problem than in law enforcement.

In analyzing the nature of enforcement versus public safety within police agencies, we have to look at the command protocols that govern patrol officers who confront civilians every day on their beats. The New York Police Department (NYPD) enforced the law with Eric Garner, confronting him about what they said was his illegal selling of "looseys," individual cigarettes. But their actions during the confrontation did not protect the public safety and, in fact, because making the arrest was most important, violated NYPD rules about the use of the choke hold in the takedown. Was the stress of Garner's refusal to be handcuffed and taken into custody such a stressor to the police who outnumbered him that they overreacted with such force that they violated their own command protocols? That is how it looked on camera. It looked like the necessity to control trumped the requirement for public safety, especially in hindsight as demonstrations broke out all over New York, two innocent police officers were murdered, and the police demonstrated public disrespect for their chief and the New York mayor. Policing is more dangerous than ever. Controlling things is even harder with conflict between young people of color in the community and the police peaking to the point of explosiveness in any encounter, whether routine or already a hot call when gangs rule the neighborhood.

Matters of occupational stress worsen in an environment of concealed weapons. When traffic stops were monitored in downtown Seattle at night, the police discovered that 70% of drivers were armed after 10:00 p.m., most of them legally. Whether the officer knows the car and driver or not, stopping a car and approaching the driver in Ferguson, Missouri, is now more dangerous and challenging for control than it was on August 8, 2014, because the public not only distrusts the police, but has become hostile. As a result, the stress may become so overwhelming that the fear factor, an officer's need to protect his or her own life, becomes greater than the officer's requirement to protect the public. Every officer knows, however, that he must function to protect his career and livelihood as well as the public. But the occupational stress factors can overwhelm an officer's judgment in the moment.

In the case of NYPD rookie officer Peter Liang who fired into the darkness in an unlit New York housing project stairwell that he and his partner were patrolling, the stress factor clearly was too high for the officer. Liang shot and killed an unarmed Alex Gurley, who had ventured into the stairwell, unlit because there was no power and the New York building or housing authority had not made the repairs. Liang fired his weapon without knowing at whom or what he was shooting. We can sympathize with an officer in fear of his life, but it is a matter of training, too. A police department is an agency. An agency operates on behalf of its clients whose interests, according to agency laws in almost every state, should be placed at a higher level than those of the agent. Thus, a police officer must think of his or her client first—the public the agency protects—even before the officer's own safety. Accordingly, police agencies must do a better job in training officers how to handle job stress so that it does not put the public at risk, as it did in the case of unarmed Alex Gurley. Liang has since been indicted by a Kings County grand jury for his killing of Alex Gurley.

Similarly, in the case of 12-year-old Tamir Rice, shot to death by a rookie Cleveland police officer who was released from a previous job at a neighboring police department because he was assessed as psychologically unfit to handle a weapon, the stress of responding to a dispatch call about a "guy in here with a pistol," triggered a bad reaction. As the police unit pulled up to Rice, standing in an open area and wielding a pellet gun, officer Tim Loehmann opened the right front door of his unit and fired within seconds of pulling up to Rice. There was no threat, but Loehmann did not wait to assess the situation before firing and killing the 12-year-old. Was Loehmann in so much fear for his own life and the occupational stress so high that his professional judgment—requiring an assessment of the situation first—submerged by that stress and fear? This is a training and hiring issue as well, because departments cannot put officers on the street absent training that enables them to wait and see before firing. Moreover, police agencies must assess their own officers psychologically, making sure that they do not shoot first and face a grand jury later.

Most police officers do not enter law enforcement in order to kill somebody, and, if they do kill a citizen, they usually suffer what is known as postshooting trauma. This is a unique form of posttraumatic stress disorder (PTSD) wherein the officer is fixated on the shooting and cannot get beyond it to really be safe on the street. They return to duty but are fearful of having to draw their weapon. The gun is an intimate extension of a police officer's self-image. It is his ultimate protection, even if he will rarely shoot anyone or even fire it in the line of duty. The average police officer can expect to complete his career without firing his weapon—or certainly killing anyone. In fact, the majority of police officers report that in their respective 20-plus years on the job they have not even drawn their weapons. Thus, when an officer even has the face of citizen in his gun site and feels the slightest pressure of squeezing the trigger, this is oftentimes traumatic enough to panic him, regardless of whether or not shots are fired. Although police shootings, whether they involve officers getting shot or their shooting a citizen, are high profile and seemingly common, they are rare within the statistical universe of all police encounters with citizens.

As with all professions, of course, there are good cops and bad cops. Bad ones tend to seek locations and shifts where they have the opportunity to have physical encounters like New Mexico police officer Keith Sandy en route to Boyd's bush, bragging that he would shoot off the guy's penis. These types of officers expect to get in gun battles and even shoot a bad guy. That is a common public perception of the police officer, but it is not the true makeup of the vast majority. In fact, a Los Angeles Police Department (LAPD) study years ago found that lethal and near-lethal shootings of suspects were confined to a very small percentage of officers, a significant number of whom were repeat shooters. For officers not looking to get into physical encounters with suspects and hoping to deal with them with reason—and even sometimes sympathy—the ability to control must be there. It also must be accompanied by a sense of personal accomplishment from being able to do so alone and with little time for decision making or support to decide. Nobody can do this job without it.

In fact, most officers have been found to have a deep-seated need to rescue people, the fantasy that one day in a 20-year career they will dive into the icy waters and rescue a drowning child. It happens, but rarely. Far more likely is the inevitable deadly confrontation with another human being where they have license to kill. Until they do so, however, they are unaware how traumatic that will be for them, unless they are cowboy cops or simply sociopaths not yet detected by internal investigations. Excitement does go with the job, and the adrenaline pumping can be motivating. It can also, as in combat, wear the officer down. Those retiring without emotional or physical scars know they were lucky, but they also knew how to "walk slow" and avoid dangerous confrontations without shirking their duty. The good beat cop can tell when confronting a citizen who is a threat. It is in the citizen's eyes and the expressions of the citizen's mouth. The citizen who is yelling and mouthing off is not as dangerous as the one with a blank stare who does not talk. What is the citizen thinking? "Grab my gun and get me to shoot him?"

## THE THREAT OF COPACIDES

One of the major stresses facing police are what we addressed earlier, "copacides." Copacides, a suicidal act perpetrated by an individual seeking death by a police bullet, are not uncommon as a way to go out in a blaze of glory that shows the suicidal man's wrath for the whole world to see. Copacidal individuals are especially dangerous because it is axiomatic that, when they're suicidal they are convinced that there is nothing to lose; death is at that moment is not a fearsome thing. The St. Louis police shooting of Kajieme Powell is our case in point here because Powell's behavior illustrates the problems police face. Powell, who was wandering back and forth on a street corner, talking to himself, was obviously delusional. He was mentally ill, according to people who knew him. When police approached him, he was wielding knives and dared police to shoot him. They did. It was a suicidal act as much as it might have been perceived as a criminal act. What we need to assess are the stress factors such as police confronted with a knife-wielding suspect. Was he a real threat? Could Powell have been talked down? Could police have called for more backup and a police negotiator to defuse the situation? Did the department have a police psychologist or psychiatrist on call who could have engaged him in a conversation so as to lower the stress level between police and their suspect? Similarly, according to witness statements, Michael Brown was reported to have challenged Darren Wilson to the effect that, "are you going to shoot me?" If so, was that an invitation for the shooting? It is an important part of the equation explaining the nature of their confrontation. Absent the facts of the field interrogation of Big Mike and Dorian Johnson, along with the clinical psychology of Officer Wilson, it will likely be impossible to ever judge the nature of this seemingly routine incident in Anywhere U.S. going sour and nationally viral.

Without knowing the specific psychology underlying these stressful situations, we can still dissect what we do know from them and draw some conclusions to help public safety officers maintain their emotional balance, perform effectively, and complete their careers with some degree of pride, the sense of accomplishment, and as few scars, either emotionally or physically, as possible.

Many retired officers go on to second careers and live apparently normal lives. Many departments have retired guilds where officers gather periodically and have fellowship and collegiality. Getting to either of these places, however, requires that the shooting of copacidal individuals is understood, both in terms of its necessity, as well as its consequences.

When looking at the activities of police departments from big cities to small towns, one has to realize that every police department is stretched thin in terms of manpower and support because of budget restraints caused by the great recession. Ferguson, Missouri, is no Bellevue, Washington, with an affluent population willing to pay for adequate force and equipment. For such affluent departments, the concept of community policing is appropriate. In these communities the officers are not like armies of occupation, as they are perceived to be in many poor and minority communities nationwide. The officers are encouraged to become helping people in the neighborhoods. In this way, they are trusted by most and get information about crime that can lead to arrests and prosecutions. Community policing sounds wonderful, but it can only be implemented when the police are adequate in numbers and training. It is also possible when the police are accepted by most in the neighborhood. That has not appeared to be the case in Ferguson, where deadly force, whether properly executed for purposes of public safety or not, lit the fuse of festering rage among many and kindled an explosive riot with massive deadly consequences not forgotten quickly.

Community policing also means that the department has protocols in place to defuse situations in which the community itself confronts the police. This is another occupational stress issue, because, when crowds become infuriated and ultimately unmanageable, people can get hurt, police officers' lives can be put in danger and any trust between police and the community quickly dissolves. What we saw in Ferguson, for example, was the inadequacy of the FPD's ability to control the landscape—both that of the postshooting and aftermath of the grand jury decision. Although the legal pundits on the cable news channels dissected and criticized the grand jury results, the community policing issue rarely came up. In fact, the FPD chief acknowledged the number one issue; his department could not even protect one of its own following lethal use of deadly force. Is that not a total admission that his streets are not only dangerous for his officers but uncontrollable? Was that why the chief called out the heavy equipment to patrol the streets as demonstrators gathered and fired tear gas into crowds, pointing assault weapons at unarmed protestors and to occupying the streets as if the Russians were rolling into the Ukraine? Did the stress and fear level on the part of the police and police administration rise to the point where the only response was to bring in military equipment? If so, this, again, points to bad training, bad police protocols and bad communication with the community.

Law enforcement training and administration need to be realistic and not simply propagandized with idealism that stokes academic criminology programs. There can be no community policing without a community to police. Simply stated, it means that local residents have to be in control of their own police departments to enable local police officers to have the community's trust to control incendiary situations. If departments have the trust of the community, if community members do not feel threatened by police who are going after the low-hanging fruit of quality of life misdemeanor offenses, as championed by former New York Mayor Rudy Giuliani. Police operating under these rules tend to focus on minorities, people of color, and communities already struggling financially. Thus, individuals become frustrated and more apt to confront police; this raises the occupational stress levels to the point where even the necessary routine stops for questioning can escalate into violence. We are not arguing that police should not enforce the law. Instead we are suggesting that when law enforcement becomes perceived by the community to be especially harsh on one particular group, the individuals in that community no longer trust that there is equal justice under the law, and that spells danger. Ferguson is an integrated black/white community. Perhaps it is not harmoniously integrated, but it was not an impoverished black slum of St Louis; most residents, black and white, are likely supportive of police for protection from gangs and criminals. Thus, we suggest that when assuming risk is the issue, officers need to know how and when to pick their fights—particularly in communities like Ferguson, where they are the thin blue line, desperatedly needed by the majority of residents struggling for a better life and threated by street violence from which only the police can protect them.

When we review confrontations between police and civilians, the interactions between white officers and African American young men are in the forefront. Would black officers fare better in these situations? Not necessarily. There is evidence that black officers in white communities and white officers in black communities actually are less incendiary in potentially explosive situations. Black officers in a city like Ferguson might actually have long standing personal ties to young blacks and respond more emotionally than Dorian Johnson alleges Wilson did. It gets complex, but just putting more black officers on the streets is not the only answer—as is evident in critical incidents in Baltimore—although in a city like Ferguson it would have helped. Certainly better—more realistic—training is. And, monitoring officer health is important, too. Ironically, the St. Louis Police Department was an innovator in early identification of problem police officers. After two resisting arrest incarcerations, the officer was interviewed by a police psychologist to determine if these two arrests were necessary or simply a response to losing control and covering up excessive use of force. Whether the program is still in effect or not, certainly it was known within law enforcement in adjoining Ferguson—or, it should have been.

## THE TRAUMA OF USING LETHAL FORCE

Critical incident stress debriefing was developed by former fireman, Jeff Mitchel, who became a clinical psychologist. Although studies show that group therapy and debriefing led by peer counselors reduces the risk for PTSD to a significant degree, the statistics for outcome are not robustly positive or negative versus control groups. It is the rare first responder, whether fireman, medic, or police officer—even mortician—who is not impacted by critical incidents such as mass casualty incidents, ambiguous shootings of suspects witnessing such shootings investigating them, and then responding to any community unrest in the wake of the shooting. Of course, the loved ones of the deceased are just as traumatized, but this chapter is about occupational stress and those professionals forced to encounter such critical incidents as the Ferguson, Missouri police shooting and its aftermath. Eventually that routine police encounter with an unarmed and nonthreatening citizen brought the U.S. Army on to the streets of a lower middle class and integrated U.S. suburb! Many of the guardsmen patrolling the streets in the wake of the riot were in a form of combat, because they were facing unknown dangers from crowds that were hostile to them. Many had survived the threats and dangers of urban combat in Iraq, but would confrontations with their own citizens, for whom they went to war, cause reliving of war and blur the boundaries between this discussion and that of the veteran? This very extension of combat trauma did occur when Vietnam veterans were recruited by police departments during the urban riots in the late 1960s.

Police officers who may have adjusted from Vietnam did not completely heal emotionally because of incidents in confrontations with rioters in many urban departments without mandatory police academy training—sometimes within weeks of returning from Vietnam. Some, of course, may have adjusted better by becoming policemen after their war experiences, proving to themselves that they could face threats and conflict without killing. We do not know about them, but some did make retirement without serious incident while serving as police officers; many, however, did not. In the latter case their combat PTSD was lit up by traumatic encounters with citizens or crowds in the inner cities or on campuses during race riots and "days of rage" on campuses in the late 1960s and early 1970s. In either case, they returned home to expressions of shame and then had to confront with deadly force their peers who did not go.

We are once again ripe for such complex post-traumatic syndromes in the police and other frontline public safety and health professionals, many of whom have, as Chief Masterson informed Congress, been at war too. They may have returned from Iraq and Afghanistan to a public more receptive to them than the Vietnam veteran, but such improved public acceptance is not immunization for post-traumatic stress as policemen, emergency medical personnel, or first responders. Chief Masterson complained to Congress of his concerns that combat veterans on his force would have to kill their comrades on the streets of Boise if Washington, DC, did not start taking care of veterans from the War on Terror. There is generational change, but the problem remains the same with combat veterans in law enforcement as in 1970.

It is no surprise that the firefighting service is dangerous. No fireman retires without being exposed to extremely traumatic incidents. Few retire without either serious injury or intimate knowledge of a friend disabled by serious injury. Recurrent training, camaraderie, trusted command leadership, adequate equipment, and control over the destruction of fire can be improved. Never, however, can it be 100%, because training can never replicate the next situation encountered. Most fire departments require all firefighters to also serve as emergency medical technicians. With little training, oftentimes they are first on the scene of serious illness and injury. They feel responsible for saving people, but, if untrained to do that, they cannot. Many factors affect their ability to save the injured and ill, but remoteness of site is oftentimes a critical factor. Working with mass casualties or in remote sites requires triaging decisions and lengthy prehospital transport where they oftentimes must make life and death decisions without expert support. Many develop skills that require little expert support, and many know both their limits and the limits of the job—life support and safe transport to the nearest hospital with adequate resources and census. Seemingly simple—it is not. Some states require hospitals to notify ambulances that they are filled or have no resources—such as surgical suites; this prevents the wasteful drive and diversion from one hospital to another with a critically ill patient on board. Nonetheless, medics still must drive around large regions with seriously ill patients seeking an ER that will accept the patient. We have lost 20,000 ERs since 9/11, and they continue to fold—particularly where they are most needed. That is in rural areas and the inner cities, where costs, security and malpractice risk far outweigh reimbursements.

Nowhere is this a more serious problem than with the severely impaired psychiatric patient. Emergency rooms do not want them, because psychiatric patients require a lot of care due to necessity of having to board them for days as inpatient psychiatric beds have been eliminated faster than ER beds since 9/11. Once the ER accepts the patient, they are stuck with the patient's care, now called the "psychiatric boarder," and they can rarely decline to accept under federal law unless proving that all beds and resources are 100% utilized. The Emergency Services Act, designed and implemented under the leadership of David Boyd under both the Nixon and Ford administrations, has created a system for emergency medical services. Calling 911 today, one likely takes it for granted without knowing that hospitals resisted its implementation in the 1970s. The sooner patients arrived at the hospital, administrators and medical staffs were thinking, the higher their risk of dying. Hence, the hospital dead on arrival (DOA) rate would increase. Such archaic and inhumane administrative thinking is no longer voiced. Nonetheless, hospitals need to run in the black and conform to increasingly complex rules for reimbursement or close.

Our Emergency Medical System still needs a lot of work. EMTs and firemen rescue people, but what good does it do to save a life if that life cannot be spared within that Golden Hour given by Mother Nature to either sustain life or lose it to death or permanent disability? That is prehospital care and transport, the responsibility of first responders, whether policemen, firemen, or EMTs. Emergency departments are mandated for expansion under the Patriot Act, but funding has not followed and remains in dispute between departments of Homeland Security and Health and Human Services. Accountable Care Organizations promise sustainability for rural hospitals and reduction in unnecessary ER visits, but unnecessary ER visits are increasing under Obamacare. People get one-stop service in the ER and have to be seen under federal law by a physician. Most working people cannot afford time off to be running from one specialist and lab to another, which means they go to the ER—even if insured under the novel universal health care of ACA. They go in increasing numbers, and ERs are the highest-cost beds in our system; they have to be highest tech to save all lives—not the majority who are walking wounded. First responders have a tough enough job at the scene of an accident or fulminating illness. They know what to do in first response and during prehospital transport, and they get high marks for doing it well. They cannot, however, be driving around looking for an ER bed or emergency psychiatric crisis bed.

It is a hard enough job stabilizing a patient at point "A," boarding him onto the ambulance and getting him as quickly and safely as possible to the closest ER to preserve the Golden Hour. They must be provided the resources, if we are to expect good people to apply for an oftentimes sacrificial style of life. They have a hard enough job to do under the best of circumstances; they do not need constant disruption of support services and loss of necessary resources—like ERs close to their emergency scene on diversion due to inadequate resources like emergency Imaging from MRIs or a surgical suite and excessive census reducing beds appropriate for necessary level of care for patients with certain specific emergency needs. The federal government has totally defaulted on the demands for just this in the wake of 9/11, failing to fund ERs as mandated by Congress to protect us from what they warn is the inevitable second terrorist attack. The case of Thomas Duncan in Dallas, Texas, proved we were not prepared for either the potential of a known epidemic of Ebola or for bioterrorism. First responders must work in a post-9/11 world that is prepared only for 9/10/2001.

One of the challenges facing police emergency responders is the way they have to change their responses to different situations. Rolling on a call for a traffic accident with injured victims is very different from rolling on a car chase. Responding to assist EMTs traveling to a cardiac arrest call is different from responding to a domestic violence/shots fired call. But sometimes police must respond to different situations back to back with little or no time to reset themselves. This is stressful, because it presents a challenge to the ways police have to manage themselves without any decompression time. Regarding the Ferguson case, it is interesting that Officer Wilson was responding to a sick call just before the life threat leading to his killing Michael Brown. Such a sudden change in emotional states, from caretaker to enforcer, is extremely stressful and wears out the neurochemical system of the brain from that of nurturing to fight and flight.

Firemen and EMTs are no longer universally considered good guys either. Ex Con William Spengler set up an ambush in West Webster, New York, by lighting his house on fire and calling 911. Known as a madman, he lured, then entrapped, first responders into a suicidal mass murder on Christmas Eve just 3 weeks after the Sandy Hook Elementary School massacre.

Emergency responders, and particularly the police in violent confrontations, sometimes suffer from a syndrome called "survival guilt." A vivid portrait of survival guilt is recorded in a recent interview of Oklahoma State Patrol Officer Betsy Randolph who arrested Alton Nolen in 2010. Nolen is another madman, like Spengler, prematurely released from prison without any rationale. Such releases seem almost random rolls of the dice in corrections today. Nolen had an extensive history of drug dependency. He reportedly converted to Islam in prison. His Facebook abruptly changed from posts featuring harmless song lyrics, talk about football, and other topics to posts almost exclusively related to violence in the name of Islam in April 2013 shortly after he was released from prison. He began posting pictures of Osama bin Laden and an image of beheading, as well as condemnation of the United States as "wicked" for failing to help Palestine when bombed by the Israel Defense Forces (IDF). His last posting demonstrates a mind cracking from either crack cocaine or psychotic illness. He condemns masturbation. Later he incites verbal racial conflicts with fellow employees at Vaughn Foods in Moore, Oklahoma. He was suspended from his job at Vaughn Foods; he immediately returned to the company with his own knife and beheaded a female employee before attacking one of the complainants of his racially disruptive behavior before being shot by the company's chief operating officer. By miraculous coincidence, this CEO was a reserve deputy!

Oklahoma Highway Patrol Officer Betsy Randolph broke into tears when describing the events of the arrest of Alton Nolen (aka Jah'Keem Yisrael) in 2010, saying, "had I known then he had assaulted an officer and could have done this, I wish I had shot him." Instead she stopped him for driving a vehicle without a proper license showing. He did not slow down right away when she turned on her light bar and turned off the highway. Eventually he did stop. She approached the car and could see he had a woman and child in the car. She had no reason to suspect he was a dangerous felon. She continuously repeats that she only expected him to comply with her procedures. He seemed calm, and the presence of whom she believed to be his wife and child were disarming for her. She had him sit in the front of her patrol car, evidencing her lack of perceived threat from Nolen. He could see her bringing up his criminal record on her computer. There were warrants out for his arrest. Seeing the data come up on her screen, she left the car and went to his side of the car, opened the door and told him he was under arrest. She clasped handcuffs on his wrist, and then, for the first time, he exploded and ran, ripping the chain from her hand, tearing a piece of flesh from her finger and leaving her hand scarred from the encounter. He fled into the woods. Backup was called with a helicopter, and Nolen was arrested several hours later. He did 2 years and was released from prison, allegedly very early under condition he receive anger management—a poorly defined cookie cutter remedy with no outcome studies or clinically standardized protocols. Obviously he needed a lot more than just that! He obtained employment at Vaughn Foods where he used a knife to cut food. But the story of Nolen's encounter with authorities did not end after his release and hoped-for or anticipated reintegration into society.

Leaders at the mosque he sometimes attended said he was quiet, not outgoing, and that there was no sign of violent tendencies in his personality, according to KOCO and *The Oklahoman* newspaper. "The only time I ever said anything to him was one time," Saad Mohammed, spokesman for the Islamic Society of Greater Oklahoma City, told KOCO. "He was in the mosque and he had his Quran and prayer rug on the floor. And I said, 'Hey, pick it up because I don't want the Quran on the floor.' And he picked it up and he sat down. That's it.'" The Imam reported that he was a bit odd and isolated, but, when told to pick up something near his prayer rug, he complied. No problems were described, but one member in disguise for fear for his life described this mosque to be radical and supportive of ISIS.

Nolen had converted to Islam in prison. Prison records show that Nolen has a tattoo reading "Assalamu Alaikum," an Arabic greeting that translates to "Peace be with you." He tried to convert employees where he worked. That, however, was not the source of problems at work. He complained of white racism. An employee reported he told her that he did not like white people. He was suspended, went home, and returned with a food-cutting knife from home. He crashed into a car, entered the building, and accosted the first employee from behind, carving her head off. Her fellow employees fought him off, but he was able to get to the employee he thought to be responsible for complaining and began cutting her throat, when Vaughn, the owner, appeared with a rifle. He charged Vaughn with the knife. Vaughn fired three shots, wounding Nolen with one shot. Although only targeting the employee who reported him, this was reportedly a large crime scene. Those attacked were not all white. Shouting in Arabic during his rampage of beheadings, he did nearly behead the complainant who got him fired. He was apprehended after being wounded and confessed to detectives in the hospital that he did it.

For Officer Randolph, the history will be flashbacks nearly every day of her career when making an arrest, fearful of both overreacting with deadly force this time, or underreacting again. Will she make it to retirement? She will only make it with support of the department, her peers, and expert psychotherapy addressing her survival guilt. She could have prevented this beheading, but she would have had to shoot an unarmed black man, and she would likely have had to shoot him in the back as he fled. Such use of lethal force would have violated *Garner v. Tennessee*, the U.S. Supreme Court decision that set forth the rules for the use of deadly force by police. She would have been in far worse trouble than Officer Wilson. That is not much of a choice. She had no choice at the time. The human mind, however, does not allow such discretion when it comes to deadly force to protect the public safety. Nolen posed no threat to her. His escape may have been critiqued for error. That was 2010, and his insanity does not surface until 2014 on his Facebook, although it should have been detected in prison.

The stress that Officer Betsy Randolph felt at her encounter with Nolen was palpable. Now imagine the stress Cleveland Police Officer Tim Loehmann must have felt encountering Tamir Rice in a park and not knowing that he was only 12-years-old and wielding a pellet gun. Now, a child is dead for no reason whatsoever, bereaved parents must confront the unthinkable, and, unless Loehmann is completely remorseless, a career in law enforcement has been ended. And, depending on the results of a number of likely investigations, the state may file criminal charges. How could this have been avoided?

Could Loehmann have waited before firing? Should Loehmann's partner that day, department veteran Frank Garmback, have ordered him not to fire? Loehmann's father, who had been an officer on the NYPD, told a story about his own experience when a man had brandished what he believed to be a gun, but he did not fire. The gun turned out to be a cigarette lighter. Are police now trained to shoot too fast? Is there such a generational gap between police that we are looking at a new breed of young officer who is not trained in virtualized "shoot–no shoot" training labs? Are we asking too much of our public safety officers? We expect them to perform under budget and understaffed. We are also asking too much of our ER and hospital staffs. According to the Bureau of Labor Statistics, in 2010 some 60% of all nonfatal assaults and violent acts in the workplace occurred in the health-care industry. Yet, health-care professionals are not trained like police officers to defend themselves. Emergency rooms, however, are a very dangerous workplace, second only to mining for incidence of serious injury to staff—almost always from assaultive patients. Challenger Corporation now teaches a course with a martial arts instructor for taking down the aggressive, threatening patient without injury to either staff or patient (Figure 7.7).

A recent article in the *Minneapolis Tribune* responds to the eruption of a paranoid patient mistakenly admitted through the emergency room into a general medical bed without psychiatric supervision. This patient had no history of serious mental illness but changed following minor surgery at another hospital days before presenting to the St. John's Hospital ER with confusion. A nurse noted that he had episodes of confusion since his admission 3 days before for sudden onset of delusional thinking. It is unknown at this time how far his workup had proceeded for this reportedly episodic confusion in a man never before reported to be either violent or suffering any psychiatric impairment. It is not known how he presented, but likely he was brought to the emergency room and admitted from there. A family confrontation likely escalated his violence when his attorney challenged his wife and daughter over the patient's sudden desire for divorce and change of will. The attorney tried to obtain an order for emergency conservatorship, but the judge refused to hear him until the following workday. After the family confrontation at bedside, the patient went on a rampage with a metal bar, attacking everyone in his sight, reportedly nurses, two of whom were seriously injured and required hospitalization. A postsurgical patient, awakened by the violence, got up and saw his own nurses lying in a pool of blood and another patient running down the hall, clad only in a hospital gown. He told the press that it was horrible his own caretakers had no security. Nor did he. This was a hospital ward. Police found the patient three blocks away in his hospital gown and had to Taser him, but the weapon did not work. They had to take him down physically, and he went limp. They returned him to the ER from which he had been originally admitted, where he was pronounced dead on arrival.

In chapters on rapid assessment we have addressed the needs to carefully and methodically work up altered states of consciousness to determine both potentially lethal medical conditions causing them or clinical states of unremitting human destructiveness. Clearly, this patient was not just confused. He was paranoid and feared for his life due to delusions. Most likely he was suffering from an organic psychosis that was aggravated by a family bedside confrontation over his mental capacity for making financial decisions along with probable late night delirium. There is no record of his having been under psychiatric management, although the hospital publicizes its psychiatric resources on grounds. There is no mention of security responding either. This rampage was between local police and nursing staff left to their own devices with an obviously volatile patient on a medical unit with little or no apparent psychiatric supervision or security—i.e., a sitter could have been ordered at minimum with orders barring family from arguing over his money at bedside. It is not clear if he had any workup in the ER before admission or if there were "prn" as-needed tranquilizers ordered for his known sudden onset of paranoia and delusions, most likely of medical-surgical origin at this age, having no prior history. The chaos and bloodshed in this setting was shocking and brought attention of both the press and state legislators.

According to a recent *Star Tribune* analysis, nurses are being attacked in record numbers. This year, Minnesota nurses have filed 46 workers' compensation claims for attacks and intentional injuries suffered while on duty in hospitals, the analysis found. The number of attacks is on pace to double that of 2012 and 2013. The problem goes beyond Minnesota. A 2011 U.S. Justice Department study found that more than 400,000 nurses and other health-care professionals are the victims of violent crimes in the workplace every year. According to the American Nurses Association, one in every four nurses listed physical assault as their top job safety concern. Extreme verbal abuse has been reported by nearly half of nurses in the line of duty.

The crisis in law enforcement and violence perpetrated against health care and first responders is escalating. Those needing control over their worksites and situations for which they are responsible, whether remote camping site, urban street, or hospital grounds have increasing challenges in exercising control. These sites, whether remote, urban, or even within the supposed sanctity of a hospital, are becoming more dangerous. Frontline professionals, whether doctors, police officers, nurses, medics, or police, need to know both the rules of rapid assessment as well as physical techniques for restraining threatening people while reducing risk of injury.

"No," as one ER doctor retorted after 9/11 in response for calls of preparedness in ER, "we are not commandos." Yet even psychiatrists in outpatient practice debate whether they should carry firearms while seeing patients. Certainly ER staff debates it or simply does carry. According to Tony York, former president of the International Healthcare Security and Safety Foundation, there have been at least 206 cases of guns being fired inside health-care facilities since 2006. Similarly, a 2012 study in the *Annals of Emergency Medicine* found that 154 hospital shootings occurred from 2000 to 2011, killing or injuring 235 people. Forty-four of those incidents took place in an emergency department, but no medical ward is safe anymore from the violent and insane poorly screened at admission and, for lack of better word, simply internally dumped for lack of appropriate psychiatric resources and avoidance of diversion to other facilities that would risk EMTALA violation.

When doctors and nurses arrived at Room 834 just after 11 a.m., a college student admitted to the hospital hours earlier lay motionless on the floor, breathing shallowly, a sheet draped over his body. A Houston police officer with a cut on his head was being helped onto a stretcher, while another hovered over the student.

Blood smeared the floor and walls. "What happened?" asked Dr. Daniel Arango, a surgical resident at the hospital, St. Joseph Medical Center.

The student, 26-year-old Alan Pean, had come to the hospital for treatment of possible bipolar disorder, accidentally striking several cars while pulling into the parking lot. Kept overnight for monitoring of minor injuries, he never saw a psychiatrist and became increasingly delusional. He sang and danced naked in his room, occasionally drifting into the hall. When two nurses coaxed him into a gown, he refused to have it fastened. Following protocol, a nurse summoned security, even though he was not aggressive or threatening.

Soon, from inside the room, there was shouting, sounds of a scuffle and a loud pop. During an altercation, two off-duty Houston police officers, moonlighting as security guards, had shocked Pean with a Taser, fired a bullet into his chest, then handcuffed him.

"I thought of the hospital as a beacon, a safe haven," said Pean, who survived the wound just millimeters from his heart last Aug. 27. "I can't quite believe that I ended up shot."

Like Pean, patients seeking help at hospitals across the country have instead been injured or killed by those guarding the institutions. Medical centers are not required to report such encounters, so little data are available and health experts suspect that some cases go unnoticed. Police blotters, court documents and government health reports have identified more than a dozen in recent years.

They have occurred as more and more American hospitals are arming guards with guns and Tasers, setting off a fierce debate among healthcare officials about whether such steps—along with greater reliance on law enforcement or military veterans—improve safety or endanger patients.

The same day Pean was shot, a patient with mental health problems was shot by an off-duty police officer working security at a hospital in Garfield Heights, Ohio. Last month, a hospital security officer shot a patient with bipolar illness in Lynchburg, Virginia. Two psychiatric patients died, one in Utah, another in Ohio, after guards repeatedly shocked them with Tasers. In Pennsylvania and Indiana, hospitals have been disciplined by government health officials or opened inquiries after guards used stun guns against patients, including a woman bound with restraints in bed.

Hospitals can be dangerous places. From 2012 to 2014, healthcare institutions reported a 40% increase in violent crime, with more than 10,000 incidents mostly directed at employees, according to a survey by the International Association for Healthcare Security and Safety. Assaults linked to gangs, drug dealing and homelessness spill in from the streets, domestic disputes involving hospital personnel play out at work, and disruptive patients lash out. In recent years, dissatisfied relatives even shot two prominent surgeons in Baltimore and near Boston.

To protect their corridors, 52% of medical centers reported that their security personnel carried handguns and 47% said they used Tasers, according to a 2014 national survey, more than double estimates from studies just three years before. Institutions that prohibit them argue that such weapons—and security guards not adequately trained to work in medical settings—add a dangerous element in an already tense environment. They say many other steps can be taken to address problems, particularly with the mentally ill.

Massachusetts General Hospital in Boston, for example, sends some of its security officers through the state police academy, but the strongest weapon they carry is pepper spray, which has been used only 11 times in 10 years. In New York City' public hospital system, which runs several of the 20 busiest emergency rooms in the country, security personnel carry nothing more than plastic wrist restraints. (Like many other hospitals, the system coordinates with the local police for crises its staff cannot handle.)

"Tasers and guns send a bad message in a health care facility," said Antonio D. Martin, the system's executive vice president for security. "I have some concerns about even having uniforms because I think that could agitate some patients."

Kelly Brinson Jr., a schizophrenic patient, died after he was shocked three times with a Taser in the psychiatric unit at the University of Cincinnati Medical Center in 2010.

But many hospitals say that with proper safeguards—some restrict armed officers to high-risk areas such as emergency rooms and parking areas—and supervision, weapons save lives and defuse threatening situations. The Cleveland Clinic, which has placed metal detectors in its emergency room, has its own fully armed police force and hires off-duty officers as well. The University of California medical centers at Irvine and San Diego and small community hospitals are among the more than 200 facilities that use stun guns produced by Taser International, which has courted hospitals as a lucrative new market.

"I've worked in systems where everyone has a firearm and an intermediate weapon, and I've worked in systems where a call to security meant the plumber and every able-bodied man would respond," said David LaRose, past president of the health care security association. "How much has your system thought about safety and security? In some places that's a 2 or 3; in some places it's a 10."

After Pean's shooting, St. Joseph's chief executive, Mark Bernard, said the officers were "justified." The hospital said it was reviewing its practices but declined to respond to questions. The Houston Police Department, citing an internal investigation, declined to comment or to make the officers available for interviews, and only released a heavily redacted version of its report on the shooting. This account is drawn from a review by federal health investigators, medical records, criminal complaints, and interviews with medical personnel and family members.

## WEAPONS IN HOSPITALS

More than half of hospitals surveyed have security guards who carry guns. 96% handcuffs, 56% baton, 52% pepper spray, 52% handgun, 47% Taser, and 12% K9 unit.

Pean had expected an apology after the shooting. Instead, during four days in intensive care, prosecutors charged him with two counts of felony assault on a police officer. They accused him of attacking with four "deadly weapons"—an unspecified piece of furniture, a wall fixture, a tray table, and his hands. James Kennedy, a lawyer representing Pean, says his client disputes that he was the aggressor and other allegations by the police, but cannot discuss specifics until the charges are resolved. His family has filed complaints with the Justice Department and healthcare regulators, including the Centers for Medicare and Medicaid Services, which provides funding to most American hospitals.

After an emergency investigation, the Medicare agency faulted St. Joseph for the shooting, saying it had created "immediate jeopardy to the health and safety of its patients." Threatening to withdraw federal money, the agency demanded restrictions on the use of weapons.

A family with Haitian and Mexican roots who settled in McAllen, Texas, the Peans were shocked that Pean's effort to get medical aid ended so badly. Though his father, Harold Pean, and a half-dozen other relatives are physicians, they said they had no idea that guns could be used against patients. After watching the nation roiled by the shootings of unarmed black men by police officers over the last year or so, the family now wonders whether race contributed to Alan's near-fatal encounter.

"We never thought that would happen to us," Dr. Pean said.

'I'm Manic!'

In his family of high-achievers, Alan Pean (pronounced PAY-on) is the soft-spoken and mellow middle sibling, into yoga, video games, and pickup football. Christian, 28, now a medical student at Mount Sinai in New York, is the Type A leader; Dominque, 24, is following his path, applying to medical school while pursuing a master's degree. Alan, who had never been in any sort of trouble, is "probably the nicest of us three," Dominque said.

Like many people with mental health issues, he did not get a clear-cut diagnosis. After a brief delusional episode in 2008, he was hospitalized for a more severe recurrence the next year, at the end of his second year at the University of Texas. He was kept for a week and told that he had possible bipolar disorder, though his symptoms did not reappear for years even after he tapered off medication.

He was prone to bouts of sadness and anxiety, he recalled in an interview, but had attended college, taking breaks from time to time, and worked for a while as a medical assistant back home in McAllen, near the Mexican border. Though he had smoked marijuana regularly to help tame his symptoms, he said in an interview, he quit last summer when he enrolled at the University of Houston to complete his bachelor's degree.

Just days into the semester, though, he barely slept and found himself increasingly agitated and delusional.

On August 26, he talked repeatedly on the phone with his parents and brothers, who tried to calm him but worried that he sounded disoriented. Christian had been concerned enough that he called the Houston police to do a "welfare check" on his brother at his apartment, though no one answered the door when officers arrived.

Alan Pean's white Lexus. He struck several cars after driving himself to St. Joseph Medical Center for treatment of possible bipolar disorder. Prosecutors later charged him with reckless driving.

When Pean sounded worse in the evening, his family summoned a fraternity brother in Houston to take him to an emergency room; his parents would fly in the next morning. But Pean did not wait. His mind vacillating between the knowledge that he needed psychiatric medication and encroaching delusions that he was a Barack Obama impersonator or a "Cyborg robot agent" who was being pursued by assassins, he said, he got into his white Lexus and drove at high speed to St. Joseph Medical Center, the only major hospital in downtown Houston.

Turning into the parking lot just before midnight, he crashed, nearly totaling his vehicle. As Pean was helped into the emergency room and onto a stretcher by paramedics and nurses, he recalled, he yelled: "I'm manic! I'm manic!"

He was seen immediately by a doctor from the trauma team to assess his injuries (scans and exams showed none). The physician's initial note, minutes after arrival, lists the young man's history of bipolar disorder. His father and brother, in separate phone calls to the emergency room, and a family friend who came to the hospital, alerted the staff about his psychiatric issues, they recalled.

Nonetheless, Pean was admitted for observation to Room 834 on a surgical floor. The diagnoses were hand abrasion, substance abuse, motor vehicle accident. His toxicology tests were negative for alcohol, opiates, PCP or cocaine, records show. (They did disclose some THC, the active ingredient of marijuana, but the chemical remains in the body for many weeks.)

While St. Joseph does have a psychiatric ward, Pean was never seen by a psychiatrist or prescribed any psychiatric medicines before the shooting. Because he had complained of back pain, he was given Flexeril, a muscle relaxant, which can exacerbate psychotic symptoms.

In interviews with the Medicare investigators and notations in medical records, the nurses who cared for Pean describe a man who had flashes of lucidity, but was increasingly restless and bizarre.

He pulled out the IV in his arm. He thought it was 1989. He could not remember the car crash or why he was in a hospital. But even in the throes of his illness, he was polite. When a nurse told him to return to his room after he repeatedly emerged naked into the hall, he complied, she told investigators, with a "Yes ma'am, righty-o, O.K. ma'am."

## "NO CLEAR GUIDANCE"

Though the trauma team had planned to discharge Pean that morning, his parents were so alarmed when they arrived about 10 a.m. that they insisted a psychiatrist see him. As they waited for doctors to discuss their concerns, the Peans went to their nearby hotel to try to rent a car and drive their son to a psychiatric facility. In their 30-minute absence, a nurse made a call to security.

At St. Joseph Medical Center, the security force included armed off-duty police officers as well as unarmed civilian officers. Who responded to a call depended only on availability, according to the investigators' interview with the chief nursing officer.

The two men who arrived were Houston police officers. Roggie V. Law, 53, who is white, and Oscar Ortega, 44, who is Latino, each had decades on the force. They supplemented their base salaries of about $64,000 by moonlighting at the hospital. Their records were unremarkable. Both had some commendations and Officer Ortega had one distant four-day suspension for failing to submit an accident report.

Houston police officers get 40 hours of crisis intervention training, according to the department. The NAACP and the Greater Houston Coalition for Justice, a civil rights group, have complained that local officers too often use their weapons, and repeatedly requested the appointment of an independent police review board. From 2008 to 2012, there were 121 police shootings, in which a quarter of the victims were unarmed, according to an investigation by *The Houston Chronicle*.

At right, Room 834 at St. Joseph Medical Center, where Alan Pean was shot in an encounter with armed security personnel, two off-duty Houston police officers. The two off-duty officers had signed on with Criterion Healthcare Security, a four-year-old staffing agency based in Tennessee whose executives had previously managed prisons and owned gyms. Their training at St. Joseph consisted of an orientation and online instruction, which investigators found inadequate. "The facility had no clear guidance for the role, duties and responsibilities of the police officers they employ to provide security services," the Medicare investigators' report said.

Like many other security firms, Criterion encourages applicants with law enforcement or military backgrounds, who are trained to use weapons and to deal with volatile situations. But working in healthcare settings requires a different mind-set, security experts emphasize.

"If they come from law enforcement or the military, I ask them directly, 'How would you respond differently here than if you encountered a criminal on a street in L.A. or when you are kicking down a door in Iraq?'" said Scott Martin, the security director at the University of California, Irvine, Medical Center. "You have to send the message that these are patients, they're sick, the mental health population has rights—and you need to be sensitive to that."

Many mental health professionals strongly object to weapons in hospitals, saying they have numerous other means—from talk therapy to cloth restraints and seclusion rooms to quick-acting shots of sedatives—to subdue patients if they pose a danger. State mental health facilities typically do not allow guns or Tasers on their premises; even police officers are asked to check weapons at the door. (Twenty-three percent of shootings in emergency rooms involved someone grabbing a gun from a security officer, according to a study by Dr. Gabor Kelen, director of emergency medicine at Johns Hopkins Medical School.)

Uniforms and weapons may, in fact, exacerbate delusions, since many psychotic patients are paranoid and, like Alan Pean, believe they are being pursued. Anthony O'Brien, a researcher at the University of Auckland, in New Zealand, said, "That's not a good thing, pointing something that looks like a gun at a patient with mental health issues."

When the two Houston officers arrived on St. Joseph's eighth floor, they headed for Room 834. Unannounced, and unaccompanied by doctors, nurses, or social workers, they went in, the door closing behind them.

## ANXIOUS PATIENT TO FELONY SUSPECT

Racing upstairs to a Code Blue in Room 834, Dr. Arango found a cluster of about 20 Houston police officers in the hall, according to his interview with investigators.

When he pulled back the sheet covering Pean, he saw that the patient was in handcuffs, his torso dotted with Taser probes and a bloody wound on his upper chest. It was only after the doctor noted the blood pooling around the young man, who began shouting that he was Superman as the physician tried to examine the wound, that someone mentioned he had not only been hit with the Taser, but also shot.

"Take the damn handcuffs off!" Dr. Arango yelled, according to an employee.

Initially combative and flailing, Pean allowed a staff member to start an IV as she told him: "It's O.K., Alan, I'm a nurse. We're here to help." Within minutes, doctors placed him on ventilator, inserted a tube into his chest and whisked him away for a scan, which showed that the bullet had fractured his fifth and sixth ribs, scattering metal fragments and causing extensive bleeding as it ripped through his chest.

According to a statement on the Police Department's website, Alan struck one officer in the head, causing a laceration, when they arrived in the room. Officer Law shocked the patient with a Taser, to no apparent effect, and then Officer Ortega, fearing for their safety, shot Pean.

After the shooting, his father said officers asked over and over if Alan had a criminal record. The next day, Christian Pean asked Sgt. Steve Murdock, a Houston police investigator, why the officers had to shoot his brother. In a phone conversation, Christian recalled, the sergeant replied, "Let's just say the term 'Tasmanian devil' comes to mind."

"It was like a big whirlwind," he went on. "Everything was fair game. Objects, chairs, eating trays, everything was being thrown."

An ambiguity in Medicare rules allowed Alan Pean's conversion from delusional patient to felony suspect. If a patient throws a tray at a nurse and the staff responds with restraints, it can be considered a healthcare incident. If the same patient throws the same tray at a police officer, even one off-duty, who shoots in response, the encounter is subject to a criminal investigation.

While Pean was in the intensive care unit, he was handcuffed to his bed, even though he was heavily sedated, with a Houston police officer standing guard. His family had to post $60,000 bail days later so he could be discharged from the hospital.

Pean's felony case is likely to go before a grand jury in the coming months. Under the care of a psychiatrist and on medication, Pean left Texas behind. Living with his brother in New York, he is finishing his degree at Hunter College and planning to go to graduate school in public health.

But the day before Christmas, Pean learned that prosecutors had brought a new charge—reckless driving—against him, referring to his race to the hospital.

Accompanied by his father, he flew to Houston. In five hours of processing at the Harris County Detention Center, Pean was interviewed by a detention officer, photographed for a mug shot and fingerprinted. "Being paraded around was really stressful," he said. "Did they not understand what I'd gone through? I'd been shot in a hospital room by an officer" (www.nytimes.com/2016/02/14/us/hospital-guns-mental-health.html).

Whether on the racially tense streets of Ferguson, Missouri, the rural roads of Oklahoma, or the medical ward in St. Joseph Medical Center, Houston or John's Hospital in upscale Maplewood, Minnesota, our frontline public safety and health-care professionals are out there, usually on their own with little support or security, trying to keep us safe and well. Legislation can be introduced to raise the ante for assaults, but we know that most go unreported. It takes only a matter of hours practicing in the locked psychiatric units of California County Hospitals from the East Bay to Ventura and central valley to learn to take care of yourself, because nobody's going to do it for you. All veteran health-care workers know that—especially veterans of inpatient psychiatry. Things are getting worse with budget cuts. As a result, police officers, nurses, and firefighters can expect little in the way of help on their jobs during the duration of their careers. But, we can learn from these critical incidents.

In these difficult security situations, in situations where the level of stress can cloud judgment, protocols can save lives. And the protocol of Rapid Assessment is a good way to start. Rapid Assessment begins with medical causations, rather than criminal and possibly insubordination. Medical screening should be the first priority. Subjects in police interactions acting strangely need not be handled violently. They need to be talked down, outnumbered by many officers, or EMTs called in to perform full emergency psychiatry if necessary. When possible and medically necessary, they need to be taken to the hospital ER. How would Brown and Johnson have responded to an ambulance with EMTs showing up? We do not know. Perhaps they would not have been provoked into confrontation as they were by an aggressive acceleration of a police car blocking their path. "Apparent Intoxication" is an evidence-based clinical presentation; so, Officer Wilson should have been informed or known that he had the option, given his belief he could not simply leave the scene, to call for EMTs to perform medical screening on the street; he certainly could not rule out that both had been exposed to toxins. Sure, this is unlikely, but far from impossible. Most cord blood of babies within a short radius of an LA hospital test positive for PCP. The mothers are not on it, or they could not deliver; it is likely in the atmosphere. Is it in the atmosphere of Ferguson, Missouri? We do not know, and neither did Officer Wilson. He assumed these two young men to be healthy males simply behaving with disorderly conduct or fugitives from a robbery—a very high-risk assumption for any first responder out there today. In this way, should police officers confronting difficult individuals be thinking differently than the nursing staff at St. John's? Actually, the nursing staff was probably in more jeopardy starting out with their patient than most police are with their subjects. Most times, difficult individuals acting strangely need medical assessment for altered states of consciousness that could be harbinger of dangerous medical problems. But, looking at street confrontations versus hospital confrontations, the settings for these engagements are so different that it is hard to see them in similar context. Yet, they are. Law enforcement could not stop any of them from risking the lives of others and themselves. It is doubtful, for example, that Big Mike and Charles E. Logan in their respective states of mind were concerned about the legal consequences of their aberrant behavior. Limits cannot be set in such circumstances. Smart management is necessary—tranquilization for Logan and diverting traffic while calling for EMTs for Brown and Johnson. It is very possible that in all three cases, some form of intoxication, whether from alcohol or from another substance, was the underlying cause of lethal escalation into ultimate use of deadly force that was not necessary, given our times of budgetary constraints and shortage of public safety and frontline health-care resources today.

For Oklahoma Highway Patrol (OHP) Officer Randolph, she herself admitted to the press that she prejudged Nolen, because he was riding with a woman and child. Her rapid assessment should have started with dangerousness, and this man fit the profile of "Dangerousness." Could anything she had done differently made a difference? She would agree it could have prevented a 12-hour manhunt for a fugitive. She should be extremely relieved she did not shoot him. For this type of suspected dangerousness, she should have been able to keep a close watch on him in the event he took off while she checked her computer for his record. She should not have trusted him so much to sit in her front seat and view his record with her. He could have hijacked the car with her. He could have gone for her gun. She did not know if he was armed. Therefore, as soon as she saw his record, she should have called for backup, maybe from the county sheriff likely closest by. A helicopter did show up, and maybe a high-speed chase would have occurred. With such a pursuit, perhaps Alton Nolen would have been examined more carefully in prison. Whether he was primarily a sociopath, psychotic on drugs, or an addict at this moment is not the important point. Officer safety and public safety are; bringing him into her car was risky, as she acknowledges. "It's a dangerous job," she said. Yes it is, and perhaps one counters fear with sense of omnipotent safety; recognizing who was in that car with her in 2010, she said that she learns, like everyone, from the scars. Nolen stripped flesh from her hand when he took flight with only one hand cuffed. Her hand is functional but visibly scarred from this violent encounter with one of the most insane of madmen ever released from our prisons.

The other was a suicidal killer we talked about here, William Spengler. The response to him was late, because he did not officially break the law after being released from parole. Boasting to a neighbor about killing his grandmother was chilling evidence that things would not stay peaceful, if they ever were really stable after release from prison. Spengler started a fire in his own home and began shooting firefighters as they tried to put the fire out, killing multiple first responders before killing himself. William Spengler should have been well known to everyone in public safety in Rochester, New York. West Webster lakeshore is not too big a community to know of a dangerous madman like Spengler who should not have been in the community in the first place, at least not without thorough psychiatric and clinical psychological examination before even sent to prison. Again, in this case, as studies show—and likely Ferguson is one more example—these people on the frontlines of public safety and health care today need to know what they are going into.

The case of William Spengler was like another Shawcross for Rochester, New York. Neither one of the worst of serial killers in history nor Spengler were undetectable. They were undetected. Failures in communication not only raise the risk for occupational stress in first response and health care but are also lethal. Clearly, public safety and public health institutions need to know who is in their domains, whether an officer's beat, ER admitting desk, or hospital ward. With knowledge and communications come better control. Such knowledge and communications will not bring us to zero violence for frontline clinicians and officers of the law, but extremely costly turnover of valuable staff and needless psychiatric and physical damage to our protectors can be significantly reduced by getting smarter and beginning to face the facts of life out there.

We live in a new era in which a large city police chief has to beg Congress to stop federal agencies from dumping undiagnosed and untreated combat veterans on his streets, and the judiciary has ruled that there is no such medical entity as psychotic disease; then what just happened at St. Joseph's Medical Center in Houston? (www.nytimes.com/2016/02/14/us/hospital-guns-mental-health.html). Thus, no more Red Roofs needed to humanely care for those who cannot cope with the demands of freedom. Our founding fathers certainly did not consider it the right of gravely disabled patients to be sleeping on the streets or obviously dangerous felons to simply do their time with determinate sentences, regardless of mental state at time of release. Such release should not be based on time or—too often, early, due to warden's authority to reduce overcrowding of prisons however he deems necessary. Even one of the deadliest serial murderers of our times, Ed Gein, subject of the movie *Psycho*, was paroled from prison to family in Seattle. Only a one in a million chance occurrence stopped the parole; a Bundy task force member recognized Gein's name by pure coincidence in a Rolodex file, simply because he recognized the name from growing up in Wisconsin. Nobody else in the department recognized the name, although they remembered the case and they know the corrections game of sunsetting—shipping the problem offender toward the setting sun.

We are asking our police, frontline medical professionals, and corrections officers to be responsible for far more than they are either equipped or trained to handle, and at the same time asking them to handle their own stress management as the requirements of the job change. Is this where we're going? Is this where we want to go?

> Milwaukee County Sheriff David A. Clarke Jr. set off alarm bells Friday with a radio spot some view as a call for citizens to arm themselves. In the radio ad, Clarke tells residents personal safety isn't a spectator sport anymore, and that "I need you in the game …… With officers laid off and furloughed, simply calling 911 and waiting is no longer your best option," Clarke intones."You could beg for mercy from a violent criminal, hide under the bed, or you can fight back." Clarke urges listeners to take a firearm safety course and handle a firearm "so you can defend yourself until we get there…. You have a duty to protect yourself and your family. We're partners

> now. Can I count on you?" (www.jsonline.com/news/milwaukee/sheriff-clarke-urges-residents-to-arm-themselves-with-guns-o38h47h-188375091.html)
>
> The suicide of Phoenix police officer Craig Tiger has city management taking a look at its policies and training regarding post-traumatic stress disorder issues.
>
> City Manager Ed Zuercher has announced the assembly of a panel to review the city's policies, at the request of the police unions, which have blasted Police Chief Daniel Garcia for his handling of Tiger's case.
>
> The Phoenix Law Enforcement Association (PLEA) and the Phoenix Police Sergeants and Lieutenants Association (PPSLA) announced Monday that they're going to hold votes of no confidence against Garcia. PLEA president Joe Clure said Garcia has "zero credibility" with Phoenix police officers on the issue of PTSD.
>
> Tiger committed suicide on November 8 after being fired from the department for a 2013 DUI arrest. Tiger was pulled over on June 5, 2013, on his way to a family cabin, where he planned to commit suicide. In the subsequent treatment he was ordered to undergo, Tiger was diagnosed with PTSD, stemming from his involvement in a fatal shooting the year before.
>
> According to Clure, Garcia ordered a termination hearing for Tiger, even though Garcia's policy on DUI doesn't call for automatic firings of officers busted for drunk driving.
>
> Clure says that at the termination hearing, he and Tiger provided medical proof of Tiger's PTSD diagnosis, and both pleaded with Garcia not to fire him. (Hendley 2014)

With so many people armed, and so many of them legally able, but too psychologically dangerous, to carry, the public cannot expect the police, EMTs and frontline clinical staff to keep them safe. It is their streets. Citizens must make them safer, and they can, as the parents of Newtown victims and Virginia Tech massacres are trying to do by suing firearms manufacturers and the state, respectively, for reckless endangerment.

Memorials are a posthumous honor, and expensive as well. It is time to pay forward and hold politicians and officials responsible for our public health and safety. From failures in Centers for Disease Control and Prevention (CDC) oversight of Ebola entering the ER at Texas Presbyterian Hospital to faulty practices at St. John's Hospital in Maplewood, Minnesota, the impossible must be removed from police, first responders, and frontline clinicians' unspoken job descriptions. The public does not want them to be disposable anymore than it wants our troops to be. But they are, and will continue to be, as long as accountants decide what is necessary for them to do their jobs, instead of competent leaders following best practices and professionals who know how to reduce the occupational stress our frontline emergency providers experience.

## REFERENCES

Dionne, E. J. 2015. FBI director offers "subversive" speech. *Washington Post* (Op-Ed), *Miami Herald* February 18, www.miamiherald.com/opinion/op-ed/article10647695.html#storylink = cpy

Hendley, M. 2014. Phoenix cop's suicide has city leaders looking at police PTSD issues. *Phoenix New Times*, November 18. www.blogs.phoenixnewtimes.com/valleyfever/2014/11/phoenix_cops_suicide_has_city_leaders_looking_at_police_ptsd_issues.php

Liebert, J., Smith, D., and Holiday, W. 1991. Prevention of stress disorders in military and police organizations. *Proceedings of Critical Incident Conference, Critical Incidents in Policing*. Federal Bureau of Investigation, Quantico, Virginia, 1989.

# 13

# Innovations in psychiatric criminology

Providing health-care insurance has been one of the major social goals of a handful of American presidents for over a century, beginning with Theodore Roosevelt. President Lyndon Johnson's Medicare moved the country forward in providing a form of health insurance for older Americans. First Lady Hillary Clinton's push to get more children covered under a form of health insurance also moved the ball forward. And President Obama's Affordable Care Act moved the ball up to the goal line, albeit, plagued with irrelevant riders from special interest groups. Though some may scream about socialized medicine, the real truth is that if a portion of the population cannot afford health care, especially mental health care, and emergency rooms (ERs) become the de facto family medical practice, American society itself will suffer, will bifurcate into the medical haves and have nots, and, ultimately, all taxpayers will wind up on the hook for the costs of public safety and emergency response, either at a state or local level. Thus, like it or not, we are in an era when public health will have to be publicly financed, ideally through an insurance mechanism rather than through property, local, state, and federal taxes, as it is now for the uninsured and underinsured as previously cited by the Detroit News for its metropolitan Wayne County.

The challenge for physicians in the era of the Affordable Care Act, though, is to make it work to solve problems we have identified, such as the evaluation and emergency treatment of those persons who are dangers to themselves and others, particularly in the workplace, on school campuses, and on the streets. "Going postal" is not just a term to describe a person acting with insane fury, it is a real phenomenon that grew out of the spate of workplace shootings over the past two decades, especially in post offices and other warehouse-type facilities where workers felt powerless, frustrated, and abused by their superiors. The problem with veterans suffering from untreated mental illness and having to navigate through the public sector as potential threats to their families and to the police is another challenge to public health under the Affordable Care Act as they are enrolled in private insurance plans due to the Department of Veterans Affairs (DVA) waitlist scandal.

The promise of the Affordable Care Act was that it would create a demand for more jobs in the health-care industry. But, professional health-care jobs require professional training, usually at the professional and graduate school level, and such job candidates are slow in coming online. As a result, even as the insurance industry experiences a boom from the federal medical insurance mandate, there are still scarce professional clinical resources that must be leveraged against the needs of medical consumers. And nowhere is this more evident than in the field of emergency psychiatric health care where, according to the Orange County Register in California, psychiatric patients are "packing" emergency rooms to the point where patients are simply "parked" waiting for attention while the ER nurses pay the price (Wolfson, staff writer, 2014).

The article reports that a severe shortage of psychiatric hospital beds, tight space in residential facilities, and less help at community clinics has turned Orange County emergency rooms into virtual boarding houses for psych patients. "'If you had a family member who had a psychiatric emergency, what would you do? The reality is you wouldn't know what to do'," says Steve Moreau, chief executive officer (CEO) of St. Joseph Hospital in Orange County, California, which is one of the county's designated psych facilities. "'There is no psychiatric emergency system in place. The default is for the police or a family member to take them to the nearest emergency room, and I can tell you that none of the ERs, including ours, is built or equipped to deal with psychiatric emergencies'."

Typical of many localities across the country, the newspaper reports, for almost a decade, hundreds, if not thousands nationwide, of psychiatric beds were lost, in Orange County alone over 20 years—over half its psychiatric beds. And just in the past couple of years Orange County alone had less than one-third of the psychiatric beds needed to house the county's population, according to mental health experts.

One of the major factors generally has been the shrinking and consolidation of the hospital industry itself. It stands to reason that as hospitals lose the ability to keep their doors open, as states cut public health-care budgets and underfund hospitals, one area of shrinkage is the emergency psychiatric facility. Gang violence, crime, domestic terrorism, and accidents all require emergency trauma centers which states have to fund to some degree and too often are in the public view after mass shootings today. But, not coincidental to increasing visibility of trauma centers for shooting victims is the marginalization of budgets for Psychiatry beginning in the 1970s. Before the Affordable Care Act, the lack of patients with health insurance also prevented hospitals from expanding their psychiatric treatment facilities, because the patient population simply could not afford it. Thus, a form of criminalization of psychiatric patients took place in which emergency first responders and public safety officers became the de facto custodians of the mentally ill behaving strangely or dangerously—a form of cost and administrative shifting.

The bottom line, according to directors of hospital-based psychiatric services, is that hospitals lose money on psychiatric, beds because the reimbursable costs under insurance policies for the most part do not cover psychiatric evaluations, absent hospitalization. Thus, unless patients can pay, hospitals don't have the means to pay attending psychiatrists. The medical specialty of psychiatry, therefore, is underfunded, and its work force is shrinking at a time when the country itself is in psychiatric crisis threatening both its national public health and safety. Moreover, because psychiatrists are not paid by insurance companies for consulting in the Emergency Rooms, the hospital itself must subsidize such psychiatric consultation services via salaries to have consultation for medical/surgical inpatients, whether in medical unit beds or the ER. With shrinking budgets, hospitals can't afford such overhead—thus the absence of emergency psychiatric ER consultation services. We still do not know how the Affordable Care Act will address this problem, if at all.

Even the context of inpatient psychiatric beds is different from that of trauma-focused emergency room. Because an ER is a place where patients are brought in from car accidents or heart attacks, it is often a chaotic environment with speakers blaring for on-call physicians, bright lights, and corridors filled with medical crash carts slamming back and forth, it is not the peaceful setting for psychiatric patients in distress. Imagine an agitated paranoid patient at the end of his or her tether having to wait for an interview with a Psychiatrist while the world around the patient looks like it is going to explode. This is not the facility where you want an emergency psychiatric patient to wait for help. And because time is of the essence for an emergency psychiatric patient due to worsening prognosis for increasing Duration of Untreated Psychosis (DUP), the standard trauma ER is exactly the wrong facility. Yet, ironically, a countertrend for survival in emergency medicine is to provide appointments by phone. This is oxymoronic. If a patient can make an appointment to come to the ER, the most expensive clinical site in town, he or she is simply not likely to have an emergency medical condition—or hopefully not calling for an appointment if considered an emergency! So, emergency medicine is perhaps giving up trying to be what it should be: inpatient emergency medical services for bona fide patients in need of Emergency Medical clearance and/or intervention, along with disaster preparedness. Instead it is encouraging patients to use it for their routine care; some insurance companies, including one of the federal government's own largest carriers TriCare for military dependents, pays 100% for any ER visit, while paying almost nothing for far greater needs of outpatient psychiatric care. Hopefully that is not the federal insurance program that veterans are receiving to overcome dangerous wait-time manipulations of the past, because even more psychiatric patients will be diverted then from acute and chronic outpatient care to ERs!

We need a new model to get us out of the box, and that model, we argue here, is telehealth and smart computers that embed clinical decision support into diagnostics and treatments via user-friendly screens—intuitive screens that move with the flow of the clinician's demand for decisions based on the artificial intelligence of best clinical practices—not just the "optimized patient flow by throughput in lean managed healthcare." The cornerstone for lean managed workflow is the Toyota Way, and this family business long ago embedded human decision-making every step of the way in manufacturing cars by enabling every worker on the assembly line to stop it to prevent errors, followed by brainstorming to fix the source of errors to prevent recurrence. This, in part, explains the reason for the explosion of the Japanese car market in the 1970s as the assembly-line procedures in American automobile manufacturing facilities resulted in so many defaults that many cars had to go right from the line to the repair shop to fix the faults created by the assembly line.

The same quality-control throughput must be accomplished with electronic healthcare records (EHRs) if the ambitious goals of improving outcomes under the Affordable Care Act—namely Meaningful Use—are to be accomplished. Unfortunately, Lean Managed Health Care is too often bastardized as cutting costs without comprehension of the Toyota Way for quality control. Hundreds of millions invested in an electronic medical record may reduce costly and cumbersome storage of paper medical records some day in the future. But, if it cannot prevent—or it actually causes—medical errors, value is simply rhetorical and marketing hype.

Also, along with the development of telehealth resources, there is a great need for psychiatric consultation liaison training for state, regional, and large municipal law enforcement, and emergency response agencies. Law enforcement agencies may argue legitimately that police should not be clinical psychologists, psychiatric nurses, and social workers, but we have argued just as legitimately that well trained and experienced police officers already are operationally active in those functional capacities in one form or another. The street smarts they developed over the years to keep them safe has imparted a significant degree of psychological expertise, both in the identification of problems and the means to solve them nonviolently and reasonably. Any good street cop will tell you that; they all know the good cops and the bad cops on their forces.

From the physician's point of view, one can view the Affordable Care Act (ACA) from two perspectives: the first is primarily political, top-down, both externally and internally, while the second is tactically. In the former case, the law has met great political resistance, for which the party passing it puts blame on partisan Republicans simply looking for a cause to block any progressive legislation. Of course, this is true to a great extent, as would be any legislation imposed so quickly following another in a recent series of polarized elections based on dramatically different views of how the economy and the government should work. Opposition to ACA, however, has justification in both the fact that, although it was a campaign issue promulgated by both candidates, its passage by a Democrat-controlled legislature caught the public off guard. The first target of the new act was the dramatic reform of the health-care insurance system. Because there was little or no drawn-out public debate on the subject due to embroilment in ideology having nothing to do with health care and everything to do with misunderstood notions of what a free marketplace is, America woke up one morning to what amounted to a new health-care tax camouflaged by a mandate. The Supreme Court unraveled any confusion by correctly holding that under Article I of the Constitution, the legislature has the power to "tax and spend" for any legitimate purpose that Congress so defines. Now, years after its passage and as the country enters its next enrollment period, we need to look at statistics with respect to how the ACA deals with the issue of community mental health, particularly community mental health as a firebreak to stop the spread of psychopathogens causing an epidemic of violence in society and a counterepidemic of police overreaction by lethal criminalization of mental illness.

Regardless of how one views the benefits or drawbacks of the ACA, it is clear that it has changed the landscape of health-care provision in the United States in ways that it may take a decade or so to understand or fully appreciate. One can argue the validity of subscriber numbers and demographics back and forth, but with successive enrollment periods amid the graying of the American population, we will soon be able to gauge the longer-term success. For our purposes, though, the impact of the law should be looked at as it applies to addressing the problem of mental health, something that President John F. Kennedy argued for so passionately early in his term in office. It was an issue he passionately supported because of his sister, Rosemary, who was mentally ill, institutionalized by her father Joe Kennedy, and then lobotomized into a kind of oblivion. Jack Kennedy sought better solutions, but it was an issue that died with him in 1963 (Fuller Torrey 2013).

No matter what one's position is about the ACA, both sides can agree that it has changed the consumer landscape of health care in America. From the view of the practicing physician, hospital director, and public health official, however, the perspective from the ground up is quite a different matter. Those intending to stay in the game are learning the new rules and struggling, as well as maneuvering, to adapt. Finding the smooth flow of reimbursables to deliver the best quality health care while avoiding the shoals of claims denials, is the mantra today. Those not adjusting to the new landscape will flounder as their patients and clients feel the pain. Entrepreneurs are mushrooming across the landscape to find out how to take advantage of the new law's requirements and get on its right side. They include clinicians and MBA's alike, both in numbers never seen before.

For example, the federal government estimated that this country needs 30,000 MD/Intensivists to safely man intensive care units (ICUs) across the nation. There are only 8000. There is a need for 6000 more child psychiatrists, but without massive funding invested for training now, this quota will never be reached in this century. At the same time, Congress, decrying the federal deficit, has cut billions from community health programs, the National Institutes of Health, and the Centers for Disease Control for both enlarging emergency medical capacity and preventing the violence threatening its effective function. Is it any wonder, then, as the first stirrings of the Ebola epidemic reaches our shores that the lack of medical personnel training at the local and municipal levels—as well as the lack of research in epidemiology—is having an effect on the incidence of Ebola in the United States, the incidence of which should have been zero. The very politicians screaming about unpreparedness are the same ones who cut the budgets in the first place. Congress could not even bring itself to confirm a new surgeon general as the Ebola crisis exploded in West Africa, because President Obama's candidate, Vivek H. Murthy—also an MBA who was finally confirmed in December 2014—spent a year in the shadows of waiting for his vote because of a statement he'd made about gun violence being a matter of public health. Of course C. Everett Koop, a previous surgeon general, had said that as well, but it made no difference to the National Rifle Association (NRA) who lobbied against him and kept his nomination in limbo for a year, regardless of the Ebola crisis reaching our shores. This was never about the right to own guns. It was about how the gun lobby terrorized craven legislators into putting Americans at risk for disease and violence.

We are behind the curve on many emergency medical issues. For example, medical education has not expanded nearly enough to meet the demands of equitable care for everyone under the intent of universal care of ACA. But, something else has happened, whether due to ACA or coincidental to it, and that is mobile communications and computing, which in many ways facilitate the intent of ACA so that it takes health care to the patient. It is not that different a trend than brick-and-mortar shopping, which is evolving into online shopping. Many states, like those in the four-corner region of Utah, Colorado, Arizona, and New Mexico, concentrate over 80% of their populations in just two cities. Rural areas have been neglected by health-care planners and providers alike. Small-town hospitals in these states cannot deliver quality care and must depend on diverting patients at great cost and great risk to one or two cities for their care. And some state governors, so adamantly opposed to the ACA that they will punish their own constituents by denying them federally funded Medicaid, watch and applaud while some of the small hospitals in their states that serve the underprivileged and minority populations simply close for lack of Medicaid support and funding; so much for public emergency medical response and public health. Long ago this was noticed as a problem, and the University of Arizona began a program to read interpret frozen sections in Tucsson during surgeries in remote areas, enabling general surgery to be safely performed in remote regions. Nobody knew of ACA then, but now the Four Corner Telemedicine Consortium is seeking ways to implement, benefit from and change certain provisions of state and federal law to remedy the situation.

Internet connectivity also enables specialists to diagnose and treat many of their patients at virtually any point on the globe from a fixed position. Geography, for the most part, is no longer a barrier to many highly specialized clinical services, such as neurology, ophthalmology, dermatology, clinical psychology, and psychiatry. Only political and legal barriers obstruct taking many valuable services, such as psychiatric diagnosis and treatment, to patients in remote locations. The ability to take health care to the consumer, rather than having the consumer come to health care, is part of the change in ACA. Prisons and colleges alike are experimenting with secure video screens in cells and dorm rooms, respectively, to facilitate the prompt assessment of at-risk populations profiled in this book. Patient satisfaction also becomes "meaningful use" for which providers are rewarded. The younger patient wants to connect with health care using his cell phone. Now, for many channels of care, such as psychiatry, such delivery of care is feasible via telepsychiatry and teleneurology.

Billions in private venture capital, along with billions in federal grants, are going into this burgeoning field of medicine once called telemedicine, then e-health—and soon, simply "medicine"—that is neither outpatient nor inpatient. It is too young to have a title as it encroaches from the margins of care delivery to the core. You can now sit in a chair anywhere and look into a binocular-like apparatus that can be adjusted by someone without a lot of training and have the retinae of your eyes examined as well as, if not better than, the quick exam in a darkened office. Cannon brings its high-quality photo technology to the patient-doctor relationship, creating a better visualized retina to find possible brain disease that manifests in changes of the optic nerve as visible as Mt. Fuji on a clear day. Arteries to the eye that are traditional signatures of hypertensive cardiac disease and diabetes can also be scanned this way once the pupils are dilated to allow a specialist to see the retina. Furthermore, the images can be archived and seen later, if not urgently, or sent to another specialist in order to track the all important change depended on in medicine to establish a baseline for measurement that can help distinguish wellness from disease. One shot, for example, may not be enough. Serial images, whether hourly, as in head trauma, or monthly in serious cases of essential hypertension and diabetes, are brought to the screen as easily as your children's photos on a smartphone.

> Ralph Lauren is leading in early detection of disease with smart sweaters. Doctors will be following the lead of fashion designers for early detection of such conditions as Hypertension, when early detection and clinical intervention means the difference between a relatively healthy life and one of costly debilitation with suffering and premature death. (Sanders, 2014)

What does Sanders mean? This sounds like heresy, but he explains. There is "white coat" hypertension. You walk into the doctor's office, and your blood pressure is above the norm of 140/90. Based on that one reading, you are prescribed antihypertensives, which you may take for the rest of your life with risk of side effects, unnecessary costs, and possible adverse reactions. But, your sweater was monitoring you while sitting on the deck listening to the birds, and your blood pressure was 110/70. You do not have essential hypertension, but, rather benign labile hypertension that does not require treatment—just mindfulness of your health. You do not have to read your blood pressure every 15 minutes and become a hypochondriac. People need to be educated. The flip side of this is the highly functional person, perhaps the high school basketball player. His pulse transmits variability of heart disease, particularly when exercising. He needs treatment, but he never had an electrocardiogram (ECG). He drops dead in the middle of a game. We call it "Sudden Death." But, was it that sudden? Today, his sweater from Ralph Lauren and shirt from Under Armor showed him to have fatal cardiac disease with exercise intolerance for years prior to his sudden cardiac arrest. His Apple watch that monitors his pulse may not only warn him of circulatory problems, it may also have the ability to transmit his heart rate via a WiFi hub to his team doctor. This is just an example that allows the consideration of the possibilities for optimizing health-care services via technology alone with no new law required. This is not the world of Dick Tracy, but, rather, the real world now. Why now? Because ACA has, by intelligent planning in some cases and pure luck in others, made it harder for providers, whether hospitals or doctors, to do it the old way.

"Meaningful Use" can be the justification for getting paid by Medicaid or Medicare for taking care of somebody you refused to care for the old way. Now, you can get paid to meet your patient in his home, take his blood pressure, look into his eyes, and check abnormalities of his pulse and heart rhythms without the patient or you traveling anywhere. It is all done via your tablet and the patient's large-screen smartphone. By and large, pathologists do not recognize such electronic changes early on in the at-risk person as disease. We are stuck with a norm that one blood pressure (BP) reading was not essential hypertension, but benign labile hypertension.

Could that 16-year-old star basketball player have been spared his athletic career—or more importantly his life? Most likely, but we need to follow our smart apparell. This is the coming new world of iMedicine—smart watches that read your blood pressure, blood glucose, and take your pulse while working out or at rest. Connect the device wirelessly to a physician's EHR database and you can be diagnosed on the fly without making an office visit. As clinicians, think about how it can work for both the health–care provider and the health of the patient, as well as the community. Ideally, there will not be those shocking sudden deaths, because the disease is detected before the apparently healthy person simply drops dead (Dolan 2014).

The devil, of course, is in the details, and there is a myriad of devils in ACA. For example, if a hospital discharges a patient and that patient is readmitted for any condition, whether related to the original disease or not, the first hospital is penalized. Think about the Texas Presbyterian Hospital in Dallas where Ebola patient Thomas Eric Duncan was released by an emergency-room clinician, even though he was spiking a 103-degree fever and reported he had just come from Liberia. Days later he was readmitted and quarantined and infected other people as well as requiring the evacuation and cleanup of the apartment where he was staying. Think of the costs that entailed. The intent, therefore, is to reduce readmissions by getting it right the first time without cost-plus utilization of expensive inpatient services and testing. That is worthy, as demonstrated by the catastrophic Duncan discharge and readmission.

Hospitals must keep their beds filled with higher numbers of new patients every year to avoid bankruptcy. They must do it within evidence-based parameters of effective hospital days. This is called diagnostic related groups. So, you discharge the patient a day early, and you keep the money. You do not, and you pay the extra days out of somebody else's days, or your own reserves. Fair? Arguably not. Safe? Not always. The way it is going to be? Most likely. So, we learn to operate with what is not too unfair or unsafe and lobby to get rid of the devils in the details. Hospitals cannot be responsible for everything that can go wrong with a patient after discharge unless they were initially negligent in that discharge.

Hospitals can be responsible for some of what happens after discharge. For example, delirium, particularly in geriatric patients, affects most inpatients at some time during their inpatient stays. Too often it is missed, and when not missed, it is minimized euphemistically as "sun-downing." But, research shows that undiagnosed and untreated delirium results in higher posthospital mortality, as well as chronic disability, or "morbidity." So, hospitalists and nursing staffs must be alert for delirium and monitor it with evidence-based tools now available to diagnose, measure and monitor it.

Treatments are not proven yet, but there is an evidence base for clearing delirium. It is not the norm for the frail and sick patient to forget where she is and who she is just because the sun goes down. Treat it, or there may be a readmission in 30 days to your hospital or another. Had Charles Logan been monitored by a nursing technician on a CAM Scale for Delirium at St. John's Hospital in Maplewood, Minnesota, very likely his confusional state could have been detected before he exploded with paranoia and a bloody rampage that injured his nurses and resulted in his death at the hands of police outside the hospital. Similarly, Thomas Duncan, when his temperature spiked, very possibly had mental status changes detectable with current bedside monitoring tools, but too often, in the fast-paced ER, such monitoring is not available. It may have prevented admission of Charles Logan to a medical bed had his confusional state been detected and diagnosed in the ER, rather than postmortem with probabilities from severe febrile disease state—if even then. Hospitalization is costly and bed time an increasingly scarce resource that must be used wisely, and in cases like the Maplewood, Minnesota disaster, safely also.

What is new and driving innovation and best practices is that the hospital gets financially penalized for bad outcomes. Hospitals run on thin profit margins, and the government knows that. Thus, the requirements of the ACA will impact hospitals where it makes them think about best practices as it relates to their bottom line. A local hospital might be a "Charity Hospital," but, unless it has the Harvard endowment underwriting its losses for research and overstays in teaching hospitals, the facility will close in bankruptcy. And many smaller hospitals in rural areas are closing. Mobile technology can save them. They can also save the big guys—particularly in the ERs that are under stress for being penalized for long wait times on the one hand and failure to have an MD effectively examine and treat the patient on the other, which was the case with Thomas Eric Duncan, who ultimately died from Ebola.

With liability issues on the rise in the midst of an epidemic of violence, as well as a potential epidemic of infectious pathogenic diseases, the ER waiting room where, traditionally, patients sat waiting interminably in varying degrees of misery and discomfort, is soon gone, and along with it the triage nurse. With the new trend of optimizing patient flow, every patient is to be taken back and bedded down in the ER where they undergo rapid assessment, a form of triage in which the credentialing, experience and training are undefined, as are the rules and knowledge base. In this chapter, we define rapid assessment and illustrate it, using mobile technology applications coming on-stream in health care faster than new products on supermarket shelves. We examine the evidence-based rules for rapid assessment generated, by the intent of—or despite—the ACA, one step beyond the patient's home or a clinical facility's bed, and we advocate for reimbursement to do this. Money drives the bus in health care, just as it does in any other business. We demonstrate rapid assessment's promise as it relates to encounters from on the street, in prison, in the dorm room, to the little school nursing office of the next potential Sandy Hook, Isla Vista, Columbine—or the gang incubators in inner city at storefront clinics. And we illustrate its effectiveness as well in the counseling and health centers of Northern Illinois University (NIU), Pima College, and Milwaukee School of Engineering Nursing School, all of which incubated suicidal mass murderers—Kazmierczak, Loughner and Haughton, respectively—and unwittingly cut off from their educational attachment to assumedly be picked up in some undefined way in the community. They weren't; so, there is no longer a choice. The risks of denying reality or an epidemic more deadly than Ebola—that of neuropsychiatric emergencies converting through negligence in the community into disaster medicine from the very sick going berserk, as with Kazmierczak at NIU, Loughner in Tucson and Haughton at Azuza Spa, Wisconsin, respectively—is now unacceptable. There is a threshold of public consciousness simply no longer mollified by pundits and their assertions that school massacres are random acts that simply go with living on our planet; the public will not watch another school evacuation with their kids marched from school, hands up. Congress will be forced to act. This will be the promise of change we can believe in.

The next weekend of shocking body counts from gang violence will be here soon. Just look at the recent spate of homicides in Baltimore after the Freddie Gray riots. Another veteran has probably shot himself to death since reading this far in the present chapter, and there are millions more at high risk. Even the FBI knows now that school shootings are not random but expected anywhere and anytime without limits. More police scandals will be headlines as psychotics and the marginalized—particularly minorities—are shot down in the street whether they present a lethal threat or not. ERs will be packed with patients, many posing threats of violence to staff and should not be there, particularly when the dreaded surge of a multicasualty incident, whether accident, terrorism, or storm hits, as in the case of Joplin, Missouri, Hospital; it was literally blown away and had to be managed mostly via telehealth by its partner hospital in St. Louis. As more seriously ill psychiatric patients tie up ER staffs due to nonavailability of any other care besides jails, more patients with pneumonia and heart attacks will have delayed preadmission treatment that increases their posthospital risk of serious and chronic disability—or even death. More patients will disgracefully suffer worse and longer from severe pain in the ER due to overcrowding. More psychotics will die in prison from nothing other than correctional practices predating unchaining of the mentally ill of Paris in the eighteenth century, thus regressing public psychiatry to the Colonial practices. And this is where we are with our mental health system in America. Violence is all around us, and even medical professionals do not have a clue about stopping it or responding personally.

Should they get a gun and go to the range? Should they tell anyone they are armed? A psychiatrist recently killed an intruder who shot his colleague. This is a rare event, but one that got most psychiatrists' attention; should they worry about this any more than they have throughout their careers? Most psychiatrists have been assaulted during their careers, and murder is one of the most common—if not the most common—cause of death in the young psychiatrist. Is that changing for the worse? Psychiatrists and therapists—and since the murder of a cardiac surgeon in a Harvard teaching hospital, increasingly all doctors in general—are worried.

Violent assaults by patients in hospitals is surging, risking both their own lives from security officers who shoot them when they are agitated and unaware of their environments—or increasing numbers of clinical staff are seriously injured, if not killed while attending to patients!

This is not change we can believe in. It is simply the unvarnished reality of public health and safety today. It is not even the political changing of society in favor of one constituency or another. School shootings have been favoring the richer communities and not the ghettos of our cities or rural poor. Ebola does not discriminate. Guns, knives, fists, or rape do not discriminate. Change is not a political choice. It is a public health and public safety responsibility that can be accomplished without another round of legislation and election debate.

The recent death of a Liberian citizen from Ebola in a Dallas Hospital is also the marquee case for time-determined and epidemiologically informed clinical decision making. This patient presented to this ER of Texas Presbyterian Hospital in Dallas where he informed clinicians that he had just arrived from Liberia. This, in itself, should have been a red flag. His symptoms of abdominal pain, dizziness, a headache, decreased urination, and a spiking temperature were all indicators, in light of his recent arrival from Liberia, that he was suffering from Ebola and was contagious. Though attending physicians ruled out appendicitis, stroke, and cardiac disease through differential diagnoses, they did not flag him for Ebola and instead prescribed antibiotics and a weak painkiller, discharging him nonambulatory on a stretcher to a medically naïve fiancé with diagnosis of sinusitis, despite a normal CAT Scan of his head. Then, in spite of his fever, a physician's note dated September 26 said Duncan was "negative for fever and chills."

This is a huge problem with point-of-entry diagnostics in all encounters with the unknown patient today, whether the ER or college counseling center. Attending clinicians, whether triage nurse, crisis counselor, EMT or emergency medicine specialist, fly by the seats of their pants. This patient was very sick coming in and discharged as stable—a magical recovery! The printout from the Epic Electronic Medical Record controlled this patient's throughput at some robotic level, likely matching hundreds of others printed out with the touch of a finger and handed to the patient for discharge—in and out. Compare this to flying. Flight surgeons became knowledgeable about the cockpit's warning lights; they want to live to practice another day. Sometimes in wild and dangerous situations, it is necessary to take chances and take off before getting blown up—but, not when taking off from Love Field, Dallas-Fort Worth. All the lights have to be on, off, and not blinking wrong before takeoff. Now apply this to medicine.

It has been repeatedly found that physicians need more information every day in their practices than they can access from memory—particularly in these days when in and out fast is very important for purposes of financing such points of entry, such as the ER. There is tremendous pressure on staff to get people in and out of the ER for the next patient to bed down. Patient satisfaction is primo, and patients do not want to wait. The old model of a packed waiting room with an ER nurse experienced in clinical triage is giving away to zero wait times and rapid assessment by staff with unknown qualifications and experience—sometimes even a lay volunteer. The result can be a tragic misdiagnosis. How could disastrous outcomes such as these have been prevented?

The answers lie in the concept of time-determined and epidemiologically informed clinical decision making. What does "Working smart" by knowing "Likelihood" mean in classical emergency medicine triage? Now, as pushed down from experienced "pivot nurses" in the waiting room to anybody selected by the director of the ER to greet patients like Thomas Duncan, the trend is to have them put an ID tag on the patient and send them back to be admitted to an ER bed. This is the trend, with no options such as long wait times, diversion to urgent care, or otherwise. These terms are critically important to understand what went wrong in this routine local emergency medicine presentation that converted to a potential case of disaster medicine globally. The case of Thomas Eric Duncan caught the nation's attention and became politicized by the left and the right, driving their respective pundits to the frontlines. But suicidal students and veterans do not—at least to the degree that anything will change within the institutions responsible for changing, as with CDC, American Hospital Association, DVA, Department of Defense (DOD), Substance Abuse and Mental Health Services Administration (SAMHSA), and the myriad others in the bureaucratic alphabet soup too numerous to list.

When have we read before that patients were discharged before a meaningful time-determined diagnosis was assembled? Eddie Routh, who shot and killed "American Sniper" Chris Kyle at a Texas gun range was shoved out of the Dallas Veterans Affairs Medical Center (VAMC) 2 days before the shooting in total disregard of the terrified pleadings of his parents. He was grossly delusional. Documentation records the fact that he was so confused the clinician discharging him home alone had to communicate instructions to his mother. Aaron Alexis was shoved out of two VAs until, finally, complaining of a microchip embedded in his brain commanding him to do things against his will, likewise, in short order, terminated the mind control of the microchip in his brain by committing the Navy Yard massacre. He left many dead, but the mind control was finally extinquished as he graphically engraved in psychotic terminiology of controlling microwaves on his rifle butt. It was tragically late to decode his motivation, but any clinician having read Freud's Influencing Machine about paranoia could now belatedly understand at an inexcusably what was engraved on the rifle butt had been written on the wind for years.

Seung-Hui Cho was discharged from emergency detention with the most cursory workup and sent back to campus. Nobody even knows to this day how he got back there, and—his delusions of suicidal mass murder compounded every day until shocking the world following unspeakable bloodshed on a college campus with his unintelligible manifesto on NBC News and appearance of martyred Korean warrior.

The records of his critically important commitment hearing were intentionally destroyed; the records from his court-ordered treatment at the university health center mysteriously disappeared, only coincidentally to resurface following the conclusion of the governor's investigation. Most curious is the fact that this investigation concluded that Cho, and only Cho, pulled the trigger, but the

Cho case remains under investigation to this day—as does, perhaps by no coincidence, civil litigation against the Commonwealth of Virginia.

Where have we heard this before—case closed, but not cleared? It was Mirage Man, Bruce Ivins, who was tried and convicted posthumously in the press and civil court following his suicide as highly publicized person of interest for dispersing weaponized anthrax. But we already know for an indisputable fact that the 9/11 hijackers were walking around with a suitcase full of weaponized anthrax as they sought a Small Business Administration loan for a crop-dusting company start-up in Florida (Liebert and Birnes 2011). All this was considered random and unpreventable, as was the Eliott Rodger case in Santa Barbara, when sheriff's deputies investigated this young man who was making threats of mass murder/suicide on the Internet. But, a policeman decided he was neither sick nor dangerous enough to transport to the hospital under 5150 probable cause order for emergency psychiatric examination.

Our nation's points of entry, whether ERs, clinics, jails, prehospital care on the street, or forward operating bases overseas (FOBs) for war on terror can no longer be deaf, dumb, or blind to the threats of the viral spread of pathogens, whether in the form of a deadly virus, chemical warfare agents as in Gulf War Syndrome or from ISIS—or diabolically learned nerve pathways turned pathogenic like a virus to spread mass violence and suicide from Oslo, Norway, to Newtown, Connecticut. Most recently two girls died from a murder suicide on the grounds of a Glendale, Arizona High School campus! Most likely they had a suicide pact driven from social media. All points of entry need to be intelligent for surveillance of problems identified as epidemic—whether infectious diseases or suicidal psychosis. Staff can no longer fly by the seats of their pants, ignoring the clear and convincing evidence that they can no longer diagnose and treat everyone without the technological extension of Computerized Clinical Decision Support Systems built into their EHR—along with smart mobile applications. Mobile communications now facilitate clinicians and first responders' access to all information needed for care of a person anywhere the at-risk populations identified in this book takes us.

The task embodied within the ACA—or any other approach to universal health care—besides bringing the best health care to consumers and keeping costs as low as possible, is to assess threats to health, both the physical threat of a viral epidemic and the psychopathological threat of a person possibly approaching the point of the spear for dangerous behavior. We have seen in the Duncan case that this has failed, just as we have seen in the epidemic of mass shootings, one occurring every few days in America, that the old ways of workup in first encounters with unknown people are failing. We understand that in terms of physical medicine, the ACA provides for electronic medical records shared among physicians treating the same patients. Now we have to use that same type of technology for psychiatric cases; the psychiatrist at University of Illinois had no knowledge of Kazmierczak's serious mental illness requiring institutional care in high school, and nor did the US Army or NIU. But, it has to work, create valid alerts with less dumbing white noise, and truly be interoperable; more often than not, despite the marketing hype of computer software makers and their DC lobbyists, it fails in all of these needs for intelligent clinical computing. Nowhere is this more important than in the patient cohort of veterans who are already stamped with approval to be in the VA medical services system via the DVA Compensation and Pension adjusters and PEBLAs in military hospitals.

Our case-in-point here is the rather long-standing telepsychiatry practice of Milwaukee VAMC to evaluate patients in the remote upper peninsula (UP) of Michigan. Many combat veterans seek out remote sites to live for both peace of mind and financial survival. The UP is such a place, sparsely populated and rich in game and fish. A veteran can survive on little income, such as a partial disability for posttraumatic stress disorder and traumatic brain injury. Veterans living in the UP can see as many people in a day—or none, as he/she wishes. Combat nurses from Vietnam likewise sought out such remote areas to live. Their PTSD was way under-assessed too, because, unlike female soldiers today, they were supposedly not exposed to combat—a glaring deficiency in DOD administration's understanding of that war also. They were exposed to combat, and even worse—its casualties, and they were least experienced and youngest of the military nursing corps.

In the case of remote medicine in the "UP," the veteran goes to a clinic that is staffed with a nurse or physician's assistant trained in neuropsychiatry—perhaps a former combat nurse or medic with additional training. These are telepresenters who meet with the patient and perform selective examinations directed by medical staff at Milwaukee VAMC 600 miles away. The patient is assessed, diagnosed, and treated on the spot. This is synchronous telepsychiatry. The presentation can also be archived for further assessment later. In the case of remote areas and such skittish patients known as "tripwires," veterans seemingly addicted to living hand to mouth in the forests—like jungles of Asia—it is best to treat them on the spot. They are simply not going to—nor capable of—travel to Milwaukee. Although this program predated the ACA with accountable care organizations (ACOs) and meaningful use (MU), it would be a model for achieving outcomes, rather than "reimbursable patient visits." This is meaningful use in the VA EHR, known as VISTA—and connectedness via telehealth, hopefully portending the future for ACOs under the Affordable Care Act. In this case, Milwaukee VAMC is the hub, and UP VA clinics are the spokes. The technology for such consultations has vastly improved since this project was first implemented. Now the psychiatrist and neurologist can see the retinae of their patients' eyes 600 miles away with images, oftentimes more clearly than they could with the patient in their examining room. Likewise with auscultation of the heart, perhaps they can get better resolution or rhythm and clarity of heartbeat than they could in their examining room. And, with wearable sensors, they can monitor blood pressure, pulse, and oxygen and glucose of the veteran's blood 24/7. They can monitor his ECG, too, if necessary, and in the not too distant future, economically monitor his brain waves while awake and sleeping—all by broadband transmission of signals from a nonintrusive, durable, and wearable computer embedded in the veteran's hunting uniform—or even winter steelheading vest—and a sophisticated wired helmet.

For these veterans and players, Under Armor may be the innovator. These vets hunt and fish all year around. That is the way they survive and find peace of mind.

Their behavior cannot be changed. They are not going to live the way we expect them to live and receive their medical care the way we think they should—i.e., downtown, close to the Milwaukee VAMC. Basketball jerseys may also monitor ECG rhythms, pulse, blood oxygen, and blood pressure, thus preventing many sudden deaths on the playing fields and courts; routine pediatric exams to date have not been able to detect these cardiac diseases early enough to prevent sudden death during athletic events.

The DVA already has the capability for meeting the requirements of the ACA. Their failures to do so are mainly embedded in their moronic dual missions—hence culture—of both caring for and adjudicating entitlements of 20 million beneficiaries. This is impossible to juggle, so, until the Commander in Chief and Congress recognize this fact, there will be major incident after major incident, preventable disaster after preventable disaster, and scandal after scandal among our veteran population. The DVA administration is incentivized to generate numbers that show results. They must also stay within budget. Again, this is a mission impossible, because counterproductive incentives at cross-purposes to each other require cooking the books, and this demoralizes clinical staff while it kills off veterans who survived war but not the claims processing maze created by the kindly Uncle Sam.

There are challenges in time-determined diagnoses:

> One is our health-care system's reliance on computerized technology that is too often unfriendly to clinicians, especially those who work in stressful situations like a crowded emergency room. . . .
>
> Long promised as the panacea for patient safety errors, electronic health records, in fact, have fragmented information, too often making critical data difficult to find. Often, doctors or nurses must log out of the system they are on and log into another system just to access data needed to treat their patients (with, of course, additional passwords required); that is the case with the four different systems in the Army that track each soldier's care. Worse, data is frequently labeled in odd ways. For example, the results of a potassium test might be found under "potassium," "serum potassium level," "blood tests," or "lab reports." Frequently, nurses and doctors will see different screen presentations of similar data, making it difficult to collaborate.
>
> Another technological issue is the "flatness" of electronic medical records: much of the information looks the same—a series of boxes to check and pre-formatted text that makes highlighting an urgent or important issue difficult. Electronic records, with their cut-and-paste functions, create what doctors call "chart bloat." The announcement that Thomas Duncan's electronic records totaled 1400 pages illustrates this phenomenon. Poor record presentations may well have contributed to the hospital spokeswoman's initial statement that Duncan's temperature was only 100.1, when in fact the hospital's records show it increased from that to

> 103 by the time Duncan was discharged four hours later. (Koppel and Gordon 2014)

The electronic medical record in the Duncan case probably did not cause this catastrophic failure in rapid assessment, as alleged by some, but it is certainly not the tool the president promised members of the American Medical Association (AMA) listening to his address to prevent malpractice. We do know that electronic medical records in use today have little or no intelligence and would not pass the first screen of quality control at Apple for intuitiveness. They are simply recordkeeping devices that either take garbage in and give garbage out—as in the 1400 pages of digital records of Thomas Duncan—or distract and add burden to already overburdened ER staff, too frequently desensitizing attendings with dumb alarms not really passing an FDA smell test for meaningful use. But, where is the Food and Drug Administration (FDA) on this? Is the FDA hamstrung by lobbyists for medical software makers under both the billions allocated to them under the Financial Stimulus Act of 2008 or The Affordable Care Act? They made sure they would be well taken care of by Uncle Sam, although they way oversold their "flat" digitized solutions to both the needs of our economy and then our healthcare system in both legislative acts. How, then, can they be simplified and truly be meaningful to optimize service, and not just blind in supporting "throughput" of the hospital administration's six sigma dashboard?

Here's how. First there must be evidence-based clinical defaults like this one for "Contagiousness"; this has been known, and essentially ignored, since the anthrax attacks associated with 9/11.

Save the patient, then yourself by immediately doing the ABCDE of classical Emergency Medicine Triage and observing for contagiousness and contamination (Figures 13.1 and 13.2).

> And, now protect yourself, and, *if slightest suspicion of contagiousness,* take precautions from standard infectious disease protocols available in Dictionary of Dictionary and Text from The Digital Clinician®

Software developers will have to go back to their drawing boards to make their systems effective tools for managing patients and patient flow—not just storage devices for 1400 virtual pages of clinician documentation and data useful now in the Duncan case, only to plaintiff attorneys and corporate counsel making a deal largely invisible to the public—and even politicians and officials who need to know what went wrong that fateful day at Dallas Health Presbyterian Hospital ER. EHR salesmen should start working with democratically elected representatives from all clinic or hospital constituencies to make certain that their software supports all stakeholders in a healthcare ecosystem—not just the hospital CIO. Such consensus before the ink is dried on an irreversible multimillion dollar EHR contract in a CEO's office is the Toyota Way that, as in the Toyota family enterprises through generations created unity In production. And, yes there can be Unity in Health Care the Toyota Way, but for healthcare IT to be the master of its synonymously and more preferred management testimonial, lean managed health care,

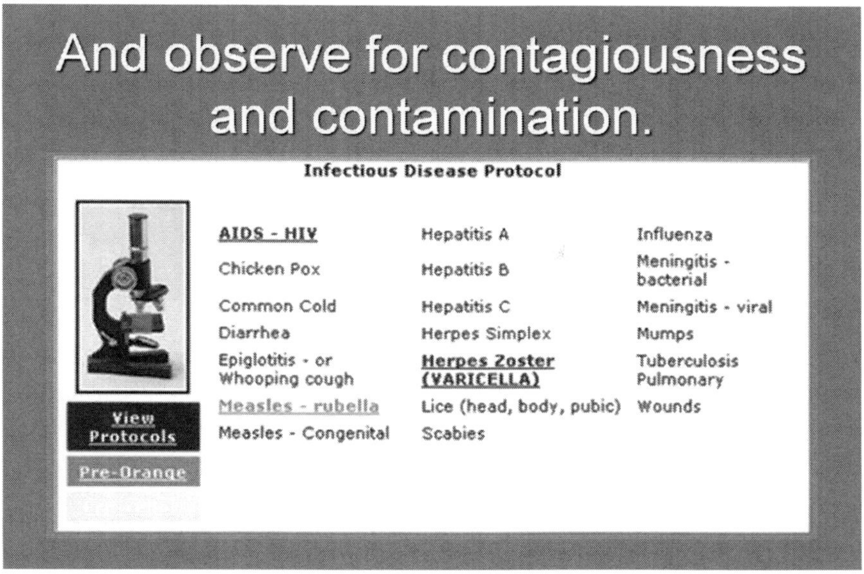


Figure 13.1 Contagiousness screen.

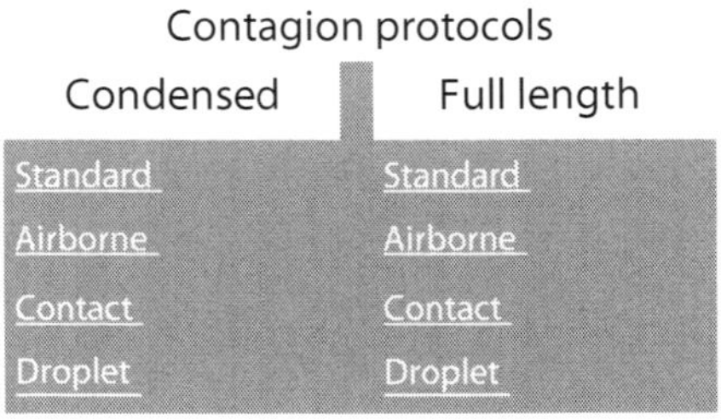


Figure 13.2 Contagiousness protocols.

medical software companies and hospital trustees with their CEOs must read the book—The Toyota Way; they can no longer simply dazzle stakeholders in the labs, ERs, imaging, accounting, nursing, and hospitalist staff with PowerPoints from General Electric's Six Sigma that transformed an old GE into a highly functional company. Health care is not manufacturing locomotives and light bulbs, and these are multimillion, multiyear subscription sales that have made large medical computing companies the darlings of Wall Street and the White House alike. They can be functional as tools for clinicians and hospital or clinic staff, but not if the contracts are between marketing folks and chief information officers whose knowledge is almost entirely computer networking and mobile computing—both essential skill sets for purchasing decisions. But, their shortfall is that that these systems do not work well in an emergency at 2:00 a.m. when they might not work at all or have way too much control at any time over complex patient pathophysiology and its than they are designed to have. Electronic medical records (EMRs) have to be smarter with a more comprehensive knowledge base that rapidly narrows the range of differential diagnoses for rapid assessment so patients in ER admissions can be triaged and specialized resources brought in when clinically indicated; not every patient who comes to the ER with a headache, for example, needs a CAT Scan of the head. The medical clearance of Thomas Duncan failed, because he had a normal CAT Scan. That may be helpful, but it did not assure safe passage through the door for discharge as depended upon to do. In his case, a CAT Scan of the head was not only useless, but it distracted clinical staff from the obvious presentation—Very Sick Adult! EMRs are not under the user's control to the degree necessary for exempting them from evaluation and approval of the FDA, just like any other device or drug controlling the patient's welfare, whether taking control of a patient for a minute or a lifetime.

Unity in Health Care the Toyota Way is now enabled by the advent of omniscient mobile computing and telehealth. Workstations with desktops are diminishing in their power over patient care, and both hospital administration and medical software companies must be in the new millennium of mobile computing—rather than mass marketing "flat" EMR computing that chokes on data, spitting out printed diagnoses with *International Classification of Diseases* (ICD) codes for a patient like Thomas Duncan. He was wheeled out so seriously ill he could not stand on his own and was recklessly handed over to a medically naïve fiancé on a stretcher with the robotic clinical support of clinically deaf and dumb computing. Clearly, it has already been discovered in the 1400 virtual pages of EMR documentation that he was too ill for discharge—but discovered far too late to mistakenly prevent converting Emergency Medicine into Disaster Medicine. Clinical Medicine is time determined, and oftentimes—and more often unpredictably—time is of the essence. So it is about time—time to demand radical improvement in medical computing, because it is about time—time-determined clinical decision-making. Low blood sugar can kill immediately, but high blood sugar does not; clinicians need that knowledge to survive, and so do EMRs.

Above all, at an ER in this day of potential pandemics that can reach the United States from any country in the world, contagiousness should be screened for protective measures instituted early on in the admission process. That was not considered in the case of Thomas Duncan. In addition, a patient's mental status and pain level should be continuously monitored via wearable device, like an Apple watch—not just a dumb wristband from the mid last century—so that a patient's family and neighbors do not become victims of a deadly viral epidemic, as well as the next carriers. Again, there is no evidence that Thomas Duncan was monitored on The Pain Ladder, whose metrics could have been the tell-tale of a deadly infection, if not specifically Ebola.

Mobile computing, supported by intelligent EMR software designed like an airplane—with all constituents at the table before the multimillion dollar contract is inked—can clinically clear the unknown patient for most high-security and medical/surgical risk before admission to an inpatient bed. That is what is meant by the comprehensive mnemonic, clearing the "ABCDE" of emergency medicine; the WWHHHIMPES, GUNS, and SOAP of emergency neuropsychiatry and the ACT MYSELF and MAS TACO SALAD of forensic psychiatry, security, and suicidology. Such rapid assessment with clinical clearance must be performed with consistent discipline before the patient is left in the hands of helpless and mostly naïve transport staff to be wheeled on the elevator for admission or rolled out the door to be checked another day at another place; the authors have documented case after case where such clearance has been neglected with disastrous results from Marysville, Minnesota to Houston, Texas, and Dallas to Blacksburg, Virginia.

In the wake of the Ebola scare, screening for potentially epidemic contagiousness—or even the early warning signs of a bioterror attack on the homeland, as occurred in the anthrax attacks associated with 9/11—can be routinely performed at security gates in our airports. Are these now clinical sites and points of entry, like possibly our football fields and hockey rinks, to our health-care system? Better believe they are, because what happens when that traveler from West Africa coming in on KLM has a fever with or without symptoms? An elaborate medical intervention must be made for which, despite billions spent for such preparedness since 9/11, we know way too little about. That person becomes a patient immediately. That patient must now be on an EHR from some hub capable of monitoring his or her clinical course from the airport through prehospital transport—and then through an ER or other hospital triage area to labs and x-ray until securely bedded in an infectious disease or ICU bed that has isolation precautions. This is done through connected health. It is not just for rural and inner-city hospitals, as was the intent of ACA. It is for the patient, and that patient, whether Thomas Duncan or mentally ill veteran Omar Gonzalez, is not in a licensed bed or home with a registered home-care provider. Duncan and his girlfriend were without case follow-up and not even close to a valid or reliable diagnosis. Omar Gonzalez was in his car and obviously had no valid psychiatric diagnosis or case management. Both had encounters with officialdom that could have, following evidence-based rules of classical, evidence-based triage, resulted in turning portending disaster into Emergency Medical Triage that should prevent disaster.

It is no different in the case of University of Illinois Healthcare Center with Steve Kazmierczak. Connected health should have forced the psychiatrist to go back into past history. He obviously was evaluating an unreliable source—a patient not wishing to take antipsychotics while purchasing weapons, accompanied by a girlfriend who was uninformed of his true past health status from Chicago to Beaumont Hospital at Fort Bliss and back. The unreliable historian is an emergency. So, like Flight 93 highjacker, Jerah, accompanying al Hazwani to Fort Lauderdale's Holy Cross Hospital, sporting an infected skin abrasion more likely than not contracted from anthrax, a seemingly low grade and localized chronic infection presenting as emergency can portend disaster. Similarly with Cho's first clinical presentation early in his matriculation to Virginia Tech; he complained of being infested with mites, a somatic delusion, and was cavalierly brushed off by the family doc as acne instead of being referred for emergency psychiatric evaluation of his fulminating psychosis that, without antipsychotic medication, would culminate in The Virginia Tech Massacre. We need smarter points of entry! This is a dangerous world with many moving parts not controllable as they are by The Great Leader in Pyongyang, North Korea where everyone is in step or tortured to death in prison.

We argue, Fourth Amendment protections against arbitrary search and seizure notwithstanding, a patient's privacy does not matter at points when personal and public health and safety are more probably or not at risk. That was the intent of the Tarasoff Decision handed down by the Supreme Court in California; common sense must prevail in some encounters where threat and risk of harm are medically certain. Where was Steven Kazmierczak—just like Duncan, Cho and al Hazwani—coming from in their first encounters with clinicians in Dallas, Blacksburg and Fort Lauderdale, respectively? He had just flunked out of NIU after receiving the top award in his graduating senior class. Is that not cause for contacting his family, who would have opened up the Pandora's box to his history of psychosis before his disastrous failure at NIU and resultant transfer to University of Illinois? All of his records could have been in the psychiatrist's computer before the patient had a chance to leave. Why was James Holmes' diagnosis of a mental illness and whatever ideations of violence he had manifested not red-flagged? That is the intent of ACA: outcomes depending on secure interoperability of EHRs.

As psychological testing would have shown, as cited in campus safety chapter, Kazmierczak was an unreliable historian, negating his history from that point on in the evaluation at University of Illinois; nothing can be taken at face value from either him or his girlfriend. This is an emergency demanding more information than the patient is either willing or able to provide—including his girlfriend who was unaware of his history of serious mental illness during high school and at Beaumont Army Medical Center, Fort Bliss, Texas. Inpatient evaluation with further testing and observation, whether involuntary or voluntary, could have, like Elliot Rodger, turned up the wrathful vengeance brewing in the cauldron of a psychotic mind; Steve had already been collecting an armamentarium that likely could have been discovered. The mnemonic "Wash with SOAP" could have picked up psychosis and paranoia (Figure 13.3).

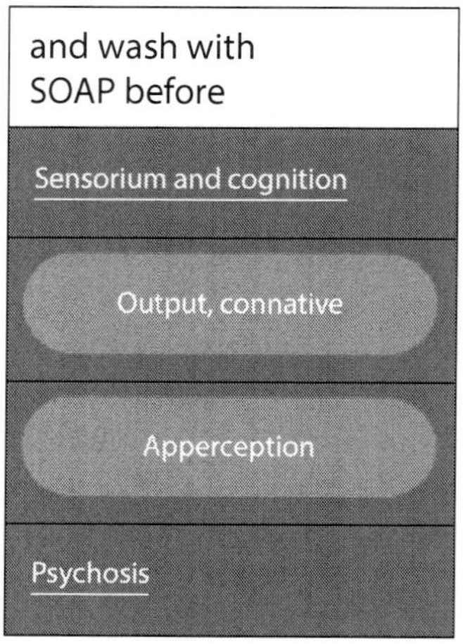


Figure 13.3 Consciousness screen.

## WASH WITH SOAP

- S = Sensorium: If disoriented, this is medical, rather than psychiatric emergency. You must manage until qualified physician takes over care. Rarely should psychiatry be the primary for this patient, but may help as psychosomatics consultant.
- O = Output: Is connative output volitional or involuntary? Is it too high, as in mania; too low, as in (CD[D]DC) complex? Or is it disorganized for speech, motor or psychomotor.
- A = Apperception: Is patient paranoid? If so, better have sound reason for release without evaluation or treatment.
- P = Psychosis: This is the most common call for psyche consult in the ER. The main differential, again, is functional versus organic brain syndrome. Most cases can be differentiated in the ER with adequate time and attention to determine whether medical or psychiatric intervention is necessary. Prematurely concluding the confused patient is "Psych" risks inevitable wait these days for psychiatric inpatient care that is simply asking for a sentinel event either waiting for or upon arrival at the psyche unit. Medical clearance must be zero defect, and it can be, unless throughput pressures cause the internal dump in the guise of "med psych" transfer with inevitable risk of sentinel medical/surgical event.

Checking "S" for sensorium, you begin to gather demographic information for the first time. In fact you are also checking first element in Mental Status Examination, Orientation.

"What's your name?" "What's the date?"—An answer of "Abe Lincoln, 1850," tells you to go back and throw out the WWHHHIMPES before proceeding, because you have a disoriented patient who could immediately die on you. With mobile and wearable computer technology, patients like Duncan and Logan should have had a smart watch on their wrists monitoring their sensorium within the context of the diagnostic cross for determining causation of confusional state (see "Diagnostic Cross"). Lean managed hospitals should follow the rules of the Toyota Way and prevent any change in mental status from escaping detection from initial evaluation in the ER through transport and ultimate admission. All parties responsible for such a patient, whether doctor, x-ray tech, or transport staff, must have the authority, as in the Toyota Way, to stop the assembly line where changing pathophysiology is on the conveyor belt of "Throughput for Optimization of Patient Flow." That euphemistic testimonial to best practice may save money up front but collide with the rhetorical intent of the Affordable Care Act—namely "Service Optimization," which is "better outcomes" at "lower costs" (www.johnliebert.com/johnliebert/pdfs/ToyotaWay_BulletinFeb2008.pdf).

The front-end costs of caring for Kazmierczak at University of Illinois, Urbana, and Beaumont Army Hospital, Fort Bliss; Thomas Duncan at Texas Health Presbyterian Hospital, Dallas, and Charles Logan at St. John's Hospital,

Maplewood, Minnesota, were likely cheap. The costs, both human and financial, following disastrous discharges were astronomical but probably only accounted for in the clinical sites' budget as legal costs picked up under insurance or government attorneys. This is cost shifting at its most nefarious extreme; it is not the intent of ACA and should be part of the changes expected in amending this law after the presidential election, regardless of party selected to implement it from the White House. We assume it will, survive the 2017 Congressional debate on its repeal.

After you have done that, note the connative "O"utput; that is, the level of person's psychomotor and behavioral production. It is either too high, as in mania or agitation; disorganized, as in impaired coordination, dysphasia, or psychosis; or too low, as in depression or central nervous system obtundation.

At this step of progressing through the triage rules by following mnemonics, you can discipline yourself to ask the crucial question. Is this patient presenting as overcontrolled or undercontrolled? In either case, try quickly to walk in the patient's shoes. The police will usually take the violent person who is controlled to jail and the out-of-controlled one to the ER. You are not usually a target with the hyperkinetic patient, unless your own behavior exacerbates his fear, either imagined or real.

The overcontrolled patient brought in by the police, however, must be approached cautiously. He did something violent or he would not be here; delusion is the key. The guy who started a silent countdown appeared very cool at time of presentation, but routine questioning began irritating him. It shocked all who had to interview him that he had done time for murder. Then, you can see him isolating, preoccupied with an inner world while cleaning the tables and arranging books on the shelves, and you read the police report. They brought him to the ER when he started yelling at them about how his body was the temple of God and they are in its presence. Beware, therefore, the over-controlled and otherwise healthy male; keep your distance. He is not doing anything; so, time is not of the essence for a formal mental status that could set him off with you as his next target. He does not want you to know about him; find out what you can from others and let inpatient psychiatry sort it out. The police have already sorted it out; he probably is a real patient—and a really dangerous one, too. Do not try to melt his cool.

The intermittently explosive disordered patient usually destroys property. Again, if he is cool now with you, do not melt him down. He can go off any time on a rampage, tearing up your worksite when handing him an emergency detention notice. Find out why police brought him from others or the paperwork and let inpatient psychiatry sort it out; they have the structure to prevent and contain a rampage.

There is political controversy over the threat posed by temporal lobe epileptics (TLE) and seriously mentally ill patients. Statistics are not robust supporting one side or the other, but in either group, the overcontrolled TLE case with intermittent dyscontrol and the undercontrolled with mania or schizophrenia, you should heed that small body of literature focusing on past violence. If a patient from either of these two groups has been violent before, you need to be supercautious in your approach, decision making, and clinical management.

Get a reliable history from somebody about recent or past violence; that is the key during your short time frame. Here is the place for the formal violence questionnaire, and following the rules of this or respecting a majority of positive answers from it will serve you well for the next 24 hours, whether you decide to admit or discharge the patient. It is not perfect, but it is as good as it gets with our current state of knowledge. It is adequate for purposes of determining conditional voluntary admission, or, short of that option, emergency detention, until inpatient psychiatry can sort it out in the cooler light of day.

Here, as in the case of Logan, the horizontal axis of the CD(D)DC complex is fluid and must be metered and monitored by dashboard just like all critical elements of optimized patient flow, such as time spent in imaging. And, anyone in control of the patient at any minute must have the authority to enter "Confusion" into the networked EMR; would that have helped after the family conference with Charles Logan, were an aide entering his room and noting something different in his response to her, been authorized to enter "Confused" into the EMR, thus automatically demanding thorough investigation with a CAM monitoring that could have prevented a later suicidal rampage murder in the sanctity of a quiet medical unit housing the most acutely ill?

Examining Apperception, "A." You find out if this patient has a perceptual distortion? Quickly determine whether the patient seems either paranoid and/or autistically preoccupied. You can ask softly and politely in clinical tone of voice whether he is frightened or hearing voices. You can usually tell from the response whether patients are either paranoid or hallucinating.

You, as the physician, are entering their world if they are either or both, but they can usually hear simple communications when not intoxicated. When intoxicated on drugs like meth or cocaine, however, do not try to contract with them. On the other hand, the hallucinating and paranoid patient will contract with you, unless you enter their perceptually distorted world as a threat. These patients—by the very fact of Emergency Psychiatry presentation—will have to be admitted and likely treated with antipsychotics or Ativan before admission, preferably po with informed consent.

The paranoid patient also can be overcontrolled, hiding extreme and intense feelings of vindictiveness and hatred—ready to attack in order to make certain that victims get what they deserve—e.g., the man making that armored bulldozer in Colorado. And do not forget to rule out paranoia in that tough young male who seems so aloof and arrogant; he is very likely paranoid, or reasonably frightened about the "S"ituation outside. What is the situation outside? Are enemy gangsters out there on verge of attacking him, whether he comes out or they come in to get him?

And, remember that the patient who is not eating frequently is likely not eating because he believes his food is poisoned. He may not tell you that, because he has been hospitalized before when talking about his paranoia. Such paranoid patients can be controlled in situations threatening to restrict their freedom; they oftentimes know what to say and what not to say in order to stay the way they are.

Paranoia is grandiosity; who would want to take antipsychotics and land on earth a mere mortal not really worthy of a minute of time from either the FBI or CIA.

And work smart: "Voices with seeing things" is a very common chief complaint in ERs; always think cocaine, and never forget a toxic drug screen.

This should have been carefully monitored and managed with Logan; was it the reason for admission, and was it checked in the ER at admission, or was Logan simply "put through" to an insecure medical bed with high risk intoxication from some source?

If you have not determined yet whether the patient is psychotic, "P" disciplines you to clear this first major state of mental disorganization previously shown on the JAL Triage Algorithm, https://www.linkedin.com/pulse/preventing-medical-errors-from-acute-newborn-disaster-liebert-md?trk=prof-post. By this, we are trying medically to clear the organic from the functional psychoses. The latter is debilitating for nearly 1% of Americans at either some point or throughout most of their lives and, along with brain damage and abuse in childhood, remains a major risk factor in violence. Psychosis is treatable with access to and availability of adequate psychiatric resources and modern psychopharmacotherapy. Unfortunately, however, despite its inclusion within the seven critical categories targeted under EMS legislation listed above, acute psychosis was mandated but never equitably funded or supported, if at all, compared to other categories like "acute cardiac."

This is the core, therefore, of emergency psychiatry; like in the case of temporal lobe epilepsy, violence within this population stirs heated controversy. Discriminating studies do show, however, that psychotic patients who have presented in the past as violent must be taken seriously. Their past violence will, more than any other factor, predict future disruptive behavior within clinical, community, family, or residential settings. We believe that this is due to frequent noncompliance or partial compliance with medications that results in recurrence of acute psychosis embedding destructive command hallucinations that must be obeyed by the patient—as in "you must now strike."

By now, you should have determined whether this patient is too cognitively impaired to rule out organic brain syndrome and simply internally dump on inpatient psychiatry as "psychotic." That is not a safe disposition. You may think it should be, but, unless you have worked inpatient psychiatry a lot, you may not realize that patients are almost always ambulatory and there is little medical support available—i.e., IVs, telemetry, med-surg consultation and ironically including restraint, which has a much higher standard for implementation than in either the ER, where the legal threshold for restraint is low, or a medical bed where it is higher, yet not as high as in Psychiatry, where patients are supposed to be talked down. Yes, perhaps there should be more MedPsyche beds in every hospital, but there are not; that could be a cause for taking up arms. But, it is a cause for hospital meetings and not slam-dunk admissions that guarantee maximum staff disruption and jeopardize life and limb.

Medical clearance is medical clearance. An organic brain syndrome admitted to inpatient psychiatry as "psychosis," for whatever reason, is not emergency psychiatry; it is very sloppy emergency medicine—all considerations of hassles and jeopardy of EMTALA aside—when med-surg beds are not readily available.

When no med-surg beds are available and you believe, on a more likely than not Basis, that the patient's altered mental status is caused by medical-surgical disease, transport the patient with your stated purpose, intent, and documentation to the nearest med-surg bed appropriate for care—not to inpatient psychiatry just to avoid any risk whatsoever of EMTALA.

It is not good for the patient with an acute brain syndrome to be on the inpatient psychiatry unit unless there are special circumstances previously understood by both emergency service and admitting psychiatrist for this admission. What is good for the patient—not what is expedient at the time—will rule in the event the case goes sour, e.g., EMTALA investigation for dumping an ER patient at another ER when beds are available on psychiatry. Ask yourself, when dumping the patient on inpatient psychiatry, whether you would do the same with a patient who has a GI bleed? Why not? Might the GI bleed require more acute care resources than available on an inpatient psychiatric unit and die?

Ask yourself why you believe the acute brain syndrome you intend to admit to inpatient psychiatry is any different before simply cloaking admission of a neatly dressed man with sudden onset of confusion, disorientation, and visual hallucinations in a diagnosis of psychosis NOS to avoid the legal risks of sending him to another hospital that is safer for his care when your med-surg beds are full.

---

### Case study: Jason

Jason was recovering from quadruple bypass surgery and had no psychiatric history. He was a religious man but never known for religiosity or crazy behavior. For the first time, at the age of 67, he ran out of his house at 3:00 a.m. screaming at the stars to give him the sign of the Messiah's return. He was admitted to psychiatry and immediately determined to have an acute brain syndrome. It took 5 days to get the man a medical bed that provided adequate physiological support for this hypoxic state and recurrent CVS decompensation.

This is not emergency psychiatry, but should be consultation Liaison psychiatry in the ICU. Otherwise, it is simply bad medicine. And, if oriented and psychotic, treat ASAP. This is not the place to be differentiating between affective disorder, schizophrenia, or brief psychosis. More likely than not, you are confronted now with a psychotic patient wherein you are best off clearing psychosis; the risk-reward ratio for such intervention favors antipsychotic treatment. Once again, you either declare an emergency and treat with or against patient consent or you admit to inpatient unit on a 72-hour hold. If patient consents at this point, you have a wide spectrum of options—assuming that patient is not escalating or currently disruptive.

Here are some options, and, because you are treating psychosis instead of dangerousness and disruptive behavior, you might try IM or PO Geodon—IM between 2.5 and 20 mg, depending on frailty and physical status. Caveat: if you think this is more an affective rather than some other psychotic process, best go higher on Geodon, where risk, we have discovered, is less for aggravating mania.

Here consider 40 mg po in the patient who consents to treatment, because less is not best in case of Geodon, we are learning. For that distinctive change in behavior, like acute onset of pacing, offer oral Ativan, Geodon, Zydis, or Risperdal M Tabs to reduce the intense psychotic anxiety driving crystallization process that incorporates distortions of ER experiences into a patient's evolving delusional system—thus enabling escalation into disruptive behavior and violence from over-stimuation.

Charles Logan was obviously psychotic, and the "P" should have been front and center on all dashboards of St. Johns' EMR for close monitoring by any staff engaging him—particularly those not familiar with him, like, perhaps, a new nurse on the unit who did not come to know him until whacked over the head with a steel bar. In the case of Kazmierczak, the psychiatric staff at University of Illinois had to dig deeper for other comorbid conditions associated with obsessive-compulsive disorder (OCD) and anxiety; this could have been done with simple testing like the Minnesota Multiphasic Personality Inventory (MMPI) or SCL 90 as previously discussed; a simple call home, as in the case of Cho Seung Hui when committed to St. Albans psychiatric unit, would have found a powerful past psychiatric history demanding at least a 2-week intense psychiatric inpatient evaluation. Had that occurred with Cho at St. Albans, the involuntary commitment hearing records would not have been intentionally destroyed, leading to potentially dire consequences for a lot of professionals and one or more vital institutions.

---

The nemonic for Neuropsychiatric Clearance continues. After washing with SOAP, you may now eat "MAS TACO SALAD." This color-coded mnemonic can guide you reliably via time-determined clinical defaults through the assessment of impulse control—first, imminent behavioral dyscontrol, particularly suicidality, in the first 10 minutes of presentation, then more in-depth assessment of any unmitigating process of human destructiveness in a less critical state of clinical awareness, the yellow zone, allowing 1 hour for safe evaluation from the first encounter with the patient (Figure 13.4).

Of major significance in this screen for Unremitting Clinical States of Human Destructiveness is the relatively rare screen for Triad—that is enuresis, cruelty to animals, and illegal fire-setting. Steven Kazmierczak was + for this, thus predicting high likelihood of future homicide. The finding of this history in psychiatric patients bodes ill for prognosis and informs of extreme caution in management—in this case thorough past psychiatric history, including suicide attempts, military history, and history of serious mental illness. Steve, after thorough inpatient psychiatric evaluation, would have proven a young man requiring the closest of supervision that can be provided under assisted treatment, or barring that, return to long-term inpatient care, as was the requirement when he was in high school. The patient in this case presented to a college psychiatrist accompanied by his girlfriend with the complaint of compulsive behaviors. This was an unreliable patient accompanied by

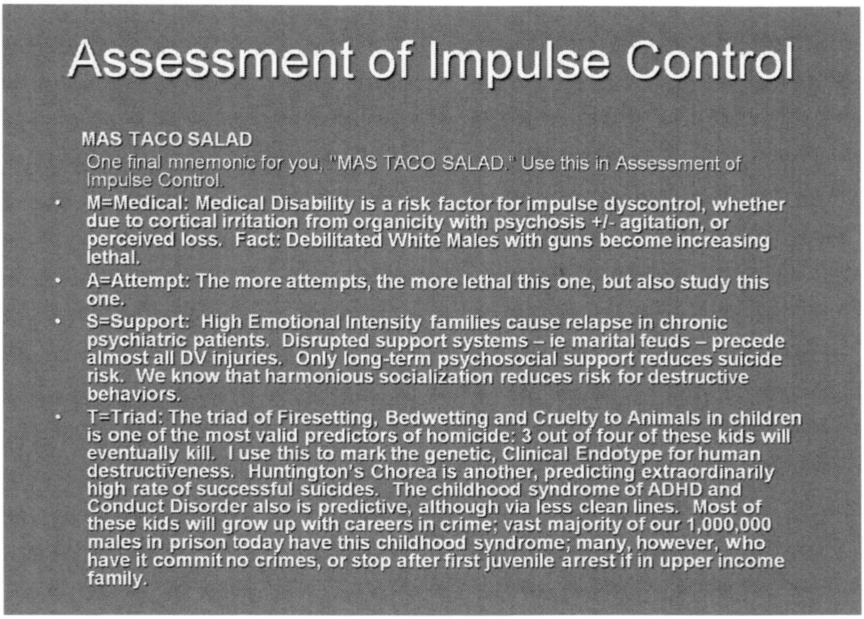
Assessment of Impulse Control
MAS TACO SALAD
One final mnemonic for you, "MAS TACO SALAD." Use this in Assessment of Impulse Control.
M=Medical: Medical Disability is a risk factor for impulse dyscontrol, whether due to cortical irritation from organicity with psychosis +/- agitation, or perceived loss. Fact: Debilitated White Males with guns become increasing lethal.
A=Attempt: The more attempts, the more lethal this one, but also study this one.
S=Support: High Emotional Intensity families cause relapse in chronic psychiatric patients. Disrupted support systems – ie marital feuds – precede almost all DV injuries. Only long-term psychosocial support reduces suicide risk. We know that harmonious socialization reduces risk for destructive behaviors.
T=Triad: The triad of Firesetting, Bedwetting and Cruelty to Animals in children is one of the most valid predictors of homicide: 3 out of four of these kids will eventually kill. I use this to mark the genetic, Clinical Endotype for human destructiveness. Huntington's Chorea is another, predicting extraordinarily high rate of successful suicides. The childhood syndrome of ADHD and Conduct Disorder also is predictive, although via less clean lines. Most of these kids will grow up with careers in crime; vast majority of our 1,000,000 males in prison today have this childhood syndrome; many, however, who have it commit no crimes, or stop after first juvenile arrest if in upper income family.

Figure 13.4 Impulsivity screen.

an unreliable collateral providing anamnesis. Minimal psychological testing, such as a computer-scored MMPI, would have likely demonstrated this unreliability. These means of presentation tell you much immediately, and, as stated before, the unreliable patient presenting by himself or an unreliable person accompanying the patient = "Inappropriate History" = immediate switching in your mind to the red zone of Clinical States of Awareness—you can assume nothing based on history.

The disaster of the suicidal mass murder at NIU was as bad an outcome as could have been imagined. School health and counseling centers must be spokes within ACOs. This psychiatrist should have had immediate access to Kazmierczak's past medical history, but school health and counseling, like Sandy Hook Elementary School wrestling with Adam Lanza's psychosis that was way over their heads, are not connected. They need to be. Certainly personality changes in Alton Nolen were detectable in prison where he reportedly converted to radical Islam; yet he was paroled early. Then, he, as an ex-convict, was aggressively trying to convert employees at the meat processing company in Moore, Oklahoma, to radical Islam. Is that not strange behavior? Is the only solution release from prison without proper follow-up parole management or firing without necessary neuropsychiatric examination? Of course prisons and employers cannot be responsible for vetting every case of strange behavior they wash their hands of.

But Alton Nolen? Maybe public safety officials, if not public health officials, are taking the "behavioral health" of prisoners and workers more seriously now. Not only do we have our first two U.S. citizens testing positive for Ebola due to the failure of preparedness in U.S. ERs, but now we have a beheading by someone who should have been known to have the motivation and means to carry out such a horrific act. So, both the occupational nurse and prison cell must be spokes connected to the hub of an ACO; they must have telehealth technology to make it work.

We have seen that some prison cells have secure telehealth presentation screens in the inmates' cells. A case could be made for that being as necessary as a locked door. Despite the political rhetoric of prosecutors and hard-nose politicians, most of these guys in prison for violent crimes will be getting out. Charles Manson may be a rare exception. Ed Gein, the butcherer and cannibal from Plainfield, Wisconsin, and subject of Hitchcock's *Psycho* was never to get out, but, in fact he was paroled to Washington State. Only a serendipitous discovery of his identity during the Ted Bundy investigation stopped his release so that he died, as promised by the judge and prosecutors, in prison. But, he was on his way to parole transfer from Wisconsin to Washington State.

We can be sure that as ACA settles in to American society over the next 5 to 10 years, things will get worse in many ways before they get better. There will be bureaucratic interference with success, as in the case of the disastrous roll-out of the healthcare.gov enrollment website. Senior doctors will retire early from practice, thus degrading scarce resources even more. Technologies, like the EHR at Texas Presbyterian, will fail. As the reimbursement pie becomes more restricted, there will be internecine warfare among providers, both among institutions and health-care disciplines. There will be confusion over who should be the primary care provider—a nurse practitioner, a physician's assistant, or a medical doctor? When will specialists be called in to take charge of a case at higher cost but promised better outcomes? When will the culture of health care adopt telehealth, not as an ancillary tool for the odd situation and patient, but as a core best practice? There is inpatient health care. There is outpatient health care. Now there must be telehealth care, and it should be called "medicine" to stop marginalizing it.

Unless ACA, MU, and ACOs work because of parallel surge in mobile communications, we will end up with a two-tier system like England, with its dysfunctional and ossified NHS and Harley Street for the privileged. Mobile communications, computerized clinical decision support systems (CDSS) and data storage technology with analytics can now take specialized and highest-quality health care to the patient, not just at home computers or WiFi—but the person in the dorm room, the school health nurse, the prison cell, the Forward Operating Base (FOB), such as the recent U.S. Liberian Military mission for fighting and containing Ebola at its source, the EMT, policeman, and first responder. To fix health care in this nation, ACA must drive quality to the patient, and, as can be seen in this book, the patient in most critical need is not always at home and accessible to a home-care provider or immobile in a licensed clinical bed. But, without intelligence embedded into the telehealth platform in the form of computerized clinical decision support, the intent of the law—improved outcomes—will not be realized. Again, it can be done and is being done; Figure 13.5 presents an example from McGill University's Telehealth platform for remote worksite (www.johnliebert.com/johnliebert/pdfs/talisman_arnaert_11%2012%202012_final%20final2.pdf).

Translational research allows technology transfer of such innovation from lab, to remote arctic mines to prison cells, dorm rooms, ambulances, and ERs,

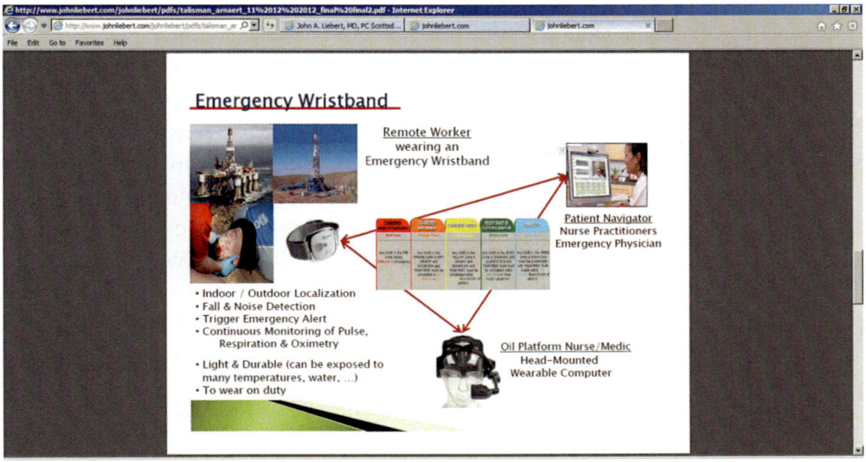


Figure 13.5 Talisman telehealth project of remote worksites integrates a CDSS from www.digitalclinician.com.

whether overcrowded in big cities or understaffed in rural areas. It will take time for legislators, authorities already with powers to act, and regulators to realize: It's about time. It's all about time—both for innovation to make health care reform work for us and not against us, and it's about time in rules-based triaging of patients to save lives in the cases cited in this book—from helpless passengers exposed to Ebola to helpless students and faculty unknowingly awaiting their fate in Cole Hall on the Northern Illinois University campus.

## REFERENCES

Dolan, B. 2014. iHealth unveils wearable ECG, pulse ox, BP devices. *mobihealth news*, January 7. www.mobihealthnews.com/28547/ihealth-unveils-wearable-ecg-pulse-ox-bp-devices

Fuller Torrey, E. 2013. *The American Psychosis*, 1st edition. Oxford University Press, Oxford.

Koppel, R. and Gordon, S. 2014. Koppel and Gordon: Learn, don't blame, after Dallas hospital's Ebola diagnostic failure. *The Dallas Morning News*, October 14. www.dallasnews.com/opinion/latest-columns/20141014-ross-koppel-and-suzanne-gordon-learn-dont-blame-after-dallas-hospitals-ebola-diagnostic-failure.ece

Liebert, J. A. and Birnes, W. J. 2011. *Suicidal Mass Murderers: A Criminological Study of Why They Kill*. Taylor and Francis, Boca Raton, Florida.

Sanders, J. 2014. President, global telemedicine group, transformational trends in the Telehealth Service Industry: Planning for change. *Arizona Telemedicine Program's First Annual Telemedicine/TelehealthService Provider Showcase Conference*, SPS, Phoenix, AZ, October 7.

Wolfson, B. J. 2014. Psychiatric treatment in Orange County Part 1: Psych patients pack emergency rooms. Staff writer, *Orange County Register*, October 25.

# 14

# Special forensic issues

The attempted assassination of Congresswoman Gabrielle Giffords in the Tucson Safeway Plaza massacre taught us a lot about the state of public psychiatry today, perhaps more than psychiatrists want to know. Public psychiatry is totally controlled by the judiciary who may ask for the opinion of a psychiatrist or clinical psychologist, but has been left to run what is left of any public psychiatric system. Gabby Giffords' assassin, Jared Loughner, had a rap sheet, which should have been a page long, but too many charges were dismissed or simply not filed. Multiple encounters with security officers on Pima College Campus should have been filed as at least misdemeanors. He was able to wiggle through the college's security monitoring system and even through the justice system.

Loughner was stark raving mad and extremely disruptive on campus. Students and faculty alike were scared of him. Accordingly, when he was arrested in the bloodbath he created in the Safeway Plaza, his criminal record was the bare tip of an iceberg. Even his acquaintances, when they heard about the shooting, remarked to themselves that it sounded like Loughner. Yet, like the officers on watch in the wheelhouse of the Titanic, it seemed nobody was looking hard enough, because a catastrophe was in view of officers and counselors who chose not to see it—or could not. The Pima County Sheriff, en route to California, when hearing the news from the Safeway Plaza shootings, said, while making a U-turn, that there would be many psychiatrists on one side saying he is insane and just as many saying he is not. He was essentially predicting that the person committing the massacre was insane. He never said he suspected it was Jared Loughner, but he had reason to believe it was. Tucson is not that big a city and makes up the majority of his county's citizens. His department should have seen the looming catastrophe in full view before it but did not. An officer even stopped him running a red light shortly before the massacre, at which time Loughner reported being really scared, because he was in the act of committing suicidal mass murder, as he already pretty well had spelled out on his Facebook page. Like the officer who stopped Keller between serial arsons and let him go because he did not fit the FBI profile of a serial arsonist, the officer could not see Loughner fitting any profile. Of course, there was no profile, because the officer in Tucson was unaware of any threat to homeland security.

He should have. Pima College campus was roiling with turbulence and obviously psychotic, disruptive behavior by one student on this large state college campus—namely, Jared Loughner, recently suspended for behaving and talking with megaphone on campus with obvious and gross insanity. Inevitably, therefore, there soon would be a threat, and when that threat was over and Safeway Plaza soaked in blood of the dead and wounded, a chronically, severely ill young man was diagnosed for the very first time by the Department of Justice with paranoid schizophrenia in the Federal Medical Facility in Springfield. Long after lawyers and judges negotiated the solution for this massacre in Tucson, it was discovered that Loughner had two targets in mind and The Arizona Republic would obtain extensive emails about Loughner's disruptive behavior from Pima College administration; The Tucson Safeway Massacre, it turns out, should have come as no surprise and we were lucky he was stopped during his first mass murder; total denial and selective blindness to Loughner's fulminating psychosis left Tucson's well-liked congresswoman with a bullet in her frontal lobe and a federal judge dead. A psychiatrist finally did examine Jared Loughner, but not until judges and attorneys argued back and forth about his being medicated. Judges were spread from Tucson to California, and attorneys from Phoenix and Tucson to California and Washington, DC, while the high-profile insane man who caused the catastrophe was in Missouri. The president of the United States spoke at the memorial as if the assassination attempt on Congresswoman Giffords' life was a conspiracy from the radical red district of Scottsdale, then new home to Governor Palin. Tucson is a blue district. We never saw the psychiatrist in Springfield, Missouri who ordered an antipsychotic medication for Loughner, but we heard Loughner's reaction to it on the court record in Tucson. "Had I been on this medicine years ago, I would not have done this," he asserted in his signed statement.

In addition to the horrific cost of life, the trauma to loved ones and witnesses alike—and our entire political system, where a dedicated congresswoman was doing her job, meeting in person with her constituents—there were millions in legal bills, court costs, and travel expenses for Air Force One to bring the president to memorialize the tragedy. The political hype all quieted like the poof of air from a balloon popped with a pin, that pin being one word, "Schizophrenia." Tucson has relatively effective case management for Schizophrenia, but nobody on the bench, law enforcement, or Pima College security and administration was either knowledgeable enough or courageous enough to call Jared Loughner's "psychosis" a serious neuropsychiatric disease requiring emergency medical attention, the very attention publicized as a priority of the State of Arizona in its Pima College student/parent handbook (Liebert and Birnes 2014). Instead Loughner's grossly exhibited insanity was left to the courts, which ultimately would determine the fate of this obviously insane man loose on one of the largest public campuses in the nation and city of a half million.

Tucson is home to sensitive military and border operations, as well as a hightech industry and the state's primary university, the University of Arizona. Whoever had suspicions of the final outcome of Jared Loughner's obvious and fulminating psychosis in Tucson understandably expected he would meet a judge one day who would order intervention to protect both him and the community from his disruptive insanity. Nobody, however, expected it would happen after he tried to assassinate his congressional representative, murdered a federal judge, and killed or maimed many others for life, leaving popular Safeway Plaza soaked with blood from ordinary people either coming to hear their representative in Washington or just picking up some groceries. Nobody expected the recent Federal Bureau of Investigation (FBI) report stating that Loughner planned another massacre after Safeway.

The trauma of the Safeway Plaza massacre is still a topic not open to much public discussion in Tucson. It was up to the courts to solve it in the end, and it ended in a moment of legal competency determination that must have made our Department of Justice and all judges involved praying. They got a guilty plea with life in prison from an insane suicidal rampage mass murderer who luckily got a legally accepted window of competency; that had to draw a sigh of relief after all the hype and complex legal maneuvers of great value for The Law Review at Harvard. Certainly, however, this plea was hardly reassuring as a model for the public's health or safety which would be jeopardized over and over again by such suicidal rampage murders for years more to come with no preventive solutions in sight except faster police interventions when the bullets start flying. If there is one case that shows why law enforcement, college counseling services, attorneys, and the judiciary should not be managing serious mental illness, it is the case of the Tucson Safeway massacre, a catastrophe extreme enough to bring the president of the United States to Tucson, Arizona, for purposes of healing the nation.

Healing the nation from what? There was no Red-Blue conspiracy. There, of course, could have been in a state so polarized and heavily armed. But there was not. There was undetected psychosis in places where there should have been detection. There was severe neuropsychiatric impairment, totally ignored before judges and academic professional alike, and in the end there was the diagnosis of paranoid schizophrenia, clearing to considerable degree with a pill called Risperdal, an antipsychotic, which Loughner himself said he should have been on years before his suicidal rampage.

The local hospital where Loughner should have been taken years ago is Kino/UAZ, now owned and operated by University of Arizona under the new title, Banner University Health Sciences/South. For years it was essentially run by the state superior court which held court there every day. A high-cost social service company managing psychiatric services was layered in between incoming University of Arizona and the court. It boasted of its ability to enhance the hospital's reputation with the Pima County Superior Court. This company made sure that psychiatrists, regardless of their medical duties, dropped everything when paged to testify in the courtroom at Kino/UAZ. Psychiatrists bowed to the pressures from young attorneys finding an easy start out of law school with a steady flow of cases every day. Often staff psychiatrists muttered, "we're really not doctors anymore." No, they were primarily expert witnesses and emergency medicine doctors "on the fly" on behalf of the courts requiring their testimony—namely predictions of future threat to self and others for which they have been notoriously scalded for not possessing.

The University of Arizona certainly medicalized Kino/UAZ, but was the judicial shield and inappropriate presence of too many dark-suited attorneys compared to white-coated clinicians too intimidating for Pima College staff to take Loughner? Were families and college counselors or security officers made to feel unwelcome bringing psychotic people in for treatment? We will never know, but access to Kino/UAZ was actually among the best in the nation for first-break psychosis, as was the case with Jared Loughner. He should have been there probably near a hundred times before finally detained at the Federal Medical Facility in Springfield, Missouri, again, a hospital run by attorneys and not psychiatrists (Liebert and Birnes 2014).

How did this flip flop in public psychiatric care occur? There were many converging forces that have left public psychiatry in shambles. One was deinstitutionalization of the seriously mentally ill, which was more a financial decision made by states to get out of the business of running large hospitals for the sickest psychotic patients. Then there was the withdrawal of funding from the federally funded community mental health center movement initiated and built by JFK. It lived and died with him. Finally, in what appears to have been an anomalous circumstance, it was the *Lessard* decision that opened the floodgates known as criminalization of the seriously mentally ill. Unfortunately, polls of Americans show that the majority agree that what is severe neuropsychiatry impairment has nothing to do with genetics or abnormal neurocircuitry in the brain. Although 10% do, that was not enough to stop this train of denial of the existence of mental illness when it left the station in Wisconsin nearly 50 years ago (Liebert and Birnes 2011; Stahl 2013; Torrey 2012).

With all these winds and cross-winds of recent history, it is not surprising that public psychiatry is now controlled by the courts, its judges, and attorneys on both sides of the case. Diagnostics and treatment, unless a patient is well insured with insight into his distress and inability to adapt in society, are now adversarial. Kino/UAZ was a product of that legacy when Loughner needed it (Liebert and Birnes 2014). Milwaukee County Crisis Center is constantly in the headlines and basically on life support: "Chronic Crisis: A system that doesn't heal. Milwaukee County mental health system traps patients in cycle of emergency care; Shortage of community treatment means police are called to handle those in crisis while doctors face legal hurdles to providing adequate care" (Kissinger, journal sentinel staff, Imminent Danger Series).

Nationwide, the judiciary has taken over management of whatever is properly called serious mental illness, or inherited it from court decisions made far away in places like Milwaukee, Wisconsin, and Sacramento, California, decisions successfully muddling the psychopathology of millions suffering from psychotic illnesses to the point that the courts became medical practitioners dictating diagnostics and treatments. This is the stuff of law: adversarial, case based, muddied, and clarified trial by trial. They did take charge in the case of Jared Loughner, but there is not a judge in this nation who would not agree that it was a tragic ending with a pathetic denouement: "competent to stand trial, first degree murder plea accepted by Attorney General Holder and state prosecutors waived jurisdiction" (Martinez and Lah 2012).

Law students might find this case of great interest. For everyone else, the case of Jared Loughner came to a catastrophic conclusion, one preventable, as the most insane of all involved, Jared Loughner himself, stated after taking a medication—antipsychotic Risperdal, available with good safety and low side effects when injected once every 2 weeks—although too toxic, many will assert, even though, when properly managed it is not.

There have been scores of suicidal mass murders since Loughner. The courts are still managing the seriously mentally ill. And the public still questions whether psychiatrists can predict dangerous behavior even when the evidence of hindsight into suicidal mass murderers is as conclusive as it possibly can be that certain suicidal and violent ideation pose extreme danger to others. It is time for the judiciary to consider that they are not qualified for the job of assessing dangerous mental illness and should bow out. The legal system is too jammed up with trial attorneys who have a steady diet on their dockets for arguing diagnostics and treatment plans before a judge and expecting psychiatrists always to be available on either side of the argument. How would this work in the case of coronary artery insufficiency, where clinical intervention is a life and death matter? A beating brain is in fact no different than a beating heart, and the morbidity and mortality are just as great from its neglect. The judiciary and legal profession has its place in oversight of cardiac care, just as it does over serious neuropsychiatric impairment wherein the patient loses insight into existence of his impairment through anosognosia which in lay terms means "denial of impairment" (Liebert and Birnes 2011). Simply stated, the technical aspects of a criminal trial for a defendant pleading insanity are often beyond the capacity of a jury of laypersons to sift through the arcane medicalese put forth in the testimony of adversarial expert psychiatric witnesses. To wit, the battling psychiatrists testifying in the case of Aurora, Colorado, shooter James Holmes is an example.

Here is a young man diagnosed as insane who was living within the virtual reality of Batman villain, the Joker, who, after being diagnosed with a severe mental illness by a psychiatrist at the University of Colorado, progressively devolved before the eyes of his professors of neuroscience and University of Colorado counseling center staff into psychosis. Driven by his delusion to cause mass murder, he was methodical; the planned police chase following the shooting, state's expert psychiatric witness attested, was evidence of his ability to discern right from wrong thus his murders were not the product of insanity under the increasingly rigid terms of the Not Guilty by Reason of Insanity Defense, requiring offenders to know right from wrong. The defense's psychiatric witness testified that a methodical plan is certainly within the capacity of a schizophrenic, especially one suffering from paranoid delusions. How can a jury figure out who is scientifically correct? Our advice to defense attorneys is that, unless there is a set of clear-cut evidence showing that your client is so delusional he or she believes the victim is an extraterrestrial, go with a bench trial and rely on a judge's expertise.

# CRIMINALIZATION OF THE MENTALLY ILL

## The courts and serious mental illness

There are approximately 6 million incarcerated mentally ill individuals. Cook County Jail is now America's largest psychiatric hospital.

One must question the perception of the public health crisis caused by ignoring the needs of many millions of seriously impaired neuropsychiatric patients. This question applies to the first encounter with an unknown person behaving strangely on the street in Los Angeles. Consider the social media statements that shocked peers with threats of suicide and/or violence in Marysville, Washington; parole hearings assessing prisoners undergoing profound personality changes in an Oklahoma prison, such as conversion to violent Jihadist beliefs before release to work in Moore, Oklahoma; corrections officers subduing the hallucinating psychotic yelling back at his voices in a jail cell at Rikers Island; neighbors awakened by illumination of their entire neighborhood to prevent an imagined enemy's penetration of the wire in Kileen, Texas; supervisors confronting a worker actively proselytizing extremist jihadi before having to shoot him before he beheaded a second victim of his persecutorial paranoia; and ER nurses being assaulted just about anywhere and every day in this country by violent psychotic patients.

The existential or epistemological nature of what psychiatrists diagnose as mental disorders must be left to philosophy classes if we are to really be epidemiologically informed at so many points of entry to our health-care system that were not considered within current health reform legislation. To wit: the most seriously impaired patient, such as Eddie Routh who murdered the American Sniper, is unlikely to be at the family home because they are either exhausted or terrified of him. He is not in a licensed medical or nursing bed because such beds have disappeared as fast as the need for them surges. Politicians, health professionals, hospitals, and the public are waiting for some entity to stop the human rights violations of neuropsychiatric patients wrongfully incarcerated in the most brutal condition. We have documented how these patients are in Riker's Island in New York, or "boarded" in overstimulating emergency rooms where, by definition, they are not considered patients in need of treatment but, rather, "boarders in crisis" only in need of transfer to the effective and secure inpatient psychiatric bed that hardly exists anymore. If medication can help clear the problems causing their admission to the emergency room, why are they not patients, just like stroke and cardiac patients (Zun and Liebert 2010)?

When addressing the American Medical Association to gain support from doctors for his Affordable Care Act, President Obama told members not to expect changes in malpractice legislation. He told a stunned audience of physicians that malpractice was generally good for health care, presumptively as a purge for bad practices as well as a recourse for patients who have suffered from bad medical practices. But, not to worry, he stated, "we will provide the tools to help you prevent malpractice." One could take this as hubris, naiveté, or the poster child for successful DC lobbying by the Trial Lawyers Association. Depending upon the area of litigation, such as OB-GYN, medical devices or appliances and certain types of surgery, malpractice insurance companies predict increasing tort action due to increasing volumes of patients having fewer options for placement in the right settings for evaluation and definitive care along, ironically, with higher expectations for their improved outcomes dictated by the Affordable Care Act. As reverse psychology, perhaps the president was laying the groundwork for a crescendoing crisis from an international Human Rights Report that shames the United States for excessive incarceration of the wrong people, including the severely impaired neuropsychiatric patient.

> The recent *New York Times* undercover report on July 14 detailing the "brutal and routine" violence by Rikers Island Correction's officers upon 129 inmates with serious mental illness over 11 months should have rocked a nation in disgust. One would expect outcries for immediate action, given the extreme urgency of this new revelation. This news, coming on the heels of the grotesque death of 56-year-old homeless veteran, Jerome Murdough, who was arrested on a simple trespass charge and then simply "baked to death" in his Riker's Island Jail cell. Mr. Murdough reportedly suffered from two psychotic disorders, Schizophrenia and Bipolar Affective Disorder and was unable to post a $250.00 bond. To be fair, the abhorrent abuse and neglect of persons with serious mental illness and other neurological disorders is so deep and widespread in the U.S. that in 2003, Human Rights Watch, a major international human rights policy center, published a Special Report, "Ill-Equipped," documenting wide spread human rights violations in U.S. super-max prisons. Many articles have been authored by renowned international disability law and human rights scholar, Professor Michael L. Perlin, the late Professor Bruce J. Winick, Professor David Wexler, and other law and policy experts who have long sounded the human rights alarm. So, why is this significant? First, we must take a lesson from successful corporate leaders who have followed the teachings of leadership guru, former Harvard Professor John P. Kotter, best known for his eight-step evidence-based framework for effecting social and institutional change. According to Kotter, first you must establish a "sense of urgency." (Lerner-Wren 2014)

The wind is blowing in the institutional sails for change now, because health experts—as well as government policy experts—are arguing that, like medical treatment for other diseases, treatment for the mentally ill should be considered a human right. According to E. Fuller Torrey,

> A distinguished group of International and U.S. mental health experts, including NAMI's distinguished medical director, Dr. Ken Duckworth, issued its policy report, "Time to Commit to Policy Change, Schizophrenia." This report, declared that delivery of

> mental health treatment is a human right. Most shaming for a nation claiming to lead the civilized world in morality, it echoes the United Nations Convention on the Rights of Persons with Disabilities. Anyone involved in mental health care today knows of Dr. Thomas Szcaz who really does not speak so much to rights, but simply makes insanity an existential matter for philosophers to debate—rather than a medical issue. Many have heard of John Monahan, who supported deinstitutionalization of the seriously mentally ill by his publications and aggressive lectures on the inability of psychiatrists to predict behavior. Monahan has backed up on this, now acknowledging that there may have been flaws in his research. (Torrey 2012; see also Liebert and Birnes 2011)

This places him closer to forensic psychiatry expert Seymor Halleck, who supports caution in predicting behavior but makes clear that some psychotic patients are predictably dangerous and must be treated, or detained if untreatable on an outpatient basis (Liebert and Birnes 2011).

The literature of international disability law and human rights scholars, Professor Michael L. Perlin, the late Professor Bruce J. Winick, Professor David Wexler, and other law and policy experts are less known. They have alerted the legal profession of human rights violations caused by criminalization of the seriously mentally ill; Thomas Szasz is no longer here to comment. Nor does he know the force of his book, *Myth of Mental Illness*, in shaping public policy, particularly government treasuries delighted to get out of the expensive and politically unrewarding business of caring for the seriously mentally ill. Harvard Professor John P. Kotter is best known for his influence on corporate management believing in the need to change their corporate cultures. It must start by establishing a sense of urgency.

> Since 2008, that sense of urgency has been successfully raised by Pew Center in its groundbreaking report on the crippling costs of mass incarceration in the U.S. Finding that "policy drives growth," Pew together with other major justice policy centers have worked steadily to help sway public opinion and drive legislation, largely through the attack on The War on Drugs, institutional racial bias and the inequities of federal drug sentencing laws. Further, evidence-based recommendations have effectively promoted a range of smart problem-solving criminal justice sentencing strategies to reduce length of sentencing, promote rehabilitation and begin to reduce recidivism and direct downwards the collateral costs of mass incarceration. (Lerner-Wren 2014)

After shocking headline after shocking headline of the neuropsychiatric patient, whether going on a suicidal rampage murder spree or being gunned down by police is seems almost a process of de facto genocidal elimination of our bad seeds; what is the tipping point? Is it another video of police shooting down a mentally ill man, as they did in Pasco, Texas, just recently? Will the urgency come when attorneys representing the rights of the mentally ill sue the governors of states responsible for cost-shifting emergency neuropsychiatric treatment from specialized hospitals and clinics to jails and prisons? A few such lawsuits could, in justification for the president's resistance to capping malpractice, create Professor Kotter's "sense of urgency" very quickly. After all, the Department of Justice is both suing Arizona's Maricopa County Sheriff, Joe Arpaio, for racial profiling and investigating events in Ferguson and Albuquerque. Why not sue states and prison officials for violation of patients' rights to treatment and discrimination against the mentally ill? That is exactly what brought Dr. Green to Pelican Bay Prison under the *Madrid* decision.

In terms of legal liability, the vulnerability of any clinician encountering a patient with neuropsychiatric impairments is about the same as that for psychiatrists. That means, if agents of the government, such as prison guards and police officers, are functioning in the role of psychiatrists—as most currently are—they should expect to be held liable for negligence, recklessness—or, if they are de facto clinicians handling the mentally ill, held to the same standards of clinicians with respect to malpractice. How better to up the "sense of urgency?"

The president advocates for doctors accepting higher-volume patient flows and higher administrative costs without relief of capping malpractice awards by tort reform, although that is probably a matter for the states and not the federal government, in as much as there is no constitutional issue in play. This requirement for higher patient flow, he said, is justified by his administration providing them with more advanced tools to better their practice skills and clinical effectiveness. Presumably these tools are embedded in the Affordable Care Act and stimulus package funding health-care information technology (IT) research and development (R&D) with $20 billion of awards. But there is still an obvious lack of ER preparedness, caused in large part by federal and state policies that criminalize the mentally ill, while medical computing, although promising and inevitably a wave of innovation for the healthcare industry in the future, is like a Model T Ford contemporaneously being promoted as a Tesla Model S in the automotive industry. As discussed in detail in the previous chapter, medical computing was imposed on clinical sites like hospitals before it was proven effective for either improving outcomes in general or preventing fatal medical errors; the latter were proven by Health Research Quality studies within the U.S. Department of Health and Human Services to be in inexcusable numbers nationally. Then, criminalization of mental illness drives millions of psychiatric patients into ERs for care where the questionably accepted policy of "boarding" them drains routine emergency service, dulling its cutting edge when really needed and draining resources of mandated preparedness in the wake of 9/11. This nation's emergency services, despite the multibillions spent after 9/11 still flunk across all states for measures of preparedness. Texas Presbyterian Health is case in point of that long known failure in both emergency services and homeland security (TimH 2014; *HealthDay News* 2005).

We can improve the system confronting police and emergency service personnel by looking at the flaws in the system and addressing them. For example, we can look at the lapses taking place in the area of veterans' affairs and see what immediate steps can be taken while the agency ramps up to manage the soldiers currently on waiting lists for Medical Evaluation Boards or, following discharge, for Pension and Compensation examinations by Department of Veterans Affairs.

## VETERANS' AFFAIRS

We can begin by making sure every returning veteran has immediate access to health care under the Affordable Care Act, requiring each veteran to register with the act as part of his or her initial application for benefits. During the waiting period, Platinum level health insurance would immediately kick in, allowing the veteran to seek care from private physicians, who would be compensated by the insurance company. Also, all veterans would be entitled to a living stipend for support based on sound actuarial statistics predicting duration of unemployment following discharge. The authors acknowledge the high incidence of disability among veterans; so, for those not healing with adequate medical and financial support in the private sector, additional Veterans' Courts need to be established under Social Security to hear their cases and adjudicate long-term disability through specialized SSI. We do it for criminal offenses by veterans; so, we can do that for long term disability claims also. These two steps alone: (1) Immediately upon military discharge—with few military jurisprudence exceptions—buy out recruitment contracts of this all-volunteer army with adequate money in trust for them to immediately have traction to integrate into the civilian world, and (2) provide free Platinum-grade Obamacare medical insurance guarantying healthcare access wherever they chose to live, would provide emotional security to veterans, their families and every community in America, from Menasha, Wisconsin to Dallas, Texas.

## CORRECTIONS

Because we are criminalizing the mentally ill, our jails have become de facto psychiatric wards staffed by personnel acting as properly trained and experienced clinicians, but, in fact, with little or no training or understanding of the people they are guarding. If we look at the human and civil rights context, incarceration of the seriously impaired neuropsychiatric patient can be judged a violation of his or her rights, because the Supreme Court of California ruled that any clinician treating a psychiatric patient is in fact the same as a physician diagnosing and managing a patient with a contagious disease. This clinician, the court ruled, has special knowledge—that is ability to diagnose and predict likely spread of a pathogen—and ability to control—that is doing what is necessary to protect a potential victim and the community of the patient's unremitting clinical state of human destructiveness. Clearly, the Supreme Court of California believed that neuropsychiatric impairment was no myth and required medical management as reliable and effective as contagious infectious diseases. Accordingly, if corrections officers are placed in the shoes of the clinician—as they currently are as caregivers of those judged to be mentally ill—what goes on in corrections facilities, like Rikers Island, should come under the auspice of the *Tarasoff* decision insofar as the "peculiar ability" of special care is applicable. For those now wearing the hat of de facto psychiatric clinician within a correctional facility, here are the elements necessary for successfully remediating the conditions contributing to festering mental illness, neuropsychatric impairment, and risk of untimely death. First, understand and seek competent diagnosis. Eliminate entirely solitary confinement for the mentally ill. Seek psychiatric consultation for those inmates who seem to manifest psychiatric impairment above and beyond the psychopathology of antisocial personality disorder—aka criminal. And most of all, ask whether there is dereliction, whether improper departure from accepted practice or inept application of accepted practice. Solitary confinement for managing disruptive behaviors caused by auditory hallucinations, as with Murdough's killing at Rikers, is a flagrant example. And we suspect that what is happening at Rikers is happening all around the country.

## SCHOOLS AND CAMPUSES

Merely reviewing the cases of Cho, Lanza, Holmes, Loughner, and Rodger should indicate enough "don'ts" or red flags for any professional. For example, accepting an involuntary committed patient at a state university counseling center having no psychiatrist and, therefore never offering him medications—as in the case of Cho—is a flagrant example of professional negligence (Liebert and Birnes 2011). The same can likely be argued in the case of Loughner at the state of Arizona's Pima College, resulting in the Tucson Safeway Plaza Massacre. Dereliction is rampant in both state and federal systems responsible for the care of the impaired neuropsychiatric patient. Cursory reviews of students acting strangely from Pima College in Arizona with Loughner to University of Connecticut with Adam Lanza—absent any medical review—is also a red flag of negligence. Students acting strangely or with aggressive hostility should at least be the subject of counselor-parent conferences, and Internet; social media postings should be reviewed. Students who make threats should be taken very seriously, and if the threats continue—freedom of speech notwithstanding—law enforcement should be notified. At a minimum, the most flagrant and potentially dangerous cases like Cho at Virginia Tech, Holmes at University of Colorado and Loughner at Pima College will be flagged early.

Identify and manage the delinquent child within the juvenile justice system, informed by Wolfgang's classic findings that clinical intervention following the third offense can significantly reduce major adult felony violence in early adulthood.

First-episode psychotic breaks for schizophrenia are not uncommon; there are 300,000 per year in this country. They are in most cases unpredictable based on family histories, but warning signs are oftentimes clear—unfortunately, too often in retrospect; early recognition of pre-psychotic deterioration, as in the case of Adam Lanza, must prevail over rights to privacy to prevent sick kids from dying with their rights on as adults, too often taking total innocents with them. We know morbidity in chronic, unremitting clinical states of human destructiveness peaks following that first psychotic break; epidemic suicidal mass murderer makes that case without room for doubt, rights to privacy on campuses oftentimes being held up retroactively as a defense to hide both incompetence in recognition and diagnosis of psychosis and/or suicidality and negligence in management (Liebert and Birnes 2011, 2014).

But, what about the 100 people shot in Chicago over the July 4 weekend in 2014? These perpetrators knew what they were doing and at least had plans for escape and evasion in order to fight another day. They may be self-destructive, but they were not imminently suicidal if able to escape and evade the police. They represent a different cohort of unremitting clinical states of human destructiveness—a dangerous one, unique in the developed world for the United States and its North American neighbor, Mexico. Their victims, whether known competitors in trafficking—or simply targets for gang initiation to prove solidarity and commitment, had no chance.

Reiterating the landmark research by Marvin Wolfgang on repeat offenders in the 1970s clearly showed a progression of criminality among a cohort of randomly selected juveniles in Philadelphia. It also showed a distinctive dropout rate from police records. In fact half of Wolfgang's 10,000 juveniles followed from early teens into their twenties were arrested once, and one-half of them were arrested again. Wolfgang studied these arrests and found them too scattered and oftentimes minor to call for in-depth investigation. One-half of the group arrested a second time recidivated; that is the cohort from their third offense where Wolfgang found a high concentration of high-risk young males who could be red flagged for going on to commit serious felonies. In the end, he found 1% of his original cohort of 10,000 young males—or 100 of them—were ultimately responsible for more than 90% of major felonies in the community!

It is this default discovered by Wolfgang long ago that must be translated from research to judicial best practices. The third offense is the time that every judge in this country needs to order thorough psychological, social, and family assessment. This was certainly the case of Steven Kazmierczak whose parents could not get him examined at school when he had been arrested three times. It was the case of Jared Loughner within the community also—even separate from the numerous encounters with Pima College police on campus.

Had either Kazmierczak or Loughner been evaluated, even with simple screening devices such as the MMPI and an interview with a clinical psychologist, they would have been found to be psychotic; that is now clear in retrospect, although not clear to the courts on the occasions of any court appearances. This must change if this nation is to stop the violence, whether psychotic suicidal mass murderers or young gangsters (Liebert and Birnes 2011).

Only the judiciary can get at the roots of the violence in our society, but they need to heed the advice of Wolfgang, or at least educate themselves to his research. They may not have known about all three offenses in the Kazmierczak and Loughner cases that could have led to the reliable and valid diagnoses of chronic psychotic neuropsychiatric impairment in all three of them, but they could have known had they asked or searched. Certainly, none of these individuals presented in any court or before any officer, for that matter, as ordinary people with minor offenses.

The massacres at NIU and Safeway Plaza were preventable, had both perpetrators been ordered into treatment for psychotic illness—schizoaffective disorder in the former and schizophrenia, paranoid type in the latter. Both were so diagnosed, but one was allowed to get out of treatment, enter the military, learn how to kill, and then commit the massacre at NIU. The other was never diagnosed before his suicidal rampage shootings at Safeway Plaza in Tucson; tragically he is on the court record as saying that he would not have committed the massacre had he been on the antipsychotic medication forced by the court to be taken in federal prison.

Are we simply going to leave it to fate, allowing disenfranchised kids, regardless of race or ethnicity, to grow up on the street and leave gangs—which some do—age in prison or die from gunshot wounds? Black teens growing up near the U.S. Capitol had a better chance of surviving from multiple deployments to Iraq than they did on the streets of Washington, DC, where they had a 10% chance of being shot before reaching adulthood. And, if they are shot, what is done? One pediatrician battled Medicaid agents to hospitalize a black teen on the psychiatric ward for evaluation after being treated in the ER for a gunshot wound. That is discriminatory. Those agents were essentially implying that this black kid had thicker skin and did not need psychiatry. Too often that is the thinking. The progression of teens arrested from Wolfgang's research follows very closely the arrest records for attention deficit hyperactivity disorder (ADHD) and also showed 50 years ago the heightened risk for ultimate incarceration of young black adults who were ignored within the juvenile justice system as children. One-half of boys with ADHD will be arrested once, regardless of socioeconomic class. One-half of those arrested once will be arrested again; those arrested the second time, however, are heavily weighted toward lower socioeconomic status. That might explain Wolfgang's finding decades ago of a disproportionate number of young black offenders at each progressive cut-off point.

## ADHD AS INDICATOR OF BEHAVIORAL DISORDERS

California Corrections prohibited diagnosing ADHD in prisoners evaluated under the *Madrid* decision. Of course, they are reasonably afraid of having stimulants in the prison. There is no answer for that, but maybe we need to turn the clock back. Is it not a bit late to diagnose fulminating paranoid schizophrenia in Loughner after he goes on a suicidal rampage murder in totally delusional state of mind? Is it not a little late to be diagnosing prisoners with ADHD in prison? ADHD, unlike schizophrenia, is diagnosable in elementary school. But, like psychotic illnesses and medications effective in clearing much of their psychopathology, there is so much prejudice toward medicating children that schools and families alike avoid looking too deeply at the child, like Kazmierczak, who is not efficiently learning in elementary school. Adult attention deficit disorder (ADD) afflicts millions. It does not, however, start in adulthood, except in cases of traumatic brain injuries. The 20 million people with reliably diagnosed attention disorder in this country are born with it and are diagnosable in elementary school without thousand dollar workups. Women slip through the cracks, because they are rarely hyperactive and disruptive in class. They show up later in drug programs with DUI's and in divorce courts.

Not all untreated ADHD kids go on to troubled careers, and a small percentage end up in prison. Some ADHD-disordered kids go on to be very successful, but they do so at high cost in having to overcompensate for their distractibility and frequently associated learning disabilities. Conversely, however, the yield of ADHD in prison from valid testing would be very high. Before our prisons filled with chronic psychotic patients declared by our judiciary not to be sick but simply making bad choices, Pincus and Tucker found that the vast majority of these violent youthful offenders have robust evidence of brain damage (80%, including epilepsy in 20%), paranoid ideation (frequently misdiagnosed as callousness), and histories of either witnessing or experiencing extreme child abuse in their families (Pincus and Tucker 2002). These are all diagnosable conditions, and, if associated with later-onset conduct disorder, can be effectively treated in more than half of the cases with family therapy—rarely provided to this highest-risk population. The highest risk for a young adult male ending up in one of those special mental health courts is being a male growing up in a single-parent home without a father (Kessler et al. 1994). What, therefore, is being done in public health to address the known problem of the single mother with an impulsive teenage son? Nothing. Also, not only is ADHD frequently associated with comorbid learning disabilities, it is frequently associated with conduct disorder. The genetics and epidemiological correlation of these frequently co-occurring diagnoses is not understood but demands better research if we are to get at the roots of delinquency, whether individuals, like Michael Brown, stealing for drugs or kids, like his accomplice in Ferguson, at war on our city streets with each other and the police.

The prevalence of conduct disorder is 10% in males and 2% in females (*Clinical Psychiatry News*, 1994.) Follow-up research on 300 children referred to a child guidance clinic in St. Louis for antisocial behavior (conduct disorder) showed that in 35 years 71% were arrested and 50% had multiple arrests and incarceration. Nearly one-third were diagnosed in adulthood as having antisocial personality disorder, while almost all committing four offenses went on to adult criminal careers. Only 16% were ultimately found to be free of psychiatric illness. The severity and number of antisocial behaviors in childhood conduct disorder predict adult behavior better than any other variable, including social class and family background (Kay and Kay 1990).

If it were not for this progression of conduct disorder in comorbidly ADHD males to a malignant form of adult sociopathy defying current corrections efforts, our streets—when curfewed from adolescent reoffenders and drug dealers—should be safe. But, presently nearly 20 million people move in and out of jails in the United States each year, most with past violence-related injuries and high risk of future violent injuries or death; 26% of those jailed had survived prior gunshot wounds. Furthermore, statistics demonstrate combat strategies to deliberately wound rather than kill in this cohort of youthful offenders going to jail; the non-fatal-to-fatal ratio is 12:1 in drive-by shootings (Northrop and Hamrick 1990).

Twenty-five years later, this translational research is dead on arrival in the clinics and streets of America. Worse yet, this is the tip of the iceberg. Ninety percent of illegal acts in juveniles are undetected (Anderson 1994). And nonpsychiatric dispositions in the criminal justice system are now, at best, politically expedient, despite the fact that the metro jails are among the largest psychiatric inpatient facilities in most states. Ultimately, presentence investigation will have to once again become an integral point of entry into the healthcare delivery system, unless we are prepared to write off a generation of young males, now mostly low-income minorities, and mortgage our childrens' future to pay for life and health care for millions of men behind bars with three strikes (Liebert and Wright 1977).

## EMERGENCY ROOMS

We have already argued that corrections departments must differentiate between prisoners who are sick and those who are not, and we recognize that most of the seriously impaired neuropsychiatric prisoners have already turned up as patients and have been hospitalized in ERs at one time or another. Let's begin there. The ER of today is becoming, more and more, the clinic of street people cared for by the police and jailers. The concept of boarding of this population of patients is controversial, because some ER specialists believe that they are patients like any others and should therefore be treated, rather than boarded, like any other ER patient—such as the stroke patient who is not boarded. That, however, is a minority opinion that has gained little traction in the real world of emergency medicine.

The primary focus of this book, therefore, is the emergency room, where many psychiatric patients are transported when the police believe they are too sick for jail. In the current paradigm shift of emergency medicine for optimizing patient throughput away from initial triaging to immediately bedding all ER patients with rapid assessment to reduce wait times—thus improving patient satisfaction ratings, while paradoxically upping the stakes for diversion to another hospital—gridlock in patient flows will likely occur at some point.

Since the supposed awakening of 9/11—also paradoxically—there are 200,000 fewer inpatient beds for admitting any patient and 20,000 less ERs for diversion of patients in the event of such gridlock; adding to the inevitable forthcoming gridlock, inpatient psychiatry is all but gone. That leaves "discharge lounges," the latest innovation, as a gray zone between being homeless on the street and actually being a patient in a hospital in the frequent event somebody does not pick up the discharged patient and take him or her home. Within this paradigm shift from a crowded waiting room with an experienced "Pivot Nurse" triaging patients for timely need of clinical intervention to an empty waiting room with even volunteers greeting patients, as if they are walking into Walmart, everyone encountering the patient needs to understand and appreciate the concepts of "time-determined" and "epidemiologically informed" clinical decision making. This is what clinicians do every day they practice or take call in acute care medicine regardless of clinical discipline or specialty.

Nancy Auer stated in 2002 that ERs were now ground zero. Although recognized as such by Congress following the attacks of 9/11, the CDC was not provided the funding to prepare them for anything; an ER physician must examine and diagnose everyone coming in by federal law. Nothing else, however, is done to make certain that they can or that they will be there for us in the event of another attack by weapons of mass destruction, whether airplanes, anthrax—both of which we have already witnessed—or chemicals and radiation—which we have not yet witnessed, but fear from both The Great Leader's seeming intent on terrifying us from Pyongyang with long range missiles tipped with nuclear warheads and chemical warfare agents attributed to causing Gulf War Syndrome threatening our soil from infiltration of North America by ISIS.

Given the confusion in events in the emergency management of Thomas Duncan at Texas Presbyterian Health, as well as the recent decision on the ground by a fire chief to wave off medevac helicopters in Marysville, Washington to better their chances for survival by ground transport to the local ER instead of nearby Harborview Trauma Center, clearly protocols are required for rapid assessment at all points of entry, whether the more common disaster scenes of our school campuses or overwhelmed ERs. Doctors do not listen to nurses telling them important data. Communications in general in ERs are chaotic. One thing that is certain is that the electronic medical record, presumably a tool the president is promising for best practices to reduce fatal and disabling medical errors, was at best a hindrance in diagnosing and managing a patient like Thomas Duncan. With 1400 pages of electronic reports for a case that required immediate diagnosis and clinical intervention—namely emergency precautions for contagiousness in the ER and transfer to isolation for Ebola—the system was clogged from the outset, and procedures to contain his contagiousness were not followed. How can this communication be simplified? Here is how.

Whether a first responder in the field, as in the case of Marlene Pinnock on I-10, jailer of Jerome Murdough at Rikers Island, or "intake worker" in Texas Presbyterian greeting Thomas Duncan in the ER, there is a requirement that all these people know the taxonomy and lexicology of classical emergency medicine triage. Are we advocating that the street and jail cell become emergency rooms? No, because, with aid and abetting of our judiciary, they already are. Immediate frontline personnel need training, therefore, in what to do until the entire debacle of deinstitutionalization and criminalization of the seriously mentally ill caused by eccentric federal court decisions, in tandem with the current degradation of care for discharged soldiers runs its course and politicians are forced to declare, "enough's enough."

There is acknowledgement of this imminent terminal crisis, but awareness is at the margins. Boise's police chief went to Congress to plead for better care of veterans so his officers do not have to shoot sharpshooters discarded on to his streets with impaired nervous systems from combat. Emergency room doctors in San Antonio are building a mental health center with inpatient beds like all those advocated by JFK and rejected by President Reagan after President Carter's ineffectual efforts for their sustainability. The Los Angeles Police Department (LAPD) does not want to simply train more SWAT teams to shoot students on campus before they kill more kids and shoot themselves. Their program follows kids from initial threat all the way to their bedrooms, regardless of school status, and find out what the kids are up to. They do it legally, usually with parents' consent, but the courts will have to back up from taking charge of a public psychiatric system it neither understands nor demands its judges to anything about in law school. A tip from a student in Traverse City, Michigan, allowed police to interdict mass shootings by a fifth-grader who entered school with a loaded weapon and a hit list of students he wanted dead. Awareity Inc. has installed a sophisticated TIPS system in schools so that anonymous tips about threatening students can be processed and triaged according to salience of threat; interventions are layered according to seriousness, all the way from simple surveillance to psychological assessment—or finally, aggressive intervention to assure the student—or even faculty member—receives adequate psychiatric treatment.

The judiciary could have and should have had Jared Loughner diagnosed and treated with antipsychotic medication at Kino/UAZ Hospital in Tucson before his Tucson Safeway Plaza massacre—not afterward in federal prison to make him competent to agree to a plea in lieu of the death penalty. Like Cho, students had expressed their fear of Loughner on Pima College Campus, but nothing was done until he was simply suspended and forcibly removed from campus, absent perceived authority by administration to do anything else but removal from campus.

Educators and clinicians alike in Newtown avoided acknowledgement and responsibility for Adam Lanza's progressive deterioration into psychosis, likely fearing invasion of his or his mother's rights. School nurses and counselors need authority to force students to receive psychiatric treatment when it is obviously needed—not simply suspend them from school until they have been evaluated by a psychiatrist. This is what was done with Loughner. There has to be a better legal solution to assure that Lanza and Fryberg in Marysville get properly assessed, rather than simple school suspensions considered safely within the legal domaine of school administration. Suspension alone did not work with Fryberg in Marysville High School, Schick at Duquesne, or Loughner at Pima College, and only made things worse. Cases that ultimately sour with severe death and injury are sometimes preceded by visible behavioral change. Most mass shooters showed gross behavioral changes on school campuses. Instead of simply ignoring these changes or hoping the student will go away, school health personnel must be proactive like the Western Kentucky Awareity Program or LAPD school shooting prevention program and track that student even if he leaves, is suspended, or flunks out. All schools need to have that legal authority to find out a student's psychosocial background when strange behavior rises to a threshold all but screaming psychological decompensation with ultimate high risk of suicide—and worse, psychosis with or without violence to others. There has to be a limit to privacy for such students. The vast majority of faculty and students alike deserve a safe learning environment.

Laura's Law was passed in California to provide assisted treatment to involuntary committed patients as the condition for their being allowed to reside within the community and receive outpatient care instead of indeterminate institutionalization. Counties had discretion to implement the law. Except for few in the nation-state of California, they did not. Grossly psychotic individuals were shot dead, committed suicide, or were beaten down by police instead of being intercepted, assessed, and committed for observation. Perhaps Laura's Law will help stem the violence. Laura's Law is expected to be implemented because of this carnage early next year, but, other than Los Angeles, San Francisco, and Orange counties, county supervisors have been curiously resistant to its implementation. Even if it is implemented, it must be enforced so that psychotic patients like Marlene Pinnock do not wander in harm's way with grandiose mystical delusions of being impervious to tons of metal crushing them and piling up in an inferno on her preferred barefooted walkway—I-10 at La Brea. There was no excuse for the judiciary in Los Angeles to fail in management of her case under Laura's Law.

In New York, despite Kendra's Law, a man with an extensive record of violence and known psychosis was allowed to wander freely and once again defy the very law made to prevent such horror. Kevin Darden pushed a father of two into an oncoming subway train. He is suspected of having done it before, too. A short time later a homeless man, Rudralall Baldeo, pushed a man on to the tracks of an oncoming train, but the victim was saved just in time. New York is fortunate to both have Kendra's Law and have implemented it. With these lethal shovings onto New York's subway platforms, obviously it is time to enforce the law; the judiciary must take the lead in setting the example, as they have the ultimate power to prevent such disastrous tragedies. Certainly if Eric Garner can be taken down for resisting arrest, then psychotic homeless men like Darden and Baldeo can be supervised or detained in secure hospitals for the criminally insane if it is the case that they are unmanageable under Assisted Treatment of Kendra's Law.

Seattle did have somewhat a kangaroo court of justice for involuntary commitment before involuntary commitment was essentially gutted of its powers in Washington State. Every psychiatrist in Seattle knew that some people were being detained under family pressure who should not have been. Two psychiatrists had too much power to detain people; it was known as the Klein-and-Reilly Show at Harborview Hospital, named after the two psychiatrists examining people brought to them by the police as 220s for detention. The police slang for strange behavior on Seattle's streets is still 220 and stands for the overtime pay of $2.20 received back then for the officer's transport of patients to Harborview Hospital—then King County Hospital, like Kino Hospital, without university affiliation. Klein and Reilly were believed by most psychiatrists to be doing a fair and ethical job of deciding who was too insane and dangerous to be on the streets, but they needed more judicial oversight. They did not, however, need the revolving door now allowing psychotic people like Ian Stawicki roaming the streets with the knowledge of both the police and his own family that serious damage was inevitably going to be done. It is out of control now, and order must be restored to a system totally failed.

Clearly, the public is going to have to be better informed about the near total absence of societal control over psychotic patients who either deny their neuropsychiatric impairment or are nonadherent to medical management. A major test case is now in the hands of the San Diego County Board of Supervisors to decide whether Laura's Law for court-ordered treatment of psychotics in the community believed to be a threat to self or others will be implemented. Of interest is the fact that only one supervisor has voiced support; others are undecided or not available for comment. This is likely a microcosm of political thought and expected action on proactive judicial intervention into unremitting clinical states of human destructiveness. Walter Stawicki and other families like the Klebolds of Columbine share the grief of inevitable tragedy from psychotic loved ones—including threats to their own safety—are speaking out. "In A Mother's Reckoning, Sue Klebold writes about how well she knew—and didn't know—her son, Dylan, who was one of two gunmen who killed 13 people at Columbine High School in 1999" (Susan Dominus, NY Times, February 15, 2016). But such informing voices are few and far between, always following a headline event of massive bloodshed—then ignored in the news cycle until the next disaster recalls the last one—and so on, hopefully not forever.

The first thing that needs to be done, therefore, is for the San Diego County Supervisors to learn the consequences of their political legacy from the Reagan era embodied in the Lanterman–Petris–Short (LPS) Act. Whether Ronald Reagan had anything to do with this disabling of involuntary commitment in California or not, clearly his understanding of psychotic illness was not good. His naiveté was demonstrated by his amazingly well-intentioned request to meet personally with his assassin, John Hinckley, and forgive him. Fortunately Hinckley's psychiatrist said no, and that such a conversation would not be wise. In the politically more liberal northern part of California, San Jose police are now clearing an encampment of homeless people numbering in the four figures. While relocating these people, they should demand of the court the authority to at least subject them to medical examinations to determine if they are gravely disabled and helpless in finding shelter on their own due to psychotic illness or devastating post-traumatic sequellae from combat. These are not people choosing to camp out in San Jose and create an eyesore or public health hazard for Santa Clara County, one of the richest places in the world; nor are they transients. These are people native to Santa Clara County and San Jose who are likely in need of medical assessment and treatment, whether inpatient when too treatment resistant for adherence under Laura's Law—or close supervisory outpatient management under Laura's Law. Some certainly need social services, but they are probably in the minority and not the core of chronic homelessness in San Jose—or anywhere else for that matter. But, in bulldozing them away, they are considered moles needing "whacking," as their tents will pop up elsewhere; "don't ask, don't tell" is the unspoken policy for finding out why they spend their lives in squalor homeless. Seattle is going the other direction and helping build tent cities, but, again, the city has not a clue who these people are or why they are chronically homeless—or, if they do, they are not saying. Their policy is to let them live in tents, but not such that they disturb the hustle and bustle of this rich and prospering young city. Like San Jose, the largest in the Bay Area, Seattle is the largest in the Pacific Northwest.

This is a huge responsibility for the courts, but these are the facts of life in a nation that is closing ERs, hospital beds, and psychiatric resources faster than the population generates increasing demands for services—even beyond those of preparedness from another 9/11 terrorist attack, all but promised us by officials.

There are solutions to the psychiatric interactions between officialdom and the neuropsychologically impaired, but it will take a focus on specific solutions to move, albeit slowly, the logjams from the judicial system and recognize that all mentally impaired persons are not criminals, just as all criminals are not mentally impaired. In trial after trial, from Routh in Texas to Holmes in Colorado, we get the opposite—prolongation of obfuscation of reality by professionals either prosecuting or ruling on cases, whether out of clinical naivete or sheer political expediency, catering to threat of the crowds on the streets outside the courthouse following acquittal for Not Guilty by Reason of Insanity. The judiciary now controls public psychiatry, whether by intent or default; so, it is their responsibility to face up to Lessard and LPS and face the deficiencies in those eccentric laws in order to enable reform of public psychiatry and stop the blood of innocents from flowing on our campuses and public places.

## REFERENCES

Anderson, D. 1994. The crime funnel. 'lock em up' can't possibly cut crime much, a few cold facts show why. *New York Times Magazine*, 56–58, June 12.

Conduct disorder-still a therapeutic challenge. *Clinical Psychiatry News*, April 1994, p. 8.

*HealthDay News*. 2005. U.S., most states get failing grades for health emergency preparedness. *Pharm Daily*, December 6. www.pharmdaily.com/womenshealth/u.s.-most-states-get-failing-grades-for-health-emergency-preparedness.html

Kay, R. L. and Kay, J. 1990. *Adolescent Conduct Disorders in American Psychiatric Association Psychiatry Update Annual Review*. American Psychiatric Press, Inc., Vol. 5. pp. 408–496.

Kessler, R. et al. 1994. Lifetime and 12 month prevalence of DSM-III-R psychiatric disorders in the United States: Results from the national comorbidity survey. *Archives of General Psychiatry*, 51, 1, January.

Kissinger, M. Journal Sentinel staff, "Imminent Danger Series" www.jsonline.com/news/milwaukee/Milwaukee-County-mental-health-system-traps-patients-in-cycle-of-emergency-care-206806341.html, www.jsonline.com/watchdog/watchdogreports/reporter-wins-polk-award-for-investigation-into-milwaukee-county-mental-health-failures-b99203508z1-245774731.html

Lerner-Wren, G. 2014. The criminalization of the mentally ill in America—Have we reached a flashpoint? *Huffington Post*, September 21. www.huffingtonpost.com/ginger-lernerwren/the-criminalization-of-th_b_5607820.html

Liebert, J. A. and Birnes, W. J. 2011. *Suicidal Mass Murderers: A Criminological Study of Why They Kill*. London, UK.

Liebert, J. A. and Birnes, W. J. 2014. *Hearts of Darkness*. New York, New York.

Liebert, J. A. and Wright, C. 1977. *The Washington State Pre-Sentence Unit*. American Academy of Psychiatry & Law, New Orleans, Louisiana.

Martinez, M. and Lah, K. 2012. *CNN Loughner Pleads Guilty to 19 Counts in Tucson, Arizona, Mass Shooting*. August 8.

Northrop, D. and Hamrick, K. 1990. Weapons and minority youth violence. *United States Department of Health and Human Resources*, Centers for Disease Control and Prevention, Atlanta, Georgia.

Pincus, J. H. and Tucker, G. J. 2002. *Behavioral Neurology*, 4th edition. Oxford University Press, October 3.

Stahl, S. M. 2013. Neuroscience Education Institute. *Principles of Psychopharmacology*, 4th edition. Cambridge University Press, Cambridge, UK, May 27.

TimH. 2014. Grading the nation's support for emergency care. *Physician's Weekly*, July 10. www.physiciansweekly.com/grading-countrys-eds

Torrey., E. F. 2013. *American Psychosis: How the Federal Government Destroyed the Mental Illness Treatment System*, 1st Edition. Oxford University Press, October 1.

Torrey, E. F. 2012. *The Insanity Offense: How America's Failure to Treat the Seriously Mentally Ill Endangers Its Citizens*, 1st Edition. W. W. Norton & Company, January 2.

Zun, L. and Liebert, J. A. 2010. Boarding the psychiatric patient. *World Congress on Optimization of Patient Flow*, Chicago.

# 15

# Suicidal pilots in the aviation industry

With astonishing suddenness, although this phenomenon has been on the edges of our awareness for some time, the suicidal/mass murder perpetrated by the mentally impaired pilot has broken into the headlines with the crash of Lufthansa's Germanwings Flight 9525 into a mountainside at Prads-Haute-Bléone, Alpes-de-Haute-Provence, France. The flight had originated from Barcelona's Prat airport in Spain en route to Dusseldorf, Germany, when, according to crash investigators and prosecutors from both France and Germany, the copilot Andreas Lubitz, alone in the cockpit after pilot Captain Patrick Sondenheimer, took a bathroom break and left the cockpit.

Copilot Lubitz, according to investigators, now alone in the cockpit and in control of the aircraft, which was on autopilot, reprogrammed the autopilot into a rapid descent to 100 feet allowing the aircraft to accelerate. Lubitz had flown this route before as a private pilot and knew the area well. Meanwhile, Captain Sondenheimer, in the bathroom, noticed the plane's rapid descent, realized something was obviously wrong, and made his way back to the cockpit only to find the door locked and Lubitz, on the other side, unresponsive to the pilot's orders to open the door. As airspeed increased, the pilot, frustrated at first, became increasingly agitated, and the passengers, fully aware that the aircraft was descending at a steep angle and accelerating, were seized by panic. One can only imagine, from the sounds on the cockpit voice recorder, the chaos that ensued in the Airbus A320-211's passenger cabin. We also now know that Lubitz had actually rehearsed his suicide attempt earlier in that same flight from Barcelona to make sure he could input the proper commands into the plane's computer quickly enough while the pilot was out of the cockpit.

It was also apparent that he either manipulated—or at least knew of the Captain's not going to the men's room prior to boarding the aircraft.

This was not the first time a pilot or copilot in control of a commercial airliner deliberately crashed, killing all aboard—Lubitz not the first suicidal pilot. There are some high-profile cases that provide both evidence and facts for suicidal autopsy. Other suspected pilot suicides causing commercial airlines disasters included Japan, 24 killed, February 9, 1982; Royal Air Maroc, 44 killed, August 21, 1994; EgyptAir, 217 killed, October 31, 1997; SilkAir, 107 killed, December 19, 1997; LAM Mozambique, 33 killed, November 29, 2013; and FedEx attempted pilot suicide, April 7, 1994.

## EGYPTAIR FLIGHT 990

On October 31, 1999, EgyptAir Flight 990 crashed into the Atlantic just 60 miles south of Nantucket after having taken off from New York's JFK, the second leg of a flight that had originated in Los Angeles (LAX), en route to Cairo. At the time of the crash, the plane was under the control of a relief first officer, a crew member designated to fly the route over the Atlantic until the primary crew took over for landing. Shortly after takeoff from JFK, relief First Officer Gameel Al-Batouti entered the cockpit, though he was not scheduled to do so, and convinced the first officer, who at first refused to do so, to allow him to fly for awhile. Soon after he took over the controls, investigators playing the cockpit voice recorder heard him say to the pilot Ahmed Mahmoud El Habashy that he should return the active first officer's pen to him. Habashy then asks to be excused because he has to go to the toilet. There is a sound of the cockpit door opening and closing, and then Al-Batouti is left alone in the cockpit. Then as the plane begins to descend and warning sounds are heard on the tape, Al-Batouti keeps repeating over and over again, "I rely on God"—even as the voice of El Habashy can be heard saying, "what's happening Gameel, what's happening?" El Habashy then asks again, "what's happening? Did you shut the engines?" While Al-Batouti says, "it's shut," investigators could hear El Habashy yelling to him, "pull with me, pull with me." Then the plane hits the water and all on board are killed.

The U.S. National Transportation Safety Board (NTSB) ruled the crash a suicide murder while the Egyptians disputed the finding and said it was a mechanical failure. But it was no mechanical failure because the NTSB, which had called in the Federal Bureau of Investigation (FBI) because it believed a crime had been committed—but then had to relent when the Egyptian investigators balked at the FBI's presence—said they could find no evidence of any mechanical failure. To this day EgyptAir Flight 990 is officially listed by the NTSB as a murder/suicide while the Egyptians list it as a mechanical failure.

## MALAYSIA AIRLINES FLIGHT 370

In March 2014, after the disappearance of Malaysia Airlines Flight 370 over what was assumed to be a remote area of the southern Indian Ocean, the world seemed to hold its collective breath. The new Boeing 777, en route from Kuala Lumpur, Malaysia, to Beijing, and piloted by an experienced captain, simply dropped off radar after making an unexplained deviation from its assigned flight plan, turning toward open water. There was speculation all over the media that the plane had been hijacked or the pilot was trying to land the plane somewhere because of mechanical trouble. The pilot, who eventually became the subject of a police investigation, was Captain Zaharie Ahmad Shah from Penang. He had publicly expressed his unhappiness with the political situation in Malaysia and, in the absence of search teams' finding any evidence of the crashed plane in the Indian Ocean or of the flight data or voice recorders, remains the subject of speculation that he initiated the course change, cut off all communications with Lumpur after he was directed by flight control to contact air traffic control in Ho Chi Minh City before they were set to enter Cambodian airspace. But the plane never entered Cambodian airspace. After radar detected that the plane made a turn, departing from the flight plan without notifying air traffic control, radar and automated satellite communications with the plane were lost. The mystery remains. Speculation still runs high. But the bottom line is that the pilot is suspected of having made the turn off course, cutting off all verbal and electronic digital communication, and crashing the plane and all its passengers into a spot in the southern Indian Ocean where the countries in the area would have to expend vast resources in order to search for the remains. Perhaps this was Captain Shah's final statement; "Find it" (Wilson 2014). They did; wreckage was discovered on the beach of Reunion Island. "Investigators learned Thursday that a series of numbers found inside the plane flaperon matches records held by a Spanish company that manufactured portions of the component, linking the debris to MH370, the office of Paris Prosecutor Francois Molins said. 'Consequently, it is possible today to affirm with certainty that the flaperon discovered at the Reunion Island on July 29, 2015, is that of MH370,' the office said" (Hanna and Vandoorne, 2015).

## JETBLUE FLIGHT 191

The passengers on JetBlue Flight 191 from New York's JFK to Las Vegas McCarren Airport were lucky. When pilot Captain Clayton Osbon experienced a psychotic breakdown in the passenger cabin, started rambling about Al-Qaeda and Jesus and threatened that the plane would never reach its destination, he had to be subdued by passengers while the plane, now piloted by the first officer, was diverted to Amarillo, Texas, where Captain Osbon was removed from the plane and arrested. He suffered, what observers said and what a court ultimately ruled, a psychotic break.

The incident began when Osbon missed the preflight briefing. He was late. Then, in the cockpit at wheels up, Osbon began talking to his first officer about "being evaluated," something the first officer did not understand. Then Osbon began talking about his church and about how the plane was headed for a sinful city, Las Vegas, and, after he asked the first officer to take over the controls, said that things simply "didn't matter" anymore and then told his first officer that the plane would not go to Las Vegas. This was not only confusing behavior, it began to confound and then frustrate the first officer. The pilot's erratic conversation continued off and on for the ensuing 3 hours as the plane made its way across the country, and then the pilot left the cockpit to use the bathroom, banging on the lavatory door to urge the female occupant to get out. Now the first officer's desperation over his captain's behavior heightened, and he asked another JetBlue pilot, who was deadheading as a passenger to Vegas, to enter the cockpit and assume the role of active crew. They locked the cockpit door to keep Captain Osbon out, leaving him for the cabin crew to attend to.

But Osbon began to decompose mentally in the passenger cabin, first trying to reenter the cockpit using his security code. When that did not work, he started banging on the door. With what seemed to be a psychotic person at loose and acting out just aft of the galley, the first officer asked passengers in the cabin to subdue Captain Osbon, who was now ranting about 9/11, Iran, terrorists, and Jesus. He again ran toward the cockpit door, screaming, "throttle back" and "we gotta bring this plane down." At this point, a number of the passengers and cabin crew restrained him, grappled him to the floor, and subdued him, holding him for federal officers who removed him from the plane in Amarillo. Fortunately there were security professionals on board traveling to Las Vegas for a conference; one was able to disable the dangerously agitated pilot with a choke hold or passengers could have been injured or the flight more threatened.

This was a frightening incident, especially for the passengers and cabin crew, one of whose members was slightly injured in the melee as they tried to subdue Osbon. Subsequently, because under the doctrine of *res ipsa loquitur*, or "the thing speaks for itself," flight crews do not become psychotic on board and commercial flights are supposed to be safe and as uneventful as possible. Accordingly, some of the passengers sued the airline. Osbon himself is also suing Jet Blue for failing to screen him for fitness of duty before allowing him to board and take control of the aircraft.

## MOZAMBIQUE AIRLINES FLIGHT TM470

In a pattern eerily similar to what Andreas Lubitz would do 2 years later, Captain Herminio dos Santos Fernandes, the pilot of a Mozambique Airlines flight en route to Angola during a heavy rainstorm programmed his automatic pilot to bring the plane down in Namibia's Bwabwata National Park on November 29, 2013, killing all on board. Captain dos Santos Fernandes had locked himself in the cockpit, locked his copilot out, and, despite his copilot's demands for reentry as the warning sounds of danger echoed throughout the cabin, forced the plane to crash into a swampy area. Investigators called this crash a deliberate suicide. One has to wonder during Andreas Lubitz's research into methods of suicide and the technology of cockpit door security locks post-9/11, whether Lubitz had also researched pilot suicides such as Flight TM470.

## JAL FLIGHT 350

On a February 9, 1982, flight from Fukuoka, Japan, to Tokyo, Japan Airlines Flight 350 crashed on its approach to landing when pilot Captain Seiji Katagiri shut down the automatic pilot and pushed the yoke forward to bring the plane's nose down below the glide path while, at the same time, pulling back on the throttles allowing airspeed to bleed off and, possibly, stall the aircraft. He was not alone in the cockpit at the time, but although his first officer and flight engineer tried to restrain him while at the same time attempting to reengage the controls, it was too late. They could not bring the plane back under control in time to prevent a deadly crash, landing in the water just short of the runway. Not all of the passengers were killed, and the pilot, who had crashed the plane, got himself into one of the first rescue boats, claiming to rescuers that he was not the pilot and only a passenger. But he was later identified and prosecuted for murder. He was found not guilty by reason of insanity, because it was determined that his suicidal mass murder attempt was the result of serious mental illness.

## SILKAIR FLIGHT 185

Although there is still some dispute about the cause of this December 19, 1997, crash—either a defective servo valve controlling the rudder on the Boeing 737 or a deliberate suicide act by the pilot—the NTSC, Singapore's National Transportation Safety Committee, ruled the results of its investigation inconclusive even though the evidence suggested deliberate acts by the pilot Captain Tsu Way Ming. The captain had reportedly suffered devastating financial losses as the result of stock trades he had made. He was depressed and was looking at severe financial hardship.

The evidence inculpating Captain Tsu in the crash centers around the shutdowns of the cockpit voice recorder and flight data recorder, both of which were disconnected so as to stop recording. Investigators speculated that Captain Tsu first manually tripped the cockpit voice recorder's circuit breaker before he left the cockpit. Then, after he returned, he suggested his first officer use the lavatory and then, when alone in the cockpit, tripped the circuit breaker on the flight data recorder. He could not have tripped that breaker with the first officer in place, because a warning light would have blinked on the console. The plane, then at its cruising altitude of 35,000 feet, began a steep, almost vertical, dive, descending almost 35,000 feet in just over a minute, exceeding the speed of sound. As a result, stress on the plane's hull exceeded its structural integrity, and the plane began to break up during the dive. One wing actually sheared off. The plane crashed nose first into Musi River in Sumatra, killing all on board.

Investigators from the U.S. NTSB reasoned that the tell-tale indicators of pilot deliberate activity centered around the circuit breakers. They argued that if a mechanical default tripped the breakers on both the voice and data recorders, there would have been an audible click on the voice recorder before it shut down. Because there was no click, they believed, the circuit breaker was manually pulled, and only the pilot could have done that. Hence, the pilot shut the recorders down and then put the aircraft into a vertical dive from which there could have been no recovery—especially because the plane broke up prior to impact.

However, other investigators examined the servo valves on the rudder control and found minute defects. They reasoned that as a result of these defects, hot hydraulic fluid hitting the cold surfaces of the rudder controls could actually make the rudder deflect in a direction opposite to that commanded by the autopilot, thus causing loss of control. In Los Angeles Superior Court, a judge ruled that the arguments and evidence of the NTSB regarding the deliberate actions of the pilot could not be admitted as evidence. Therefore, no finding of pilot suicide/homicide was held by the court. Nevertheless, there is a strong belief that it was the pilot, who not only suffered from severe financial losses, but had taken out a hefty life insurance policy that went into effect on the day of the crash. He had also been disciplined by the airline for manually and improperly tampering with the cockpit voice recorder. There were also complaints that had been lodged against him by other pilots and cockpit crews claiming he was unfit for command. A picture emerged, therefore, of an individual facing extreme hardship, in danger of losing his job, who had practiced with manipulating the cockpit voice recorder's controls and who had bolstered his family's ability to survive his death by taking out a large insurance policy. This could well have been an act planned well in advance.

## ROYAL AIR MAROC 630

Pilot Younes Khayati had an important passenger on board on August 21, 1994, when he took off from Agadir, Morocco, en route to Casablanca. His royal passenger was the Kuwaiti prince whose brother was the kingdom's defense minister. Whether his passenger's presence was the reason Khayati disconnected the plane's automatic pilot 10 minutes into the flight, after the aircraft had reached 16,000 feet, or whether there was another reason, investigators believe that the autopilot disconnect was no mechanical failure. It was deliberate. As the plane neared a desolate area of the Atlas Mountains, pilot Khayati placed the aircraft into a steep dive, never pulled up, and plunged the craft into the ground, killing all onboard, including the prince and his wife. There was some dispute about the pilot's motives, and the Moroccan authorities believed that it had to have been a mechanical failure, lest they incur the wrath of the Kuwaiti royal family. But, the truth was that only the pilot could have disengaged the autopilot, disregarded warning lights that would have illuminated, and then disregarded indisputable warnings as the plane entered its dive. There was little follow-up information regarding Khayati's mental condition, but some theorists believed that the crash was a terrorist act.

## FEDERAL EXPRESS FLIGHT 705

On April 7, 1994, FedEx Flight 705 took off from the company's Memphis, Tennessee hub headed for San Jose with a load of cargo. Also on board was Auburn Calloway, a FedEx cockpit crew employee who was deadheading to the West Coast. But Calloway was harboring a desperate plan. Because he was about to be disciplined—if not fired—because he had been lying on his flight reports, he had decided to take over the cockpit, crash the plane, make it look like the whole thing was an accident, and have his family collect on the company's insurance policy. As an employee, he carried insurance.

His plan was diabolical, even if not completely well thought out. He had brought a collection of hammers on board, as well as a speargun, a weapon being an otherwise benign piece of equipment for someone going scuba diving. But he was traveling to San Jose, California. His plan was to use the hammers to render the pilot and copilot unconscious and then beat them to death, take over the controls of the plane, and then crash it. The injuries the cockpit crew had suffered from his beating them would look to crash investigators as if they were injuries incurred in the accident. And, of course, Calloway would die in the crash and his family would be the beneficiaries of a generous life insurance settlement.

Calloway was an experienced Navy pilot as well as a martial arts expert and believed his sudden surprise attack would overwhelm the unsuspecting crew. Thus he attacked. But the crew, despite injuries from being repeatedly struck with the hammers, was able to fight back just enough to subdue Calloway and land the plane. Calloway was arrested and charged with hijacking and attempted murder. He pled insanity, but because it was clear he had planned everything in advance, including his having made a substantial cash transfer to his wife, the prosecution was able to refute his insanity claims and Calloway was sentenced to prison.

If, as has been reported, Germanwings flight officer Andreas Lubitz had been carefully researching suicides as well as cockpit door security, it is likely that his time on the Internet also included research into the very suicides and attempted suicides we have described above, especially the ways in which the suicidal pilots manipulated their pilots or first officers out of the cockpit to enable them to reprogram the autopilot. Lubitz also displayed other psychiatric impairment including his obsessive need for control. His behavior was also erratic, according to his live-in girlfriend, Kathrin Goldbach, who said she recently had to drop the news on him that she was pregnant with his child.

Protecting himself from anticipated rejection by her, Lubitz was already having an affair with a flight attendant when she separated from him on March 22. She told friends that she could no longer tolerate his control of her. The *Daily Mail* reporter interviewing her friends revealed that "he tried to order her what to wear, what men she could speak to, even the length of her skirts. He was a control freak of the highest order." She was afraid of him also, they reported; so, she was searching for a new place to stay to get out of his life. Two days later, he carried this same obsessive observation for the details of human life to work, noting that his pilot, Patrick Sondenheimer, did not go to the lavatory before takeoff in Barcelona and thus would need to visit the lavatory during the flight, the same scenario that other suicidal pilots noted.

It is unlikely Lubitz had ever met Sondenheimer before, because crew members are traditionally not scheduled to fly together on a regular basis. But he knew that Sondenheimer had not gone to the bathroom before takeoff that morning. Then, when reaching cruising altitude of 38,000 feet, the pilot prompted Lubitz to prepare for landing. Had he known Lubitz well he may never have left the cockpit, because his copilot's responses to preparation for landing were peculiar and described by French prosecutors as "laconic" with use of prescient terms "hopefully" and "we'll see."

Sondenheimer took Lubitz's bait 2 minutes after routine checks for landing were completed, when Lubitz reminded him a second time, "You can go now." On the cockpit voice recorder, the pilot seat is heard sliding back followed by the sound of the cockpit door's click, when Sondenheimer presumably left and headed for the lavatory. Once inside, he detected the sharp change in aircraft attitude and heard the distinct sounds of increasing speed as the aircraft descended rapidly. He most likely clasped the hand bar in the lavatory as he finished his pit stop under force of accelerating negative G forces before heading back to the cockpit. Most passengers would have felt the aircraft nose over into a dive, prompting anxiety throughout the cabin.

But Sondenheimer would never get back into the cockpit during the ensuing multiminute plunge at thousands of feet per minute terminating in an unspeakably apocalyptic disintegration of life, limb, and metal. As the plane descended, all codes Sondenheimer desperately entered to get back into the cockpit failed, because Lubitz deactivated the emergency entry coding installed following 9/11 and fixed the controls for crash landing, setting off automatic alarms built for warning rational pilots. "Sink Rate" first, and then "Ground! Pull up! Pull up!" They were of no use with a suicidal mass murderer solely in control of the aircraft.

The final minutes of the recording picked up Sondenheimer cussing out Lubitz to open the door. Then there was the terrifying last seconds of life aboard Flight 4U9525 with what sounded like the adrenaline-powered hacking of a fire axe smashing at the cockpit door and screams of all on board aware of the seconds left in their lives and the horrors of their imminent death. It happened fast, but 10 minutes during a steep descent from 30,000 feet with obvious terror at the cockpit door was likely an eternity as the sheer rocky mountainside zoomed into vision. Their plane was hurtling at 450 mph into the rocky spire of an alpine peak. The stress was so great on the aircraft that, for the final few seconds of the descent that the wing cracked, a sound marking a final death knoll just before the plane, now spinning like a missile, plowed into the mountain crag and came to rest disintegrated into pieces in a barren mountainous ravine. Seconds after the wing tip cut the escarpment, the sudden silence of human life was horrifying; there were no more screams.

The first helicopters to spot the crash site saw 6 acres of slate and limestone escarpment strewn with pieces of wreckage, personal effects, and human flesh. Soon a crude path for ATVs would be cut from the mountain village of Seyne-Les-Alpes into the crash site. Hundreds of first responders would soon crowd into the remote mountain terrain in search of tell-tale signs of what happened in this catastrophe, looking, especially, for the cockpit voice recorder and flight data recorder—then DNA or personal effects for identification. There were no intact bodies—just fragmented charred flesh and body parts. Lubitz probably did not care or even relished the likelihood the whole world could hear what he did. Ironically, his DNA was the first to be identified.

As so often is the case in suicidal mass murders, the press gets little personal history of prior psychiatric problems in perpetrators, but then they leak out, all the red flags possibly missed for preventing such catastrophic events. The *Daily Mail* reported this from Lubitz's friends: "he was very kind and attentive, but he had problems with mood swings. And I think we sensed that she (his pregnant girlfriend) became more fearful over time."

His second girlfriend, anonymously known only as "Maria," described Lubitz as insecure, saying, "He was always seeking assurances about the way he looked and the way he was viewed by others." She painted a portrait of a tormented and erratic man who would wake up from nightmares screaming: "We're going down, we're going down!" She added: "He once told me he would do something to change the whole system, that the world would know his name and remember him" (Gallagher and Hall 2015).

Caution is, of course, necessary in suicide autopsies, but a catastrophe such as the Alpine crash of Germanwings Flight 4U9525 demands, as at the crash site forensics, examining reliable comments by witnesses and piecing fragments of small facts together. That is what is being done by investigators at the crash site and command center in Marseilles. Assuming the prosecutors' case for suicidal mass murder is the cause of this aviation disaster, then crew health is necessary to examine, best we can. Intimates of Andreas Lubitz describe a rigidly but fragile man with narcissistic traits. Having been grounded from pilot training for 7 months for clinical depression with suicidal thoughts in 2009 and antidepressant medications having been found in his apartment, a significant mood disorder—very possibly bipolar in type—is also more probable than not. That is the standard for medical certainty. Also reported is the history of 35% retinal detachment, a condition virtually guaranteed to ground a commercial pilot. Eyesight is to pilots as hearing is to musicians. Loss of these senses is usually disabling. Visually impaired pilots are grounded. Among pilots, competence and physical ability are deeply embedded in personality structure. He flew as an attendant when disabled with depression from pilot training; he could not, in his own mind, likely take that step down or be grounded again but had to be in control. He had to be the pilot.

Lubitz loved to fly, and his love for flying came at an early age when an active member of his local glider society. The interruption of his flight training by a bout of severe depression in 2009 did not stop him. He came back and pursued it again, this time succeeding with pure documentation of his health and fitness with Lufthansa. "Lufthansa Chief Executive, Carsten Spohr, a former pilot, said Mr Lubitz had been deemed by the airline to be '100 percent flightworthy without any limitations'" (Kulish and Ewing 2015).

Mr. Spohr said last week that candidates for flight school were chosen not only on the basis of their technical ability but also their psychological fitness. He said that Lufthansa's screening process was considered state of the art "and we're very proud of it" (www.nytimes.com/2015/04/01/world/europe/lufthansa-germanwings-andreas-lubitz.html). However, Spohr is going to have a tough time explaining the receipt of Lubitz's removal from flight training in 2009, at which time he had to serve as a flight attendant due to severe and obvious impairment from a mood disorder; this meant he had been physically cleared for a Federal Aviation Administration (FAA) Flying Class III Medical certificate as flight attendant. Reports of his suicidality, however, are absent any timeline, as are their severity. Sucidal tendencies can range from relatively transient ideation without intent to intent with finalized plan (www.nzz.ch/feuilleton/flug-ins-nichts-1.18519591).

Now that this is a murder investigation instead of an aviation accident investigation, the uniquely rigid privacy laws for post-Nazi Germany will be brought down by French prosecutors. He was reportedly being treated by a neuropsychologist, but he must have also seen a psychiatrist to be prescribed antidepressants, which are not automatically prohibited by aviation regulations as long as the drug is one that is an approved selective serotonin reuptake inhibitor (SSRI) and dosed within Food and Drug Administration (FDA) guidelines for major depression. We now know that Andreas Lubitz was far sicker than simple depression. He was more likely suffering from manic depressive illness—or, bipolar affective disorder—with axis II personality trait problems of narcissism. With blindness threatened on axis III, the medical surgical parameter of multiaxial diagnostics in psychiatry, this commercial pilot was high on the stress scale of axis IV, his livelihood and self-esteem severely threatened by anticipation of losing his vision. Although his ophthalmological problems are discussed as possibly psychosomatic—thus purely his personal experience without hard findings on examination of retinal detachment—they were more likely than not very real for him—and very threatening with the power to bring his axis V impairment rating down to near zero—that is high likelihood of suicide or homicide.

Let's revisit the Mnemonic for *Unremitting Clinical States of Human Destructiveness*: Lubitz should have scored high on psychological testing, assuming he was examined, as reported, by a neuropsychologist.

"After washing with SOAP, you may now eat MAS TACO SALAD"; this mnemonic can guide you reliably through your assessment of impulse control—first, imminent behavioral dyscontrol, particularly suicidality, in the first 10 minutes of presentation—then more in-depth assessment of any unmitigating clinical states of human destructiveness in that less critical state of clinical awareness, the yellow zone, which allows 1 hour for safe evaluation from first encounter with patient. The number of +'s roughly quantify the reported evidence on Lubitz's profile for an unremitting clinical state of human destructiveness.

- A = Attempt: must be assumed from history, so +
- S = Support: failing, so +++++
- T = Triad of enuresis, fire-setting and cruelty to animals: unknown, so –
- A = Affect: ++++, mood swings described; diagnosed with burnout, suicidality, and depression
- C = Culture of violence: no evidence –
- O = Organization: described as erratic as well as overcontrolled ++++
- S = Separation: +++++ +
- A = Alone: about to be +++++
- L = Loss: +++++, career, girlfriend, vision, and child
- A = Alcohol: unknown –
- D = Drugs: reportedly nonadherent with antidepressants

Had Lubitz been competently assessed, had he been forthcoming in the fears that were plaguing him, had any of his doctors—and he was seeing doctors—stepped forward to say to the airline that this guy should not have been sitting in a commercial airliner cockpit, all those lives would have been saved. Had Lufthansa, knowing their pilot had suffered from depression, demanded a full-scale psychiatric workup, including the requisite personality profiles, and had they interviewed his friends and girlfriends, they would have discovered his lurking illness.

The dynamics of the *Diagnostic and Statistical Manual of Mental Disorders* (*DSM*) multiaxial diagnostic system does not prove anything about the crash of Flight 4U9525, but it supports the initial opinion of French prosecutors that the crash was a suicidal mass murder caused by Andreas Lubitz. It is a circumstantial case, because the only people who know what happened are dead, but such a suicidal autopsy is of more than heuristic value. It is empirical, based on credible reports from one flight recorder, knowledge of the aircraft, and witness reports of the copilot; thus it is operationally of necessity to reduce the risk of suicidal mass murder from other than terrorists in the post-9/11 world—namely the mentally impaired pilot.

Suicidal mass murder by aircraft is as old as aviation itself and will always be a threat to society. There were kamakaze pilots in World War II. Islamic extremist terrorists have a predilection for air transport as a vehicle for wracking both terror and economic burdens in way of security demands on contemporary society; about 1% of private aviation crashes are caused by suicidal pilots. The high-profile suicidal mass murder by Andrew Stack on February 18, 2010, is the classical example. He deliberately crashed his single-engine Piper Dakota into the Austin, Texas, Internal Revenue Service (IRS) headquarters housed in the Echelon Office Complex, killing himself and IRS manager, Vernon Hunter. Thirteen others were injured—two of whom were seriously injured. Prior to the crash Stack posted a suicide note that referred to greed, insanity, and the IRS on his business website following his torching his house in North Austin in a suspected arson.

Although the civil aviation industry—even the extreme risk military aviation enterprise—are relatively safe from pilot suicide compared to other life and vocational hazards, such as highways, workplace violence, and gang shootings, nearly a thousand people have now been killed in commercial air crashes caused by pilot suicide (if Flight MH370 is included). Although a relatively low mortality figure for such a vulnerable mode of transportation that literally defies gravity, it is too significant to warrant complacency. Already the post cockpit entry prohibitions contributing to Lubitz's suicidal mass murder are to be reexamined so that both crew and passengers can be protected from suicidal pilots who are not terrorists. Still, some obvious barriers to pilot fitness in the cockpit must be examined.

The current $15 million lawsuit by retired JetBlue pilot Clayton Osbon could be an opportunity to shine some light into the murky self-regulatory system of commercial pilot health and safety to fly, suddenly lit up by assertions by French prosecutors that the Alpine crash of Germanwings Flight 4U9525 was a criminal act of suicidal mass murder by first officer, Andreas Lubitz. On March 27, 2012, Captain Clayton Osbon alarmed JetBlue First Officer Jason Dowd not long after takeoff of Flight 191 from New York to Las Vegas, telling Dowd, "We need to take a leap of faith." Again, as with Lufthansa crews, most likely they had never met until now, and critically important in Osbon's case is the fact that he was late for the flight and missed preflight check-in. Captain Osbon was obviously insane and was yelling at air traffic controllers. "We're not going to Las Vegas," he told his First Officer. "Things just don't matter," Osbon said; "we need to focus." The pilot was able to turn off the radios in the Airbus 320 after admonishing the First Officer for trying to talk on them. Clearly Osbon was intent on doomsday. Dowd either lured the crazed pilot out of the cockpit, or Osbon bolted out and grabbed a flight attendant's hands en route to the lavatory. Then he banged on the lavatory door for the woman inside to get out. As the plane continued its ascent to cruising altitude, the melee aboard continued. The deranged captain then reportedly yelled at passengers about Al-Qaeda, bombs, Afghanistan, and Iraq. The plane may have been somewhere near Shanksville, Pennsylvania, where UAL Flight 93 was crashed by its hijackers on 9/11. He then began pounding on the cockpit door, demanding to get back in. It was three and a half terrifying hours in the air when attendants requested assistance from passengers with the crazed captain. Like Flight 93, there were security officers on board headed to the International Security Conference in Las Vegas, and they were ready to roll. Osbon continued to scream about Iraq, bombings, and Afghanistan, pounding on the cockpit door. Helpless flight attendants desperately requested assistance from passengers. A corrections officer came forward and told Osbon, "This is Afghanistan and Iraq," and put him in a choke hold, telling investigators later that he was not going to let him out of it. Osbon was so pumped in the fury of psychosis that he broke a pair of plastic handcuffs; so, passengers finally sat on him and bound his flailing hands with leather belts. He was restrained by passengers for the final 20 minutes of flight. An off-duty pilot was able to get into the cockpit to assist in flight and its emergency landing in Amarillo, Texas, where it was met by the FBI and an ambulance. Osbon was removed and restrained in a gurney to be transported to the hospital where he was charged with interfering with a flight crew, a felony charge, which if convicted carries up to 20 years in prison and a $250,000 fine. He was later booked into jail and stood trial but was found innocent by reason of insanity—brief psychotic reaction caused by sleep deprivation was the diagnosis testified to by the expert witness neuropsychologist. There was no mention of a possible anniversary reaction; Osbon's father died in a plane crash nearly 17 years to the date of his psychotic break aboard JetBlue Flight 191. Osbon was ultimately freed and medically retired, but, following the events of the Germanwings catastrophe, he filed a civil lawsuit against JetBlue.

Osbon is now claiming that he suffered brain damage from a childhood head injury that was asymptomatic until his first epileptic seizure struck around the time of his in-flight psychotic break. "Osbon's lawyers say the seizure caused Osbon to hallucinate and promoted extreme feelings of paranoia. Because of the seizure, Osbon missed a critical pre-flight meeting where attorneys argue JetBlue would have been able to assess his behavior and prevent him from flying."

JetBlue issued the following statement to FOX6 News: "While we can't discuss the specifics of what happened that day due to ongoing litigation, we stand behind the heroic actions of the crew who followed well-established safety and security procedures both before and during the flight" (CNN Wire Service and Lemoine 2015).

Following this terrifying in-flight emergency, Diane Sawyer interviewed Aviation expert, John Nance. His understated comments are more salient today in the wake of the Germanwings catastrophe. Nance said that screening was good for airlines—presumably he meant U.S. airlines—and that after a year of probation the "neural networking" of airline crews becomes an effective regulatory device. "It could be ratcheted up," he concluded in the aftermath of Clayton Osbon's in-flight psychotic break. How can this be accomplished with resistance from all parties involved, including clinicians caring for crew members and bound by privileged communication, pilots' unions protecting the careers of members and patient rights advocates concerned about increasing stigma of mental health if flight crew members lose privacy of communications with their doctors.

Clearly now the subdued recognition for ratcheting up health and fitness evaluations needs tightening and enhancement, but how? "Suicide to psychiatrists is like snow to Eskimos; we've got 40 words for it," said Dr. Paul Summergrad, president of the American Psychiatric Association and the chairman of the psychiatry department at Tufts University School of Medicine. He added that suicidal tendencies can range "all the way from someone who, at one extreme, has transient thoughts of self-harm, to people who have intense and relentless thoughts of killing themselves" (www.nzz.ch/feuilleton/flug-ins-nichts-1.18519591).

So, what can be done without clashing outright with special interest groups that will oppose selecting out flight crews for closer psychological and medical screening for what is a rare but significant existential threat to society—namely, the suicidal pilot. A solution that could work would be that of imposing the model of aviation medicine from the military to civil aviation—at least commercial aviation, in which so many lives are at risk on board. Clearly in the cases cited so far, these pilots were not invisibly flying under the radar of competent clinical oversight. They were simply missed. Or, more seriously, the culture of flying, like that of the military, is resistant to intrusions of psychiatrists and psychologists possibly finding mental weakness in those, who by nature, are born of "The Right Stuff."

In the military model, MDs are specially trained in unique problems of aviation and are expected to fly with their crews on any type of mission flown, whether high-performance tactical fighter jets, air transports, or long-range bombers. University of Texas has such a postgraduate residency program; so, it is not a wheel that needs reinvention. It would not be difficult to attract doctors to the field of aviation medicine, because so many are attracted to flying and would find it a unique way to get paid for what they love to do—fly.

In the U.S. Air Force model, physicians receive training in the special physical and psychological stresses inherent to the field of aviation. They undergo simulation training in decompression chambers in which they experience exactly the sudden threat to their consciousness and life as theorized by Wilson in Good Night M 370. They learn the most extensive occupational screening likely ever created—that is medical and psychological screening for stealth bomber pilots. The examination was developed for stealth bomber pilots at Brooks Air Force Base, Texas, and is to be learned by residents in aviation medicine and implemented for flight crew screening. But now a few questions about mental health are asked in the initial pilot screening that Nance claims to be effective.

The stealth B2 bomber is a billion-dollar aircraft requiring the soundest of bodies and minds at its controls—two at all times. But, money should not be the determining factor. If the government believes such thorough examination is necessary for stealth bomber pilots, then why not for commercial airlines pilots, too? Human life is as valuable as a billion-dollar aircraft. No airline CEO is going to deny that with a straight face. In fact, I cannot think of any plausible denial. So far no suicidal pilots are known to have crashed a stealth bomber. No suicidal pilot should be able to crash a commercial airliner either. The random theory of mass murders defying measures of prevention must be tossed out in aviation now, or those promulgating it from academic silos of research from big data should be required to fly a million miles per year to back up their data-driven opinions. Germanwings proved it. Because of this same silo mentality that supports underfunding of preventive psychiatry, universities will also be allowed to keep going without adequate psychiatric services for their 20 million students under the specious arguments that suicidal rampage murders are rare and unpredictable, random events. The authors uncover the mythology underlying this rhetorical argument in case after case in their series of books, *Suicidal Mass Murders*, *Wounded Minds*, and *Hearts of Darkness* (Liebert and Birnes 2011, 2013, 2014). Similarly, the cases of Lubitz, Shah, and Osbon clearly are not simply rare and unpredictable events in a small universe of international flight crews; the large universe from World Health Organization (WHO) statistics should not apply to flight crews, anymore than surgeons, both of whom need monitoring that entails more scrutiny than the average working adult.

Flight surgeons should be stationed in occupational health clinics at all airlines hubs internationally. This can be done voluntarily by the airlines who simply do it and then are certified with the International Organization of Aviation in Montreal. The flying public can then decide for themselves if they wish to fly with a carrier not certified for medical monitoring of crew health by flight surgeons or not. This will not eliminate the risk of impaired pilots in the cockpit, but it will significantly reduce it by penetrating the culture of silence dramatically described decades ago. Nothing obviously has changed since this was written: "From flight schools to safety seminars the story of the plane that ran out of fuel while timid crew members kept silent has been told again and again" (Lavin 1994).

This is the culture of flying—sort of macho culture, not unlike surgery, demanding perfection. Commercial flying is not for the weak of ego, but narcissists like Shah and Lubitz must be confronted and eliminated from the cockpit. Osbon will likely prevail in a lawsuit; he missed pre-check briefing because he was grossly psychotic. It is not that airlines management does not know this or did not know that these were problem pilots, as we learn from information gradually leaked out. Malaysian Airlines may remain in denial, whether internally, externally, or both, unless the clear and convincing evidence—maybe not beyond reasonable doubt—becomes the reality of the mysterious disappearance of their Flight 370. Some commercial aviation cultures are less penetrable than others due to autocratic regimes infiltrating the management and cockpits of their airliners. But, 9/11 proved to Condoleezza Rice when starting as national security director that airplanes can be used as weapons of mass destruction, just like the Japanese had so successfully used them. She learned a costly lesson, but they can also be used as such, not only by terrorists, but by psychotic and mood-disordered suicidal pilots. After recognizing the threat from a suicidal pilot commandeering a commercial airliner, she, in particular, would likely support the need for flight surgeons assigned to the FAA having the authority for boarding any flight at any time to monitor crew health and safety; this would be an adjunctive layer of protection supporting the industry's implementation of aviation medicine as high a priority as selling its credit cards. With airline profitability at its all-time high because of a reduction in seat mile availability and energy costs, the time is now.

Flight surgeons in the navy and air force integrate well with their crews. They take care of them and fly with them. They can be trusted, but they also have the authority to take a pilot out of the cockpit for health and safety reasons. They likely would have grounded Lubitz and unlikely would have missed Osbon's extreme psychotic agitation before boarding. Flight Surgeons must balance their engagement with air crews to be honest and caring, but they also, unlike private clinicians, have no responsibility to keep secrets that can cause a disaster. The Human Reliability program in the air force was developed for just such a purpose—to prevent a nuclear weapons accidents. So far it has worked well, and it could also work in commercial aviation. The Lubitz's pastor poignantly asserted a need for such balance between privacy and public safety in the Lufthansa first pilot's hometown.

> The Rev. Michael Dietrich, pastor of a Lutheran church on the edge of Montabaur where Mr. Lubitz's mother sometimes played the organ, tried to address the spiritual quandary during his regular sermon Sunday morning. "Where should we go?" he said. "Where should we go?"
>
> The question posed itself for families of the victims, Pastor Dietrich said, "and also for the family of co-pilot Lubitz who many of us knew personally."
>
> The glider club has received death threats for its role in teaching Mr. Lubitz to fly, the club president, Klaus Radke said.
>
> At the other church, Pastor Dietrich nailed a plain wooden cross below the bell tower, and invited people to pin slips of paper to it with their thoughts. "Family L.," one slip read Sunday morning, "there are no words," said Saturday.
>
> Pastor Seemann said he planned to erect a sort of wailing wall in his church, with the names of all the victims inscribed on it.
>
> "Finding the balance is very difficult," he said. (Ewing 2015)

Finally, more people in this world think like this person now than last month:

> Yesterday, a distraught Philip Bramley visited the monument erected close to where the Germanwings Flight 9525 crashed. His son was one of three Britons who lost their lives. Fighting back tears in Digne, close to where his son perished on Tuesday, Mr Bramley

> said: "What is relevant, is that it should never happen again. My son and everyone on that plane should not be forgotten, ever. I don't want it to be forgotten, ever." He added: "I believe the airlines should be more transparent and our finest pilots looked after properly. We put our lives and our children's lives in their hands. I want to see this cloud over this town lifted and the natural beauty be restored and not to be remembered by the action of a single person."

On the nihilistic side is this aviation expert's comment (at www.aviation-business-gazette.com…enter-Lubitz-Rheinland-Pfalz-.html):

> What to do? There are good reasons to lock the cockpit door (although I think the so-called terror threat is exaggerated by the authorities), but that alone was the enabling factor with LAM and Lufthansa (Germanwings). I don't think a three man crew would help, if one guy goes to the toilet then it's easy for one guy to hit the other with the fire extinguisher. I am positive that psychiatric screening wouldn't catch these guys, one in a million and probably in some cases perfectly sane on the outside. The Lufty FO who has downed the Germanwings flight was cited by the FAA for outstanding airmanship. Is this just an intractable problem of the human condition we have to live with and be vigilant for? I cannot think of a single concrete step that could help.
>
> Japan Air Lines 24 killed, 9 Feb 1982
> Royal Air Moroc 44 killed, 21 Aug 1994
> Egyptair 217 killed, 31 Oct 1997
> Silkair 107 killed, 19 Dec 1997
> LAM Mozambique 33 killed, 29 Nov 2013
> Lufthansa (Germanwings) 150 killed, 24 Mar 2015
>
> Fedex attempted pilot suicide, 7 Apr 1994
> Malaysia suspected pilot suicide 239 killed, 8 Mar 2014
> (www.origin-www.airliners.net/aviation-forums/general_aviation/read.main/6354843)

The authors disagree. No there is no screening system for the one in a million suicidal people in a randomly selected population, but commercial aviation is not randomly selected, and flight surgeons and FAA examiners not looking for the one in a million. They should be looking for the one in a hundred within an originally well-screened and selected population who is at high risk of causing a crash when mentally impaired. If this cannot be done, then stop the extensive crew screening for the stealth bomber pilots. There is no difference, unless a higher value is placed on the cost of replacing the plane and two pilots than replacing an Airbus with its crew and paying off claims for hundreds of dead passengers, while ignoring the true scope of the catastrophes reported above.

The Lubitz case is an example of how public safety and public health, as we have indicated above, tends to run smack into privacy laws promulgated and enforced by the government. From *Lessard* to the rigid strictures of California's 5150 involuntary detention statutes, whose LPS manual's protocols caused sheriff's deputies to allow Elliot Rodger to finalize his suicidal plan for mass murder, it is becoming clear that, in the face of a changing neuropsychiatric paradigm of mental impairment, not only in the United States, but around the world, we are failing those who would, and will, become the innocent victims of suicidal rampage violence.

Aviation is a special case, in which we know since 9/11 that we must detect dangerous crews, whether on ground or in the air—as well as dangerous passengers boarding at all points in the world. Error rate in all the elaborate detection screens available and implemented cannot be zero, but it can be significantly reduced, just like the risk of a nuclear accident has been from five major nuclear militaries. The risk of such accidents is increasing because of rogue nations acquiring nuclear weapons, but the record to date has been absolutely excellent. And that has not been by chance; human reliability programs have worked in military aviation in preventing nuclear accidents and rogue attacks. They can also work in commercial aviation once airlines have to make the necessary investment and the FAA is empowered to demand healthy pilots in the cockpits, healthy attendants in the cabin, and healthy ground crews keeping them flying. As in college campus and military populations, there must be compromise made between the rights and responsibilities of those choosing to be there. These are not, as Virginia Tech is arguing in civil court in defense of its response to the Cho massacre, simply shopping centers where anyone can choose to go and security is minimal and mainly on site to catch thieves.

## REFERENCES

Airliners.net. 2015. What to do about pilot suicide. Airliners.net discussion forum, post from cedarjet. March 26.

CNN Wire Service and Lemoine, B. 2015. Former JetBlue pilot from Mequon suing airline after his 2012 in-flight meltdown—but why? March 31.

Ewing, J. 2015. Andreas Lubitz's home city is left to clear away emotional wreckage. March 30. International Edition of NYT, New York.

Gallagher, I. and Hall, A. with Linning, S. and Glanfield, E. 2015. Is killer co-pilot's teacher ex-girlfriend pregnant with his child? Couple found out "weeks before crash" as it emerges she left him because of "erratic" behavior.

*Daily Mail*, May 12. www.dailymail.co.uk/news/article-3016420/Killer-pilot-Andreas-Lubitz-planned-marry-teacher-girlfriend-broke-relationship-just-weeks-Alps-crash-police-small-mountain-anti-depressants-flat.html#ixzz3VudzthD2

Hanna, J. and Vandoorne, S. 2015. CNN, September 4, http://www.cnn.com/2015/09/03/europe/mh370-investigation/

Kulish, N. and Ewing, J. 2015. Lufthansa now says it knew of co-pilot Andreas Lubitz's history of depression. *The New York Times*, March 31. www.nytimes.com/2015/03/27/world/europe/andreas-lubitz-germanwings-co-pilot-showed-no-warning-signs-before-crash-airline-says.html.

Lavin, C. 1994. When moods affect safety; communication in a cockpit means a lot a few miles up. *The New York Times*, June 26, p. 18.

Liebert, J. A. and Birnes, W. J. 2011. *Suicidal Mass Murderers: A Criminological Study of Why They Kill.* Taylor and Francis, London, UK.

Liebert, J. A. and Birnes, W. J. 2013. *Wounded Minds: The Menace of Post-traumatic Stress Disorder.* Skyhorse, New York.

Liebert, J. A. and Birnes, W. J. 2014. *Hearts of Darkness*. Skyhorse, New York.

Wilson, E. 2014. Good night Malaysian 370: The truth behind the loss of Flight 370. www.bbc.com/news/magazine-31736835

# 16

# Prevention in the era of optimized patient flow, criminalization of serious neuropsychiatric disease, and anemic occupational and student health services

When it comes to public health in the United States, we spend entirely too much time cleaning up damage instead of preventing damage in the first place. This chapter, therefore, is about prevention. Prevention is like protecting people on our bridges. Primary prevention is keeping them from falling off. Secondary prevention is detecting them after they drop off the bridge and as far upstream as possible. Tertiary prevention is salvaging people before they flow under the last bridge and drown at sea.

## PRIMARY PREVENTION: FIND CAUSE OF DISEASE AND ELIMINATE THE CAUSE

As we grapple with the core elements of our social safety net system, we need to understand what public safety and health agencies can do to support community health and reduce the threat of confrontations resulting in lethal force and spread of disease, whether that of natural epidemic or from weapons of mass destruction. These are public awareness issues designed to make public safety agencies and frontline health-care services more trustworthy in the eyes of local citizens. We have to understand that our health system is a dichotomy. Individuals can receive the best health care in the world while, at the same time, preventive medicine runs smack up against individual rights as set forth in the Constitution's Bill of Rights in the cases of the lethal threats from serious mental illness and contagiousness. Nowhere was this better illustrated than in the case of the nurse who returned to America from treating Ebola patients in West Africa. The governor of New Jersey, on his own say-so absent a hearing, absent a court ruling, confined her to a tent-based quarantine on the grounds of Newark Airport, even though she was not diagnosed with the disease. In this "Age of Lessard" that protected Alberta Lessard's rights to refuse psychiatric treatment for psychosis in Wisconsin, where were this nurse's Fourth and Fifth Amendment rights? Did fears of the spread of Ebola simply trump those rights? How easy was it for a governor to discard the Constitution arbitrarily in the face of panic over an epidemic? Governor Christie dramatized the issue of prevention of the spread of disease in the age of Ebola at a time when weekly headlines of suicidal rampage murders worldwide have the public awaiting answers from public health officials—"what in the World is going on?" (Liebert 2015).

The foundation of prevention in public health is recognition and understanding disease threats—particularly those that are communicable, like measles—so that designated authorities and professionals, whether in public safety or health care, can take the appropriate steps to resolve an issue. Principles of prevention apply to management of pathogenic viruses, just as they do to untreated suicidal and dangerous people cut loose on the public, whether via military discharge in the case of Eddie Routh who killed the American Sniper; early release from prison, like Alton Nolen whose beheading rampage in Moore, Oklahoma, reminded us of the daily horrors of ISIS, or simple expulsion from college, as in the case of Jared Loughner in the Tucson Safeway Plaza massacre. For the purposes of our argument that law enforcement, first responders, and even emergency rooms are ill-equipped to assess and manage either threat, we suggest that the problem is much bigger than simply a few random cases headlined in the news cycle. We argue that there is an epidemic of rampage violence taking place in the United States, as well as in the rest of the world. Our level of preparedness for terrorism, whether from weapons of mass destruction or the suicidal mass murdering lone wolf, psychotic, or more sophisticated Islamofascist, remains poor following both the events of 9/11 and massacre at Columbine High School in 1999.

The recent Ebola outbreak has reawakened us to the threats of deadly epidemics, whether bioterrorism, as in the case of the anthrax attacks of 2001, or spread from anywhere in the world in this day of rapid global transport. Complicating the traditional role of public health in monitoring and managing communicable diseases, we now have an epidemic of rampage suicidal violence, traceable to both mentally deranged individuals who have not been properly identified and case managed, as well as politically motivated terrorists. If the recurrent stories of school and campus suicidal rampages are not enough to spark concern, workplace shootings should. If that is not enough, look to the rest of the world where suicidal mass murder has been politicized by pseudo-governments. Mexican drug cartels do not just eliminate their competition or seek revenge in the good old way like Cicero, Illinois, in the 1920s. They attack schools, murder children, torture their rivals, and seemingly enjoy the public carnage they inflict. Think of Boko Haram, which has now pledged its fealty to the Islamic State, copycatting it in its perpetration of violence, beheading those they seek to punish for not worshipping the way they do. This copycatting has spread to Libya, Tunisia, and Yemen—now even Moore, Oklahoma, where an ex-con and recent parolee, Alton Nolen, just beheaded a coworker following Islamofascist conversion in prison. Such deranged and drug-impaired minds can now compete on our own soil and in our own media with ISIS and their shockingly high-definition global images of an ever more unspeakable and horrific bloodbath. Nolen did not know his boss was a deputized police officer, or the horrific scenes of his cold-blooded pseudo-religious rampage at Vaughn packing company in Oklahoma would have brought the blood-soaked beaches of Libya right into the heartland of this country, with the ISIS message, "there is no place to hide from our mass terror; so, convert or get your head chopped off."

Look at the math and the trends. Something very big, something socially seismic, is going on, and police, at least in the United States, are the frontline defenders. Next are EMT emergency responders and after them come the emergency rooms (ERs), with their only backup resource now usually being jail and prison for the seriously mentally ill who are officially "boarded" by them without active treatment. The trends are disturbing for a variety of reasons. In the case of the Islamic State, like a viral pathogen, their methodology has infected social media and the psychologically at-risk and politically and socially marginalized individuals, like Nolen, who thrive on it. We live in a new era where unfiltered fantasies of violence—once the private and secret domain of snuff films—and ritualized hatred flow freely across the Internet. Our own reliance on free speech in the First Amendment protects the rights of people to express their views, as long as these views do not pose imminent threats of violence. Hate groups of all stripes are free to wander there. But the problem is that these same social media sites—Twitter, Facebook, and others—are also recruitment tools. The federal government, as we now know from Edward Snowden's revelations, monitors these sites. They are exempted from Fourth Amendment protection, because there is no expectation of privacy on behalf of those who post. The at-risk parolee and suicidal mentally ill, however, slip through the net, as did Elliot Rodger who massacred college girls at University of California, Santa Barbara following his clear and convincing postings of intent to do just that. His family knew he could act out his fantasies, but the police turned deaf ears to his parents' concerns for both his and the public's safety, because they reported he was able to explain himself away in a polite and reasonable manner.

Street gangs, too, enforcing their own brand of loyalty and fealty on their turfs, may communicate via graffiti as well as via social media kites to green light rival individuals and groups for execution, whether on a barrio street corner in Los Angeles or a Chicago park on July 4. Police may monitor their activity, but gang violence spreads, taking over neighborhoods, and recruiting new members at increasingly younger ages. Although not overtly suicidal at first, these gang members almost always wind up behind bars, running their gang enterprises—usually drugs—from behind bars, as in the Security Housing Unit (SHU), and enforcing their brand of law on those outside of prison until they go down when "green-lighted" themselves by a "kite," whether inside or outside jail for execution.

And then there are the lone at-risk psychotics like Adam Lanza, James Holmes, and Seung-Hui Cho who go untreated until their mental illness metastasizes into lethal self-destructiveness. They, too, often rely on social media but also manifest themselves as avatars in single-shooter online games, only dealing with their ilk in shared violent ideations. But online single-shooter games, just like violent motion pictures and television shows glorifying violence against women and children, are protected as elements of free speech under the First Amendment. In a world of free speech and the open transmission of ideas, where is the prevention of violence? We are not in Kansas anymore, nor are we living in the idealized world of President Bill Clinton's Andy Hardy, *Father Knows Best*, *Ozzie and Harriet*, or even *The Waltons* (Lertzman and Birnes 2015), especially when just hearing that two girls committed a planned murder-suicide on a high school campus in Glendale, Arizona just days after the Super Bowl there.

What has happened and what can we do about it? Humans are mostly made up of water, but both soluble and insoluble particles are in motion as a super complex biochemical machine individualized by DNA. Our organic and skeletal structure is determined by our genes. We are bridges over troubled waters, some with more durability and tensile strength than others, and like bridges humans need maintenance for their genetically determined structure and biochemical processes to endure the stresses and traumas of life. We argue that humans need more maintenance now, because the corrosive powers of their social environments are no longer protective. It is easier for that next loaded semi or spring flood to knock them down into unremitting states of human destructiveness or psychosomatic vulnerability to disease. Holmes and Rahe demonstrated how the accumulation of excessive life change units within an 18-month period can predict serious breakdown into serious mental illness, cancer, or a cardiovascular event. Dlin found that waiting for a dreaded deadline in life was more conducive to heart attacks than any known risk factor, such as smoking, weight, or cholesterol. He compared two well-matched groups of 100 patients admitted to Philadelphia General Hospital orthopedic and cardiac care units. The only difference he found between these two patient cohorts was the expectancy of a fatal deadline in life—an "Anniversary Reaction" anchored in their own personal histories of lost loved ones (Weiss et al. 1957).

We are, therefore, "psychosomas," hence, protoplasm integrating complex regulation, both from the brain down to the tissue and from the tissue up through the spinal cord to the brain. We are not mind and body, but both, an aggregation. Holmes, Rahe, and Dlin et al. present clear and convincing evidence of that. And that is what we know as psychosomatic medicine. It is not, therefore, just the mind that must be protected from the troubled waters of societal change, whether hardly visible in the Internet of Things, or apocalyptic like war. We can do little about the genes that determine our durability and tensile strength, because those genes are ever present. We can, however, understand what may be our predispositions to certain types of diseases, like alcoholism, and avoid the environmental stimulus by not drinking. We can, however, start examining the psychosocial rust we have and take the required steps without rupturing the fabric and structure of our society, but reinforcing it, just as we know another bridge is going to cave into the Mississippi if public works neglects our infrastructure. Hilary Clinton has written that we need a village for our children's protection from rapid social change. She is, likely without knowing it, echoing Holmes and Rahe's research that informs public health and safety institutions about primary prevention of both malignant decompensation into clinical states of human destructiveness and psychosomatic breakdown. Primary prevention must start, therefore, with awareness of the winds of social change.

As a visual example of how our social fabric has weakened, consider the difference between "The Waltons" and "The Simpsons," fictional representations, but idealized portraits, of two American families portraying two different eras: the 1930s Depression and today. Where the Walton family lives in a multigenerational farm household in which Grandpa and Grandma Walton serve as buffers for the children, taking the stress off them from their parents who struggle to make a living, the Simpsons live in front of their television sets and grandpa is relegated to an old-age home where he festers on the border of a laughable dementia. Sure, the Simpson family is comedy, satire, a distorted depiction of the modern family, but there is too much truth behind this satire. It evidences a big difference between the world of Jeff on "The Donna Reed Show" and Bart on "The Simpsons." Entertainment does not just reflect society as it is, it refracts it, bending the reality to create a future for its viewers. Former president Bill Clinton remarked on his parents' love of the Andy Hardy movies of the 1930s and 1940s, motion pictures that depicted American family life before the war. The Hardys comprised a multigenerational family headed by patriarch Judge Hardy who reigned over his son, Andy, whenever the teenager, played by Mickey Rooney, strayed too far out of bounds. This was the fictionalized family President Clinton remembered that his family looked to as an ideal, but it was only a projection written by a screenwriter, who, by the way, was a card-carrying member of the Communist party. The Hardys was produced by studio head Louis Mayer who had a very difficult family environment in Russia, where his family was persecuted by Cossacks. It portrays Mickey Rooney, who grew up in what amounted to a "no-parent" environment and was then thrust onto a burlesque stage at age one and a half (Lertzman et al. 2015).

Simply stated, our American family has changed, and the generations born into that changed family are slowly decomposing from the corrosive distress of the modern family with both parents out of the home and children socialized into day care very early. There is a seismic adjustment in family structure that has been taking place over the past four decades. If growing children are expressing forms of aggression driving the consumer audience for violent online gaming, among other media inputs and outlets, then that aggression needs to be addressed without limiting the free speech of either game developers or gamers themselves. If social media is a conduit for violent ideation and politicized violence, then parents need to spend far more time in front of their children's computers than they currently do. We suggested, hypothetically, what if Nancy Lanza had manifested her own avatar into Adam's online gaming chat groups? If that was his primary means of communication, might Nancy have related to him in a channel that gave him comfort from a world he viewed as hostile and threatening? Hardly the stuff of PTA meetings or clinical consultations, of course, but the new reality of a social structure rusting from the corrosive forces of social change seemingly beyond our control.

At the extreme is what former Secretary of Defense Hagel asserts as one of the greatest threats to national security: cyber warfare. He alerted us. We are not dealing with it internationally. Perhaps his ominous warnings should extend metaphorically into our living rooms and children's bedrooms. Certainly it did in the Lanza home, where Adam downloaded a video game titled, "School Shooter," which provided his chaotic psychotic mind with a solid and detailed template for focused execution: the Sandy Hook Elementary School massacre.

We now know that Nancy Lanza was not affluent. She was living over her head and probably could not afford all that needed to be done with her son, namely mid-range seven-figure legal bills to involuntarily commit him, assuming that was her final desperate act to save him and herself (Liebert and Birnes 2014). So, are the requirements of maintaining a two-income career-dominated family the very things that are compromising the necessary emotional support of children in the foundations and girders of our most basic psychosocial infrastructure, the contemporary family? If so, how does society protect itself from the violence inflicted on it by a small minority of those at-risk children? Does that responsibility fall to the schools and, if so, are our teachers themselves, the caregivers in charge, at risk from state and local governments looking to cut budgets as well as tenured positions? That is the understated memorialized cries of martyrdom from the Sandy Hook Elementary School massacre. Those teachers did not have a chance and were mowed down just like the children they were helpless in protecting (Liebert and Birnes 2014).

We believe that what we are seeing before our very eyes are the initial outcroppings of a tectonic generational shift, social climate shift, with violence, like the advance of a glacier or the friction between two clashing tectonic plates, as a manifestation of that change, with more fulminating mental illness accompanying an upswing in suicides as symptomatic of that seismic shift. If the melting ice in Antarctica is evidence of global climate change, then the violence we are seeing is a form of social climate change. We cannot—nor should we—require all of our children to undergo psychological testing to determine sequestration requirements for primary prevention, but we can look for signs of trouble, as the Los Angeles Unified School District (LAUSD) does. We can make sure that schools, in addition to requiring vaccinations to protect the public health, also hire more school counselors, maybe requiring Masters of Social Work (MSW) with family counseling backgrounds to talk to children. And parents should closely monitor their children's Twitter feeds and Facebook postings. We must be aware that because society is changing and violence is one of the indicators of that change, we should recognize it for what it is, understand the causality, and confront the issues posed by that change. Only then can we confront what looks to be a growing menace of suicidality and the homicidal violence associated with it; Department of Justice statistics showing a decrease in homicides over the decades are simply that—raw statistics taken out of context. They did not lead us to expect a sixth-grader to walk into a school with a loaded gun and hit list for students to be assassinated that day in Michigan. At-risk children should be evaluated with validated psychological testing, but it all begins with awareness. The police were tipped off about that boy in Michigan, or there could have been another Sandy Hook. Public awareness and education is the most basic form of primary prevention in public health today, whether early manifestations of malignant neuropsychiatric psychopathology in schizophrenia or morbid obesity that promises early death or disability from metabolic syndrome progressing into debilitating and deadly complications of cardiac disease and diabetes.

We have a great individual health-care system. The Shah of Iran, the young Pakistani victim of a vicious attack Malala Yousafzai, Ann Romney, all can get the best health care in the world. But, a mentally ill Miriam Carey or an Ezell Ford are shot to death in the streets by the police while our seriously mentally ill and combat vets walk around digging food out of garbage cans and looking for steam vents to sleep on during frigid winters. Meanwhile, our troubled youth huddle around their computer screens at night, and shooting avatars, fantasizing about shooting up their schools by day. Concurrently, our health-care system is plagued by gimmicky industrial process solutions and dysfunctional electronic medical records that are turning the art and science of medicine and nursing into assembly lines for "patient throughput." We live in an age of rising demand for care with escalating inflows of patients threatening to overwhelm our frontline acute, urgent, and emergency care resources. It is a time for thoughtful examination of needs, solutions, and their benefits in health care—not persuasive salesmen and politicians with silver-tongued solutions and easy fixes. Meanwhile, off the hospital grounds in our streets, the police, whom we want to protect us from bad guys, are trained to deal with the mentally ill sleeping in the gutters of America, yet still shoot them every day out of panic or pure despair. Officer Andrew did not shoot Marlene Pinnock, but how many times should a California Highway Patrolman be expected to weave through the rush-hour traffic of a Los Angeles freeway to rescue a homeless woman with the omnipotent transmutational delusion of being impervious to the phalanx of thousands of tons of metal she believes will simply race harmlessly through her body. Pinnock was certainly known in the system and was simply spun within the correctional and county hospital revolving doors to almost inevitable death and destruction for her, police officers, and commuters alike. This is the result of optimized throughput and assembly-line management, the new mantras of health-care delivery, even though ERs are not factories. It would take either a catastrophic accident or her inevitable death some other way to stop the assembly-line of ER throughput of Marlene Pinnock's challenges of oncoming commuter traffic over her home in the grotto beneath La Brea and I-10 when discharged back there again—even as a multi-millionaire now.

Clearly, the police are not the first line for primary prevention of disease in our society, nor are emergency rooms and hospitals. Both can play their roles through best practices and public affairs, but they have become the primary prevention by default for public health and public psychiatric systems that have become failed institutions. Finally, after the California Highway Patrol (CHP) officer beat her nearly to death, Marlene Pinnock was hospitalized for her psychosis, because now she needed surgical treatment also from the beating by a highway patrolman.

Complicating primary prevention is congressional interference in the Centers for Disease Control and Prevention's (CDC) research on violence. At a time when shootings take more lives than automobile accidents, Congress, under the lobbying influence of the National Rifle Association (NRA), has rendered research on violence within CDC impotent. The Department of Transportation has no such withdrawal of funding for research on automobile accidents. The NRA successfully lobbied Congress to strip millions from the CDC's budget to study violence under the rhetorical guise that such science is not legitimate.

> The Centers for Disease Control and Prevention receives no federal funding to study gun violence, thanks to a 1996 law the NRA succeeded in ramming through Congress. Now two lawmakers are sponsoring a bill to give the CDC $10 million a year to study why guns kill people (Pearson and Adams Otis 2014).

It is the blind leading the blind today, even in the wake of 9/11 and the Columbine School shooting that set off an epidemic of suicidal mass murders. The federal government passes legislation regulating health-care operations, but it is incapable of managing its own translational research in primary prevention. Emergency medical services, therefore, are as desperate for solutions to the overwhelming demands of preparedness for anything and everything today as are the police having to confront impossible situations with cameras running. The question is never raised, why are the police confronting these situations now? Similarly, why are ERs the primary care provider for millions of insured and uninsured residents alike in this country, when we need them for bona fide emergencies and preparedness in the event of disasters, whether acts of Mother Nature or terrorists? Modern management clichés of operational efficiencies have replaced medical and nursing judgment in the clinical management of ER patients. You can call for an appointment at an ER now? That is so silly that it hardly requires comment. Silly, too, we are expected to accept the concept of mental health cops because state and federal government have abdicated their responsibility for the care of the seriously mentally ill. We are expected to face crowded ERs when in dire need of care, because they must fill the vacuum created by government's failure to fund—perhaps even read—the Emergency Services Act of 1978.

Boyd, who wrote this act, laid out the solutions decades ago; they are all but ignored so that we wait for somebody else to reinvent the wheel. Read the Emergency Services Act, obey the law, and fund it. But, we are into new paradigms from MBA programs. Challenging quality control and throughput protocols from the bibles of "Six Sigma" of General Electric and Lean Management from Toyota in hospital meetings is heretical.

Jack Welch came up with Six Sigma to manufacture airplane engines, light bulbs, and locomotives, not for the diagnosis and treatment of disease. "Lean Engineering" was developed by the founding family of Toyota 200 years ago to create the culture of optimizing quality and efficiencies in the manufacturing of spinning looms. Later the family adapted its processes to the manufacture of Toyota vehicles with great success. Few in hospital administration who loosely throw these terms around in hospital meetings and conferences really know what they mean and bastardize them to perceived efficiencies that save money one place and cost lives and untold monies in another place. To understand lean engineering as an industrial process, one must understand the principles, both generated through and embedded in the Toyota Way for centuries. Ideally it could embrace health care. In practice it does not, because it demands unity in solving problems, autonomy for everyone in the process to stop the flow—and, then, when there is failure or incident, to huddle together to solve it and prevent it happening again. What lean-managed hospital does this except for postmortem patient reviews? Few, if any do this. It is too time consuming, but it is lean management. In health care, it is care of a patient and time-consuming troubleshooting of every incident to prevent recurrence. In fact, the Toyota Way with its lean management could enhance primary prevention through improved diagnostics that lead to effective clinical interventions generating improved outcomes, getting patients with severe anxiety out of cardiology and primary care clinical pathways and into psychiatric clinical pathways is primary prevention, because these patients wrongly diagnosed are at high risk for killing themselves. This is a huge problem in ERs today, and just one way emergency services can be the point of the spear in preventing costly anchoring of patients with invalid diagnoses (Liebert 2008).

This is not to say that operational efficiencies in hospitals are unimportant. Reducing wasted time in the imaging department by prohibiting all technicians to take coffee breaks at the same time might improve efficiency by optimizing patient flow. It simply is not the Toyota Way. Hence, such an efficiency in imaging is not lean managed health care, unless imaging is necessary and enhances diagnostics to inform more effective and economical treatment as part of a unified solution of health care. For example, has it been determined what patients really need imaging and when? Is imaging always a necessary window into the symptomatic patient's psychosoma or is it defensive medicine? Too often imaging replaces hands-on medicine that requires a careful history from the patient and directed and selective physical examination. Empowering one of those technicians to stop modern hospital "throughput" of a patient's discharge from CT scanning onto the stretcher and out the door to the street is lean managed health care, as we learned so tragically in the case of Ebola patient Thomas Duncan.

The case of Thomas Duncan might have been a classic for patient throughput in terms of euphemistic lean managed health care. It was not, however, the Toyota Way, and it is the classic study of how our entire system of primary prevention, from CDC, to local hospital protocols, to the ill-fated euphoric hype of electronic medical records literally caused an epidemic of a lethal virus, until then not detected in this country (see Philips eICU Program: Transforming critical care, www.healthcare.philips.com/main/products/patient_monitoring/products/eicu/).

The WHO Pain Ladder was developed in 1986 as a conceptual model to guide the management of cancer pain. There is now a worldwide consensus promoting its use for the medical management of all pain associated with serious illness, including pain from wounds. The Severe Pain of Thomas Duncan is called a General Discriminator in Emergency Medicine Triaging, and it means

"Emergency"—not the routine care that he received and unsupportable discharge. The best practice of the Pain Ladder, whether embedded in the hospital's EMR or considered a protocol in their ER, was either ignored, overlooked, or misinterpreted at Texas Presbyterian. Reasons for neglect of Best Practices of a Pain Ladder will only be winnowed out of the haystack of 1400 pages of digitalized records when the family and his nurse, who contracted Ebola herself in this debacle, are reviewed and dissected. Did they throw out the classical rules and knowledge base for triaging Thomas Duncan so as to satisfy the demands of patient "throughput" by optimizing patient flow? Certainly some process of optimization of patient flow within the lexicology of "patient throughput" ruled the care of Thomas Duncan that day. It is extremely unlikely the medical and nursing staff were simply incompetent. Contrary to rules of lean managed health care, nobody could stop the throughput of Thomas Duncan once this Ebola train left the station. Whatever that point of predetermined patient throughput, in absolute defiance and disregard for the natural laws of pathophysiology, it is likely recorded indelibly on that EMR. It will be of meaningful use only to lawyers and the public record, not medical staff operating at high ER tempo with very sick people in clinical encounters with unknown patients. Their misdiagnosis actually wound up killing the patient, starting a near epidemic of a feared virus in North America, and infecting nurses with Ebola in the process.

If the health-care information technology that government, along with the EHR industry, claims necessary for reforming health care can be depended on to come close in matching performance with the costs to hospitals "going live" with it, then computerized clinical decision support for immediately screening "Contagiousness" must be embedded under the Affordable Care Act's (ACA) rules for meaningful use. Furthermore, trained and experienced staff encountering the Thomas Duncans in our ERs and clinics must have input into purchasing decisions of these computers that have so much control over diagnostics and patient care; purchasing decisions should not be a pact between EMR salesmen and hospital information officers. A recent opinion piece in *The New York Times* addresses the oversell, both from government and industry, of medical computing for optimizing service in hospitals—that is, better outcomes at lower cost.

"I interviewed Boeing's top cockpit designers, who wouldn't dream of green-lighting a new plane until they had spent thousands of hours watching pilots in simulators and on test flights." This principle of user-centered design is part of aviation's DNA, yet has been woefully lacking in health care software design. Our iPhones and their digital brethren have made computerization look easy, which makes our experience with health care technology doubly disappointing. An important step is admitting that there is a problem, toning down the hype, and welcoming thoughtful criticism, rather than branding critics as Luddites.

> In my research, I found humility in a surprising place: the headquarters of I.B.M.'s Watson team, the people who built the computer that trounced the "Jeopardy!" champions. I asked the lead

> engineer of Watson's health team, Eric Brown, what the equivalent of the "Jeopardy!" victory would be in medicine. I expected him to describe some kind of holographic physician, like the doctor on "Star Trek Voyager," with Watson serving as the cognitive engine. His answer, however, reflected his deep respect for the unique challenges of health care. "It'll be when we have a technology that physicians suddenly can't live without," he said. And that was it. Just an essential tool. Nothing more, and nothing less. (Wachter 2015)

Of course, like the army, in the hierarchical system of hospitals, "crap rolls downhill," too. In the fallout at Texas Presbyterian, nurses were initially cited as the cause of this catastrophic failure in modern hospital throughput—probably preached during in-services as lean management. But, Pham alleged that the nurses did not wear HAZMAT suits while treating Duncan initially and that the suits only came after a few days. She also reportedly claimed that medical waste was piled up in a hospital room because the maintenance staff refused to collect it. The nurses treating Duncan wore two of everything—from gloves to gowns to booties—as well as a face shield before the HAZMAT suits arrived. She is describing the obverse side of the coin in primary prevention. She is describing in detail how to start an epidemic of a deadly viral illness in this nation, where there was none before. As in the cases of Flight 93 and the anthrax attacks of 9/11 and first missed diagnosis of Cho's psychosis, all frontline clinicians need to know what certain skin lesions look like. That includes doctors presumably well trained in infectious diseases and dermatology. They need to read an atlas of dermatology and pass a test on it so that family doctors do not magically transform the complaint of mite infestation from another delusional Cho into acne in order to pacify an anxious kid. It did not pacify Cho.

Seung-Hui Cho followed the doctor's acne treatment right up to cleaning up on the last morning of his life before committing one of the worst rampage mass murders in history. "Bites and Stings" is an emergency medicine presentation; everyone, as we cite in this book practicing emergency medicine by default today, must know what these look like when examining a person behaving strangely and likely psychotic, like Cho was. Rashes in very sick adults with even blood emanating from pores could signal early Ebola infection. Did Thomas Duncan have a rash or hemorrhage visible simply by examining the surface of his whole body? We do not know, but EMR documentation should have either findings of such or normal checked in the box for "Skin" or "Integumentary System." Wounds must be differentiated between reality of mechanism of action and cutaneous anthrax or child, adult, and elder abuse; the lesion does not lie. The patients or collateral informants, whether muscleman Jerah who slit the throats of the pilots of Flight 93 or millions of abusive parents and partners, do lie. It is the frontline clinician and public safety professional today who must determine the difference and do something about it the first time—not the third time, or at autopsy. Dermatology atlases are not for taking tests or seeking ugly images; they are for first-line prevention and preparedness. Cho and the failed investigation of Mirage Man Ivins are marquee cases of this clear and convincing need for better dermatology training on the frontline where the at-risk carrier can be first detected (Liebert and Birnes 2011b).

Everyone on the frontline of clinical medicine and public safety needs to know what the pain ladder is too. Unrelieved pain should raise a red flag that attracts the attention of the interdisciplinary team. (South West Regional Wound Care Toolkit. www.southwesthealthline.ca/healthlibrary_docs/B.5.3.WHOPainLadder.pdf)

The Duncan case is instructive, not just because it is illustrative of the administrative failures in our public preventive medicine system, but because it reveals how the best laid plans for primary and secondary prevention can easily go awry. Under the ACA, the requirements to slow the rising cost of medical care in America through the use of electronic health records and the optimization of patient flow also open up fissures in the care of patients when thoroughness in clinical assessment is compromised by throughput. Hospitals are totally clinical environments, but their policies and procedures are derailing more often with a surge, not only of unknown patients like Thomas Duncan from anywhere in the world, but a surge in hospital violence.

A lesser-known catastrophic incident occurred nearly concurrent with the introduction of the Ebola epidemic to North America in Dallas. This deadly incident occurred in the upscale St. Paul community of Maplewood, Minnesota. Although seemingly quite different, there are likely more similarities than differences—both cases sending national signals of our flawed preparedness for epidemics. The first in Dallas was recognizing contagiousness along with bioterrorism immediately and containing it. The second in Minnesota was a lesser-known epidemic, that of hospital violence.

It had been a quiet night at St. John's Hospital in the Twin Cities suburb of Maplewood. There had been a family dispute in room 310 over a patient's competency to change his will and divorce his wife. Logan was a 68-year-old man with no significant neuropsychiatric history prior to a recent minor surgery at another hospital. Following that he became confused, fearful, and reportedly paranoid. This was an abrupt change in his personality along with his mental status, both reported as normal until then. He presented in the ER of St. John's 3 days earlier with the chief complaint of confusion. It is not certain if he was worked up in the ER or simply admitted to an acute medical bed. The night of November 2, family members and an attorney had a bedside argument over the patient's competency. The patient's attorney said he was getting a protective order to prevent his client from being declared incompetent to change his will and leave all his money to his grandchildren. The judge refused to decide on this until the next working day. The family and his attorney left. There were no reported adverse effects from this bedside family dispute, but it should never have been allowed to occur with a man being worked up for sudden onset of confusion and paranoia in an acute medical-surgical bed. Like the encounter with an unknown "sick adult" at Texas Health Presbyterian Hospital, the encounter with an unknown man with sudden altered mental status demands following the rules and knowledge base of classical emergency medicine triage, rather than allowing emergency department throughput policies and attending physicians to fly by the seats of their pants. Again, almost concurrently with the Thomas Duncan catastrophe that could have been prevented in Dallas, a patient was killed and nursing staff seriously injured by defying evidence-based clinical rules (Figure 16.1).

This default should have been cleared prior to admission in the ER. It is not clear if ER staff even threw out the WWHHHIMPES; fortunately they may have been lucky, as he did not die on the elevator en route to the third floor. Did they rule out urgent altered states of consciousness that must be cleared in an hour? (See Figure 16.2.)

It is unlikely he was suffering from any of these, because he would have died in the ER or elevator en route to the acute medical-surgical unit had the diagnosis and treatment not been effected by the emergency medicine attending. But, we will not know until autopsy results are completed, because Charles Logan blasted out of his room at 2:00 a.m. wielding an iron bar from his bed and attacked the nursing station. Reportedly he had never been violent before—certainly not to this degree. His rampage was brief, but he relentlessly beat two nurses with the bar, seriously injuring them. A patient recovering from an appendectomy came out of his room because of the sudden uproar and chased Logan in unprotected in just his hospital gown and in post-op state. There was blood all over the floor, the post-op patient reported. Logan fled down the hall and through the hospital until finally subdued by police some distance from the hospital. He was combative, and they tased him.

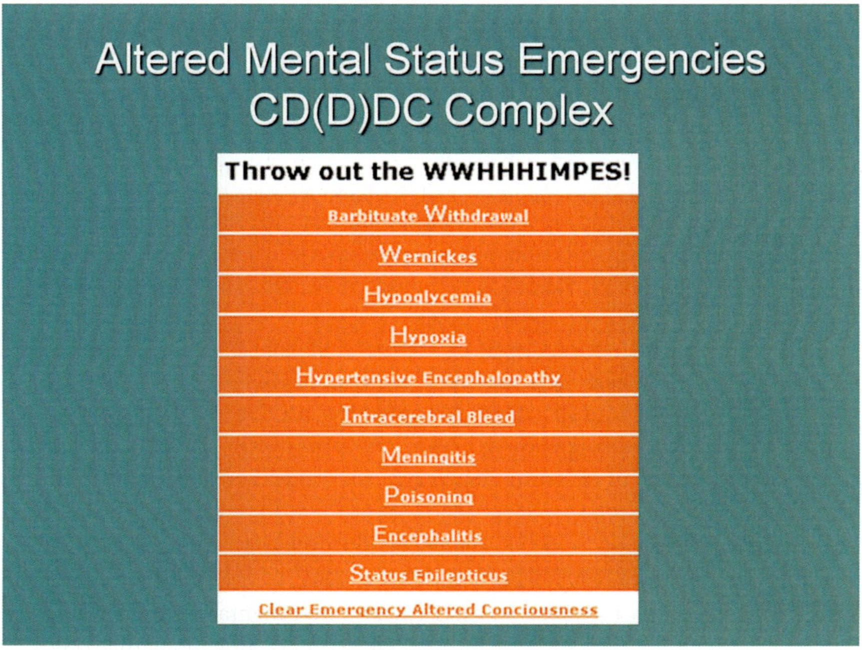


Figure 16.1 Emergency AMS.

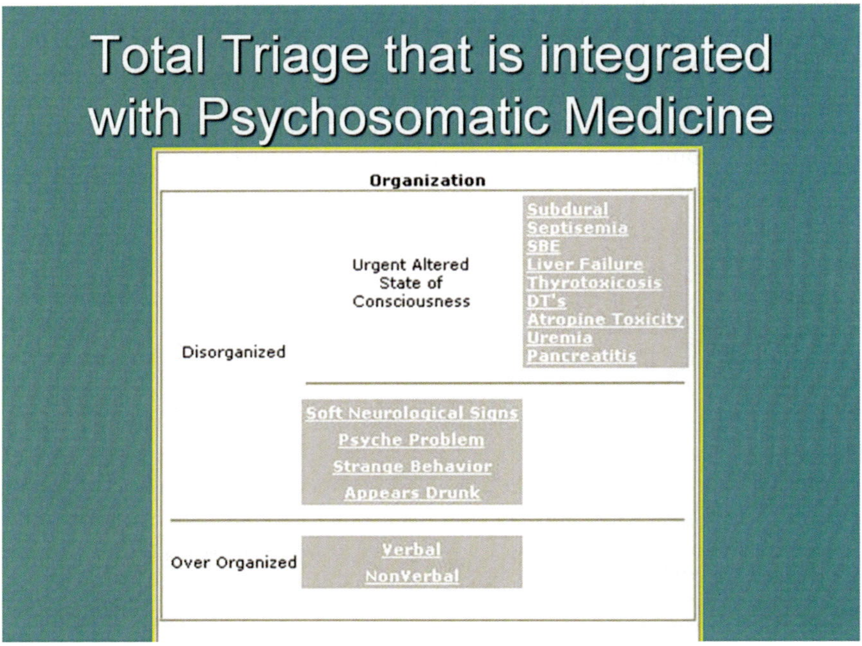


Figure 16.2 Urgent AMS.

The Taser malfunctioned, so the Maplewood Police took him down physically. Logan suddenly went limp and was returned to the ER where he was pronounced dead on arrival (DOA). All four nursing staff members are expected to survive, but two of them were critically injured, one with a collapsed lung from blows to her chest from a steel rod.

Questions will be raised about whether Logan was seen by their staff psychiatrist. Obviously, for a presenting emergency syndrome of confusion and paranoia, intensive consultation-liaison psychiatric management is mandatory. But, sadly, there is little or no reimbursement for this specialty service. St. John's, as their website clearly states, does have this specialty capability. Their administration and chief of staff will be asked how they were utilized, and, if not engaged, why not? At a minimum, this patient, like Thomas Duncan, another "sick adult" denied monitoring on the WHO Pain Ladder, should have been monitored for delirium. Failure to do so results in patient management failures of delirium leading to increased incidence of disability and even death following discharge. In Logan's case there was no discharge—at least none ordered. He simply ran away in paranoid panic and was killed by the police. Most inpatients suffer delirium during their hospitalization. Thus, what is delirium?

Delirium is best defined by fulfilling all of the criteria of the Confusion Assessment Method for a patient in the intensive care unit (CAM-ICU), as follows: (1) either the acute onset of altered or fluctuations of mental status; (2)

associated inattention; and (3) either disorganized thinking or altered level of consciousness. The CAM-ICU requires minimal training and takes only 2 minutes to administer. With this tool, intensivists can operationally define delirium based on diagnostic validity that supports prediction of outcome. Interrater reliability of serial patient assessments by different staff is also high, thus supporting diagnostic reliability.

The four elements examined and serially documented are as follows:

1. Either change in mental status from baseline or a fluctuating course. Mental status is quantified by Mini-Mental State Examination.
2. Inattention.
3. Disorganized thinking.
4. Altered level of consciousness.

Level of consciousness (4), is based on the Richmond Agitation-Sedation Scale (RASS) and provides the lower default for delirium:

0 = Alert and calm
−1 = Drowsy
−2 = Light sedation
−3 = Moderate sedation
−4 = Stupor (deep sedation)—unresponsive to voice but eye movements spared with physical stimulation
−5 = Coma—unarousable and unresponsive to voice and physical stimulation

Determination that there is "no response to verbal stimulus" concludes the exam, as the patient is diagnosed with either coma or stupor.

Element 1 is determined by comparison to admission baseline from the patient's history, his admitting documentation, or collateral sources, like family. Any change in level of sedation from baseline within 24 hours fulfills criteria 1 for change or fluctuation in mental status. And the criterion for altered state of consciousness—or, CD(D)DC and OBS—is defined operationally as any number less than 0 on a scale 0 to −5.

To identify abnormality of attention, the patient must be unable to pass simple tests for attention of either the visual or auditory versions of the attention screening exam (ASE). Neither test requires verbal interaction with the patient.

If delirium cannot either be specifically ruled in or out by now, then element 3, disorganized thinking, must be examined by most simple questions. Disorganized thinking is present if the patient is unable to answer three very simple questions—i.e., Will a stone float on water?—or the patient cannot follow simple commands—i.e., "Hold up this many fingers. Repeat with the other hand" (Show the patient two fingers on the first trial but none on the second.) By doing this, both the verbal and nonverbal patient can be tested.

There will be questions following the coroner's report on autopsy of a diagnostic workup—or lack thereof—for what turned out to be a lethal disease, only needing family uproar at bedside and a malfunctioning police Taser outside to kill an otherwise reportedly healthy 68-year-old man. In this high-paced era of patient throughput—most often absent consultation liaison psychiatric consultation in hospitals and ERs—all clinicians must have etiology in mind, because altered mental status, whether delirium or other altered states of consciousness, are so prevalent in ERs and medical-surgical inpatient units. We do not know how Logan's workup was progressing for 3 days, but from his admission to room 310, he should have had a sitter for security purposes, a CAM protocol, and a prompt neuropsychiatric workup to rule out known causes of altered states of consciousness; this could have been performed in the ER and possibly prevented admission to a medical bed, obviously ill equipped for management of altered states of consciousness due to restrictions and lesser levels of experience for restraining patients compared to the ER.

One rapid assessment tool useful for directing workup of the patient with altered mental status is the diagnostic cross—an intellectual visual icon that can be stored in any clinician's frontal lobe, instead of distracting and time-consuming trips to the computer station or dialing up the iPhone to Medscape and other Internet medical sites for diagnostic support (Figure 16.3).

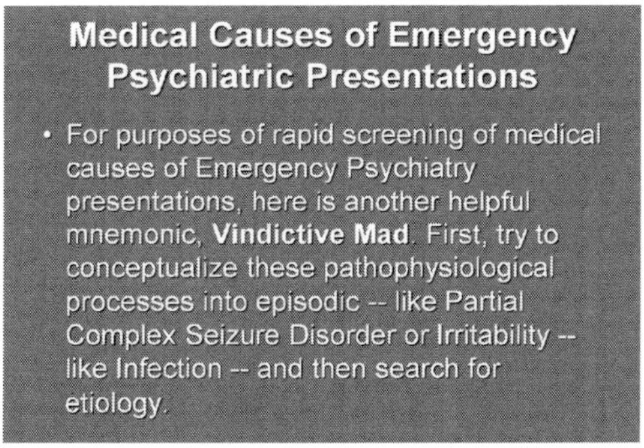
Medical Causes of Emergency Psychiatric Presentations
• For purposes of rapid screening of medical causes of Emergency Psychiatry presentations, here is another helpful mnemonic, Vindictive Mad. First, try to conceptualize these pathophysiological processes into episodic -- like Partial Complex Seizure Disorder or Irritability -- like Infection -- and then search for etiology.

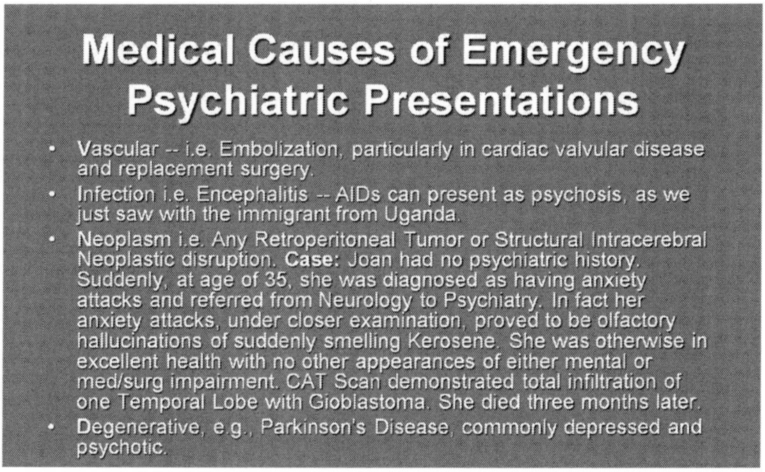
Medical Causes of Emergency Psychiatric Presentations
• Vascular -- i.e. Embolization, particularly in cardiac valvular disease and replacement surgery.
• Infection i.e. Encephalitis -- AIDs can present as psychosis, as we just saw with the immigrant from Uganda.
• Neoplasm i.e. Any Retroperitoneal Tumor or Structural Intracerebral Neoplastic disruption. Case: Joan had no psychiatric history. Suddenly, at age of 35, she was diagnosed as having anxiety attacks and referred from Neurology to Psychiatry. In fact her anxiety attacks, under closer examination, proved to be olfactory hallucinations of suddenly smelling Kerosene. She was otherwise in excellent health with no other appearances of either mental or med/surg impairment. CAT Scan demonstrated total infiltration of one Temporal Lobe with Gioblastoma. She died three months later.
• Degenerative, e.g., Parkinson's Disease, commonly depressed and psychotic.

Figure 16.3 The diagnostic cross. *(Continued)*

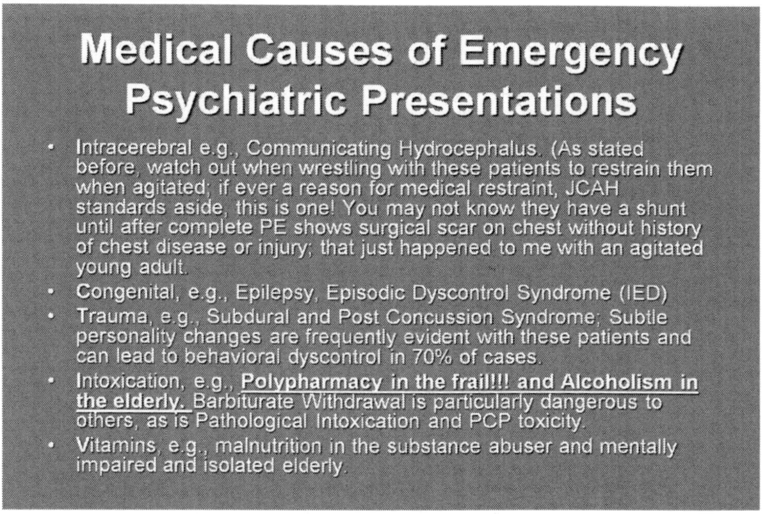
Medical Causes of Emergency Psychiatric Presentations
• Intracerebral e.g., Communicating Hydrocephalus. (As stated before, watch out when wrestling with these patients to restrain them when agitated; if ever a reason for medical restraint, JCAH standards aside, this is one! You may not know they have a shunt until after complete PE shows surgical scar on chest without history of chest disease or injury; that just happened to me with an agitated young adult.
• Congenital, e.g., Epilepsy, Episodic Dyscontrol Syndrome (IED)
• Trauma, e.g., Subdural and Post Concussion Syndrome; Subtle personality changes are frequently evident with these patients and can lead to behavioral dyscontrol in 70% of cases.
• Intoxication, e.g., Polypharmacy in the frail!!! and Alcoholism in the elderly. Barbiturate Withdrawal is particularly dangerous to others, as is Pathological Intoxication and PCP toxicity.
• Vitamins, e.g., malnutrition in the substance abuser and mentally impaired and isolated elderly.

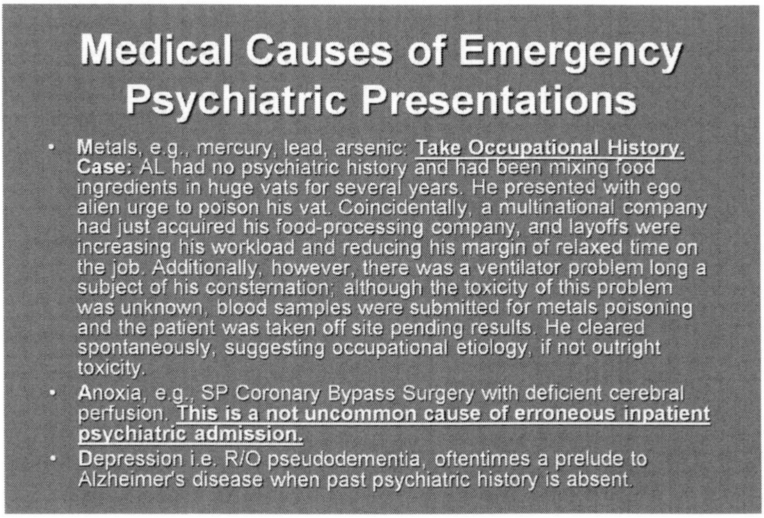
Medical Causes of Emergency Psychiatric Presentations
• Metals, e.g., mercury, lead, arsenic: Take Occupational History. Case: AL had no psychiatric history and had been mixing food ingredients in huge vats for several years. He presented with ego alien urge to poison his vat. Coincidentally, a multinational company had just acquired his food-processing company, and layoffs were increasing his workload and reducing his margin of relaxed time on the job. Additionally, however, there was a ventilator problem long a subject of his consternation; although the toxicity of this problem was unknown, blood samples were submitted for metals poisoning and the patient was taken off site pending results. He cleared spontaneously, suggesting occupational etiology, if not outright toxicity.
• Anoxia, e.g., SP Coronary Bypass Surgery with deficient cerebral perfusion. This is a not uncommon cause of erroneous inpatient psychiatric admission.
• Depression i.e. R/O pseudodementia, oftentimes a prelude to Alzheimer's disease when past psychiatric history is absent.

Figure 16.3 (Continued) The diagnostic cross.

V ascular
I nfection
N eoplasm
CD(D)DC (coma, delirium, pseudodementia, dementia, confusion)
I ntraventricular (i.e., low-pressure hydrocephalus)
C ongenital (i.e., epilepsy)
T rauma
I ntracranial
V itamin deficiency

E ndocrine
M etal poisoning (i.e., mercury and lead)
A noxia
D rugs

The central "D" in the diagnostic cross informs clinicians to think before premature diagnostic closure. The differential diagnosis of memory problems in the geriatric population is complex and oftentimes skewed toward either underdiagnoses of an early dementing process or misdiagnosis of Alzheimer's disease. Was a dementing process considered in Charles Logan? He was the right age for an early dementing process that could have been arrested, at least for several months, with cognitive-enhancing medications. Pseudodementia is a real entity, although not a recognized diagnosis; it is included in the diagnostic cross to make certain reversible causes of dementing illness, such as neurosurgical intervention for normal pressure hydrocephalus and psychiatric treatment for depression are ruled out. Alzheimer's disease is a devastating diagnosis for both patient and family. It must be made with both knowledge of its differential diagnosis and diligence in its workup; it is a final diagnosis after every other presentation mimicking it is ruled out; that is the significance of pseudodementia, which too many doctors in the geriatrics field laugh off as, "boy that's a new one on me." It should not be; it is critically important to understand and work through if both patient and family can be spared the fate worse than death that is Alzheimer's disease.

Pseudodementia is a presentation with cognitive deficits caused by a psychiatric disorder that clears with psychotropic medication. Folstein evaluated depressed patients while developing the Mini-Mental State Examination. He found so much overlap that he coined the term "demented syndrome of depression"—thus the "D" in the CD(D)DC complex. Many patients suffer both depressions with intellectual impairment without amyloid plaques in the memory centers of their brains. The prefix, "pseudo," is very misleading, because the cognitive symptoms and signs of pseudodementia are real—not false, as implied by the term. They are usually associated with a depressed patients' lack of effort caused by impaired motivation. The term, pseudodementia, lacks specificity, implying mimicry of organic brain syndromes, absent a progressive course. Heterogeneity, perhaps, is the most defining feature of pseudodementia. We are usually talking about depression with pseudodementia, because of its prevalence in the highest-risk geriatric cohort for dementia. In fact, the monoamine oxidase enzyme increases with aging, particularly in the Alzheimer's patient. Remember that 2% of patients admitted in studies of coma were depressed, catatonic, or conversion disordered. In retrospective studies of inpatient admissions for organic brain syndrome that included approximately 350 patients—nearly 10%—ultimately showed no clinical findings of neurodegenerative disease. One study of 20 pseudodemented patients found the following prevalence of purely psychiatric disorders:

1. Depression in 3/20
2. Anxiety in 3/20
3. Somatoform disorder in 6/20

4. Hysterical conversion disorder in 1/20
5. Others in 6/20

The Maudsley study of 31% of erroneous dementia diagnoses found that most had functional psychiatric illness—many with depression, and thus the (D) in the CD(D)DC syndrome. But more than one-quarter had a nonprogressive organic brain syndrome course, the majority having a profound depressive mood component. Rothschild postulated an “X” factor for this inexplicable clinical course that was neither medical nor psychiatric. Caveat: Most elderly patients referred for dementia and found not to have it improve with psychiatric treatment, but later turn out to be demented within a few years of workup. In retrospect, it was found that many of these false-negative workups ignored subtle neurological findings present at initial workup. The highest alerting signs for subtle dementias in the depressed geriatric population are as follow:

1. Cerebrovascular disease
2. Spinocerebellar signs
3. Extrapyramidal syndrome
4. Hachinski** scale greater than 4
5. Mini-Mental State Exam*** score under 8
6. Iatrogenic confusion from the anticholinergic effects of homeopathic doses of psychotropic medications like Cogentin, often prescribed for side effects of antipsychotic medications like Haldol or even the newer Risperdal in higher doses
   (Asterisks indicate scale for cerebrovasular dementia.)

The bottom line is that it is very hard to isolate these cases in large populations referred for organicity. In fact, Wells finally settled on clinical course for diagnosis. He thought that the most distinguishing factor was the inconsistency of testing results from session to session that best identified the pseudodemented (Liebert 2007).

This knowledge base is essential for points of entry like our ERs today, and, absent both inpatient psychiatry and consultation liaison psychiatry, med-surg units must have this knowledge base for differentiating altered states of consciousness manifesting neurological disease from treatable and reversible primary psychiatric disorders, like mood and psychotic disorders. In the case of Ben at North and South hospitals in the Twin Cities area, I discuss a previously well man like Charles Logan who has the rapid onset of an altered state of consciousness. He presented in all five segments of the CD(D)DC complex, because the complex is not static, but fluid. Its multiform presentations from day to day, hour to hour, and week to week, therefore, can be perplexing to physicians either unable to or simply failing to obtain a careful longitudinal history that includes past and personal history of the patient. In the case of Ben, he presented initially with confusion when traveling as a salesman. He missed flights, because his executive function was impaired. The confusion was attributed to multiple time zone changes, but then the confusion required observation in the South

Hospital ER, where the CAM demonstrated significant delirium, from which he recovered. Weeks later he was found wandering in the street, and such behavior was out of character. He was admitted this time into the psychiatric unit at South Hospital, where a dementing illness was suspected. It improved, however, with high doses of an antidepressant, and he was treated in the outpatient psychiatric clinic with the diagnosis of major depression with psychotic features, due to both his cognitive signs and response to antidepressants. He was not in remission, but he was stable for a couple of weeks before returning to this same hospital in a coma. Finally an intensivist in the ICU with experience in such multiform presentations of altered states of consciousness in this region of the nation became suspicious because of his work history: Ben was an archery salesman who spent most of his working hours in the woods testing and demonstrating bows and arrows. A Lyme disease titer returned positive. By following the discipline of the diagnostic cross, he was able to pinpoint Ben's diagnosis at (D) for pseudodementia and (I) for infection. The horizontal element of the cross clearly was a slowly progressing and fluctuating illness affecting the brain, but he also had developed other system problems, such as severe neck pain requiring a brace. Brain scans were negative all along. This presentation turned out to be the "Great Pretender of illnesses"—namely, Lyme disease, commonly occurring in people who spend a lot of time hunting in Minnesota forests; it is passed along through ticks hosted by deer.

Ben is the marquee case for caution in premature closure in altered states of consciousness. His pseudodementia that responded to antidepressants threw everyone off, until he returned to the hospital comatose. Now, clearly, Ben was a very sick man who could die. A powerful course of antibiotic with careful monitoring of antibodies to the Lyme bacteria, however, brought complete recovery to Ben. He was the fortunate one, because in parts of this country densely populated with deer, most people are still buried with it not having a diagnosis. It is the case of Ben that emphasizes the critical importance of respecting the fact that pseudodementia can in a fraction of such cases be purely psychiatric, but it should not be reason to label a man like Ben, having late-onset neuropsychiatric impairment with pure functional psychiatric diagnosis, despite response to antidepressants—neuropsychiatry is way too complex for that. Lyme disease humbles us in remembering this fact over and over again as the Great Pretender of all illnesses—particularly in areas of the country with large deer populations.

Charles Logan is the classic example of a patient where there needed to be a high index of suspicion for Lyme disease. Was it in the differential? We do not know, but it could have explained his sudden onset of altered mental status and paranoia—particularly if he was a deer hunter, for which there was a high statistical chance of his being in Minnesota. Still there are patients who appear demented at times with cognitive impairment who have reversible medical-surgical disease like was the case of Ben—and likely Charles Logan. Catatonia is more common in immigrant populations whose fear of mental illness is masqueraded as mutism with stony immobility. Oftentimes these patients are not schizophrenic, but rather traumatized and fully recover with supportive care and tranquilization. If Charles Logan was admitted to a med-surg unit for observation and workup of altered mental status, what did the differential include, having survived the initial hour of admission, whether through the ER or direct admit? In both his case and that of Thomas Duncan, primary prevention depended upon rational and time-determined diagnostics of the CD(D)DC complex, because etiology was more likely than not detectable in the emergency department utilizing the diagnostic cross. We do not even know if serial mental status examinations were performed on Thomas Duncan, but with the severity of his infection and fever, his mental status was likely to have fluctuated in a state of delirium. Valid diagnosis would have informed the necessary clinical interventions for both deadly pathophysiological processes that could have been interdicted to prevent injury and illness to others—in these two cases, nurses caring for them. That is primary prevention, even though it is not apparent as such in high-acuity treatment sites like the ER and acute med-surg bed.

The tragic deaths of Thomas Duncan and Charles Logan—as well as the collateral damage to nursing staff from failed triaging—are marquee index cases that should, like railroad signals, send deafening alarms to medical administration and public officials alike: "Stop, Look and Listen" before crossing the line again. If emergency medicine converts to disaster medicine on the grounds of two mainstream U.S. hospitals, then what can we expect from the care of the many millions of sick in the gutters of our streets and behind bars?

Clearly, as we read every day in the news, when flaws in early identification of causation for definitive clinical interventions and collateral damage to others are coupled with criminalization of the mentally ill, we see more instances of police gunning down mentally ill individuals who sometimes are so delusional they do not even realize they are being gunned down. Charles Logan tragically turned into a case of excessive force by the police, but Charles Logan should never have been physically restrained by the police. He should have been restrained by emergency medication in his hospital bed. The recent case in the DC Metro system, however, where an officer shot to death a young, scantily clad man walking on the tracks is just another example of how unprepared most police departments are in dealing with the mentally ill and how this lack of preparedness often results in the death of unarmed individuals.

Although veiled by the terrors of epidemic infectious diseases such as Ebola and shocking atrocities by ISIS in our War on Terror, the threat of death, lifetime disability, and human destruction of neuropsychiatric disease remains. They are disguised and cloaked in ignorance, denial, and ancient public prejudices toward madness that have returned diagnostics, treatment, and management of psychotic neuropsychiatric diseases to the eighteenth century, when these patients were chained in lunatic asylums. A seeming turning point for civilization and humane recognition of neuropsychiatric disease, particularly the most dramatic and threatening form presenting as psychosis, occurred when Jean-Baptiste Pussin removed the iron shackles from psychotic patients at l'Hôpital Bicêtre in Paris in 1797 and Philippe Pinel freed patients from punitive torture and restraint at the Hospice de la Salpêtrière 3 years later, after Pussin joined him there.

Have we regressed as a civilization since then? One must wonder, because too often now the management of psychosis in the seriously impaired neuropsychiatric patient is first, criminalization, followed by solitary confinement after conviction. The double homicide of the American Sniper and colleague by Eddie Routh is another marquee index case. Following serial release from three hospitals with the diagnosis of psychotic disorder and dangerousness, he is convicted as sane and sent to prison. But, then, he is once again insane—same person, same brain, in the same body in just a short period of time. Unmanageable in prison because he is insane, he is returned to psychiatric inpatient management. There was no responsibility exercised by any public facility or official in the case of Eddie Routh, a Marine Active Reservist, his life is over and two dedicated men are dead trying to help him (Liebert and Birnes 2014).

As we have seen in cities from New York, Milwaukee, Madison, to Tri Cities, Washington, Albuquerque, and Los Angeles, execution is the final common pathway when the mentally ill are acting strangely. Threatening the very fabric of our society is the tragic fact that these mentally ill people are disproportionately people of color and the police officers white. Arguably this takes public psychiatry back to prerevolutionary days when the mentally ill were not even in hospitals (Friedman 2014).

But, it is not just on the streets, as the daily headlines of our news cycle inform us. Mental illness is also punished inside correctional institutions with both violence and sequestration from the general population inside solitary confinement units or SHUs. As a case in point, a *New York Times* undercover report has detailed the "brutal and routine" violence perpetrated by corrections personnel at Rikers Island upon almost 130 inmates with serious mental illness over an 11-month period. The writer asks, "Have We Reached a Flashpoint?" (Lerner-Wren 2014).

Many articles have been authored by renowned international disability law and human rights scholar, Professor Michael L. Perlin, the late Professor Bruce J. Winick, Professor David Wexler, and other law and policy experts who have long sounded the human rights alarm. The argument is that the first step in leadership on this issue is to establish a sense of urgency, according to change advocate and former Harvard Professor John P. Kotter. The brutal treatment of the mentally ill in prisons should arouse national disgust. One would expect outcries for immediate action, given the extreme urgency of this new revelation. His wrongful death suit is like a lightning rod for the torrent of abhorrent abuse and neglect of persons with serious mental illness and other neurological disorders.

Other headline cases capture our attention as well, such as the *New York Times*' report on the brutality taking place at the San Francisco jail (Stack 2015). The San Francisco public defender called on investigators to look into what the public defender called organized gladiator-style physical combat organized by the prison guards in which, for their delight, prisoners were matched up against one another and made to battle against their will. Those that refused were beaten by the guards. What type of blood sport is this in our correctional system? Are the officers more violent and insane than the prisoners they are sworn to manage and protect?

The other case of note, according to the Washington, DC, local NBC affiliate, is the federal government's investigation into the Baltimore City detention center where juveniles awaiting trial on adult charges are sometimes kept in solitary confinement for, in one case, 143 days (Associated Press/NBC4 Washington 2015). "'This is grossly excessive and violates basic principles of Due Process', reads the February 19 Justice Department letter to jail officials. 'It is even more troubling for the 24% of juveniles in seclusion who are ultimately found not guilty under the disciplinary process.'"

After shocking headline after shocking headline of the neuropsyche patient either going on a suicidal rampage murder spree or being gunned down by police, almost in the process of a de facto genocidal elimination of our "bad seeds," what is the tipping point? Will the urgency come when creative law from the Trial Lawyers Association really does purge the system effectively by suing the governors of states responsible for cost-shifting emergency neuropsychiatric treatment from specialized hospitals and clinics to jails and prisons? A few such lawsuits could, in the justification for the president's resistance to capping malpractice, create a "sense of urgency" very quickly. After all, the federal government is suing the Maricopa County Sheriff, Joe Arpaio, for racial profiling, and the U.S. Attorney General's findings of police discrimination in Ferguson, Missouri, have also revealed disturbing results of disproportionate treatment of people of color. Why not pursue state governors and prison officials for violation of patients' rights? Like the French public over 200 years ago, the sad facts are that only a small percentage of Americans—about 5%—believe serious neuropsychiatric impairment has anything to do with abnormalities of the brain, genetic or otherwise (Stahl 2010).

The plight of the seriously impaired neuropsychiatric patient is not as simple a medical story to get across to even the highly educated American, still preoccupied with existential issues in what might be called "insanity" versus free will. We now know, however, that the millions of patients who can be reliably diagnosed with schizophrenia by psychiatrists agreeing on criteria do in fact have abnormal genetics. The genetics, however, are not simple, as they are in diseases with the high rates of suicide like Huntington's chorea, a terrible disease, but with simple genetics. In Huntington's, for example, if you have the dominant gene, you get the disease and usually die from suicide. Is suicide, therefore, genetic? Perhaps, but not all Huntington's patients commit suicide and somehow survive the untreatable torturous movement disorders until dying a natural death. Is it the disability that causes the suicide? Probably not 100%, because there are other debilitating neurological diseases that take away the essence of life without ending it. Such a disease is amyotrophic lateralizing sclerosis, or Lou Gehrig's disease. Huntington's cannot be so much worse to explain the suicidality accompanying it. There must be a suicidal aberration in the dominant gene of Huntington's.

Certainly the shocking violence of Robin Williams's suicide by cutting, and then hanging, cries out for a complex genetic matrix of aberrant genes that bore him the genius of comedy, but in tragic paradox, ultimately determined his violent death by suicide. It is well known that the devastation of uncontrolled bipolar disorder afflicting Robin Williams is robustly familial. That means it is rare to find a case without a blood relative clearly suffering it also. Many more millions suffer this potentially devastating mood swing disorder, manifesting as early as childhood, than suffer schizophrenia, but the genetic transmission is unknown and poorly researched. The mortality of this illness is high, and in some cases of rampage suicidal mass murder, can be enormously devastating. The authors wrote of the cases of Christopher Dorner and Timothy Jorden, the former a suicidal mass murderer, and the latter a famed trauma surgeon who killed his girlfriend and then himself (Liebert and Birnes 2013). The Azuza Spa suicidal mass murder by Radcliffe Haughton was very likely caused by this disease also (Liebert and Birnes 2014).

There is a crossover neuropsychiatric disease that can be reliably diagnosed as schizoaffective disorder. In this disease the patient does not deteriorate as severely as the patient with schizophrenia, so dramatically evidenced for years by Aurora Theater suicidal rampage murderer, James Holmes (Liebert and Birnes 2014). The schizoaffective disordered patient also has mood swings like Robin Williams but is far more paranoid and psychotically impaired when both manic and depressed. From a genetic perspective, this neuropsychiatric disease breeds schizophrenia, however, and not bipolar disorder.

Wade Page, perpetrator of the Milwaukee Sikh Temple suicidal mass murder, was founder of the band "End Apathy" in 2005 and a musician in the band "Definite Hate," both considered racist white-power bands by the Southern Poverty Law Center. He very likely suffered this neuropsychiatric disease and was discharged from the army because of it. Page was a highly functional enlisted man selected for psychological operations in the U.S. Army before succumbing to a suicidal psychotic illness witnessed and intimately described by his neighbor, a psychiatric nurse at a Milwaukee hospital. She reported her helplessness in getting help for him in Milwaukee. The First Family would again have to travel to memorialize the murder and mayhem—this time inside a temple of worship, instead of a shopping center (Hyler 2012).

A brief case overview highlights the problematic management of this complex and highly lethal psychiatric disorder. Robert was a high-functioning businessman with extended bouts of manic excitement, during which times he would be highly productive. Then he would seemingly disappear in a depressed state of mind. He never deteriorated as in the case of schizophrenia and successfully completed his career, although his boss exploited his highs and protected him during his lows. Unlike mood-disordered patients, he was paranoid, even when not either high or low. His diagnosis was schizoaffective disorder, but all five of his children were institutionalized with classical schizophrenia.

It is also known that certain fathers with well-diagnosed antisocial personality disorder (APD) breed sons, nearly 100% of whom develop APD. Their daughters, however, develop Briquet syndrome, a psychosomatic disorder with multiple physical symptoms that cannot be traced to medical-surgical diseases. Such gender-determined genetic transmission is so baffling that it begs for intense research. Other epidemiological studies also beg for large-scale studies into the psychogenesis of violent people. Follow-up research on 300 children referred to a child guidance clinic in St. Louis for antisocial behavior (conduct disorder) showed that in 35 years 71% were arrested and 50% had multiple arrests and incarceration. Nearly one-third were diagnosed in adulthood as having APD, while almost all committing four offenses went on to adult criminal careers.

Only 16% were ultimately found to be free of psychiatric illness. The severity and number of antisocial behaviors in childhood conduct disorder predict adult behavior better than any other variable, including social class and family background (Kay and Kay 1990).

It is well established that certain populations are at risk for psychiatric impairment, due to psychosocial risk factors. Poor, single-parent families with an adult son at home, for example, are at particularly high risk for having one of the 14% of patients who are afflicted with the most serious psychiatric disorders. In fact, in the Kentucky study, family analysis predicted future psychopathology in 82% of cases (Kessler et al. 1994).

Many of the cases of suicidal mass murder cited in this book emanate from a small fraction—less than 10%—of patients suffering from untreated schizophrenia (Torrey 2012). It has been known that genetics are a necessary but not sufficient condition for developing this devastating disease afflicting 1% of the world's population with 300,000 first psychotic episodes every year from schizophrenia in the United States. The denial of genetically determined brain abnormalities in this disease has led to philosophical debates and court decisions hampering progress in understanding causation, early detection, and treatment (Liebert and Birnes 2014). Swedish studies of identical twins raised by different parents are convincing in their high incidence of schizophrenia in both twins compared to nonidentical twins similarly raised. Yet, the numbers are small and the population studied hardly representative of the global population at risk for the disease. New light has illuminated the complexity of the genetic vulnerability in schizophrenia. There is strong evidence that many gene variants create the risk for schizophrenia. Studies are all over the place on the actual numbers, but the range to date is between a couple dozen to over a hundred genetic markers.

The epigenetics of schizophrenia is made more complex because of the likelihood of their interactions with many variables, such as age, determining being turned off or on. How the timed mix of those on and those off likely determines risk but not the emergence of schizophrenia. Additional work also found a significant correlation between autoimmune diseases and schizophrenia, further strengthening the genetic risk basis of this debilitating psychiatric disorder. The current belief is that genes nudge the person toward that first psychotic episode, but there may be environmental triggers that bring it out—thus manifesting the phenotype from the genotype. Do all children of parents who contract lung cancer get the disease? No. But do these children of parents with lung cancer who smoke have a higher probability of contracting the disease? Yes. And the same goes for heart disease and diabetes. Clearly, though genes likely predispose a person for a certain disease, they are not sufficient to cause it. Environmental factors, such as psychological trauma and loss, are necessary, although oftentimes clinically invisible from the patient's history. Few experts in the study of schizophrenia still subscribe to "sick family" or schizogenic mothering as sufficient causation for the profound deterioration and mental disorganization of this debilitating psychiatric disorder as subscribed to in departments of psychiatry during the 1960s and 1970s (Cardiff University 2014).

> Risk factors for psychosis have been identified at the level of single genes, and in relation to disorders caused by these. For example, the lifetime risk of psychosis in velo-cardio-facial syndrome is around 30%. In general, psychiatric risk is likely to be determined by contributions from many genes which are individually of small effect: genome-wide association studies are locating such genes including ZN804A which influences the risk of schizophrenia and CACNA1C which modulates the risk of bipolar disease. Variations in copy numbers are proving to be common risk factors for disorders previously regarded as distinct, for example, autism, schizophrenia and learning disability. The path leading from genotype to psychiatric phenotype will undoubtedly be a complex one in which gene–gene and gene–environment interactions will play a key role. Imaging genetics is identifying the effects of genetic variation on patterns of brain activity. (Zeman 2014)

Siblings at risk genetically who do not get the disease also fail cognitive psychological testing the same as those who develop the disease. This does not inform of early intervention to prevent the disease, because there is no known means for prevention. Certainly excessive stress is a factor. One could compare it to five rusted bridges over the same river. One day commuter traffic is heavy on all of them, but two large semis come across one of them. The first one makes it, but the second dives into the river after the bridge buckles. The other four bridges remain standing but obviously vulnerable to the same fate, and similarly with the development of the child at genetic risk of developing schizophrenia. Many simply stand without collapsing, but another gets that unique hit and does collapse with one of the 300,000 first psychotic episodes of schizophrenia occurring in this country every year. Because of the window of vulnerability being late teens to mid-adolescence, of course, a disproportionate number of cases are going to occur on campus where 20 million in this age bracket are concentrated, similarly with military bases. The unique stresses of transitioning from home to these new environments could be the necessary conditions for the disease manifesting in one sibling and not another carrying the same genetic risk markers. The paradigm of that unique hit breaking the damaged bridge therefore brings up the environmental threat. Certainly, better resilience in our population would likely reduce risk. That is a field of study necessary for addressing psychosocial risk factors caused by rapid changes in our modern society (Liebert and Birnes 2014).

In terms of prevention, reducing trauma is also necessary through better child and adult protection services. Improved equipment, training, and command for war could have some impact on reducing posttraumatic stress disorder (PTSD) and traumatic brain injury (TBI) (Liebert and Birnes 2013). James Shore studied those impacted by the eruption of Mount St. Helens and found that onset and severity of psychiatric illness correlated with severity of loss, whether family members or property. Such studies of trauma that address how a population is actually affected by extreme events outside the realm of expectable life experience are needed to find out what unique events in life break that fragile bridge. Those bridges are not checked that well. In the case of human genetic vulnerability, they are not checked at all. This will be a great area of future growth in psychiatry and neurology, just as it is in oncology and other medical specialties.

Treatments are far better now for schizophrenia than they were 60 years ago when the first antipsychotic was introduced into North America by Heinz Lehman at McGill. The transition of patients grossly psychotic in the caves of Verdun Protestant Hospital in Montreal was revolutionary. The worst of their gross psychotic behaviors were subdued without cold baths and straightjackets. It was truly a spiritual moment to witness after seeing such a seemingly endless parade of grossly dysfunctional humans who could not possibly adapt to the world above them on the streets of Montreal (Liebert 2015). The dramatic positive signs did improve and even clear, but the deterioration usually did not. We are a long way from personalized medicine that develops drugs from genetic markers, as in the case of advancing care for breast cancer or more recently lymphoma. But, it can be optimistically predicted that we are still years away, which is less than the 200-plus years since schizophrenic patients were unchained in Paris. We can be hopeful that one day they may not end up in solitary confinement, beaten, or shot by police. Hopefully, therefore, so many young men and women will not commit suicide, as is too frequently the case following the first episode when there is still insight into a terrible life to come—or they simply die of dehydration or the elements in their cells, as reported with Murdough at Rikers Island, or, as not reported, in their filthy blankets in the gutters, as was Murdough's ultimate destiny from so-called "natural causes"—natural, perhaps in Charles Dickens' London, but not in modern America.

One unique case of primary prevention could be that of Darion Aguilar, known to be a smoker and skateboarder at a Columbia, Maryland, mall. Hearing voices and distressed by his deteriorating mental condition, Aguilar sought help and was finally referred to a psychiatrist for treatment with antipsychotic medications. He never made the appointment. Instead he studied mass killings and became preoccupied with the Columbine suicidal mass murder of 1998. On January 25, 2014, he entered the Zumiez store in the mall at the exact time of the Columbine suicidal mass murder and murdered two people. He even dressed like the Columbine killers. Very likely he was a mall rat. What was he smoking? We do not know from any autopsy, but it is very possible he was smoking cannabis, certainly not a diabolical sin in itself. But, were he an at-risk person with a variant of *COMT* gene necessary for metabolizing cannabis, he could likely be one case of primary prevention of first-episode psychosis with double homicide and suicide. Had he been known to have a gene variant for *COMT*, he and his family could have been advised of his extreme risk for smoking dope. Aquilars were concerned enough about his deteriorating mental condition to have a psychiatric appointment, but he never got the help he needed. He may have abstained from cannabis, had he known. We will never know, but it is an interesting hypothetical highlighting the importance of primary prevention of neuropsychiatric disorders.

Unlike neurology, psychiatry is handicapped by the absence of biological markers for the profound clinical presentations faced with psychotic and mood disorders. Functional imaging, however, promises to once again merge the two brain-based specialties of medicine.

> The techniques are in some respects crude, and the apparent localization of cognitive activity by functional MRI (fMRI) in the brain of an animal urges caution in the interpretation of its results and relevance to humans. Yet, functional imaging approaches hold out great promise in understanding the elusive neural basis of psychiatric disorder, with notable results, for example, in the study of Charles Bonnet Syndrome, where the content of hallucinations associated with visual loss correlates with regional activations. The developing study of the human "connectome," the architecture of connections that creates the functional networks of the brain, and the novel techniques that facilitate this, such as resting-state fMRI and analysis using graph theoretical analysis, are likely to be especially valuable in psychiatry, for which the previous approach to neurological analysis—mapping the brain—small area by area—was probably inappropriate … Neuropharmacology provides a final example of the seamless boundary between neurology and psychiatry …. Neurologists prescribe antidepressants to reduce migraine and cataplexy, psychiatrists prescribe antiepileptics to stabilize mood. This is not surprising as the systems based in the brain stem that neurologists-in-training come to know as the ascending activating system regulating conscious state, overlap massively with the systems psychiatrists-in-training encounter as key regulators of motivation and mood. (Zeman 2014)

All of these cases illustrate that primary prevention involves the identification of a danger and then fixing that danger, just like a damaged bridge, before anyone goes across it. Applying this to two current ancillary medical models, aviation experts Bill Scott and Lieutenant Colonel Mike Bell, concerned over the rash of police shootings of unarmed, nonthreatening, or mentally ill individuals, presented an argument to the President's Task Force on 21st Century Policing that the policies for change include standards from the aviation industry—long in place to ensure personnel and passenger safety. The White House accepted these suggestions after Scott and Bell's 10-minute presentation for primary prevention of the type of police shootings that have made the news recently (Scott 2015). These policy procedures included third-party, independent investigations (emulating how the National Transportation Safety Board [NTSB] handles aviation accidents); citizen review boards; protocols that guarantee police officers are held accountable for their actions, and putting bodycams on every police officer in the nation. President Obama endorsed Bill Scott and Mike Bell's presentation. We argue that if police believe they are being watched by the entire world on camera and that a third-party independent review board is on constant watch to hold them accountable for what they do, they will think twice before letting emotion overwhelm their rational behavior. This is a form of primary prevention that, we believe, will reinforce the bridge carrying the truck.

## SECONDARY PREVENTION: EARLY IDENTIFICATION REDUCES MORTALITY AND MORBIDITY

Secondary prevention is identification of the at-risk person for early onset of neuropsychiatric disease. Duration of untreated psychosis, as was the case in Aguilar and many other suicidal mass murderers like Seung-Hui Cho, portends increasing impairment with more serious disability, violence, and suicide (Liebert and Birnes 2011b). There is strong evidence that early intervention in the youth and young adult showing signs of personality change and emotional distress can reduce both the severity of psychiatric disease course as well as damage to neuronal development and connectedness in the brain. Studies of brain-derived neurotrophic growth factor (NGF) show abnormalities in pathways of neuronal connections in the multibillions of brain circuits rapidly changing during adolescence and early adulthood. There is evidence that psychotropic medications increase NGF in the brains of symptomatic youth and young adults, thus likely reducing misconnections of neurons that lead to signaling deficits. Just as in the most complex of computers, it only takes damage to or abnormal connectedness between a small number of neurons to scramble computing and, thus, with the brain, too. More research on psychopharmacology and also psychotherapy will likely show healing effects of the at-risk brain deteriorating into a sick brain.

It is not possible to screen every person in this country—even students like Jaylen Freyberg of the Marysville Suicidal Mass Murder through K–12 and beyond to PhD programs where the Aurora Theater rampage mass murder of James Holmes incubated. Other than legal drivers renewing their licenses, the state is not authorized to examine anyone for simply being on the street or in a private residence. The STASSI of the former East German DDR did exactly that by turning family members into spies at citizens' dining rooms to pick up the faintest a voice signaling treason. The slightest criticism of the Moscow-based regime was cause for arrest of anyone who might never be seen again and whose fate was 100% under control of the police. Its effectiveness was both chilling and brutal—a lesson, therefore, to be learned. But, STASSI should not be a justification for lax surveillance, as it was for the undoing of Norway's Minister of Security in the wake of Anders Breivik's Utoeya Island massacre and bombing of her government's state house. She said that not even the STASSI could have detected Anders Breivik before he planted bombs in the very heart of Norway's government. Her staff was not monitoring security videos when Breivik was clearly seen parking his car, packed with explosives, in front of the Prime Minister's office, and then lumbering past the main entrance armed and strangely outfitted as a commando. Worse yet, his name was on her own security watch list, because Poland warned her office that he was importing agricultural chemicals in quantities more appropriate for terrorism than farming his small plot of land. The blindness to his paranoid psychosis continued through his trial. Norway prosecuted him as insane, but he defended his sanity and won his case, which was the height of insanity in this Norwegian suicidal rampage murder (Liebert and Birnes 2014).

We can both prepare and surveil better than that for the lone deranged suicidal rampage murderer or terrorists without restoring a dreaded East German regime that judged every German guilty before proven innocent. In the Soviet Union, anyone dissenting from the Kremlin's line could be committed to a mental hospital under the communist ideology. The state was perfect. Therefore, the protesting dissident must be insane and, by such rationale, be committed to a state mental institution and tortured with injected psychotropic drugs without medical indication, causing intolerable side effects.

Hopefully there will be no more Hutschneckers to purify our society along with carbon emissions. As previously discussed, this was considered in the Nixon administration's formal request of our nation's top health authorities to consider giving every child a Rorschach to predict delinquency, thus providing cause for removal from family and home to be sent for corrective action under preventive detention in special camps. Other than states' authority to periodically screen drivers for their health and ability to safely operate their vehicles, widespread invasive intrusive surveillance of private citizens' lives in this country is against the law and not permitted, although recent disclosures regarding National Security Agency (NSA) surveillance via telephone and the Internet seem to belie Fourth Amendment protections. This constitutional protection, therefore, makes it of utmost importance to use opportunities presenting the state to examine certain individuals when they do cross the line, whether detained for emergency prevention of threatened violence or clear violation of the law, as in probable cause for arrest.

Marvin Wolfgang's prospective study of 10,000 male children through adolescence and into early adulthood discovered that half of this cohort would be arrested once. There appeared to be a progressive, quantitative cut for further arrests. Although never studied for correlation, a highly suggestive parallel trend is observable in children with well-diagnosed attention deficit disorder (ADD). One half of these children will be arrested once and then half of them rearrested. There were no differences found between those arrested and normal controls, but there was significant difference between those rearrested, as they were predominantly from lower socioeconomic class. There are no studies to determine if these cohorts of arrests and rearrests are similar in any way to Wolfgang's studies, other than increasing percentages of poor minorities with multiple arrests, as was the case in rearrests for attention deficit-hyperactivity disorder (ADHD). It would be both intriguing and valuable to find out, because ADHD does have reliable clinical signs relatively easy to detect in school settings with teacher and parent rating scales of behaviors that can be computer scored (Figure 16.4).

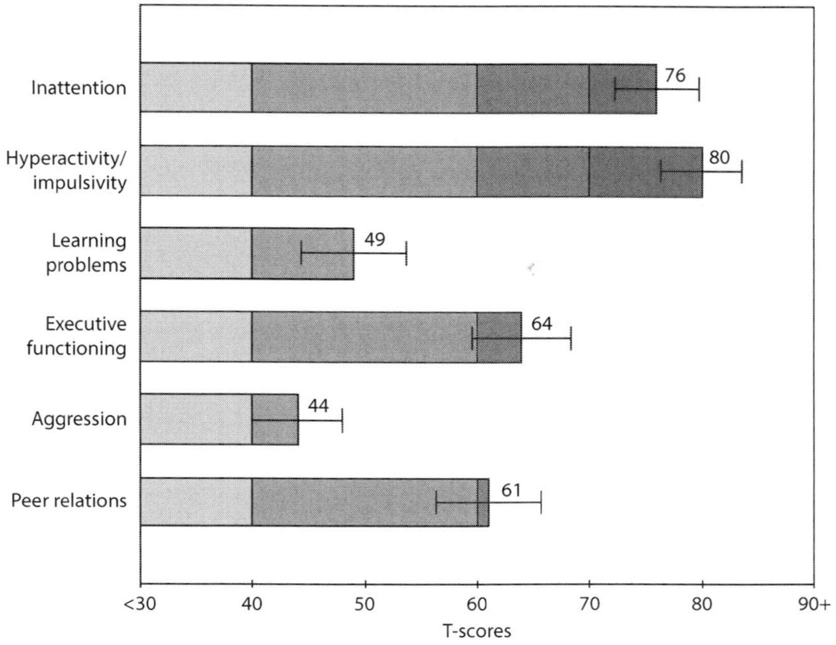


Figure 16.4 ADHD testing. (From Conners. *Conners Comprehensive Behavior Rating Scales™ (Conners CBRS).* 3rd Edition. Copyright © 2008 Multi-Health Systems. Reproduced with Permission from MHS.)

Wolfgang convincingly demonstrated that effective diagnostics were not economical until the third offense. With knowledge of similar progression in ADHD, the third offense, therefore, would be the most economical point of detecting and possibly diagnosing correctible psychopathology and neuropsychiatric deficits predictive of future antisocial behaviors. ADD oftentimes has considerable comorbidity, such as conduct disorder, whether socialized in gangs or nonsocialized in solo antisocial behaviors. Family therapy can reduce severity of conduct disorder, but too infrequently is ordered for children called "delinquents"; they are ultimately declined due to severity of their offenses, as in the previously reported Baltimore scandal, and then labeled "felons," regardless of their age. ADHD is also frequently associated with debilitating learning disabilities and substance abuse that guarantee failure in school but, with remedial attention, can facilitate graduation from high school and further educational programs that enhance both adult careers and reduce risk for incarceration.

Only a small percentage of antisocial acts in our society are trapped by arrest. Fewer are trapped by convictions or pleadings of guilt. Therefore, it is critically important to invest in evaluation when that third offense does present, as it did with Kazmierczak, before he required commitment for serious mental illness as a ward of the state of Illinois while a high school student, and then was permitted to acquire expert combat skills in the military and as a corrections officer. When Kazmierczak's teachers did detect failure to perform at his expected level in school on two occasions, nothing was done, other than to give his parents a booklet on learning disabilities. Had Kazmierczak been evaluated by a clinical psychologist, undoubtedly severe psychopathology would have been dramatically evident via computerized Conners Testing for behaviors, Symptom Checklist (SCL-90) for emotional distress and aberrant thinking, and the MMPI that picks up deception with uniquely low or high scores through an embedded validity scale. Kazmierczak even had the rare triad of arson (planting bombs on neighbors' porches), cruelty to animals, and bedwetting, anyone minimizing the risk of homicide in young males with this full triad is flying in the face of clinical experience. But, the triad was never identified with Kazmierczak, and memorials are posthumous honor to the many promising and innocent lives taken that bloody Valentine's Day in 2008 (Figures 16.5 and 16.6).

Kazmierczak could have been identified in grade school, likely preventing multiple serious suicide attempts in high school. He certainly could have been picked up with such testing in high school, when his parents asked the school for help; this could have diverted him from his brief and disastrous military and corrections careers where he was trained to be a killer with multiple weapons that he ultimately

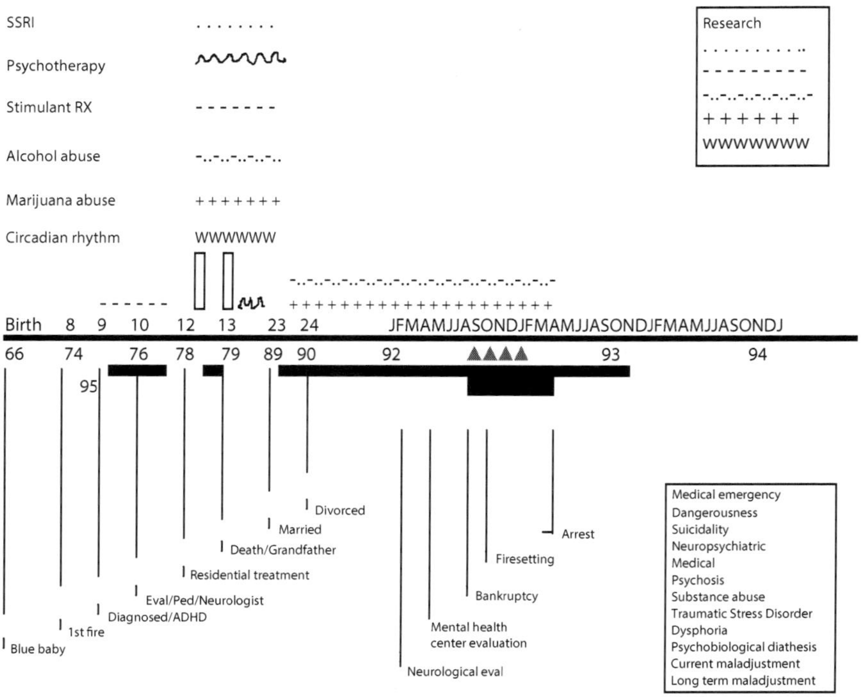


Figure 16.5 The JAL Triage Algorithm.

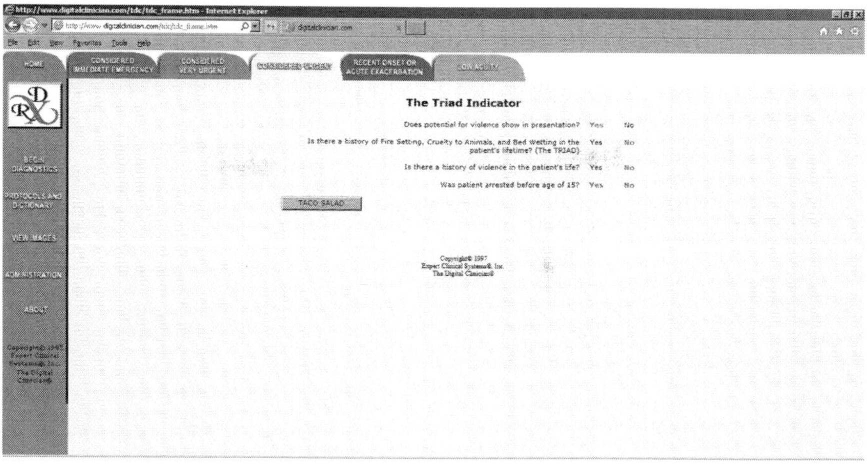


Figure 16.6 www.digitalclinician.com MAS TACO SALAD where T = Triad in assessment screening for dangerousness and suicidality.

used on helpless students in Cole Hall at Northern Illinois University, that deadliest of 2008 Valentine's days in Illinois history. Ideally in the future, genetic studies at the time of his first psychiatric hospitalization for a suicide attempt could have detected his genetic diathesis for schizoaffective disorder, ultimately diagnosed by process of elimination after multiple suicides and nearly fatal violent incidents of ambushing cars with a pellet gun and planting explosives on a neighbor's porch. There is suggestive evidence for genetic testing that identifies a patient's need for the psychotropic medication Clozapine.

> Brain-derived neurotropic factor (BDNF) is involved in the development of the brain, and likely influences the neuroplasticity in schizophrenia. BDNF is also believed to interact with other neurotransmitter systems implicated in schizophrenia, such as dopamine, glutamate, serotonin and GABA. Therefore, BDNF is a candidate gene for schizophrenia. ..., different drugs have been reported to have different effects on BDNF protein levels. A cross-sectional survey revealed that serum BDNF levels in chronic schizophrenic patients treated with clozapine exceeded those of patients treated with risperidone or with typical antipsychotics. (Huang 2013)

Clozapine was in fact the drug Kazmierczak ultimately was prescribed for schizoaffective disorder, a robustly genetically transmitted neuropsychiatric disease. Although he was nonadherent with this medication, court-ordered assisted treatment could have required and accurately monitored his adherence. This could have been of great value in translational research, too, particularly were personalized medicine advanced enough to match his genetic vulnerability to the disease to a brain-derived NGF deficiency likely causing his extreme vulnerability to paranoid and disorganized thought, along with wide mood swings. These signs, obviously recognized by psychiatrists in high school, are the signature of this disease. Indeed, there are side effects from Clozapine, even lethal adverse reactions that require routine blood counts for the very uncommon depression of white blood cells providing humans with immunity to disease. All drugs have their cost in risks and side effects, which must be balanced. In this case Kazmierczak's suicidality was known to be extreme, with four unsuccessful attempts in high school alone. The last known attempt was successful at Northern Illinois University (NIU) when he took his own life and shot 25 students and faculty, five of whom died.

For purposes of understanding the true damages of such suicidal rampage shootings in this country, however, it must be remembered that besides those injured and physically disabled for life, the loved ones, and those simply exposed to the murder and mayhem will have a 100% lifetime incidence of PTSD (Rynearson 1987).

The disability, therefore, is far, far greater than the numbers cited. Such suicidal rampage murders have a ripple effect across generations and upon the lives of victims' families, as well as upon survivors and their families—thus the importance of this index case from the 2008 NIU massacre. There were so many points where this seriously impaired young man could have been accurately diagnosed and maintained in court-ordered assisted treatment, likely with Clozapine supported—at least some day—by personalized medicine to detect his neuropsychiatric genetic predisposition to the suicidality and paranoia intrinsic to this disease. Ultimately he slipped through the public psychiatric system as a ward of the state in high school, military psychiatry at Fort Sill, and University of Illinois Health Services Psychiatry in Champagne/Urbana during grad school. None of these institutions had full knowledge of the cumulative data on Steven Kazmierczak until it was too late, with many dead—including him, and many more injured and disabled for life. Opportunities, therefore, are rare for valid diagnosis leading to effective treatment. In this case, he likely had a valid diagnosis in high school that led to effective treatment, but it was way too easy for him to get off of it. Nonadherence and denial of illness are part of the neuropsychiatric impairment in psychotic illnesses due to anosognosia, a defective functional deficit in the parietal lobe region of the brain necessary for our own detection of being well or disabled.

Opportunities for legal intervention in secondary prevention for earliest possible identification of progressive neuropsychiatric impairment, therefore, are not frequent and continuous. Kazmierczak is the classic example of one seriously impaired and whose disease reportedly only popped into view on occasion. Unfortunately, due to anosognosia, the patient himself may consider himself sick at the earliest stage, as did Aguilar, the suicidal rampage shooter in the Columbia Mall. But, if the disease is not trapped with valid diagnosis to inform and allow earliest intervention, the patient deteriorates and ultimately lives in the cocoon of self-deception and delusion.

Jared Loughner, for example, went before a judge three times for antisocial behavior as a juvenile. This should have informed the court of Wolfgang's classical research and conclusions. But his progressive disease was missed over and over again when there were opportunities to intervene. His behavior on campus at Pima College was so disruptive that he should have at least been charged more times. Maybe with a dozen appearances in Pima County Court a judge would have discovered his severe impairment and ordered a diagnostic workup that led to treatment with antipsychotic medication. Unfortunately, despite good access to inpatient psychiatric care at Kino/UAZ Hospital (Banner University Health Center-South) in Tucson from Pima College health and security services, his psychosis was not identified, even when it was detected, and there is a difference. Detection led to suspension. Identification should have led to voluntary or involuntary commitment to the large and relatively good psychiatric services of the local county psychiatric facility instead of, like the army's ultimate disposition of Kazmierczak, simply dumping him on his parents' doorstep. In the case of Jared Loughner, Pima College ignored its own testimonials for providing liaison services for its student with all necessary community health and social services. Not once, however, was he offered such liaison services, so uniquely available in the city of Tucson (Liebert and Birnes 2014).

The authors believe that the official and clinical Pima College and Illinois University encounters with suicidal mass murderers having robust histories of serious mental illness, although not officially identified with Loughner, should inform boards of trustees of higher education on the legal and successful means for avoiding another Virginia Tech and NIU massacre on their campuses. The policies and procedures of both Pima County Court and Community College fueled such extended duration of untreated psychosis that a massacre occurred at the Tucson Safeway Plaza. Loughner's statement on the record during the opportunistic moment of mental lucidity to get a guilty plea is proof of what could have been accomplished medically before the shooting. Having been diagnosed for the first time with schizophrenia following the Safeway Plaza suicidal rampage murder, the judge ordered that he be administered an antipsychotic medication in federal prison. His psychosis cleared, and he said that had he been on this medication years earlier he would not have committed this massacre. Even as Gabrielle Giffords tours the country on behalf of gun safety and preventing violence, perhaps Loughner himself could be a more effective spokesman for secondary prevention and early detection of the suicidal psychotic collapse in the adolescent and young adult. His relative normalcy following treatment with an antipsychotic medication is the strongest testimony to date for enhancing public health surveillance for suicidality and psychosis with dangerousness—particularly in our schools and campuses of higher education (Liebert and Birnes 2014).

Since the Virginia Tech massacre, suicidal rampage murders have become epidemic—particularly in schools and college campuses. Many, many millions have been spent on memorials in their wake. The president or first lady have traveled to three of them including Loughner's Tucson Safeway massacre, the Sandy Hook Elementary School suicidal mass murder by Adam Lanza, and the Sikh Temple suicidal mass murder by Wade Page in Milwaukee County. Memorials are a posthumous honor, serving the living more than the dead (Liebert and Birnes 2011a). It would have been far better had those committing suicide/murders been diagnosed and treated, or at least sequestered until treatment, so that there would have been no victims to honor. Instead the many millions of dollars for such memorials need to be invested in both primary and secondary prevention of suicide and violence, the number 8 and number 16 leading causes of death in this country, respectively—and likely way underreported.

Practically speaking, what can be done in a free and open society based on the rule of law for purposes of prevention, especially in light of our constitutional protections of privacy and due process? This is the essential conflict between constitutional protections and the need for preventive medical intervention. The simple arguments right now concerning mandatory vaccinations are an example. Does the government have the authority to require all children to be vaccinated, even over the parents' objections? Does a governor have the authority *sui sponte* to order the mandatory quarantine of a private citizen because the governor believes that person may have been exposed to an infectious disease and is a carrier of that disease? Where is the red line drawn between protecting an individual's right against arbitrary search and seizure and for due process and the need for government to protect the public from disease, even if that disease is a mental illness that can cause dangerous behavior? This is a discussion that will come to dominate medicine and public policy over the next decade as suicidal mass murder rampages become even more prevalent.

There are solutions when at-risk people present at various points of entry to our polymorphous health-care system, having such heterogeneous and multiple points of entry. For example, most women are murdered or seriously injured by intimate partner violence. Yet, the statistics of detecting early cases in the emergency room setting is poor. Injuries from domestic violence are among the most frequent of the hundreds of millions of ER visits every year. Studies show that male physicians on the average pick up domestic violence on the third visit, while female doctors pick it up much earlier on the average—more often the first visit (*Psychiatric News* 1994). Ultimately, too many of these female victims will be seriously battered or killed.

There is no excuse for this epidemiological blindness to domestic violence at points of entry to our health-care system. We are the United States fighting the medieval caliphate of ISIL in Syria and Iraq and, in the process, defending otherwise defenseless women and children from persecution and slaughter. But, what about the statistics indicating violence against those same populations at home? And because, as most law enforcement spokespersons will tell you, domestic violence calls are among the most dangerous for responding police officers, and we must find a way to protect our officers as well as the primary victims of domestic violence. The news today is far from promising; that Thin Blue Line is fading and blurring with the police being investigated for racism, while our institutions are failing all around us in their responsibilities to the sick, the children, the women, and the veterans—even the nurses caring for them being unable to care for and also protect themselves.

Let us begin at home and protect women in dangerous relationships. Even before violence occurs, marital conflict can be predictive of battering and murder in crisis counseling settings. Primary care providers need to be more observant for detecting the at-risk relationship. Frequently the female is helpless to speak out or get away. Intervention is necessary through adult protective services or child protective services earlier, rather than later. The case of Timothy Jorden in Buffalo, New York, details the professional blindness to a man losing it over narcissistic injury from rejection in love and, as a result, killing both himself and his ex-lover (Liebert and Birnes 2013). Does any academic department of emergency medicine, therefore, address this known disparity in diagnostic blindness and teach male trainees how to recognize and diagnose intimate partner violence before it progresses to murder—even familicide and suicidal mass murder?

Adam Lanza began his suicidal rampage murder in domestic violence when he became psychotically incommunicado with his mother. Hiding behind his computer screen in a room with the shades drawn and only messaging his mother via e-mail was a disaster waiting to happen. Yet, Nancy Lanza, his mother at her wits' end, had no means to reach him and became his first homicide victim before he drove to Sandy Hook Elementary to commit mass murder. Was there a way to use Adam's own obsessive use of his avatar-based computer gaming preoccupation to communicate with him via a channel he understood and appreciated? That may have been a viable form of intervention, but nobody to this day is focused on how this young man deteriorated, like Cho, before the eyes of school staff, school psychologists, and private therapists of unknown credentials and even University of Connecticut faculty and staff. The civil action by surviving parents of this needless massacre of children is going after the manufacturer of assault rifles, a likely fruitless pursuit even under the legal standard for the manufacture of dangerous products because the gun lobby has successfully pushed through legislation in a number of states to protect gun manufacturers. Worse, in some states, unsuccessful plaintiffs in suits against gun manufacturers must bear the defendants' cost of defense when state laws protect weapons manufacturers from lawsuits and require plaintiffs to pay for the gun manufacturers' legal costs.

Although a worthy cause in and of itself, the case of Adam Lanza, just like Eddie Routh posttrial for double homicide in the case of the American Sniper, cries out for better secondary prevention when clear and convincing evidence of dangerous psychosis is so overwhelming. In both cases, intensive case management with psychotherapy and antipsychotic medication, whether inpatient or outpatient, voluntary or involuntary under assisted treatment, were deferred. Some reckless shooting range therapy was allowed, if not actually prescribed. This all but guaranteed to get people killed—a lot of them, including now the lives of the patients, whether by self-inflicted bullet to the head, as in the case of Lanza, or life without parole, in the case of Eddie Routh (Liebert and Birnes 2014).

Pre-employment screening and better surveillance for circumstances conducive to workplace violence need to be instituted. Alton Nolen aggressively tried to convert employees in Moore, Oklahoma, before going on a rampage of beheading them. It was fortuitous that his massacre was limited to one beheading, because he was shot by his manager, a reserve deputy police officer. Is proselytizing a religion for the purposes of converting friends and coworkers illegal in this country? Of course it is not. But is there a legal line between proselytizing and forceful conversion? Yes. Nolen had recently been released from prison, and certainly his personality change and radical conversion must have been observed by corrections staff. Yet he obtained an early release which will be hard for the state Department of Corrections to both explain and justify. Workplace violence is increasingly serious as an occupational and public health problem; ironically, ERs themselves are the second most dangerous place to work in this country, second only to mines (Liebert and Klauer 2013).

The evidence of yet another school shooting, this time in Marysville outside of Seattle by Jaylen Fryberg, a member of a Native American tribe, reminds us yet again, that for all the superior health care in the United States, we still have no mechanism for preventive community emergency psychiatric care. Fryberg even shot his own cousins because, he tweeted, his cousin stole his girlfriend. We do not recognize the red flags, ignore troubling signs of dangerous behavior, and mostly look the other way when the at-risk and person acting strangely is someone we know or a family member. In the school setting, oftentimes the first response to disruptive and threatening behavior is suspension, as in the case of Fryberg after he assaulted another student and Loughner after displaying continuously alarming behavior. This might be followed, as appears to have been the case with Fryberg, with a visit to a hospital emergency room, which is poorly staffed and configured for the psychiatric patient.

Law enforcement, too, is often a first responder to psychiatric emergencies, although all too often the police, as a result of their training and current criminalization of serious mental illness, assess the mentally ill acting strangely as violators and not sick. This was the scenario causing the suicidal mass murder by Elliot Rodger at University of California, Santa Barbara, wherein the family's concerns about his violence were left to a police officer to judge. Police officers are not trained to examine psychotic people and determine their future behaviors, even those police, as in the Los Angeles Police Department (LAPD), who are trained in dealing with the mentally ill. That is the job of psychiatrists in selecting treatments most likely to reduce impairment—in this case suicidal mass murder, killing many and impairing even many, many more. As Donald Klein stated, "for what use diagnosis if it does not predict outcomes from treatment?" (Klein 1993). And, so neglect of this warning caused the deaths of many helpless students and the suicidal, psychotic Elliot Rodger who clearly met probable cause standards of a 5150 preventive detention at Ventura/UCLA Medical Center.

The ER is a primary focus of secondary prevention, because that is where many emergency psychiatric patients are transported. The paradigm shift of emergency medicine's optimizing patient throughput away from initial triaging to bedding immediately all ER patients without option for diversion, reinforces ER clinicians' needs to understand and appreciate the concepts of "time-determined" and "epidemiologically informed" clinical decision making. This is what all clinicians do every day they practice or take call in acute care medicine—regardless of clinical discipline or specialty—but they do it intuitively and learn it primarily by experience and not via formal training.

Given the throughput requirements of a modern ER, especially during a disaster such as a school campus shooting, health-care workers need to reduce their clinical decision making to the bare minimum that can be remembered for immediately saving the patient's life—then making sure they save themselves, associate staff, and others. The implementation of the ACA, although intending to broaden and ease access to primary care physicians, is by no means guaranteed to accomplish this anticipated goal and thereby reduce overcrowding and misuse of ERs for nonemergent problems. Early evidence shows paradoxically increased utilization of ER services. After all, for busy Americans, the ER is one-stop shopping that requires by Emergency Medical Treatment and Labor Act (EMTALA) the examination by a physician. So, initially, we discover an increasing shortage and maldistribution of primary care physicians with concomitant increase in demand for their services. Wait-times for appointments will likely increase, regardless of increased insurance coverage of our population. Those who chose to pay the fine or tax under the ACA and do not qualify for extended Medicaid will probably utilize the ER for primary care even though they know they are nonemergent. Such a result to the new legislation portends such paradoxical overutilization of ERs, counter to the intent of the law. The federal government's own medical insurance for military dependents encourages such overutilization by paying 100% for ER evaluations and almost nothing for psychiatric evaluations. Who is in charge here? Where are we being led by the very authorities initiating massive change in the health-care system?

We saw in the Thomas Duncan case that, in these modern times of instant global communications and travel, failed first encounters with unknown patients can lead to an epidemic, whether one of extreme contagiousness, or nearly as calamitous, national hysteria. In our lean engineered health-care assembly lines of today, where inpatient time is money—whether length of stay (LOS) is short and likely profitable, or long and guaranteed unprofitable—there is push from hospital administration to move patients fast by either admitting them or discharging them. Time is money, as cost-plus contracts with insurance companies to temporize and see how patients do over time become vestiges of another era. Finally, for those accustomed to immediate care via the ER, where they are guaranteed to see an MD under federal EMTALA law, we simply do not know what any population of newly insured patients is going to do with improved access to routine acute and chronic outpatient care. It is wise, therefore, to plan for the paradoxical collision course of financial pressures to increase patient flow through the ER with actual increasing demand for emergency services for nonemergent care.

## TERTIARY PREVENTION: TRIAGE AS PREVENTION

Triage is time-determined and epidemiologically informed clinical decision making in both first encounters with unknown patients and mass casualty incidents (MCIs). We know that primary prevention is keeping them from falling off a bridge. Secondary prevention is detecting them after they drop off the bridge.

Tertiary prevention is salvaging people before they flow under the last bridge and drown at sea. As discussed, primary prevention for neuropsychiatry, although holding great promise in preventing serious mental illness is in its embryonic stage of development. Secondary prevention is better. At all the sites discussed in this book, ultimately lethal psychopathology emitted strong signals that should have informed clinicians, security, and first responders of inevitable calamity to come. Tertiary prevention is treating those detected, identified, and diagnosed with neuropsychiatric illness to prevent progressions of clinical states of unremitting human destructiveness to suicide, murder, and mayhem. Similarly with medical-surgical illness, tertiary prevention is selection and clinical intervention with medications, radiation, or surgery having the best evidence base for reducing disability or effecting remission in treatment and recovery after it.

Under tertiary prevention, time-determined clinical decision making is who gets worked up and treated first, how and for how long, based on severity and "safe time" for waiting to clinically intervene, whether diagnostically or therapeutically. Epidemiologically informed clinical decision making is based on likelihood of occurrence of injuries and illnesses. Today, ER sites are informed for Ebola infection. Therefore, the issue that confronts our changing emergency health-care system is time. It is all about time—the time every patient spends in the ER waiting for evaluation and treatment and the time it will take for the emergency health-care system to ramp up to handle the increased load under the ACA. It has already failed its first test in the Thomas Duncan Ebola case just as law enforcement intervention for involuntary commitment failed in the Elliot Rodger case in California.

It has been shown that clinicians lack necessary information for clinical decision making during every day of their practice. This argues for utilization of computerized clinical decision support systems (CDSS) increasingly embedded in the electronic medical record. By definition, however, rapid assessment in emergency medicine does not allow time for depending on accessory sources of information. The electronic health record at Texas Health Presbyterian Hospital proved to be more an obstruction to timely and effective care than supportive and enabling. It is, therefore, necessary to embed some rules and clearly reduced clinical protocols into the best system of artificial intelligence yet discovered—the experience and expertise of the diagnosing clinician. And, because his or her clinical assessment within first encounters will almost exclusively be with the unknown or unremembered patient, it is important to judge the time frame that is safe for definitive intervention.

In emergency medicine, one needs to replicate at least one of those varied, yet seamless, ER racks of intake presentation-based templates within the front of one's brain, i.e., "Truncal Injury," "Altered Mental Status," or "Violence." Such templates match the broadest of our diagnostic spectrum, usually falling far short of codable specificity of syndromic diagnostics—i.e., chest pain or vomiting—too nonspecific, sensitive, and all-inclusive diagnostically to constructively drive any specific intervention, such as ordering a magnetic resonance imaging (MRI) scan or billing an insurance company for reimbursement of time spent and services rendered. The longer one judges the safety margin for time of definitive intervention, the more specific should be the diagnosis. A common example in ERs is differentiating between a panic attack and chest pain from heart attacks. Both can be lethal without appropriate treatment, and cardiology examinations are very expensive. The differential diagnosis of coronary artery disease and panic attacks in the ER is one of the most serious problems facing emergency medicine today. Repeat examination of the psychiatric patient for cardiac pathology is prohibitively expensive and counterproductive, yet premature diagnostic closure in the presentation of chest pain can mean discharging the patient to a certain lethal fate.

Furthermore, because pathophysiology is rarely stable, a patient's clinical status from initial point of entry through definitive interventions and discharge is rarely static and almost always fluid, thus subject to reassessment (www.digitalclinician.com). The time for intervention in an actual nonurgent presentation should always be expected to change, demanding reassessment. And, reassessment may be infrequent, yet unanticipated, or it may be continuous. But, the margin of safety for judging time for definitive intervention cannot be selectively lengthened for real emergency and very urgent presentations at any time or for any patient for purposes of optimizing patient flow and running "lean." Somebody could die or be maimed for life. Nature controls pathophysiology, not computerized lean engineered solutions for optimizing patient flow, although these can help. Therefore, the clinician must be responsible for the former while utilizing the latter as thoughtfully as possible. The computer is a tool for the physician and not a robotic clinician that, were it not for Luddite doctors, can reduce fatal medical errors.

For rapid assessment, clinicians must also work smart, knowing the likelihood of certain presentations at their sites. This is epidemiologically informed clinical decision making, which doctors do all of the time when either practicing or on call. Doctors and evaluating nurses must know what are the most likely causes for certain types of presentations at their respective sites. To illustrate "epidemiologically informed" in most reduced form, one only has to say the obvious: ER staff need not overthink about scorpion bites in Seattle but must in Phoenix. Epidemiologically informed clinical decision making is site dependent. Therefore, it has also become time dependent following the events of 9/11, as first alerts of terrorism may be both an acute medical presentation like cutaneous anthrax, and therefore related to the vigilance of color-coded alerts of homeland security, rather than those of emergency medicine (Liebert and Birnes 2011b).

Rapid assessment is therefore all about time and likelihood. That means it is all about immediate clinical decision making with diagnostic validity to predict treatment outcomes rather than perseverative coding predicting little more than clinical chronicity or prompter reimbursement. Diagnostic coding for purposes of coding to effect prompt and reliable reimbursement should be reserved for later with the discharge diagnoses. Being on the frontline of acute care medicine, clinicians find the validity of interventions is more in the public spotlight. Emergency rooms are way overexposed to and unprotected from the utilization review crisis caused by their being the primary care point of entry to the healthcare systems for a large percentage of our population, while simultaneously pressured to clear the beds in preparation for anything and everything that can go wrong, such as the Boston bombings or a catastrophic multivictim campus or workplace shooting.

A dramatic report from one Texas hospital highlights the crisis of overutilization of ERs by the wrong patients. The report cites that just nine patients accounted for almost 2700 ER visits from 2003 to 2009, with the majority of those visits resulting from drug abuse and mental illness. The taxpayers in Texas footed the bill. This story out of Texas is likely more the norm for metropolitan ERs nationwide and not just a statistical fluke. Therefore, as more patients can be expected to enter our ERs and be taken back to keep the waiting room clear, whoever is assigned to initial rapid assessment must think fast and first categorize patients. An iconic image like this must light up the frontal lobes of anyone responsible for rapid assessment in this new era of optimizing patient flow in and out of the ER (see Figure 3.1, the red zone of www.digitalclinician.com).

Saving lives by knowing the ABCDE of Emergency Triage is critical, but believing that neuropsychiatric patients simply should not be queueing in the same line as those clearly medical and surgical is counterproductive and potentially lethal. Regardless of the numbers, neuropsychiatric patients are coming to ERs, and they will be coming in large numbers for as far out in the future as one can see. There is no other place for them to get medical care, because the states have shut down hospitals for the seriously mentally ill and the federal government has gutted the community mental health system of the last century.

One must question the perception of the public health crisis caused by ignoring the needs of many millions of seriously impaired neuropsychiatric patients. These encounters, as we have seen, occur on the street in Los Angeles; in social media, where students are shocked by threats of suicide and or violence in Marysville, Washington; at parole hearings with profound personality changes, such as conversion to jihadism in an Oklahoma prison; with guards subduing the hallucinating psychotic yelling back at his voices in a jail cell at Rikers Island; when neighbors are awakened by illumination of their entire neighborhood to prevent an imagined enemy's penetration of the wire in Kileen, Texas; when supervisors confront the worker actively proselytizing Islamofascist beliefs in Moore, Oklahoma; and when ER nurses are assaulted just about anywhere and every day in this country.

The existentialism of whether there is such a thing as mental illness or what psychiatrists should diagnose as mental disorders must be left to philosophy classes if we are to really be epidemiologically informed at points of entry to our health-care system, especially those not considered within the scope of health reform legislation—i.e., jails and field interrogations by police officers. Whether such a thing as mental illness exists or not should not be the key question asked at a point of entry into the emergency medical system. Treating the patient is the key issue. The most seriously impaired patient is unlikely to be at home. The family is either exhausted or afraid of him, as was the tragic opening of the final scene to the double homicide of the American Sniper (Liebert and Birnes 2014). The vast majority of patients in need, as was Eddie Routh over and over again, are not in a licensed medical or nursing bed, because such beds have disappeared as fast as the need for them surges. Meanwhile some politicians, health professionals, hospitals, and the public are waiting for some policy to stop the human rights violations of neuropsychiatric patients wrongfully incarcerated in the most brutal of conditions. These conditions exist in solitary confinement at Rikers Island or in overstimulating ERs where they are not treated, but, rather, "boarded" until transfer can be arranged to an effective and secure inpatient psychiatric bed that usually exists only in the minds of health-care dreamers waiting for Godot.

NAMI's distinguished medical director, Ken Duckworth, issued its policy report entitled "Time to Commit to Policy Change, Schizophrenia," in which he declared that the "Delivery of mental health treatment is a human right." This report takes the position that human beings have a right to mental services as a form to remediate a disability. We already recognize the human right of those with physical disabilities, the report argues. Thus, we should extend our scope of rights to include those with mental health issues, also a form of disability. Imagine what this policy change would mean for correctional institutions, for county jails, and for the police on the street.

Some police departments are cognizant of the need for specially trained officers to deal with the mentally ill. LAPD Chief Charlie Beck spoke about this in the wake of a police shooting in downtown LA's skid row, where a homeless mentally ill man whose street handle was "Africa" and who had recently been released from prison on a robbery charge, was shot to death by LAPD officers during an altercation outside his gutter tent. Officers, Chief Beck said, were part of a special unit trained to deal with the mentally ill, but that they had to defend themselves when one of the rookie officers yelled out that the homeless man had taken his gun away. And in Phoenix, after another shooting death of a mentally ill individual who threatened police with a hammer, Police Chief Joseph Yahner announced new community outreach programs, which include a specialized squad, trained to deal with the mentally ill. A sergeant will be tasked to supervise officers on what Chief Yahner is calling a "Crisis Intervention Squad." These are positive developments, but, like emergency medicine physicians, there is a caveat: young people do not select either law enforcement or emergency medicine as careers to be psychiatrists, psychiatrists do. The ultimate mission, therefore, should be to get the psychiatric patients off the streets and out of the ERs and into psychiatrists' offices. That is the way it used to be. Psychiatric patients have not always been boarded in our gutters and ERs. This is a new phenomenon, one that requires clear and decisive action from government. Local communities like San Antonio are starting to carve out new community mental health centers from the rubble of the past, because the ER doctors cannot take care of emergencies and trauma cases while replacing state hospital psychiatrists at the same time. And cities in Florida, which has a large homeless population, have engaged outside contractors to construct a form of "come and go as you please" homeless camps where homeless people can seek shelter with no questions asked.

The president has advocated for doctors accepting higher volume patient flows and higher administrative costs, but he is doing so without relief of capping malpractice awards by tort reform because, he stated, malpractice claims will assuredly be reduced with modern tools to enhance their skills. Presumably these tools are embedded in the ACA and stimulus package funding health-care information technology (IT) research and development (R&D) with $20 billion of awards. We have seen the fallacy of this grand strategy proselytized to the American Medical Association with the launch of the Affordable Care Act (see Obama AMA speech: full video, full text at www.huffingtonpost.com/2009/06/15/obama-ama-speech-full-tex_n_215699.html).

These tools are digitalized medical records, prematurely promoted and sold as solutions in their infancy. Texas Health Presbyterian Hospital's Electronic Medical Record either caused or obstructed in the failed diagnosis and treatment of Thomas Duncan. It was allegedly one of the best, tailored to hospitals' needs. With 1400 pages of documentation from an unknown number of clinicians caring for one patient, the question must be raised: how was this helpful in either informing best practices for time-determined and epidemiologically informed clinical decision making? The answer is sobering after the president's upbeat address to an audience of practicing physicians. It was not helpful at all in any way, other than as a ghost digital recording of inchoate staff communications in their failure to follow standard practices of Emergency Medicine Triage and catastrophic proof that robotic medicine is not even close to being here yet.

Billions have been wasted, and billions more will be wasted, because companies producing medical software have succeeded far greater in lobbying government and selling to hospital CIOs than they have in R&D. It is time for the Food and Drug Administration (FDA) to get in the ring with them before impacting clinical practices—even influencing them—from computer software purchased without input from those most controlled by it, clinicians, which is the law with drug treatments approved by the FDA.

Tort reform and, thus, capping malpractice awards by statute is also championed by self-described health reformers. But, tort reform notwithstanding, from a trial lawyer's perspective, how does one value the life of a Joan Rivers? Here, in the wake of her death in an endoscopy clinic in New York, facts coming to light thus far point to a lack of patient consent for a biopsy, a question regarding the medical license of the practitioner, and a possible delay in transporting Rivers to a trauma center for resuscitation after cardiac arrest. Admittedly, the facts have not yet come to light at trial, whether in a malpractice suit, a wrongful death suit, or even in a suit for battery because of nonconsensual touching, touching exceeding the consent signed by the patient. But we can be sure those facts will come to light if there is no settlement prior to trial. However, in valuing the life of the decedent for settlement or judgment, what metrics can be applied? Do we look at the projected income from the E network's Red Carpet telecasts each year? How about Joan's *Fashion Police* series? Was she contemplating more sales appearances on QVC with her line of jewelry or more nightclub engagements or television appearances? And was she planning to write another book? How do these potential events, some ongoing, some projected, factor in to a settlement under tort reform? Capping medical malpractice awards under the euphemistic term, "reform" is not as easy as it sounds, is it? Nor is it a catchall remedy. It is a means of recruitment of doctors to states having shortages and states like California having rebellion in their medical ranks. For the cold winter state of Wisconsin, recruiters' phones stopped ringing when the state supreme court ruled that capping malpractice was unconstitutional.

## TERTIARY PREVENTION OF NEUROPSYCHIATRIC DISORDERS BECOMING DEADLY

When confronted with an epidemic, our health-care system does not seem to respond rapidly enough for primary and secondary prevention. We still cannot eradicate the highly lethal virus of AIDS or Ebola, but treatments came fast, fast enough to save many lives. For that 22% of our population seriously impaired by psychiatric disorders, the treatments are not accepted as effective or made accessible as in the cases of serious contagious diseases, strokes, heart attacks, trauma care, or cancer. Nonetheless, psychotropic medication and psychotherapy both have significant bodies of literature for interrupting progression of the course of neuropsychiatric illness, whether antidepressants and mood stabilizers for mood disorders; antipsychotics for schizophrenia and other psychotic disorders, such as bipolar affective disorder; or tranquilizers for panic attacks, PTSD, emergency agitation, some disturbances of consciousness, and severe anxiety. Cautious use of sedatives for sleep disorders and, similarly, the same in the case of stimulants with ADD is merciful and likely restorative of overall health in allaying the suffering from insomnia and distractibility, respectively. Both chronic insomnia and distractibility come with debilitating comorbidity, oftentimes promising serious psychosocial consequences, such as increased risk of accidents, delinquency, and suicide. Some psychiatrists are skilled and prefer to provide psychotherapy and psychotropics by themselves, whereas some prefer collaborative therapy, coordinating their medication management with a psychotherapist.

There are many variants of psychotherapies, and no size fits all. Conduct-disordered children usually require family therapy to help parents support and set limits on impulse disordered children, whether medicated for ADD or not medicated. It works too, but these children and families are too often deprived or unaware of this modality of treatment of impulse disorders—particularly self-harm, such as cutting, and assaultiveness. Similarly, the families of patients released from hospitals following their first psychotic breaks need supportive therapy for their returning loved one. There is significant evidence that the high expressed emotion (HEE) family milieu that is critical of the returning psychotic patient usually portends relapse that could result in suicide and/or violence if not rehospitalized. The evidence is convincing that hospitalization does not prevent ultimate completed suicides, although it may prevent it from occurring during the hospitalization. The evidence is equally convincing that partial daycare for the seriously mentally ill and chronically suicidal patient is effective in reducing suicide risk. For now, however, this point is a moot one. We have neither. When and if rebuilding the community mental health system from the rubble left by governors, federal officials, and politicians alike, it will be wise to look at the evidence. Emergency hospitalization with discharge to the gutters does not prevent suicides; prevention is far more complicated and expensive. To say suicide is a moral decision is reiterating the conviction from another era too, as well as from a theory base that obfuscates the reasoning of good medical practice.

A walk through Williamsburg, Virginia, is as enlightening as a visit to one's state department of social and health services, although the stocks and pillories are absent from our streets. Such social consensus, regressed to Colonial social attitudes toward the mentally ill, is extremely confining. Benjamin Rush, the recognized founder of American psychiatry, was morally outraged by the institution of slavery, but he thought that slaves had a disease that pigmented their skins. His solution to this nation's legacy from the horrors of slavery was to depigment freed slaves, thus curing them of their disease of being black. Obviously, policies and procedures for morally and philosophically charged issues of mental illness—like race—must be examined in context. We cannot find schizophrenia on a brain scan today. What will happen—perhaps decades from now—when it is clearly and reliably visible? The social context of psychiatric diagnostics will change, just as did race relations when being black became a normal human state. That was not so long ago either. Rush, as we all are, was shaped in large part by both knowledge and social consensus.

With this in mind, the question that must be asked for tertiary prevention is, what could have been done to pick up the bodies in cases we presented above before they flowed to the sea of suicide and murder? Seung-Hui Cho was rescued very late in the course of his psychotic deterioration in paranoid schizophrenia. His duration of untreated psychosis was probably the most neglected of cases we have presented. He presented at the Virginia Tech counseling center as ordered by the hearing officer following emergency detention at St. Albans, but he had been discharged with the ambiguous two-headed monstrous diagnoses of serious mental illness by a psychologist (not specified as to what type and not even an accepted diagnosis, but rather a lay term) and depression NOS (psychiatric diagnosis). His behavior on campus, however, was that of florid psychosis requiring antipsychotic medication. He was committed to Virginia Tech's counseling center against clinical advice of both examining psychiatrist and psychologist, but for what purpose? There was no psychiatrist at Cook Counseling Center to see him; so, he was never medicated. His treatment has been a mystery because his assessment and therapy records disappeared from Cook Counseling Center at the time of the governor's investigation of the Virginia Tech massacre. There is no doubt, however, that he showed up for assessment as ordered and was adherent with scheduled appointments. He simply was never medicated, and that is the only treatment that could have prevented the consolidation of his delusional thinking from his earliest preoccupation with Columbine in middle school to the massacre in 2007 and his bizarre, terrifying video on NBC the night after. His family was never contacted by either Cook Counseling or by the school. His parents found out about his problems at Virginia Tech the same as all of us seeing the apocalyptic image of a Korean warrior proclaiming his final stand against a world of persecution. In fact, there is little evidence of persecution in his entire childhood and young adult history. It was Cho's paranoia. His parents naturally were devastated and said that the hospital or university should have called them. They knew nothing. They would have simply come to Blacksburg, picked him up, taken him home, and obtained treatment for him. They had done that before in middle school and should have been considered reliable again to have done it again. Cho had been in psychiatric treatment in childhood and was adherent with his appointments and taking medication that did help him. He likely would have been adherent again had the parents not been excluded from the fragmented and unskilled circle of clinical supervision at Virginia Tech by raising insubstantial claims of protecting Cho's privacy (Liebert and Birnes 2011a,b).

Like Cho, Adam Lanza should have been intensively case managed and medicated with antipsychotics instead of being nursed at Sandy Hook to prevent bullying while walking with his back to the lockers, clutching his computer, and later cast adrift as a precocious college student from Southwestern Connecticut University. His father has said that his son was underdiagnosed. Were that true, in fact preventing intensive case management with supervised antipsychotic medication or inpatient psychiatric care, the Sandy Hook massacre is simply one more marquee case of failed diagnostics leading to oversimplified treatment and case management, leading inevitably to no case management or treatment. The only person who had the answers to the fatal errors in Adam Lanza's treatment and case management met the same fate as computers and cell phones containing secrets. Adam destroyed all of them, including her, leaving investigators to only guess what went wrong in the Sandy Hook Elementary School suicidal rampage murders (Liebert and Birnes 2014).

Most egregious were the fates of James Holmes and the other victims of the Aurora Theater massacre. He demonstrated the classical deterioration of schizophrenia at typical age of onset in his early twenties. His first graduate neuroscience professor at Scripps Institute commented on his negativity and inability to function anywhere near the capabilities later rewarded with a rare graduate PhD scholarship from the National Institutes of Health (NIH). This neuroscience professor was already complaining of a personality change never noted before in either high school or college. He was captain of his high school soccer team. His deterioration would continue progressively, as is typical of schizophrenia, at University of Colorado until he was either forced to seek treatment at the student health center or did so on his own. His treatment, as in the case of Cho, is murky at this college counseling center, although he did see a psychiatrist and likely was prescribed medication, as was Adam Lanza. Again, however, there was no case management. None of these patients were adherent with prescribed medication, nor did they have case management following identification of serious mental illness on campus. In fact, by the time James Holmes showed up for his final oral exam and flunked, he was already deep into the planning of his suicidal rampage murder in Aurora. Any slender thread he had with the university counseling center, however, was abruptly cut when simply flunked out of grad school without any follow-up treatment, his access to any therapy on campus terminated with removal of his access to campus (Liebert and Birnes 2014).

Because it is argued in academia that behavior cannot be predicted, the university psychiatrist did not believe he could be involuntarily committed. His neuroscience professors, however, had no problems in predicting his future behavior far, far into the future. They told him, after such a stellar academic career, to find a different career after failing one oral examination. That is certainly a dire and likely deadly prediction to make for a graduate student in state of mental decompensation from malignant neuropsychiatric decompensation, the very field of their own expertise (Liebert and Birnes 2014).

Loughner was never medically evaluated, despite many opportunities before the judiciary for juvenile offenses, failure of military enlistment examination, and grossly psychotic behavior on the campus of Pima College, one of the largest community colleges in the nation. After his suicidal rampage murder in Tucson, he finally was diagnosed with schizophrenia and treated with antipsychotic medication. Not only did he clear enough from his florid psychosis to plead guilty in lieu of the death penalty, relieving authorities by muting a public scandal for the State of Arizona with potential for generating the same civil lawsuits as occurred in the wake of the Virginia Tech massacre, but he went on the court record asserting he would never have committed the Tucson Safeway massacre had he taken the antipsychotic prescribed for him in prison, finally offered or forced on him after the fact in federal prison (Liebert and Birnes 2014).

Steven Kazmierczak was likely diagnosed correctly with schizoaffective disorder in high school and treated with a mood stabilizer and antipsychotic, Clozapine, that could have maintained his sanity at least adequately to have prevented the Northern Illinois University suicidal mass murder at Cole Hall. Like Adam Lanza, however, he was allowed to control his own fate when he was incompetent to do so. He prided himself in nonadherence to case management as a ward of the state of Illinois and slipped out of supervision to actually join the army. He made it into advanced training in the army but was detected as being unfit for duty due to psychotic illness. Instead of treating him and taking responsibility for his case management, the army simply discharged him without any benefits, literally dumping him on his helpless parents' doorstep for them to take responsibility. In fact, the U.S. Army should have discharged him through a Medical Evaluation Board. Such a disposition could have substantially reduced the risk of his going berserk (Liebert and Birnes 2013). He should have been transferred to the care of the Department of Veterans Affairs and restarted on Clozapine for his schizoaffective disorder. Further failure to restart him on Clozapine occurred after he flunked out of Northern Illinois University grad school and resumed studies at University of Illinois in Urbana. Under urgings of his girlfriend, he made an appointment to see the psychiatrist at the counseling center. But, as is the case so often in these young adults, barely capable of covering over their deterioration into apocalyptic suicidal murder and mayhem, there was no coordination of care between the state of Illinois, for which he had been a ward following four serious suicide attempts in high school and a failed fitness for duty examination for psychosis at Beaumont Army Medical Center, Fort Bliss, Texas. Prozac and Xanax would not stop Steven Kazmierczak's march toward madness. In fact, given his history, certainly no psychiatrist would have knowingly prescribed this combination of medications. He was already planning his attack and collecting armaments. Whatever help the medications may have been, he simply stopped them on the advice of a military recruiter for enlistment into the navy. He had done this before with the antipsychotic and mood stabilizer during high school. It would not be long before another star student, NIU's senior of the year at graduation, would, like academic wizard, James Holmes, commit an atrocity no one, except a peer or two sitting next to him or rooming near him, could have anticipated. He showed no emotion as he mowed down helpless students and faculty in Cole Hall before killing himself. There was no emotion, because he was totally enshrouded in a delusional state of the ruthless warrior he claimed so comforting to him in army basic training. It is also believed by some that the psychotropics caused the Chos, Lanzas, and Kazmierczaks of the world to go berserk. Tragically, this is social ignorance or propaganda by antipsychiatric institutions. More often than not, those who need psychotropic medications are simply deprived of them until it is too late, or they do not take them in the first place.

Colleges are not clinical environments, even though the incidents of undergraduate and graduate students decomposing mentally on campus are on the increase. Accordingly, college campuses need far better clinical services and far more authority in dealing with students facing emotional challenges. Simply expelling them back into the community is not the answer. Colleges are environments for learning and emotional growth, and not, as the president of Virginia Tech asserted in his testimony in defense of his policies and procedures with Cho during testimony in a civil trial, simply shopping centers for students purchasing education. Anyone making the sacrifices required for a college education today should not be conned by such defensive testimony into believing that either students or faculty are simply like shoppers and retail clerks for purposes of their health and safety on campus.

Suicidal rampage murders do occur in shopping centers, as was the case at Von Maur Department Store in the mall at Omaha, Nebraska. There is no comparison between the random victims of that suicidal mass murder and the victims at Virginia Tech who repeatedly complained of Cho's threats to their security. One of Cho's classes was nearly emptied by his grossly psychotic behavior due to his peers' fear of him. Such incidents were repeatedly ignored by higher administration at Virginia Tech and delegated, seemingly, and skillfully, without a paper trail to teachers and student dorm proctors. If we expect cops to be more intelligent in their encounters with the seriously mentally ill, presidents of our institutions of higher learning should be the model. The model set by Virginia Tech University, and its multimillion dollar whitewash from the Governor's Conference in the wake of Cho's massacre only help to freeze the management of our seriously mentally ill in colonial American attitudes, policies, and procedures more appropriate for historical viewing to the east in Williamsburg than on a twenty-first century university campus in Blacksburg (Liebert and Birnes 2011b).

Tertiary prevention is where the investment in health care is today as skimpy and inadequate as it may be. Therefore, we must take it as it is, while trying to push diagnostics upstream to earlier identification and even discovery of causation. The cases presented so far show how important this is, whether the terminal failure in tertiary prevention of death and transmission of injury or illness to their caretakers with Thomas Duncan and Charles Logan or the missed opportunities for identification of fulminating psychosis of students on the campuses of NIU, Pima College, University of Colorado, or Virginia Tech.

Sadly, for all the superior health care in the United States, we still have no mechanism for preventive community emergency psychiatric care—even within the supposedly best managed health-care environment in the world, our own medical-surgical wards of affluent communities like Maplewood, Minnesota. We do not recognize the red flags, ignore troubling signs of dangerous behavior, and mostly look the other way when the at-risk and the person acting strangely is someone we know or a family member. Can it get any worse than this when encountering patients outside the supposed sanctity of an inpatient hospital ward at St. John's Hospital, where people, patients, staff, and visitors alike are supposed to be monitored by trained and experienced health and security professionals?

It gets worse when outside the hospital, although there is less and less definition of what constitutes best practices inside a dorm room or behind bars or outside on the street. In the case of Charles Logan, as apparently was the case at Texas Health Presbyterian with Thomas Duncan, a patient came through the ER and contemporary pressures of throughput likely rushed him into the elevator for admission without adequate evaluation. The outcome of this throughput was suicidal mass murder, except, fortunately for potential victims, only the perpetrator died. The four nurses were not killed, thus not qualifying this incident as a mass murder, even though, more likely than not, it was suicidal mass murder. But it does get worse outside the hospital, as in the case of Marlene Pinnock who did suffer a serious head injury from the beating by CHP.

Homicidal psychotic patients like Charles Logan represent a minority of the seriously mentally ill, probably less than 10% of that population of several million seriously impaired patients. Doing the math, however, it is not hard to understand how they are responsible for 10% of our homicides. Only Lady Luck spared the lives of the four nurses in his path and many others between him and his escape outside the hospital with a dangerous weapon, a lethal metal bar. Less than one month before the Marlene Pinnock case, Elliot Rodger went on a suicidal rampage murder to the north in Santa Barbara, killing six people and injuring thirteen others before committing suicide. About 3 weeks before his killing spree, Rodger's parents contacted police after becoming alarmed by his behavior and YouTube videos. He wrote in his manifesto that he had already planned the killings and purchased his guns by that time, and that officers who interviewed him at his apartment would have found the weapons if they had conducted a search of his bedroom. The deputies determined he did not meet the criteria for an involuntary hold. Rodger told them "it was a misunderstanding."

Under the Lanterman–Petris–Short Act, the so-called California Magna Carta for the mentally ill, the Law's LPS Handbook enables a police officer to detain a subject when the officer has observed the qualifying symptoms in the routine process of a response. This is commonly used to allow the officer to process a subject into the psychiatric facility without requiring criminal processing. The basic foundation of this law is that it requires neither psychiatric nor clinical psychological training or credentials to effectively examine a seriously mentally ill person and judge whether this person is safe to be unsupervised in the community. Police judged him safe despite his ravings, but believed him to be polite and calm and rational. Inside, though, he was seething. He was able to trick the sheriff's deputies, who did not take him to a psychiatrist for an evaluation and thus enabled a dangerous person to roam free. He met all the criteria for psychosis and dangerousness and more likely than not would have been detained for emergency psychiatric assessment at Ventura/UCLA Hospital, sparing the lives of young students in the path of his murder and mayhem. In terms of tertiary prevention, Rodger was already psychotic, thus passing primary prevention. He was not under treatment for that psychosis and had begun his targeting list of victims, hence passing the secondary prevention level. All that was left was tertiary prevention, keeping him from drowning while he was already under water in the context of the bridges metaphor. But that, too, failed when sheriff's deputies believed him when he said he was all good.

The prevention problem for psychiatry is that it relies on a false view of the nature of mental illness, criminalizing it instead of evaluating it clinically. If strange-behaving people are not medical, then criminalizing their aberrant behaviors in the name of "deviancy" and throwing them in jail if nuisances on the street—or, if really breaking the law, throwing them in prison—becomes normative for our society. Like the repeated alarms from the electronic medical record that numb clinicians into a state of complacency in the face of high clinical risk, the alarming news of suicidal rampage murders and police shootings on the news numbs the public into complacency. After all, pundits say, "these things happen." But these things do not simply happen. There is a reason, and many of them can be stopped. The police have progressed in sparing lives since Columbine. Public health, particularly in psychiatry, continues backward on a slippery slope, because politicians took advantage of patient rights to cost shift care of the seriously mentally ill from hospitals and community mental health centers to the gutters for the police to take care of them, or failing that primitive solution, jails and prisons. That is where we are now. It is the same normative conceptualization of deviancy historically witnessed in the historical context of colonial America.

Where are these sick people now? Thomas Logan was in a private room in the med-surg ward of one of the premier hospitals in the Twin Cities. How could he possibly have been transported from the ER so deep into the most vulnerable heart of acute medical care? It turns out he was delirious and paranoid, thinking it necessary to escape. He was admitted that way in spite of obvious signs of serious neuropsychiatric impairment and was killed by the police just like homeless psychotic James Boyd in Albuquerque. Certainly Logan was not killed execution style like Boyd, but what should have been a medical emergency became, once again, a police emergency and wrongful death piled atop likely medical negligence. There apparently was no disciplined emergency neuropsychiatric clearance in his case. Had there been a psychiatric inpatient unit, he may have been admitted there, too, with medical problems way too severe for staff to manage. But, blind throughput, not real assessment, likely trumped disciplined and thorough patient evaluation and care. What obviously was not clocked during throughput was his mental status, as nighttime brings on delirium and terror in the brain-damaged patient. Presumably he was in that CD(D)DC complex. His mental status must be clocked, just like length of stay and all the other metrics of throughput determining the fates of patients and staff alike today. Hopefully it did not trump a Lyme disease antibody screen. This is an aspect of prevention obfuscated today by hospitals' strivings to survive financially through optimizing patient flow instead of optimizing health-care service—that is better outcomes at lower costs, and not just lower costs alone. The dashboards of modern business management even track the time required for transporting patients to the lab and back, as well as how long it takes to change the sheets and clean a room for a new patient. Where are the fundamental time-determined and epidemiologically informed rules of classical emergency medicine triage on the dashboards of hospital management today? Time is of the essence in transporting patients back and forth to the lab and cleaning up a room, but so is constant assessment and reassessment of the patient's clinical state, particularly at shift changes, as in the case of Charles Logan in Maplewood, Minnesota, or in hospital transport and throughput in the case of Thomas Duncan in Dallas.

We as humans are bridges over troubled waters. Our tensile strength and durability are determined to a large extent by our DNA, maintenance of which and early signs of cracking, whether in our bones or our neurocircuitry, can reduce corrosive rusting. The threats of troubled waters and corrosive rusting are no longer those of archaic medical technologies, such as surgeons scrubbing their hands after operations instead of before, or maiming farm injuries far from effective trauma care. They are more subtle winds of change threatening our social fabric, accompanied gusts from the seemingly increasing fury of our weather and social chaos of cult-like organizations calling themselves nations and recruiting our youth to take us back to the Middle Ages. Amid these corrosive forces and turbulent waters, we have a public health and safety system that is crippled by failures in leadership, politicization, and budgetary restraint. Psychiatric criminology is a means to capture these changes in order to target areas of need for public health and safety, more and more the same today. The Roadmap for Rapid Assessment places in the hands of those making first clinical encounters today with the nation's sickest the rules and knowledge base for primary, secondary, and tertiary prevention.

## REFERENCES

Associated Press/NBC4 Washington. 2015. DOJ says Baltimore illegally jailing juveniles in solitary. March 27. www.nbcwashington.com/news/local/DOJ-Reports-Says-Baltimore-Jail-Keeping-Juveniles-in-Solitary-297834011.html

Cardiff University. 2014. Understanding schizophrenia. *News View*, July 22. www.cardiff.ac.uk/news/articles/understanding-schizophrenia-13272.html

Friedman, R. A. 2014. A solution that now looks crazy 'American Psychosis' attacks mental health care. The New York Times, January 13.

Fuller Torrey, E. Treatment Advocacy Group. www.treatmentadvocacycenter.org/

Huang, T. L. 2013. Effects of antipsychotics on the BDNF in schizophrenia, *Current Medicinal Chemistry*, 20(3), 345–350.

Hyler, L. 2012. The Wisconsin tragedy: What the gunman's neighbor saw. *Time*, August 8. www.nation.time.com/2012/08/08/the-wisconsin-tragedy-what-the-gunmans-neighbor-saw/

Kay, R. L. and Kay, J. *Adolescent Conduct Disorders in American Psychiatric Association Psychiatry Update Annual Review*. American Psychiatric Press, Inc., 1990, Vol. 5. pp. 408-496.

Kessler, R. et al. 1994. Lifetime and 12 month prevalence of DSM-III-R psychiatric disorders in the United States: Results from the national comorbidity survey. *Archives of General Psychiatry*, 51, January 1.

Klein, D. et al. 1993. Clinical psychopharmacological practice, the need of developing a research base. *Archives of General Psychiatry* 50, 491–494.

Lerner-Wren, G. 2014. The Criminalization of the Mentally Ill in America. HUFFington Post, July 22. www.huffingtonpost.com/ginger-lernerwren/the-criminalization-of-th_b_5607820.html

Lertzman, R. A. and Birnes, W. J. 2015. *The Life and Times of Mickey Rooney*. Gallery Books, New York.

Liebert, J. A. 2007. Diagnostic clearance of neuropsychiatric presentations, *The Annual Webcast Series sponsored by The American Association of Emergency Psychiatry*, August 7, National Webinar.

Liebert, J. 2008. Unity in Healthcare: *The Toyota Way. King County Medical Society Bulletin*, 87(2), 9–24. www.johnliebert.com/johnliebert/pdfs/ToyotaWay_BulletinFeb2008.pdf

Liebert, J. 2015. Suicidal rampage murders: What in the world is going on? *Presentation to Annual Conference, American Investigative Society of Cold Cases*, St. Louis, Mosby.

Liebert, J. A. and Birnes, W. J. 2011a. The strange case of Timothy Jorden. In *Wounded Minds: The Menace of Post-traumatic Stress Disorder*. Skyhorse, New York.

Liebert, J. A. and Birnes, W. J. 2011b. *Suicidal Mass Murderers: A Criminological Study of Why They Kill*. Taylor and Francis, Boca Raton, Florida.

Liebert, J. A. and Birnes, W. J. 2013. *Wounded Minds: The Menace of Post-traumatic Stress Disorder*. Skyhorse, New York.

Liebert, J. A. and Birnes, W. J. 2014. *Hearts of Darkness*. Skyhorse, New York.

Liebert, J. A. and Klauer, K. 2013. *Self Defense for ER Staff*. Challenger Corporation, Las Vegas.

Liebert, J. *The New Psychiatry*. Psychiatrist at War, Unpublished.

Pearson, E. and Adams Otis, G. *New York Daily News*, May 29, 2014.

Rynearson, E. 1987. Posttraumatic stress disorder in surviving relations of violent death. *Victims of Trauma, First and Second Annual Pacific Northwest Conference on Trauma, Separation and Loss Center*, in collaboration with Seattle Psychoanalytic Association. Seattle, Washington.

Scott, B. 2015. Law enforcement is fifty years behind aviation. *William B. Scott Blog*, January 8. www.williambscott.com/2015/01/law-enforcement-is-fifty-years-behind-aviation/

Stack, L. 2015. Deputies said to taunt prisoners. *The New York Times*, March 26. www.nytimes.com/2015/03/27/us/san-francisco-sheriffs-deputies-said-to-taunt-prisoners.html?_r=0

Stahl, S. 2010. *Neuroscience Education Institute Congress*, Neuroscience Education Institute, Washington, DC.

Torrey, E. F. 2012. *The Insanity Offense: How America's Failure to Treat the Seriously Mentally Ill Endangers Its Citizens*, 1st Edition. W. W. Norton & Company, New York.

Wachter, R. M. 2015. Why health care tech is still so bad? *New York Times Opinion*, March 21. www.nytimes.com/2015/03/22/opinion/sunday/why-health-care-tech-is-still-so-bad.html

Weiss, E., Dlin, B., Rollin, H. R., Keith Fischer, H. and Bepler, C. R. 1957. Emotional factors in coronary occlusion. *AMA Archives of Internal Medicine*, 99(4), 628–641.

Women doctors detect abuse faster than men. *Psychiatric News*, April 15, 1994, p. 24.

Zeman, A. 2014. Neurology is psychiatry—and vice versa, *Practical Neurology*, 14(3), 136–144.

# 17

# The terrorist and the suicide cult

> In the death cult of apocalyptic jihad, the final battle between the righteous and the wicked is nearly at hand. The Islamic State trades extensively in end-times ideology. It was to Abu Bakr al-Baghdadi, the leader of the Islamic State, the self-appointed caliph, that Malik dedicated her bay'ah—her pledge of allegiance—on Facebook after she and Rizwan fled the site of the attack. The Islamic State seemed not to know who these two mass murderers were but soon enough declared them "soldiers of the caliphate" and asked God to accept them as martyrs. The shooters emptied four thirty-round magazines, striking thirty-six people and killing fourteen, and then immediately fled, although they were wearing vests packed with more ammunition. They left a bag with three pipe bombs on a table—the remote-control detonator was in their vehicle—but the bombs failed to explode, perhaps because of the sprinklers. (Finnegan 2016)

The cold blooded brutality and carnage of an ordinary office Christmas party continues to raise questions of Farook and Malik's affiliations and control as the FBI challenges Apple for access to linkages either proving or disproving foreign control of this Jihadist attack on middle America. Regardless of the ultimate findings—assuming there are any—the current primary elections highlight the fear in America's heart from people who have choices as Americans but choose apocalyptic murder and mayhem. Who are these people? How do they pass through our gates of immigration screening and become vetted while behaving so strangely in an ordinary suburban community. Nobody ever saw Malik's face. They received weapon deliveries in full view of neighbors in preparation for their apocalypse. Nobody noticed. The perpetrators' personal motives are a mystery to us. Their amoral, dehumanizing actions were not rooted in ordinary criminality. We ask why?

> As the Islamic State of Iraq and Syria attempts to carve out a caliphate in the Middle East, the terror group has other ambitions: attacking the United States, according to threats and alleged warnings made by Abu Bakr al-Baghdadi, the mysterious leader of ISIS.
>
> Al-Baghdadi's rhetoric doesn't usually slam the West to the extent that the late al Qaeda leader Osama bin Laden did, but the shadowy figure gave a direct message to Americans in a 'rare audio statement' while addressing ISIS fighters in January, according to congressional testimony in February from Brett McGurk, the deputy assistant secretary of state for Iran and Iraq. (Koplowitz 2014)

Breivik, the Norwegian mass killer who gunned down teenagers at Utoya Island before being arrested by the police and convicted as a mass killer, said at his trial that not only is Al-Qaeda an eminently successful terrorist organization, it should serve as the model for right-wing revolutionary groups seeking to impose their will on recalcitrant populations.

And mass murderer Mark Lepine, a virulent and violent antifeminist who perpetrated the Montreal massacre, after which he shot and killed himself, said in a letter he wrote that his attack was political. "If I am committing suicide today … it is not for reasons … but for political reasons. For I have decided to send Ad Patres ["to the fathers"] the feminists who have ruined my life. … The feminists always have a talent for enraging me. They want to retain the advantages of being women … while trying to grab those of men. … They are so opportunistic that they neglect to profit from the knowledge accumulated by men throughout the ages. They always try to misrepresent them every time they can" (www.theguardian.com/world/2012/dec/03/montreal-massacre-canadas-feminists-remember). At the bottom of his letter, Lepine attached a list of 19 feminists whom he said he wanted to kill, but that he had started too late to include them as victims. Rather, he killed dozens of ordinary women at the École Polytechnique who bore the brunt of his psychotic fury.

Lepine, like other mass murderers before him, those who bore deep-seated grudges against a society they said shunned then, belittled and berated them, or so cast them so far to the margins of society that they felt beyond alienated, was a creature unto himself like Anders Breivik, Adam Lanza, Eliot Rodger, and now Robert Dear. They were cults of one. But what about individuals who join groups specifically to dedicate themselves to suicide for what they believe is a greater glory, a life beyond life, their version of heaven achieved in an apocalyptic moment? This defines the modern terrorist group, Al-Qaeda, the Islamic State, and to a lesser extent Hamas and Palestinian terrorists from Fatah and the Palestine Liberation Organization (PLO). And these individuals are usually younger, belonging to the 15–29 age group in which suicide is the second greatest cause of death. What defines them?

In some generational struggles where children are radicalized by seeing the horrors their parents faced or simply through hearing the stories of their parents, violence is transmitted within the family and community culture. Hamas leadership, for example, actually trains children in violence, teaching them how to don suicide vests and how to handle weapons. And so does self-styled prophet and spiritual medium, Joseph Kony, who has assembled an army of child soldiers. ISIS, too, trains child soldiers in the act of killing prisoners and inculcates them with what they claim is the glory of martyrdom—self-destruction for their political agenda. But sometimes the situation itself radicalizes new generations, for example, the deprivation within Palestinian refugee camps. As such, charismatic leaders of Hamas emerge from constituencies with family legends of being marginalized.

Jerrold Post states, "on the basis of extensive interviews with incarcerated members of Islamist Palestinian groups, we noted commonalities in the terrorists' personal histories. The boyhood heroes for the Islamist terrorists were religious figures, such as the Prophet, or bin Laden's mentor, the radical Wahhabi Islamist Professor, Abdullah Azzam. Most had some high school, and some had education beyond high school. The majority of the subjects reported that their families were respected in the community. The families were experienced as being uniformly supportive of their commitment to the cause." (Post 2008).

The recent terrorist attacks in Paris, and the follow-up raid on Abouad's hideout, all of which resulted in the deaths of the terrorists, some by suicide, some by police and special forces, and the recent attack on the Radisson Hotel in Mali in which the two attackers were killed, were actually suicide mass murders. The perpetrators did not expect, nor did they probably want, to escape alive. Part of the terror they sought to inflict on the victim population was the fear that they were willing to die. In other words, the threat of death or prosecution was no threat at all, only a badge of honor. And unlike spies, protecting their organizations and handlers, these individuals were happy to disclose their organizations' plans because in so doing, they were propagandizing and thus spreading the terror through an all-too-willing media to the victim population.

## REVOLUTIONARY SUICIDE: "WHY WE WANT TO DIE"

Harold is a specialist who served in Iraq as a gunner on a Humvee. One day his convoy was passing through a populated area and a truck approached them at high speed. Suspecting a suicide bomb attack, he fired at the oncoming vehicle; it exploded just yards away from him. An innocent bystander with a child was blown across the hood of his Humvee. "The father's intestines were hanging out. I recall that," he said with little emotional inflection in his voice.

"How about the child"?, I inquired.

"Oh, yeah. I remember him running away."

This was just one of a number of gruesome explosions he either witnessed or took directly from suicide bombers or improvised explosive devices.

"We had to back up a unit pinned down in Sadr City. The market was littered with bodies blown to pieces and awash in fresh blood. We couldn't stop and had to pass on through to back up another unit."

On the road to Mosul, a convoy driver reported the grizzly scene of entire families hanging from balconies in villages. “They refused to cooperate with al Qaeda and were hung out to show what happens if you refuse to blow up Americans with IEDs or won’t let your kid be a suicide bomber.”

In the interrogations of failed suicide bombers and their commanders in Israeli prisons, a disturbing profile emerged of the young men and women who lived briefly to die for the cause of martyrdom by exploding as human bombs in Israeli streets. In early years, they were young males with little future who were recruited—or, perhaps, forced by threatened family—to martyr themselves as bombers. They were isolated in safe houses, methodically prepared, both by extremist Muslim verse and tactics. Then they were fitted with suicide belts and either directed or taken to crowded places where, at the right time, they pushed the button that would propel nails and shrapnel into crowds of innocent people. These boys knew little beyond a hatred for those who were characterized for them as their oppressors—first Israelis, but then anyone allied with Israel and secularized governments in the Middle East—i.e., the United States in Beirut, Kenya, Yemen, Saudi Arabia, and Iraq.

Then came the attacks on the World Trade Center and centers of power in Washington, DC, on 9/11, followed by the Madrid and London subway bombings, and then by the kidnapping of young girls by Boko Haram and the ISIS attacks in Paris and Mali. How can we begin to understand people who seem so desperate in life that they dedicate themselves to sacrificing their own lives to deliver carnage to an entire community in the name of God—or simply a charismatic man-God whose cosmic agenda pales in comparison to personal charisma?

To put the events of 9/11, Paris, and our War on Terror in historical perspective, we need to see them as more of the same, as well as something genuinely threatening our traditional views on personal and national security. But we also need to view them through the lens of social psychology because to see them as solely criminal acts or solely political acts is to be shortsighted. Our national security and military analysts, looking at them with a stovepipe decision-making mandate, are suffering from linkage blindness, a form of intellectual blinders that keep them from looking at explanations outside the box. If you also add to the analytical mix of causalities for this international terrorism the idea that these individuals, even when they are raw recruits, are teetering on the edge of alienation, harboring suicidal ideations that need only encouragement and a trigger, and are looking for some form of meaning in a time beyond time—or who suffer from the delusion that they are already dead—then dealing with suicidal terrorist groups may involve looking at a broader picture.

As David Rappaport wrote in *Inside Terrorist Organizations*, “three English words—zealot, thug and assassin—trace their origins to religious terrorist groups, the ‘Zealots,’ the ‘Thugs,’ and the ‘Assassins’” (Rapoport 1988). The Zealots came from the Israelites who, in revolting against their oppressive Roman rulers, effected the spectacular mass suicide at Masada in 66–70 CE. This movement lasted less than a century but managed to inspire two more terrorist mass suicides against Roman rulers.

The Thugs, actually "Thugees," a gang of bandits who considered themselves children of the Hindu goddess of destruction, Kali, and who terrorized India for more than a thousand years, were suppressed by the British in the nineteenth century. They disguised themselves as travelers who inserted themselves into groups of otherwise innocent travelers or merchants, winning their trust, and then strangling their victims with garrotes, hence the term *garroting*. The modern English word "thug" derives from the Hindi language "thuggee."

The Assassins were a radical Shia Islamic Sect who considered themselves divinely commanded to repel the Crusaders for more than 200 years during the Middle Ages. The modern English word *assassin* is derived from the drug hashish that the assassins were given to provide them with greater strength and endurance and resistance to pain. Convinced their sacrificial and murderous violence would not only protect their sacred lands from alien invaders, they believed "assassination" would secure them a higher place in paradise. It is interesting that the assassins were given hashish while modern ISIS fighters are given Captagon, an amphetamine derivative. More interesting, still, methamphetamine in the form of the drug Pervitin was routinely prescribed to Adolph Hitler by his physician Theodore Morrell and was also distributed to both the Luftwaffe and the RAF during World War II to keep pilots awake on long combat flights. The formula for the methamphetamine distributed throughout the war was based on the concoction widely distributed by German doctor Max Jacobson who practiced in Berlin until the middle 1930s when he fled the Nazis, was turned into a Soviet operative in Vienna, migrated to the United States, and became the ad hoc physician prescribing methamphetamine injections to President John F. Kennedy (Lertzman et al. 2013).

Suicide cult terrorist groups, whether leaning more toward traditional criminality or turned toward a political or military purpose, are not new. Some have even argued that the fundamentalist sect called the Essenes, described by historian Flavius Josesephus and linked to the Dead Sea Scrolls, was also a type of zealotry who believed that because they were the caretakers of the Ark of the Covenant, they were therefore responsible for the purification of the Israelites even if that meant engaging in acts of murder to expunge what they saw as impurities from the group. Some modern scholars argue that Jesus belonged to the Essenes and was thus martyred as a member of this sect.

When Iranian Ayatollah Khomeini suddenly showed us the power of Shia Martyrdom in the violent takeover of our Embassy in Teheran in 1979, we began to learn how he co-opted 1500 years of Shia cultural traditions. These were the martyrdom and the persecution, torment, suffering, powerlessness, and insecurity we have in images from the fountains of blood in Tehran. These hemorrhaging fountains honor families sacrificing sons in the Iraqi-Iranian war. We also see them massed en route to Iraqi shrines, flogging themselves throughout their way of pilgrimage. We learned, and now face this ancient terrorist threat having just tested a surface-to-air missile. Khomeni made no reservations about using the ultimate power of ultimate weakness—martyrdom—to overthrow the superior power of the West and make the entire world one Shia nation.

As characterized by al-Baghdadi, the self-proclaimed leader of the Islamic State caliphate, when the flag of the caliphate flies over the government buildings of Western capitals, then and only then will the world be ready for a type of armageddon, the return of the Mahdi, the Twelfth Imam, who will save the righteous believers and condemn the infidels. Hence, the timeline of radical jihad points to a moment beyond time or after the end of time when the universe itself will be destroyed. At that point, those who martyred themselves in the act of suicide or copacide for the faith will be among the saved.

Imagine the effect of this promise to alienated youth, those looking for a cause to believe in, those believing that members of their own religion are being hunted down and killed—whether Sunni or Shia—or even westernized Muslims who feel ostracized in society like the recent San Bernardino mass murder suspect Syed Rizwan Farook. When all else seems either hopeless or too distant, it is a promise of eternal life through the gateway of martyrdom, and it is, of course, not a new idea. This idea propelled the advance of Christianity under Roman emperors who persecuted Christians even though Jesus Christ never saw Himself as anything other than a Jew. In fact, for the first three hundred or so years of Christianity, it was not even regarded as a separate faith, but instead a Judaic sect. Nevertheless, how different from those early Christians who willingly sacrificed themselves on the altar of Roman law for their faith are some of today's members of extremely fundamentalist Christian sects who would rather go to jail than observe the law regarding same-sex marriage or engage in terrorist plots against abortion clinics or Planned Parenthood, as recent shooter Richard Dear did in Colorado Springs just after Thanksgiving in 2015? Certainly there is a line between going to jail to stand up for one's religious beliefs, a form of social and political martyrdom, and opening fire on victims inside a Planned Parenthood facility, but on an individual level, is it a shifting line and what are the triggers to force a person over it?

On a mass scale, we have witnessed the martyrdom of thousands under religious/political leaders like Ayatollah Khomeini, who put his money where his mouth was when he shocked America with the seizure of the U.S. Embassy in Tehran and then waged war on a traditional enemy, Iraq, by forcing the sacrifice of hundreds of thousands of young men, by sending them out in human wave attacks into the face of Saddam Hussein's poison gas. And, now, in the face of ISIS, Al-Qaeda, and Boko Haram, it is this vast chasm of thought disruption that to this day we are barely beginning to grasp. That is the global threat of megalomaniacal cultists like the self-proclaimed caliph Al-Baghdadi and general of the children's Army of God, Joseph Kony, imposing an ancient cultural tradition on a world that is physically shrinking, and whose citizens, for the most part, are both internally and externally driven to live better lives, rather than die for them and their Medieval interpretation of the Koranic scripture. Though we may find it hard to believe that these suicidal/political cults are inspired by the tenets of mainstream Islam, enough converts and recruits are willing to use Islam itself as a rationale for their own apocalyptic ideations. With such sacrificial violence in the name of Muslim scripture, we must look back to cults like the Assassins and the Thugees, the Medieval forebears of modern terrorism, whether Hamas in Palestine, Hezbollah in Lebanon, or Al-Qaeda and ISIS globally.

We have argued above and in our previous books on the subject of suicidal mass murder, especially in the discussion of the Unabomber, Ted Kaczynski's manifesto as an influence on Anders Breivik's manifesto, on Adam Lanza, and on Eliot Rodger, that suicidal mass murder is not just psychopathological, it is also contatigious in that pathogenic ideations are transferred from one individual to another, usually through the mass media. This is like an epidemic of Ebola or the plague, but there need be no physical contact whatsoever, just contact through the media that touches the psyches of at-risk individuals. Is that what happened when the Paris attacks possibly inspired the attacks in San Bernardino? Did a workplace dispute between Farook and his coworkers set the trigger? This is where the modern suicide cults of Al-Qaeda and ISIS excel in their understanding of the mechanism or meme of ideation transference. Arab television, the Internet, and our own major media outlets project the militant power of martyrdom embodied in the omnipotent Al-Baghdadi, bin Laden, or Nasrallah via constant primetime portrayal of his image throughout the Arab world. And for those individuals looking for a cause for which to die, for a type of glory of the apocalyptic moment, what better image than that of Jihad John, all robed in black and wielding a sharp sword, beheading those he calls the infidels. It is the execution of the infidel and conversion by the sword, something with which alienated at-risk violence-prone youth can identify.

The designated Islamic terrorist organization, Hamas, like the Revolutionary Guards of Iran and Hezbollah, also derives power from contextual distortions from Muslim scripture, but its followers need less God-man inspiration from men like Khomeini. The Palestinians have suffered marginalization from their own people, from defeat, incarceration in refugee camps, allegedly widespread corruption by their own leadership, and despair. Even though the Israelis correctly argue that Palestine, such as it is, is actually the Kingdom of Jordan, which has turned its back on its own people, it makes no difference to those who see themselves as dispossessed. Jessica Stern, author of *Terror in the Name of God,* quoted one elderly Palestinian resident: "Look how we live here, then maybe you'll understand why there are always volunteers for martyrdom. Every good Muslim understands that it's better to die fighting than to live without hope" (Stern 2004).

There is a difference in the military and political approaches of these suicidal cults, some, obviously, less suicidal than others. The charismatic leadership of Hamas, for example, depends more on defensive operations that could be applied from individual to social psychology—that is the defense of projective identification. The message seems to be that individuals and their families live in desolation because they have been deprived politically of their homeland. Thus, the motivation for suicidal violence and martyrdom is to sacrifice one's life in a war to take back the homeland from which they have been exiled. Though this is propaganda fed to the population, it is nourished by poverty, joblessness, hunger, and a sense of loss at the hands of another party. Hence, to sacrifice one's hopeless life, to give it hope of an afterlife better than this, to remove an occupying force from the homeland is a legitimate argument for suicide.

Al-Qaeda originally had a similar, but larger goal, throwing the occupier out of all Muslim lands. Whether the Soviets in Afghanistan or the Americans in

Afghanistan and Iraq, the goal was a war against the occupiers or, as they were termed, the Crusaders. This is vastly different from the Islamic State caliphate that seeks to conquer the world in the name of Islam for the specific purpose of preparing it for the end of days, the end of time when the Mahdi will come. However, in all three entities, the goal of the suicide terrorist is (a) to inflict harm and fear upon a target population; (b) to convince the occupying government that there is no victory in sight, only continual punishment of the target population; (c) to sow fear and confusion among the target population so they distrust the government's ability to protect them and in so doing weaken the occupying government; and (d) through their bold and heroic initiatives, recruit more members by providing the disillusioned, alienated, and hopeless, actual hope of glory through martyrdom and an afterlife in bliss. And the more the occupying government cracks down, the more the occupied population sees itself as at war and thus joins the ranks of the terrorists. Thus, there is a psychological and social as well as a political approach, melding a political agenda to a psychological approach. We see this, in a more benign approach with our own politics.

In the Palestinian refugee camps that created the fertile soil for growing violent young men, boys repeatedly stated that they found a sense of security in the Mosque, perhaps the only transitional object of security to help them emancipate from a mother who had to be protective and a father stymied in career. In such a social environment, Suicide Bomb Commanders said that they had no problems finding recruits and actually had to be selective. And, the same security of brotherhood prevailed again, as the young boy—or girl—found support from peers and idealized mentors. The latter always made certain that their final commitment to suicide bombing was a videotape of their final commitment, assurance that they could not renege for fear of public humiliation and burying their families further into poverty and despair. They took the flip side, foreseeing their photos embedded on public posters, green birds flocked above their heads.

Moreover, as is always the case with radicalized, monotheistic religious sects, whether Jew, Christian, or Muslim, the fruits of life are sacrificed by contextual distortion of scripture. In this case the young victim about to be sacrificed like an artillery shell has it inculcated into the final vision of his future. It can be extracted from the Koran that the soul of a martyr is carried to Allah in the bosom of the green birds of paradise. The rage of hopelessness and despair can now be projected onto the enemy—as is the case with projective identification, which we discussed in detail in our book *Suicidal Mass Murderers* in 2011.

The evil does not lurk within—neither killing innocents nor suicide is supported within Muslim scripture. In their vision of the world, the evil resides in the occupier, and thus the leadership of Hamas needs only to mobilize the rage of youth growing up with no future vision of success as we know it in America and project it onto the evil outside them. In this case, the identification of their rage is about to be innocent Israeli citizens merely going about their lives, oftentimes with less political conviction than believed.

As with all political upheavals involving terrorism, there appears to be a point where the leadership can negotiate, as with South Africa and Northern Ireland. It seems the problem is that the very leader who can have an impact on the security of a powerful nation like Israel is the very person who too often cannot let go of either the omnipotence or projective identification so effective to a point. In the case of Hamas, it is hard not to see the basic premise of its leadership as paranoid.

"The enemy planned long ago and perfected their plan so that they can achieve what they want to achieve. ... They (Jews) are behind the French Revolution, the communist revolution... they formed secret organizations throughout the world to destroy societies and promote the Zionist cause.... They are behind the First World War in which they destroyed the Islamic Caliph.... There is not a war that goes on here or there in which their finger was not playing behind it," this according to the Hamas Charter. Thus, is there any doubt that this is about a religious war?

In a most ominous summary statement of Hamas terrorist psychology, Ariel Merari, terrorism researcher, minimizes the individual psychological problems motivating the suicide bomber within the context of the suicide terrorist assembly line of Hamas. "First the volunteer or recruit is identified, usually by friends or relatives in the organization, and commits himself to becoming a shabid. Then he is publicly identified as a living martyr, a member of the 'walking dead'. This gives great prestige both to the prospective martyr and to his or her family. Finally, just before the mission, he is videotaped reading his last will and testament, in which he explains his motivations and his goals. This cements his commitment, and makes it nearly impossible for him to back out, for it would bring unbearable shame and humiliation to either him or her and family alike. These videos then are disseminated on Hamas Websites, where they glorify the martyrs and contribute to further recruitment" (www.books.google.com/books?id=IMTu5gwWE0kC&printsec=frontcover&dq=Hamas+Terrorist+Psychology,+Ariel+Merari&hl=en&sa=X&ved=0ahUKEwiGw7vstIvLAhVO3mMKHQ4LA0MQ6AEINDAA#v=onepage&q=Hamas%20Terrorist%20Psychology%2C%20Ariel%20Merari&f=false).

From an existentialist perspective, the stated mission of the suicidal martyr is reminiscent of the feeling of relief and security Mersault describes in the concluding pages of Albert Camus' *The Stranger* in which the narrator is comforted by the surety of his impending death by execution. The narrator of the novel lived amid uncertainty, not even remembering the day his mother died, this day or yesterday, and not knowing the direction of his life until he murders an Arab. At that point, his fate is sealed. From uncertainty, he is guaranteed a certainty: he will be executed. And that certainty, the determined end point of his life, gives him security. So might this literary conceit also apply to the alienated hopeless Palestinian youth living in refugee camps or on the West Bank in that the meaning of certainty is provided to his life through his mission of suicide guaranteeing him status as a martyr.

As Jerrold Post responds, however, to the dire hopelessness of the fate of potential suicide recruits, "these youths must have a better alternative to living than blowing themselves up to destroy primarily innocent human beings who are not that different than they in desires, fears and needs. And, from the cultist brainwashing that proceeds to final closing of the deal to die a violent death, they must, as in any cult, be provided a viable—not deceptive—way out" (Post 2008).

And, to make matters more complex, there are those equally destructive in their leadership ambitions and totalitarian human engineering skills. Justification for jihadist suicide bombings were provided by Baruch Goldstein when he killed or wounded 130 Palestinian Muslims praying in the Tomb of the Patriarchs in Hebron in 1994. Suicide bombings had already started, but now Hamas leadership, as on Black Sunday in Northern Ireland when British soldiers fired on civilians with combat efficiency, claimed it had justification. Before this tragic ignition of a tinderbox, Rabbi Zvi Yehuda Kook formed Gush Emunim, the Movement of the Faithful, dedicated to fulfilling the biblical prophecy of Eretz Israel, the land of Israel, and not yielding a single inch of the God-given land of Israel. This only served Hamas with further claims of justification for their actions because political statements were perceived as psychological and political incitement.

Lest American readers become complacent in their superiority, we have our own native-born terrorists, just not jihadists. In America we have the Aryan Nation who, like Muslim terrorist leaders, extract and twist scripture to justify their violent means. From the Bible book of Genesis they extract the following, "Aryans are descendants of the last tribes of Isare and are the true chosen people. They have a special calling and are on earth to do God's work. It is the God given task of the Aryans to warn of the dangers represented by the Jews and the blacks and to destroy them." Another nominal Christian, former Catholic priest, David Trosch, extracted and divined the pro-life tenets of Cannon Law to dehumanize those performing legal abortions. "Defending human life is not murder. You're comparing the lives of morally guilty persons (doctors and nurses) against the lives of manifestly innocent persons (the unborn fetus)" (www.books.google.com/books?id=3nALAQAAMAAJ&q=,+David+Trosch,++%E2%80%9CDefending+human+life+is+not+murder.&dq=,+David+Trosch,++%E2%80%9CDefending+human+life+is+not+murder.&hl=en&sa=X&ved=0ahUKEwiO8JPst4vLAhUK-GMKHfKnBIIQ6AEIITAB). And we wonder why alienated individuals like Richard Dear wind up getting arrested for opening fire in a Planned Parenthood facility, killing at least two people and a Colorado Springs law enforcement officer who was a co-pastor in his church. Then there was Wade Page, a psychotic drifter trained by the U.S. Army with Psy Ops skills, whose career was white supremacist rock bands. Finally, he crashed and committed the Sikh Temple Suicidal Mass Murder in Milwaukee. And, of course, the alienated and disturbed Dylan Roof who, though he had African American friends, nevertheless, saw himself on a mission to protect what he saw as Aryan culture by killing parishioners in one of this country's most historic black churches in South Carolina. Wearing the symbols of the Confederate battle flag and the South African flag of Apartheid, he fought a lone war of psychotically driven racism.

Those who have interviewed both policemen and offenders who had killed have come to realize that one of the most frightening things is the ease of taking another life. If the deep prohibition of guilt is there, it can be devastating psychologically, even for the "best" police shooting. If not, the joy of it can be terrifying. And the charismatic cult leader, whether in name of Abrahamic scripture or "other deities" can project the violence embedded in his omnipotent narcissistic state of borderline insanity with chilling complexity.

Shoko Asahara predicted a nuclear attack by the United States by 1998 in his book, *The Land of the Rising Sun Is Headed Toward a Bitter Fate.* Asahara, a former con man who had felony convictions, a failed election bid for the Diet and two failed attempts to create a global messianic cult of his own, provides us with the portrait of pathological narcissism bordering on full-blown insanity. We do not know whether any psychiatric examination ever found him clinically psychotic or insane, but, needless to say, he had to be sane enough to accomplish what he finally did on his path to becoming the last coming of Christ.

Asahara introduced the civilized world to the reality of weapons of mass destruction controlled by a nonsanctioned madman, when he released Sarin nerve gas into the Tokyo subways. It was not weaponized adequately to kill en masse, but a dozen were killed and 5500 injured. He later burned enough cyanide in bags to kill ten thousand people in a train station had they been ignited properly. Of somewhat terrifying significance was his ability to recruit high-level scientists to his cause. Not only did they dedicate their lives and careers to producing biological warfare agents like weaponized Ebola virus, chemical warfare agents, and a nuclear weapon for him, they paid him thousands of dollars to drink his bath water and eat tiny samples of his DNA. He amassed a fortune estimated to be over a billion dollars and had 50,000 loyal members, 10,000 of whom were in Russia. With offices throughout the world, he could recruit from the best and brightest. Amazingly, like the Nazis, intellect was no protection from his cunning ways and madness. And, there was no way out. One couple trying to escape was incinerated alive in one of his giant high-tech microwave ovens.

Asahara, like our Western zealots before him, prostituted Buddha in his name. His knowledge derived, he claimed, from his "astral vision, intuitive wisdom, and knowledge inferred from Jnana Yoga." He claimed to be the only Japanese man to achieve the stage of Satori. He found Buddhism to be too ethereal for his temporal existence on earth, but then found the ultimate truth in the Bible's New Testament. Noting his own similarities to Jesus Christ, he announced that he was Jesus Christ and warned against false prophets. He was the last coming—hence the founder of a millennium cult, Aum Supreme Truth. Increasingly preoccupied by threats to himself and his followers from the U.S. military, his grandiosity escalated to messianic proportions. He decided to preempt the prophesy with his own apocalypse, wherein only he and his 50,000 believers would have salvation.

Closer to home, a similar cult of high-rolling extremists, the Rajneeshnees, followed the orders of Bhagwan Shree Rajnees and committed biological warfare in Oregon restaurants by contaminating salad bars and creameries with salmonella. That such megalomaniacs can capture the hearts and minds of the educated and the affluent that have choices in their lives puts visible backlighting on the stage of America's attempts to democratize the world. Caveat: there are some problems democracy cannot solve, even though we believe it can. In many ways, it only feeds terrorist groups in countries where, historically, democracy is not native to the area and the conflicts between heterogeneous populations forced into politically determined borders forged by former colonial powers result in endless war. When we intervene, the danger is that we unite the population against us, the common invader, until we leave and they get back to warring among themselves. Just look at Iraq and Syria today, a mix of tribal and religious communities that were better left to form their own societies rather than forced unification into a nation state. Out of that mix come terrorist groups who vie vengeance upon each other, but also upon us.

It will take an approach of highest intelligence, rather than more purely defense forces, to secure our futures from messianic madmen achieving reigns of political power, including the far right within both Israeli and U.S. political spectra. The 1972 Kent State shootings fueled Bernadine Dohrn's violent ambitions for the Weathermen, as did Baruch Goldstein did for Hamas in Hebron, and the British Paratroopers on Black Sunday in Ireland. We may ultimately pull back only to see the rise of new jihadist groups as well as homegrown terror groups populated by otherwise "normal" American citizens like Farook and his wife Malik in San Bernardino or the Tsarnaev Brothers who bombed the Boston Marathon.

In the playbook against terror groups, in addition to targeting the group militarily by direct confrontation and cutting off its financial and logistic supply lines so as to starve it, intelligence personnel from different agencies, including local police, have to think about the individual recruit just as they think about the group. In the case of ISIS and their actions in France and Belgium, the individuals who perpetrated the violence were home-grown even if they were of non-European descent. They were radicalized through sophisticated demographic marketing, message targeting, and through a network of individuals who knew how to bring other potential radicals into the field. And here is where preventive measures can run afoul of the Constitution, because even belief in the need for a revolution, albeit violent, is still considered free speech, as is freedom of assembly. Time and place restrictions apply to free speech cases, but for the individual alienated and hostile, a message of hope for a meaningful existence unless inciting immediate violence would likely be deemed protected speech. However, friends, family members, and even those involved in judicial and juvenile intervention have the best chance to sway a potentially radicalized individual away from violence.

We know from the friends and relatives of those who have gone to Syria to join ISIS that the recruits were attracted to the ISIS either by friends or by the prospect that the organization promised them a meaningful life through its online media operations. Sometimes using the dark net so as to cloak itself from government surveillance, the savvy media techs at ISIS seek to brand the organization as they would a product. They do so in a way that promises to potential recruits that the organization will provide something their lives lack, a meaning and purpose to their existence. Though alienated and adrift, there is a cause for them, a life after life that will welcome them, and a relationship that will supersede even their deepest abhorrence to acts of horror and bloodshed. ISIS is a case study in Marketing 101: create a need within a demographic and a means to fill that need. This is how IBM sold office automation in the 1970s. This is how Apple sells the iPhone today. The challenge for parents, relatives, and friends when it comes to ISIS, however, is to understand the need of a child or loved one and to find alternative ways of filling it.

We suggest that parents, who are actually the first line of defense here, address a child's feelings of alienation, even when the child is an adult. If there is an emptiness, what will fill it other than violent adherence to a cause? Why will violence, even in the name of a religious afterlife, satisfy a need in an otherwise not at-risk individual? These are the early assessments parents and family members can make. Is a child immersed in the Internet to the exclusion of everything else? Then take a tour of his or her Internet wanderings and searches. Figure out what the child, or in most cases the teenager or young adult, finds so engaging about the sites he or she is visiting. Learn what the child is reading, absorbing, and be prepared to discuss it. Parents who abandon their young adult children to the Internet are simply ignoring danger signs.

Friends, too, can be helpful. Taking a careful look at the Dylan Roof Mother Emanuel Church shooting, investigators learned that Roof had spent time in a trailer with a group of friends to whom he confided his feelings and his ideations of violence. Yet they did not take him seriously. They did not go to the police about things he said, because they thought he was just mouthing off under the influence of booze and drugs. Yet, had they taken him seriously and thought seriously about preventing violence, people would be alive today that he would have been prevented from killing.

Sometimes when people are acting out strangely, even the police and justice system are hamstrung, because those who can testify refuse to do so. Look at the troubled life of Planned Parenthood shooter, Richard Dear. How many run-ins with the law did he have, how many charges of sexual abuse and rape, how many times were women simply too afraid to voice their complaints in the form of formal charges? He was a time bomb who was allowed to remain free, until he killed.

Far from arguing that we should turn the United States into a nation of informants, we are simply pointing out that when people make threats, they should be expected to make good on those threats. Threats of suicide and threats of violence are not to be taken lightly.

Another source of influence on the at-risk personality to violent behavior on behalf of a cause is some political rhetoric that can be interpreted as incitement to violence. When Jared Loughner, for example, sought out Congresswoman Gabby Giffords at her planned public meeting at the Safeway Plaza shopping center in Tucson, he had a personal grievance in that he felt somehow she was dismissive of his complaints about life being a "sham." But at about the same time, former Alaska governor and vice presidential candidate Sarah Palin was telling her followers in the most specific terms that, when challenged by liberal politicians, "don't retreat, reload." Taken at its literal meaning, was she telling her followers to go for their guns to make their point? She denied it, but commentators in the media saw her remarks as a not-so-veiled threat of a militia-style resistance to the government. Is it any wonder that when groups like Operation Rescue, and the politicians that support them, call abortion doctors and the facilities that house them "murderers" and post films of fetal tissue from so-called aborted fetuses online that at-risk individuals like Richard Dear mumbling about "no more baby parts" strike out when they see the opportunity?

This may indeed characterize the case of Richard Dear, a loner, drifter, serious malcontent, and a person who had been in and out of trouble with the police and who had manifested violence toward women and likely suffered from severe psychiatric impairment. He was likely just functional enough to support himself, but still very paranoid and susceptible to any kinds of messages that fed his paranoia. Thus, when he likely saw the footage of an aborted fetus over which the discussion at a Planned Parenthood facility regarding the disposition and sale of that fetal tissue took place, he was likely energized. Worse, that footage, now shown to have been a hoax, because it was edited as if it were a piece of propaganda and the fetus in question had not been the result of an abortion at all, was trumped up by presidential candidates for purely political purposes so as to energize their radical pro-life base. Worse, that footage, mixed with the message that abortion clinics had to be closed by any means possible and urgings from the rabid pro-life radicals to perpetrate violence upon abortion providers, was tantamount to a recruitment message for the potentially violent to take matters into their own hands.

Yes, this was all free speech, and political speech is for the most part protected speech, just like violent song lyrics and violent single-shooter video games are free speech, even though they have effects on at-risk individuals that could lead to violence. Like the shortcomings of public preventive medicine in the United States, political messaging that can be interpreted as a call to violent action runs smack up against the protections of individual rights set forth in the Constitution. Thus, protections against epidemical disasters, the spread of pathogens, must be laid out against individual protections in the Constitution. And this is a good thing, but it does require that we take a hard look at some of our assumptions about the free speech we take for granted. For example, the U.S. Supreme Court in *Brandenburg v. Ohio* (1969) set a standard for determining when the content of speech can be constrained by the state, holding that even inflammatory speech cannot be punished unless that speech leads directly to incitement, which incitement must be immediate—not a distant threat. Hence, calls by the anti-abortion fringe groups to punish providers, in this case Planned Parenthood, are not punishable unless a specific and immediate threat to incite violence is the content of the speech. Inciting anger simply is not enough. And this applies not only to politicians, but to inflammatory speech by ISIS or Al-Qaeda as well.

We cannot end violence by constraining free speech, but as a society we can monitor inflammatory speech to see how at-risk individuals, juveniles or adults who have had run-ins with the law enforcement, are affected by the content of that speech and intervene early in their lives if the courts determine that they may be a future threat to others or themselves. Clearly, Richard Dear, with multiple arrests, was a potential threat. Yes, this is the only solution. There are evidence-based practices for this, and thus we marry the above historical narrative with rapid assessment.

While there is no likely fix-all solution to the kinds of violence, suicidal mass murders, violent reactions by police officers against those acting strangely, or violence against the homeless, there are steps society and law enforcement can take on the margins to reduce some of the incidents of violence. These steps include, for example, closer monitoring of the media to pick up messages of incitement of violence; a sharper red line to be drawn between religious speech and speech that deliberately invokes a call to violence; better training for police officers and front-line clinicians, as in ERs, urgent care clinics and primary care—as well as judges, along with parole and probation officials who do have authority and control over a person following an illegal act in handling the mentally ill or even those acting strangely we need special emergency units composed of paramedics and police to restrain potentially violent mentally ill individuals using less than deadly force. We need racial sensitivity training to be required at police academies; state special prosecutors required to investigate all police-involved shootings so flagged by citizen review boards when the victim of the shooting is unarmed; clear protocols for rapid assessment of individuals acting strangely, whether that assessment takes place on the street, in a private residence, or in emergency rooms; and early identification of violence-prone individuals, even starting at elementary school age, so that early intervention can prevent the onset of dangerous psychiatric disorders. The case of Steven Kazmierczak, described in detail above, is the gold standard, because it fits Murphy's Law. Everything that could go wrong in respect to him throughout his life did go wrong, and the parents were helpless. It is the same with Seung-Hui Cho at Virginia Tech whose psychosis was allowed to progress untreated until he killed himself and over 30 other people.

We recognize that in America, people are actually free to act eccentric, even crazy. And for some people, crazy is not all that bad. But we have to draw the line between eccentricity and danger to self and others, and, if that line is drawn thoughtfully and is respected, individual rights can be protected, as well as the larger rights of society to be safer from violent individuals. This is a job we can do. We reel from the sights and sounds of the San Bernardino, and Orlando Colorado Springs massacres, covered as they were on the 24/7 cable news cycle. We recoil in horror as a police officer guns down 17-year-old Laquan McDonald on a Chicago street as the teenager seems to be walking away, posing no threat, and keeps on shooting when the boy's body twitches on the ground as more rounds hit it. We watch, perhaps with fury, as Eric Garner, tackled by police, screams out, "I can't breathe" 11 times before he dies. Do we need to be reminded about Walter Scott, shot while running away from police? Although all these cases have a commonality, a white officer killing a black offender who poses no threat, there is another commonality that brought these cases to public attention. It is the camera.

We live in the age of the digital smartphone camera, an all-seeing eye, a McLuhanesque universe in which all is seen, all is recorded, and all is broadcast. Surveillance cameras hang from street lights and store fronts, police will be wearing body cams and mount cameras on their dashboards; passers-by to any event only need to pull out a smartphone and hit the record button on their camera app. Nothing escapes us. We argue here that in this new universe, interactions that would be suppressed, filed away never to be reopened, and abuses never to be disclosed are part of the past, and police and other first responders need to be trained with this in mind.

Worse, not only do cameras record, they also distort. Like a classical drama, what comes before the video and what comes after it are only to be discerned from the video itself. Thus, the moment captured on video is, by definition, a distortion of reality. This is what cameras do, they distort what they report. And police and first responders need to be mindful of that, which is why the protocols we set forth herein for rapid assessment and thoughtful observation need to be employed by all who encounter individuals displaying strange—whether psychotic or threatening behavior on the street.

## REFERENCES

*Brandenburg v. Ohio*. 1969. 395 *U.S. 444* [1969].

Finnegan, W. 2016. Last Days: Preparing for the apocalypse in San Bernardino. The New Yorker, February 22.

Koplowitz, H. 2014. ISIS to attack America? Leader Abu Kakr Al-Baghdadi makes threat but issues few warnings to the West. *IBT*, June 19. www.ibtimes.com/isis-attack-america-leader-abu-bakr-al-baghdadi-makes-threat-issues-few-warnings-west-1606252

Lertzman, R. A., Birnes, W. J., and Azevedo, D. F. 2013. *Dr. Feelgood: The Shocking Story of the Doctor Who May Have Changed History by Treating and Drugging JFK, Marilyn, Elvis, and Other Prominent Figures*. Skyhorse Publishing, New York, New York.

Post, J. M. 2008. *The Mind of the Terrorist: The Psychology of Terrorism from the IRA to al-Qaeda*, 1st Edition. St. Martin's Griffin, New York, New York, December 15.

Rapoport, D. 1988. Inside *Terrorist Organizations*. Columbia University Press, New York, New York.

Stern, J. 2004. *Terror in the Name of God: Why Religious Militants Kill*. Harper Collins Publishing, New York, New York, August 17.

# Index

## A



## B

## I



## K



## L



## M

## N



## O

## R



## S

## T



## U



## V

## W